D1756244

Eoin MacNeill: The pen and the sword

Eoin MacNeill: The pen and the sword

CONOR MULVAGH

AND

EMER PURCELL

EDITORS

NUI

CENTENARY PUBLICATION

First published in 2022 by
Cork University Press
Boole Library
University College Cork
CORK
T12 ND89
Ireland

Library of Congress Control Number: 2021932768
Distribution in the USA: Longleaf Services, Chapel Hill, NC, USA

British Library Cataloguing in Publication Data
A CIP record for this book is available from the British Library.

ISBN: 978-1-78205-460-3

Printed by Hussar Books in Poland.
Print origination & design by Carrigboy Typesetting Services
www.carrigboy.co.uk

COVER IMAGE – 'Portrait photograph of Eoin MacNeill seated at a desk with an open
book.' [c.1900-09] (UCDA LA30/PH/325).

www.corkuniversitypress.com

Contents

REVOLUTIONARY

HISTORY, MEMORY, LEGACY

List of Abbreviations

ALI	*Ancient Laws of Ireland*
AOH	Ancient Order of Hibernians (Board of Erin)
BMH	Bureau of Military History
CSO	Chief Secretary's Office (Ireland)
DFA	Department of Foreign Affairs (Ireland)
DIAS	Dublin Institute for Advanced Studies
DIB	*Dictionary of Irish Biography*
DIFP	*Documents on Irish Foreign Policy*
DMP	Dublin Metropolitan Police
DT	Department of the Taoiseach
EIHM	*Early Irish History and Mythology*
IBIS	Institute for British-Irish Studies
IHS	*Irish Historical Studies*
IMC	Irish Manuscripts Commission
IPP	Irish Parliamentary Party
IRA	Irish Republican Army
IRB	Irish Republican Brotherhood
JRSAI	*Journal of the Royal Society of Antiquaries of Ireland*
MAI	Military Archives, Ireland
MSPC	Military Service Pensions Collection
NAI	National Archives, Ireland
NEBB	North Eastern Boundary Bureau
NLI	National Library of Ireland
NUI	National University of Ireland
NYU	New York University
ODNB	*Oxford Dictionary of National Biography*
OSA	Ordo sancti Augustini [Order of Saint Augustine]
QUB	Queen's University Belfast
PMLA	*Proceedings of the Modern Language Association*
PRIA	*Proceedings of the Royal Irish Academy*
PRONI	Public Record Office of Northern Ireland
RIA	Royal Irish Academy
RIC	Royal Irish Constabulary
RUI	Royal University of Ireland

SJ   Societas Iesu [Society of Jesus]
TCD   Trinity College Dublin
TCDA   Trinity College Dublin Archives
UCC   University College Cork
UCD   University College Dublin
UCDA   University College Dublin Archives
UVF   Ulster Volunteer Force
WS   Witness Statement

List of Plates

11. Róisín, Brian, Eibhlín MacNeill (seated L–R) with a dog and (standing) Turlough MacNeill in uniform and an unidentified man [*c.*1921–2] (UCDA LA30/PH/359).

12. Photographed on the steps of the Club House and Commercial Hotel, Kilkenny, MacNeill accompanies Cosgrave on the latter's first visit to his constituency of Carlow-Kilkenny since his election as President of the Executive Council. Cosgrave will use this visit to launch Cumann na nGaedheal's 1923 general election campaign. L–R, front row: Vincent White, Mayor of Waterford; Peter de Loughrey, Mayor of Kilkenny; W.T. Cosgrave, President of the Executive Council; Hugh Kennedy TD, Attorney General; Senator John MacLoughlin; MacNeill. Back row (not in order) includes Dan McCarthy TD, Chief Whip and President of the GAA; James Dolan TD; and Colonel-Commandant J. O'Reilly [27 May 1923] (UCDA LA30/PH/395).

13. Members of the Boundary Commission on the first day of their tour, Armagh, 9 December 1924. L–R: Dr Eoin MacNeill, Free State; Mr J.R. Fisher, Northern Ireland; Mr T.E. Read, OBE, JD, Secretary to Armagh County Council; Mr T.E. Montgomery; and Mr Justice Richard Feetham. Photographer: W.D. Hogan (NLI, National Photographic Archive, HOG 181).

14. MacNeill and members of the Catholic University of America, Washington DC [May 1930] (UCDA LA30/PH/398).

15. Máire Sweeney (MacNeill) and Michael Tierney standing underneath a portrait of Eoin MacNeill, 1964 (UCDA LA30/PH/105).

16. Group photograph on the occasion of the publication of *The Scholar Revolutionary: Eoin MacNeill, 1867–1945*, edited by F.X. Martin and F.J. Byrne, 1973. L–R: Thomas Murphy, President of UCD; Éilis McDowell; Francis John Byrne; Máire Sweeney; Séamus MacNeill; Eibhlín Tierney; F.X. Martin; Róisín Coyle (UCDA LA30/PH/377).

Author Biographies

Mairéad Carew is an archaeologist and cultural historian. She is author of *Tara and the Ark of the Covenant: A search for the Ark of the Covenant by British Israelites, 1899–1902* (2003); *Tara: The guidebook* (2016) and *The Quest for the Irish Celt: The Harvard Archaeological Mission to Ireland, 1932–1936* (2018).

Ruairí Cullen received his PhD in history from Queen's University Belfast in 2017. His doctorate was entitled 'Contention and Innovation: The medieval period in late nineteenth- and early twentieth-century Irish historiography'. Ruairí now works in policy and public affairs in London.

Diarmaid Ferriter is Professor of Modern Irish History at UCD. His books include *The Transformation of Ireland 1900–2000* (2004); *Judging Dev: A reassessment of the life and legacy of Éamon de Valera* (2007); *Occasions of Sin: Sex and society in modern Ireland* (2009); *Ambiguous Republic: Ireland in the 1970s* (2012); *A Nation and Not a Rabble: The Irish revolution 1913–23* (2015); *On the Edge: Ireland's offshore islands, a modern history* (2018); *The Border: The legacy of a century of Anglo-Irish relations* (2019) and *Between Two Hells: The Irish Civil War* (2021). He is a regular television and radio broadcaster and a columnist with the *Irish Times*. He was elected a member of the Royal Irish Academy in 2019.

Ted Hallett is a graduate of Aberystwyth University, 1965–71. He joined the Foreign and Commonwealth Office (FCO) in 1971 as a research analyst. He was posted to the British embassy, Bonn 1972–5, the British embassy, Dublin 1984–5 and seconded to the Northern Ireland Office (NIO), 1988–91. He was attached to the Northern Ireland Office political talks team, 1996–8. He was head of the FCO Western & Southern Europe Research Group 1998–2003, and deputy head of mission, British embassy, Dublin 2003–6. He retired from FCO in 2006. He was re-employed as a sensitivity reviewer at the FCO (2007) and the NIO (2010), reviewing departmental files prior to their transfer to the National Archives.

Brian Hughes lectures in the Department of History at Mary Immaculate College, Limerick. His edition of Eoin MacNeill's memoir was published by the Irish Manuscripts Commission in 2016 as *Eoin MacNeill: Memoir of a revolutionary scholar*. Other recent publications include *Defying the IRA? Intimidation, coercion, and communities during the Irish revolution* (2016 [repr. 2019]) and, with Conor Morrissey (eds), *Southern Irish Loyalism, 1912–1949* (2020).

Elva Johnston is an associate professor in the School of History, University College Dublin. Her monograph *Literacy and Identity in Early Medieval Ireland* (2013) was awarded the Irish Historical Research Prize (2015) for the best new work of Irish historical research. She was general editor of *Peritia: The Journal of the Medieval Academy of Ireland* and currently edits *Analecta Hibernica*, the periodical of the Irish Manuscripts Commission, of which she is a member.

Michael Kennedy has for almost three decades written and published widely on modern Irish history, in particular on Irish military and diplomatic history and on Irish foreign policy. He has been the executive editor of the RIA's *Documents on Irish Foreign Policy* series since 1997 (12 volumes published to date). Previously he lectured in Irish and European history at Queen's University Belfast and received his doctorate from the NUI in 1994 on the early history of Ireland's relationship with the League of Nations. As well as having published twelve volumes as executive editor of *Documents on Irish Foreign Policy* to date, Michael's wide range of books and articles include: *Ireland, the United Nations and the Congo* (2014) (with Art Magennis); *Guarding Neutral Ireland* (2008); *Division and Consensus: The politics of cross-border relations in Ireland 1921–1969* (2000); *Ireland and the League of Nations, 1919–46* (1996). Edited volumes include: *Irish Foreign Policy* (2012) (with Noel Dorr, Ben Tonra and John Doyle); *Reconstructing Ireland's Past: A history of the Irish Manuscripts Commission* (2009) (with Deirdre McMahon).

Michael Laffan studied at University College Dublin, Trinity Hall Cambridge and the Institute for European History in Mainz. Having lectured briefly at the University of East Anglia he took up a post in UCD, where he taught for over three decades and served in various positions, including as head of the School of History and Archives, before retiring in 2010. From 2010 to 2012 he was president of the Irish Historical Society; he is now an emeritus professor in UCD. He has published widely on modern Irish history. His writings include *The Partition of Ireland 1911–1925* (1983); *The Resurrection of Ireland: The Sinn Féin party, 1916–1923* (1999) and

Judging W.T. Cosgrove and the Foundation of the Irish State (2014), and he has edited *The Burden of German History: 1919–1945* (1988).

Liam Mac Mathúna is Professor Emeritus of Irish at University College Dublin. He has published over a hundred articles on Irish language, literature and culture. His book publications include *Béarla sa Ghaeilge* on Irish/English literary code-mixing 1600–1900 (2007); a new edition of Peadar Ua Laoghaire's ground-breaking novel *Séadna* (2011); *Saothrú na Gaeilge Scríofa i Suímh Uirbeacha na hÉireann, 1700–1850* on the cultivation of written Irish in urban areas (co-ed., 2016); *Douglas Hyde: My American journey* on Hyde's highly successful tour of America in 1905–6 (co-ed., 2019) and *Éigse*, vol. 40, 2019. He is editor of *Éigse: A Journal of Irish Studies*, published by the National University of Ireland. He delivered the NUI/UCD Hyde Lecture/Léacht de hÍde in 2019. Together with Dr Máire Nic an Bhaird, he is currently researching the life and work of Dr Douglas Hyde. His monograph *The Ó Neachtain Window on Gaelic Dublin, 1700–1750* was published in 2021.

Michael McDowell is the youngest grandson of Eoin MacNeill. He graduated from King's Inns in 1974 and is currently a senior counsel and an adjunct professor in the UCD Sutherland School of Law. He was elected as a TD for Dublin South-East (now the constituency of Dublin Bay South) in 1987, 1992 and 2002. He served as Attorney General from 1999 to 2002, as Minister for Justice, Equality and Law Reform from 2002 until 2007, and as Tánaiste from 2006 until 2007. He was first elected to Seanad Éireann in 2016 as an Independent member on the NUI panel and was re-elected in 2020.

Conor Mulvagh is an associate professor in modern Irish history at the School of History, University College Dublin with special responsibility for the Decade of Centenaries (2012–23). His research centres primarily on British and Irish political history and the history of Ireland during the decade of the Irish revolution and the First World War. His current research focuses on a comparative study of partitions. He lectures on memory and commemoration; the Irish revolution; and Northern Ireland. He is the author of *Irish Days, Indian Memories: V.V. Giri and Indian law students at University College Dublin, 1913–1916* (2016) and *The Irish Parliamentary Party at Westminster, 1900–18* (2016), which was awarded the 2017 NUI Special Commendation Prize in Irish History. He is a contributor to the *Cambridge History of Ireland* (Cambridge University Press, 2018).

Kevin Murray lectures in the Department of Early and Medieval Irish (Scoil Léann na Gaeilge), University College Cork. He is one of the editors of the *Locus* Project (www.ucc.ie/en/locus) which is engaged in producing a new historical dictionary of Irish placenames and tribal names; eight volumes of the dictionary have been published to date. His other research interests include editing and analysing medieval Irish legal and literary texts. He is the author of *Baile in Scáil* (2004) and *The Early Finn Cycle* (2017).

Shane Nagle attained his PhD from the University of London with a thesis on the comparative study of nationalist history writing in Ireland and Germany in the nineteenth and twentieth centuries. This was published as *Histories of Nationalism in Ireland and Germany: A comparative study from 1800 to 1932* by Bloomsbury Academic in 2016. He has also published on Eoin MacNeill and nationalisms in Ireland and Germany in *History Ireland, European History Quarterly* and *Labour History Review*.

Dáibhí Ó Cróinín is Professor Emeritus, National University of Ireland, Galway. Among his numerous publications are *The Irish Sex Aetates Mundi* (1983); *Cummian's Letter De Controversia Paschali: Together with a related Irish computistical tract De Ratione Conputandi* (1988); *The Songs of Elizabeth Cronin, Irish Traditional Singer* (2000; repr. 2021); *Early Irish History and Chronology* (2003); vol. 1 of the Royal Irish Academy's *New History of Ireland: Prehistoric and early medieval* (2005) and, most recently, *Whitley Stokes (1830–1909): The lost Celtic notebooks rediscovered* (2011). Since 2015 he has been chief-editor of *Peritia: Journal of the Medieval Academy of Ireland* (with Elva Johnston, UCD, and Máirín MacCarron, UCC). He is a Member of the Royal Irish Academy and chairman of a number of RIA committees and a former Member the Irish Manuscripts Commission.

Emer Purcell is an administration officer in the Publications Office of the National University of Ireland with special responsibility for the commemoration of the Decade of Centenaries. She has published widely on Viking-Age Ireland and medieval Dublin. She is the general editor of *Clerics, Kings and Vikings: Essays on medieval Ireland* (2015), a collection of forty-four essays in honour of Donnchadh Ó Corráin, and co-editor with Carrie Griffin of *Text, Transmission and Transformation in the European Middle Ages, c.1000–1500,* Cursor Mundi Series 34 (2018). She is also a coordinator of the Forum for Medieval and Renaissance Studies in Ireland: https://fmrsi.wordpress.com/.

Regina Uí Chollatáin is Senior Professor of Modern Irish and former head of the UCD School of Irish, Celtic Studies and Folklore (2015–2021). She has published widely on Irish language revival, media and print culture. Recent publications include chapters in *The Edinburgh History of the British and Irish Press*, vols 2 & 3 (2020). She was awarded the Nicholas O'Donnell Fellowship, Melbourne University (2019) and ICUF Senior Visiting Professor (2011–12). She is a member of the Irish Language Scholarship, Irish Literature and Celtic Culture Royal Irish Academy committee (2015–); the National Academic Advisory Board of the Museum of Literature of Ireland (MoLI), the National Folklore Commission, former Chair of the National Newspaper and Periodical History Forum of Ireland (2015–18) and a former board member of TG4. She is the current president of the Global Irish Diaspora Congress, which she co-founded in 2017. She was appointed Chair of Foras na Gaeilge, the North South Irish language state body, in 2021.

Niamh Wycherley lectures in medieval Irish history, culture and literature in the Department of Early Irish, Maynooth University. Her current research focuses on a philological approach to history, in particular in relation to the role of the Church in medieval society. She is a former Irish Research Council and NUI awardee and has completed postdoctoral research fellowships in UCD and NUI Galway. She won the NUI Publication Prize in Irish History 2017 for her monograph *The Cult of Relics in Early Medieval Ireland* (2015).

Acknowledgements

This collection of essays is born of a collaboration between the National University of Ireland and the School of History UCD in the publication of lectures given as part of a UCD History Hub series in 2013 and a symposium held in NUI in 2016; the titles of both focused on Eoin MacNeill as scholar and revolutionary. With the addition of some invited essays, the structure and themes of the book took shape. Five years later, as editors we would like to express our sincere thanks to the sixteen scholars who have contributed to this volume. Each essay presented here has helped realise our aim to produce a book that would do justice to the complex figure of Eoin MacNeill.

We are very grateful to the National Library of Ireland and UCD Archives and Special Collections, for their permission to reproduce the images used in this book, which help contextualise and bring the subject matter to life. We would also like to thank the staff of the following libraries and repositories: Military Archives, Ireland; National Archives of Ireland; National Library of Ireland; Parliamentary Archives, House of Lords, UK; UCD Archives; and United Kingdom National Archives.

We acknowledge with thanks the grant received from the NUI towards publication.

We would also like to thank: Attracta Halpin, Elva Johnston, Maurice Manning, Kevin Murray and Dáibhí Ó Cróinín for their support and assistance with the text. It remains to record our sincere gratitude to the two readers who reviewed the text as part of the Cork University Press peer review process. They both made invaluable suggestions which have greatly enhanced the book; in particular, their recommendation to reorganise and retitle some sections proved central to the cohesive presentation of the multi-faceted Eoin MacNeill you will find here.

We are very grateful to Cork University Press for the guidance and advice we received from Maria O'Donovan, Mike Collins and all the team in bringing this volume to publication.

Chronology

Chronologies of the life of Eoin MacNeill can be found in F.X. Martin and F.J. Byrne (eds), *The Scholar Revolutionary: Eoin MacNeill, 1867–1945 and the making of the new Ireland* (Shannon: Irish University Press, 1973) and Michael Tierney, *Eoin MacNeill: Scholar and man of action, 1867–1945*, ed. F.X. Martin (Oxford: Clarendon Press, 1980). Additionally, the published writings of Eoin MacNeill have been compiled, first as F.X. Martin (comp., ed.), 'The Writings of Eoin MacNeill', *Irish Historical Studies*, vol. 6, no. 21, March 1948, pp. 44–62 and subsequently in an expanded version in *The Scholar Revolutionary* (pp. 327–53).

What follows amalgamates information from the previously published timelines of MacNeill's life with information from his biographers – Michael Tierney, Patrick Maume, Thomas Charles-Edwards and Brian Hughes – along with further information from the present volume and additional primary sources.

The most comprehensive bibliography of MacNeill's scholarship and journalism is 'The Published Writings of Eoin MacNeill' (in *Scholar Revolutionary*, pp. 325–53). Although some additional writings by Eoin MacNeill have been uncovered since 1973 (notably MacNeill's chapter in the *Handbook of the Ulster Question*, co-authored (anonymously) with J.W. Good and published by the North Eastern Boundary Bureau in 1923), the editors have not attempted to incorporate MacNeill's writings into the present chronology with the exception of his four major monograph works (1919, 1921, 1934 and 1935).

1867 15 May: John (Eoin), sixth child of Archibald and Rosetta (née McAuley) McNeill born in Glenarm, County Antrim.

1869 James McNeill, younger brother to Eoin, born.

1872 Archibald McNeill is indicted on criminal charges following Catholic protests over an Orange Order demonstration in Glenarm but, represented by prominent Belfast Presbyterian barrister Hans McMordie, he is acquitted.

1881 Eoin enters St Malachy's College, Belfast.

1885 Secures a modern languages scholarship and begins studies for a degree at the Royal University of Ireland. As the RUI is solely a degree-awarding body, MacNeill will later study at TCD and the King's Inns.

1887 Obtains a junior clerkship by competition (first place) at the Accountant-General's Office at the Four Courts, Dublin. MacNeill is the only Catholic on the permanent staff of the office when he enters; places an advertisement in the *Freeman's Journal* for a tutor in Irish and engages a tutor for two lessons per week for a month; exhausts his tutor's limited knowledge of Irish after eight lessons.

1888 Awarded BA (Hons) in Economics, Jurisprudence and Constitutional History; begins to study Modern Irish, then Old and Middle Irish, under the Jesuit scholar Edmund Hogan, UCD Professor of Irish Language and History and RUI examiner in Celtic.

1889 15 May: Archibald, Eoin's father, dies of oesophageal cancer at Glenarm.

1891 June: first visit to the Aran Islands (Inis Meáin) to learn spoken Irish.

1893 March: moves to Hazelbrook, Portmarnock, north County Dublin with his mother and other members of the family; his unsigned article 'A Plea and a Plan for the Extension of the Movement to Preserve and Spread the Gaelic Language in Ireland' is published in *Irisleabhar na Gaedhilge / The Gaelic Journal*. Becomes a founder member of the Gaelic League (Conradh na Gaeilge) and is appointed its first honorary secretary.

1894 Takes over editorship (–1897) of the *Gaelic Journal* (monthly); sits on the committee of the first Feis Ceoil.

1897 On the invitation of Archbishop of Dublin William Walsh, MacNeill is invited to teach Irish lessons at the Catholic Archdiocesan Training College at Drumcondra two evenings per week; December: MacNeill meets P.H. Pearse for the first time when Pearse invites him to address the New Ireland Literary Society.

1898 8 January: first issue of *Fáinne an Lae* (weekly) published, MacNeill is the paper's first editor (–1899); 19 April: at All Saints parish church, Ballymena, County Antrim, MacNeill marries Agnes (Taddie) Moore, of Ballymena, sister of his schoolfriend Brian Moore, signing his legal name, 'John McNeill', Eoin lists 'journalist' as his profession on the marriage certificate. Eoin and Agnes' first home together is 14 Trafalgar Terrace, Monkstown, but they will return to Hazelbrook, Portmarnock, to live with Eoin's mother and his brother Charles by 1901.

1899 5 February: first son, Niall, born; Eoin becomes first editor (–1901) of *An Claidheamh Soluis* (weekly), which appears for the first time that March. March 1899 marks the peak of stresses which had been building on Eoin since he took on the editorship of *Fáinne an Lae* the previous year. MacNeill suffers a nervous breakdown requiring medical treatment. The episode leaves MacNeill with a lifelong dislike for writing letters; August: goes on a cycling holiday in Normandy with his brother-in-law Brian Moore and two other friends.

1900 8 March: Brian, second son, born.

1901 Assists Douglas Hyde in preparing evidence for the Robertson Commission on Irish university education on behalf of the Gaelic League. The Commission reports in 1903; 23 September: Eibhlín, eldest daughter, born.

1903 25 April: Toirdhealbhach (Turlough) MacNeill born.

1904 On the suggestion of his mentor, Edmund Hogan, MacNeill is invited to deliver a series of lectures on early Irish history at UCD by Rev. Dr William Delaney SJ; 7 December: Máire MacNeill born.

1906 Gives evidence (–1907) to the Fry Commission on Trinity College and the University of Dublin, Hyde sits as a commissioner; his lectures on early Irish history appear in *New Ireland Review*; 7 August: Róisín and Giollaspuic MacNeill (twins) born; three days later, Giollaspuic dies as a consequence of a birth defect.

1907 Elected Member of the Royal Irish Academy (RIA).

1908 1 April: Séamus MacNeill born. The family (Eoin, Agnes, their seven children, and Eoin's mother) move to 19 Herbert Park which will be their home until late 1915; appointed to the first Senate of the NUI; takes on personal responsibility for a bank overdraft occasioned by losses sustained by *An Claidheamh Soluis*. Payments amount to £50 per annum over six years on his £600 salary at the Accountant General's Office.

1909 Appointed Professor of Early (including Medieval) Irish History at UCD.

1912 31 March: Alongside Pearse, MacNeill makes a speech in Irish from platform number four ('the students' platform') at a massive pro-Home Rule demonstration on O'Connell St, Dublin. An estimated 100,000 people attend the rally.

1913 1 November: publishes 'The North Began' as an editorial in a new series of *An Claidheamh Soluis*; 25 November: presides over the opening meeting of the Irish Volunteers and is appointed president and chief of staff.

1914 7 June: Éilis MacNeill born; 24 September: in reaction to John Redmond's Woodenbridge speech, MacNeill and nineteen other members of the Provisional Committee of the Irish Volunteers sign a statement expelling John Redmond's twenty-five nominees from the Provisional Committee, reaffirming the original manifesto of the organisation, and calling a convention of the Volunteers on the anniversary of its foundation (25 November). Approximately 12,000 Volunteers remain with MacNeill while an estimated 158,000 side with Redmond forming a separate organisation: the National Volunteers. MacNeill takes over editing the *Irish Volunteer* newspaper, which had first appeared on 7 February.

1915 The MacNeill family move to Woodtown Park, Rathfarnham, County Dublin with Eoin's brother James who has just returned to Ireland having retired from the Indian civil service.

1916 Attempts to stop the 1916 Rising; arrested and sentenced to life in prison by field general court martial in its aftermath; transported to Dartmoor prison in Devon; expelled from RIA; elected president of the Gaelic League in absentia; becomes legally ineligible to hold his professorship at UCD under the Forfeiture Act (1870) following his conviction in the aftermath of the 1916 Rising. By coincidence, 1916 was the year all NUI professorships and lectureships became vacant under the Irish Universities Act (1908). MacNeill reapplied for his professorship from Dartmoor and a decision on the vacant chair was twice postponed by UCD's governing body.

1917 January: transferred to Lewes Prison, East Sussex; June: released from prison on amnesty; 6 July: Rosetta McNeill, Eoin's mother, dies of heart failure aged eighty-nine years at Woodtown; 2 October: applies to be reinstated to his professorship at UCD as MacNeill is no longer subject to any civil disabilities owing to the terms of the release warrant that freed the remaining 1916 convicts. UCD's governing body decides to take no action on the professorship at its October meeting; 25 October: MacNeill is elected to the Executive Committee of Sinn Féin; 6 November: UCD's governing body resolves to advertise the vacancy for the Chair of Early (including Medieval) Irish History; the MacNeill family move to Netley, South Hill Avenue, Blackrock, County Dublin which will be their home until 1932.

1918 10 January–28 March: lacking a salary from UCD and with the assistance of Bulmer Hobson, MacNeill delivers a series of twelve lectures on early and medieval Irish history to large audiences at the Rotunda, Dublin. The enterprise nets £100 and MacNeill will subsequently publish the lectures as *Phase of Irish History*; 23 April: UCD's Faculty of Arts and Faculty of Celtic Studies unanimously recommend the appointment of Eoin MacNeill to the Chair of Early Irish History at UCD. The appointment is not officially confirmed until 17 December, at which point MacNeill's reinstatement (and pay) is backdated to 24 May 1918; 14 December: elected MP for the constituencies of Derry City and NUI in the Westminster general election. Made a freeman of Limerick city.

1919 21 January: attends the first sitting of Dáil Éireann; appointed (22 January) minister for finance and subsequently (1 April) minister for industries for the Dáil Éireann government; publishes *Phases of Irish History* (Dublin: Gill).

1920 26 November: arrested with his son Niall during a raid on the family home in which all papers and documents are seized but the boys' arms cache is not discovered, Eoin is released on 28 November and Niall a fortnight later; 30 November: the family home is raided for a second time and Eoin is rearrested, this time with his son Turlough, and interned without trial in Mountjoy prison.

1921 23 April: the MacNeill family home is raided for a third time. Eoin and Turlough were still in Mountjoy and Niall and Brian were by then on the run. Nothing is found and no arrests made; 24 May: Eoin MacNeill elected for Londonderry and NUI (uncontested) in the simultaneous Northern and Southern Ireland general elections thus nominally becoming a simultaneous member of the Northern Ireland, Southern Ireland, and second Dáil Éireann parliaments while still in prison; 30 June: released from Mountjoy in advance of the truce on 11 July; receives DLitt from NUI; publishes *Celtic Ireland* (Dublin: Martin Lester); elected speaker of Dáil Éireann, presides over the debates on the Anglo-Irish treaty (14 Dec. 1921–7 Jan. 1922).

1922 7 January: presides as speaker of Dáil Éireann over the vote on the Anglo-Irish treaty; 21–28 January: attends the Irish Race Conference in Paris; June: elected pro-treaty TD for NUI in the third Dáil; August, appointed minister for education in Cosgrave's second provisional government (retains the position with the formation of the Free State Executive Council in 1923); 20 September: Brian

MacNeill is shot dead following capture by National Army troops in County Sligo. He is buried in the family plot at Kilbarrack cemetery, Sutton, County Dublin.

1923 4 April: Edith Crilly, former member of the UCD branch of Cumann na mBan, marries Niall MacNeill; 28 June: Michael Tierney, Professor of Greek at UCD, marries Eibhlín MacNeill; 27 August: Eoin MacNeill elected TD for Clare and NUI at general election (sits for Clare); 31 August: travels to Geneva as part of the Irish delegation to the League of Nations; visits Bobbio, in Emilia-Romagna, northern Italy, for the thirteenth centenary of St Columbanus; appointed Free State representative to the Boundary Commission.

1924 Commences work on Irish Boundary Commission alongside chairman Richard Feetham and Northern Ireland representative J.R. Fisher.

1925 November: collapse of the Irish Boundary Commission; resignation as commissioner; resignation as member of the Executive Council.

1927 Choses to contest NUI but not Clare constituency in June general election; loses NUI seat and retires from active political life.

1928 Appointed chairman of the newly founded Irish Manuscripts Commission which he was largely responsible for founding; awarded DLitt (*Honoris Causa*) by University of Dublin.

1930 Embarks on a lecture tour of the United States; awarded DLitt (*Honoris Causa*) by the Catholic University of America, Washington DC.

1931 Elected corresponding member of the Académie des Inscriptions et des Belles Lettres.

1932 Moves to Hatch Street, Dublin, which will be Eoin and Agnes MacNeill's home until 1941; begins dictating (–1933) his memoir to Leila Carroll.

1933 Delivers the Rhys Memorial Lecture on 'The Picts in Ireland'.

1934 Publication of *St Patrick, Apostle of Ireland* (London: Sheed & Ward).

1935 Publication of *Early Irish Laws and Institutions* (London: Burns & Oates).

1936 Inaugural president of the Irish Historical Society (–1945).

1937 President, Royal Society of Antiquaries of Ireland (–1940).

1938 September: undertakes (with Agnes) his final trip abroad to attend an international conference on Christian archaeology in Rome hosted by Cardinal Eugenio Pacelli (who was elected Pope Pius XII the following March). Upon arrival in Rome, the MacNeills find out the event has been postponed owing to the Munich crisis; 8 October: has an audience with Pope Pius XI at Castel Gandolfo.

1939 Resumes dictating his memoir (–4 January 1940), this time to Ita Mallon.

1940 President, Royal Irish Academy (–1943).

1941 Retires from UCD, moves to 63 Upper Leeson St, which will be home to Eoin and Agnes until their deaths in 1945 and 1958 respectively; 7 November: receives the final version of his memoir from Ita Mallon.

1942 11 April: Éilis MacNeill, architect, marries Anthony Gerard McDowell, barrister-at-law.

1944 Awarded Gregory Medal by the Irish Academy of Letters; 21 June: Róisín MacNeill marries David Donovan Coyle, Galway businessman; August: travels with his extended family to the Aran Islands on what will be his final holiday.

1945 May: diagnosed with abdominal cancer; 15 October: dies at home, 63 Upper Leeson St.

Foreword

The National University of Ireland has always been proud of, and has greatly valued, its relationship with Eoin MacNeill. He was a strong supporter of the idea of a national university long before it became a reality in 1908, was a member of the first university Senate and remained an active member and supporter for many years thereafter. He was foundation Professor of Early (including Medieval) Irish History in the university and was elected to the first Dáil from the NUI constituency in 1918.

NUI planned an ambitious and broad-based commemorative programme for the Decade of Centenaries. From the outset it was decided that, as part of the programme, the university would honour figures associated with NUI who had made significant contributions to the building of the new Irish state. Four names stood out – Douglas Hyde, Eoin MacNeill, Éamon de Valera and Patrick McGilligan.

This series began in 2013 with a seminar 'Douglas Hyde: The professor who became president of Ireland', and these proceedings were published in 2016. In 2013 NUI published a facsimile reproduction of *Lia Fáil: Irisleabhar Gaeilge Ollscoil na hÉireann* launched by President Michael D. Higgins. In 2018 the inaugural Hyde lecture/Léacht de hÍde (in partnership with UCD) took place when a paper 'The Legacy of Douglas Hyde' was delivered in UCD by President Higgins. The second Hyde lecture 'Douglas Hyde's American Tour 1905–6' was delivered by Professor Liam Mac Mathúna in UCD in 2019.

In 2016 two additional travelling scholarships in Mathematics were offered to honour Éamon de Valera, the second chancellor of the university who presided over its affairs from his election in 1921 until his death in 1975. In that year also a special Éamon de Valera medal was commissioned and presented to each of the 2016 NUI award winners. 2021 marks the centenary of de Valera's election as chancellor. A lecture series, 'DevTalks: towards an assessment of his legacy', was jointly hosted by the NUI and DIAS.

Two events were held in the National Gallery in 2018. In March, 'John Redmond and the Irish Party: A centenary symposium' was a state commemoration to mark 100 years since the death of Redmond. A book based on the symposium is in preparation. In December, in collaboration with Maynooth University, NUI marked the centenary of women's suffrage with a symposium, 'Political Voices: The participation of women in Irish public life, 1918–2018'.

Publication is at an advanced stage of the 'National University of Ireland World War 1 Honour Roll', an extended reproduction of the original 1919 volume accompanied by a collection of essays, one of which examines the contribution of NUI women to the war effort.

Future events will include a seminar to examine the contribution of Patrick McGilligan who succeeded MacNeill as TD for NUI in 1923. He also served on the NUI Senate. McGilligan was a key player in two of the major developments of the 1920s: the establishment of the ESB and the constitutional developments that led to the Statute of Westminster in 1931.

Given his very strong personal and continuing family connections with NUI, the university felt it particularly appropriate to honour Eoin MacNeill. To mark the centenary of the publication of MacNeill's 'The North Began', HistoryHub.ie, UCD's public history website, produced an eight-part online series, 'Eoin MacNeill: Revolutionary and scholar' beginning on 1 November 2013. In 2016, NUI held a seminar 'Eoin MacNeill: A reassessment of the scholar revolutionary'. These two programmes combined provided a ready-made framework for a publication that, with the addition of some invited contributions, forms a fresh re-evaluation of MacNeill's contribution to the shaping of modern Ireland and Irish academia.

This volume commemorates Eoin MacNeill. Indeed, the volume is not so much a reassessment as a rediscovery of MacNeill. As never before we get a fuller picture of his personality, MacNeill the family man, the pride and delight he took in his wife and family and the hardships and dangers his life inflicted on them, the long absences due to various imprisonments, the frequent house moves, the military harassments and, most of all, the personal anguish of the Civil War, which saw his son Brian killed by the soldiers of the government of which he was a member. We get a sense of MacNeill the man, gentle but steely, absent-minded but clear-headed when there was a job to be done, wily in the ways of academic politics, good at getting his way and always with a quiet sense of humour.

The emphasis in this book is, quite rightly, on MacNeill the scholar, for that is, first and foremost, what he was and that was how he saw himself. His scholarship has had its detractors and what this volume seeks to do is to put both his achievements and its critics into a wider context. Some of the criticisms were indeed justified, others not, but the overall conclusion of this volume is just how substantial and innovative the bulk of his work is and how well it has stood the scrutiny of time and of a newer generation of scholars.

MacNeill was a public intellectual long before that phrase came into vogue and he probably would not have approved of it. He was prepared not just to contribute but to lead on the great public issues of the day: education and the university question; nationality and identity; language; and self-government. Revelling in public debate, he was a clever debater and could strike a low blow if he thought it necessary in an era when rough and robust public exchanges were not uncommon. But he was not just a talker, he was prepared to get stuck in and lead, whether as a driving force in the Gaelic League, as the inspirer of the Irish Volunteers, as a gunrunner, as a man with a price on his head, as a man who went to jail, fought elections, served in government at a dangerous time, arrived on the scene shortly after his colleague and friend Kevin O'Higgins was assassinated and ultimately accepted the poisoned chalice that was membership of the Boundary Commission.

He could never be accused of being, in Belloc's words, 'a remote and ineffectual don' or of living in an ivory tower. The accepted wisdom has been that he was not a success as a politician and we can see why this has been so. The two major black marks against him are the countermanding of Pearse's orders in 1916 and the failure of the Boundary Commission to meet the expectations of nationalist Ireland. It is unlikely that this view will greatly change, but both issues were more complex than first appears. Each is examined in this volume and each helps explain why he did as he did.

It is important to note that in neither case – nor elsewhere over a long career – was MacNeill's integrity ever questioned, not by his colleagues or his opponents. His judgement was sometimes questioned, but never his honesty or patriotism.

The fact that he felt obliged to resign after the Boundary Commission fiasco was to have very important consequences for Irish historical and legal scholarship. Such was his standing, and the genuine respect there was for him, that he was the only politician who could possibly have persuaded a beleaguered and cash-starved administration – and against the entrenched advice of its civil servants – to establish the Irish Manuscripts Commission. It was an unparalleled deed of foresight which did so much to ameliorate the consequences of the destruction of the Public Record Office at the Four Courts. But not alone did he cause it to be established; he led it for the rest of his life and did his best to protect it against its enemies in the civil service. For this alone, Irish history and those who study it will forever be in his debt.

This volume, so superbly edited by Dr Conor Mulvagh and Dr Emer Purcell, is a hugely important and timely contribution to the scholarly and personal rediscovery of Eoin MacNeill.

MAURICE MANNING,
Chancellor, National University of Ireland,
25 February 2021

Introduction: reassessing
Eoin MacNeill

CONOR MULVAGH AND EMER PURCELL

T he story of the Irish revolution cannot be told without Eoin MacNeill. From its long gestation through its protracted dénouement to its muffled cadence with the collapse of the Boundary Commission, Eoin MacNeill played a central role in shaping the cultural, political, military and even geographical development of the island of Ireland in the early twentieth century. The present volume provides fresh insights, and applies new methodological approaches, to the life and times of MacNeill. It builds upon, and reacts to, both the small body of work on MacNeill himself and the broader historiographical trends in scholarship on medieval history, the Gaelic Revival, the Irish revolution, and the history of state formation on the island of Ireland. The images on the front cover and flyleaf of this book depict two different MacNeills: one the scholar, clean shaven, posing with his book; the other the bearded man of action, uniformed and armed.[1] This encapsulates the enigmatic, multi-faceted, mercurial MacNeill which this book sets out to understand.

The contributions to the present volume strike a balance between respect and iconoclasm. Our collective endeavour in this centenary volume has been to try to reconceptualise and comprehend a three-dimensional version of MacNeill. We have drawn upon scholars who know him through his academic writing, those who know him as a politician, and even one who knew him as a departed grandfather, a figure who loomed large in the family history. At all times, the written word of MacNeill himself has been to the fore as the contributors collectively re-engaged with his private papers, his scholarly publications, and his journalism.

The other image of MacNeill, which is dominant in the minds of many of the contributors to this volume, is a literal backdrop: the portrait of MacNeill which now hangs in the boardroom of the UCD School of History (see plate 15 in this volume). It is a gigantic, almost life-sized portrait of a seated MacNeill, holding a green hardbound volume in his

hand and dressed in his professorial robes. For as long as any of the current
staff of the school remember, it has loomed behind seminar speakers, heads
of school chairing meetings, and students bravely presenting their work
to their professors and peers. In the most literal sense, MacNeill has cast
his presence over generations of Irish historians. Beside him is the portrait
of another of the founding historians of the National University, Mary
Hayden, first Professor of Modern History at the National University. They
stand guard over the UCD History department and its visitors, MacNeill
given the central place his successors allotted to him while Hayden, in
a much smaller portrait, sits to the side, nowadays often occluded by a
large presentation screen, a statement, conscious or subconscious, by the
successors to these two professors on the relative hierarchy between them
and the gender politics of the department since the 1940s. Recently, this
imbalance has been greatly redressed by the publication of Joyce Padbury's
Mary Hayden: Irish historian and feminist, 1862–1942 (Dublin: Arlen
House, 2021).

The complexity and variety of MacNeill's life has proved a challenge
to biographers to date. The definitive biography of MacNeill is Michael
Tierney's posthumously published *Eoin MacNeill: Scholar and man of
action, 1867–1945* (1980). A shorter biography of MacNeill was published by
Tierney during the latter's lifetime as part of a thirtieth anniversary edition
of Eoin MacNeill's *Saint Patrick*, which had originally been published in
1934.[2]

Tierney opens his biography by stating that 'In Eoin MacNeill three
strands of history meet: he came of historic stock, he was a pioneer
historian, and he made history'.[3] One of the great values of *Scholar and man
of action* is in its frequent and extensive use of quotation from MacNeill's
papers, not only in the provision of evidence but as a means to give the
reader a first-hand impression of the subject's voice and reasoning. It is to
Tierney's credit that he stuck rigorously to the evidence in front of him. It is
to his wife Eibhlín's credit that this evidence was available to her husband.
She was cataloguing her father's papers simultaneous to Tierney's writing of
the biography.[4]

Tierney was cognisant of the fact that he was close to the subject of his
work. In opening the book, its editor F.X. Martin absolves its author of any
perceived bias, stating that 'there were sufficient differences between them
[MacNeill and Tierney] to make Tierney examine aspects of MacNeill's life
with a fresh eye'.[5] At its best, Tierney's biography is written with a keenness
to get to the heart of the matters MacNeill was best known for but about

which he spoke least. Tierney explains that this curiosity about his father-in-law drove the book: 'From that year [1923] on I met him and talked with him constantly, and found him unlimited in his interests and inexhaustible in discussion. But though we discussed almost everything, he was reticent about the ordeals he had undergone.'[6] At its weakest, Tierney's writings on MacNeill lack sufficient distance and dispassion from their subject and can be seen to have been written defensively, an apologia for a revered father-in-law, colleague, mentor and friend. Tierney justified his writing saying, 'I hope ... to have put in a fairer and more useful perspective the life-work of a remarkable man who has undergone both in life and afterwards a strange and systematic denigration.'[7]

The other indispensable work on the life and work of MacNeill is F.X. Martin and F.J. Byrne's *The Scholar Revolutionary: Eoin MacNeill, 1867–1945* (1973).[8] *Scholar Revolutionary* stands both as a loose template and a historical challenge to the present volume. Nearing fifty years since its publication, the dozen essays contained therein paint a vivid picture of MacNeill by scholars, many of whom personally knew MacNeill as friends, students and colleagues. Essays like Brian Farrell's 'MacNeill in Politics' left the present editors asking themselves what more could be said on such a subject. Essays like Robin Dudley Edwards' 'Professor MacNeill' and Francis Shaw's 'MacNeill the Person', meanwhile, reveal such a deep personal knowledge of their subject that the present generation of scholars could not hope to replicate them.

In contrast to Tierney's often rose-tinted view of his father-in-law, some of the contributions to *Scholar Revolutionary* do not hold their punches when it comes to assessing MacNeill. Farrell takes aim at the gap between MacNeill's aspirations and achievements in his essay. He delivers a cutting but accurate assessment of MacNeill's life in politics, noting how MacNeill

> ... was concerned more with cultural unity and freedom than with geographical and political unity and freedom. His interventions in active politics marked a series of diminutions and failures for his own best ideals. The man who had found it impossible to stand aside when the north-east moved was to be the man who would be held responsible for the loss of the six counties. The moderate leader who sought to impose a policy of realistic restraint on the Volunteers became the cover behind which a revolutionary conspiracy launched an armed revolt. The political theorist who thought of public affairs purified of partisanship in a post-war world was to help launch one

Irish party leader and himself to become titular head of another party. The educationalist who had such high hopes of liberalising the schools became the minister who pioneered a continuing conservatism in Irish education.[9]

Farrell, however, points out that to multiply these ironies in MacNeill's career is to 'ignore the real achievement of MacNeill and the men of his generation'. In assessing MacNeill's political contribution, Farrell asserts that it was as an intellectual that MacNeill left his greatest, but not always identifiable, mark on the Irish independence movement.

> '[J]ust as important as his role as a critic and destroyer of the *ancien régime* was MacNeill's positive contribution to the new order. In the task of acquiring acceptability, legitimacy and stability the participation of men like MacNeill might well be regarded as critical. His willingness to become identified with the Irish Free State that emerged was more important than any specific act performed or policy promoted.'[10]

The long (1980) and short (1964) Tierney biographies alongside Martin and Byrne's *Scholar Revolutionary* (1973) are three sources that have informed all subsequent scholarship, not just on MacNeill but on a wider span of history pertaining to the Gaelic Revival, the Irish revolution, the formation of the Irish state, and the partition of the island. They have also informed scholars and historiographers of medieval Ireland seeking to understand one of the founders of the modern study of early and medieval Irish history.

The other indispensable source that has informed historical under-standing of MacNeill is the vast trove of his papers that is now held by UCD Archives. Tierney wrote how

> The story of his [MacNeill's] papers is a saga in itself. They had been carefully preserved by his wife through several changes of residence and his two imprisonments. In November 1920 he was arrested in a night raid on his house by the Crown forces, and every document he possessed was 'bundled into sacks, boxes, baskets, or any container that was handy' and taken to Dublin Castle, where, as indications show, they were extensively examined. Probably because the bulk of the documents were his own scholarly writings and correspondence going back to the early days of the Gaelic League, they were subsequently

returned to his house. They must have presented the decipherers at Dublin Castle with a formidable task, lightened perhaps by discovering among them crayon drawings by his youngest child Éilis, then six years old, which were returned with the other documents. Before her death in 1953, Mrs. MacNeill gave them into the possession of my wife [Eibhlín], to whose devoted and skilful work of classification and arrangement I owe the possibility of undertaking this work.[11]

Tierney points out that many of the letters within Eoin's papers consist of 'drafts of his own, some of which were never dispatched. They often provide valuable insights into his thinking on problems and events'.[12] Transferred in tranches between 1973 and 1982, MacNeill's papers run to fifty-six archival boxes and additional outsize material, making this one of the largest collections of personal private papers among the deposited collections currently open to the public at UCD Archives.[13] One of the key sources within those papers has been MacNeill's memoir, written between 1932 and the end of his life. One of the single largest developments in scholarship on MacNeill in recent years has been the publication of a scholarly edition of this memoir by Brian Hughes in 2016.[14] Writing in the present volume, Hughes reflects in depth on the meaning, the content and the context of MacNeill's memoir and what it can tell us not only about MacNeill's life but about how MacNeill had begun to craft an image of himself for posterity in his final decades; moving from the realm of history into the world of memory, legacy and posterity.

This book brings together multiple generations of Irish scholars – from well-established historians such as Michael Laffan and Dáibhí Ó Cróinín to a new generation including Ruairí Cullen, Hughes, Shane Nagle and Niamh Wycherley. The Bureau of Military History [BMH], Military Service Pensions Collection [MSPC], and Dublin Metropolitan Police [DMP] 'Movements of Dublin Extremists' files all provide new and complicating insights into the activities and perception of MacNeill. However, the advances in scholarship which this book builds upon arise not so much from the opening of new archival sources but more from the new methodologies and approaches which are brought to bear here in assessing MacNeill's scholarship, his political outlook and alliances. The nature of biography itself is also central, with particular focus on memory, posterity, and the challenges posed by an individual who left a very clear picture of himself through the deposition of an archive and the cultivation of an image of 'scholar revolutionary' which can obscure more complex and less positive traits in someone who was frequently at the centre of matters but not always, it seems, in the driving seat.

MacNeill's life and work defies the format of a traditional biography – the study of a figure as complex as MacNeill requires the expertise of the medievalist and the modernist, the cultural, social, political and revolutionary historian not to mention expertise in philology, historiography, power and politics. This collection opens with a biographical portrait of MacNeill written by his grandson Senator Michael McDowell and offers a family perspective on the main events in his life, not least the impact of the Civil War on the MacNeill family. The book then nestles around a series of broad themes within MacNeill's varied life; as a 'Scholar', a figure central to the long history of the Gaelic Revival in 'Language and Culture', and a 'Revolutionary'. The final section of this volume, 'History, Memory, Legacy', looks at MacNeill's influence and reflects on his life from the privacy of his home to the cut and thrust of the political arena into which MacNeill cast himself.

'Scholar' examines MacNeill and the way in which he shaped the discipline of Irish history from new perspectives. Kevin Murray begins with a reassessment of his contribution to early Irish law, Wycherley explores his influence on our understanding of the church in medieval Ireland and Ó Cróinín looks at his scholarly achievements through the lens of MacNeill's academic contemporaries, who were often his most ardent critics. Elva Johnston places his work as a historian within the broader context of contemporary historical debate and interpretations of the Irish past. Michael Kennedy outlines MacNeill's lasting institutional legacy with a study of the establishment of the Irish Manuscripts Commission and MacNeill's foresight in his attempt to preserve and publish historical documents.

'Language and Culture' begins with two papers that come from different perspectives to examine MacNeill's contribution to the Irish language and the Gaelic Revival. Liam Mac Mathúna argues for MacNeill's pioneering role in the Irish language movement, while Regina Uí Chollatáin's essay centres on MacNeill's journalistic writings, exploring the ideology behind the Gaelic Revival and how it shaped the formation of the early state. Cullen undertakes the first dedicated analysis of MacNeill's role in the final years of the Irish university question, asserting MacNeill's prominence in these debates. Mairéad Carew brings this section to a close with an innovative paper demonstrating how MacNeill created and promoted at home and in the US what she describes as an 'Irish Cultural Republic'.

MacNeill as 'Revolutionary' begins with Michael Laffan's detailed examination of 1916 and the countermanding order. Nagle then places MacNeill and nationalism in a European context, blending his scholarship with his wider contribution to a definition of Irishness during a period of state formation. Ted Hallett gives an authoritative and fresh examination of the Boundary Commission.

The concluding section, 'History, Memory, Legacy', opens with Conor Mulvagh's study of the domestic world and private life of MacNeill. He charts the ways in which scholarship and politics interacted with MacNeill's home life and family. Hughes explores MacNeill's memoir, examining how MacNeill himself interpreted this period in a text which broke uncharacteristically from his convention of remaining relatively silent on his role in the independence struggle and state-formation. Finally, Diarmaid Ferriter concludes the volume with an analysis of MacNeill's life in politics, one hundred years on from his political decade. He situates MacNeill within the Irish revolution before going on to explain how MacNeill's place in that revolution was minimised and misrepresented before being slowly and fitfully rehabilitated from the early 1960s onwards.

MacNeill is much championed as the founding father of the discipline of early medieval Irish history. As one of his successors at UCD, F.J. Byrne (Professor of Early (including Medieval) Irish History from 1964 to 2000) declared: 'To MacNeill belongs the credit of having dragged Celtic Ireland practically single-handed from the antiquarian mists into the light of history.'[15] Similarly, Donnchadh Ó Corráin in his introduction to the 1981 edition of MacNeill's *Celtic Ireland* stated: 'Eoin MacNeill was the founding father of the scientific study of early Irish history.'[16] He continued:

> Highly original studies on all aspects of early Irish history – Ogham inscriptions, tribal origins and nomenclature, source criticism of the annals, genealogies and early historians, law and the structures of early society and institutions, and latterly, Patrician studies – flowed from his pen. In these years, he laid out the foundations of his discipline and struck out almost all the lines which subsequent research was to follow.[17]

In 1996, Colmán Etchingham, in a survey of the discipline of early medieval Irish history, commented:

> It may seem inconceivable that serious study of this most fascinating and vital period of Irish history should cease to take place, yet one

has mixed feelings, to say the least of it, about the fate of MacNeill's inheritance. While it would be an exaggeration to say that it has been squandered, its potential has hardly been thoroughly exploited.[18]

In the twenty-five years since that essay, some progress has been made in terms of the edition and translation of sources, and the provision of textbooks – two of 'the plethora of desiderata' outlined by Etchingham as essential to the development of the field.[19] However, over a century on from MacNeill's appointment as professor in UCD, it is interesting to survey the current institutional standing of early Irish history across NUI colleges and note that there are currently no occupied Chairs of Early Irish and/or Medieval History; extend that search to non-NUI colleges across the island of Ireland and there is one occupied chair: Trinity College Dublin's Lecky Professorship.[20]

Standing on the shoulders of the work of scholars such as Geoffrey Keating and Roderick O'Flaherty, and 'the erudite but uncritical' Eugene O'Curry and John Donovan,[21] and armed with linguistic skills influenced by the school of German philologists, there is no denying that MacNeill was a pioneer in the field of early Irish history. Not all of his work has stood the test of time as essays by Murray, Wycherley, Johnston and Ó Cróinín in the present volume show. Indeed, as Ó Cróinín discusses, his work drew much criticism from contemporaries: his writing on St Patrick was rightly challenged by Thomas O'Rahilly. In addition, there were considerable disagreements with Osborn Bergin and Daniel Binchy on matters of interpretation of early Irish law. Of more interest, however, is Ó Cróinín's observation that, although MacNeill was part of a small coterie of Irish scholars in Dublin in the early decades of the twentieth century who fashioned early Irish studies, he was not of them and stood apart from them. This is echoed in Ferriter's essay where MacNeill's political legacy is likewise seen as that of an insider on the outside.

Academically, MacNeill most certainly set out the framework for our understanding of the political, social and economic organisation of early medieval Irish society. His study of early Irish population groups was unparalleled and is still very much the starting block for dynastic history. He may have made errors in transcription and/or interpretation, he may have misdated texts (such as *Lebor na Cert*), or misrepresented the reliability of the earliest layers of the Irish annals, but his signal contribution was the very way in which he sought to translate and interrogate primary sources.

His work is replete with mention of 'the revising hand'; of interpolations; he sets forth and demonstrates his understanding of the layers of accretion in Irish texts and manuscripts; and, most importantly, he attempted to establish and to synchronise relationships both within and between texts. MacNeill's often-times critical analysis of the synthetic historians of early medieval Ireland is interesting and could be read as a reflection on his own work:

> Stories could not pass for histories unless they fitted together, in time and in all other relations. The schools, therefore, set themselves to collect all the ancient traditions of the nation, weaving them into a single fabric, with dates and a regular succession and correlation of events. This was 'the harmonising and synchronising of all the stories', which was the part of the true *fili*. Along with the stories, it was necessary to harmonize the genealogies, which are the bone-work of history.[22]

MacNeill's historical ability was distinguished by three factors: one, as Murray discusses at length, his ability to read the primary sources, not only Latin, but most importantly those written in Old, Middle, Early Modern and Modern Irish. Second, his wide-ranging knowledge of early medieval Irish source material in all forms: law tracts, genealogies, annals, literary texts and onomastics. And the third factor, a little more ephemeral, as many have remarked, his historical intuition or flair.[23] Murray also quite rightly emphasises MacNeill's hallmark humility, which he sees as a key aspect of his scholarship: his ability to grow through his mistakes. In 1913, MacNeill wrote to Kuno Meyer that

> For my part, I find nothing so instructive or so stimulating as my own mistakes, when they are discovered. I shall probably be as proud of my scars as any duellist, and why not? I can always point to the marks where Stokes hit me, and Meyer and Thurneysen and Bergin himself and sometimes the birds of the air might have flown through the holes made in me.[24]

Where and how did MacNeill gain such a breadth and depth of knowledge of early medieval Ireland? As Murray and Johnston discuss, much of it was acquired while serving his 'professor apprenticeship' working with Edmund Hogan editing medieval Irish texts and, perhaps most importantly, his involvement with the compilation of the *Onomasticon*

Goedelicum.[25] In particular, this allowed him to link population groups with territories and map early medieval Ireland.[26] It is a map, as Paul MacCotter's work shows, we largely still follow and we are still piecing together.[27] He must have spent endless hours of research and study, while all the time in the middle (or on the fringes of) important political, social and cultural concerns of late nineteenth-century and early twentieth-century Ireland. As Laffan points out, in the run-up to the Easter Rising, MacNeill was working with R.A.S. Macalister on the Ó Cléirigh recension of *Lebor Gabála Érenn* (The Book of the Taking of Ireland).[28] At one point, just as Macalister left Woodtown, members of the Irish Volunteers arrived, among them fellow medievalist Colm Ó Lochlainn.[29] Occasionally, MacNeill's entanglement in political affairs gave him unexpected research time. Binchy noted how much of MacNeill's best work on early Irish law was conducted while he was in Mountjoy prison from late 1920 to July 1921.[30] Throughout all of this, and perhaps at the centre of it, he was a husband, and a father to eight children. This private world of the MacNeill household, the environment in which Eoin conducted so much of his scholarship and business, is explored by Conor Mulvagh.

The symbiotic relationship between his political life and his academic work has occupied historians for decades and continues to do so in this volume. Byrne first detailed the accusation of nationalist bias in his work,[31] Ó Cróinín and Johnston both touch upon this debate and his clash with that other great historian of medieval Ireland, G.H. Orpen. However, it is the interplay between his work as a medievalist and his political life that makes MacNeill such a fascinating subject. While he was mediating Ireland's relationship with Great Britain, he was simultaneously researching and writing early Irish history focusing on the very same matters: identity, nationality, and the formation of Ireland.

There is a brief glimpse of the medievalist in 'The North Began' when he talks of feudalism, and when Irish unity is viewed in terms of three famous saints of medieval Ireland:

> There is no 'homogeneous Ulster'. It is impossible to separate from Ireland the city that Saint Patrick founded, the city that Saint Columba founded, or the tombs of Patrick, Brigid and Columba. They would defy and nullify the attempt. It is impossible to separate from Ireland the 'frontier town' of Newry, the men of south Down, Norman and Gael, the Gaelic stock of the Fews that hold 'the Gap of the north', the glensmen of south Derry, or north Antrim.[32]

His examination of the Irish past was not without its faults and prejudices, but it was not the romanticised past of Cú Chulainn and a heroic Ireland that others of his generation fostered. His was a researched past, based on detailed historical enquiry and forensic analysis of primary sources. As Ferriter's essay shows, he was critical of those who were preoccupied with the drama of heroism. MacNeill remarked:

> It teaches young people to regard their country or their nation not so much as a thing which they should be satisfied to serve, but rather a stage upon which they may expect to play a part in the drama of heroism and that notion has become very widespread ...[33]

Historiography has not always been kind to MacNeill. Much of the impetus behind earlier studies of him stemmed from the publication and propagation of often unkind and sometimes two-dimensional depictions of him. Many of those who wrote the first popular histories of the 1916 Rising, some of them participants, some contemporary observers from near and far, make MacNeill out to be something of a narrative device rather than a complex historical actor in his own right. In 1937, Dorothy McArdle cast MacNeill's role in the foundation of the Volunteers as being one in which he was a mere figurehead used by others: 'an ideal name under which to launch a movement which, if openly fathered by known Separatists, would have been instantly suppressed'.[34]

By 1949, Desmond Ryan, who had been Pearse's secretary, and a former pupil and tutor at St Enda's, cast MacNeill as duped and duplicitous; honourable yet indecisive.[35] Ryan claimed to have overheard the infamous confrontation when MacNeill 'in a towering rage' woke Pearse at St Enda's in the early hours of Friday, 21 April 1916 to confront him about the deception to which he had been subjected.[36] Ryan recalled Pearse's reply to MacNeill as 'Yes, you were deceived, but it was necessary.' Of the deception, Ryan gave a vivid summary of his sentiments on MacNeill, asserting that

> MacNeill had run away from the truth that had stared him in the face if he had only the courage to face it: that Pearse, Clarke and Connolly had been bent on insurrection from the outbreak of the war. It was MacNeill's own evasiveness and refusal to come to grips with the real problem, his temperamental caution, his proneness to play for safety and non-action beyond the last possible minute that had moved Connolly to suspicion and active hostility, the astuteness with even

a touch of cunning that led him to hide in bland isolation in his study behind the barricades of platitudes and syllogisms ... MacNeill, majestic in wrathful innocence, outraged behind a flowing beard and waving mane ...[37]

Tierney rather caustically attributed this and other early unfavourable depictions of MacNeill to

... the influence of Marxist propaganda [on] so many writers about the period 1913–21 [who] are inclined to treat movements, parties, and personalities of the time as Hegelian abstractions, assigning to them only the qualities which fit their preordained role in a preconceived pseudo-history. It is more likely, however, that this is an older human tendency, and that Marxism and mythology here reinforce each other. Irish history in those years is seen as a dramatic and largely fictitious *Risorgimento*, in which the people involved are given no more reality than the characters in the *Commedia dell' Arte*. They are not characters: they are merely roles, fixed almost more by tradition than by any historical reality.[38]

In the run-up to the fiftieth anniversary of the rising, the MacNeill family were especially put out by the depiction of Eoin in Max Caulfield's *The Easter Rebellion* which was first published in 1963. Tierney lambasts Caulfield's description of his father-in-law as 'the eminently respectable Professor of Archaic Gaelic at the National University of Ireland' and describes this as an example of Caulfield's 'Punch-and-Judy method of writing history'.[39] Ryan could at least claim some credibility, as Pearse's secretary, to have been auditor, if not witness, to the exchange between MacNeill and Pearse on the night of 20–21 April 1916. Caulfield, meanwhile, without citation, provides his own alternative text for the dialogue between Pearse and MacNeill on that night with fresh flourishes and interpolations not present in Ryan's version of events.[40]

MacNeill presents a real challenge as the subject of the present volume. At various points along the journey of researching, editing and writing for this book, we have been forced to ask ourselves to what extent did MacNeill really matter? Was he really central to things or was he a sort of interested and interesting professor who turned up and was tangentially involved in various cultural, political and paramilitary movements that were steered and led by others? While this is a legitimate question to ask, the answer time and again has been that MacNeill mattered. Even more so than his leadership of movements – which at times could be decisive – MacNeill's singular contribution to the Irish revolution and the foundation of independent Ireland is that he was one of the wellsprings of its ideological underpinnings and he acted both as a creator and a guide for the ideas and the idealists of the revolution, especially in understanding and illuminating historical precedents, be they real or imagined.

Like Tom Clarke in Fenian circles, there is evidence to suggest that part of MacNeill's significance to his contemporaries had a generational element to it. The younger revolutionaries looked up to MacNeill and, for his part, he saw a role for himself within the independence movement with which he was familiar both from fatherhood and teaching. On the day of Desmond Fitzgerald's twenty-eighth birthday, MacNeill wrote to his wife Agnes from Lewes prison:

> I cannot feel myself a bit old, and among these younger men I seem to myself to be as young as they are ... I say to myself for aren't they foolish & with that comes the counterthought – am not I foolish to think so? ... what must I expect but boyishness in comrades averaging perhaps less than half my age & some of them as young as my own boys at home?[41]

These young men would go on to become MacNeill's cabinet colleagues. MacNeill's age came up again towards the end of his political career when, aged fifty-seven, he opted to be the Free State's representative on the Irish Boundary Commission in Patrick McGilligan's stead. McGilligan had been a rising star among the students at the National University and MacNeill argued that 'the ripest fruit falls first'. He insisted to cabinet that the thirty-five-year-old McGilligan had his political career ahead of him and that, if an Ulsterman must take on the role it would be him, apparently acknowledging from the outset that the Boundary Commission would 'damage rather than assist the political career of a commissioner'.[42]

Aspects of MacNeill's legacy which seemed to the editors to have fallen between the 'scholar' and 'revolutionary' include the activist, the revivalist and the theorist. Offering a root and branch reinterpretation of MacNeill's 'scholar' and 'revolutionary' personae, Johnston's essay challenges the casual yet pervasive criticism that Robin Dudley Edwards levelled at MacNeill, namely that he put patriotism over history and Volunteering over academic work. Johnston argues forcefully that Edwards has missed the point: the peaks of activity in MacNeill's intellectual life did not occur in a vacuum of splendid isolation but rather they overlapped with the phases of his greatest political (and paramilitary) activity. Johnston shows that 'Far from being an accidental activist or a disappointed scholar, MacNeill was both intensely political and intensely academic. The two went hand-in-hand.'

MacNeill somehow never became as synonymous with the foundation of the Gaelic League as did Douglas Hyde in the popular imagination but, as Mac Mathúna forcefully establishes here, MacNeill was right at the centre of language revivalism at every twist and turn in its three formative decades from the 1890s to the 1920s. Uí Chollatáin takes a deep look at MacNeill's contribution as a language activist, a newspaperman, and a wellspring of the Gaelic Revival through his pioneering journalism first with *Irisleabhar na Gaedhilge* and subsequently with *Fáinne an Lae / An Claidheamh Soluis*. MacNeill's success, Uí Chollatáin argues, was not merely in making a case for the Irish language but in cultivating a literate public through a combination of classes and print journalism so that the revival could propagate under its own momentum.

Kennedy's essay delves into one of MacNeill's lasting institutional legacies: the establishment in 1928 of the Irish Manuscripts Commission (IMC). The main impetus to found the IMC arose out of necessity following the destruction of Ireland's archival heritage in the opening salvoes of the Civil War in June 1922. However, Kennedy traces MacNeill's ideas for the IMC back even further to the preface to *Celtic Ireland* in 1921 showing that the project had a deeper intellectual basis than the reactive necessity to preserve and publish manuscript sources after the archival cataclysm of 1922.

In politics, MacNeill's habitually idealist conception of the world came up against hard-headed pragmatists both among his allies and his enemies. Laffan examines MacNeill in 1916 at arguably his most decisive. Although he did not succeed in his ultimate object of stopping the rising, MacNeill's countermanding order was the defining moment in his political life. He summoned a resolve and clarity of action that were not otherwise hallmarks of his usually pensive and pluralistic outlook, traits that had otherwise stood him in good stead in the Gaelic League and in academia. If the imbroglio of Holy Week marked a new dawn in MacNeill's political career, Hallett's essay on the Irish Boundary Commission explores the event that would ultimately extinguish MacNeill's life in active politics. Here we find a less decisive MacNeill who foundered in the chaos following the leak of the Commission's report by the *Morning Post* in November 1925.

As to how MacNeill reflected upon his own life and times, in 1932 he published an article entitled 'Ten Years of the Irish Free State' in *Foreign Affairs*. This was written for an international audience, with states within and beyond the British Commonwealth in mind. The article stands as a succinct summary of Cumann na nGaedheal's achievements during the 1920s from one who was at the cabinet table for much of that period. The article offers a rare insight into how MacNeill viewed his record as minister for education (1922–5), a subject that receives only one fleeting reference in Tierney's biography nor is it covered in his memoir.[43] In 1932, MacNeill wrote that

> The education policy in the Irish Free State has been based mainly on the principle of state aid rather than on the principle of state control. As Minister of Education in the first years of the Free State I entertained no doubt that to bring the whole direction of the education of the young under political control would be a more radical and penetrating form of state socialism than the political control of the material means of economic production and distribution.[44]

He went on to criticise his counterpart in Northern Ireland, Lord Londonderry, for adopting 'the policy of state control, with the result that his government has ever since been in continual conflict not only with the Catholics, always opposed to that policy, but with a large body of Protestant opinion which rejects the view that education is wholly and rightly a function of the state'.[45]

MacNeill's reluctance to engage with his portfolio at the Department of Education might be best explained by his admission to the Dáil in 1923 that 'To speak plainly, I assure you I have what I could hardly describe with any other word, a horror of State-made education'.[46] MacNeill had been consistent on this view throughout the years prior to independence. In the absence of state intervention, the pattern of denominational influence over Irish education, already present under the union, carried on into the Free State years and beyond. In the aforementioned *Foreign Affairs* article from 1932, we also learn that MacNeill believed that the imperial and industrial British educational model that was inherited by the Free State geared school leavers towards emigration. 'The standard of success was not the betterment of the surrounding community but the degree in which education enabled a proportion of the pupils to become sharers and helpers in the prosperity of some distant city or country.'[47] By contrast, MacNeill asserted that

Under the Free State administration some beginnings of reform,
tending to give another direction to educational purpose, have been
instituted, but it can hardly be said that the popular mind has yet been
able to recover the idea of the school as a means towards local and
thereby towards national well-being.[48]

As Mac Mathúna notes in the present volume, the educational policy with
which MacNeill is most often credited – compulsory Irish – was actually
initiated by his predecessor, Fionán Ó Loingsigh. While MacNeill was
indeed responsible for much of the rollout of the policy, his record as
minister saw his Executive Council colleagues fielding Dáil questions on
educational matters on his behalf.[49]

Finally, looking to the present day and MacNeill's relevance to it:
academically, MacNeill played a founding role in a new national university
project; politically, he offered a nuanced, even symbiotic vision of European
nationalism. To the generation who would go on to realise a form of
statehood out of the Irish national idea, MacNeill delivered a historically
rooted articulation of Irish identity that went as far back as written sources
would permit. In doing so, MacNeill redefined both contemporary notions
of identity and scholarly conceptions of the Irish medieval past. Contrasting
Ireland's history with that of various imperialisms, he asserted that, once
the Gaelic Irish had Christianised, they never 'sought domination or any
partnership in domination over other lands or other peoples'.[50] MacNeill's
vision of 'nationality' as opposed to 'nationalism' seems to have contrasted
sharply with that of European contemporaries who were at that time drifting
into totalitarianism and when members of his own party were glancing
admiringly in that same direction.[51] In 1981, Ó Corráin stressed that

> Mac Neill's enthusiasm for the national state was subtly tempered
> by a deep appreciation of the dangers of nationalism to European
> civilisation.
>
> Far from being a narrow nationalist, Mac Neill was very consciously
> a European and he saw the study of early Irish history as an invaluable
> contribution to European culture: 'Irish law is one of the most
> European things that can be known, an essential chapter in the history
> of European civilisation.'[52]

On commemoration and reconciliation too, MacNeill was ahead of his time.
In the *Handbook of the Ulster Question*, a volume produced for international

distribution by the Free State's North Eastern Boundary Bureau in 1923, MacNeill and J.W. Good concluded their historical survey of Ulster with sentiments of national reconciliation through joint commemoration. Their co-authored, but unattributed, contribution to the volume concluded that

> Within the nation the heroisms of Limerick and Derry would be the common property of the Irish people, and the victory of the Boyne would be a common inspiration as much as the victory of Benburb. All Frenchmen are heirs of the French Revolution and the wars of Napoleon, just as all Americans are heirs of Washington and the battles of the Civil War.
>
> The national idea reconciles not only differences of race, religion, character, and ideals, but even bitter domestic feuds, so that from the widest range of differences is evolved an enfolding and stimulating unity.[53]

Here, in an unlikely anti-partitionist publication, MacNeill and Good give a foreshadowing of the language of peace and reconciliation which would become intrinsic to the Northern Irish peace process seven decades later.

MacNeill's relationship with the National University of Ireland is explored by Cullen in his examination of the Irish university question, and by Mac Mathúna who demonstrates that MacNeill played a pivotal role in the success of 1908–9 campaign to have Irish recognised as an essential matriculation requirement for the NUI. This was a significant achievement for the Irish language movement and, as Cullen points out, it also shows how MacNeill helped shape higher education in Ireland. MacNeill was also a member of the first NUI Senate (1908–14). Reflecting the Ireland of the time, membership of the Senate was diverse. As Donal McCartney notes, at one end of the political spectrum were the Tories and the Unionist members, the Redmondites were in the middle, at the other extreme were the cultural nationalists. Irish Unionist James Campbell, MP for Dublin University, once complained that among them 'was a mere clerk in the Civil Service whom he had never heard of before. The only qualification which Campbell could find that the clerk possessed was that he was Vice-President of an organisation known as the Gaelic League. He was, of course, referring to Eoin MacNeill'.[54] In 1918, MacNeill was elected for the NUI constituency and for Derry City. In keeping with Sinn Féin policy, he abstained from Westminster and took his seat in the first Dáil in January 1919. He was returned for the NUI Dáil constituency in subsequent elections: 1921 and 1922 as a Sinn Féin candidate and for Cumann na nGaedheal in 1923. Having been elected for two constituencies in the 1923 general election, MacNeill opted to sit for the constituency of Clare and a by-election was held to fill his Dáil seat for the NUI constituency in which he had topped the poll.[55] Although he abstained, MacNeill was one of six Sinn Féin MPs elected to the first Parliament of Northern Ireland (1921–5) where he was returned as MP for the county constituency of Londonderry. Finally, when a general election was called in June 1927, MacNeill opted to re-contest the NUI seat he had left in 1923 rather than going for re-election in Clare. Factors including the fallout from the Boundary Commission, the automatic filling of one seat by the then ceann comhairle Michael Hayes, and a lack of support from his party meant he was unsuccessful, coming in third in a contest for the two vacant seats. This would mark the end of MacNeill's career in parliamentary politics. However, a few months later when a fresh general election was held in September 1927, Michael Tierney, who had previously sat for North Mayo, was successful in securing the final NUI Dáil seat his father-in-law had narrowly missed out upon just three months previously.

Given his association with NUI as Professor of Early (including Medieval) Irish History in UCD from 1909 until 1941, it is fitting that his successor to the chair at UCD, John Ryan, received funding from both NUI and UCD towards the publication of MacNeill's festschrift.[56] Published in 1940 and following very much in Germanic academic tradition, it was one of the first such honorary volumes in Irish academic circles. The content and contributors demonstrate both the wide range of MacNeill's scholarly interests and the esteem with which he was held both in Ireland and abroad.

The reassessments this book undertakes – deconstructing MacNeill's life and work and clearing out the mythology that has been built up by MacNeill's admirers, his detractors and the man himself – means that the present volume does a service to modern understanding of historiography, to political and cultural history, and to biography itself.

Eoin MacNeill: a family perspective

MICHAEL McDOWELL

In the decade 2012 to 2022, frequently referred to nowadays in Ireland as 'a decade of centenaries', I have been asked in a number of different ways to reflect on some of those events from the perspective of a descendant of one of the leading figures in Ireland's national struggle for independence. I do not claim any special authority for family members of historical figures; it is, however, almost inevitable that family connections colour one's views of historical events.[1] Any examination of my grandfather Eoin MacNeill and his part in the events of 1916 must start with a close understanding of his background. He was born in Glenarm in County Antrim in 1867, of Catholic parents who lived in the Glens, an enclave in Protestant east Ulster. His father Archie, a tough local tradesman, was by times a shipwright, a baker, a builder and the proprietor of the local postal service in Glenarm, a mixed community. His mother, Rosetta, was the daughter of Dr Charles McAuley also of Glenarm. Archie was prosecuted and acquitted arising out of unrest during an Orange demonstration in Glenarm when Eoin was just five years old. One of a family of eight, Eoin benefited from a family determination to seek good education for the children. Unlike three of his brothers who were sent to Belvedere in Dublin, Eoin was sent to St Malachy's in Belfast and obtained a scholarship to study for a degree of the Royal University, graduating in Constitutional History, Jurisprudence, and Political Economy in 1888. The previous year he had obtained by examination a junior clerkship in the Accountant General's Office in the Four Courts, becoming the first Catholic to have such an appointment, which previously had been made on the basis of Dublin Castle patronage.

As an undergraduate, he had begun in 1887 to study the Irish language, which was virtually extinct in the Glenarm of his childhood. From basic learning of the spoken language (on grinds for which he spent a quarter of his small starting salary), he graduated to the study of Old and Middle Irish, and quickly became an expert in matters Gaelic. Along with Douglas Hyde, he co-founded the Gaelic League (Conradh na Gaeilge) and started to develop a theory of Irish identity that was a blend of his political, linguistic and religious outlooks. In his role as editor of the *Gaelic Journal*, as co-editor of *Fáinne an Lae* and as the first editor of *An Claidheamh Soluis*, he became a leading figure in the Irish language movement. It was in this context that he met and befriended the young Pádraig Pearse, a relationship that became of central importance to later events in 1916.

At the turn of the nineteenth and twentieth centuries MacNeill became increasingly politically active and took a leading role in the debate on the university question which led to the foundation of the National University of Ireland (NUI) in 1908. He was appointed Professor of Early Irish (including Medieval) History in University College Dublin (UCD) in 1909.

THE VOLUNTEERS

Four years later, in 1913, he wrote a leading article in *An Claidheamh Soluis* entitled 'The North Began', calling for nationalists in Ireland to consider establishing a Volunteer force to counterbalance the Ulster Volunteers of Edward Carson, and describing the Ulster Volunteers as a positive step towards national self-determination.[2] On foot of 'The North Began', MacNeill was approached by a number of figures in the Irish Republican Brotherhood (IRB) and some of their associates to ask him to lead the process of forming the Irish Volunteers. When John Redmond imposed himself on the Irish Volunteers, MacNeill at first cooperated but later, when Redmond pledged the Volunteers to the Great War effort, sided with Pearse, Tom Clarke, Thomas MacDonagh, Bulmer Hobson and others in the split between Redmond's 'National Volunteers' and the 'Irish Volunteers' of which MacNeill was president and commander-in-chief.

However, a further, largely unseen, split was developing in the Irish Volunteers. A small IRB-based group consisting of Pearse, Clarke, Seán MacDermott, Joseph Plunkett and Éamonn Ceannt formed a secret 'military council' within the IRB. In 1916, they added James Connolly and MacDonagh to their number. The military council spent 1915 secretly plotting to start an armed insurrection against British rule in Ireland while the Great War was in progress. MacNeill's priority was to arm the Volunteers. With Roger Casement and others, he had planned the Howth and Kilcoole gun-running operations in the summer of 1914, which were modest in scale compared with the massive UVF importation at Larne in March of that year. MacNeill and Hobson (who although an IRB member was initially unaware of the military council's plans) had a different view from that of Pearse, Clarke and MacDonagh of the legitimate use of force. The IRB's own constitution prohibited any armed insurrection that had not the backing of the Irish people. MacNeill categorically rejected any notion of any violent coup unless it had a reasonable prospect of military success. In particular MacNeill was wholly opposed to the notion of 'blood sacrifice' as a way of polarising or catalysing the Irish people into a political struggle with Britain.

MacNeill, aware of Pearse's romantic and idealistic notion that an insurrection would be justified as a blood sacrifice, struggled to persuade the Irish Volunteers' executive that the use of force would only be justified (1) if the British attempted to disarm or suppress the Volunteers or (2) if the Volunteers were in a position, in terms of arms and organisation, to use force successfully to end British rule in Ireland.

THE 1916 MEMORANDUM

His memorandum on this issue (the '1916 memorandum'), written in February 1916, was a forceful and convincing exposition of his views. He suspected, but was not definitively aware, however, that Pearse and Clarke had already decided to stage an insurrection 'come what may', and did not suspect that they were willing to use any means, including deception, to bring about a 'rising'. This memorandum lay unpublished until 1961, when Professor F.X. Martin revealed it in *Irish Historical Studies* in an article entitled 'Eoin MacNeill and the 1916 Rising'. Martin's article makes for compelling reading.[3]

In 1961, F.X. Martin's article ran counter to the then prevalent 'national myth' of 1916 which had relegated MacNeill to the status of an indecisive, incompetent academic 'bit player' who had somehow brought about by his indecision the military failure of the rising. Hobson, though an IRB man, once he learned of preparations, attempted to alert MacNeill to the secret plotting for a rising. He and MacNeill believed that the Volunteers should not stage a rising during the Great War but should wait for its end, a scenario in which, regardless of the outcome of the war, there would be an influx of returning Irish soldiers to strengthen the Volunteers. In the meantime, MacNeill and Hobson argued that the greatest priority was to secure arms for the Volunteers. If the Volunteers were to be outlawed, they believed that a guerrilla-type campaign would be more successful (a view which Michael Collins was later to adopt and implement). Compounding this dispute within the Volunteers was the determination of James Connolly to stage a violent socialist uprising through the involvement of the Irish Citizen Army, a group that had emerged in the context of the 1913 Lockout. Because Connolly's Citizen Army revolution had no prospect of success, the Volunteers were naturally convinced that it would almost certainly be used by Dublin Castle as a pretext to disarm and suppress the Irish Volunteers. MacNeill, at the request of Pearse, met with Connolly to dissuade him from starting any armed conflict. Pearse was present at this meeting and later informed MacNeill that Connolly had been persuaded by MacNeill's argument to abandon any thought of unilateral action by the Citizen Army. But, in reality, Pearse had secretly assured Connolly that an early rising was being planned in which he and the Citizen Army could take part.[4]

It was in that context that MacNeill wrote and circulated the 1916 memorandum. It was discussed at a day-long meeting at MacNeill's residence in Woodtown Park in Rathfarnham during which Pearse expressly disavowed any plan for armed insurrection. In the opening words of the 1916 memorandum, MacNeill stated:

> The only reason that could justify general active military measures – as distinct from military preparations – on the part of Irish nationalists would be a reasonably calculated or estimated prospect of success, in the military sense.
>
> Without that prospect, military action (not military preparation) would in the first place be morally wrong – and that consideration to my mind is final and conclusive. To enter deliberately on a course of action which is morally wrong is to incur the guilt not only of that action itself but of all its direct consequences. For example, to kill any person in carrying out such a course of action is murder. The guilt of murder in that case falls on those who have planned and ordered the general course of action on the party which makes such course of action inevitable. The success which is calculated or estimated must be success in the operation itself, not merely some further moral or political advantage which may be hoped for as the result of non-success.[5]

The memorandum goes on to dismiss any policy based on 'feelings' or 'instincts' and pleas for reason to prevail. He argued strongly against any premature use of force with no prospect of military success and against any rising while the Great War was in progress simply based on the claim that 'Ireland has always struck too late'. He said, 'We must listen to nothing except proper preparation and proper calculation.'[6]

On Pearse's notion of a blood sacrifice, MacNeill's memorandum had this to say, clearly directed personally at Pearse:

> There is a feeling in some minds that action is necessary, that lives must be sacrificed, in order to produce an ultimate effect on the national mind. As a principle of action, I have heard that feeling disclaimed, but I did not fully accept the disclaimer. In fact, it is a sounder principle than any of the others I have dealt with. If the destruction of our nationality was in sight, and we came to the conclusion that at best the vital principle of nationality was to be saved by laying down our lives, then we should make that sacrifice without hesitation. It would not be a military act in any sense, and it does not come within the scope of our military counsels [sic].[7]

This passage demonstrates that MacNeill understood and was partly sympathetic to Pearse's fervour, but also underlines his conviction that it was morally wrong to drag other innocent people into a futile self-sacrifice or to kill others in pursuit of self-sacrifice. He was simply not willing to sacrifice the Irish Volunteers as a movement and all the inevitable victims of an early insurrection to 'produce an ultimate effect on the national mind'. This, then, was the line of intellectual and moral cleavage between the patriots who met that day in March 1916 at Woodtown Park in Rathfarnham.

MacNeill's memorandum had spelt out at length the inevitability of a military defeat for any rising and pointed out to the conspirators that the Volunteers' state of preparation outside Dublin was negligible. But he wrote:

> ... [W]hereas in my conscientious judgment an armed revolt at present would be wrong and unpatriotic and criminal, it is quite a different case with regard to the possession and retention of our arms. I have not the slightest doubt on the point that we are morally and in every way justified in keeping by all necessary force such arms as we have got or can get. I hold myself entitled to resist to the death any attempt to deprive me of my arms or ammunition or other military articles that I have or can protect for myself or the Irish Volunteers. If

in such resistance, any man meets his death through my act or counsel or command, I shall have no guilt on my conscience.[8]

THE 'CASTLE DOCUMENT' AND MacNEILL'S PRE- AND POST-RISING MEMORANDA

The Pearse, Clarke and MacDonagh faction affected to accept MacNeill's argument at the Woodtown Park meeting, but secretly they decided to subvert it by composing a forged document purporting to be a Dublin Castle decision to disarm, arrest and suppress the Irish Volunteers. Knowing that MacNeill would authorise the use of violence in such a scenario, all they had to do was to produce false but convincing evidence – and that is why they concocted the famous 'Castle document'.[9]

As F.X. Martin put it:

> In the light of MacNeill's attitude it is obvious that the 'Castle document' was 'a most opportune document' for the members of the I.R.B. who were trying to manoeuvre MacNeill to support for an armed rebellion ... It was the news on Holy Friday morning of the expected arrival of the *Aud* with arms for the Volunteers which decided MacNeill to support the plan for gun-running at Fenit, and thereby risk an almost inevitable armed collision with the British forces.[10]

The great historical value of MacNeill's memorandum of February 1916 is that it was written *before* the rising and is therefore completely devoid of post-factum justification or reasoning.

In a second memorandum (the '1917 memorandum') written in the latter half of 1917 at the request of Hobson, MacNeill, who had been released from a life sentence imposed on him by a general court martial in 1916 for his part in the rising, set out at length his account of what happened in the period November 1915 to April 1916. The 1917 memorandum makes compelling reading too.[11] It shows how the Pearse, Clarke and MacDonagh plan was concealed from MacNeill and how they forged the 'Castle document' to win him over to armed action. It gives a very vivid account of MacNeill's journey from Woodtown Park in Rathfarnham to St Enda's in Rathfarnham on Holy Thursday 1916 where MacNeill confronted Pearse with his knowledge of their plan for a rising. MacNeill's account shows him as having been resigned to a rising up until midday on Easter Saturday when

The O'Rahilly and Seán Fitzgibbon came to Woodtown Park and revealed to MacNeill that orders for a rising had been issued on the false basis that they were authorised by MacNeill, and crucially that the 'Castle document' was a forgery designed to bring him over to the planned rising.

It was in that context that MacNeill at last countermanded the manoeuvres that were to initiate the rising. The order was largely effective except in Dublin where the rising's planners were in control of the Volunteers. MacNeill states:

> It is also untrue that I changed my mind several times. For a few hours I was convinced that all was over with our movement and nothing left for us except to sell our lives as dearly as possible. When The O'Rahilly and Fitzgibbon came to me on Holy Saturday, we agreed that the situation was by no means so desperate and that the rising ought to be prevented, and The O'Rahilly gave more help than any other person to prevent it.[12]

But Pearse, while assuring MacNeill in a written message as late as Easter Saturday that the countermanding order would be implemented, was in reality busily re-scheduling the rising for Easter Monday. Commenting on the two memoranda, F.X. Martin said:

> Perhaps the most noticeable characteristic of both memoranda is their dispassionate line. MacNeill condemns nobody, though he might have considered himself to have reasonable grounds for resentment. Pearse, in his last dispatch from the GPO, on Friday 28th April, declared that 'Both Eoin MacNeill and we have acted in the best interests of Ireland', and MacNeill was no less courteous during his court martial to the revolutionary leaders.[13]

MacNeill actually remained unaware that a military council or 'council of four' within the IRB had pre-determined on a rising until he met with Mrs Tom Clarke in the aftermath of his release from prison in 1917 while assisting Éamon de Valera in his campaign for the Clare East by-election.[14] Mrs Clarke, Countess Markievicz and Helena Molony had previously bitterly attacked MacNeill at the Sinn Féin convention in 1917 for his action in countermanding the rising. The great majority, however, vigorously defended MacNeill. In the result, MacNeill topped the poll in the election for the Sinn Féin ard-chomhairle leaving his critics far behind him in terms of votes.[15]

Also elected on that occasion with the narrowest of margins was a young 1916 veteran called Michael Collins. Collins never doubted MacNeill's sincerity or integrity. Indeed, in 1922, when asked by American journalist Hayden Talbot to comment on MacNeill's decision to countermand the rising, Collins told Talbot that he had never discussed the issue with MacNeill, and urged him to interview MacNeill on the matter. Talbot did so and Collins, on learning of the account given by MacNeill in the interview, accepted MacNeill's explanation.

MacNeill was quoted by Talbot as having described the executed 1916 leaders as 'patriots' motivated by 'pure martyrdom'. He ascribed the result of their execution as their 'fondest dreams' being 'exceeded'.[16] Furthermore, he is quoted by Talbot as saying that, if it were argued that their pre-vision was good and his bad, he could make no comment except that even if he had known fully of their plan, he would still have countermanded the rising. He believed it was the madness of British reactive violence in suppressing the rising and executing its leaders that created the conditions for Irish independence.

It is also notable that MacNeill unreservedly backed the War of Independence. His three eldest sons became active members and officers in the 6th Battalion of the Irish Republican Army (IRA) in south Dublin. During the War of Independence his home at Netley in Booterstown was raided and searched on a number of occasions. MacNeill and members of his family were arrested. But none of the searches ever revealed the secret compartment specially built in the ground floor of the house that was the arms dump for the 6th Battalion. By using his home in this way MacNeill was again putting his life on the line for Irish freedom.

An indication of MacNeill's personal commitment to the morality of the War of Independence can be gleaned from a letter that he sent to the Archbishop of Tuam on 22 July 1920, in a context that the Archbishop was reported as saying that the shooting of two Royal Irish Constabulary (RIC) men near Tuam, although a 'dastardly crime', could not justify the subsequent sacking of the town by Black and Tans in reprisal.[17]

MacNeill, a devout Catholic, wrote to the Archbishop:

> Either we Irishmen are morally entitled to carry arms or we are not. If we are, we are entitled to defend our right and if the so-called 'police', who are well known to Your Grace to be no police but a mere branch of the British military forces, endanger our lives in the exercise of that right, Your Grace can define the extent of resistance that is morally justifiable.

It is surely not a case for vagueness, and till we know our rights supposing the present belief of the people in general and their present conscientious conviction to be mistaken – we are justified in protesting against your Lordship's use of the term 'murder' even without the qualifying adjective.

If on the other hand we have no right to bear arms, surely Your Grace ought to say so, for undoubtedly the bearing of arms, being the occasion of shooting on sight by those in command of the so-called police, will also be the occasion of the so-called police being shot at sight.

For my part I have not the slightest doubt that I am entitled to bear arms in defence of Ireland against the British forces, and that I am also entitled to resist being disarmed to the same degree as I may resist an attempt to destroy my house or my life or the lives of my family.

I am not bound to put up my hands when ordered to do so by any subordinate of the British Government. I have the clearest evidence therefore that my life and the rights I am entitled to defend unto death are <u>always</u> threatened by the so-called 'police'. Does Your Grace really believe that this state of mind implies that I am at heart and in conscience a murderer, not to say a dastard.

I am, my Lord Archbishop,
Your Grace's faithful servant
Eoin MacNeill[18]

The echoes of his 1916 memorandum are striking.

One can only assume that MacNeill had believed in 1920–2 (and rightly as it turned out) that the War of Independence had a good 'calculation of success', while in March to April 1916 he judged that a rising had none. For a man who, two years later, on 20 September 1922, was to lose his second son Brian to an on-the-spot execution by his own Irish Free State forces on the slopes of Ben Bulben, the moral complexities of MacNeill's views on the use of force are striking. Brian, like his two brothers Niall and Turlough, had enlisted in the South Dublin IRA's 6th Battalion and all three were members of an active service unit that played a leading role in the War of Independence from 1919 to 1921.

The three boys were on the run and imprisoned during that period. During the truce, Brian was sent by IRA GHQ to help reorganise the IRA in Sligo, north Roscommon and east Mayo. He was appointed divisional adjutant. When the IRA split over the treaty, Brian's division went anti-treaty. With a heavy heart, his loyalty to his division outweighed his loyalty to his father and to his brothers, both of whom became commissioned officers in the National Army.

After the death of Michael Collins, General Richard Mulcahy put strong pressure on General Seán Mac Eoin, his western commander, to bring a quick and decisive end to the Civil War in Sligo and the west. Dáil Éireann had passed a resolution giving the National Army powers to conduct field courts martial and to execute 'Irregulars' found under arms. What happened on the slopes of Ben Bulben is not certain, but it appears most probable that Brian and his comrades surrendered, were disarmed and shot by their captors. Apparently, Brian MacNeill, realising what was about to happen, attempted to run and was shot a short distance from where the other three were gunned down.

The Free State forces published untrue and highly misleading accounts of the killings and privately gave the MacNeill family a further untrue but consoling version of the shootings. 'Sligo's Noble Six', as the victims became known, became symbols of Civil War cruelty.[19] They remain embedded in the political and historical fabric of County Sligo to this day. For MacNeill, his wife Taddie, and their children, this was a cause of unimaginable grief and misgivings, which they dealt with entirely privately, and an horrendous outcome to their participation in the struggle for Irish freedom. A letter written by MacNeill at the height of the Civil War gives some insight into his grief, and his pride in and his love for his lost son. In the end, Brian's coffin was borne by his brothers and by fellow IRA comrades now wearing Free State uniforms, to his family grave at Kilbarrack in Dublin. Such was, and is, the reality of civil war.

So too was his defence of the notorious summary executions at Mountjoy on 8 December 1922, in reprisal for the shooting of two pro-treaty TDs. On that occasion he informed the Dáil that it was a case of clear legal and moral justification and invited anyone to prosecute him for murder. These events show that MacNeill's views on the morality of the use of force were based always on deep subjective conviction tempered by his strong sense of principle.

It can be argued that the two episodes of MacNeill's life that attracted most criticism from nationalist critics – countermanding the 1916 Rising and failing to obtain a border much more favourable to northern nationalists in the Boundary Commission report – have turned out, in retrospect, to be wiser in terms of Irish independence and Irish unity. A more widespread rising in 1916 would probably have resulted in a greater repression and destruction of the Volunteer movement and reduced capacity to wage the War of Independence. Likewise, if the Boundary Commission had resulted in a readjustment of the border so as to transfer large areas of nationalist Ulster into the Irish Free State, the prospect of a thirty-two county united Ireland might well have been permanently extinguished.

For all these and many other reasons, MacNeill deserves close and detached study; his influence on Irish history is significant. In more than one sense he was a foremost author of Irish history.

Scholar

Eoin MacNeill's Contribution to the Study of Medieval Irish law

KEVIN MURRAY

What set Eoin MacNeill apart as a medieval Irish historian was his facility in dealing with texts written in Old, Middle, Early Modern and Modern Irish. He was one of the first historians of medieval Ireland in the modern era who was able to deal competently with original documents in the vernacular from all periods of Ireland's past. The combination of linguistic training in the older language and fluency in the modern tongue, allied with a finely honed historical sensibility and a keen analytical mind, meant that he was able to interrogate and interpret texts in a manner altogether different from the historians who had preceded him. Those of his contemporaries and before who had possessed the linguistic skills in Irish often did not have the requisite historical nous, while many of the best medieval historians of the period – though very comfortable with Latin sources – frequently struggled when faced with texts in the Irish language.

MacNeill's multi-faceted capacities were a reflection not just of his natural abilities, but of the education and training he received, particularly under the guidance of Father Edmund Hogan SJ.[1] He was an adult learner of Modern Irish on the Aran Islands and a student of all periods of the language with Hogan, and subsequently contributed to his editions of texts such as *Cath Ruis na Ríg for Bóinn* ('The Battle of Rosnaree on the Boyne') and *The Irish Nennius*.[2] Along with his brother Charles, MacNeill later went on to assist Hogan in the creation of his *magnum opus, Onomasticon Goedelicum*.[3] This consequent grounding in the study of place- and tribal-names stood him in good stead for the rest of his academic career and led to numerous valuable onomastic publications from his pen.[4] More importantly, however, it opened up sources to him that remained central to all his work on medieval Irish history, a fact that he himself acknowledged:

> *Onomasticon Goedelicum* has and will long continue to have a value far beyond a topographical dictionary. It supplies innumerable clues to guide the research student through the labyrinths of early and

medieval Irish history. I have found by experience that, by following its references to the manuscripts or printed sources, one may often expect to discover or link up information so as to gain insight into matters of history which would otherwise be altogether obscure.[5]

This emphasis on sources permeates all of MacNeill's scholarship on medieval Ireland. He edited and analysed numerous genealogical texts, provided the standard editions of many Fenian lays, worked on *Lebor Gabála Érenn* (The Book of the Taking of Ireland) with R.A.S. Macalister, edited and translated some lengthy Middle Irish poems, numerous Modern Irish tales and a number of pieces of folklore (to list just some of his better-known work on sources).[6] The range and extent of his interests, and the competency that he displayed in dealing with texts in Irish of all periods ensured that he stood apart in the field of medieval Irish history.

Ironically, he admitted himself that his initial interest was in the language and that it was only under the influence of Father Hogan that this began to change:

> [Hogan's] own natural bent was for history, and a list of his published works in order of date will show clearly that his studies in Irish were at first only accessory to his studies in Irish history. In my case it was just the converse. Coming to him for instruction in Irish, I began to discover how little I knew of the history of my country and how little of its history was to be learned from the books of Irish history that people read.[7]

The training he received in the Irish language – and in editing, analysing and interpreting vernacular texts – was to remain at the cornerstone of his scholarship throughout his career. This commitment to sources is also evident from the central role he played in the establishment of the Irish Manuscripts Commission in 1928.[8] Many editions of primary sources were published under the chairmanship of MacNeill, and facsimiles in collotype of Irish manuscripts were also made available. The first of these was issued in Dublin in 1931, titled *The Oldest Fragments of the Senchas Már*.[9]

That a legal manuscript should be the first facsimile to see the light of day from the Commission should come as no surprise considering the significance that MacNeill attached to the study of early Irish law, more popularly known as 'Brehon law'.[10] This is reflected in his comment that the 'laws and institutions, in fact the whole civilisation of ancient Ireland, have an interest and importance passing far beyond the bounds of Irish history'.[11]

Furthermore, his BA degree – awarded by the Royal University of Ireland in 1888 – was in Economics, Jurisprudence and Constitutional History and he had long recognised the importance of legal studies to a fuller understanding of medieval and early modern Irish society.[12] However, he was well aware that the 'official' editions of the native laws – issued in six volumes as *The Ancient Laws of Ireland* (*ALI*) – were deeply flawed and unreliable;[13] they were famously referred to by Whitley Stokes as 'Curiosities of Official Scholarship' in the article of the same name.[14] Before undertaking any detailed work on the law texts, MacNeill published a paper on succession to kingship in medieval Ireland which was to kick-start a protracted debate on the topic which is still ongoing.[15] His major contribution to this debate was to recognise that the term *rígdomna* did not mean 'royal heir' or 'crown prince' but referred instead to those who were eligible for the kingship. His essay, despite its title and though significant in legal terms, did not draw in any detailed way upon the corpus of law in its formulation.[16] However, he did place particular emphasis therein on the correct interpretation of kinship nomenclature in medieval Ireland. One of his major legal achievements subsequently was the development of this analysis of the terms for near kindred – *gelfhine* ('bright kin'), *derbfhine* ('true kin'), *íarfine* ('after kin') and *indfhine* ('end kin') – which revolutionised our understanding of the structure of medieval Irish society.[17] The model he developed laid the foundation for all subsequent work on the topic,[18] and underpins the most convincing interpretation of the evidence thus far advanced.[19]

His detailed work on the Brehon laws only commenced with his incarceration in Mountjoy jail from late 1920 until July 1921 when he worked his way through the first five volumes of *ALI*;[20] this meticulous textual endeavour formed the basis of much of his subsequent pronouncements on the topic. At an early stage in the undertaking, in December 1920, he wrote a brief introduction to the laws, which was subsequently annotated, referenced and published by Daniel Binchy nearly fifty years later.[21] The fact that Binchy – a scholar of formidable academic standards – believed that this was worth publishing substantially unchanged after such a long interval bears witness to the high esteem in which he held MacNeill and his legal scholarship.[22] For the modern reader, what stands out most about this article – apart from his beautifully controlled writing style, which permeates this contribution and his other academic publications – is the author's readiness and ability to speculate openly and to draw general conclusions from a limited amount of evidence.[23] His willingness to take such intellectual chances was informed by the following attitude:

For my part, I find nothing so instructive or so stimulating as my own mistakes, when they are discovered. I shall probably be as proud of my scars as any duellist, and why not? I can always point to the marks where Stokes hit me, and Meyer and Thurneysen and Bergin himself and sometimes the birds of the air might have flown through the holes made in me.[24]

One very significant legal publication – perhaps the most important to come from his pen – emerged from this intensive period of study: this consisted principally of re-translations of *Críth Gablach* ('The Forked Purchase') and *Uraicecht Becc* ('The Small Primer'), two of the central tracts on status in medieval Ireland.[25] Because of his in-depth knowledge of the Irish language of all periods, these translations were a major improvement on those offered in *ALI* and were welcomed, for example, by the foremost scholar of medieval Irish of the era, Rudolf Thurneysen.[26] Similar legal endeavours did not follow, however, and the possible transformative nature on the field of a succession of revised translations by MacNeill was never realised. No clear reason has been established as to why he did not pursue such research further; the preparatory work had been done and substantial gains for the study of medieval Irish history would have ensued. Binchy has suggested that MacNeill may have adopted this approach

[p]artly, perhaps, because he felt that the subject could henceforth be safely left to Thurneysen, whose celebrated articles and papers [on the Irish laws] began to appear shortly afterwards, whereas he himself had to concentrate on the vast area of early Irish history that still remained unexplored.[27]

This indeed may be true. I suspect, however, that his work on status in the law tracts also convinced him that new editions were a desideratum before fresh translations could be undertaken with confidence, and that he was minded not to undertake such work while he had other duties to attend to. Whatever the reasons, he did not pursue this particular avenue of research further, though the laws – along with the annals and genealogies – remained central to his subsequent outputs in the field of medieval Irish history.

Though he produced no further translations (or editions) from the medieval Irish legal corpus, he still remained active in the area. In 1927, MacNeill published a two-part article reviewing T.P. Ellis' study of Welsh law and custom.[28] He brought comparative material from Ireland to the fore in his analysis, restating many of his fundamental tenets derived from a close reading of the sources such as

> ancient Irish literature, including the Laws, has not revealed any consciousness of the existence of a "clan system", and the *derbfhine* ("true kin") or joint family extending to second cousins was ... an institution common to Ireland and Wales, and must be regarded as the prehistoric Celtic form of the joint family.[29]

MacNeill was also very struck by the contrasts between medieval Irish and Welsh law. For example, he notes the more dominant position assigned in the Welsh laws to the king and the concomitant prestige of the royal court, which is quite well developed in legal sources from Wales.[30] Nevertheless, he was also interested in making links between medieval legal practices in both countries. As well as drawing attention to materials that he thought had shared origins such as the joint family (mentioned above), he also highlighted the importance of the kingdoms in south Wales, which had rulers of Irish origins in the early medieval period and which, to his mind, helped 'to explain why south Wales retained a system of judicature closely comparable to the Irish system'.[31] Nevertheless, he argues that, despite the close ties between Ireland and Wales over the centuries, 'there is not much evidence of interacting influence between Irish and Welsh jurisprudence'.[32] Notwithstanding his strictures against Ellis' work,[33] MacNeill absolved him of some of his uncritical handling of Irish law because he was making use of *ALI* in which he says that 'the laws of Ireland ... have not merely not been made intelligible but have rather been obscured and confused by inadequate translations and still more by the prepossessed expositions of a series of wholly incompetent modern editors and commentators'.[34] His criticisms echo those of Whitley Stokes and were later re-echoed by Daniel Binchy.[35]

MacNeill devoted two further publications to the laws.[36] One was a short piece that he wrote for an encyclopaedia of social sciences. Though theoretically dealing with the field of Celtic law, he dispensed with Welsh law in a few lines, choosing to focus solely on the Irish material instead, arguing that these 'law tracts are more purely Celtic in tradition, much wider in scope and richer in detail, and they go back in written form to the seventh century and to a Celtic regime undisturbed by any external force except the peaceful invasion of Christianity'.[37] In this short account, MacNeill deals with the nature and structure of medieval Irish society with particular emphasis on clientship, contracts and the roles of the *rí* ('king') and *brithem* ('jurist'). A further part of his treatment focuses on the status of women in medieval Irish law, a topic of much scholarly debate at the time, as Thurneysen had conducted a seminar in the Royal Irish Academy, Dublin, on marriage law in 1929.[38] MacNeill suggests in his contribution that the 'favourable status which it [Irish law] accords to women ... may be traced to a pre-Celtic population of Ireland and Britain, the Pretani, better known by the name of Picts, among whom the family and kin were based on maternal ... descent';[39] however, such a suggestion has found very little purchase in the discipline. Nonetheless, his willingness to speculate in order to offer a possible interpretation of the facts is noteworthy once again.

In both size and scope, MacNeill's major legal publication from this period is *Early Irish Laws and Institutions*, which comprises, in essence, reprints of general talks delivered in New York University and initially published as articles in the *New York University Law Quarterly Review*.[40] In this book, he revisits many of the topics that he had treated in more detail elsewhere, such as the codification of the Irish laws; the political framework of medieval Ireland; the importance of the king and *túath* ('petty kingdom'); and the significance of clientship. Overall, however, the volume contains very little that is new and is presented in a very discursive style with little accompanying analysis; consequently, Binchy has referred to it as being 'far from satisfactory'.[41]

Outside of the medieval Irish law tracts, MacNeill also contributed much to the study of *Lebor na Cert* ('The Book of Rights'),[42] a text with a strong legalistic element.[43] This is a composition concerned with detailing the rights of – and relationships between – the king of Ireland, the main overkings and their local kings. The rights in question are the tributes that the local kings pay to their overkings; with the payments that the overkings obtain from the king of Ireland; and with the stipends that the overkings pay in turn to their local kings. These are first detailed in prose and then in verse.[44] *Lebor na Cert* is a text that MacNeill drew upon frequently in his publications. However, because he dated it earlier than modern scholarship would allow, he was inclined to attach more importance to it than it merits, believing that the text 'begins with Cashel, for the compilation was drawn up in its existing form in the interests of the claim of Brian [Boru] to the high-kingship'.[45] He further thought that the extant work was underpinned by an 'original *Book of Rights*', which he dated to *c*.AD900.[46] Subsequent scholarship has not accepted these views and the consensus would now see the main sections of *Lebor na Cert* as dating to the late eleventh century.[47] Needless to say, the redating of the text has served to lessen the significance of *Lebor na Cert* as a witness to the early historical period and consequently to undermine MacNeill's view of it as a source that can help us reconstruct 'the prehistoric background of history, and so to attain a firm basis and reliable starting point, from which we can follow clearly and without confusion the whole development of our subsequent history'.[48]

Overall, MacNeill's scholarship in the field of medieval Irish law is best understood and analysed within the context of his achievements in the broader field of medieval Irish history.[49] He was 'a pioneer of nations', to adopt the title he himself used in his article on Cenn Fáelad mac Ailella;[50] nevertheless, it took a long time before he was fully accepted into academia and his scholarly reputation only began to be secured in his forties. As late as 1909, Kuno Meyer was content to say in a letter to James G. O'Keeffe that '[Douglas] Hyde and MacNeill ... are both amateurs, as Hyde will and Mac N. ought to admit'.[51] However, Meyer's attitude changed over the following decade as the nature, scale and quality of MacNeill's contribution to medieval Irish learning became evident.[52] The extent of his ultimate acceptance may be measured by the fact that Binchy placed him alongside Thurneysen and Charles Plummer, naming them as the three scholars responsible for initiating the scientific study of medieval Irish law, and lauding MacNeill's 'pioneer work in early Irish history [which] led him to investigate the evidence supplied by the law tracts on the social and political framework of ancient Ireland'.[53] As Francis John Byrne has said, '[t]o MacNeill belongs the credit of having dragged Celtic Ireland practically single-handed from the antiquarian mists into the light of history';[54] his researches into medieval Irish law comprise a central part of this accomplishment.

Though some of MacNeill's scholarship may now seem dated, much of it has stood the test of time. The parts that have not fared so well are those where his nationalist outlook served to influence his analysis. For example, his aversion to the concept of tribalism (which he rightly felt had colonial overtones in its articulation), his adherence to a belief in the archaic nature of the institution of high-king of Ireland (*ardrí Érenn*) despite the evidence to the contrary,[55] and his insistence on the national nature of the medieval Irish legal system weakened some of the positions he held. Nevertheless, as Donnchadh Ó Corráin has pointed out, MacNeill 'laid the foundations of his discipline and struck out almost all the lines which subsequent research was to follow'.[56] This assessment, with which I fully concur, is as succinct a judgement as is possible on the continuing importance of MacNeill's scholarship to the study of medieval Ireland.

Eoin MacNeill and a 'Celtic' Church in Early Medieval Ireland?

NIAMH WYCHERLEY

On the occasion of the fifteenth centenary of St Patrick, in 1932, Eoin MacNeill made, not a 'call to arms' but a 'call to scholarship' in 'A School of Irish Church History'.[1] As the title suggests, this was an exercise in advocating for the timely establishment of a 'school', in the sense of the 'conscious collaboration' of scholars, researching the history of the Church in Ireland.[2] His dedication to early Irish history dominated his later life and 'post-political' career. Given his explicitly expressed desire that the history of the Church in Ireland be studied on a large scale, as a dedicated effort, one could wonder why MacNeill did not tackle the subject himself as a distinct object of study. Although his work played a pivotal role in forming our modern understanding of many areas of early Irish history, including the Church, he barely mentions this institution in his three popular book-length publications *Celtic Ireland, Phases of Irish History* and, perhaps most curiously, *Early Irish Laws and Institutions*.[3] The impression is that he felt it was important to determine certain 'truths' first, for example to establish a firm foundation of the history of Ireland before the arrival of Christianity. He stated that a general history of Ireland was something requested of him, but that such an undertaking was 'still premature'.[4] He referred to J.F. Kenney's great bibliographic work on the ecclesiastical sources for early Irish history as one of the vital contributions that would make such a work feasible.[5] Kenney's book, despite its age and limitations, is still a useful starting point for students of early Ireland and it has only recently been superseded by Donnchadh Ó Corráin's monumental survey of written sources produced by medieval Irish writers, the *Clavis Litterarum Hibernensium*.[6] At three volumes and over two thousand pages, the *Clavis* epitomises the challenges and opportunities facing the scholar of early Irish history. MacNeill was, perhaps, one of the first scholars with the skill and desire to take on these sources and demonstrate their worth. This paper will explore MacNeill's contributions to our understanding of the history of the early Irish Church and how this influenced the development of the field in subsequent decades.

ST PATRICK AND RELIGION

The fifteenth centenary was an apt opportunity to publish his entreaty for a 'School of Irish Church History', as the vexed problem of Patrick was the subject of many of MacNeill's academic publications.[7] Indeed, MacNeill believed Patrick was the key to unlock early Irish history, claiming in advance of the centenary that the people of Ireland would 'prepare to do honour to Patrick and to the nation which began through him a new and glorious life, honouring him and Ireland in a manner that will bring the world to honour them'.[8] Patrick's feast day of 17 March has since become a vast international festival, ostensibly celebrating this patron saint of Ireland, all things 'Irish', and the occasion of Tourism Ireland's hugely successful Global Greening campaign. Patrick continues to act as a portal to Irish history. There are ongoing attempts to accurately discern all those pesky disputed historical details, such as his birth and death dates, his place of birth, locations of his activities in Ireland, and even his motives.[9] MacNeill's arguments on some of these details have generally been disproven.[10] What MacNeill did clearly demonstrate, however, was that Patrick left an indelible mark on Irish history through his composition of the earliest surviving sustained written sources. MacNeill revealed the immense worth of these two fifth-century documents, the *Confessio* and the *Letter to the Soldiers of Coroticus.*[11]

Through Patrick's allusions to his ministry and daily evangelical activities MacNeill developed an image of the formal establishment of the Church in fifth-century Ireland. Central to this was Patrick's tireless effort in conferring the sacraments of baptism, confirmation and the ordination of priests.[12] 'It requires no great exercise of imagination to form an idea of how much organisation and care was necessary.'[13] While MacNeill erroneously claimed that Patrick was the first to bring Christianity to Ireland,[14] his work on language and literacy clearly shows that the Irish had extensive contacts with Christianity and Latin culture for centuries before Patrick's mission.[15] He also conceded that 'some parts of Ireland remained wholly or largely heathen after St Patrick's time'.[16]

While there is an unfortunate lack of contemporary written sources for a century after Patrick, we can infer that the Church in Ireland grew steadily in the fifth and sixth centuries, given its sophisticated nature by the seventh century. In particular, as MacNeill argued, the convening of synods and the deliberations on the Easter controversy reveal this maturity.[17] The boom in archaeological research over the last couple of decades fills out the sixth-century 'gap' we have in the documentary sources. Contributions to just one of the volumes produced on the topic show ample evidence for ecclesiastical sites, such as Caherlehillan (John Sheehan), Lorrha (Teresa Bolger and Colm Moloney) and Trim (Matthew Seaver), that were founded in the fifth century.[18] Carbon 14 dates obtained from burials and materials on some of these sites tally with dates given in later documentary sources for the foundation of these communities. Dates of 545–660 obtained from Lorrha, for example, coincide with the era of the reputed founder St Ruadán (d.585) according to later written sources.[19] A similarly early date for Trim tallies with later documentary traditions that it was founded in the fifth or sixth century by the Briton Lommán. These early sites show physical evidence of extensive economic and agricultural activity. Certainly, the increased number of archaeological investigations, partially facilitated by 'boom-time' development in the early twenty-first century, has increased our knowledge of the early Irish Church and society further than even MacNeill may have hoped.[20] Perhaps most useful, and a promising avenue for future research, is the growing number of multidisciplinary collaborations.[21]

While the Church was well developed by the seventh century, MacNeill's idealised image of a (w)hol(l)y Christian island has been challenged by recent scholarship, which suggests that some medieval Irish communities may have had limited regular contact with Christianity.[22] MacNeill promoted the idea, for example, that Patrick and the Church ended slavery in Ireland: 'Tradition here, as often elsewhere, represents by prophecy what was believed to be fact: that Patrick had brought freedom to slaves and that the Church paid no regard to those distinctions of race and kindred which were so much alive in the national memory.'[23] While there is much work to be done on this topic, the legal, annalistic and archaeological evidence from the seventh to twelfth centuries suggests that slavery continued to be an integral part of Irish society.[24] What was of primary concern here, for MacNeill, was marking out this period as the most formative one in Ireland's history, and one identifiable as distinctly Christian and 'Celtic'.[25] The term 'Celtic' with a capital letter or when used as an adjective is a topic of continued debate. The term is appropriately applied, especially in linguistic contexts, when referring to Celtic languages spoken historically (and to this day) by definable populations in geographically distinct areas, such as Ireland, Scotland, Wales, Cornwall, Brittany and the Isle of Man. Misunderstanding arises when the term is used to describe broad topics without being specific about time and place. A phrase such as 'the Celtic woman', for example, implies that there was such a type of woman, distinct from those in all other societies, across all Celtic-language-speaking lands, in some vague period in history. There was not. The legal rights of women, burial customs, gender stereotypes, economic activities, etc. varied across jurisdictions and time periods. Vague notions of a 'Celtic Ireland', a 'Celtic religion' or the 'Celtic Church' implies a distinct shared identity and defined set of characteristics, which is not borne out by the archaeological and historical evidence. The classification of this period of Irish history has undergone various revisions, which move it further away from MacNeill's 'Celtic Ireland' of the fifth to twelfth century. Throughout much of the later twentieth and early twenty-first centuries, the time of Patrick until the 'vikings' (approximately the years 400 to 800) was referred to as 'Early Christian Ireland', preserving MacNeill's idea of a religious country, the isle of saints and scholars.[26] Such nomenclature marks out Ireland as peripheral to a European mainstream, and the terms 'late antique Ireland' and 'early medieval Ireland', corresponding with the same periods in other jurisdictions, are now much preferred.[27]

A major concern throughout MacNeill's work on early Irish history was an eradication of baseless notions that Ireland was wild and barbarian, lacking in order and culture. Criticising those who considered Ireland a blank canvas, and home to a communal social and economic order,[28] he signalled his exasperation at their folly: 'Ancient Ireland, as it happens, is no vacant region for free speculation. The materials for its study are remarkably copious, and the method of its study must be by way of research, analysis, and synthesis.'[29] He went on to demonstrate that Ireland had a hierarchical social system and that land was privately owned.[30] This comprehensive, and influential, reassessment of pre-Norman Irish society was explicitly framed in the context of the unionist and colonialist perspective of G.H. Orpen.[31]

MacNeill sought to redefine and uphold a distinct Irish culture by presenting the superior nature of the early Irish sources and reinvigorating the Irish language. At times this verged on extreme nationalism: 'In ancient Ireland alone we find the autobiography of a people of European white men who come into history not moulded into the mould of the complex East nor forced to accept the law of imperial Rome.'[32] Central to this distinct Irish culture was religion: 'A comprehending inquirer cannot fail to recognise that the writing or the study of Irish history is a vain conceit unless the history of Ireland is understood to comprise in a very ample measure the history of religion in Ireland.'[33] But for MacNeill religion clearly meant Catholicism.[34] The 'Catholic Church' of seventh-century Ireland, however, was not the same thing as post-Tridentine Catholicism, even though many Catholic scholars – MacNeill included – often regarded it as such. Influenced by his upbringing, having grown up as a Catholic in a predominantly Protestant area, MacNeill's work reflects clear tension between his skill as a historian and his own inherent biases and agendas. In 'The North Began', his influential *An Claidheamh Soluis* article that precipitated the foundation of the Irish Volunteers, he expressed his belief that the Irish nation's future was firmly rooted in its fifth- and sixth-century 'Christian' past.[35] While dismissing the separatist demands of the Ulster Volunteers, MacNeill invoked the might of the famous triumvirate of early Irish saints, who would rail against the notion of a divided island: 'There is no "homogeneous Ulster". It is impossible to separate from Ireland the city that Saint Patrick founded, the city that Saint Columba founded, or the tombs of Patrick, Brigid and Columba. They would defy and nullify the attempt.' Modern scholars of the early Irish Church might well be amused at such a depiction of unity, given the nature of the struggle for primacy of the seventh-century Irish Church between Patrick's Church of Armagh, Brigid's Church of Kildare and, to a lesser extent, Columba's Church of Iona.[36]

Mere months before MacNeill's appeal for a school of Irish Church history in 1932, in a series of seven weekly newspaper articles, while eviscerating the work of Archdeacon Kerr,[37] he detailed the form, early history and character of the early Irish Church.[38] Nowhere in MacNeill's extensive range of academic publications does he engage with the organisation of the Irish Church in such a schematic manner. These newspaper articles encapsulate MacNeill's fundamental understanding of the Church, implicit in many of his publications but most clearly consolidated for the first time here, that the Irish Church was primarily about two things: St Patrick and Roman Catholicism.

The basic premise of these well-researched and strongly argued articles was a reaction against a so-called Protestant claim to be the legitimate successors of Patrick, and a repudiation of Kerr's theory that Patrick established a separate, schismatic, Irish Church, independent from Rome.[39] Labelling Kerr 'a kind of anti-Papal Sinn Feiner',[40] MacNeill claimed Patrick's own writings did not convey 'the slightest hint that the relations of Armagh to Rome' were any different to the relations of Auxerre or Arles to Rome.[41] He references sources such as the late sixth-century and early seventh-century letters of Columbanus, which clearly elucidate the respect for Rome as the head of the Church. (Mis)quoting Columbanus, MacNeill argued that all early Christians were united in faith:[42] 'For we are all joint members of one body, whether Franks or Britons or Irish or whatever our race be',[43] a timely reminder of our shared history. In recent years, Columbanus has been popularly hailed as patron saint of a united Europe, and the 'first European' by the Irish media.[44] In his own work, MacNeill shares Columbanus' traits of promoting Ireland and Irish interests while acknowledging that Ireland was very much part of the wider world.

This question of Ireland and the Irish Church's extensive contacts with the rest of the known world has formed one of the biggest historiographical themes in recent decades. Research in this area is exemplified by the work of scholars published as part of Michael Richter and Próinséas Ní Chatháin's excellent *Ireland and Europe* series, which ran from the 1980s until the early 2000s.[45] The bulk of Dáibhí Ó Cróinín's publications also illustrate the pioneering activities of early Irish churchmen and their extensive networks on the continent.[46] Indeed, such was the popularity of these studies, that scholarly debate is beginning to swing in the other direction, with scholars such as Sven Meeder, Roy Flechner and Emmet Marron arguing that the contribution of Irish clerics to early medieval European culture has been overstated by modern scholars.[47]

The notion that the Irish Church was unique and original, developing at odds with the dominant Roman model, has now been all but abandoned. Nevertheless, vestiges of such an interpretation survive. In fact, recent research on the Church, in Ireland, as elsewhere, has shown that it was anything but monolithic, and that there was great variation in practice. MacNeill demonstrated that early Irish authors such as Columbanus and Cummian explicitly expressed respect for Rome as the head of the Church, and this same deference is articulated in Frankish and Anglo-Saxon sources from Avitus of Vienne to Stephen of Ripon.[48] But it is a misnomer to refer to any standard church practices in the fifth, sixth and seventh centuries. In Rome, a succession of popes shaped church policy over centuries. In the 'provinces', enterprising bishops and church leaders pioneered practices that were not always officially sanctioned by the administrative and spiritual capital. There was no single Roman way.[49] In relation to burial practices, for example, there was no discernible shift towards a degree of homogeneity until the eighth century. Eric Rebillard's innovative work on burial in Late Antiquity argues that Christians did not cultivate exclusive cemeteries until centuries after many scholars previously thought, and that there were manifest regional variations.[50] Gregory the Great attempted to dictate policy in relation to the cult of relics in the late sixth century but the work of Julia Smith, on relic tags in particular, shows there was genuine tension regarding the relic practices that Gregory was sanctioning in Rome and actual practice in other jurisdictions.[51] Effectively, there were a number of different devotional and organisational models being worked out within the Church from the fourth to the eighth centuries. While jurisdictional control of the Church was administered from Rome, Roman practices are not indicative of wider trends, and Roman treatises and prescriptions were not always followed. The enduring power of the Church lay in its ability to adapt to local politics and cultures.

PHILOLOGY AND AUTHORSHIP: 'SECULAR' VERSUS ECCLESIASTICAL LEARNING

One of MacNeill's greatest academic triumphs was exposing the breadth and depth of the vast early Irish source material, composed not just in Latin but also in considerable quantities in the native (vernacular) language, Old Irish. He proudly glorified early Irish scholars as a beacon of light in a dark age:

> Then, almost suddenly, a national written literature arises in the common speech of the people, rich in poetry and in prose, widely various in scope, the work of many writers. The country in which this singular development took place was Ireland, the language Irish. No mere passive evolution produced the phenomenon of a national literature, unexampled in that age.[52]

We can forgive MacNeill some patriotic fervour here. Other vernacular cultures in medieval Europe did not seem to produce the same volume of texts. The early Irish law texts, for example, are claimed to be the largest vernacular compendium of legal material in early medieval Europe.[53] The literary culture in early medieval Ireland developed simultaneously in two languages: one imported language with an already highly advanced literary style and form; the other a native vernacular, which some Irish scholars explicitly sought to promote as equal, if not superior.[54]

This bilingual nature of the Irish sources has deterred some researchers from early Irish history. MacNeill, however, was one of the first to demonstrate the full potential of a philological approach to Irish history. His detailed analysis of individual terms enabled non-linguists to gain a better understanding of legal and social structures in early Ireland.[55] Indeed,

MacNeill warned other scholars that our understanding of history is limited without an appreciation of historical languages:

> Those whom philology does not interest may be apt to think that the study of the development of languages leads nowhere beyond itself and does not increase our knowledge about other things. This would be a very grave error. The history of the wonderful phenomenon of European civilisation is in part dependent on philological studies. For the understanding of Irish history, except in a late ultra-political phase, the aid of the philologist is indispensable, and those students who, like the present writer, have to rely on the philological guidance of experts, find that guidance necessary in their historical studies almost at every hand's turn.[56]

The advances in technology in recent decades, including the digitisation of manuscripts and the development of online dictionaries and lexicographical databases, have greatly enhanced the ability of scholars to adopt MacNeill's approach on a grand scale. Scholars such as Elva Johnston, Anthony Harvey, Immo Warntjes, Elizabeth Boyle, Jacopo Bisagni, Paul Russell, Sharon Arbuthnot and Pádraic Moran (and that list is by no means exhaustive) have recently published research that proves there was a highly developed intellectual culture in early medieval Ireland.[57] Indeed, it is a subject area that is attracting much of the most innovative research in early Irish history. Nike Stam and Jacopo Bisagni's work on code switching, for example, details how this culture was deeply bilingual, an element that makes a holistic approach to the early Irish sources challenging, but equally more rewarding.[58] Pádraic Moran's new edition of *De Origine Scoticae Linguae*,[59] Anthony Harvey's ongoing publications on Hiberno-Latin, and David Stifter's investigations into the development of the vernacular[60] reveal both the direct influences of ancient and late antique Greek and Latin texts on Irish authors and the confidence and ability of these authors to innovate as a result of this cross-fertilisation.

Our understanding of the identity of these authors has undergone serious revision since MacNeill. He understood the early Irish sources as the work of a separate class of secular learned native poets, claiming, for example, that the tales of the 'Ulster Cycle', such as the *Táin*, preserved accounts of 'pure paganism and primitivism', 'proof that it was committed to writing very early in the Christian period'.[61] These stories, however, were written within an ecclesiastical milieu and many betray an Armagh bias, even the ones deemed 'authentic' or 'secular' by MacNeill.[62] While he transformed the understanding of Irish identity by revealing that texts such as *Lebor Gabála Érenn* (The Book of Invasions of Ireland) were legends created by a school of 'synthetic historians',[63] he incorrectly trusted the annals as genuine historical records from an early period.[64] He mentioned cases where individual annals err or were not contemporary; however, in general, he deferred to J.B. Bury, who counted these annals as authentic historical records.[65] He, rightly, discredited texts relating to Patrick preserved in the ninth-century Book of Armagh as biased accounts from the seventh century and unreliable as historical sources for the activities of the fifth-century saint.[66] But he did not exercise that same level of scholarly critique when dealing with the annals: 'Of less questionable authority are the events of St Patrick's mission recorded without embellishment in the ancient annals.'[67] While debates over the historicity and reliability of various sections of the vast corpus of Irish annalistic texts are ongoing, it is certain that it was at least centuries after Patrick before events were recorded contemporaneously.[68]

The question of authorship dominated one of the major debates of the twentieth century – the so-called 'nativist' versus 'revisionist' approach to early Irish history. There is no need to rehash this debate, as the new generation of scholars has benefited from the research stimulated by the arguments, without being directly affected by the intricacies. However, suffice it to say that, broadly speaking, scholars in the 1980s such as Kim McCone, Donnchadh Ó Corráin and Liam Breatnach, following the work of James Carney in the 1950s, argued against attitudes championed in particular by Daniel Binchy, following MacNeill, that Irish written sources preserve pagan, prehistoric and Celtic traditions.[69] 'Revisionists' held that the sources, regardless of subject matter, could not be clearly divorced from the ecclesiastical context in which many of them were composed. Scholarship has since moved significantly on from these debates to a more nuanced understanding of the exact milieu in which the sources were produced. Elva Johnston's work, for example, argues that the Church did not have a monopoly on learning, but it was the main provider of literate education in early Ireland, and from the tenth century onwards this became more centralised within the larger ecclesiastical schools.[70] It is surprising, therefore, in MacNeill's works, that there is little discussion of the ecclesiastical institutional contexts in which many of our surviving historical sources were produced. The sources, as they come down to us, present a society in which the power structures, both secular and ecclesiastical, became inextricably linked.

THE ORGANISATION OF THE CHURCH

The exact form of these ecclesiastical structures has made up one of the other major debates concerning the Irish Church in the last century. Without providing a detailed study of the process, MacNeill often referred to the great monastic development of the sixth century.[71] He went so far as to claim that 'in the centuries that had elapsed since St Patrick's time the great development of monasticism in Ireland had eclipsed and well-nigh obliterated the episcopal constitution of the Irish Church'.[72] This understanding of the structure of the Church held sway for many years. It was fully expressed by Kathleen Hughes, whose account of a major change in the sixth and seventh centuries from an episcopal system to a predominantly monastic church was the accepted model for much of the twentieth century.[73] Despite the undoubted excellence of Hughes' work, this view upheld a notion of a distinctly 'Celtic' Church developing at odds with an episcopal norm. In 1971 Patrick Corish raised the issue of pastoral care, which was not accommodated within Hughes' monastic model, but it was Richard Sharpe's pivotal 1984 paper on the organisation of the early Irish Church that inspired a whole slew of studies.[74] Scholars such as Thomas Charles-Edwards, Ó Corráin, Thomas Clancy, Craig Haggart, Westley Follett and Paul MacCotter reappraised the provision of pastoral care and the role of the bishop in the early Irish Church.[75] Perhaps most comprehensive is Colmán Etchingham's argument for considerable continuity through the first centuries of the Irish Church.[76] His analysis elucidates a complex organisational system in which the major Irish churches employed three models of authority (episcopal, abbatial and 'coarbial') to varying degrees. Part of this debate has been a re-evaluation of the Céli Dé, who played an important role in the displaced model as articulated in 1929 by J.F. Kenney, who described them as a reform movement organised to combat secular encroachment on the Church.[77] Recently scholars such as Haggart and Follett, following Clancy and Brian Lambkin before them, have shown that the Céli Dé were not an organised reform movement, but regular religious dedicated to ascetic ideals, chastity, charity, excellence in learning, and pastoral care.[78] More importantly, these studies show that there was no overriding perception in the Irish sources of a corrupt and degenerate clergy that needed substantial rehabilitation in the eighth century. All of these considerations of the organisation of the Irish Church illuminate a complex ecclesiastical system.

Evidence in myriad Irish documentary sources shows that this system was established by the Church working within existing power structures. Despite this, there is no section on the institution of the Church in MacNeill's *Early Irish Laws and Institutions*. As early as the fifth-century writings of Patrick we get a glimpse into an Irish society in which one could not travel or preach freely without permission and support from the local kings and judges.[79] The sources indicate that both kings and church leaders attended *óenaig* (assemblies) and synods and that there was active cooperation between secular and ecclesiastical rulers in the promulgation of laws, the collection of revenues, the promotion of relics and the overall maintenance of power and control.[80] This is alluded to by MacNeill in *Phases of Irish History*. He mentions, for example, a 737 meeting between Cathal, king of Cashel and the high-king, Aedh Allán, at Terryglass, where apparently an agreement was made between them securing the claim of the church of Armagh to revenue from all Ireland.[81] We get another concise insight in *Celtic Ireland*, where MacNeill briefly discusses ecclesiastical ownership of land and the grant system in early Ireland.[82] MacNeill, however, despite his in-depth knowledge of early Irish law and his influential theories on the structure of Irish society, did not engage with the full extent of cooperation between the Church and existing centres of power. This topic has received more attention since, though it is still a relatively untapped area of medieval Irish history. Ó Corráin's analysis of the Dál Cais and David Thornton's study of the Conaille Muirtheimne, for example, detail the extent of so-called 'lay' and religious political involvement.[83] Furthermore, Clare Downham's analysis of the career of Cearbhall of Osraighe shows the close links he fostered with certain Leinster churches such as Seirkeiran and Leighlinn, and the work of Tomás Ó Carragáin on the ecclesiastical estates around Fermoy illustrates how Christianisation was often a political process as well as a religious one.[84] It is not easy to separate secular and ecclesiastical politics in early medieval Ireland. The Church owned a great deal of land and wealth and maintained many of the power structures within society.[85] Members of the ruling dynasties or aristocracy often filled important church positions, maintaining the status quo in terms of hierarchy.

It is in his *Standard* newspaper articles that we discover MacNeill's most incisive, though necessarily short, theories on ecclesiastical-politics. Here, he argued against the notion that the Irish Church was independent and corrupt on such a scale that it was unrecognisable from other European churches in the twelfth century.[86] In this instance he was primarily responding to the claims of Archdeacon Kerr that the Irish Church system had lasted unchanged since the time of Patrick, needed 'scrapping' in the twelfth century and was replaced with a 'foreign' one.[87] MacNeill clearly demonstrated that the Irish Church went through extensive development and change in the seven centuries between Patrick and the twelfth-century reforms, something that is still not always fully appreciated today.[88] His argument, however, partially centres on his belief that the Irish Church was too disorganised and headless by this stage to be considered as acting in opposition to Rome and Canterbury. Referencing compromises in the Irish Church, such as an allowance for a married clergy and hereditary succession in compliance with civil law, MacNeill surmised:

> Thus there was a gradual tendency towards confusion and anarchy in the government of the Irish Church, and this tendency was aggravated by the invasions and inroads of the Northmen during the ninth and tenth centuries.[89]

More recent empirical data shows that the Irish Church before the eleventh century was highly organised and based on an extensive parochial network, at least in certain areas. P.J. Duffy's research, for example, reveals that 78 per cent of parish names in Meath and 70 per cent in Dublin were pre-Anglo-Norman in origin. Duffy suggests that the conquerors were 'inheritors rather than creators of ecclesiastical structures'.[90]

MacNeill discussed the political and legal landscape of Ireland before and during the Anglo-Norman 'invasion' in *Early Irish Laws and Institutions* with surprisingly little reference to the corresponding ecclesiastical politics. In the *Standard* articles, however, he devoted much space to exactly this topic. Essentially, MacNeill argued that the Church founded by Patrick was beyond reproach (it was clearly episcopal in nature, in line with the 'Roman' Church), and that after Patrick the Irish Church changed in character and deteriorated in organisation to the extent that it needed various reforms over the centuries, but, crucially, these reforms were all implemented within the Irish Church itself. Despite excellent research undertaken on this subject in recent years, there is no consensus on the condition and reforms of the Irish Church before the twelfth century, and MacNeill's insights remain relevant.[91]

On the question of Irish clerics of the twelfth century having little awareness of the wider Church, MacNeill wrote: The Archdeacon may be assured that the ecclesiastical conditions of other countries in their time were much better known and understood by Irish Churchmen of the twelfth century than the ecclesiastical conditions of Ireland and before it are known and understood by himself.[92]

While these newspaper articles are naturally journalistic, polemical and populist, it would be easy to argue that they reveal MacNeill's true limitations, or perhaps hesitations, when it came to a full analysis of Irish Church politics, organisation and administration. He was hampered by his faith in Patrick as an Irish Catholic hero, and this led to an uncritical evaluation of the extent of Patrick's role in the establishment of the Irish Church. His theories on Patrick were superseded within his own lifetime, but it has taken much longer for scholarship to gain a clearer understanding of the Irish Church and its role in early Irish society.[93] It is unfortunate that many students of early Ireland would not have been aware of his entertaining exposition of the Irish Church in his series of newspaper articles in 1932. While the influence of the Church of Armagh is clear in these articles, he only hints at this importance in his widely read and studied *Celtic Ireland*.[94]

On a number of occasions MacNeill bemoaned the lack of funding that kept many talented and much-needed scholars out of academia:

> If so few are in the field where there is room for so many, experience has convinced me that the deterrent forces are mainly economic ... for at present, the student, howsoever capable, who would give the time required for preparation in these studies, would find himself, when the time for research and publication had come, face to face with the prospect of having to do the work at his own expense, and in most cases to engage in other and wholly different tasks to provide a livelihood and the surplus required for this work.[95]

Given the discussion above, there have clearly been many important advancements in the study of the Irish Church, and early Irish history in general, since MacNeill. But the developments may not be as far as one would hope given the lapse of time. MacNeill's exhortations for further study certainly remain relevant today.

Eoin MacNeill: the scholar and his critics

DÁIBHÍ Ó CRÓINÍN

O n the morning of Tuesday, 28 September 1943, at the height of what was termed 'the Emergency' in Ireland, but what was known elsewhere as the Second World War, readers of the *Irish Press* woke to the dramatic front-page news that the massed forces of the Soviet Red Army had made a smashing breakthrough against the German *Wehrmacht* on the eastern front at Dniepropetrovsk, in the Ukraine, and were cascading westwards.[1] The momentous nature of that news was nearly matched, however, on the inside front page of the same newspaper, with the almost equally dramatic headline announcing that 'Dr. MacNeill Answers Prof. O'Rahilly'. The article, penned by A. de B. (= Aodh de Blácam),[2] was intended to reassure the *Irish Press* readers that, whatever might be happening in the outside world, the Catholic Christian heritage of the country was safe from the shock it had lately received from a potentially catastrophic native assault on the nation's dearest-held traditions. 'At last the long-awaited reply by Dr Eoin MacNeill to Professor Thomas O'Rahilly's astonishing theory about St Patrick has appeared.'[3] Though the earth might be shaking in the faraway Soviet Union, the nation at home could sleep safely again in their beds: 'It is, as we expected, an unhesitating condemnation of the attack upon our accepted national tradition.'[4]

> Need we recall the sensation caused when Professor O'Rahilly last summer published a book,[5] through the Dublin Institute for Advanced Studies,[6] which claimed to demonstrate these propositions? –
>
> (1) That St Patrick was not the first Bishop of Armagh, nor Armagh originally the Primatial See.
>
> (2) That St Patrick was not a national apostle by whom the conversion of Ireland was accomplished.
>
> (3) That St Palladius really was the missionary to whom the conversion of most of Ireland was due, while St Patrick only completed the work by a mission in the North and West.[7]

It is hard for today's readers to comprehend the degree of 'shock and awe' that had resulted from the first appearance of O'Rahilly's heretical views about the national saint. Writing in 1962, the great Irish scholar D.A. Binchy remarked: 'The publication of O'Rahilly's lecture *The Two Patricks* in 1942 [*sic*] had the effect of an atomic bomb dropped on the orthodox school [of Patrician Studies], and even today the "fall-out" is still active.'[8] The popular (as distinct from the scholarly)[9] reaction was seismic:

> Dismay, even indignation, arose from the publication of this subversive theory. Not only did it purport to destroy the Patrick of tradition and devotion, but it represented that tradition as a thing established by the clergy of Armagh by means of a persistent propaganda in favour of the prerogatives of their church. The Armagh clergy, we were told, 'never lost sight of the idea that to magnify St Patrick was in effect to magnify themselves', and so the deeds of Palladius were assigned to Patrick, 'as a necessary preliminary' to a claim for Armagh which could not be made with success if Patrick of Armagh was merely the successor of a greater man. In a word, the National Apostle was a fiction produced at Armagh and meekly accepted by the rest of Ireland.[10]

Modern scholarship on the subject of St Patrick would concur unanimously with O'Rahilly's view, at least in so far as it related to the role of the Armagh clergy in manufacturing a case for the saint's supposed association with that church.[11] For the readers of the *Irish Press* in 1943, however, the matter was a good deal less certain and a great deal more traumatic. After all, O'Rahilly's 'attack on tradition' could be seen to strike at the very foundations of Irish Catholic belief. All the more reason, then, for the faithful to wonder, in the plaintive tones of Aodh de Blácam: '"What does MacNeill say about it?" – for Dr. MacNeill is the admitted chief of our living historians, and has made several contributions to Patrician study.' MacNeill's more popular publications about Patrick, it must be said, would not rank among the best things that he ever wrote. On the other hand, his detailed textual studies of the Patrician sources (in particular the texts preserved in the Book of Armagh) reveal him at his forensic best.[12] His riposte to O'Rahilly's damaging lecture, however, was neither comprehensive nor crushing,[13] and the closing statement 'for the defence' in de Blácam's *Irish Press* piece gives the impression of one 'whistling past the graveyard'. 'Only in our own age, one thinks, could fable be invoked to overthrow history, tradition, and devotion.' Whatever faults there may have been in O'Rahilly's 'attack', they were neither exposed nor refuted by MacNeill at the time.

Binchy pointed out that O'Rahilly's *Two Patricks* 'was not intended to be more than a first instalment ... and he reserved several questions for detailed treatment in a larger work'.[14] That larger work, when it appeared, in 1946, turned out to be his mammoth *Early Irish History and Mythology*,[15] but though he did amplify a number of minor points of Patrician controversy in that book arising from his previous discussion, his death in 1953 prevented him from publishing the full fruits of his Patrician researches.[16] However, running throughout O'Rahilly's great book of 1946 is a steady drum-beat of anti-MacNeill comments; a perusal of *Early Irish History and Mythology* makes clear that he had little regard for MacNeill's scholarship (with one exception that I have noted)[17] and he lost no opportunity to criticise MacNeill's ideas about all kinds of matters, mostly linguistic and philological, but also including St Patrick. O'Rahilly appears to have been particularly irked by the high regard in which MacNeill was obviously held. At one point[18] he bursts out: 'Rev. Dr. John Ryan, like MacNeill, asserts that the name *Fir Bolg* means "bag men", and was applied to "a caste of bag-makers". (I may add here that it would be superfluous to give further references to the views expressed in Dr. Ryan's book [*Ireland to AD 800*], which, so far as it concerns us here, is merely a rehash, without acknowledgement, of MacNeill's "Phases of Irish History").'[19]

Such views about MacNeill appear to have been simmering for a good many years before the publication either of *The Two Patricks* or the much more detailed *Early Irish History and Mythology*. In the prefatory note that he added to the *Two Patricks*, O'Rahilly pointed out that it provided 'in summary form, the results of a detailed study of the subject made during the years 1934–35'.[20] Clearly, he – and some other scholars – were not quite so in awe of MacNeill's reputation as the Irish public evidently was. In an article of a few years previously,[21] that other doyen of early Irish studies, Osborn Bergin, issued a mordant response to a paper published the year before by MacNeill on 'The mythology of Lough Neagh' in the pages of *Béaloideas*, the journal of the Folklore of Ireland Society. A harmless enough preoccupation, one would think, but enough to provoke 'the prince of native scholars'[22] to take up the cudgels against his University College Dublin colleague. Harking back to a statement that MacNeill had made in 1921 in his *Celtic Ireland*, to the effect that 'Ancient Ireland, as it happens, is no vacant region for free speculation. The materials for its study are remarkably copious, and the method of its study must be by way of research, analysis and synthesis',[23] Bergin remarked sardonically: 'While the materials for the study of Irish mythology are but meagre in comparison with those available for the study of the social organisation, the same method may and ought to be applied here, and the unduly large proportion of free speculation seems to me to lessen the value of his interesting article.'[24] Having prefaced his essay with the warning that 'the object of the following notes is to test the conclusions he [MacNeill] has arrived at in the light of important material that he has ignored', Bergin then proceeded to demolish MacNeill's various 'speculations' one by one. The conclusion is pretty damning:

> Kuno Meyer used to say that the errors of scholars are often instructive. While I believe Professor MacNeill's arguments to be quite erroneous, they have a certain value. When an acute and brilliant scholar can be so wide of the mark through ignoring indispensable documents, the extent of his, shall I say, deviation may serve as a measure of the wide margin of error that must be allowed for in cases where documentary evidence is scanty ... I am still open to conviction, though I admit that his uncritical attitude towards his material, and his confidence in stating as fact what half-an-hour's search in a library would show to be fancy, have prejudiced me against speculations which may after all prove fruitful.[25] Is it too late to ask Professor MacNeill to consider the problem afresh, using the precautions without which knowledge can never advance, and noting what other scholars have done in kindred fields during the last forty years?[26]

What induced Bergin to write those words? A man not always given to invective or polemic, those strictures on MacNeill appear extraordinarily ill-tempered. True, his admirers often remarked on Bergin's near-maniacal obsession with accuracy. 'Accuracy was indeed the outstanding characteristic of his scholarship,' Binchy remarked,[27] and he further added that he himself remembered 'the last lecture that he gave to a post-graduate class within these walls [in UCD], with its concluding words of advice to present and future scholars in Irish: "accuracy, more accuracy, and still more accuracy"'.[28] But the answer to the question: whence the origin of the animosity displayed both by Bergin and by O'Rahilly towards MacNeill, is perhaps to be found in another observation about Bergin in Daniel Binchy's brief memoir of that scholar.

Binchy recalled that Bergin first came to prominence as 'Bergin of Cork' and 'Bergin the Gaelic Leaguer', the ardent worker in the Irish Language Revival movement during its early years (the 1890s), disciple and friend of Canon Peter O'Leary, and, at a later date, a promoter (together with Shán

Ó Cuív and T.F. O'Rahilly) of the *Litriú Simplí* campaign to simplify the spelling of Irish.[29] The first time that MacNeill and Father O'Leary met was on 27 March 1894, at a *Feis Mhór* (Congress) held by Conradh na Gaeilge (the Gaelic League) in the Lord Mayor's House in Dublin.[30] Father O'Leary travelled from Cork for the occasion and stayed a week in Dublin, where he observed the League members at work; they included Michael Cusack, Douglas Hyde, Father Eoghan O'Growney,[31] Seosamh Laoide and MacNeill. By the end of that first week they were all good friends, though the amity between MacNeill and Father O'Leary was not to last.

From November 1894 until the end of February 1899 MacNeill was editor of the League's newspaper, *Irisleabhar na Gaedhilge* (*The Gaelic Journal*). During those years Father Peter had articles in almost every issue, and in the subsequent League journals, *An Claidheamh Soluis* and *Fáinne an Lae*.[32] The first sign of difficulty emerged after Father Peter's best-known story, *Séadna*,[33] began to appear in the *Irisleabhar* in November 1894, but whose serialisation came to an abrupt halt in April 1897. The editor (MacNeill) offered the following by way of explanation:

> We want a few more writers who, like Father O'Leary, having known Irish from their infancy, have taken a keen delight in studying and bringing to light its endless resources. His story of 'Séadna' has added more to the general knowledge of those resources than any other recent publication. If there are any readers of the *Journal* who have not revelled in the deft and sinewy and versatile Irish of his narrative, we do not envy them. In our pages, perhaps, the story showed to the least advantage. Published in little driblets, month by month, its action was made to lag where it did not lag. Serial stories are always under this disadvantage, especially when their instalments appear not weekly, but monthly, and only a few pages at a time. A glance at the monthly journals of today will show that the days of the serial are well nigh numbered. In future we do not contemplate the publication of contributions extending over many months.
>
> 'Séadna' accordingly comes to an abrupt and unfinished break-off with the end of our last volume. We hope, however, soon to see the whole story published in book-form, when its high merits will be much more conspicuously seen. Meanwhile its author has kindly consented to enrich our columns with a collection of idiomatic phrases systematically arranged, which will be most valuable to the student.[34]

Father Peter's (mis)understanding of the situation, however, was that *Séadna* had been thrown out of the *Irisleabhar* because it was deemed to be of no value – 'an Irish Mick McQuaid', in his words.[35] The truth of the matter, however, was that MacNeill loved the story and had encouraged publication from the start, and indeed had resisted Father Peter's suggestions that the story might be curtailed. 'Why would you shorten *Séadna*'s life? Give it its head. The pity is that we can't give more space to it in the *Irisleabhar* every month. But don't you go shortening it in any way. Let it go and follow it!'[36] But when it began to appear that the story might go on indefinitely, MacNeill apparently took fright and announced that serialisation was to cease. Father O'Leary's response was ominous: 'If you drop *Séadna* from the *Irisleabhar*,' he wrote to MacNeill, 'I'm telling you that you'll be making a mistake.'[37] The situation was further complicated by the fact that, at exactly the same time, difficulties had arisen between the Gaelic League headquarters in Dublin and the Lee Branch (*Craobh na Laoi*) in Cork, which had been founded by Bergin and Donnchadh Pléimionn. In the early years of the League, the Cork branches were inclined to value their initial independence and autonomy, but the League's headquarters officers, almost overwhelmed by the rapid and unexpected expansion of branches all over the country,[38] were anxious to impose order on the way that their activities were to be conducted nationwide. The antagonism towards the Cork membership and its activities came to a head and resulted in the suspension of *Craobh na Laoi* and its dissolution in January 1899.[39] MacNeill was in charge of the Coiste Gnótha (Executive Committee) at the time (his brother Charles was secretary). Here too, then, was another stone to throw at MacNeill in later years: first the Lee Branch (headed by Bergin) had been disbanded but, even worse, An tAthair Peadar – who was an almost God-like figure to Munster (but especially Cork) speakers of Irish – had been thrown out of the Gaelic League's principal newspaper, apparently by MacNeill.

It may be hard to believe that such seemingly hard-headed men as Bergin and O'Rahilly could have hero-worshipped Father Peter, and held against MacNeill that he had 'evicted' him from the pages of *Irisleabhar na Gaeilge*; but the description is not exaggerated.[40] For example, in the correspondence (most of it unpublished) that was exchanged around the Castlelyons cleric's project to translate the New Testament into Irish, O'Rahilly famously remarked at one point: 'I don't want the Word of God in Irish, I want the word of An tAthair Peadar!'[41] Two years before the canon's death, one of his most ardent followers, Shán Ó Cuív (mentioned previously as one of the originators of the *Litriú Simplí* campaign to simplify the spelling of Irish),[42] published an encomium entitled 'Canon O'Leary's part in the making of Irish prose' in which he wrote the following:

> The development of Irish prose for literary expression belongs essentially to the twentieth century. In this respect Irish differs from all the other living languages of Western Europe. Once the vernacular languages began to take the place of Latin as a literary medium, the living language of each country in which there was any intellectual life began to undergo a new development. The language of ordinary speech is inadequate to the expression of complex and continuous thought. Thus, when the living languages began to be used as a vehicle for the expression of such thought, they received an impetus to growth in new directions ... It is to the continuous efforts of many great minds to express themselves in this exact sense that we owe the highly polished literary languages of Western Europe ... Literary English is a highly effective medium for the expression of every distinction of thought. This literary English is the growth of the last three hundred years. The same period has witnessed the rise of the other great languages of Western Europe ... The writing of prose in Flemish and Welsh has also undergone great development ... The nineteenth century has been a century of continuous growth for all these languages as literary media. For Irish it was the blackest that the language has ever known ...
>
> The century was drawing to a close when the greatest writer of Irish prose that has ever lived burst forth and astonished all with the vigour and freshness of his style, and the wonderful flexibility of the language which he employed. Canon O'Leary was born in 1830, but he really belongs to the twentieth century[43] ... I have called Canon O'Leary the greatest writer of Irish prose that has ever lived. I do not wish these words to be understood in any other than a literal sense ... Any person who analyses Canon O'Leary's style cannot fail to observe certain characteristics in it. The words and the sentences seem to dovetail into each other, and, when read aloud, his writing gives a harmonious stream of sound. There are no jolty, rugged sentences, no awkward voice checks. All his writings exhibit the true *legato* quality of the Irish language ... It is that above all else that distinguishes Canon O'Leary's style ...[44]

Here is the pure milk of the unadulterated Canon O'Leary cult in all its heady glory. Nor was Ó Cuív's encomium the unique outburst of a deranged

fanatic. Only two years later, on the death of the great man himself, Bergin
published an obituary piece on Canon O'Leary not much different in tone
and content from Shán Ó Cuív's:

> Tá an tAthair Peadar san uaigh. Agus mé im sheasamh ar bruach na
> huaighe san,[45] dubhart liom féin, 'Tá an seana-shaol againn dá chur
> anso'. Ní abraim ná gurbh fhíor dom an méid sin. Ní hamhlaidh
> atá Éire folamh ó Ghaelaibh. Ní dheaghaidh sliocht Ghaedhil
> as, agus ní baoghal go raghaidh. Ach is 'mó cor a chuir an saol de i
> gcaitheamh céad blian. Tá atharrú tagaithe san uile bhall, agus béidir
> gur mó an t-atharrú a tháinig ar Éirinn 'ná ar éin tír eile san Eóraip
> go dtí an cogadh mór ... Do chaill Éire a maithe agus a mór-uaisle
> agus a haos dána dá chéad bliain roime sin. Ach mar sin féin d'fhan
> na "miondaoine" sa bhaile. Bhí a seana-chaint féin aca, agus a seana-
> nósa agus a sean-intinn Ghaelach. Beatha na ndaoine ar an dtuaith,
> deireadh an tAthair Peadar gur mhar a chéile í agus an bheatha a bhí
> agá sinsearaibh míle bliain ó shin, agus bhí a lán den fhírinne aige ...
> Airighim daoine uaireanta, a fáil locht ar an Athair Peadar, de bhrígh
> ná faghaid siad 'na sgéaltaibh na smaointe doimhne feallsamhanta
> agus na cruadh-cheisteanna a thaitneann leó i litríocht Shasana agus
> i litríocht na Frainnce. Bíodh aca. Tá slí sa Ghaolainn do gach aon
> tsaghas litríochta ... Thug an tAthair Peadar dúinn an ní a bhí aige
> féin ... Tá sé féin imighthe, ach d'fhág sé a chuid Gaolainne 'na dhiaidh
> mar oighreacht ag muintir na hÉireann. Níor fhág éin sgríbhneoir eile
> oighreacht chomh mór ná chomh maith.[46]

There are clear echoes here of Shán Ó Cuív's earlier grand (not to say
grandiose) claims for Canon O'Leary's greatness, but in Bergin's obituary
there is only a hint at the other sore point regarding the canon that was a
source of lasting grievance for his devout followers, mentioned specifically
by Shán Ó Cuív in his encomium, one that may have influenced Bergin's
and O'Rahilly's view of MacNeill: the belief that An tAthair Peadar's
publications had been deliberately blocked by Conradh na Gaeilge and
then, as a consequence, excluded from the curriculum of Irish education at
all levels, from the national schools to the Royal University. The case was
made explicitly in a pamphlet published in 1907, *The Exclusion of Father
Peter O'Leary from Irish Education*:

> Father Peter O'Leary made his first notable appearance as a writer of
> Irish when he began his story of 'Séadna' in the *Gaelic Journal* of the

1st of November, 1894, just thirteen years ago. Since that time he has published a number of Irish works of varied character, which have been received with admiration and with gratitude by readers of Irish throughout the country. But while the general Irish reading public are free to enjoy the study of Father O'Leary's works, the youth of the country, upon whom the future of the language depends, are being deprived of that advantage, owing to the fact that Father O'Leary is, to all intents and purposes, excluded from Irish education, through all the grades, from the National School to the Royal University.[47]

In actual fact, the canon's insistence that he be allowed supply text for publication that was written in his own orthography and without editorial 'interference' inevitably led to the editorial staff of the various Irish language periodicals deciding to exclude his material.[48] So far from being the victim of some imagined conspiracy, Father O'Leary was, in fact, the author of his own undoing – a point made explicitly by his biographer.[49]

Hand in hand with the supposed conspiracy to exclude Canon O'Leary's publications from the schools was the perception among his admirers that his Irish translation of the Bible had likewise been blackballed by sinister forces in authority (in this case, of course, Church authorities). Whether or not that was the case, the canon's long-term project to translate the New Testament into Irish was never realised, though much of the manuscript material (which incorporates translations of almost the entire Bible text) has survived.[50] But the Bible project was always ancillary to his other activities and, though Bergin and O'Rahilly were enthusiastic supporters of the undertaking, there is no evidence to suggest and no reason to assume that MacNeill was felt to have had any sinister input into the decision not to publish.

Of more immediate interest to us as a possible explanation for the later antagonism expressed by those two scholars in particular towards MacNeill is the role that Bergin, MacNeill and Binchy played in a series of famous fisheries legal cases that came to prominence during the 1930s and '40s. In a series of landmark judgements handed down in the Irish Free State during those decades, Irish courts drew on the evidence of early Irish ('Brehon') law for their interpretations of the modern (Common Law) provisions regarding fishing rights in Irish inland waterways.[51] Three cases in particular, the 'Moy Fishery case', the 'Bann Fishery case' and the 'Erne Fishery case', caught the imagination. The earliest of these, the Erne Fishery case, arose out of an incident in June 1925 when a group of six Donegal fishermen, all from the village of Kildoney, rowed their currach to the mouth of the tidal estuary of the river Erne in order to poach salmon. The exclusive fishing rights on the Erne estuary were owned by the Erne Fishery Company, which had been in existence since the time of the Ulster Plantation in the seventeenth century, if not before. The fishermen were intercepted by the Erne Fishery Company motorboat, which rammed their currach and sank it.[52] The case that resulted was known as *Moore and others v. the Attorney General and others*. The Erne case is of historical legal interest because it turned out to be the final instance of an appeal by an Irish court to the British Privy Council in order to establish whether or not the Irish Free State had the power to change a provision of the Anglo-Irish treaty (and thereby establish full judicial sovereignty). Of more immediate interest to us, however, is the fact that the defendants called on the expertise of the two leading native authorities on Brehon law at the time, MacNeill and Binchy, to provide evidence of a supposed medieval Irish public right to fishing. The Erne case also had a sequel, the Moy Fishery case, which, on foot of a radical change of opinion on Binchy's part, saw him and MacNeill pitted against each other as they gave evidence for the opposing sides.

The controversy continued into the late 1940s, when (after MacNeill's death in 1945) the Foyle and Bann Fisheries case also raised the issue of native Brehon law and its proper interpretation. MacNeill had published a famous study of early Irish law two years previously. This comprised translations, with commentary, of three of the most important early (i.e. seventh-century) law texts, *Uraicecht Becc*, *Críth Gablach*, and the archaic poem *Má be rí ro-fesser*.[53] In MacNeill's view, exclusive fishery rights of the kind that were claimed by the fishery company did not exist in Gaelic society but were held in common by the local inhabitants, and as the leading authority on early Irish Law at the time (Binchy was still a relative novice by comparison), his view carried considerable weight. He was supported in this view by Binchy. Mohr records that James Hamilton Delargy (Séamus Ó Duilearga), then director of the Irish Folklore Commission, was also called to give evidence in the case, 'but did little more than agree with MacNeill's conclusions'.[54]

The two scholars began by supplying the court with a summary description of the nature of early Irish society, outlining the political and social structures of the pre-Norman period. 'They described a country divided into numerous small states, each roughly the size of a modern barony. Each petty state or *túath* formed a separate jurisdiction and had its own king, who in turn recognised the authority of superior over-kings.

According to MacNeill, the inhabitants of each *túath* enjoyed common fishing rights within the bounds of that petty state, and claimed that individuals, or groups of individuals, could not own exclusive fishing rights such as those claimed in the twentieth century by the Erne Fishery Company.[55]

To support his position, MacNeill then drew the court's attention to an early law tract on the subject of land and property ownership (*Di fhastud dligid 7 chirt* 'On the confirmation of entitlement and law'),[56] the details of which need not detain us here, as it involved the interpretation and analysis of individual words and phrases in legal Old Irish that exercised the ingenuity of the scholars but, in the end, failed to produce a consensus among them. Bergin's testimony, for example, at one point involved a minute discussion about the function of the letter *h* in the phrase *háe áite* (variously interpreted as 'the salmon of the place' by MacNeill, or 'the salmon of every place', which was offered as an alternative rendering).[57] The learned judge was not impressed. On precisely that (obscure) point, Mr Justice Johnston, presiding, declared himself unconvinced by the interpretation of it offered by MacNeill and Binchy, describing it as 'a very interesting superstructure of speculation', but one that he felt could not be sustained, arguing that it was impossible to arrive at a true construction for the passage in the Brehon law text by 'taking a few sentences out of context which seem to support a preconceived thesis, leaving the rest of the passage out of consideration'.[58] In spite of the formidable authority of MacNeill and Binchy, then, in matters relating to early Irish law, Mr Justice Johnston held that none of the evidence given by them (and others) was sufficient to displace the presumption of lawful origin, or convince him that the several fishery rights on the Erne were of modern origin.

The failure of the two eminent professors to convince the presiding judge that the Brehon law had not recognised private fishing rights was a central pillar in his eventual decision that there was no defect in the Erne Fishery Company's exclusive title to the fishery. Given that decision, we may suspect that Bergin (who had argued against MacNeill's interpretation of the Old Irish text) enjoyed a certain degree of satisfaction at the outcome. We might also suspect that it convinced him (if he needed convincing) that MacNeill's linguistic scholarship left something to be desired.[59] But if Bergin and the owners of the Erne Fishery Company felt vindicated by the outcome of the case (in 1929), their satisfaction was short-lived. The Attorney General, initially disinclined to appeal the court verdict, then changed his mind and lodged an appeal with the Supreme Court. Such was the quantity of historical evidence submitted by both parties, however, that the matter was not eventually decided until the middle of 1933. The case subsequently took on a legal significance of its own as the verdict this time went against the defendants (the Erne Fishery Company), who then declared themselves dissatisfied with the legal representation that they had received in Dublin and decided to take their case to London. It was the last such case to be appealed to the Privy Council. The resulting political controversy (which even saw Edward Carson, himself a Queen's Counsel, expressing that view that 'if ever there was a case that wanted investigation not merely by a judicial tribunal but by some great impartial tribunal, this is one')[60] was to cause considerable friction between the Irish Free State and Great Britain.[61]

The eventual outcome of the appeal to London is a subject that would take us too far away from the object of our present discussion. Suffice it to say, however, that the matter of Irish fishery rights and their basis in Brehon law did not go away with the resolution of the Erne Fishery case and, as a result, the same group of Irish scholars were to face each other again, but this time with a significant difference. On foot of the Supreme Court verdict in the Erne Fishery case (and before the matter came to a decision by the United Kingdom Privy Council in London) 'an immediate dash was made by members of the public to interfere with the proprietorial fishing rights of persons along the whole western seaboard of Ireland'.[62] This led to the Moy Fishery company in County Mayo instituting legal proceedings against these perceived poachers. The matter was finally litigated in the case of *Little v. Cooper*, which was heard before the Irish High Court in 1936.

However, an important change had taken place since the conclusion of the Erne case three years previously. In that case MacNeill and Binchy had been at one in arguing that a fishery could not have been held in private ownership on the Erne estuary in the pre-Norman period, since the existence of such a privately owned fishery was forbidden by Brehon law. Since that time, however (and under the influence of Bergin?) Binchy had come to completely revise his position on the subject. Under cross-examination he admitted that his previous views had been formed by his reading of the existing published texts of Brehon law. In the intervening years, however, he had familiarised himself with a much wider range of law texts, some of them unpublished, as a result of which he had come to change his mind. MacNeill, on the other hand, had no such change of mind, so that it transpired that this time the two scholars now faced each other across the courtroom as adversaries, rather than as allies. 'Much of

MacNeill's subsequent evidence focused on undermining the translation of the word *inber* offered by Binchy and Osborn Bergin [then Professor of Old Irish at University College Dublin], which had proved central to much of their evidence that the Brehon law had recognised extensive private fishing rights'.[63] The judge found for the Moy Fishery plaintiffs and in the process dismissed MacNeill's various arguments from Irish law. Again, we may assume that Bergin was silently pleased at this further vindication. How Binchy felt about the outcome of the case is less easy to conjecture.

The Moy Fishery case was not the last occasion on which early Irish Brehon law was invoked in order to decide the rights and wrongs of Irish fishing rights. In the 1940s the Foyle and Bann Fisheries Ltd, whose fishery was situated on an arm of Lough Foyle in County Donegal, and 'weary of the open defiance of poachers from the local community on their fishery',[64] decided to take legal action in order to secure their claim. Once again the plaintiffs called on Binchy to give evidence on their behalf. By this time, however, death had robbed the defendants of MacNeill's expertise, and so Binchy's evidence went more or less unchallenged.[65] The presiding judge, however, like the poet 'coming out knowing not much more than when he went in', gave the following verdict on the deliberations of the scholars:

> The data were inevitably slender and scrappy and the very learned witnesses whom I heard were unable to agree upon material conclusions. I need say no more. I refrain from attempting to formulate any judicial opinion on the theories of ancient fishery law advanced in evidence. Mr FitzGibbon [a barrister for the plaintiffs] caustically exacts of an expert witness on fishery law that he should know whether a salmon swims with his head first or not; thus far (pace the experts) I go with him.[66]

Thomas Mohr, whose brilliant discussion of these fisheries cases is a vital witness in this investigation, has remarked that the Erne, Moy and Bann Fisheries cases were of exceptional interest – and the Moy case in particular – 'because it pitted two of the greatest authorities on early medieval Ireland, Eoin MacNeill and D.A. Binchy, in direct opposition to each other'. But he also pointed to another comment by Binchy, that 'the most serious criticism of MacNeill's work is that his scholarship was deeply (though doubtless unconsciously) coloured by his political views ... Even his brilliant reconstruction of ancient Irish society tends to become an *apologia* for the Gaelic civilisation against its "enemies" among modern historians'.[67] Binchy added, however, that 'no breath of controversy was ever to mar his personal relations even with those who differed from him most widely; his kindness, charm, and courtesy made him universally beloved'.[68] Whether Bergin and O'Rahilly were quite so eirenical in their attitudes to MacNeill may be doubted. O'Rahilly's 1946 acknowledgement of MacNeill in the preface to his great *Early Irish History and Mythology* was clearly added after the book had been printed, with the news of MacNeill's death in 1945.[69]

MacNeill seems to have cut an isolated figure in the academic world in the two decades after his retirement from politics. Unlike Bergin, he appears not to have produced a 'stable' of younger scholars who could carry on his legacy. Apart from James Hogan (later a professor in Cork) and John Ryan, who succeeded him in 'MacNeill's Chair' in University College Dublin, there was no 'MacNeill School' of early Irish historical studies to set against the 'revolutionary' school of 'New History' that T.W. Moody and Robin Dudley Edwards claimed to have brought back from London in the early 1930s. More is the pity! Had he done so, the 'Ireland Under' approach to Irish history in the medieval period that MacNeill had previously lampooned might have followed a completely different path and the modern study of the subject would probably have looked very different.[70]

Though MacNeill was among that small coterie of Irish scholars in Dublin in the early decades of the twentieth century whose activities fashioned the modern edifice of early Irish studies as we know them today, he was not of them. MacNeill the scholar had his critics, but he appears at all times to have stood apart from them. Perhaps the last word should be given to Canon Peter O'Leary – one of his best friends, to begin with, then one of his bitterest adversaries – in a letter that he wrote (in 1899) to MacNeill's brother, Charles: 'The principal trouble is to know who are the individuals who would turn out to be cranks and who the individuals who would work away "absorbing all the inequalities". The latter sort of individual is rare. But they are to be found. John MacNeill has beaten all the men I ever met in that power of absorbing roughness, combined with an iron firmness of purpose.'[71]

'By blood and by tradition': race and empire in Eoin MacNeill's interpretation of early Ireland

ELVA JOHNSTON

BETWEEN ACTIVISM AND ACADEMIA

Robin Dudley Edwards, one of the most influential Irish historians of his generation, remarked of Eoin MacNeill:

> ... that his patriotism came before his devotion to history. This is why he put the Gaelic revival before scholarship, why Volunteering came before academic work and why the organization of historical studies only emerged in the frustrations of politics and the return to private life.[1]

This judgement on black and white choices between academia and activism is widely accepted.[2] Nevertheless, it contradicts MacNeill's own clearly expressed relief at leaving political controversies behind him upon his retirement from government. He presents politics as a distraction from what he loved most – academic research. Towards the end of his unfinished memoir, he declares:

> Personally I was glad to escape from politics and get back to my own congenial work. I had never pushed myself into politics and never taken any part in them except at the request of others.[3]

However, this dichotomy between politics and scholarship is misleading, whether articulated by Dudley Edwards or MacNeill, although it did help shape the carefully crafted persona adopted by the latter. His image as a patriotic high-minded scholar was a necessary counterbalance to the problems that dogged his public career.[4] And this scholar has been much admired. For example, Francis John Byrne, a successor to MacNeill's Chair of Early Irish History in UCD, judged his predecessor in the following terms:

To MacNeill belongs the credit of having dragged Celtic Ireland practically single-handed from the antiquarian mists into the light of history ...[5]

He would never claim to have said the last word on a topic: it was his glory that he had so often said the first.[6]

Byrne's MacNeill is a pioneer, not a man clinging to a life-raft of scholarship while tossed in seas of political failure.

Yet, MacNeill did suffer lingering political disappointments. While describing the assassination of Kevin O'Higgins, a key Free State minister, MacNeill remarked that there was little sympathy between the men and that he was the one responsible for his resignation from government.[7] Far from being an accidental activist or a disappointed scholar, MacNeill was both intensely political and intensely academic. The two went hand-in-hand. Throughout his memoir MacNeill interweaves descriptions of multiple incarcerations by the British state with his ever-evolving research into the history of early medieval Ireland as well as alluding to his writing and reading activities.[8] The great Swiss Celticist Rudolf Thurneysen jokingly remarked that MacNeill should never be freed because prison seemed such a productive research space.[9] Furthermore, an examination of MacNeill's publication record demonstrates that the high point of his involvement in nationalist revolutionary politics between 1913 and 1925 was especially academically productive, including the appearance of influential papers on law, politics, genealogies and what he referred to as 'synthetic histories', the latter constituting extensive textual traditions created by the early Irish learned classes to explain their past.[10] The energy that MacNeill devoted to politics was equally applied to scholarship. There is no reason to believe that MacNeill was reluctantly plucked from an austere world of scholarship and plunged into the maelstrom of nationalist struggles or vice versa.

They were intertwined, almost from the beginning, and played off each other, creatively and productively, until the end. Both were significant inspirations for his foundational contribution to the Irish Manuscripts Commission.[11] The Commission's focus on the preservation and publication of the sources for Irish history, in order to place that history on a recognised international footing, institutionalised a cultural national politics that consciously resonated with other great European enterprises such as the *Monumenta Germaniae Historica*.[12] Thus, it would be surprising not to see MacNeill's political passions encoded into his life and literature. Indeed, their echoes haunted him to the day of his death. On that day, the very last thing he wrote was a phrase from a seventh-century Life of St Patrick, found in the ninth-century manuscript known as the Book of Armagh:

Endeus autem dixit Patricio. Tu filio meo babtismum da, quia tener est.

Énde said to Patrick: 'Give baptism to my son, for he is of tender age'.[13]

This phrase movingly goes to the heart of one of the great tragedies of MacNeill's life and of his politics, the death of his son Brian, fighting for the anti-treaty forces during the Irish Civil War, pitting father against son on opposite sides.[14] Brian died on the slopes of Ben Bulben, County Sligo, while Conall, son of Énde, whose baptism is described in the early medieval text, is associated with the relatively nearby north Mayo.[15] They share a landscape of death and rebirth, as MacNeill understood baptism was a sort of death leading to the affirmation of new life. MacNeill never came to terms with the circumstances of Brian's killing. This deathbed meditation on fathers and sons, itself a powerful motif in the medieval source that he was quoting, seems to show MacNeill reaching backwards into the world of scholarship, into a past that he had done so much to unravel, in order to find comfort from the inevitable regrets of a life lived during revolution and change.

Given these circumstances, it is remarkable that MacNeill the historian tends to be considered in isolation from the politician. The extent to which his politics had a profound and lasting influence on his scholarship has been under-explored.[16] This has not only impacted upon assessments of MacNeill in the round, as shown by Dudley Edwards' comments, but has obscured identification of the politics underpinning his scholarly vision. Early Irish historians still work in MacNeill's long shadow, often unconsciously, such is the extent to which his interpretation of the organisation of early medieval Irish society is normative. Scholars broadly accept MacNeill's structural analysis of pre-Norman society while rejecting his judgements of events and even processes, especially in relationship to Christianisation.[17] The debt is thematic rather than lying in specifics, where MacNeill's knowledge has been decisively outstripped by generations of new scholarship and discovery. It is time for this dynamic to be reassessed, starting with a reconsideration of the basic assumptions that animated MacNeill's research. There is a great deal of source material for this investigation. MacNeill's published scholarly output is voluminous and this was heavily supplemented with works of popular history and commentary that were intended for wide dissemination.[18] For the purposes of this paper three studies, in particular, will be considered.

These are *Phases of Irish History*, published in 1919 and based on public lectures delivered in the Rotunda in 1919, *Celtic Ireland*, published in 1921, but drawing on his lectures on early Irish history in UCD in 1904 and, finally, 1935's *Early Irish Laws and Institutions*, the printed version of the public talks that MacNeill gave in New York University in 1930.[19] These volumes share striking similarities: they are all book-length, in contrast with the vast majority of MacNeill's publications, which consist of articles and shorter essays; each one aims to distil his research for a popular audience with one eye to academic supporters and rivals; crucially, all three books are extended and discursive attempts to explain the origins of early Irish civilisation and, as a result, provide the clearest evidence for his principal beliefs as a scholar. They also span a long portion of MacNeill's career, allowing a broad overview. In them, he frequently argues that the interplay of blood and tradition created the Irish story.[20] However, this story is heavily coloured by the legacies of empire and colonialism that shaped MacNeill. It is shot through with his anxieties around race, barbarism and culture, anxieties that were in constant dialogue with MacNeill's understanding of the early Irish past.

OF EMPIRICISM AND EMPIRE

MacNeill was a scholar of nation and of empire in an age of self-conscious modernity. He was a product of that liminal era when antiquarian enthusiasm gave way to the beginnings of history as a professional discipline.[21] In a warm appreciation of the great Jesuit scholar Edmund Hogan, the man who was effectively his teacher and lifelong inspiration, MacNeill gives a fascinating insight into his beginnings as a historian – his origin story.[22] MacNeill makes it clear that he came to Hogan for Irish language training, not history. In fact, Irish was, and remained, one of his great passions. Without love of the language, MacNeill would never have become a historian. Beginning in 1890, under Hogan's guidance, MacNeill learned the value of primary source analysis, became skilled in palaeography and started to master medieval Irish, the same skills that are today necessary for an early Irish historian. Hogan, author of the monumental *Onomasticon Goedelicum*, an enormous gazetteer of early Irish place-names running to tens of thousands of items that is yet to be surpassed, was well suited to the task.[23] It was the making of MacNeill, who described his training as being the equivalent of working in a laboratory, adopting the language of scientific rigour.[24] But there can be no doubt that MacNeill was highly self-directed. Perhaps recognising a kindred spirit, as well as a star, Hogan materially advanced MacNeill's career, acting as his first academic mentor and sponsor. He was responsible for his major academic breakthrough, recommending that MacNeill provide a series of lectures on early Irish history in UCD, which were eventually published as *Celtic Ireland*. It is worth remembering that during this time MacNeill was a clerk in the Four Courts and a founder member of Conradh na Gaeilge. He served as editor of *An Claidheamh Soluis*, a key newspaper for Irish cultural revivalists.[25] None of these activities took place in isolation of the others.

MacNeill as a scholar was firmly within the empiricist tradition. This can be seen most clearly in his deconstruction of the historicity of the great and complex work of medieval Irish synthetic history, or pseudo-history, *Lebor Gabála Érenn*, popularly known as the Book of Invasions.[26] Before MacNeill, the dominant view of early Ireland was heavily influenced by the desire of the early Irish to position themselves as part of the wider Christian world. They formulated an all-encompassing history of the island, stretching back to before the Flood, one envisaged as a series of legendary invasions culminating in the arrival of the sons of Míl, ancestors of the dominant pre-Norman dynasties. It was a high point of the medieval learned tradition and is represented in some of the most important surviving Irish manuscripts. The scheme was so all-encompassing that the temptation to accept it as real was accepted by generations of scholars and their public. The term 'Milesian' came to be shorthand for someone claiming native Irish ancestry or identity.[27] MacNeill may have idealised early medieval Ireland but he was no romanticist: he showed the *Lebor Gabála* to be completely legendary and fabricated:

> The fact is that the whole story of the origin of the Gaels in Scythia or in Armenia, their wanderings by land and sea, their settlement in Spain, and their landing in Ireland, is an artificial product of the schools and does not represent a primitive tradition.[28]

This artificial history of *Lebor Gabála* was to be contrasted with real history, which he believed to be based on original documentation and archaeological investigation. As he appositely remarked in *Celtic Ireland*, in words that still remain relevant:

> Ancient Ireland, as it happens, is no vacant region for free speculation. The materials for its study are remarkably copious, and the method of its study must be by way of research, analysis, and synthesis.[29]

Thus, MacNeill's technical skillset fitted him to be the first academic historian of early medieval Ireland in an almost modern sense. This was a role which he assumed willingly, as he believed that the early Irish past showed the potential for a modern Irish future, free from British imperial rule. Yet, one must be wary of viewing MacNeill's training as a guarantor of academic disinterest. In fact, he did not believe that such disinterest was possible: for him, history flourished through the nutrients of engaged empathy in a soil of academic rigour.[30] He doubted the power of impartiality, famously remarking that 'neither apathy nor antipathy can ever bring out the truth of history'.[31] It has been argued that this engaged empathy with the past played a major role in MacNeill's debate with G.H. Orpen, a pre-eminent and celebrated scholar of pre-Norman Ireland.[32] This debate reverberates in MacNeill's public lectures and subsequently in the pages of his extended popular works of history.[33] *Phases of Irish History*, in particular, gives Orpen a starring role. The reason for this is that Orpen, a mirror to MacNeill in his embrace of the value of primary documents,[34] had a negative view of early Irish society. He painted it as an anarchy that was saved from itself by the arrival of the Normans, by what he termed a civilisation 'more advanced' than anything that the island had previously enjoyed.[35] As MacNeill knew, Orpen's comprehension of the pre-Norman period was hampered by his complete lack of expertise in the medieval Irish vernacular sources. Furthermore, Orpen's politically unionist persuasion coloured his belief that the native Irish were unable to govern themselves without the helping hand of British paternalism.[36] Therefore, MacNeill's increasingly vitriolic responses to Orpen were inspired by scholarly and political antipathies. Even more fundamentally, however, Orpen's treatment of early Ireland was emblematic of a colonialist approach to the Irish past as primitive and tribal, a vocabulary that was typically used of subjugated peoples throughout the British Empire.[37] MacNeill not only rejected these ideas, as expressed by Orpen and others, but responded through arguing that early Ireland was far from primitive and that it was one of the glories of early medieval European civilisation. The Irish past was a source of pride rather than of shame.

Moreover, lying at the heart of MacNeill's response to Orpen was a deeply rooted and intense curiosity about how Ireland was organised before the intervention of the English. What was the island like when its native inhabitants governed themselves? This was the focus of his ground-breaking work on early Irish population groups, their names, their structures and their inter-relationships.[38] I have suggested elsewhere that

MacNeill envisaged an early medieval Ireland whose institutions were refracted through the prism of his experience as a subject of the British Empire.[39] It is worth revisiting here in the context of his over-arching and highly influential interpretation of early Irish society. MacNeill suggested that the original political organisation of Ireland was a pentarchy of five connected but largely independent kingdoms, arguing that the Irish word for province, *cóiced*, literally a fifth, pointed towards their ancient reality.[40] These were superseded soon after the introduction of Christianity by the political frameworks of what he regarded as a golden age. MacNeill argued that early Irish society existed through a network of small interdependent communities that recognised an emblematic but limited national monarchy.[41] The political and social landscapes were systematically and locally organised, flourishing in the absence of an overly tyrannical central authority. MacNeill remarked that 'a centralised authority is an instrument of civilisation, not an essential' and that societies thrived when bureaucracy was limited and subservient to group and individual needs.[42] In a moment of rhetorical hyperbole, grounded in the political fears engendered by communism and fascism, he described adherence to a monolithic state as 'the worship of the beast and his image'.[43] He favourably contrasted early Irish institutions and communities with Norman feudalism, which he decried.[44] Intriguingly, however, he mapped these small Irish socio-political communities, known as *túatha*, onto the political world with which he was familiar. His early Ireland is strikingly similar in outline to the British Empire, similar but perfected, lacking the flaws of imperialism and a heavy-handed state apparatus. In a telling passage of *Phases of Irish History*, he explains the relationships between different types of *túatha*, which could be classed as free and unfree, among other things, by analogy with the British Empire.[45] As MacNeill put it:

> The status of the unfree communities, roundly speaking, was similar to that of the natives of British India at present; and the status of a tributary state would be comparable to a country possessing self-government but subject to what is called an imperial contribution. The non-tributary states might be compared to the existing autonomous dominions of the British Empire.[46]

Early Ireland is the British Empire writ exquisitely small in minute and ornamented cursive rather than monumental and plain capitals. How much of this is analogy? How much is filtered through MacNeill's personally

driven reading of the early Irish sources? Few scholars today accept the
ineluctability of the pentarchy or follow MacNeill's confident forays into
the politics of the island's ancient prehistory. Yet, few seriously question
the reality of MacNeill's elegant dance of *túatha*, the interplay of proto-
dominions, communities and kingdoms or 'how all the different elements
of society fitted together into a functioning whole'.[47] It is now clear that
early medieval Ireland was not Orpen's anarchy.[48] It is perhaps less clear that
neither was it a forerunner of late imperial Britain.

ON RACE AND CULTURAL HYBRIDITY

MacNeill believed that these social structures had emerged through the
intertwined but unequal influences of a people and its traditions, with
the latter being by far the more significant. The idea of a people, what
constituted it and how it changed over time, resonated with MacNeill's
present circumstances and flowed within the cross-currents of Western
academic scholarship. Here the histories of peoples, ethnicities and races
had become mainstream.[49] The language of primitive tribalism, which
he objected to in Orpen, came from this same well-spring. Allied to this,
MacNeill had a distinctive, if unsystematic, interpretation of history as
the outcome of processes powered by culture and tradition. These were
not impersonal but created by human actions within social structures.
He revealingly states: ... the historian or the archaeologist will set himself
an impossible task if he undertakes to explain every fact of history or
archaeology as a sort of mechanical resultant of pre-existing forces.[50]
History, he argued, should be about people of all social standing, not just
the celebration of great leaders. For example, in a radio broadcast he stated:

> Nothing is trivial which gives us a better knowledge of what people
> were doing or even what they were thinking about before our time.
> It used to be thought by historians that everything was trivial except
> the achievements of statesmen & military chiefs ... more and more the
> business of history is recognised to be the full biography of peoples ...
> [that] tells us something about Irish families of every grade and station
> in life.[51]

Furthermore, he strongly believed that cultures coalesced into nations
which, ideally, should coexist in harmony and mutual respect.[52] This is

not particularly unusual and the impulse towards national histories was widespread, although it is telling that MacNeill stressed communities over individuals.

More contradictory is MacNeill's attitude towards race and how racial distinctiveness related to the formation and development of a people. Like most educated Westerners of his era he believed in the existence of different races. However, he frequently argued against the grain of the racial (and racist) essentialism that was coming to dominate many academic circles.[53] This essentialist position viewed races as having fixed characteristics, often read relative to each other as being either inherently superior or inferior. Thus, in *Phases of Irish History* MacNeill wrote that every people had two lines of descent, 'one by blood and one by tradition'.[54] Throughout his work he argued that descent by blood was the less important of the two, a clear rejection of crude assumptions of heredity.[55] Instead it is shared tradition that creates a people and through them vitalises a culture. Inherent racial attributes are not a factor. As he told his audience, gathered in Dublin's Rotunda in 1918:

> There is no existing Latin race, no Teutonic race, no Anglo-Saxon race and no Celtic race. Each of the groups to whom these names are popularly applied, is a mixture of various races ... and for the most part they are a mixture of the same races ...[56]

For MacNeill, nationality had little and perhaps nothing to do with race but everything to do with tradition. But even this was not infallible and had limitations. It could be improved by new peoples and new ideas.[57] Ireland was a nation made up of several groups, populations or races, terms he uses interchangeably, bound together by their habitation of the island. In this spirit he was willing to acknowledge the important role that the Vikings and the Normans had played in the unfolding history of the Irish people and the story of their island, although this was always achieved through integration with the earlier inhabitants.[58] A report published in *An Claidheamh Soluis* in 1907 describes how MacNeill publicly affirmed that a nation was a brotherhood of blood and of adoption, showing just how consistent he was in formulating this strand of thought through his entire career.[59] There can be little doubt that MacNeill's rejection of a Celtic mist-enshrouded Ireland positively shaped the discipline of early Irish history although it has proved more tenacious, generally, than MacNeill might have expected. MacNeill's views on race are core to his historical interpretation. His comment in *Phases of Irish History* that Ireland was 'one nation, composed of diverse peoples'[60] was echoed years later, and in dramatically different political circumstances, in *Early Irish Laws and Institutions*, based on lectures given in 1930 to the American Irish Historical Society in New York.[61] He told his well-connected audience that the Irish and Americans were both racially composite peoples and all the better for it. MacNeill argued that it was important not to think within the single and limiting dimension of racial categorisation.[62] Moreover, in the introduction that he wrote to accompany the publication of the lectures in a single volume, he stated that:

> I suggest that nearly every generalisation that has passed current about things Celtic or things supposed to be Celtic – the Celtic race, the Celtic temperament, Celtic art, the Celtic Church, Celtic society – stands equally in need of revision and rectification.[63]

However, MacNeill's views were not static and were frequently contradictory. For instance, his absolute rejection of interpretations of early Ireland as tribal and primitive was based on his racist acceptance that the communities of the 'head-hunters of New Guinea and the Hottentot' were accurately described by these terms.[64] MacNeill refused to accept that the Irish were like other so-called primitive peoples governed by the British. Therefore, while MacNeill's dismissal of the tribal paradigm can read as a forerunner of post-colonialist critiques, it is mired in his own assumptions about the superiority of what can be broadly described as Western and Western-derived civilisations. In addition, MacNeill does occasionally echo the language of scientific racism. He makes reference to 'Nordic' and 'Mediterranean' races and even suggests that early Irish history is valuable because it allows for the study of the European white man uninfluenced by the mould of the 'complex east'.[65] There are a whole series of prejudices here combined with racist orientalism. The viewpoint is strongly nativist, suggesting that Ireland was untouched by the great civilisations that emerged in the Mediterranean. However, such statements are relatively rare in MacNeill's published work, although they are more pronounced by the 1930s. Like many academics he was complicit in articulating a world view where races were believed to incarnate specific developmental characteristics. These sentiments are most important in *Early Irish Laws and Institutions*, although that text also explicitly celebrates racial hybridity as a driver of cultural strength.[66] MacNeill suggests that it is better to be the product of a mixture of peoples. Cultural dynamism is a gift from hybrid populations. However, it is hard to escape the conclusion that these hybrid populations were primarily coded as being 'white'.

It is hardly coincidental that this publication coincided with MacNeill's support for the Harvard Mission to Ireland of 1931–6.[67] This Mission was a combined anthropological and archaeological survey of Ireland led by Earnest Hooton, the influential Professor of Anthropology at Harvard who promoted racial typology and eugenics.[68] His legacy included work on racial classification, influencing pseudo-scientific fields such as craniometry and phrenology, none of which were value neutral. For example, Hooton believed that measuring cranial dimensions gave insight into degeneracy and advocated the use of eugenics and the sterilisation of 'undesirable' types.[69] Hooton apparently never visited Ireland but he was a guiding inspiration.[70] The Harvard Irish Study had enthusiastic support from the Irish political and academic establishments. It was regarded as a modernising force and at the cutting edge of scientific method. Measuring the skulls of individuals, including MacNeill's own, was a basic element of the so-called scientific processes engaged in by the researchers.[71] Ironically, in terms of MacNeill's support for the Mission, it was founded on Hooton's view that Ireland had a racially identifiable 'Celtic population' created from an admixture of Nordic and Mediterranean physical types.[72] Affluent Irish-Americans, who supported the Mission, believed it to be an invaluable counterweight to the image of degenerate Irishmen as seen in the infamous *Punch* cartoons.[73] The Mission did have undoubted success, particularly in archaeology: Hugh O'Neill Hencken's digs at Lagore and Ballinderry remain important and a generation of Irish archaeologists were introduced to new methodologies through the training introduced by the survey.[74] Furthermore, the anthropological work of Arensberg and Kimball in County Clare is still mined by scholars, both for what it reveals about the society of the recently independent state and about the assumptions made by the researchers themselves.[75] But other aspects have proved far more controversial and none more so than simplistic race-based interpretations of the past. Nevertheless, despite worrying echoes of the language of race and its disastrous mis-measurement, MacNeill rejected race as a meaningful historical category. As he remarked:

> History everywhere shows clearly that racial character is but the habit of a people, that can be changed as a vesture ... Nothing in history is explained by mere heredity. Acquired habits, events, institutions, education, external associations can degenerate and recreate a nation.[76]

UNDER COLONIALISM'S SHADOW

MacNeill is widely celebrated as the founder of early Irish history as a discipline reliant on fact-based approaches and grounded in the best scientific methods. To put things in perspective, MacNeill was born in 1867. Leopold von Ranke, regarded by many as the first recognisably professional historian in the modern sense, died in 1886. The Rankean revolution, which emphasised the importance of primary sources and the absolute centrality of archival research, was not even a generation old when MacNeill embarked on his scholarly journey. MacNeill, by the standards of his day, was cutting-edge, using empirical techniques and applying perspectives that were supported by historical best practice. Even more remarkably, much of his multi-faceted work remains of value. MacNeill contributed enormously to understandings of early Irish institutions, politics, genealogies and ideologies, to the extent that the political drivers of his opinions are often forgotten. Furthermore, he was passionately devoted to bringing history to the wider public. MacNeill strove to give the Irish public a taste for a history sharply distinguished from misguided mythologies. Throughout his career MacNeill dragged early Irish history into the mainstream, rejecting antiquarianism, exoticism, romanticism and racial essentialism. Understanding the past was pivotal to his career.

He was also a man of his times and these times profoundly shaped all aspects of his life. This was one lived under the influence of empire, one lived with the clear political aim of proving that the Irish in the past, and by analogy in the present and the future, were a people capable of self-government. The once and future Ireland was a full member of the European community of nations. It is, perhaps, inevitable, therefore, that experiences of the British Empire moulded MacNeill's early Ireland. They helped structure his interpretation of early Irish communities and informed his attitudes towards bureaucracy. The wider legacies of colonialism, especially as articulated through the rise of scientific racism, were more problematic for MacNeill. He accepted that the Irish people were essentially mongrels, a mixture produced by the many groups who had settled on the island, each one contributing their chapters to a glorious story. But he was careful to show that this mongrel mixture was white and European. He rejected race as relevant to historical analysis while, at the same time, sharing in the racist prejudices of British administrators towards those presumed to be primitive and in need of civilisation and government. He wrote under colonialism's shadow. But he also wrote out of a passionate belief that history was a force for liberation and self-knowledge. We cannot understand MacNeill the nationalist, the politician, the revolutionary, with all his contradictions, unless we appreciate the centrality of scholarship to his life. Understanding the origins of early Ireland was a political, a personal and a public act for MacNeill. He was also telling a story, contributing to a long narrative told by many voices stretching far into the past. As he puts it, bringing *Phases of Irish History* to its end:

> If only I have succeeded in convincing you that Irish history must contain life, movement, colour, coherence, and human interest, beyond anything depicted of it in many books [...] with that and the recollection of your kind support I make a well contented conclusion.[77]

'Bold and imaginative': Eoin MacNeill's Irish Manuscripts Commission[1]

MICHAEL KENNEDY

I

The Irish Manuscripts Commission (IMC), Ireland's primary publisher of historical source material, was Eoin MacNeill's major post-politics venture. The IMC is, arguably, MacNeill's lasting legacy to historical scholarship and the writing of Ireland's histories. MacNeill alone was the inspiration behind the creation of the IMC, which was established by W.T. Cosgrave in 1928 in the cash-strapped post-Civil War years. Its establishment was the culmination of pressure brought by MacNeill on Cosgrave and his Executive Council colleagues, many of whom MacNeill had been in government with, to address the loss of documentary sources for Ireland's histories arising out of the destruction of the Public Record Office at the Four Courts in Dublin during the Civil War of 1922 to 1923. Thus the view of MacNeill's IMC and UCD colleague Professor Robin Dudley Edwards that it was 'probably due to Eoin MacNeill than to anyone else that [the IMC] was established' is as accurate today as it was in 1973 when it was written.[2]

Edwards made a second point, also equally valid: it was due to MacNeill 'that Irish historical studies developed so impressively' from the 1920s. The academic climate for history in the first years of the Irish Free State was bleak. There were few outlets for aspiring academics, in particular those interested in publishing manuscripts. It was a cyclical problem: there were few outlets for research and, because there were few, there was little research. MacNeill knew from his own career path the difficulties facing those wishing to become professional historians in Ireland. He lamented the situation. While there was, he felt, 'a certain modicum of publication' in the *Proceedings of the Royal Irish Academy* and in *Ériu*, the journal of the School of Irish Learning, 'their scope left little room for the publication of manuscript material'.[3]

The IMC was based on MacNeill's vision for a Monumenta Hiberniae: a library of Irish historical source material in the style of the *Monumenta Germaniae Historica* founded in 1819 to edit and publish sources for German history to 1500. MacNeill's ideas found initial expression in the preface to his 1921 *Celtic Ireland*:

> Should any benefactor be inspired to promote work that will make our Nation's ancient story attractive to young Irish intellects and that will also give it the place it deserves in the world's history, my appeal would be for the endowment of research based strictly on the joint study of Irish history and archaeology and of Irish philology, and for such endowment as will ensure the publication of any piece of research work well done.[4]

He returned to the idea in an article in the Jesuit journal *Studies* in June 1924, calling for 'the institution of a Library of Monumenta Hiberniae, in the form of a continuous series of uniform volumes to be published under the direction of a corporate body of competent scholars with a suitable endowment to be administered under the terms of a permanent definite trust'.[5] This body was to make the primary source material for Irish history available. Elsewhere in the article MacNeill declared that 'for Irish History what is needed most and is severely needed, is the publication of documents, the raw material of historical study'.[6] MacNeill knew that access to original documentation was essential to developing History as a professional discipline in Ireland.

MacNeill's vision has, through the IMC, created a massive publicly available exploration of Ireland's past. Since 1928 the IMC has discovered, recovered, protected and made more accessible the sources underpinning Irish history from the earliest to modern times. It has published more than 150 individual volumes and, based on MacNeill's model, has established a tradition where IMC members give their services pro bono.

II

The destruction of the Public Record Office at the Four Courts in Dublin in June 1922 was a massive shock to the study of Ireland's history. Primary sources for over 700 years of Irish history went up in flames. It was a cataclysm that had 'torn whole chapters out of Irish history'.[7] From this national calamity emerged the immediate impetus for the IMC and its primary task of publishing original historical source materials. Though the majority of the original documents destroyed in the Four Courts could never be replaced, copies of some of them existed as researchers in the Four Courts had copied some documents out by hand and in other cases copies existed in the major research libraries of western Europe, in particular in the Bodleian in Oxford.[8] They could be found, assessed, edited and published. By publishing these original sources from which to write the history of Ireland, historical research in Ireland in the mid-decades of the twentieth century would be vastly improved and the 'pseudo-history' of Ireland, often politically inspired or religiously biased, could be effectively challenged in solid source-based academic writings.

For the next four years MacNeill worked on his plan for an Irish historical manuscripts commission. Success came a step closer after an informal meeting held in August 1927 between W.T. Cosgrave and his Executive Council colleagues Ernest Blythe, John Marcus O'Sullivan, Patrick McGilligan and Richard Mulcahy.[9] They agreed to set up an 'Irish Historical Manuscripts Commission for the publication of Irish Historical Records especially in the Irish language'.[10] MacNeill was to be the 'chief' of the Commission. The decision of the five members of the Executive Council might not have been a formal Council decision, but it represented the acceptance of MacNeill's plan by the Executive Council.

In March 1928 Blythe announced in the Dáil, in answer to a parliamentary question from Cumann na nGaedheal deputy for Donegal Hugh A. Law, that the government intended to establish an Irish Manuscripts Commission 'entrusted with the publication of Irish manuscripts and other documents of literary and historical interest to the people of Ireland'.[11]

The initial membership of the IMC had a substantially wider frame of reference and experience than MacNeill had first envisaged, its personnel a mixture of senior professors, senior civil servants and senior university administrators, and it crossed the religious and political divides in post-Civil War Ireland. The combined experience of the IMC's personnel brought to its work a greater concentration on modern Irish history, something MacNeill had not initially envisaged. However, this did not present him with a problem; MacNeill's mind 'moved easily' between the centuries and in moving the IMC's personnel to a wider base the IMC could range with unparalleled expertise from early Christian Ireland to the late seventeenth century, the latter date being that at which the academic investigation of modern Irish history normally ended in the early twentieth century.[12]

On 8 September 1928 the Executive Council agreed to set up the IMC 'for the study and publication of Irish Manuscripts and other documents of Irish literary and historical evidence'.[13] MacNeill had strong views on the membership of the Commission. To him the IMC should be made up primarily of professors of Irish and of Irish History. He favoured including Professor Osborn Bergin, Dr Richard I. Best, Professor James Hogan, Professor Tomás Ó Máille and Professor Thomas O'Rahilly. The IMC membership was based on the list of those who gave evidence to the 1924 Seanad Commission on Irish Manuscripts. MacNeill later dropped Bergin, Ó Máille and O'Rahilly when it was agreed at government level that the future the IMC would concentrate on historical rather than linguistic material. This shift showed the input of the Department of the President into deciding the Commission's personnel.

The Department of the President favoured a wide remit to the IMC – its nominees included Professors of Archaeology and of Education as well as History. It also ensured TCD representation on the IMC, making sure that TCD Provost Edward J. Gwynn was appointed to its ranks. His name had not appeared on MacNeill's original list of possible members. The department also included a strong Catholic input on the Commission with the president of Saint Patrick's College Maynooth and the Professor of Education at UCD included. The seven personnel suggested by O'Hegarty to MacNeill were:

> Professor Eoin MacNeill (Professor of Early Irish History, UCD) (Chair);
> Dr Richard I. Best (Assistant Director, NLI);
> Professor the Reverend Timothy A. Corcoran SJ (Professor of Theory and Practice of Education, UCD);
> Professor E.J. Gwynn (Provost, TCD);
> Professor James Hogan (Professor of History, UCC);
> Professor R.A. Stewart Macalister (Professor of Celtic Archaeology, UCD);
> Monsignor James McCaffrey (President, St Patrick's Maynooth).

MacNeill told O'Hegarty that he found these personnel 'in every way satisfactory', though he suggested the addition of J.F. Morrissey, Assistant Deputy Keeper of Records, 'so that there might be direct contact with the State Paper and Record Offices'.[14] It was an important choice as Morrissey's 'intimate knowledge of Irish records, both public and private, was ever at the disposal of the Commission, and those engaged in its editorial work'.[15] Finally there was William Butler, with his 'exceptional knowledge of the materials and sources of medieval and modern Irish history' and who, with Hogan and MacNeill, would be essential to the development of the Commission in its first years. Butler's sudden death in 1930 deprived the IMC of an able supporter.[16]

The members of the Commission were appointed when president of the Executive Council W.T. Cosgrave signed the IMC's Warrant of Appointment on 10 October 1928. The names of the nine commissioners and the terms of reference of the IMC were announced by Cosgrave in Dáil Éireann seven days later. It was 'an unusually imaginative and comprehensive government response to the disaster of 1922'.[17]

III

The Irish Manuscripts Commission held its first meeting on 15 January 1929. Their expertise was enhanced by MacNeill's energy as chairman. Already central as instigator and inspiration for the creation of the IMC, he had his role institutionalised in the position of the Commission's chairman. From its first meeting, the IMC began to move with the speed and urgency that characterised its first decade. There was a great willingness to work unleashed, with a sense of a job to be done and an evident delight in doing it. The IMC, through its publication of major sources in book form, would provide an outlet for research, and, by publishing sources, would act as a multiplier, enabling additional research to be undertaken from those sources.

Shorter documents would be published in the Commission's occasional journal, *Analecta Hibernica*. Established in 1930, *Analecta* was edited by UCC Professor of History, James Hogan, and MacNeill, though Hogan was the driving force behind the journal. It was the backbone of the Commission's work through the 1930s and 1940s. Hogan and MacNeill provided the impetus for the IMC for its first decade. Through MacNeill's inspiration, Dudley Edwards described the real achievement of the IMC as the 'development of Irish history in the critical years in which it has become professionalised and internationally respected'.[18]

The first years of the IMC saw it undertake a rich and full agenda with an array of important texts being published. The initial focus was on Irish sources from pre-1500, coalescing around MacNeill's early Irish texts and

1. Eoin MacNeill and Agnes Moore's wedding, Ballymena, County Antrim,
19 April 1898 (UCDA LA30/PH/346).

2. Rosetta McNeill, Eoin's mother, with her grandchildren (L–R) Brian, Eibhlín and Niall, on the steps of Hazelbrook House, Malahide, County Dublin, 1902 (UCDA LA30/PH/349).

3. Eoin MacNeill at his desk in the Accountant General's Office, Four Courts,
Dublin [n.d., pre-1908] (UCDA LA30/PH/378).

4. Photograph of a sketch of Eoin MacNeill attributed to his son Séamus [n.d.]
(UCDA LA30/PH/322).

5. Eoin MacNeill teaching a class at the Irish College in Omeath, County Louth [*c.*1911–13] (UCDA LA30/PH/386).

6. Group portrait of released 1916 prisoners outside Mansion House, Dawson Street, Dublin, MacNeill seated near the centre of the group with his arm around de Valera's shoulder [June 1917] (UCDA LA30/PH/392).

Correspondents are requested to address all letters on official business to—
THE SECRETARY,
CORK COUNTY COUNCIL,
COURT HOUSE,
CORK.

Number of Enclosures..................

THE NATIONAL UNIVERSITY OF IRELAND
No. 3.
Received 11 MAR. 1918
Answered

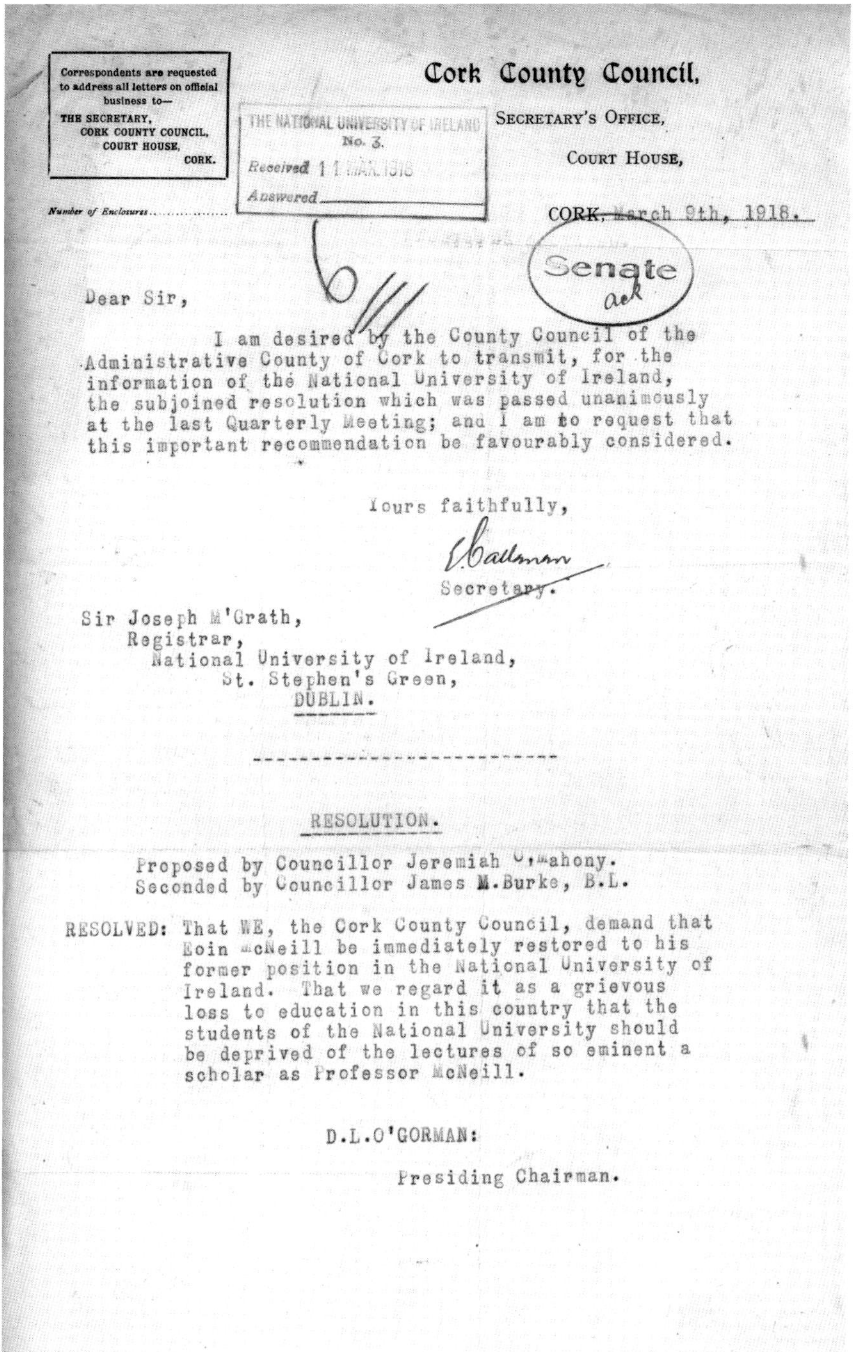

Cork County Council.

SECRETARY'S OFFICE,
COURT HOUSE,
CORK, March 9th, 1918.

Senate
ack

Dear Sir,

I am desired by the County Council of the Administrative County of Cork to transmit, for the information of the National University of Ireland, the subjoined resolution which was passed unanimously at the last Quarterly Meeting; and I am to request that this important recommendation be favourably considered.

Yours faithfully,

E. Callanan
Secretary.

Sir Joseph M'Grath,
Registrar,
National University of Ireland,
St. Stephen's Green,
DUBLIN.

RESOLUTION.

Proposed by Councillor Jeremiah O'Mahony.
Seconded by Councillor James M.Burke, B.L.

RESOLVED: That WE, the Cork County Council, demand that Eoin McNeill be immediately restored to his former position in the National University of Ireland. That we regard it as a grievous loss to education in this country that the students of the National University should be deprived of the lectures of so eminent a scholar as Professor McNeill.

D.L.O'GORMAN:

Presiding Chairman.

7. Letter to the Senate of the National University of Ireland from Cork County Council demanding that Eoin MacNeill be restored to his professorship at University College Dublin, 9 March 1918 (NUI Archives).

8. Eoin MacNeill at a picnic on Rostrevor Mountain, County Down [*c.*1919–20] (UCDA LA30/PH/324).

the key sources of medieval and early-modern Ireland. The IMC's work was made up of prestige long-term multi-volume projects, such as the *Calendar of Ormond Deeds*, the *Commentarius Rinuccinianus* and the *Civil Survey*, and single-volume publications, these, along with *Analecta*, being the core of the IMC's publication programme. The Civil Survey volumes attracted considerable interest from genealogical, historical and antiquarian societies and were extensively reviewed in the national and local press as well as academic journals. Reviews of the first volume of the *Ormond Deeds* and of the *Red Book of Ormond*, which the IMC published at the same time, were excellent. *The Times* and the *Times Literary Supplement* were particularly glowing. In an editorial article on both volumes *The Times* declared that 'scholars, indeed, have no cause to complain of the riches lavished upon them from the new Ireland'.[19]

The Commission's early years saw lively growth, and an eager, if over-optimistic, publishing programme. MacNeill 'took an active part in the mechanics' of the organisation of the IMC and 'in the routine of which its office was the centre'.[20] He was more likely to solve any problems facing the IMC with a discreet letter to Cosgrave or through a private off-the-record chat with Minister for Finance Ernest Blythe.

This can be seen when the IMC began the reproduction of one of the most important codices in Irish, 'the famous vellum Codex known as the Book of Lecan'.[21] Published in 1937, Lecan would be 'the first of a series of facsimiles to be reproduced in Ireland', with the work being undertaken by the Ordnance Survey.[22] To get the project up and running, MacNeill met with his former cabinet colleague and friend Minister for Finance Ernest Blythe, and unofficially discussed the production of Lecan with him. Even though it was not possible to give any figure as to the cost of Lecan, Blythe gave MacNeill a virtual open cheque to go ahead with publication, stating he was simply 'in agreement with' MacNeill's plans.[23] MacNeill's contacts with Blythe are revealing of his view of the Commission and its work. MacNeill explained to Blythe:

> I want to keep you personally interested, if I can, in the work of the Manuscripts Commission. From experience of the meetings of the Commission, I believe that we have secured a very good body of men, who understand the possibilities and are all zealous to have the work done. I have no doubt that their programme, if they can carry it out, will work well for the national reputation and for the reputation of the Government. They are all extremely anxious, and feel it to be especially

urgent, that the Commission should achieve something worthy of its institution during its first year of operation – that it will be judged upon that by our own people and others. Already the prospects of its work are exciting attention widely, and we have correspondence and inquiries from various countries, including several American universities, mostly in a spirit of approval and co-operation. The most important part of the programme is the facsimile reproduction of some of the principal MSS and we have decided to begin with the Book of Lecan.[24]

In the event, *The Oldest Irish Fragments of the Senchas Már* preceded it by six years as the IMC's first facsimile publication. Lecan nevertheless remained MacNeill's favourite IMC project and, for him, a labour of love.

IV

Fianna Fáil's arrival in power in March 1932 changed MacNeill's working relationship with government and civil service. Like Cosgrave, de Valera was a supporter of the work of the IMC, and MacNeill had recourse to him at important junctures. However, the change of government removed MacNeill's comfortable channel to Blythe. In Blythe's successor – Seán MacEntee – the IMC found itself dealing with a minister with academic leanings and interventionist views. MacEntee was supported by civil servants who 'harboured a deep resentment' that the IMC and similar bodies 'were absorbing public money that might have been put to "better use"'.[25] In part this attitude stemmed from thinking in a period of overall cutbacks and economies but, as O'Brien argued, 'historians, the officials quickly came to believe, did not understand the value of money'.[26] This view dominated Department of Finance thinking on the IMC at all times. Regardless of their minister's viewpoint, the department harboured a pathological distrust of the workings of the IMC and went to absurd lengths through the 1930s to query its financial practices. The academic and the civil servant simply did not understand the other's way of working and an accommodation was to prove impossible. Indeed, the Department of Finance was to act as the first strategic overseer of the IMC, challenging the Commission's over-optimistic publications programme by seeking not a more achievable output, but straightforward cutbacks.

Nevertheless, early production schedules began to bear fruit by the mid-1930s. *Analecta Hibernica* appeared regularly and the catalogue of

IMC publications grew substantially. The IMC's long-term projects – the *Calendar of Ormond Deeds*, edited by Trinity College Professor of History Edmund Curtis, the *Civil Survey*, edited by Dr Robert Simington, and the *Commentarius Rinuccinianus*, edited by Father Stanislaus Kavanagh OSFC – were also underway.

To the *Irish Times*, the IMC was 'trusted with a task of momentous importance', publishing history and literature 'hidden away in manuscript form in libraries in Ireland, in England and on the continent'.[27] The *Cork Examiner* wrote that the IMC was 'doing excellent work in publishing these old records, which are in danger of being lost. Possibly someone may be inspired to write a really good history of Ireland.'[28] The *Standard* hoped that for those 'who endeavour in a distracting and trying atmosphere of jazz, "sport", radio and chatter to remain anchored to such studies as general and local history' the Commission's publications 'may witness the beginning of a new era in Irish scholarship and Irish historical studies'.[29]

Under MacNeill's chairmanship the 1930s became one of the most productive decades in the history of the IMC with the publication of forty-three volumes, including eight volumes of *Analecta Hibernica*. Big projects like the *Civil Survey*, *Commentarius Rinuccinianus* and the *Calendar of Ormond Deeds* maintained a steady rate of publication with three volumes of the *Commentarius*, five of the *Ormond Deeds* and four of the *Civil Survey* appearing in the 1930s. The *Civil Survey* was largely the work of the remarkable Robert C. Simington, who had been an official at the Quit Rent Office until he was transferred to the IMC in January 1934. This was done at MacNeill's behest as he had great respect for Simington's scholarship and the two men maintained a regular correspondence down the years to MacNeill's death.

MacNeill's determination that the Commission stimulate postgraduate study continued through the 1930s. Behind the formidable array of IMC publications in the 1930s were dozens of researchers, transcribers and indexers. In the preface to *Genealogical Tracts I* (1932) by Toirdhealbhach Ó Raithbheartaigh,[30] MacNeill wrote 'this book comes from the hands of a young University graduate of the National University and offers an example of the kind of work that may be expected more and more from our University students in bringing the rich sources of Irish historical lore before the public'.[31]

At a time when there were few women academics in Irish universities, it is striking to note how many IMC researchers were women graduates from TCD, UCD, Galway and Cork. For example, Dr Kathleen Mulchrone worked on the *Book of Lecan*; Pauline Henley was assisting Hogan on the *Letters and Papers Relating to the Irish Rebellion 1641–46*; Jocelyn Otway-Ruthven, later Lecky Professor of History at TCD and a member of the IMC, worked with Curtis on the *Ormond Deeds*, as did Hilda McGuire, another Curtis student. Margaret Griffith worked on a transcript of Council Roll 16 of Richard II. Griffith would in time become Deputy Keeper of the Public Record Office and, like Otway-Ruthven, a member of the IMC. The gathering and expansion of this skilled group of academics began to fulfil one of MacNeill's goals for the IMC. The Commission created a wider academic skill base in Ireland and even in the handful of individuals mentioned; a number would play leading roles in developing the disciplines central to the development of the study of Irish history.

Most gratifying to MacNeill was the advent of young scholars whose involvement with the Commission would last for the next five decades. Robin Dudley Edwards had been a student of MacNeill's at UCD and subsequently went to the Institute of Historical Research at the University of London where he obtained a PhD. He had already met Theodore Moody, a graduate of Queen's University Belfast, who also obtained his PhD at the Institute. In a talk on Irish history which he gave to the Dublin Rotary Club in 1934, Dudley Edwards emphasised that, as long as the sources of modern Irish history remained unpublished, few scholars would be able to use them. The IMC had been set up to publish these sources but the extent of its activities would depend on the availability of qualified scholars, few of whom could 'earn even a modest livelihood at Irish historical research'. By 1936 Moody and Edwards were laying the foundations for *Irish Historical Studies*.[32] The IMC agreed to give them a list of IMC publications for the first issue, which appeared in 1938. MacNeill warmly welcomed the new journal and relations between the journal and the IMC remained close, if occasionally fractious when an IMC work received a poor review.

v

In the years before the outbreak of the Second World War MacNeill's main concern was the protection, should war come, of documents in the keeping of the state and the main cultural institutions like the National Library, Trinity College Dublin and the Royal Irish Academy. The threat of another Four Courts disaster was all too possible. The Cabinet Committee on Emergency Measures, which was set up in 1938 as a major European war appeared imminent, contacted MacNeill in December 1938 about the protection of state records against loss or damage from air raids on Dublin. He was asked to draw up a list of the most important documents. When Simington went to an Air Raid Precautions meeting he was concerned that there appeared to be no guidelines about the safety of documents in government offices and suggested that the IMC draw up guidelines that would alert government offices to the importance of particular records.[33] Simington started to compile a list but soon realised that there was a basic lack of awareness of what constituted historical records. A two-page draft questionnaire on Protection of Documents was sent by the IMC to the Department of the Taoiseach.[34] However, it soon got bogged down in inter-departmental wrangling between the Departments of Education and Finance.

The battles of the 1930s between the IMC and the bureaucrats of the Department of Finance were superseded by the pressures of life in neutral Ireland during the Second World War. The war seriously circumscribed the IMC's work. There were fewer meetings as members from outside Dublin found travel to the capital difficult. This particularly affected Hogan in Cork, with train journeys now taking hours longer. However, he still managed to make regular trips to Dublin as the publication schedule of *Analecta* demonstrated.

Shortages of paper, chemicals and type, and the return to an almost exclusively military role of the IMC's facsimile printer, the Ordnance Survey, dealt a severe blow to the IMC's plans and extinguished a vibrant publication programme. The Commission would have to wait until the return of normality in peacetime to restart a regular publication schedule.

The IMC developed a greater advocacy role during the Second World War, a role that it would carry through into the post-war years. It highlighted the need to prevent a 'second Four Courts' by asking government departments to safeguard papers of historical value at the same time as they were preparing to safeguard strategically important papers against destruction through invasion or air attack. The war brought other opportunities as the IMC responded to the paper shortages of the Emergency with appeals for people across Ireland to check their attics for valuable papers and not to destroy these papers by handing them over for pulping by greedy paper merchants. For example, in a Radio Éireann broadcast, MacNeill urged listeners not to regard family papers as somehow trivial and unimportant:

> Nothing is trivial that gives us a better knowledge of what people were
> doing or even what they were thinking about before our time ... for
> us in Ireland, among the classes of old papers of special importance
> are those that tell us something about Irish families of every grade and
> station in life.[35]

The Commission initiated a related survey of papers in private hands
to report on material held in family collections. Undertaken by Edward
MacLysaght and John Ainsworth, it would run to the 1960s when it was
taken over by the National Library.

VI

MacNeill was diagnosed with cancer in May 1945 and went into hospital
shortly afterwards. IMC secretary Eileen Brereton told James Hogan that
'Dr MacNeill sees a number of visitors and I am told that he takes the
same interest as heretofore in current events'. He died in October 1945.
An editorial in de Valera's paper the *Irish Press* declared that 'his country's
history, her literature and her folklore would still be partially enveloped
in darkness were it not for his genius and his labour'.[36] MacNeill's widow
Taddie affirmed the importance of the Commission's work to her husband;
it 'was his foremost interest and a source of great satisfaction to him in his
later years even to the last days of his life'.[37] MacNeill's brother, Charles,
echoed her; to MacNeill 'the work of the Commission was an absorbing
interest, work of high public interest under several aspects, and it was his
earnest wish that it should contribute towards the growth of a serious and
well-informed spirit of dealing with the matters within its scope'.[38]

In an article written in 1929 MacNeill declared that the proper function
of the state 'was to serve and defend the civilization of the people'.[39] He
saw the IMC as a vital instrument to achieve this because, as he wrote in
the foreword to *Phases of Irish History*, 'neither apathy nor antipathy can
ever bring out the truth of history'. He was a very remarkable man whose
contradictions were a fruitful source of stimulus. As Dudley Edwards, his
former student and IMC colleague, noted with perception:

> ... he was a great artist – and he knew it. He loved learning but he
> enjoyed life. He loved Ireland and he loved people. But his Ireland
> was linked to traditional learning, and his patriotism came before

his devotion to history. That is why he put the Gaelic revival before scholarship, why Volunteering came before academic work and why the organisation of historical studies only emerged in the frustrations of politics and in the return to private life.[40]

It was the IMC's great good fortune to have MacNeill's services in this last great phase of his career. An obituary in *Analecta Hibernica* remembered his wide range of interests, his kindness and tact in dealing with IMC members. It explained that 'by the death of Eoin MacNeill ... the Irish Manuscripts Commission has lost something more than a revered and beloved Chairman. It lost as well the man to whom, more than to any other, it owed its being.'[41] The post-war years would be hard and trying ones for the IMC as it slowly adjusted to the harsh new environment it faced into without MacNeill's energy and guidance. MacNeill's death in 1945 was probably more catastrophic than all of the preceding difficulties the IMC had endured through the 1930s and the Second World War. It removed the IMC's driving force and left the remaining Commissioners, who regrouped under Richard Best, director of the National Library, without direction. It would take IMC over a decade to get over the loss of MacNeill and the economies enforced by the war.

The IMC was established as a post-independence cultural statement in troubled times when the Irish Free State was still a fledgling democracy. It became an essential building block in the development of history as a profession in Ireland. The IMC also helped to give independent Ireland a secure historical foundation. It was a bold and imaginative move by an administration only five years on from having fought a divisive and expensive Civil War. The IMC provided a library of materials for the young historians who profited from the expansion of higher education in Ireland since the 1960s, just as MacNeill had hoped for with his 'Monumenta Hiberniae' proposals of the 1920s. That a vibrant history research community exists in Ireland today and is prospering is the visible success of MacNeill's vision for the IMC.

Language and Culture

Eoin MacNeill's Pioneering Role in the Irish Language Movement

LIAM MAC MATHÚNA

INTRODUCTION AND EARLY YEARS

Three, perhaps four, people can be said to have had a particular involvement in the establishment of the Gaelic League in 1893: Father Eugene O'Growney, Dr Douglas Hyde and Eoin MacNeill, to which group we might add J.H. Lloyd (Seosamh Laoide). Three others soon came to play prominent, if somewhat different, roles in the early development of the language movement. These were Father Peter O'Leary (An tAthair Peadar Ó Laoghaire), Father Michael O'Hickey and Patrick Pearse. All of these pioneers had varied experiences of acquiring Irish and becoming interested in the well-being of the language.

Eoin MacNeill, or rather John MacNeill, as he was then and very often later known, was born in Glenarm, County Antrim on 15 May 1867. Accounts of his early life suggest that he would have had an awareness of the existence of the Irish language, if little occasion to hear it being used. As to schooling, he was educated privately at home, first by governesses, and later received tuition from a teacher from a local school. An old nurse called Peggie Carnegie from Glenariff is said to have called Eoin and his siblings by the Irish versions of their names, and used to say *Bí 'do thost!* ('Be silent!') to keep them quiet.[1] As MacNeill maintained cordial, indeed close, relations with the Catholic Church throughout his public life, it is worth noting that his father, Archibald, was the contractor for building the local Catholic church in Glenarm, when he was a youngster.[2] However, despite being included by Father John Ryan in *The Scholar Revolutionary*, edited by F.X. Martin and F.J. Byrne (1973), pertinent references made by MacNeill himself (about 1907) to personal and family links with traditionally spoken Irish in Antrim seem to have been generally overlooked. This is perhaps because they are to be found in a previously unpublished response to a review of Professor J.B. Bury's book entitled *Life of St Patrick*, published in 1905. In this draft and unsent letter with no addressee mentioned, MacNeill recalls: 'In McKeown's Town lived within my recollection an old man,

95

Michael McLoughlin, who said his prayers always in Irish, being the last Irish speaker known to me south of Glenariff.'³ He goes on to say:

> The last Irish poet in County Antrim was a Protestant, an uncle of Sir Daniel Dixon. My mother knew him well, and says that on every possible occasion he tried to interest people in the Irish language and would rather talk about it than about anything else. His name was John McCambridge. I managed to rescue and print one of his songs, *Árd Í Cuain* a really beautiful little lyric, which I printed in an old number of the *Gaelic Journal* [vol. 6, 1895, p. 108]. I am told that the air of it is still known in Glenariff. Lest you may not have the printed copy, I wind up by writing it for you from memory. It is as if spoken by an Irish emigrant in some wild part of America.⁴

MacNeill then proceeds to quote four verses and the refrain from the song in question, beginning *Dá mbeidhinn féin i nÁrd Í Cuain.*

Whatever about his early awareness of Irish, when MacNeill came to Dublin to take up a position as a clerk in the Accountant General's Office in the Four Courts in 1887, he set about learning the language, depending initially on books such as Neilson's *Grammar* and Canon Ulick Bourke's *Easy Lessons.*⁵ However, tellingly indicative of the low public visibility of Irish in the city at the time, he had to resort to placing an advertisement in a newspaper, seeking to find someone who could teach him the language. The reason for this, he recalled in 1932, was that 'in the city of Dublin in 1887 I had not the faintest notion where to turn to get tuition in Irish'.⁶ Two lessons a week for a month at a cost of £1 exhausted the capabilities of the teacher, who knew little more than the pronunciation of Irish words.⁷ Thus, MacNeill's initial difficulties in accessing Irish contrast somewhat with the experience of two other pioneering revivalists, namely Douglas Hyde (1860–1949) and Eugene O'Growney (1863–99).⁸ Hyde had come upon Irish spoken as a vernacular by some of his neighbours in Frenchpark, County Roscommon, in 1874 at the age of fourteen. He began to learn the language from them and to keep a diary, mainly in Irish, from that time on. Father Eugene O'Growney is reputed to have made initial contact with both written and spoken Irish in his teens. At any rate, it was O'Growney, whom MacNeill contacted on the recommendation of Dean O'Loan in Maynooth, another Antrim man, who advised MacNeill to visit Inis Meáin in the Aran Islands.⁹ MacNeill followed this advice, spending June 1891 on the island. He went on to study various periods of Irish under Rev. Edmund Hogan SJ at University College Dublin.¹⁰

FOUNDING THE GAELIC LEAGUE

Inspired by earlier articles by O'Growney and Hyde,[11] in December 1891 MacNeill wrote an essay on Irish entitled 'Why and How the Irish Language is to be Preserved' in the *Irish Ecclesiastical Record*.[12] In this piece, as well as demanding that Irish be taught in the schools, and arguing that young men's clubs should establish Irish classes for themselves,[13] MacNeill urged the Catholic clergy to champion the language. As editor of *The Gaelic Journal*, Father O'Growney asked him to expand on these views, which he did just over two years later. By then MacNeill had become a regular visitor to the Royal Irish Academy's house, where he had been first admitted in order to consult manuscripts on 12 March 1892.[14] There in the reading room he used to meet others with an interest in the living language, men such as John Hogan, James Cogan and Thomas O'Neill Russell.[15] Hyde delivered his famous address 'The Necessity for De-Anglicising Ireland' to the National Literary Society of Ireland on 25 November 1892 and this may have acted as a further stimulus for MacNeill to write the follow-up article sought by O'Growney, viz. 'Toghairm agus Gleus Oibre chum Gluasachta na Gaedhilge do Chur ar Aghaidh i nÉirinn' / 'A Plea and a Plan for the Extension of the Movement to Preserve and Spread the Gaelic Language in Ireland', which was a call to action on behalf of Irish in *Irisleabhar na Gaedhilge / The Gaelic Journal* in March 1893.[16] This was published anonymously, but correspondence with Hyde and others confirms that it was written by MacNeill.[17] In his thirteen-point plea, MacNeill stresses the positive factors associated with Irish (or rather 'Gaelic' as he terms it), especially that it was still being spoken by 700,000 people, in fully one-third of the country. He argues that the language is now held in higher esteem among the middle classes than at any time since the seventeenth century and maintains that an organisation is needed to address the central challenge.

Then in June 1893, after consulting Eugene O'Growney and J.H. Lloyd, MacNeill issued a circular about establishing a society to further the position of Irish, asking interested parties to contact any one of the three.[18] He wrote what appears to have been a copy of this circular letter (in English) to Douglas Hyde on 12 June 1893, inviting him to attend a meeting to establish a society to maintain spoken Irish. The letter read as follows:

Hazelbrook, Malahide.
12 June 1893

Dear Sir,

It is proposed to arrange, by agreement between persons interested
in the preservation of Gaelic as a spoken language, for a preliminary
consultative gathering of an informal kind to initiate practical steps
towards the formation, on the lines indicated in a recent article in the
Gaelic Journal or otherwise as may be determined, of an organization
to maintain and promote the use of Gaelic as a *spoken language*
in Ireland. Also to discuss the means by which the aim of such an
organisation may best be attained.

Your cooperation is very earnestly desired, as also that of any friends
of the movement with whom you may have influence.

Kindly communicate early with Rev. E. O'Growney, M.R.I.A.,
Maynooth College or with Mr J.H. Lloyd, 8 Waterloo Avenue, Nth
Strand Road, or with me at above address or at the Office of the
Accountant General, Four Courts, Dublin.

Yours very truly,[19]

Hyde replied with a four-page letter of support in Irish, dated 26 June 1893.
While Hyde says he had seen MacNeill in the Academy, it is clear from his
reply that the two had not yet spoken.

The meeting to set up the new organisation duly took place in a room
at 9 O'Connell Street, then officially Lower Sackville Street, on 31 July. The
event was attended by ten persons, with Hyde in the chair. The group of
men attending the meeting decided to found a society called 'The Gaelic
League'. Those present 'resolved themselves into a society for the sole
purpose of keeping the Irish language spoken in Ireland. It was agreed
that the literary interests of the language should be left in other hands,
and that the new organization should devote itself to the single purpose
of preserving and spreading Irish as a means of oral discourse'.[20] MacNeill
was elected honorary secretary, and at a later meeting Hyde was elected
president.[21] Other officers appointed in 1893 were J.H. Lloyd as treasurer
and the Rev. Euseby Digby Cleaver as vice-president. The main aims of the
organisation were subsequently articulated as (1) the preservation of Irish
as the national language of Ireland, and the extension of its use as a spoken
tongue, and (2) the study and publication of existing Gaelic literature, and
the cultivation of a modern literature in Irish.[22]

The burden of work involved in launching the new organisation effectively must have been considerable, as is clear from Donal McCartney's summary, based in turn on MacNeill's own 1930s 'Memoirs':

> For the first few years of its existence much of the work of running the organization devolved on the secretary as the growing volume of correspondence indicates. Some of this work he did more or less furtively at slack moments in the Four Courts where he was employed as a clerk. Frequently he had to attend meetings or give addresses far from Dublin and this involved a good deal of travelling by night trains. He bore all the expense of the postage and much of the travelling expenses in these years. Besides giving classes and talks to the Gaelic League branches he was also teaching 'two evenings each week and two lessons each evening' in Drumcondra Training College at the instance of Archbishop Walsh. An impressive list of publications was also mounting up in these years, and he was editing a weekly, *An Claidheamh Soluis*, and a monthly, the *Gaelic Journal*. He attempted to establish an Irish printing establishment – An Cló Cumann – and put all the money he could scrape up into it. When it collapsed he was left considerably in debt. The effect of the overwork was a break-down which left some permanent effects on him, notably a dislike for writing letters which he was never able to overcome.[23]

McCartney makes his overall point well, although his account rather telescopes activities together: they were not all actually being conducted simultaneously; some such as the newspaper and periodical editing were consecutive.

EDITING *THE GAELIC JOURNAL* AND *AN CLAIDHEAMH SOLUIS*

MacNeill's entry into editing was more or less contemporaneous with his moves to found the Gaelic League. He took over the editorship of *Irisleabhar na Gaedhilge / The Gaelic Journal* temporarily from Eugene O'Growney in July 1893, due to the latter's illness. In fact, O'Growney was suffering from tuberculosis and emigrated to the US towards the end of 1894 in the hope that drier climes, such as those of Arizona and California, would counteract the disease. However, O'Growney did not recover, and passed away in 1899. MacNeill was appointed as permanent editor in October/November 1894,

and Tierney observes that 'the journal became almost the official organ of
the League'.[24] He continued as editor of *The Gaelic Journal* until 1899,[25] the
year he became the founding editor of *An Claidheamh Soluis*.

MacNeill proved to be a dynamic editor of *The Gaelic Journal*, which
became linked to the Gaelic League, of which of course he was secretary,
while he was also editor of the journal. The periodical proclaimed that every
effort would be made to be lively and standard-bearing:

> The GAELIC JOURNAL will be at once the organ of the Irish
> language movement, the willing medium of interchange of knowledge
> among the students of Irish. The record of much of our literature
> and traditional lore, and the clear and indubitable witness that our
> language is still a living tongue, a great instrument of thought, with
> a living literature, *and with its powers of creating a living national
> literature unimpaired.*[26]

Writing in 1935, Torna (Tadhg Ó Donnchadha) felt that *The Gaelic Journal*
had made great strides under MacNeill's editorship, especially in helping
native speakers and others throughout the country to master the art of
writing in Irish:

> Ar feadh na gcúig mbliadhan 'na raibh an tIrisleabhar fá chúram
> Eoin Mhic Néill do déineadh mórán treabhtha agus fuirste ar son
> na teangan. Bhí daoine óga idir Ghaedhilgeóirí dúthchais is eile ar
> fuid na tíre ag foghluim ar a ndícheall agus ag dul i dtaithighe na
> scríbhneóireachta. Do méaduigheadh go mór orthasan, agus do
> bhí an chaoi aca ar a ngaisceadh do theasbáint, nuair do cuireadh
> an tOireachtas ar bun san bhliadhain 1897, agus 'Fáinne an Lae' i
> bhfíorthosach na bliadhna 1898. Do tharraing an dá nídh sin bail thar
> meadhón ar shaothrú na Gaedhilge.
>
>   Acht do bhí an obair ag dul i ndéine, agus an chuid ba chruaidhe
> dhi ag luighe ar Eoin Mhac Néill, go dtí gur dhírigh sí ar bheith ag
> goilleamhaint ar a shláinte, agus gurbh éigin dó cúram an Irisleabhair
> do chur de. I Mí na Bealltaine san bhliadhain 1899, tháinig an páipéar
> amach, agus Seósamh Laoide mar eagarthóir air, fá árdchoiste
> Chonnradh na Gaedhilge.[27]

Throughout the five years during which the Journal was the
responsibility of Eoin MacNeill much ploughing and harrowing was
done on behalf of the language. Young people, both native speakers

and others throughout the country, were learning as best they could and becoming accustomed to writing. Their number increased greatly, and they were able to display their prowess, when the Oireachtas was founded in the year 1897, and 'Fáinne an Lae' at the very beginning of the year 1898. These two things were of great benefit in the cultivation of Irish.

But the work was getting more arduous and the hardest part of it was falling on Eoin MacNeill, until it began to affect his health, and he had to relinquish the responsibility of the Journal. In May of the year 1899, the paper came out, with Seosamh Laoide as its editor, under the executive of the Gaelic League.[28]

MacNeill's period as editor is remembered in particular nowadays for the warm welcome he gave An tAthair Peadar Ua Laoghaire's *Séadna*, the first novel-like tale of the revival, perceptively drawing attention to its linguistic strengths. However, he is also remembered as the editor who decided that the *Journal* had had enough of *Séadna* by April 1897, and wished it continued success – elsewhere. Ironically, An tAthair Peadar turned to MacNeill for help to publish the second third of the novel in 1898. The final third appeared in the *Cork Weekly Examiner* in 1900, with the entire work being published as one volume by The Irish Book Company in 1904.

Father Shán Ó Cuív published lively excerpts from the correspondence of the author to the editor in his contribution to *The Scholar Revolutionary*, covering this period.[29] The letters exchanged make for fascinating reading, hot friends cooling, as Shakespeare might have put it, with the priest proving himself to be petulant and peevish. Furthermore, in a letter to an unnamed priest friend, An tAthair Peadar observed in 1899: 'Our friend John MacNeill is turning out a complete crank on our hands.'[30] In the absence of MacNeill's side of the correspondence, his attitude to the affair must be inferred from An tAthair Peadar's own letters to him and from his public comments as editor of the *Gaelic Journal*.[31] He would seem to have held to his position politely, but unwaveringly.[32] The stance adopted by An tAthair Peadar was especially ironic, as he had initially been lavish in his praise of the young northerner. He came to Dublin to attend the Irish Language Congress being held there on 27 March 1894 and was so impressed by what he saw that he wrote:

Do bhidheas ag Feis na Gaedhilge i m-Baile-atha-Cliath agus ó shoin a lcith tá sé buailte isteach am' aigneadh go n-déanfaid fir óga na

h-Éireann an Ghaedhealg do choimeád beo, agus nach baoghal duinn
feasda, le congnamh De, an masla agus an míochlú a bheidheadh i
n-dán dúinn go deo dá n-imthigheadh an Ghaedhealg as an saoghal
le n-ár linn.[33]

I was at the Irish Language Congress in Dublin and since then I am
quite convinced that the young men of Ireland will keep Irish alive,
and that, with God's help, we are no longer in danger of incurring the
opprobrium and shame which we would face if Irish were to disappear
from the world during our time.[34]

An tAthair Peadar happened to visit a class being taught Irish by MacNeill
when he attended the Irish Language Congress and had this to say of the
impact it had on him:

Bhidheas cúpla uair an chluig 'sa sgoil ag éisteacht leo, agus do thánag
uatha lán d'iongnadh agus d'áthas.[35]

I was a few hours in the school listening to them, and I came away
from them full of wonder and joy.[36]

Admhuíghim ó chroídhe go raibh mo mhisneach féin nách mór
imighthe go dtí an oidhche úd i mBaile Átha Cliath, nuar chonac tusa
air aghaidh an chláir dhuibh amach agus do bhlúire cailce agat ... 'Dar
bhríghe na Mionn!' arsa meise, am aigne féin, 'dá mbeidheadh aon
deichniúmhar amháin de'n t-saghas san i n-Éirinn bhídh an gnó déanta.'[37]

I heartily admit that my own courage was almost gone until that night
in Dublin, when I saw you out in front of the blackboard with your
piece of chalk ... 'By my oath!' said I, in my own mind, 'if there were
just ten of that kind in Ireland the task would be done.'[38]

MacNeill had earlier been central to the publication of Father O'Growney's
renowned series of *Simple Lessons in Irish*, having supervised the issuing of
Parts I–III, and the continuation of the series in Parts IV and V, which he
himself wrote.[39] Brian Ó Cuív has pointed out that by publishing An tAthair
Peadar Ua Laoghaire's *Séadna* in *The Gaelic Journal* with – in MacNeill's
own words – its 'deft, sinewy and versatile Irish', 'he demonstrated beyond
all possible doubt the suitability of what came to be known as *caint na
ndaoine* as a basis for literary usage'.[40]

On 15 October 1898 MacNeill proposed that P.H. Pearse be co-opted
onto the Gaelic League's Executive Committee, its Coiste Gnótha. He had

met Pearse at the end of 1897 when he was invited to give a lecture to the
New Ireland Literary Society, founded earlier that year by the eighteen-
year-old Pearse and his friend Eamonn O'Neill. In his dictated memoir,
MacNeill records: '... in the end of the proceedings I made an earnest
appeal to these young men to join up with the League, which needed all the
workers it could enlist. A number of them, including Pearse and O'Neill,
came into the Gaelic League some time afterwards.'[41]

MacNeill was clearly extremely busy at this time, although his duties in
the Four Courts seem to have left him with plenty of opportunity to pursue
his other interests. However, in the 1890s the Gaelic League was already
expanding in size and influence and MacNeill relinquished the position
of secretary in 1897. Bernard Doyle, the printer who had brought out
Séadna Part II, founded a bilingual newspaper called *Fáinne an Lae* in 1898,
closely allied to the Gaelic League. MacNeill was one of those who formed
an editorial board.[42] There were policy tensions from the start, however,
which led the League to establish its own paper, *An Claidheamh Soluis*, in
1899, and Doyle subsequently agreed to amalgamate his paper with that
of the League, and this was reflected in the expanded title of the League's
newspaper, namely *An Claidheamh Soluis agus Fáinne an Lae*, which first
appeared on 4 August 1900.[43] The League had already fallen out with
Doyle, who was supported by members of the Cork Lee Branch. MacNeill
penned a forceful article on the first pages of the January 1899 issue of the
Gaelic Journal, complaining *inter alia* that Doyle had the support of 'a small
knot of gentlemen belonging to one branch of the League in Cork city',
who had already shown themselves to be discontented with the Dublin
executive. MacNeill went on to describe them as 'this little clique', a phrase
that, naturally enough, rankled with them.[44]

Séamus Ó Cathasaigh and Donal O'Connor were appointed assistants
to MacNeill as honorary secretary of the League in 1898 as he struggled
with all his commitments.[45] In December 1898 MacNeill's brother Charles
was made secretary of the League, a position he held for just a year.[46] The
arrangement whereby MacNeill continued as honorary secretary of the
Gaelic League, while allotted a joint honorary secretary and an honorary
treasurer, only lasted three years. Salaried full-time staff were now needed.
Stiofán Bairéad was appointed treasurer and Pádraig Ó Dálaigh secretary.
At the beginning of 1899 Tomás Bán Ó Concheanainn was appointed
as *timire* ('organiser') and William Shanley as business manager of *An
Claidheamh Soluis*.[47]

MacNeill was the founding – and of course part-time, voluntary – editor of *An Claidheamh Soluis* from March 1899 to September 1901.[48] He had had a health breakdown at the start of 1899, and eventually relinquished the editorship, realising that the position should be a full-time salaried one, which recommendation of his was accepted. Thus, when the pressure of all his duties caught up with MacNeill, he relinquished the editorship in September 1901, being succeeded first by Eoghan Ó Neachtain (October 1901–February 1903), and then by Patrick Pearse (March 1903–November 1909).[49] A further change in the League's officers took place when MacNeill accepted Hyde's proposal, made in a letter dated 26 April 1903, that he become vice-president along with Father O'Leary, whose tenure was nominal.[50]

IDEOLOGY

While this is not the occasion to attempt a thorough analysis of the various components of MacNeill's understanding of the ideology of Irish-Ireland, a few points may be noted. Father Peter Yorke, of Galway and San Francisco, caused a great stir in 1899 with a forceful lecture delivered to the newly formed Central Branch. Hyde was happy enough with this because he felt Yorke had been able to say things that were worth saying, but that he, as president of the Gaelic League, was reluctant to do, for fear of losing allies. Yorke stated that 'Nationality in the true sense is a totally different thing from politics'. Replying to warnings in the *Freeman's Journal* about the fate of earlier Irish language societies, he said they had died 'because they were not of the people, and only the people can make a Gaelic movement prosper ... The Gaelic League is a *volksbewegung*,[51] not an academic organisation'.[52] Tierney writes of the effect of this insight on MacNeill: 'MacNeill himself had not hitherto so clearly formulated the philosophy which underlay the movement he had founded. In effect it was a new form of nationalism, which unlike the commonly received ideology known by that name did not begin with the concept of the nation-state.'[53]

With regard to the theoretical relationship of Irish language literature to Ireland's English-language literature, Tierney argues that MacNeill was at one with Pearse vis-à-vis Anglo-Irish literature, etc. Pearse, for instance, wrote a letter to *An Claidheamh Soluis*, expressing his considered and uncompromising opposition to Anglo-Irish literature:

> The Irish Literary Theatre, is in my opinion more dangerous, because less glaringly anti-national than Trinity College ... Mr. Yeats' precious 'Irish' Literary Theatre may, if it develops, give the Gaelic League more trouble than the Atkinson-Mahaffy combination. Let us strangle it at its birth.[54]

Tierney opines:

> At any rate, the rejection of the literary revival by MacNeill and those who thought like him was absolute ... MacNeill agreed entirely with Yorke. Impervious as he was to the revolutionary nationalist ideology, he had no abstract or absolute definition of an Irishman, but he was convinced that an Irish nation could only be built upon, and derive its identity from, the Irish language. This was so because for most of its existence the Irish people had expressed itself in Irish. An English-speaking Ireland, for MacNeill, could not be an Irish Ireland; it could well be a nation, but another kind of English-speaking one like America or Australia, not an Irish one in any real sense of the word.[55]

Less sympathetically perhaps, and from a different perspective, Tom Garvin has made more or less the same observation: 'Eoin MacNeill, a fine scholar with a genuinely scientific mind, never seems to have questioned the Gaelic League view that the true Ireland was the Gaelic Ireland.'[56]

MacNeill was resolutely committed to giving priority to indigenous industry. When William Martin Murphy, proprietor of the *Irish Independent*, set about organising an international trade exhibition in Dublin in 1904, MacNeill took the lead in opposing the effort. Writing in his memoir, he says:

> The effect of an international exhibition would be to advertise foreign goods. Although as I have said the Gaelic League did not take [up] a formal stand on matters outside of its programme, the interest of its members in economics caused a sense of indignation among them regarding the proposed International Exhibition.[57]

MacNeill and a number of others attended a public meeting being held in support of Murphy's proposal. Their intervention broke up the meeting, which was dispersed by the police. MacNeill was criticised in the *Irish Independent*, which denounced him as 'a British civil servant masquerading as Robert Emmet' and he was brought up for questioning by Sir Antony

MacDonnell, the under-secretary, but no action was taken.[58] When the accusation was made that the League's members were afraid of foreign competition, MacNeill replied: 'We are not, but we object to expending £150,000 on advertising the goods of our industrial rivals. [...] The extension of their Market here means the contraction of ours.' In this, as Regina Uí Chollatáin's work on *An Claidheamh Soluis* ably demonstrates, MacNeill was at one with that paper's then editor Patrick Pearse, who stated in an editorial: 'Féadfam Taisbeánadh Idir-náisiúnta bheith againn nuair a bhéas ár dteanga, ár mianach agus ár náisiúntacht againn' ['We can have an International Exhibition when we have our language, our resources and our nationhood.'][59]

MacNEILL AND PEARSE

Pearse held MacNeill in the highest esteem, as two passages of his from *An Claidheamh Soluis* demonstrate. He expressed his high regard for MacNeill on 5 October 1907 in an account of an address the latter had given at the first session of Coláiste Chomhghaill in Belfast:

> Eoin MacNeill is always careful to explain that he is not an orator. There are some, nevertheless, who hold him to be the finest orator in the League. At his worst he is always worth listening to; at his best he is an inspiration. Every sentence he utters stands for an idea, and the only trouble is that the sentences he utters are so few. There come to him, however, moments when he 'lets himself go', when he throws back, or unconsciously drops, his habitual mask of reserve – and then you see into the most interesting mind in Ireland.[60]

When MacNeill stated in another address, this time at Coláisde Laighean on 24 October 1908, that he wished to retire from the League and concentrate on his books, Pearse reacted as follows:

> But the disappearance of Eoin from the propagandist platform would mean the ceasing of the finest expositions of the inner spirit of the League that have been given by any amongst us. It is An Craoibhín's part in the movement to inspire the many with enthusiasm; it is Eoin's to expound the philosophy of the movement to the few. Let us hope that he will find it possible to reconcile his two allegiances – that to his books and studies on the one hand and that to the movement which he conceived and set going on the other.[61]

Fortunately for Pearse, MacNeill did not withdraw totally from League activities. For instance, he accepted the post of principal at Omeath Irish College, near Carlingford, County Louth which opened in 1912 and Tierney tells us that 'there he and his family spent many happy summers despite the interruptions caused by war and imprisonment'.[62]

NATIONAL UNIVERSITY OF IRELAND: IRISH IN MATRICULATION

In 1909 MacNeill had stepped forcefully into the intellectual debating arena during the great Gaelic League campaign on behalf of Irish as a requisite subject for matriculation in the NUI, alongside English and Latin. Cardinal Tomás Ó Fiaich held his contribution to have been the most cogent of all: 'By far the best argued case in favour of the League's policy on this issue was Eoin MacNeill's pamphlet, *Irish in the National University of Ireland*, and it must have convinced many a waverer who took time to study it.'[63] On the other hand, Ó Fiaich went on immediately to observe: 'It was not the cold logic of MacNeill's words, however, but the whirlwind campaign of lectures and letters, embarked on by the Professor of Irish in Maynooth, Father Michael O'Hickey, that roused the country.'[64] MacNeill set out his views over sixty-three pages in the pamphlet mentioned by Ó Fiaich, whose full title was *Irish in the National University of Ireland: A plea for Irish education*.[65] In the preface he outlined his thesis:

> The case stated in the following pages is, that Irish *is* an essential factor in Irish higher education. Higher education without Irish may be English or cosmopolitan, or what you please. It certainly is not Irish. Those who have a difficulty in accepting this view are invited to ask themselves, in what respect such an education differs from non-Irish education.[66]

In setting out his case, MacNeill references Hyde's ground-breaking lecture of 1892, which in a way had started it all:

> It need not be inquired whether a free national university ought rather to throw in its lot with that sterile and inglorious convergence of forces summed up by Dr. Douglas Hyde in the term 'anglicization', or with the fruitful, hopeful, and inspiring activities that spring from the idea of a self-centred Ireland.

This then is the position: the University is bound, alike by duty and by interest, to take a leading part in the reconstruction of a veritable national life and culture; the national language is an indispensable element in this reconstructive work.[67]

1915 ARD-FHEIS IN DUNDALK

However, a few years after the success of the League's matriculation campaign, national and international military considerations began to sideline cultural concerns. The Irish Volunteers were founded in Dublin in November 1913, inspired by MacNeill's important article 'The North Began', published in *An Claidheamh Soluis* earlier in the month,[68] while the Great War broke out on the continent the following summer. In fact, the founding of the Irish Volunteers, and the subsequent split into Irish and National Volunteers, had the unintended consequence of weakening the language movement by shifting the focus and energy of the younger activists from cultural to military matters.[69] The Irish Republican Brotherhood, which was intent on staging a rising against British rule in Ireland during the war, decided to flex its muscles and put pressure on the Gaelic League's ard-fheis in Dundalk in 1915. While the imminent election of some of the IRB's imprisoned members to the Coiste Gnótha was the immediate cause of Hyde's resignation, the backdrop was a resolution to amend the League's constitution in order to state that one of its objects was an independent Ireland. Following Hyde's departure, the delegates unanimously decided that the presidency should remain vacant for the time being, with power granted to the Coiste Gnótha to restore Hyde to office, if he would consent. However, he did not do so and at the ard-fheis of the following year MacNeill, then serving a sentence of penal servitude at Dartmoor imposed by a British court martial after the rising of Easter week, was elected president of the Gaelic League.[70]

With regard to MacNeill's attitude to the events at the 1915 ard-fheis, we have the benefit of his own retrospective assessment from his 1930s memoir. Although his view at the time of the ard-fheis was strongly opposed by Agnes O'Farrelly and others, MacNeill had come to the conclusion – wrongly, as he felt in retrospect – that the work of the Volunteer movement and 'national defence' should take precedence over all else:

> Till the Volunteer movement came along, my only public activity was connected with the G[aelic]. L[eague]. After the Volunteer movement

began, the annual Oireachtas of the G.L. was held in Dundalk. I was so strongly convinced that we were in the middle of a national crisis that would concern the future of the G.L. movement as well as other things that I thought everyone else as well as myself should throw all our weight into the work of national defence and I spoke to the G.L. Oireachtas to that effect. Other leading members took a different line. The majority sided with me. Douglas Hyde who had been Pres[ident] of the League from the outset felt bound to resign. I was also strongly opposed by Fr. Matthew Maguire and Miss Agnes O'Farrelly and no doubt by many others. I now believe that those who opposed me were right and that I was wrong. The fact was that the G.L. had drawn to its membership many who regarded the League as a political instrument. In fact I was aware at the time that the League was being used by certain of its members though not openly as a recruiting ground for the I.R.B.

And of course there were many like myself [who] believed that the whole national interest was in a very critical condition. But the main result was that the political aspect of Irish nationality got the upper hand within the G.L., and it became for a time a semi-political organization. This was a complete departure from its whole principles and policy.[71]

MacNEILL AND HYDE

Writing recently, Patrick Maume notes that, although Douglas Hyde was only one of several individuals involved in organising the Gaelic League, admirers of MacNeill complained that the role of Hyde had overshadowed MacNeill's centrality to the hard work of the organisation.[72] In reality, the success of the Gaelic League is best attributed to the manner in which Hyde and MacNeill complemented each other's strengths and were willing to work together over an extended period. Donal McCartney's assessment seeks to capture the essence of their collaboration:

> Hyde produced the battle-cry of de-anglicization. MacNeill invented the machinery of the Gaelic League and made it work, and each was prepared to give much of the credit to the other. Hyde made the wider impact but MacNeill went deeper in the search for a philosophy of what they were both about.[73]

McCartney felt that this complementarity was understood by Pearse, citing the passage already quoted from *An Claidheamh Soluis* from the end of 1908 when MacNeill signalled his wish to turn from the public arena to his books.

In Hyde's own memoir (1918), held in the National Folklore Collection, UCD, he gives the background as to why MacNeill withdrew from being active in the League, yet again laying the major share of the blame on the Munstermen. Hyde explains how MacNeill had acted as an arbitrator in a quarrel about the appointment of a teacher in Ring, County Waterford and was roundly vilified in various journals by members of the League for his trouble, and tells of the effect this had on him:

> These attacks had their natural consequence. MacNeill gradually dropped out of the League, ceased apparently to take any interest in it, and finally though he was vice-president deserted the meetings altogether. This played into the hands of his attackers, for MacNeill if he had continued to attend could have kept things pretty straight. He was the longest-headed and most clear-sighted man in the Gaelic League, and had great moral influence with the members.
>
> In vain I went to his house over and over again to beg him to attend some meeting or other where ticklish questions of politics or something of the kind were on the agenda, and implored his assistance in helping me to keep things straight, but all to no purpose. He would say he would come if he could and then in the end he would not come, and would leave me to do the best I could by myself. This was I believe the consequence of the open and shameless abuse showered on him by people who were not fit to tie his shoe-strings. When having got rid by this simple process of abuse first of O'Hickey and then of MacNeill they proceeded to play the same game with me I turned on them furiously and appealed to the branches of the League all over Ireland to protect me, and succeeded in quenching them for a time, for the branches rallied round me almost to a man, and the mischief-makers were really people of no account, only good at writing letters, anonymous or other, to papers that would print them.[74]

SCHOOLS

Tierney and McCartney repeatedly dwell on MacNeill's antipathy towards what he perceived as relying unduly on the school system in the effort to revive Irish. I suspect that MacNeill's views were more complex and ambivalent than these scholars appreciate. After all, he did write the long pamphlet arguing for compulsory Irish in the NUI matriculation examination, knowing full well the effect that would have on the secondary school system. But there is no gainsaying the import and passion of a draft letter to An tAthair Peadar contained among the MacNeill family papers, which provides an animated exposition of MacNeill's seemingly lifelong conviction as to the limitations of excessive dependence on schools to revive Irish:

> The fruit of all the anxious thought about saving the Irish language seems to be nothing but a cry for schools, schools, schools, teachers, teachers, teachers. Can a language be saved by schools? Do we realize what a language means? It means the way that people express themselves in happiness, in misery, in anger, in affection, in triumph, in anxiety, in resolve, in perplexity, in fear, in caution, in wisdom, in folly, in prayer, in rebuke, in remonstrance, in disgust, and in a thousand other moods and passions. I know how most of these uses of language would come to me in English. Would they come to me in Irish? Pshaw! Does anyone out of Bedlam imagine that they can be taught in schools or classes? Not even a teacher with the dramatic powers of Garrick or Kemble could make these uses of language an adhering reality in the minds of little boys and girls or of adults. What is language without them? A mere scratchy caricature – you know it well.[75]

In fact, as far back as his groundbreaking call for action, *A Plea and a Plan* of 1893, discussed above,[76] MacNeill expressed doubts about the efficacy of relying on schools for the language revival:

> The movement to preserve Gaelic in Ireland has so far confined itself almost solely to education.
> No language has ever been kept alive by mere book-teaching.
> Special conditions make the attempt to preserve Gaelic by book-teaching alone specially futile.
> Some additional means must therefore be employed.[77]

It is therefore somewhat ironic that MacNeill himself was *in situ* as Minister for Education in the Free State in 1922 when the position of Irish was being determined, although in fact it was his predecessor Fionán Ó Loingsigh/

Lynch who was actually responsible for Public Notice No. 4, issued by the Minister for Education of the Irish provisional government on 1 February 1922, ordering 'that the Irish language shall be taught, or used as a medium of instruction, for not less than one full hour each day in all national schools where there is a teacher competent to teach it'. This came into effect on 17 March 1922.[78] MacNeill was Minister for Education from 30 August 1922 to 24 November 1925. Maume holds that as Minister for Education 'MacNeill was largely inactive, because he saw the primary responsibility for education as lying with the churches rather than the state; his principal legacy was the stringent implementation of compulsory Irish. In these respects he set a pattern for state education which lasted until the 1960s.'[79] MacNeill was succeeded as minister by fellow UCD historian John M. O'Sullivan.

CONCLUSION

The uneasy and somewhat fragile position which MacNeill is often deemed to have in Irish history is strange. To my mind the Boundary Commission debacle, and even the 1916 countermanding order, are offset by the enduring significance of the two organisations and movements he may be said to have set in motion, viz. the Gaelic League and the Irish Volunteers. The one resulted in the Irish cultural awakening, the other led to the foundation of an independent Irish state. It is a commonplace of business thinking that the founder of a company or institution is not necessarily the most appropriate person to lead or guide it through later stages of its life cycle. No more than Michael Cusack's short-lived but crucial role in the history of the Gaelic Athletic Association, subsequent failings and falling-outs cannot diminish the legacy of the pioneering part Eoin MacNeill played in the Irish language movement.

Eoin Mac Néill: scríobhaí forásach agus iriseoir fadradharcach i bpróiseas na hAthbheochana

REGINA UÍ CHOLLATÁIN

> One of the plainest facts we have to face is that Irish has absolutely no chance to hold its own as a spoken language, unless it also holds its own and makes good its position as a cultivated, that is, a read and written language. One of the chief objects in view in establishing a weekly paper in Irish was this – the creation of an Irish-reading public, which is an absolute necessity if the language is to be maintained.[1]

Is léir ón phíosa seo a cuireadh i gcló nuair a bhí Eoin Mac Néill ina eagarthóir ar *An Claidheamh Soluis* i 1900, gur thuig sé tábhacht na scríbhinní iriseoireachta i gcur chun cinn fhís na hathbheochana. I nóta beathaisnéise Eoin Mhic Néill, deir Breathnach agus Ní Mhurchú gurb 'í eagarthóireacht na n-irisí an saothar ba thábhachtaí dá ndearna sé ar son scríbhneoireacht na Gaeilge'.[2]

Sa chaibidil seo tabharfar spléachadh ar na scríbhinní sin agus déanfar iad a mheas i gcomhthéacs an ionchuir a bhí aige mar scoláire, mar intleachtóir, mar cheannródaí agus mar cheannaire athbheochana. Déanfar scagadh áirithe ar scríbhinní agus ar rólanna eagarthóireachta Eoin Mhic Néill a léiríonn an ról eiseamláireach a bhí aige in athbheochan chultúrtha na hÉireann a tharraing cuid mhaith de na háiteanna nach raibh aird tugtha orthu, isteach i bhfís nua na hathbheochana.

Tamall gearr tar éis bhronnadh Uachtaránacht na hÉireann ar Dhúbhghlas de hÍde ar 14 Deireadh Fómhair 1938, scríobh sé litir oscailte do *Féil-sgríbhinn Eóin Mhic Néill*. Le téarmaí cairdis mar 'Chara na nGaedheal', mar 'Mháighistir dhílis', agus 'do shean-chara', léiríonn de hÍde an cairdeas agus an tuiscint a bhí eatarthu agus aithníonn de hÍde ionchur Mhic Néill i saol cultúrtha agus i léann na hÉireann:

> Ba tú an stairidhe is mó leig an solus isteach ar shean-stáid na tíre seo, ba tú an cómhairleóir nach raibh a chómhairle i gcúrsaibh Connartha

na Gaedhilge riamh gan tairbhe, ba tú an t-oibhrightheóir d'oibrigh de ló agus d'oidhche ar son na tíre seo, agus indiú tá tú ar mhór-sgoláiribh an Domhain.[3]

Tugann an tagairt a dhéanann de hÍde do shaothar Mhic Néill ar son 'ár ndaoine', aitheantas do ról Eoin Mhic Néill i gcur i gcrích na poblachta mar chloch mhíle thábhachtach i stair na hÉireann. Tugann ábhar na Féilsgríbhinne an t-ómós a bhí ag dul do Mhac Néill chun solais: aistí agus ailt ó níos mó ná caoga scoláirí aitheanta domhanda i réimsí a chlúdaíonn teangacha Ceilteacha, seandálaíocht agus réamhstair, luath-stair agus stair mheánaoiseach na hÉireann, béaloideas agus cuid mhaith táblaí gineolaíochta, mar aon le hailt faoi iliomad teangacha ar fud an domhain. Aithníonn de hÍde tóraíocht gan staonadh Mhic Néill chun ceantair, a d'fhan faoi chuing dhorchadas na hanchumhachta agus an bhochtanais rófhada, a threorú i dtreo an tsolais:

> Níor staon tú d'obair ar son na teangan agus do rinne tú níos mó ná aon duine eile chum solais do leigean ar na h-áiteachaibh dorcha do bhí go flúirseach i stair an oileáin. Ar tóir na fírinne do bhí tú de ghnáth, agus ní thug tú cead do aon rud, olc nó maith, seasamh eadrad agus í.[4]

Bhí tionchar mór ag fís Mhic Néill ag iarraidh 'na h-áiteachaibh dorcha' a tharraingt isteach sa ghile, ar a chuid oibre in athbheochan na Gaeilge agus é ag iarraidh na ceantair bhochta ina labhraítí an Ghaeilge a tharraingt isteach i ré úr an fhichiú haois. I scríbhinní iriseoireachta Mhic Néill in uirlisí poiblí Chonradh na Gaeilge, aimsítear an cur chuige a glacadh mar aon le cúlra na tuairimíochta agus na gcinntí a bhí mar bhunús do cheann de thréimhsí eiseamláireacha na hÉireann, ré na hAthbheochana.

SÍOLTA TOSAIGH NA hATHBHEOCHANA

Foilsíodh cuid den óráid a thug de hÍde ag Cumann na Gaedheilge, Nua Eabhrach, 16 Meitheamh, 1891, i nuachtáin na hÉireann. Spreag ábhar na hóráide Eoin Mac Néill le tuairimí a roinnt agus tús a chur le díospóireacht sna meáin scolártha ar cad a bhí i gceist le suaitheantas agus le labhairt na Gaeilge i gcomhthéacs fhéiniúlacht na hÉireann.[5] Tá an chéad fhóram a roghnaigh sé spéisiúil, mar léiríonn sé an tábhacht a bhain le tionchar na Cléire Caitlicí ar ghluaiseacht na hAthbheochana Gaeilge agus an gá le tacaíocht dá leithéid chun plean a chur i gcrích. Sa chéad alt 'Why and How the Irish Language is to be Preserved' i *The Irish Ecclesiastical Record* i 1891, cuireann sé teoiric ar leith i láthair, bunaithe ar an bhfís atá aige do chur chun cinn ghluaiseacht na Gaeilge mar aon le moltaí praiticiúla do thogra dá leithéid.[6] Is fiú mionscagadh a dhéanamh ar ábhar an ailt seo, mar is ionann é agus tráchtaireacht ar phlean athbheochana a chlúdaíonn idir ghnéithe praiticiúla agus theoiricí saoil. Mar shampla, tuigtear ón alt seo nach samhlaítear gluaiseacht na teanga mar ghné imeallach d'fhéiniúlacht úr na hÉireann, ach mar ghné idirnáisiúnta nach mbaineann teorainneacha tíreolaíocha léi. Ba ghné lárnach de chur chuige tosaigh na hathbheochana é seo atá soiléir ó óráidí tosaigh de hÍde agus scríbhinní eile ó cheannairí eile athbheochana agus tíre (Pádraic Mac Piarais, mar shampla), in irisí eile na linne ina dhiaidh sin.[7] Is léir go raibh siad ag súil go nglacfadh Éire a háit i measc náisiúin an domhain agus gur samhlaíodh Éire mar thír a raibh naisc aici le ceantair agus le pobail idirnáisiúnta a thuig cultúr na hÉireann agus an teanga mar ghné chomónta idirnáisiúnta, mar aon le huirlis chumarsáide. Féiniúlacht láidir chultúrtha agus léannta atá á míniú aige sa chéad alt seo a bhfuil tús curtha lena saothrú cheana féin i dtíortha eile timpeall an domhain a bhfuil Éireannaigh lonnaithe iontu. Mar shampla, déanann sé comparáid idir cur chun cinn bríomhar na Gaeilge i measc na nÉireannach sna Stáit Aontaithe, san Astráil agus i Sasana, agus na Gaeil in Éirinn atá de réir dealraimh, 'under a spell of impenetrable apathy':

> Submitting the question of the Irish language to this test, we ask ourselves, if we permit the Irish language in this generation to be extinguished, or to be weakened beyond hope of recovery, what will the Irishmen who come after us think of us? Perhaps we may infer the answer from the spirit of Ireland beyond the seas. In America, Australia, and even England, we find Irishmen, under the impulse of something akin to the pain of loss, turning lovingly and earnestly to the cultivation of their mother-tongue; while those at home, who enjoy every opportunity, seem to lie under a spell of impenetrable apathy – the better their opportunities, in fact, the greater their apathy. So, in America, our countrymen have societies, and classes and periodicals devoted to the culture of Irish, whereas we in Ireland cannot decently support a quarterly journal devoted to the same purpose.[8]

Ar bhonn teoiriciúil, ceanglaíonn sé an ghné thíreolaíoch idirnáisiúnta leis an bhunús teoiriciúil nuair a leagann sé téarmaí athbheochan na Gaeilge amach go sonrach mar chuid de 'greater Ireland'. Tógann sé sin ar na naisc atá cruthaithe cheana ag Éireannaigh thar lear le cultúr léannta na hÉireann. Críochnaíonn sé an sliocht seo le béim ar an ghá le gníomhú láithreach ionas nach gcaillfear Gaeilge bheo na ndaoine, Gaeilge na glúine reatha, mar thréith luachmhar suntasach na hÉireann:

> Of the thousands upon thousands of Irish books published within the last generation, a fraction only remains in Ireland; the rest has been exported to satisfy the still unsatisfied demand of greater Ireland. It cannot then be deemed an exaggeration to say that if it were possible that any body of Irishmen, through their action or inaction, should cause the national speech to pass into the list of dead languages, they would forfeit the esteem and affection of posterity ... Let us prefer to believe that the cause of inaction is only a hope for better times, and that there is still the will to act, when an easier way is found ... The duty of the moment is, therefore, immediate action, energetic action, united action, individual action.[9]

Cheangail sé na gnéithe praiticiúla agus teoiriciúla le chéile arís agus athlonnú na Gaeilge i struchtúir oifigiúla na hÉireann, státseirbhís agus institiúidí poiblí an Aontais mar shampla, á phlé aige. Shainmhínigh sé go raibh athbheochan na teanga ag brath orthu siúd a raibh cumhacht agus deiseanna acu chun í a chur i bhfeidhm. Aithníodh láithreach mar sin an gá le gréasán agus le plean poiblí struchtúrtha a chuirfeadh an Ghaeilge ar ais i mbéal an phobail agus i struchtúir oifigiúla na tíre:

> The students of Irish are usually men of little means and much work. The leisured classes do nothing, and nothing is expected of them. Once, then, that the duty of preserving and cultivating the language is recognised, its obligation must be seen to affect those most that have most power and best opportunities towards its fulfilment.[10]

Struchtúr lárnach i sochaí na hÉireann ab ea an eaglais Chaitliceach agus cuireann sé béim an-mhór ar an chaidreamh idir an Chléir agus an teanga mar 'a tie as sacred as any that can hold between men and things'.[11] Léirigh sé ón tús, fosta, go raibh sé i gcoinne aon ghníomhaíochtaí foréigneacha, ainneoin an naisc idir tuiscintí náisiúnaíocha polaitíochta agus teanga. Is cineál tairngreachta é an sliocht seo ar mheon na linne as ar eascair buntuiscintí agus bunfhealsúnacht na hathbheochana:

One of the main aims of Roman Policy was, we are told, to extinguish the national language of the Gauls; the Romans, with their keen political insight, plainly discerning the importance of language as a political factor. With the loss of their language, the Gauls lost their nationality; with the loss of their nationality, they lost their national spirit and their other splendid characteristics; so that at the break up of the empire they were left nerveless, inert, helpless, at the mercy of their barbarian neighbours ... Politics will not form such a defence, for politics follow the forces of the time. Physical hostility is not to be dreamt of.[12]

Ag teacht chun deiridh, deir sé go bhfuil lucht labhartha na Gaeilge ag iarraidh an Béarla a fhoghlaim toisc go bhfuil siad ag iarraidh gotha oideachais a chur orthu féin nó dul ar imirce. Deir sé go neamhbhalbh nach bhfuil an Béarla á fhoghlaim ag cainteoirí dúchais ar son cúrsaí eacnamaíochta nó gnó na tíre agus ar an ábhar sin nach bhfuil aon leas ábhartha le baint as foghlaim an Bhéarla a thuilleadh. Críochnaíonn sé an t-alt le spotsholas ar thábhacht na tréimhse féin, an phointe ama seo mar phointe le gníomhú láithreach:

The time is critical. The language may reach a certain stage of decay that may cut it off from all its past or may suffer a diminution in the numbers of those who speak it that may make restoration almost impossible. If there is cause for congratulation, there is also cause for apprehension. Politics are now all absorbing, and there is no greater enemy of the Irish language than the Irish politician, of whatever section. Every piece of special legislation affecting the Irish-speaking districts of Ireland is like a fall of rain on a badly roofed dwelling. If the house be put in order there will be nothing to fear from the rain. Those who already have been workers in the movement should exert themselves still more, and the apathetic should at last bestir themselves. The advantages of the time should be availed of, and its dangers guarded against. If the Irish clergy step into their rightful place, they will assure the success of the Gaelic movement, and add one more to their claims on the affection of their countrymen.[13]

Tá dáta an ailt suntasach agus thuig Mac Néill go raibh cumhacht na Cléire tagtha in inmhe in Éirinn le beagnach leathchéad bliain anuas agus go raibh meas ag an bpobal uirthi. Ní mór timpeallacht pholaitiúil na linne seo a

chur san áireamh fosta. Tagann na scríbhinní seo le tuairimíocht na Cléire
Caitlicí a bhfuil scannal Pharnell agus turnamh an dara Bille do Rialtas
Dúchais, ach go háirithe, mar chúlra dóibh. Ní dócha gur aon chomhtharlú
é ach an oiread gur iarr Eoghan Ó Gramhnaigh, sagart a raibh ról lárnach
aige in athbheochan na Gaeilge, ar Eoin Mac Néill an t-alt seo a scríobh. In
ainneoin go raibh neamhaird á déanamh ag pobal óg intleachtúil na tíre ar
chomhthéacs polaitiúil na tíre, tá idir fhís athbheochana agus pholaitíocht
na linne le braistint go smior sna scríbhinní seo i dtréimhse a raibh fís
Pharnell ina smidiríní thart orthu:

> After the Parnell Split there was no interest taken in politics by the
> young folk. There were too many divisions. The Gaelic League where
> there were no politics spoken was a mecca for everyone. The people
> learned that they had a country with a language; they learned the
> music, the dancing, the games, they were encouraged to use Irish-
> manufactured goods.[14]

Ar an ábhar sin is léiriú suntasach iad na scríbhinní seo ar an nasc idir Cléir
Chaitliceach na hÉireann agus gluaiseacht na hathbheochana. Bhí meitheal
tuairimíochta agus intleachta ag borradh. D'fhéadfadh gluaiseacht na
Gaeilge feidhmiú mar uirlis phobail chun muinín mhuintir na tíre as a dtír
féin a chothú le tacaíocht ón eagraíocht ba chumhachtaí sa tír ag an am,
an Eaglais Chaitliceach, go háirithe i measc chosmhuintir na gceantracha
tuaithe. Cé nach mairfeadh an tacaíocht sin i bhfad ina dhiaidh sin, nuair
a bhí an ghluaiseacht ar thairseach cumann nó struchtúr nua oifigiúil a
bhunú mar shuaitheantas na gluaiseachta athbheochana agus cultúrtha, ar
bhonn íorónta chuidigh suaitheantas na hEaglaise Caitlicí le híomhá agus
le hidéal an 'mecca' a bhí á saothrú ag aos óg na linne:

> It is the privilege of the writer to place before the Irish Clergy, through
> an exceptionally favourable medium, a few considerations embodying
> a portion of the views of a large number of thinking Irishmen, and
> concerning an object instinctively dear to the hearts of the whole
> people.[15]

Anuas air sin, ba theist ar luach an ábhair agus ar mholtaí an ailt i
gcomhthéacs an naisc seo, gur iarr an tAthair Eoghan Ó Gramhnaigh ar
Mhac Néill alt níos cuimsithí a chur le chéile. Foilsíodh leagan Gaeilge agus
Béarla den alt seo in *Irisleabhar na Gaedhilge / The Gaelic Journal* i mí an

Mhárta, 1893. Ghlac sé claonadh níos sainiúla sa dara halt le teachtaireacht láidir faoi labhairt na Gaeilge chun í a choinneáil beo. Cuireann Mac Néill in iúl go bhfuil beagnach 700,000 duine a labhraíonn Gaeilge in Éirinn agus gurb ionann ceantracha labhartha na Gaeilge agus aon trian den tír, a thugann le fios go bhfuil sé indéanta an teanga a shábháil, dar leis. Leanann sé ar aghaidh le dhá phointe déag i nGaeilge agus i mBéarla a leagann amach an bunús le slánú, le caomhnú agus le hathbheochan na Gaeilge. Cé gur chuir sé béim i gcónaí ar luach an oideachais, sa tríú pointe is treise an bhéim a chuireann sé ar bhealaí eile agus ar chumarsáid na Gaeilge sa bhaile ach go háirithe:

> No language has ever been kept alive by mere book-teaching ... The language cannot live at all that does not live in the homes of the people. Special conditions make the attempt to preserve Gaelic by book-teaching alone especially futile. Some additional means must therefore be employed ... Whatever is worth doing is worth doing speedily.[16]

Leagann sé an-bhéim ar thábhacht na gcainteoirí dúchais agus mar a rinne sé san alt i *The Irish Ecclesiastical Record*, pléann sé an dúshlán a bhaineann le nasc a chothú idir pobal an iarthair agus grúpaí uirbeacha an oirthir nó 'The East and the West' mar ar thagair sé dóibh i *The Irish Ecclesiastical Record*. Aithníodh Baile Átha Cliath mar phríomhchathair na hathbheochana, cé go mbeadh na himeachtaí ar bun ar fud na tíre, 'The organisation would probably be centred in Dublin but its main activity would be provincial'. Mar sin féin, b'fhís fhíorúil í mar níor fíoraíodh gníomhaíochtaí athbheochana go hiomlán ar bhonn réigiúnach.[17] Aithníonn Mac Néill gur gá pobal meánaicme na Gaeilge atá ag saothrú na teanga ag leibhéal léannta, agus an gnáthphobal labhartha, a tharraingt le chéile. Bhí gá le hathrú treorach:

> The Gaelic movement in Ireland has hitherto appealed directly only to the middle classes. The language is now in higher esteem among those classes than at any time since the 17th century. The masses are as open to the claims of truth, and beauty, and strength as the classes. They have never yet been directly appealed to on behalf of the Gaelic Language. It remains to appeal directly to them.[18]

D'fhorbair sé an pointe ón alt i *The Irish Ecclesiastical Record* faoin ghné idirnáisiúnta le moltaí praiticiúla. Níor ghluaiseacht chúng ar imeall iarthar na hEorpa a bheadh inti ach eagraíocht dhomhanda le fís ilghnéitheach, idirnáisiúnta a tharraingeodh ar iliomad foinsí airgid mar aon le feachtais agus pobail éagsúla:

> Funds would come from three sources:
> From members' subscriptions,
> From private donations,
> From the proceeds of meetings and addresses in Irish centres of
>   population at home and abroad.[19]

Ag tógáil ar an chomhfhreagras a tháinig isteach tar éis fhoilsiú an ailt, shocraigh Seosamh Laoide (J.H. Lloyd), agus Eoin Mac Néill go ndéanfaidís teagmháil le neart daoine tábhachtacha a cheap siad a mbeadh suim acu i mbunú a leithéid de ghluaiseacht. Bhí Seosamh Laoide ina bhall de Chumann Buanchoimeádta na Gaeilge ó 1886 agus ba scoláire mór Gaeilge é. Nuair a bunaíodh Scoil Ard-Léinn na hÉireann faoi stiúir Kuno Meyer i 1903, bhí Seosamh ar na chéad mhic léinn ann agus toghadh é ina bhall den Acadamh Ríoga i 1909. Tar éis ghairmscoile Mhic Néill agus Laoide, tháinig an grúpa seo le chéile ar 31 Iúil, 1893 agus bunaíodh Conradh na Gaeilge / the Gaelic League. Ní raibh Seosamh Laoide i láthair i 9, Sráid Saicfil ar 31 Iúil nuair a bunaíodh Conradh na Gaeilge, ach faoi fhómhar 1893, bhí sé ina chomhchisteoir le Seán Ó hÓgáin sa ghluaiseacht nua. Bhíodh sé ag scríobh in *Irisleabhar na Gaedhilge / The Gaelic Journal* ó 1891 ar aghaidh agus ceapadh é ina eagarthóir air in 1899.[20] Cuireadh an tríú alt tábhachtach i gcruthú an pholasaí athbheochana, dar teideal 'The Gaelic League', i gcló in *Irisleabhar na Gaedhilge* i mí na Samhna, 1893, a bhfaightear ceann de na cuntais is cruinne ar bhunú an Chonartha ann.[21] Tugtar liosta ainmneacha bhaill an choiste agus luaitear Eoin Mac Néill mar rúnaí oinigh *pro tem*. Cuirtear béim arís ar obair Bhaile Átha Cliath agus ar thábhacht an tsuímh uirbigh:

> For the present, this work is of necessity confined to Dublin and consists in enlarging the membership of the society and in holding the weekly conferences ... The object of this feature of the meetings is not the cultivation of Gaelic literature as such, from which the Gaelic League dissociates itself; but to demonstrate to the public the actuality and existence at the doors of the living Irish language and to show that there are, even in Dublin, men who can speak Irish freely and masterfully, and who can exhibit the powers of the language as

still alive and vigorous; and also that there is in Dublin a large number of people who understand Irish well enough to form an intelligent audience for a speaker of Irish.[22]

Léiríonn an sliocht seo fosta gur cuireadh an oiread céanna béime ar chruthú an phobail éisteachta agus scríbhneoireachta sna ceantair uirbeacha agus a cuireadh ar neartú an phobail labhartha. Ionas go mbeadh rath ar an obair seo, bheadh fóram pinn de dhíth ina gcruthófaí plé ar ábhair chasta na sochaí a d'ardódh réim na teanga ó phobal tuatach a raibh téarmaí bunúsacha maireachtála in úsáid aige, go pobal a d'úsáidfeadh an Ghaeilge i ngnó theanga oifigiúil na tíre. Cuireadh clabhsúr leis an alt sin le haitheantas láidir a thabhairt do bhunaitheoirí Chonradh na Gaeilge: 'In the noted Bismarckian phrase, it is abundantly clear that the founders of the Gaelic League have "seized the psychological moment."'[23]

Anuas air sin agus ag filleadh ar cháineadh Mhic Néill ina alt i *The Ecclesiastical Record*, ar an dóigh ar theip ar Ghaeil an bhaile 'to decently support a quarterly journal devoted to the culture of Irish', bhí fórám dá chuid féin aige anois chun an bhearna seo a líonadh le tógáil ar athrú mheon na ndaoine. Bhí taobh siceolaíoch na hathbheochana fite fuaite i saothrú scríbhneoireacht an phobail intleachtúil agus bhí Mac Néill chun tosaigh i saothrú an fhóraim sin, fiú nuair nach raibh airgead le saothrú as an obair a bhí le caitheamh le cur i gcrích an 'psychological moment'.

Nuair a ghlac Conradh na Gaeilge cúram *Irisleabhar na Gaedhilge / The Gaelic Journal*, bhí Eoin Mac Néill ina eagarthóir ó mhí an Mhárta, 1895 go 1899, a chinntigh aistriú gan cham. Ina dhiaidh sin, ghlac sé cúram eagarthóireachta tosaigh nuachtán dhátheangach an Chonartha, *An Claidheamh Soluis*, ar bhonn deonach idir Márta, 1899 agus Meán Fómhair, 1901. Cé nach féidir a bheith go hiomlán cinnte cén 'moment' go baileach a bhfuil Mac Néill ag tagairt dó, tríocha bliain ina dhiaidh sin ina chuimhní cinn, tagraíonn sé do thábhacht agus do ghangaid an 'moment' seo. Tá sé spéisiúil go luann sé ról na meán agus na hiriseoireachta mar uirlis chumarsáide san anailís a dhéanann sé ar an tréimhse:

> The main feature of the Parnell crisis was its bitterness. This was imparted to it by the speeches and the journalism on both sides and strange as it may seem, my recollection about it is clear that the bitterness of that time was deeper and sharper; and more widespread than anything we experienced afterwards even at the height of the Civil War in '22.[24]

EAGARTHÓIR *IRISLEABHAR NA GAEDHILGE*

Nuair a fógraíodh go raibh Eoghan Ó Gramhnaigh tinn i mí Iúil, 1894, ba é Eoin Mac Néill a tháinig mar chomharba lánaimseartha air agus cuireadh tús lena thréimhse eagarthóireachta ar *Irisleabhar na Gaedhilge* leis an eagrán dár dáta 1 Meán Fómhair, 1894.[25] Leag sé a phlean eagarthóireachta amach go soiléir agus cuireadh in iúl ón tús go mbeadh an t-ábhar dírithe orthu siúd a raibh ar a gcumas an Ghaeilge a léamh agus a scríobh agus go gcuirfí cuid mhaith focal úr i gcló. Cuireadh in iúl fosta, go gcuirfí amhráin i gcló mar aon le staidéir ar chanúintí na Gaeilge i Maigh Eo, Iarthar Chorcaí, Co. an Chláir agus Cúige Mumhan. Bheadh seanfhocail, 'Gaelic Notes', 'Foilseacháin nua', 'The Gaelic Papers' (ábhair ó cholúin in Éirinn agus thar lear) ann agus ba chur chuige é seo a chuir na 'háiteacha dorcha' a luaigh de hÍde ina litir d'Fhéilsgríbhinn Mhic Néill san áireamh. Chuir sé na háiteanna seo a bhí faoi thionchar na hoidhreachta traidisiúnta a raibh pobal na hathbheochana ag iarraidh greim shiceolaíoch nó 'psychological moment' a fháil orthu, faoi spotsholas na dtuiscintí úra. Dá mbeadh baint ag Mac Néill le bunú Stát úr na hÉireann, bheadh sé le tuigbheáil ón tús go mbeadh an oidhreacht Ghaelach lárnach ann.

Sa chomhthéacs sin, is fiú cúpla rud suntasach a lua ón *Irisleabhar* a chuir go mór le léann na Gaeilge agus le caighdeán na hiriseoireachta scolártha ag an am. I mí na Nollag, 1894, cuireadh dán i gcló le P. Standún dár teideal 'Athbheoghudh na Gaeilge' a chuir fís na hathbheochana i láthair faoi sheanfhoirm na filíochta agus bhí cúpla alt ag Mac Néill féin ar 'Irish in Co. Antrim' ar cuireadh tús leo ar an chéad lá de mhí Mheán Fómhair, 1895.[26] In alt eile, aithnítear tacaíocht na mban do bhunú an chumainn úir le cur chun cinn na Gaeilge. Cé go mbaineann an eagraíocht atá á plé le ceantar Bhéal Feirste, tuigtear go raibh mná na nGlinntí an-ghníomhach ina lán slite le cur chun cinn na Gaeilge. Aithníodh an tábhacht a bhain le tacaíocht na mban sa tionscnamh seo: 'It has the sanction and support of some of the most influential ladies and gentlemen in the city'.[27] Foilsíodh alt spéisiúil eile uaidh i mí Aibreáin, 1896, dar teideal 'Irish Studies III' mar aon le litir ó Dhubhghlas de hÍde i mí an Mheithimh, 1896.[28] D'aithin sé feidhm an fhóraim iriseoireachta fosta i saothrú na nualitríochta agus thug sé ardán scríbhneoireachta don Athair Peadar Ó Laoghaire nuair a cuireadh an t-úrscéal *Séadna* i gcló i sraith sheachtainiúil ó mhí na Samhna, 1894, ar aghaidh.[29]

Ag cloí leis an bhfís tosaigh a leag sé amach, cuireann sé béim ar ghníomhaíochtaí na nGael thar lear agus ar thionchar ghréasán na Gaeilge

Issued

Branch: Dublin City Ballyfermot
Date: 10/09/2022   Time: 4:03 PM
Name: Donnelly, John

ITEM(S)   DUE DATE

The lives of Eoin MacNeill 01 Oct 202.
XCPL800009/09/
Item Value: €39.00

Total value of item(s): €39.00
Your current loan(s): 6
Your current reservation(s): 0
Your current active request(s): 0

To renew your items please log onto My
Account at https://dublincity.spydus.i

Thank you for using your local library

ag leibhéal idirnáisiúnta ar an ghluaiseacht in Éirinn. Tugann liosta na n-irisí sa cholún 'The Gaelic Papers' ag deireadh gach eagrán *d'Irisleabhar na Gaedhilge* le fios go bhfuil gréasán idirnáisiúnta á chothú agus go bhfuil an eagraíocht ag brath ar na naisc idirnáisiúnta seo. Ar an chéad lá de mhí Eanáir, 1895, tugadh spás ar leith do thuras Eoghain Uí Ghramhnaigh go Nua Eabhrac agus cuireadh an dileagra a thug sé i gcló. Is cuntas maith é a léiríonn tábhacht na gcumann Gaeilge i Nua Eabhrac agus tacaíocht na Cléire do ghluaiseacht na Gaeilge sna Stáit Aontaithe:

> In writing home, Father O'Growney has expressed great delight at the spirit and earnestness manifested by the friends of the Gaelic tongue in America. He says that those working in the same cause at home should take increased courage from the attitude of their American fellow-workers, who are watching eagerly the progress of the movement in the old land.[30]

Ba eilimintí spreagúla forásacha iad na naisc idirnáisiúnta, ach thuig Mac Néill go raibh údarás ar leith ag *Irisleabhar na Gaedhilge* mar ghuth pobail intleachtúil do na Gaeil thar lear fosta. Ar an chéad lá de mhí an Mhárta, 1895, tugtar buíochas do Mr P. O'Farrell, Sebastopol, Victoria, a chuidigh le daoine a bhí ag déanamh fiosrúchán faoi *Irisleabhar na Gaedhilge* sa *Melbourne Advocate*; luaitear alt sa *Catholic Times* i Philadelphia a chuireann síos ar ghluaiseacht na teanga i Philadelphia agus tugtar liosta daoine a bhfuil síntiús acu *d'Irisleabhar na Gaedhilge* ach a thugann breis airgid do Chonradh na Gaeilge fosta. Seo mar a chuirtear síos ar thacaíocht na gcairde Gael thar lear agus in Éirinn, a thugann flúirse na tacaíochta chun solais agus a thugann le fios nár samhlaíodh aon difríocht idir an dá phobal:

> We are sincerely grateful to many friends in the Press for their kind commendations of our efforts to the public. To mention all the journals in which the *Gaelic Journal* has of late been favourably noticed is out of the question. The list would include leading papers, daily and weekly in Ireland, Great Britain, the United States and Australia. The friendliness which prompts these notices will feel sufficiently rewarded by the assurance that this journal, supported and conducted wholly by unremunerated and volunteer work, is steadily growing in popularity and influence.[31]

Ar fhaitíos fosta go mbeadh aon amhras faoi thacaíocht Stáit Aontaithe Mheiriceá, cuirtear in iúl i mí na Samhna, 1896, go mbeidh laghdú ar an

phraghas (a chuirtear i bhfeidhm mí na Nollag, 1896) mar thoradh ar
shíntiús £10 a sheol Mr M. A. Byrne i Nua Eabhrac ar aghaidh a bronnadh
air ó Hon John D Cummins agus Mr Edward Eyre ó Nua Eabhrac.
Sonraítear gur iarradh go rachadh an t-airgead chun tairbhe laghdú an
chostais d'*Irisleabhar na Gaedhilge* chun seachadadh na hirise a neartú agus
gur baill de Chumann na Gaedhilge, Nua Eabhrac a bhí freagrach as an
bhfláithiúlacht seo.

Nuair a thóg Conradh na Gaeilge cúram na hirise in 1895, leag Mac Néill
ról na hirise amach go soiléir le seilbh a ghlacadh ar *Irisleabhar na Gaedhilge*
mar uirlis oifigiúil Chonradh na Gaeilge:

> The Gaelic Journal will be at once the organ of the Irish language
> movement, the willing medium of interchange of knowledge
> among the students of Irish, the record of much of our literature
> and traditional lore, and the clear and indubitable witness that our
> language is still a living tongue, a great instrument of thought, with
> a living literature, *and with its powers of creating a living national
> literature still unimpaired*. The existence of the *Gaelic Journal* will in
> this way be a protest and a testimony against the national crime, by
> whomsoever perpetrated, whether by design or neglect perpetrated, of
> ignoring our national language and literature, and abandoning them
> to disuse and oblivion.[32]

Faightear macalla anseo de réamhrá *Bolg an tSolair* in 1795, nuair a cuireadh
in iúl go raibh feidhm ar leith ag an iris mar chur i gcoinne na n-údarás,
ach léiríonn an bhéim ar chruthú na nualitríochta beo go bhfuil treo eile
á ghlacadh i ngluaiseacht na teanga. Bheadh tábhacht nach beag leis an
chur chuige seo agus leis an litríocht féin i múnlú an mheoin úr chultúrtha
a mbeadh luach á chur aige ar litríocht na Gaeilge i measc litríochtaí agus
teangacha an domhain. Leag sé seo na bunchlocha fosta do chur chuige
intleachtúil na hathbheochana le béim ar an Ghaeilge anois mar 'a great
instrument of thought' mar a luadh cheana. Dá samhlófaí an nualitríocht
mar scáthán ar an tsochaí, shamhlófaí na hirisí mar aghaidheanna le
guthanna beo na linne ag labhairt iontu. Cé nárbh fhear mór litríochta é
Mac Néill – a mhalairt agus é ag plé le cúrsaí staire go príomha – tuigtear
forbairt a mheoin trí na scríbhinní seo. Bhí foghlaim na teanga chun
tosaigh i gcónaí le foilsiú 'Easy Lessons in Irish' Eoghain Uí Ghramhnaigh,[33]
agus is suaitheantas ar leith é gur ceanglaíodh obair Uí Ghramhnaigh le
scoláireacht, le sagartóireacht, le saothrú phobal na hÉireann agus phobal
inimirceach na Stát Aontaithe, seachas le cúrsaí teanga amháin.

San alt a luadh cheana dar teideal 'Irish Studies III', cuirtear béim an athuair ar an chur chuige intleachtúil:

> It is assumed that those who read these hints really wish and have decided to make the Irish language a part of their own intellectual being; that they wish to regain their lost place in the intellectual continuity of the nation; that, in short, they are determined to master Irish as a living language.[34]

San eagrán céanna, déantar cur síos ar dhul chun cinn na gluaiseachta agus na gcraobhacha agus luaitear go bhfuil dhá chraobh agus fiche bunaithe anois. I mí an Mheithimh, 1896, san eagarfhocal, déanann sé iarracht léitheoirí a ghríosú chun gníomhú trí bhéim a chur ar an chomhthéacs áitiúil agus ar an ghá le seilbh a ghlacadh ar an ghníomhaíocht féin:

> No point demands more pressing attention than the necessity for the *local effort*. Local sympathisers with the movement are too apt to wait till other people do things for them ... Those who live in places where Irish is in full vigour have usually been most apathetic, not stirring themselves until, in a few years time, they find that the language is getting into a really sick state, the youth of the country beginning to forsake it generally. Intelligent men ought to remember that they are endowed, under Providence, with the power of moulding the course of events around them, and that it is a poor thing for them to live the purposeless lives of vegetables.[35]

I ndiaidh an phíosa seo, tagraítear do chruinniú i Leitir Ceanainn le litir a léadh ó Easpag Ó Domhnaill, Rath Bhoth agus ceann ó Dhúbhghlas de hÍde ar tagraíodh di cheana. Ar ndóigh ba phearsa thábhachtach é Ó Domhnaill ag leibhéal náisiúnta agus áitiúil, go háirithe i gcomhthéacs an róil a ghlac sé mar chisteoir sa Pháirtí Rialtas Dúchais san fhichiú haois.

Tá cur chuige intleachtúil na hathbheochana chun tosaigh i gcónaí i rith eagarthóireacht Mhic Néill ar *Irisleabhar na Gaedhilge*. Tugtar léargas suntasach ar thuairiscí nuachtán ar ghluaiseacht na Gaeilge in Éirinn agus thar lear i ngach eagrán, a thugann spleáchas an dá phobal – áitiúil agus idirnáisiúnta – ar a chéile chun solais. Anuas air sin, tá a lán eolais faoi chruinnithe agus eagraíochtaí eile cultúrtha agus an Ghaeilge. Sampla maith de seo ná tuairisc ar Chumann Buanchoimeádta na Gaeilge i mí Aibreáin, 1896.[36] Is i gcomhthéacs chruthú an náisiúin nua is mó a leagtar an bhéim ar oidhreacht luachmhar na hÉireann seachas ar chomhthéacs athbheochan na teanga amháin:

> What pleased us most in the 1895 report of the 'Society for the Preservation of the Irish Language' was the address of Dr Holgher Pederson [sic],[37] of the University of Copenhagen. He said: – First of all, I look upon the preservation of the Irish language as an act of justice due to that part of the Irish people who still speak the Irish language; for the intellectual and moral development of a people cannot be promoted, as it should be, by any other means than the mother tongue. But besides this the preservation of the Irish language should be considered as a part of the National cause by the whole Irish nation, whether they speak English or Irish; lest they should lose the ties connecting them with the great past of Ireland. Of course the great thing aimed at by patriotism must be the future prosperous state of the country ... Therefore I think that the oldest monuments of the Irish language ought to be studied, the wonderful tales in the ancient Irish manuscripts ought to be read, and the development of the Irish language and literature ought to be carefully traced down to our own time in all the high schools of Ireland.[38]

Taobh leis an bhéim ar an bhforás intleachtúil agus oidhreachta, tá cuid mhaith de scéal agus de bhunchlocha na n-imeachtaí ceannródaíocha a bunaíodh mar chuid de ghluaiseacht na Gaeilge le rianú trí thréimhse eagarthóireachta Mhic Néill. Ar na himeachtaí is tábhachtaí tá fógairt an chéad Oireachtas i mBaile Átha Cliath, Dé Luain, 17 Bealtaine, 1897.[39] Lonnaítear na forbairtí seo taobh le Feis mhór na Gaeilge i mí na Bealtaine, agus cuirtear in iúl go mbeidh sé tráthúil d'iomaitheoirí na Feise agus an Oireachtais go mbeidh an dá ócáid ann le chéile. Is i dtéarmaí idirnáisiúnta arís a chuirtear é seo i láthair:

> The Executive Committee of the Gaelic League, therefore, confidently appeals to the Irish societies in America, to the friends of the National Language, and to the Irish people generally for their generous co-operation and support in carrying out this patriotic project.[40]

Má bhí seilbh á glacadh ag Mac Néill agus a chomhaoisigh ar *Irisleabhar na Gaedhilge* mar uirlis oifigiúil Chonradh na Gaeilge, bheadh athshealbhú á ghlacadh ag muintir na hÉireann ar a dteanga dhúchais mar chuid de dhlúth agus d'inneach an stáit úir. Bheadh an suíomh uirbeach teanga a chruthaigh siad trí bhunú Chonnradh na Gaeilge tábhachtach in athlonnú na Gaeilge mar chuid de struchtúir oifigiúla na tíre:

> The significance of the celebrations that began on the 17th May lies in the fact that this National culture is brought back from its distant retreats and enthroned in the administrative centre of the nation.[41]

I dtreo dheireadh thréimhse eagarthóireachta Mhic Néill, aithnítear athruithe tuairimíochta faoi ról na meán in athbheochan na Gaeilge. I litir a foilsíodh ó 'Two Paddies' i mí Aibreáin, 1897, cuirtear moladh i láthair a aithníonn an gá le 'An Irish Weekly' mar an dóigh ab fhearr chun an Ghaeilge a choinneáil beo. Moltar an teideal 'The Gael' nó 'An tÉireannach' agus moltar an tOireachtas mar ardán plé don choincheap seo.[42] Tá freagra Mhic Néill stuama, oscailte. Aithníonn sé na buntáistí a bhaineann lena leithéid de thogra, ach tuigtear dó go mbeidh deacrachtaí le 'Free service' na n-eagarthóirí agus na scríbhneoirí, cleachtas a bhí á shaothrú aige féin le blianta anuas faoin am seo. In ainneoin sin áfach, admhaíonn sé fiúntas an nuachtáin mar uirlis teanga agus chumarsáide:

> It must be remembered that the service which is free from remuneration is also free from control. A paper which is to appear on a certain day every week must be in a position to command the services of its staff. But even this difficulty may not be insuperable.[43]

Faoi mhí na Bealtaine, 1897, fógraítear go mbeidh athruithe forásacha á gcur i bhfeidhm agus críoch á cur leis an seachtú leabhar den *Irisleabhar*. Aithnítear na gníomhaíochtaí cultúrtha agus cuirtear béim ar athrú meoin agus ar theacht le chéile an dá chultúr – cultúr uirbeach agus cultúr tuaithe na Gaeilge agus na hÉireann. Ní luaitear Mac Néill leis an alt seo ach d'fhéadfaí glacadh leis gur scríobh sé é mar eagarthóir reatha na hirise:

> Our seventh volume just completed has chronicled a continuous spreading and strengthening of the Irish language movement ... The success of this movement will prove the possibility of bringing the highest forms of mental culture home to the humblest firesides, and the Irish speaking people will in time be known to the world as a race the truest lovers and best judges of literary excellence since the days of the Athenian drama. This is no idle boast. It is an anticipation founded

on a knowledge of facts, an anticipation which is even now to some
extent realised, and which would long ago have been fully realised but
for the ban placed on our native culture by those who hated all things
Irish, and too servilely acquiesced in by our compliant selves.[44]

Tuigeadh dóibh go raibh an fhís athbheochana á fíorú agus cultúr
intleachtúil na hÉireann á fhógairt ar fud an domhain. Samhlaíodh go
gcuirfí agus go n-aithneofaí feabhas agus stádas litríocht na hÉireann ag na
leibhéil ab'airde domhanda. Bhí ról lárnach ag *Irisleabhar na Gaedhilge* mar
chroinic ar ghluaiseacht na hAthbheochana agus tagann an téarmaíocht seo
le tuiscintí scoláirí eile ar ról an iriseora ag casadh an chéid. Mar shampla,
nuair a rinne Osborn Bergin (scoláire mór na Gaeilge agus comhaoiseach
Eoin Mhic Néill), comparáid idir feidhm an fhile agus feidhm an iriseora,
cheangail sé oidhreacht agus traidisiún léannta na hÉireann ag na leibhéil
ab airde le cleachtadh na hiriseoireachta mar ghné lárnach na sochaí ar
bhonn seanda agus nua-aimseartha. Tuigtear sa chomhthéacs seo an ról
tábhachtach a bhí ag Mac Néill mar eagarthóir *Irisleabhar na Gaedhilge*,
príomhuirlis Chonradh na Gaeilge ag an am:

> He discharged, as O'Donovan pointed out many years ago, the
> functions of the modern journalist. He was not a song writer. He
> was often a public official, a chronicler, a political essayist, a keen and
> satirical observer of his fellow-countrymen.[45]

Agus plean an ochtú eagráin á leagan amach aige, tuigtear gur gá glacadh
le riachtanas an Bhéarla i gcónaí, a thacaíonn le cur chuige dátheangach
na hathbheochana. Cé gur aithníodh *Irisleabhar na Gaedhilge* mar 'the
recognised literary mouthpiece of the Irish language' dúradh nár mhór
úsáid an Bhéarla a aithint i gcur chun cinn na Gaeilge chomh maith:

> As regards the use of the English language in the journal, we shall
> continue to act as in the past. History tells us that Ireland was never
> worsted without the help of Irishmen. In like manner the help of
> English cannot be dispensed with in our efforts for the maintenance
> of our native language.[46]

In ainneoin sin, fógraíodh go mbeadh míonna na ndátaí don *Irisleabhar* i
nGaeilge amháin as sin amach mar chuid de pholasaí eagarthóireachta na
hirise. I mí na Samhna, 1897, fógraíodh go raibh nuachtán úr ag teacht.
'Fáinne an Lae' an teideal a bheadh air agus dúradh san fhógra,

> if this movement is a reality it should by this time be able to stand the
> test of supporting a weekly paper. The test is now about to be made,
> and we are confident of a successful result.[47]

Bhí gluaiseacht na Gaeilge ag bogadh ó choincheap an 'protest' go
coincheap an 'test'.

Ní raibh mórán achair idir 'test' agus 'teip' áfach. I mí Eanáir, 1899,
pléann Mac Néill bunús na conspóide idir an clódóir Bernard Doyle, a
chéadbhunaigh an nuachtán *Fáinne an Lae* as a stuaim féin i 1898, agus an
cur chuige a ghlac sé a bhí i gcoinne pholasaí Chonradh na Gaeilge. Tugtar
cúig leathanach do chuntas na conspóide agus é sínithe ag John Mac Neill.[48]
Fógraítear deireadh ré Eoin Mhic Néill i mí Iúil, 1899, agus J.H. Lloyd
ceaptha mar eagarthóir nua ar an *Irisleabhar*.[49]

Níor stad Mac Néill lena scríbhinní iriseoireachta ansin agus lean
sé ar aghaidh agus é ina chéad eagarthóir ar *An Claidheamh Soluis* idir
Márta 1899, agus Meán Fómhair 1901. D'eascair *An Claidheamh Soluis*
as an socrú a rinneadh le Brian Ó Dubhghaill chun nuachtán Chonradh
na Gaeilge a bhunú. Ba é *Fáinne an Lae* an chéad teideal a bhí ar an
nuachtán. Nuair a d'éirigh easaontas idir an dá pháirtí, scar Ó Dubhghaill
agus Coiste Gnó an Chonartha óna chéile agus mar thoradh ar an scoilt,
bhunaigh Conradh na Gaeilge *An Claidheamh Soluis*. Mhair an nuachtán
faoi theidil éagsúla ar feadh trí bliana is tríocha ansin go dtí gur bunaíodh
An Camán faoi choimirce Chumann Lúthchleas Gael agus Chonradh na
Gaeilge i 1932. Is díol suntais iad na teidil i rith thréimhse fhoilsithe an
nuachtáin a réitíonn le tuairimíocht Mhic Néill a luadh ag tús na caibidle
seo faoin Ghaeilge a thógáil amach as an dorchadas. Neartaíonn ábhar *An
Claidheamh Soluis* an fhealsúnacht sin, mar pléadh a lán gnéithe de shaol
agus de shochaí na hÉireann. Ina measc bhí díospóireachtaí teanga, a raibh
tráchtaireacht pholaitíochta, shóisialta, eacnamaíochta agus chultúrtha
ar ré na hAthbheochana agus tréimhse réabhlóideach bhlianta tosaigh an
fhichiú haois go bunú an stáit, lárnach iontu. Dála na scríbhneoirí agus
na n-eagarthóirí, ba cheannairí polaitíochta, staire agus réabhlóide cuid
mhaith díobh a leag a suaitheantas eiseamláireach ar fhorbairt an náisiúin
agus na tíre, Eoin Mac Néill ina measc.

EAGARTHÓIR *AN CLAIDHEAMH SOLUIS*

Sna heagarfhocail a scríobh Eoin Mac Néill in *An Claidheamh Soluis,*
chuir sé in iúl gur chreid sé go raibh ról lárnach ag Conradh na Gaeilge, ní

hamháin in athbheochan chultúrtha agus teanga, ach i slánú eacnamaíochta fosta. Chun é seo a phlé léirigh sé samplaí ó thíortha eile inar éirigh leo athbheochan teanga a chur i bhfeidhm agus eacnamaíocht na tíre a fheabhsú ag an am chéanna, an Ghréig, an Fhionnlainn, an Bhóihéim, an Ungáir agus Oirthear na Prúise, mar shampla:

> The people of a country are its wealth ... Enquire into the history of other nations under the rule of a people of another race and another language. One law will be found exemplified throughout, except in one or two cases. The decay of the native language is everywhere accompanied by industrial and general decadence. The converse holds equally true. Whenever a language revival has taken place material prosperity has been restored.[50]

Pléadh cúrsaí oideachais, litríochta agus polaitíochta i gcomhthéacs athbheochan teanga agus rinneadh iarracht staid na teanga a shuíomh i gcomhthéacs Athbheochan na Gaeilge. An Pholainn, an Bheilg, an Ungáir, an Bhreatain Bheag, Málta, Manainn, an Corn, an tSeicslóvaic agus Meicsiceo a luadh sa chás seo a thugann le fios go raibh dearcadh leathan domhanda á ghlacadh ag Mac Néill i gcónaí. Cé go raibh ábhar an phlé seo machnamhach seachas fíriciúil i gcónaí, is léiriú iad na hailt ar an chur chuige idirnáisiúnta agus an ceangal le tíortha Ceilteacha eile. Mar shampla, ceann de na conspóidí ba mhó a tháinig chun tosaigh i rith a ré eagarthóireachta ná an chonspóid faoin bhaint a bheadh ag Conradh na Gaeilge le cumann na bPan Cheilteach.[51] Don chonspóid áirithe seo, áfach, cuireann an plé spotsholas ar neamhspleáchas na gluaiseachta Gaeilge faoi scáth na dtionchar idirnáisiúnta a léiríonn íogair na gluaiseachta Gaeilge agus iad díreach ag céimeanna tosaigh na hathbheochana Gaeilge. Tá tábhacht nach beag leis an seasamh a glacadh don chonspóid seo, mar, cé go rabhthas ag iarraidh naisc a chothú, léiríodh an tábhacht a bhain le fís bhunaidh na gluaiseachta beagnach deich mbliana roimhe sin sna hailt tosaigh a pléadh cheana i *The Ecclesiastical Record* agus in *Irisleabhar na Gaeilge*.

Tugtar an-aitheantas d'alt Mhic Néill dar teideal 'The North Began', in *An Claidheamh Soluis* i mí na Samhna, 1913. Mar sin féin, dá thábhachtaí é, ba thrua cáil scríbhinní iriseoireachta Mhic Néill a bhunú ar an alt sin amháin, bunaithe ar sheasamh an ailt i stair na hÉireann mar chaitilís do bhunú Óglaigh na hÉireann.[52] San eagarfhocal in *An Claidheamh Soluis* 31 Márta, 1900, tagraíonn Mac Néill do ról Chonradh na Gaeilge mar cheann d'eagraíochtaí éagsúla atá ag obair chun tuiscintí cearta ar náisiúntacht a chur chun cinn. San alt seo faightear leid dá thuiscint féin ar a ról mar eagarthóir *An Claidheamh Soluis* mar uirlis oifigiúil an Chonartha. Admhaíonn sé ról *An Claidheamh Soluis* i gcóras an tsaoil agus an chreidimh. Tagraíonn sé do fhréamhacha agus do luachanna na hEaglaise Caitlicí i gcónaí amhail agus gur chreid sé in 1891 go mbeadh an Chléir freagrach as slánú na teanga. Anois, áfach, admhaíonn sé go raibh róil ar leith ag baill áirithe den Chléir Chaitliceach, ach gur fheidhmigh an Eaglais Chaitliceach mar 'cog wheel in the great machine' agus nach raibh ról gníomhach aici in athbheochan na Gaeilge i gcónaí. Tuigtear as seo go raibh fíorghá i gcónaí le ceannairí mar Eoin Mac Néill agus a chomhaoisigh:

> The League, unlike other organisations, has never claimed for itself that it is the sole depository of 'Nationality'; its position is that it is a big and necessary cogwheel in the great machine. No people are more conscious than we that when all of us speak Irish bread will still remain the staff of life, and that the Irish-speaking children of the future will be born in original sin.[53]

CRÍOCH AGUS CONCLÚID

Ag deireadh an naoú haois déag, forbraíodh ardán idirghníomhaíochta in irisí ar nós *The Irish Ecclesiastical Record* agus *Irisleabhar na Gaedhilge* le hailt cheannródaíocha Mhic Néill agus a chomhaoisigh,[54] taobh le hóráidí de hÍde agus an Phiarsaigh mar a luadh ag tús na caibidle seo. Tógadh ar an obair sin le bunú an chéad nuachtán Gaeilge agus ní haon chomhtharlú é go raibh Eoin Mac Néill ina chéad eagarthóir air sin fosta. Bunaíodh agus buanaíodh dioscúrsa poiblí daingean i bhfóram na hiriseoireachta ar cad ba bhunús le hathbheochan teanga i gcomhthéacs fhéiniúlacht na hÉireann agus idé-eolaíocht teanga agus chultúir. Faoi sheantuiscintí an scríobhaí agus léamha nua ar ról an iriseora san fhichiú haois, is fearr a thuigtear ról lárnach Eoin Mhic Néill sa phróiseas Athbheochana seo.

A Plea for Irish Education:
Eoin MacNeill and the
university question

RUAIRÍ CULLEN

The *basis* of higher education in Ireland ought to be distinctively Irish, not English or cosmopolitan. The basis can only be made distinctively Irish by the embodiment therein of some substantial factor which is distinctively Irish. The Irish language is the only such factor discoverable. The University should therefore require by regulation a knowledge of Irish at matriculation and in its non-specialized courses.[1]

This was the argument employed by Eoin MacNeill in his influential 1909 pamphlet *Irish in the National University of Ireland: A plea for Irish education*. In it, he weighed in on the Gaelic League's campaign to make Irish a compulsory element of the matriculation examination in the recently established National University of Ireland. He was informing both the public and the university's senators who would vote on the issue that there was a simple choice: to create a truly 'national' university with the Irish language as a central component, or to ape English universities and neglect Irish nationality. As a Gaelic Leaguer and Irish-Irelander – a term used for those who supported cultural ideals that they perceived as distinctively Irish – he believed this would act as a unifying basis for the inhabitants of Ireland. It would also reinvigorate Irish self-respect and society as a whole by defeating the Anglicising tendencies that threatened to turn the island into 'West Britain'. The issue of Irish nationalism and its role in an Irish university was a relatively new one in what was commonly referred to as the 'university question', namely the dissatisfaction expressed by a number of interest groups towards higher education in Ireland. MacNeill was a leading figure in the introduction and advancement of cultural nationalist aims into the question, which had previously been focused on solving denominational concerns.

MacNeill will nearly always be mentioned in any publication that covers the final years of the university question. Yet, he is usually a member of the supporting cast, eclipsed in prominence by characters who have received closer assessment like William Delany, Michael O'Hickey, Patrick Pearse and Archbishop William Walsh.[2] Provided here is the first dedicated analysis of MacNeill's role in the events and debates that accompanied the end of the university question, repositioning MacNeill as a figure of significant prominence. Examined throughout is his role in campaigns concerning university-level education in the first decade of the twentieth century and his vision of what a truly 'national' university should look like. The chapter is divided into three roughly chronological sections that each focus on a key contribution made by MacNeill. The first begins with the final years of the university question when Irish-Irelanders like MacNeill sought to move beyond the issue of merely sculpting a new university landscape approved by the Catholic hierarchy and instead promoted a university for the 'people of Ireland' in which both 'their religion and their national ideals shall have full and free scope'.[3] The key debate surrounding the creation of the new university was whether it would be Catholic, Gaelic or both in its ethos. MacNeill emerged as a shrewd operator and important negotiator in his efforts to satisfy the Catholic and Gaelic/Irish-Irelander factions. The second part looks at MacNeill and the compulsory Irish controversy, in which he balanced divisive rhetoric with behind-the-scenes peace-making between the warring factions. Finally, his academic activity in the early years of the National University of Ireland as Professor of Early (including Medieval) Irish History at UCD is explored. The changes in the university landscape from 1908 offered an opportunity for MacNeill to promote his ideal of a liberal education with Irish studies at its centre.

APPROACHING A SOLUTION: THE END OF THE UNIVERSITY QUESTION?

At the onset of the nineteenth century, the University of Dublin, with its sole constituent college, Trinity, was the only degree-awarding body in Ireland. This changed in 1845, when Robert Peel's government established the Queen's University of Ireland with three constituent colleges in Belfast, Cork and Galway. The university and the colleges were secular and did not teach religious studies. This sparked outrage and earned them the moniker of being 'Godless Colleges'. It also led to a declaration from the Irish Catholic bishops condemning entry into the denominationally mixed colleges. The university question would subsequently become a recurrent cause for political contention over the next six decades. On the initiative of the Archbishop of Dublin, Paul Cullen, the Catholic University of Ireland was opened on Dublin's St Stephen's Green in 1854, with the English priest and intellectual John Henry Newman as its first rector. However, the institution was never officially recognised by the government. Legislation to expand the University of Dublin failed in 1873, but change soon came: firstly in 1874 when the university removed tests that had forbidden non-Anglican staff and scholars; and, secondly, with the 1879 University Education (Ireland) Act. It replaced the Queen's University with the newly created Royal University of Ireland. As a purely examining body, students could present themselves for the Royal University examination at a regional centre without attending one of the Queen's Colleges. As long as a higher education institution taught the secular subjects that made up the Royal University's degrees, it could qualify as an associate. This left the door open for students of the Catholic University, which was rechristened University College Dublin (UCD) and placed under the control of the Jesuit order. These students could now attend a college that had the approval of the hierarchy and was recognised by the government. UCD also benefited from Royal University fellowships to support its staff, a move that allowed the government to provide funding to the institution by proxy without appearing to endorse a denominational college. By the turn of the twentieth century, UCD was beginning to flourish, with increasing numbers coming through its doors and a vibrant student body.[4] Despite this, the Royal University was never widely accepted as anything other than a temporary fix and the Catholic hierarchy's displeasure remained apparent. In addition, there was dissatisfaction with the fact that students could technically take a degree without ever attending a lecture. Instead many hired private tutors known as 'grinders' or 'crammers' to guide them through the exams. This conveyed an appearance of an overly functional university that struggled to give a well-rounded university experience to its students. MacNeill attended lectures in a variety of institutions while taking his Royal University exams. These included legal studies at the King's Inns and, interestingly due to its later demonisation in his public pronouncements, Trinity College Dublin (TCD). In 1888, he received a Bachelor of Arts with honours, a year after winning a competitive civil service post. Despite never formally studying at UCD, MacNeill went on to develop significant ties at the college. From 1890, he began to study informally under the tutelage of UCD's Professor of Irish, Edmund Hogan SJ, and soon became the professor's *amanuensis*. His connection with the college grew closer after the invitation of the college president, William Delany SJ, on Hogan's suggestion, to give a series of lectures on early Irish history in 1904.[5]

The university question trundled on as the nineteenth century came to a close. The turn of the century was, however, a time of significant reform in Ireland and curricular changes to national and intermediate schools were the subject of public debate and campaigning, in which the Gaelic League was prominent.[6] Education interest groups were set up and a campaign to allow women to take degrees from Trinity College (the Royal University had allowed this from its creation) achieved success in 1904. A determined effort by George Wyndham, the Chief Secretary for Ireland from 1900 to 1905, sparked what might be considered the beginning of the end of the university question, although the scheme he proposed in 1904 was abandoned after opposition from Protestants. The subsequent Chief Secretaries, James Bryce (1905–7) and Augustine Birrell (1907–16), continued to consult educationalists, politicians and churchmen in their efforts to put the question to rest at last. With such sustained government attention on the issue, it was becoming apparent that the solution to the question was edging ever nearer.[7]

The Gaelic League's educational campaigns at the turn of the century were focused upon the national and intermediate schools, rather than higher education. Letters to MacNeill over the course of 1900–1 from the then vice-president of the League, Rev. Michael O'Hickey, who would become a prominent proponent of compulsory Irish, show a mutual desire to influence the reforms in intermediate education and indicate that higher education was not yet a priority.[8] Early, if as yet undeveloped, indicators of the potential significance of universities to the Gaelic League can be found in Douglas Hyde's comments in two royal commissions. In 1899, he rejected statements made by J.P. Mahaffy (TCD's Professor of Ancient History) to the Vice-Regal Inquiry into Intermediate Education, which signified that League figures were concerned with the academic reputation of the Irish language. As a result of Mahaffy's dismissal of the value of learning or studying Irish, Hyde promoted the scholarly value of the language and included testimonials from philologists across Europe, many of whom studied the older forms of Irish.[9] The significance attached to the language by these acclaimed continental philologists helped lead to newly appointed lectureships in the Royal University colleges at the turn of the twentieth century, though student numbers remained low. The second example is found in Hyde's witness statement to the Royal Commission on University Education in Ireland in 1902, in which he stated his belief that 'the only hope of a new University doing good to Ireland will be to have it frankly and robustly national, in a spiritual and intellectual sense, from the very outset'. It would promote Irish studies and act as the 'intellectual head-quarters for Irish-Ireland'.[10] The statement was written with consultation from MacNeill.[11] Hyde's slogan would be used with increasing alacrity throughout the decade by Irish-Irelanders as interest in the university question intensified.

The concept of a national university of Ireland was in part inspired by the foundation of the federal University of Wales in 1893. It had also had roots in the promotion of Irish historical studies by John Henry Newman, with the implication that these subjects were tied to a university that represented the majority Catholic population.[12] A contrasting definition of what a 'national' university might actually mean in an Irish context became a topic for debate in the early twentieth century. For example, Sir George Fottrell, a retired civil servant and member of the Catholic Laymen Committee, published a pamphlet in 1905 entitled *What is a National University?* The answer, he argued, was a university that appealed to the majority of a nation, which in an Irish context implicitly meant the Catholic majority. The low numbers of Catholic staff and students at TCD, alongside its Anglican heritage, proved that the college was not a national university. The University of Dublin could still become national through either the establishment of a Catholic college or, in a scheme Fottrell campaigned for, founding 'dual chairs' with Protestant and Catholic professors in controversial subjects like history, philosophy and theology. Irish studies were not a visible part of Fottrell's scheme.[13] The idea of a national university was also debated at a meeting of the Catholic Graduates and Undergraduates Association in January 1905. Stephen Gwynn, Gaelic Leaguer and Member of Parliament, was challenged after his lecture as to what he had meant by a reference to a 'national university', to which he replied rather vaguely that it was one that 'aimed at making Irishmen'. Gwynn, like Hyde, was a member of the Church of Ireland and exemplified the religious diversity of the Gaelic League.[14] Thomas Finlay SJ, the UCD academic who had asked the question, then put it in starker terms: 'a National University in Ireland meant a University whose teaching was in accord with the spirit of the Irish Nation, whose teaching preserved the records of the Irish past'.[15] This was a sentiment shared by MacNeill – a national university put nationality and the study of the nation at its centre.

MacNeill took a dim view not only of Trinity College, but also of the Royal University. He framed its problems in a similar vein to Patrick Pearse in his essay on the school system, 'The Murder Machine'.[16] Government-approved education institutions in Ireland were deemed by both men to be denationalising forces that demanded uniformity and repressed liberality. MacNeill lamented the existence of 'civil servant factories' and the supremacy of 'livelihoodery' in the education system.[17] He was drawing from his own experience, as he had studied the traditional subjects (a broad mixture of classical and modern languages, English literature, philosophy, maths and science), taken the rather bland Royal University exams and won a civil service post. By discovering the Irish language outside of formal educative means, his eyes had been opened to the inadequacies of the current formalised structures. MacNeill and other leading Irish-Irelanders wanted to reshape education at all levels and bring their brand of cultural nationalism into the heart of the curriculum. From 1905, with a firmer footing achieved for Irish in schools and the continuing expansion of the Gaelic League at a rapid pace, Irish-Irelanders adopted a policy of promoting a university that would endorse their ideals. It became clear, certainly to MacNeill, that TCD would never be reconciled with nationalist plans and that the Royal University's days were numbered.

At a subsequent meeting of the Catholic Graduates and Undergraduates Association in April 1905, Pearse proclaimed his scepticism towards the idea that TCD could ever be reformed to the satisfaction of Catholics and expressed his desire for the establishment of an 'Irish National University'. Founded two years before, the Association was dominated by young graduates, many linked with UCD, such as Tom Kettle, Mary Hayden and MacNeill. All three were later hired to teach at the college after its incorporation into the National University. The Association contrasted with the Catholic Laymen Committee who were more favourable to the opening up of TCD. MacNeill thanked Pearse for his comments and stated that Catholics were denied their 'national rights' and so 'instead of compromising or lowering their demands, instead of doing anything to make things easy for their opponents, they ought to do the very opposite'.[18] Expressed here was the stubbornness and determination that would mark the Irish-Irelanders' behaviour in the coming compulsory Irish campaign.

Discrediting TCD was a key objective for the leaders of the Catholic Graduates and Undergraduates Association. This would lead to, it was hoped, either radical structural reform of the University of Dublin, or its sidelining in the university question and the establishment of a new university favourable to Catholics and nationalists. In this effort, MacNeill was a leading propagandist. MacNeill's next contribution to the growing debate was a powerful and articulate statement delivered to the Royal Commission on Trinity College of 1906. As Hyde sat as a commissioner, MacNeill was invited to provide evidence as the next most senior representative of the Gaelic League. The comments were published in the press and MacNeill was well aware of the propaganda opportunity. Reading from a prepared statement, he delivered a broadside that took aim at what he perceived to be TCD's neglect of Irish studies and its provincial mindset that 'looked on Ireland as a province – that it represented no more to Ireland than a local University, such as Birmingham represents to the district in which it is situated'.[19] His intention was to convince the commissioners that the college was simply not acceptable to 'Irishmen who identify themselves with the Irish nation or history' because of its 'rigid anti-national attitude'.[20] The only chair at the college dedicated to the Irish language was unacceptable for Catholics, he argued, because of its origins and continued connection with the Irish Society, a Protestant missionary society that proselytised among Irish-speaking Catholics. Pushed for a solution, MacNeill stated that the promotion of the Irish language and Irish history would make it 'more liberal and conciliatory towards all schools of opinion in the country', but he believed that ultimately Catholics were too disillusioned to attend in great numbers. A Catholic college within the University of Dublin was one solution, but a new separate university was preferable. His concluding words pre-empted the outcome of the 1908 Act:

> 'I myself am of the opinion that the best University work in Ireland will be done by Universities that are not exactly exclusively denominational, but Universities which recognise the denominational divisions of the people, and are very largely based on that principle.'[21]

This was the position of the Catholic bishops, who by 1897 had softened their line on denominational education.[22] MacNeill was also articulating the Gaelic League leadership's efforts to play to both nationalist and denominational interests during the controversy. MacNeill's statement was enthusiastically referenced by Pearse in an editorial in *An Claidheamh Soluis* that laid into TCD's inadequacy in representing the people of Ireland.[23]

A particular gripe of MacNeill's with TCD was its neglect of the Irish manuscripts in its collections. MacNeill noted that the Professor of Modern History, John Wardell, had encouraged the study of Irish history in his statement.[24] However, Wardell's envisioning of how to undertake historical research into the Irish past – by garnering records from collections in the United Kingdom, France and Spain – was interpreted by MacNeill as implying that Irish history was merely 'a record of English aggression'.[25] Indeed, Wardell did not express any lingering interest in the Irish language let alone its connection with historical research.[26] In addition, there were figures at the college who were hostile to an expansion of Irish language studies, though in contrast to Mahaffy's comments in 1899, the reason given was in terms of utility rather than the value of the language itself. For instance, T.T. Gray, the senior dean, stated that an honours course in Irish would be a waste of time and ultimately useless.[27] MacNeill's castigation of the college's Chair of Irish was not unfounded. The professor, J.E.H. Murphy, had connections to the Irish Society and published little in the field.[28] In addition, George Salmon, Provost from 1888 to 1904, was a committee member of the society. In reaction to the criticisms received in the commission, a Chair of Celtic Languages was founded in 1907 – though not without some opposition – with E.J. Gwynn its first holder.[29] Gwynn was an established philologist and, like MacNeill, a supporter of the School of Irish Learning. A university Gaelic Society was also formed and encouraged the study of the library's valuable manuscript collection. At the society's second annual meeting in 1908, Mahaffy acknowledged the error of his ways in 1899, though this went virtually unmentioned in the nationalist press.[30] These were all alterations that would have been met with broad approval from MacNeill, but did not transform the college into a haven for Irish-Ireland.

The 1906 commission proposed a similar scheme to the one planned by Wyndham – an expanded University of Dublin with a new Catholic-dominated college. Bryce, now the Chief Secretary, announced his intention to pursue this line of action in January 1907. Leading figures at TCD were, however, horrified at the prospect of sharing their university with such an institution as the one proposed. A 'Hands off Trinity' campaign was launched and, with help from contacts in Westminster, fatally threatened the Bryce scheme. Trinity academics responded in kind to the insults they had suffered from the likes of MacNeill. The Professor of Greek declared in a pamphlet that the Roman Catholic ideal for a university was one 'regulated by authority' whereas the Protestant origins of Trinity had endowed it with 'perfect freedom of teaching [and] research'.[31] Ultimately, the scheme collapsed shortly after its announcement with Bryce's appointment as ambassador to the United States. Over a year later, with Augustine Birrell as the new Chief Secretary for Ireland, it was decided to leave the University of Dublin in its current form. The Royal University would be replaced by the National University (with UCD and the former Queen's Colleges at Cork and Galway as constituent colleges) and the recasting of the Belfast College into Queen's University Belfast (QUB).

Birrell began to set out his plans in the winter and early spring of 1908. After years of failed negotiations and false hope, MacNeill was willing to wait and see what system would garner the approval of parliament. His willingness was reinforced by the fact that the Chief Secretary was open to compromise, had maintained close relations with Archbishop Walsh and because a new untainted university was to be launched with TCD left to its own devices. A key condition for Irish-Irelanders was that, once constituted, the university would have significant autonomy. Thus, Hyde and MacNeill were cautiously optimistic as the Irish Universities Bill went through parliament during the spring of 1908 and seemed to fulfil their aspirations. Their support of the new university would eventually earn them appointments as the respective professors of modern Irish and early Irish history in addition to places on the university Senate and the UCD governing body.[32] Some eyebrows were raised at this connection between an institution created by Westminster and Executive Committee members of the Gaelic League. One branch in Waterford even called for their resignation, though this gained little traction after a rallying call from other branches. Arthur Griffith, the editor of *Sinn Féin*, sought to rile the pair for their cooperation, labelling them 'Birrellites'. This was brushed off by MacNeill, who accused Griffith of fomenting division in the League.[33] Although they maintained a high prestige among the League's members, Hyde and MacNeill were seen by some as too moderate and close to officialdom. Attempts, like this, to undermine their authority were on their minds as they sought to direct the League during the compulsory Irish controversy.

MacNeill had made a strong case for the expansion of Irish studies and helped push the issue towards the forefront of the university question debate. The principle of nationality in Irish universities emerged as a stick to beat and denigrate TCD. The college had become an easily identifiable scapegoat with bogie men in figures like Mahaffy. The reforms surrounding Irish studies after 1906 were deemed insufficient. With MacNeill and other Irish-Irelanders' persistent attacks on the college, attitudes were hardened. The scene was set for distrust between the National University and TCD. The Irish Universities Act would mark the shift in the Gaelic League's focus from schools to university education with MacNeill and Hyde as the key men of influence. Nonetheless, the university question did not meet a satisfactory conclusion with the Act. Rather a new controversial chapter soon emerged with MacNeill and the League at its core.

IRISH AT THE NATIONAL UNIVERSITY

MacNeill's statement to the 1906 commission made the case for Chairs of Irish and Irish history in any new university and it would have been clear a year or two later that this case had been won. Even TCD was warming towards the study of Celtic languages. Gaelic League attention then turned to ensuring that the new university made the Irish language a subject of equal significance to English and Latin, through stipulations in its matriculation exam. Since the introduction of the Irish Universities Bill in the spring of 1908, a majority of Gaelic Leaguers had expressed a desire to see compulsory Irish in the matriculation exam as a means of ensuring the institution's dedication to reviving the language and Irish studies. MacNeill warned Stephen Gwynn, one of the few anti-compulsory Leaguers and later a National University senator, that the moderate leadership of the League would face a severe backlash if Irish studies were not central to the new university: 'I am certain that the League will promptly declare open hostility and will not allow Hyde or me to represent them.'[34] The Irish Universities Act received royal assent on 1 August 1908 and, shortly after, at its national congress, the Gaelic League called for compulsory Irish. A policy along this line had originally been proposed at the 1902 ard-fheis but was more symbolic than practical. The Gaelic Leaguers knew that they would have to win over the National University's Senate to secure compulsory Irish.[35] This would not be a straightforward task. Leading clerics, including the aforementioned William Delany (president of UCD) and Archbishop Walsh, but also Archbishop John Healy and Monsignor Daniel Mannix (both with a record of clashing with the Gaelic League), had been appointed to the body.

There were few developments concerning compulsory Irish for at least three months. MacNeill played a key part, if unintentionally, in altering this and sparking divisions in the nationalist community. On 27 November 1908, the final paper at a meeting of the UCD Gaelic Society was delivered by T.P. O'Nowlan on the necessity of making Irish a compulsory subject at the National University. MacNeill asked Delany, who was in attendance, for his thoughts on the proposal. Delany reportedly stated that he believed the university should do all it could to encourage Irish language and historical studies, but on the question of compulsion proffered that 'there were a great many people who did not care enough about Irish to have it taught to their children, and if they were to make Irish essential, they would have a university of a handful instead of a National University'. He cited the low attendance in the Royal University's Irish classes as proof of low popular demand, to which MacNeill countered with the impressive and rapid rise in Intermediate-level pupils taking the Irish examination, as evidence for the potential of the language at the National University.[36] Over the next two weeks, Delany was pilloried in elements of the nationalist press. A meeting in support of compulsory Irish was held in Dublin's Rotunda on 7 December and lasted four hours with speeches from Griffith, Hyde, MacNeill and others.[37] Griffith probably now approved of the publicly uncompromising line taken by those he formerly described as 'Birrellites'. A few weeks later, in a letter to the editor of the *Freeman's Journal*, MacNeill responded to criticism from Dr J.C. McWalter, who had leapt to Delany's defence and proposed a more 'orthodox' university, by accusing the doctor of wanting the National University to be a mere 'job shop degree factory' that neglected national culture.[38] In the new year, with the haranguing continuing in the newspapers, the Standing Committee of Catholic Bishops met and, while admitting that there was a 'fair argument' for compulsory Irish, refused to support the measure as it risked turning Catholic students away from the National University and towards Trinity College.[39]

Tensions had been bubbling between Irish-Irelanders and members of the hierarchy over the previous years, with mutual suspicions surrounding each group's influence in education. The hierarchy viewed the Irish-Irelanders as secularists intent on sidelining religious education while, in turn, the Irish-Irelanders saw the bishops as government collaborators on a mission to further denationalise education. Several historians have put the controversy in the context of an inter-generational struggle with younger Irish-Irelanders (particularly student activists at UCD) and nationalists on one side, and the ageing hierarchy and Home Rule politicians on the other.[40] The leadership of the Irish Parliamentary Party was particularly sceptical. Many younger members of the clergy sided with the Irish-Irelanders. A flashpoint was the Catholic seminary in Maynooth, founded in 1795, which also offered classes for Royal University degrees. By the early 1900s, it had become a site of difficult relations between students and college authorities over the perceived undermining of the Irish language by the latter. Irish-Irelanders were particularly wary of the overreach of the Catholic clergy in their roles as national school managers. For example, in a 1907 letter to an unidentified priest, MacNeill expressed support for the interests of parents in school education rather than the unchallenged supremacy of the clergy. He hoped for greater cooperation between clergy and laity in the future.[41] In an exchange of letters in early 1908 with Pearse, the two men agreed that while support from the Catholic hierarchy would be sought for St Enda's, the Irish-speaking secondary school that opened in September with Pearse as headmaster and MacNeill's three sons as pupils, it would employ only lay teachers.[42] The establishment of a university that was solely designed to obtain denominational approval was not sufficient for MacNeill. His views on the matter were published in *An Claidheamh Soluis*:

> If a University is now established which, as has been commonly and with good authority stated, will be acceptable to the Catholics of this country as Catholics, and which will not be acceptable to the Irishmen of this country as Irishmen – if any such institution at this time of the day is set up here in our midst – it will be the most portentous danger to Irish life that has ever been seen in Ireland.[43]

This was the grand opportunity for the Irish-Irelanders to secure their educational goals: in cooperation with the Catholic Church, they would place the Irish language at the centre of Irish education. If the Church hierarchy would not cooperate, they must be convinced.

For MacNeill, the hierarchy's disapproval was to be regretted but could not be allowed to ultimately compromise his ambitions for the National University. Anyway, he hoped to win round leading clerics like Delany and Walsh to see that compulsory Irish was imperative. This was not after all a question of religious belief. MacNeill's 'cold logic' on the issue contrasted with the fiery rhetoric of his Gaelic League colleague O'Hickey.[44] As Professor of Irish at Maynooth, O'Hickey had clashed with powerful clerics, including college president Daniel Mannix, over the status of the language. With the emergence of divisions in the compulsory Irish controversy debate, he took aim at the Catholic clergy on the National University Senate in lectures and in print. By targeting powerful clerics, his pamphlet *An Irish University, or Else* contrasts with MacNeill's comments on the subject which point to TCD and denationalising state education as the true enemy. The controversy was a serious embarrassment for the Catholic Church and O'Hickey was asked to resign in June 1909. After his refusal to acquiesce, the Maynooth trustees dismissed him on 29 July. Five days later, MacNeill chaired a meeting in defence of the dismissed professor at Dublin's Gresham Hotel. As Lucy McDiarmid points out in her account of the affair, MacNeill justified his appeal for clemency in O'Hickey's case by emphasising their long friendship. She argues that he had an eye on future support from the bishops and was keen not to alienate them.[45] In any case,

O'Hickey was never reinstated. By appealing to the hierarchy, MacNeill managed to remain true to the aims of the Gaelic League while keeping the Church on-side.

MacNeill comes across as quite uncompromising in some of his rhetoric. At a demonstration in support of compulsory Irish in Dublin, he characterised those against compulsion as 'the anglicisers of Ireland [...] the English faction and their sympathisers'.[46] However, in addition to this public stance, MacNeill maintained a balancing act between the pursuit of compulsory Irish, or 'essential Irish' as he and many like-minded proponents termed it, and strong links with the hierarchy. In fact, MacNeill was a key intermediary and peacemaker between the hierarchy and the League. He always sought clerical support where he could find it and claimed to possess approval from Cardinal Patrick Moran, the Irish-born Archbishop of Sydney.[47] MacNeill wrote to Archbishop Walsh a few weeks after Delany's comments to the UCD Gaelic Society of his regret about the resulting acrimony. Nonetheless, he would not back down from his position.[48] Walsh was shocked by the 'vulgar abuse' coming from Gaelic Leaguers and 'to judge by some of the language used, a vicious attempt to intimidate and terrorise'.[49]

To give the compulsory Irish movement a more respectable voice and a coherent manifesto in this context of such animosity, MacNeill wrote a sixty-page pamphlet entitled *Irish in the National University of Ireland: A plea for Irish education*, quoted at the beginning of this chapter. Appearing early in 1909, it placed the language debate within the wider context of nationality and was intended to be read by both the converted and unconverted. The pamphlet characterised the Irish language as the core component of the revival of Irish education and a force for unification for society as a whole. It did not contain any personal attacks and was significantly calmer in tone than many of the other pamphlets promoting compulsory Irish that appeared contemporaneously.[50] MacNeill's publication presented a predicament to the reader in the preface: 'Higher education without Irish may be English or cosmopolitan, or what you please. It certainly is not Irish.'[51] Framing the debate along such stark lines was an attempt to move away from the *ad hominem* nature of much of the debate and a reminder of what MacNeill believed was the real crux of the matter.[52] MacNeill viewed the detractors as blinded by their collaboration in government-controlled educational institutions such as the Royal University, or worse, Trinity College. 'The objections to Irish as a fundamental study,' he wrote, 'are made on the part of those who have adopted or yielded to the anti-Irish policy of State education, or on the part of those who think it more politic to conciliate that class than to take up a positive stand on the side of national feeling.'[53] He believed that, through a shared love and appreciation for the Irish language, Ireland's religious, political and social divisions would lose their significance and its inhabitants would unite. The involvement of Protestants in the Gaelic League was provided as evidence of this:

> 'The descendants of Elizabethan colonists, Ulster Plantation-men, and Cromwellian and Williamite settlers, one by one are joining the larger body of the descendants of the Old Irish and the Northmen, of Strongbow's Normans and Welshmen, and of the English of the Pale ... [Ireland] offers them a national culture, based on her own language, for no other basis is discoverable.'[54]

Despite the pamphlet's calls for unity, the opposing sides only increased in mutual hostility. The pendulum ultimately swung in favour of compulsory Irish from June 1909 after nineteen county councils and 130 of 170 urban and rural councils threatened to withhold funds for scholarships, as they were mandated to provide for and supervise in the 1908 Act, unless Irish was made a compulsory matriculation subject. Such support demonstrates how compulsory Irish had become an important signifier of one's commitment to the national cause. It also acted as a warning shot at leading politicians and clerics, tarnished by moderation and compromise. The declaration from the councils, as MacNeill recounts in his memoir, forced several senators to change their position.[55] On 23 June 1910, the National University Senate voted 21 to 12 in favour of compulsory Irish on the matriculation exam. It was agreed, however, that this would only come into effect from 1913 in order to allow schools and teachers to be sufficiently prepared.[56] A few days later the vote was hailed by Hyde as 'the greatest educational victory that the native race had scored since the battle of Kinsale'.[57] The Gaelic League's victory, however, had meant sacrificing some of its own. Concerned that compulsory Irish would make the language an imposition to be suffered rather than enjoyed, as well as deterring Protestants and English Catholics from enrolling, Stephen Gwynn had left the League in August 1909 and resigned as a senator of the National University in 1912.[58]

The sides of the compulsory Irish debate have been characterised as those who viewed Irish as the core component of Irish identity and those who saw Catholicism rather than the language as the cornerstone of nationality.[59] There is much to support this view as the Irish-Irelanders were not satisfied with a university that was merely acceptable to the Catholic hierarchy. In addition, as can be witnessed throughout his memoir, MacNeill often emphasised the essential unity of the inhabitants of Ireland, including Ulster unionists, despite their claims to the contrary. He believed that it would be the revival of the Irish language that would awaken the people of Ireland to this fact. His involvement in the compulsory Irish controversy was driven by a belief that the Irish language was the basis for a national culture that transcended the island's religious, political and social divisions. A national university must thus reflect this by placing the language at its heart. However, MacNeill's pronouncements often suggest that, as with many of his Catholic contemporaries, religion and culture were interwoven in the conceptualisation of Irish nationality. In one manuscript of an article in his UCD papers, he wrote:

> 'In a few years, the study of the ancient literature of Ireland will probably pass bodily into the hands of Catholic scholars, who, by their racial instincts and by their special facilities, will be in a much better position than their non-Catholic fore-runners to understand and expound the history of Church and people.'[60]

The implication here is that only Catholics – being the true descendants of the 'Old Irish' – could understand the early part of the Irish past. This came with the additional insinuation that the onus was on the non-Catholic inhabitants of Ireland to join with the Catholic majority in a shared national identity. The language was the tool that would allow the minority to join in a wider national culture. In effect, MacNeill wanted a university that promoted the language but was also reflective of the denominational majority of the island. In this he tried to reconcile the opposing factions while simultaneously pushing for compulsory Irish.

Reflecting decades later in his memoir, MacNeill declared that the real achievement of compulsory Irish on the matriculation exam was more symbolic in its importance than in the practical terms of revivifying Irish as a spoken language. 'Its chief effect', he wrote, 'was to mark a distinct change in the attitude of the Irish educational system towards the Irish language.'[61] In the pursuit of this goal, MacNeill was an authoritative advocate. He was also an important negotiator. He was keen to keep powerful members of the clergy onside. If his rhetoric can appear strong at times, it is because of his targeting of TCD, due to the sway he felt it held over many Catholics and nationalists. But it had the added effect, alongside the rhetoric of his colleagues in arms, of angering and alienating leading religious figures and other nationalists. Irish at the National University ultimately set a precedent. Although enacted outside of MacNeill's tenure as Minister for Education from late 1922 to 1925, from St Patrick's Day 1922 Irish was made compulsory in national schools, in 1927 for the Intermediate Certificate and 1934 for the Leaving Certificate.[62] The often-politicised controversy surrounding compulsory Irish has always simmered, with the occasional explosion, up until the present day.

IRISH LIBERAL EDUCATION AND THE NATIONAL UNIVERSITY

At the beginning of the compulsory Irish controversy, MacNeill was paraphrased in the *Irish Times* as saying that the 'business of the new Irish University was not to create professional men, but to fit all those who frequented it, without exception, for national and Irish life, and today no Irishman could claim to be possessed of a liberal education who was ignorant of the Irish language'.[63] He wanted to end university education that, to his mind, was denationalising the Irish as well as enslaving them to the pursuit of livelihoods and little else. This ideal for higher education was straightforward, often summed up by MacNeill in the phrase 'Irish liberal education'. His publications and papers do not suggest serious engagement with contemporary works on the theory of education; one historian has even called his concept of education 'an extremely narrow one'.[64] A liberal education at a university was a broad first degree that encompassed literature, modern and classical languages, mathematics and natural sciences. It was practised across the United Kingdom as the basis for a Bachelor of Arts degree before beginning a career or later specialisation.[65] MacNeill believed, however, that for a university to mould Irishmen into positive forces for society, it was necessary to have Irish studies as a key element. His support of this measure was a symptom of his language revivalism and nationalism, but also a reaction to the dangers, as he perceived them, of too much specialist and technical education that turned students into materialistic careerists. A liberal education with the Irish language and history at its centre would combat these forces and revive Irish society.

The Royal University's modern history and political science honours course had recommended histories of Ireland and, from 1901, Irish history made up a small but not inconsiderable part of the history pass course. On the whole, however, Irish history was always optional and marginal in a programme that promoted a British constitutional narrative.[66] The Irish historical texts recommended were generally by unionist politicians, such as J.T. Ball's *The Legislative Systems of Ireland* (1888), or the broad introductory histories of Ireland by P.W. Joyce – a language revivalist but politically neutral.[67] One graduate complained that Joyce's work was 'unsatisfying fare'.[68] A course of this nature would not do for the new National University, where MacNeill helped redraw the history curriculum to suit the needs of an Irish liberal education. In this endeavour, he was aided by his colleagues John M. O'Sullivan, Professor of Modern History, and Mary Hayden, Professor of Modern Irish History, both Gaelic Leaguers. The MacNeill papers in UCD do not reveal much about the behind-the-scenes activities in the early years of their professorships. One document, handwritten notes by MacNeill on a staff meeting, claims that an effort by a small caucus to get two graduates elected to the governing body was intended to lessen the influence of Irish-Irelanders. This is, unfortunately, only a tantalising glimpse of university politics; in any case, MacNeill was confident that the caucus had little wider appeal with college graduates.[69] It has been claimed that the postgraduate board established by the UCD history staff in 1911 rarely, if ever, convened.[70] Yet it is clear from the UCD calendars that the professors' new curriculum repositioned Irish history in a central role.

In 1910, when UCD reopened as a constituent college of the National University, its calendar included the rule that in their first year of study all students must take a course in either the Irish language or Irish history.[71] This measure had been passed by the governing body after a resolution put forward by Hyde.[72] Irish history was a prominent part of the modern history honours course, with two lectures per week for two terms.[73] The lack of suitable textbooks meant that P.W. Joyce's *Short History of Ireland* was still a core text and the now long-forgotten *A Short History of the Kingdom of Ireland* (1882) by C.G. Walpole was included from 1912, alongside chapters from Macaulay's *History of England*.[74] Some new works were deemed appropriate, such as Alice Stopford Green's unapologetically nationalist *The Making of Ireland and its Undoing, 1200–1600* (1908) and, in sharp contrast to the Royal University's curriculum, several primary source editions were included.[75] MacNeill would eventually publish his books of essays: *Phases of Irish History* (1919) and *Celtic Ireland* (1921). Hayden co-authored *A Short History of Ireland* (1921) with George Moonan. With only three MA graduates in modern Irish history in the first twenty years, the historian of UCD, Donal McCartney, has referred to graduate-level historical studies as a 'very slow starter' and it suggests a lack of success in appeal.[76] But in the context of few opportunities for academic positions in historical studies on the island, it is unsurprising.

MacNeill sought for more than just a home for the study of the Irish language and history from the National University. This put him in contrast to some Irish-Irelanders, particularly Pearse, who worried less about its academic study.[77] Throughout his career, MacNeill promoted the creation of institutions for scholarly research into the history of Ireland and the older forms of Irish. He helped found and support not only the National University, but also the School of Irish Learning in 1903, which later evolved into the School of Celtic Studies of the Dublin Institute for Advanced Studies, and his brainchild, the Irish Manuscripts Commission in 1928. Alongside the promotion of scholarly research for purely academic reasons, an explanation for MacNeill's efforts lies in his desire to create Irish institutions and end the reliance on British equivalents.

In one of his battles to expand the institutional prospects of Irish studies, he had been less successful. Concurrent with the compulsory Irish campaign, MacNeill and other Gaelic Leaguers with links to Ulster canvassed for a place for Irish studies at the new university in Belfast. Although the 1908 Act paid lip-service to non-denominationalism, it unofficially segregated QUB as a Presbyterian university, while allowing the National University to exude a more overtly Catholic ethos. By autumn 1908, MacNeill had begun to encourage sympathetic QUB senators and supply them with arguments in favour of the expansion of Irish studies in Belfast.[78] In contrast to his ambitions for the National University, MacNeill knew that compulsory Irish was out of the question in Belfast. Furthermore, there were no Gaelic Leaguers or Celticists among the statutory commissioners for QUB. Instead MacNeill hoped that QUB could at least play a role in enhancing the academic standing of Irish philological and historical studies. With little progress made towards an expansion of Irish studies by spring 1909, the Leaguers decided to act. MacNeill's was the first signature in a letter from a deputation to the QUB commissioners in May. They requested the establishment of a chair in Gaelic language and Literature and 'at the least, a Lectureship for Irish History and Archaeology, which may, as more funds come in, be advanced in the future to a second Chair'. Warning the commissioners that they faced alienating a significant number of potential students from Ulster (implicitly Catholics and nationalists) if the request was not assented to, the letter went on to assert the increasing popularity of Irish language studies across the island.[79] There was a precedent for the lectureship as John O'Donovan had held a chair in Celtic Languages in the 1850s. Eventually the statutory commissioners assented to the creation of a lectureship in the Irish language but turned down the offer of League funds for additional positions. The historians of QUB, T.W. Moody and J.C. Beckett, suggest that the establishment of the lectureship was likely a conciliatory gesture. No controversy met the appointment of Church of Ireland cleric F.W. O'Connell to the position.[80] Nonetheless, Gaelic Leaguers were ultimately disappointed with the outcome of their campaigning and the denial of an opportunity to appear before the commissioners. A co-signatory of the letter to the Belfast commissioners, F.J. Bigger, referred to a lectureship as 'totally inadequate'.[81] The Irish language therefore held a marginal place in the QUB curriculum and the study of Irish history was virtually absent. A strong emphasis on Irish history in the QUB graduate school would eventually emerge in the 1930s after James Eadie Todd hired Moody.[82] Unlike the more favourable conditions in Dublin, the political situation and the League's lack of influence with the Ulster unionist elite who made up the majority of the governing body in Belfast meant that Gaelic League efforts were always rather optimistic. They would have to be satisfied with just the National University.

From 1913 until he left the Dáil in 1927, MacNeill's political activities were a serious distraction from his academic duties. Still, he found time to encourage the administrators of University College Galway to consider making Irish the primary language of instruction.[83] Irish was eventually given an enhanced position at the college from 1929. Historical research in Ireland began to transform from the late 1930s with the establishment of *Irish Historical Studies*. MacNeill supported this but his appointment as president of the Irish Historical Society was a symbolic act – as he was by now the elder statesman of historical studies – rather than a practical one.[84] Nevertheless, many of the foundations, in terms of both research and institutionally, for the study of Irish history and the language were indebted to MacNeill by his retirement in 1941.

In terms of implementing Irish liberal education in Irish universities, the success of MacNeill's ambitions can probably be summed up along similar lines to that of the Gaelic League. The latter's objective of reintroducing Irish as the day-to-day language of the majority was not achieved, but the language was certainly revived and imbued with a renewed sense of value and importance. Similarly, the language and Irish history became subjects of significance at the constituent colleges of the National University; however, it was decades before postgraduate study took off. UCD's curriculum was much more Irish-centred than the Royal University's had been, although it has been argued by the college's biographer that Catholicism trumped nationalism as the major component of its ethos at its foundation.[85]

CONCLUSION

Unfortunately for MacNeill, his hopes that northern Protestants would embrace the language were dashed as he was unable to achieve much success in expanding Irish studies at QUB. Nonetheless, many of his ambitions for higher education in Ireland were realised in the National University. In addition to the enhanced stature of Irish studies in the new university's colleges, most obviously at UCD, compulsory Irish at matriculation level ensured that the language would be studied by thousands as schools prepared prospective students. This victory for the Gaelic League was achieved in no small part through MacNeill's skills as an intermediary between the louder elements of the Irish-Irelanders and the sceptical members of the Catholic hierarchy. As the O'Hickey affair amplified acrimony, MacNeill reached out to leading clerics and paid them due respect, while maintaining his position on the necessity of the policy. His pamphlet made a strong and coherent case for compulsory Irish, pointing the finger at Trinity College and state-run education for the failures in Irish higher education and away from attacks on the hierarchy. The policy would bring together, he argued, not tear apart. MacNeill was successful in preventing a breach between the factions. This followed on from his success at reframing the university question debate from 1905 onwards by incorporating the issues that obsessed cultural nationalists: Irish language education, the study of Irish history and the idea that the Royal University and Trinity College 'denationalised' students. He had also supported the clerical line of promoting a university that exerted a Catholic ethos, without necessarily being strictly denominational.

MacNeill's encouragement of the isolation of TCD facilitated the foundation of the National University, yet in the long term it contributed to a widening cultural breach. Although there were signs that the college was warming to Irish studies, it was never going to undertake a sufficient *volte-face* and acquiesce to the Irish-Irelanders. MacNeill's demonisation further stigmatised the college in the eyes of nationalists and Catholics as he painted it as irredeemably sectarian and provincial in its outlook. The wedge of mutual hostility and distrust that was driven between the National

University from its birth and Trinity College was damaging to Irish education for much of the twentieth century. The uncompromising view of the Irish-Irelanders on the supremacy of distinctively Irish educational and cultural mores accelerated the politicisation of educational debate. It also left a bitter taste in the mouth of many nationalists of an anti-compulsory persuasion. MacNeill's legacy in the university question is therefore somewhat mixed. His canny balancing of nationalists and clerics ultimately contributed to the elevated status of Irish studies that we still enjoy today, but some of his more fiery rhetoric anticipated greater divides that were to come in the decades ahead.

Eoin MacNeill and the idea of an 'Irish Cultural Republic'

MAIRÉAD CAREW

DE-ANGLICISING THE IRISH FREE STATE

In November 1934, the Irish poet and later director of the National Gallery, Thomas MacGreevy, delivered a paper to the Irish Society in London on the theme of 'A Cultural Irish Republic'. He claimed that 'There is no Irish cultural republic, no republic of the Irish mind'.[1] Decades later in 1992, Brian P. Kennedy agreed with this sentiment in his paper 'The Failure of the Cultural Republic: Ireland 1922–1939', considering it 'even more true today than it was in 1934'.[2] Both men defined the 'Irish cultural republic' in terms of literature written in the English language and fine art. Disciplines such as history, archaeology, folklore and Irish language were not interpreted as having equal cultural merit and cultural historians were to continue to put Irish literature in the English language at the centre of revival studies and cultural debate.[3] This resulted in the cultural endeavours of Celtic scholars, such as Eoin MacNeill, not being fully recognised for their contribution in terms of cultural state formation and modern identity politics. Gregory Castle, in his book *Modernism and the Celtic Revival*, argues that revivalists, such as W.B. Yeats and J.M. Synge, were 'acutely self-conscious of their marginal status as intellectuals in a colony moving inexorably towards some form of Catholic determination'.[4] This meant that 'they were burdened by questions of political and cultural authenticity'. Gaelic-Irish intellectuals, such as Eoin MacNeill, were challenging the status of the Anglo-Irish intellectual tradition as being an authentically Irish one. This chapter argues for the success of the Irish cultural republic on its own terms, under the auspices of the first two nationalist governments (1922–48) and widens the definition of 'culture' to include academic scholarship and the institutionalisation of Gaelic forms of cultural production, part of the continuum of revolutionary political activism both before and after independence. MacNeill's leadership role in fostering the creation of the Irish cultural republic, achieved through his modernist and internationalist approach to Irish history and culture, will be examined.

This chapter also highlights the international dimension of the important work undertaken in Ireland in the field of Celtic Studies, folklore, Irish language and archaeology in the early decades of the independent state. As a cultural ambassador abroad, MacNeill followed in the footsteps of Douglas Hyde in America, promoting Celtic Studies and attracting finance for scientific research in the field in Ireland. This was an attempt to validate the Irish cultural republic of the imagination, mirroring attempts by politicians in the pre-independence era to validate the Irish republic politically. The radical cultural politics expressed in Hyde's 1892 speech 'The Necessity for de-Anglicising Ireland' were not fully realised by the author himself. Hyde postulated that it was 'our Gaelic past' that prevented the Irish from becoming 'citizens of the Empire' while denying the political nature of cultural endeavour and, in particular, the foundation of the Gaelic League with MacNeill and Father Eugene O'Growney in 1893.[5] Hyde's own attitude subsequently caused people 'to overlook the radical and revolutionary nature of his policy of de-Anglicisation'.[6] Patrick Pearse, however, recognised the import of Hyde's cultural ideas, stating that 'when the Gaelic League was founded in 1893 the Irish revolution began'.[7] This revolution of the mind preceded and informed the armed rebellion and subsequently became central to the blueprint for an Irish cultural republic.

After 1922, culture perceived as being of Gaelic-Irish origin, expressed in disciplines such as history, archaeology, Irish language and folklore, was institutionalised and became part of a drive for authentication of the nation state. The continuation of the process of the 'de-Anglicisation of Ireland' saw the scientising of Irish history in the 1930s. Despite MacNeill's influential role in this, he admitted his 'inability to write an impartial history of Ireland',[8] a statement indicating the modernist sensibility of a self-aware Irish nationalist historian. However, MacNeill's multidisciplinary approach was to make a lasting contribution to the creation of an academic framework within which knowledge of the Irish past was enunciated and its cultural context explored. He put Ireland on the cultural map in European terms, placing the country in the context of emerging independent nation states.[9] A consolidation and legitimisation process underpinning state formation during the 1920s and '30s followed and will be explored in greater detail throughout this chapter. While Kennedy's view that the canon of Irish cultural policy was based on 'a nationality of difference and singularity' is true, his claim that it 'helped to thwart the movement towards cultural and artistic independence' is not.[10] A unique cultural heritage marked Ireland favourably in global terms. Cultural homogeneity was central to the Irish model of nationalism, which meant that the role of Gaelic-Irish intellectuals in state formation was crucial. The homogenisation of culture through institutionalisation embedded the idea of the nation as a cultural republic; it was reclaimed ideologically by the Irish Free State on independence and retained the potential to become a future political reality in a united Ireland.

Revolutionary elites were not just those involved in a military capacity in overthrowing a colonial power but were also involved in challenging perceived foreign cultural influence by establishing a type of Celtic exceptionalism based on history, ethnicity, tradition and religion. Scholars and historians, like MacNeill, were instrumental in providing the intellectual foundations for this process. He was ultimately to become a seminal figure in the cultural regeneration of the nation both before and after independence.[11] Before the independent state was established, the cultural nation was imagined[12] by writers, artists and poets of the cultural revival but it was the academic work of historians, archaeologists, folklorists and linguists that was essential to the institutionalisation of a Celtic and Christian identity for the state. Interpretation of historical, archaeological and linguistic data was controlled through museum policy documents; legislation to define and protect 'national' monuments; institutes of learning and commissions protecting 'national' culture. This was de-Anglicisation of Ireland by government decree. This formed the wider cultural milieu in which MacNeill was an influential presence. The power of national sentiment, essential to a nation-building agenda, could be harnessed through popular history, education, exhibitions and the media. Political ideas and aspirations were enshrined and authenticated in legislative and administrative practices associated with the institutionalisation of indigenous culture. It was this consolidation of Irish cultural identity at home that served as the cultural-legal platform from which the identity of the state could be secured abroad and ties within the diaspora strengthened.

THE CELTIC STATE: SCIENTISING THE NATIONAL NARRATIVE

In 1925, MacNeill expressed the view that he would not attach any great value to Irish national independence 'if Irish nationality were not to mean a distinctive Irish civilisation.'[13] In 1909 MacNeill had been appointed Professor of Early (including Medieval) Irish History and R.A.S. Macalister had been appointed Professor of Celtic Archaeology in University College Dublin. This focus on the study of the past of the nation was an expression of nationalist thought at the time and crucial to the later development and consolidation of the cultural identity of the independent Irish Free State. On a lecture tour of American universities to promote Celtic Studies in 1930, he revealed in a speech delivered in the New York University Law School that 'he did not believe in impartial national histories'.[14] This admission gives an insight into MacNeill's philosophy of history, his nationalist perspective of the past, and the expectations of his Irish-American audience. His statement, perhaps, seems at odds with his influential role in the scientising trend in writing about the Irish past at that time. Robin Dudley Edwards credited MacNeill for his 'achievements in establishing the scientific basis for the study of early Irish history, its laws and institutions'.[15] The vogue for bringing scientific language and approaches into the humanities, however, was not value-free, and was essential to the validation of a nationalist agenda expressed through the disciplines of history and archaeology in University College Dublin. According to Anthony Smith, 'nations and nationalisms were social constructs and cultural creations of modernity', and ethnicity and history were 'crucial to an adequate understanding of nationalism'.[16] The symbiotic relationship between historical scholarship and the state cultural apparatus is crucial to an understanding of knowledge creation in the service of the Irish Free State.

MacNeill occupied important leadership roles in cultural institutions such as the Irish Manuscripts Commission (IMC), which he co-founded in 1928, taking on the role as its first chairman. It undertook the important task of making historical source materials in Irish, English and Latin widely available to scholars in response to the 'national calamity' that saw the destruction of the Public Record Office at the Four Courts on 30 June 1922 during the Civil War.[17] The IMC contributed to the subsequent development of history as a viable academic discipline in modern Ireland, providing the 'research infrastructure' for it.[18] Robin Dudley Edwards and Theo Moody saw their journal, *Irish Historical Studies*, founded in 1938, as building on the work of the IMC.[19] In the 'Preface' to the inaugural issue, they acknowledged the influence of the training they had received at London University's Institute of Historical Research, described as 'an experimental laboratory of research methods'.[20] As instigators of the 'Irish historiographical revolution' in the 1930s, their motivation was to 'create an Irish history free from confessional bias and overt expressions of political prejudice'.[21] However, covert expressions of political prejudice were sometimes embedded in the selection of 'scientific' facts and the language used to interpret them. This was a use of the prestige of science to bolster the authenticity of the national narrative. The scientising of history caused problems between the disciplines of history and archaeology in the 1930s because the written national narrative was deemed more important than the material evidence for it. Celtic colonisation remained an academic construct even though archaeological evidence did not exist for invading Celts, and sites were deemed 'Christian' without the corroborating evidence of ecclesiastical objects within their assemblages.[22] Archaeology was deemed to be scientific evidence for history and did not, in general, challenge its assertions. Both disciplines were suffused with nationalist ideology and shared a similar agenda. This can be considered as 'part of the repertoire of nationalism and its cavalier use of the past'.[23]

In 1920, Éamon de Valera, during his fundraising tour of the United States, attempted to get political recognition for the Irish Republic by arguing that 'Ireland is now the last white nation that is deprived of its liberty'.[24] The following year Eoin MacNeill claimed that: 'In ancient Ireland alone we find the autobiography of a people of European white men who come into history not moulded into the mould of the complex East nor forced to accept the law of imperial Rome.'[25] MacNeill succeeded in attracting money for scientific research on the Celtic race by Harvard University, who undertook a five-year project in Ireland starting in 1932. This eugenic enterprise was an effort by American anthropologists and archaeologists to study the Celtic race to assess their fitness for immigration to the United States and was also an acknowledgement of the importance of Celtic culture to the Irish in America, who partly funded the research.[26] Large-scale excavations and the physical examinations of thousands of Irish people became part of the nation-building project in the 1930s, with an international attempt to confirm Ireland's Celtic identity using the most up-to-date practices and methods of archaeology and anthropology. Physical anthropological surveys were also carried out on potential immigrants to the United States in Belgium, Great Britain, Norway, Sweden, Denmark, Czechoslovakia, Italy, Holland, Poland and Germany.[27] In the case of Ireland, scientific proof of the antiquity of the Irish race would also mean an authenticated political validity for the nation state. MacNeill was also influential in the selection of County Clare for the Harvard Mission's social anthropological strand undertaken by Conrad Maynadier Arensberg and Solon Toothaker Kimball.[28] They studied the country people of north Clare and the inhabitants of Ennis using innovative interdisciplinary ethnographic research methods for examining the way of life of ordinary people.[29]

Archaeological monuments, rooted in the landscape, marked out the territory defined as the homeland and excavations were carried out in Northern Ireland as part of an extension of the Irish Free State anthropological survey by the Harvard Mission. Adolf Mahr, Keeper of Irish Antiquities at the National Museum of Ireland (and later appointed to the position of director by de Valera in 1934), was instrumental in the selection of sites and acted as the main advisor to the Harvard Mission archaeologists. An Austrian, German nationalist, and member of the Nazi party, he was an expert in European Celtic archaeology. Mahr believed that Ireland was 'the only self-governing State with an uninterrupted Celtic tradition, and has the duty of becoming *the* country for Celtic Studies'.[30] The Lithberg Report (produced under the chairmanship of Professor Nils Lithberg of the Nordic Museum in Stockholm) was commissioned by the government in 1927 and was the first cultural policy document for the National Museum of Ireland in the Irish Free State. It recommended prioritising the display of 'native' artefacts, in particular the Bronze Age gold objects (considered to be Celtic gold at that time) and Early Christian artefacts.[31] The National Monuments Act was enacted in 1930 and defined the meaning of a 'national monument'. Those buildings not deemed 'national', such as Lady Gregory's house at Coole, demolished in 1941, were not protected under the legislation as the term was open to political interpretation.[32]

MacNeill's emphasis on professional history broke with a previous antiquarian tradition that was colonialist in perspective. This movement from gentrified antiquarian endeavour to a more academic methodology created, improved and reshaped the history of Ireland. It was subsequently consolidated and democratised through the creation of institutes and commissions after independence. For nationalism, 'the supreme value is collective autonomy' and this requires collective unity and a distinctive identity.[33] The rediscovery and authentication of the nation using the tools of science in the interpretation of a unique ethnic past is essential to this ideological perspective. MacNeill argued that 'Nations that had long endured at least a partial eclipse found in the word *Celtic* a salve for wounded pride of race, a world-acknowledged guarantee of ancient lineage and high respectability.'[34] MacNeill straddled two traditions, becoming a transitional figure, acting as a conduit for a change of perspective with regard to Celtic history. His scholarship was essential to the state regeneration project.

In an unpublished essay on 'Celtic race feeling', MacNeill worried that 'with philological studies the whole "Celtic" notion was given the respectability of science'.[35] However, he was himself described by the Celtic scholar Julius Pokorny as 'a philologist of the first rank'[36] and his work in the field of Irish ogham inscriptions was praised by the Swiss-born Celtic philologist Rudolf Thurneysen. John Hutchinson explains that 'MacNeill marshalled the Celtic scholars of Europe to reinstate Ireland as one of the original cultures of Europe'.[37] He developed this idea of European belonging in his book *Phases of Irish History* (published in 1919), in which he argued that the Irish Celts were one of the first European peoples to create a national literature. Hyde had also stressed the Europeanness of the Irish language and people. This embedded the political idea that Ireland belonged to the European family of independent nation states and not to the British Empire. When *Celtic Ireland* was published in 1921, MacNeill had already accepted the premise that Ireland was indeed a Celtic country. He explained that he sought to 'establish the foundations of our early historical polity on a supposed Celtic colonisation coincident with the Roman conquest of Britain'.[38] He was aware of the misuse of historical sources for political reasons and wrote that 'superficial methods of expounding history are perhaps the main cause of modern race-delusions'.[39] Traditionally, Celtic colonisers were thought to have brought the Irish language to Ireland.

MacNeill's language activism included publishing an article entitled 'A Plea and a Plan for the Extension of the Movement to Preserve and Spread the Gaelic Language in Ireland' in the *Gaelic Journal* in March 1893. He has been described as 'the architect, organizer and philosopher of the Gaelic League',[40] which campaigned successfully to make Irish a compulsory subject for matriculation to the newly established National University of Ireland in 1908. MacNeill wrote that the Gaelic Leaguers were 'distinguished by the determination to treat Irish as a living tongue, its literature as the living expression of the mind of the race'.[41] According to Brian Ó Cuív, MacNeill's aim was to see that Irish as a subject was 'firmly established in all branches of education as a *living* language'.[42] MacNeill played an influential role in the promotion of the Irish language by serving as editor of the *Gaelic Journal* from September 1894 to March 1897 and of *An Claidheamh Soluis*, the Gaelic League's weekly paper, from 1899 to 1901. In his editorials in *An Claidheamh Soluis*, MacNeill discussed cultural and language revivals in other countries including Finland, Bohemia, Hungary and East Prussia. Patrick Pearse, who subsequently served as editor of *An Claidheamh Soluis* from 1903 to 1909, aimed to create 'a modernist literature in Irish'.[43] He believed that if literature in the Irish language was to grow and develop it 'must get into contact on the one hand with its own past and on the other with the mind of contemporary Europe'.[44] Brigittine French postulates that MacNeill's efforts to link the Irish language with an independent Irish people 'played an undeniably productive role in the process of achieving political sovereignty'.[45] MacNeill wrote about the Irish language policy in 1925 that its 'chief function' was 'to conserve and develop Irish nationality'.[46] Irish was established as the 'national language' in the 1922 Constitution and was also given this status in 1937.[47]

The collection of folklore in Irish also became a state activity with the founding of the Irish Folklore Commission in 1935, which succeeded in 'assembling one of the finest and most extensive collections of folk tradition in the world'.[48] The recording of the living language of ordinary people, described by its director Séamus Ó Duilearga as 'an untapped source of Irish history',[49] was also a democratisation of culture essential to a nationalist agenda. Ó Duilearga had written to MacNeill in 1928 from Sweden to discuss the folklore collections in Sweden, Finland and Estonia and wondered

> ... if our government will ever come to realize that they owe a duty to Ireland and to the civilized world to make the literature, history and folklore of our people known and respected everywhere.[50]

In his letter, he explained that he had arranged for the exchange of the journal *Béaloideas* (Journal of the Folklore of Ireland Society) with publications from Denmark, Sweden, Finland, Estonia, Latvia, Austria, Germany and Belgium. In a subsequent letter to de Valera in 1934, MacNeill recommended that Ó Duilearga be appointed to a lectureship in Folklore in University College Dublin. He wrote that Irish Folklore should be 'regarded and treated as a subject of high importance in University work'.[51] Later, Ó Duilearga and Adolf Mahr were among the founders of the German Society for Celtic Studies established in Berlin on 25 January 1937.[52] Its aim was 'to spread the knowledge of Celtic culture and languages in Germany, and to establish cultural and social relations between the Germanic and Celtic peoples'.[53] Rudolf Thurneysen was chosen as first honorary president of the society.

THE CATHOLIC STATE

Kennedy blamed 'religious and moral dictates prevalent in Irish society'[54] as one of the reasons for the failure to establish an Irish cultural republic. Ironically, it acted as the impetus for the innovative approach of Eoin MacNeill, whose historical scholarship contributed to the articulation of a Catholic identity for the state. A northern Catholic from Antrim, he took a keen scholarly interest in St Patrick. One of the important aspects of his work on this topic, between the years 1923 and 1934, was his analysis of the topography of the *Tripartite Life of Saint Patrick*. The 1,500th anniversary of the coming of St Patrick was celebrated with the hosting of the Eucharistic Congress in 1932. In that year, MacNeill contributed an article, 'The Historical Saint Patrick', to *Saint Patrick, A.D. 432–1932: Fifteenth centenary memorial book*, published by the Catholic Truth Society in Dublin.[55] He was invited by the Archbishop of Dublin to read a paper at one of the meetings of the Eucharistic Congress on the subject of 'The Blessed Sacrament in Ireland in the Celtic Period'.[56] The Eucharistic Congress was an international event, but has also been described as 'a flashpoint in the formation of a specific Irish Catholic identity' and 'a culminating event in the Irish national struggle', in which images of the past played an important role.[57] De Valera, in a St Patrick's Day broadcast to the United States, said: 'Since the coming of St Patrick, fifteen hundred years ago, Ireland has been a Christian and a Catholic nation.'[58] Adolf Mahr was commissioned to write a book, *Christian Art in Ancient Ireland: Selected objects illustrated and described*, for the Eucharistic Congress, which was presented by de Valera to the cardinal legate at Government Buildings on 23 June 1932.[59] That year, a contemporary reviewer commented on the book, writing that 'we warmly congratulate the Government of Saorstát Éireann on this new evidence of their appreciation of the vital function which art has in the life of a nation'.[60] It was Éamon de Valera's view that 'The Irish genius has always stressed spiritual and intellectual values rather than material ones.'[61]

In Ireland, between 1922 and 1948, the Catholic religion, Celtic ethnicity and the Irish language were the forces driving the nationalist agenda of the democratic governments in power. In many nation states across Europe, programmes of racial, cultural and linguistic purity were becoming essential to identity formation. These modernist regeneration projects involved the enactment of laws, which institutionalised concepts of national culture and identity. Nationalism, according to Smith, 'specifies what shall count towards collective purification and regeneration' of the historic nation.[62] In the case of the Irish Free State, Catholic purity laws, enacted in the 1920s and '30s, chimed with the cultural and racial purity of the imagined and reconstructed Celt, established through academic scholarship. Legislation that could be seen to have a social purity dimension to it was enacted under both the Cosgrave and de Valera governments and included the Censorship of Films Act, 1923; the Intoxicating Liquor Act, 1924; the legislative ban on divorce, 1925; the Intoxicating Liquor Act, 1927; the Censorship of Publications Act, 1929; the 1933 Budget tax on imported daily newspapers; the Criminal Law Amendment Act, 1935 (which prohibited the sale and distribution of contraceptives) and the Public Dance Halls Act, 1935. In 1937, Father P.J. Gannon SJ praised the Irish censorship laws which, in his opinion, were 'a simple measure of moral hygiene'.[63] Ideas such as 'moral hygiene' or 'social hygiene' underpinned attempts to control venereal disease, illegitimacy, prostitution and vice. 'Moral hygiene' was sometimes equated with racial hygiene in the 1930s in eugenic discourse.[64] However, there was only one eugenics society in Ireland and that was based in Belfast. While the Catholic Church in Ireland welcomed some aspects of eugenics such as pro-natalism, 'it was reluctant to condone the intervention in family life which negative eugenics proposed'.[65]

A year after independence, Father Timothy Corcoran SJ expressed his worry that 'we have in this country been viewing all history, all literature, all art, through the medium of the English mind'.[66] Elsewhere, he put it that 'The teaching of history must, in Irish Catholic schools, be frankly and fully Catholic.'[67] A few years later, he criticised the education system that had been imposed on the country. With regard to the subject of the teaching of history he argued that 'Religion and its natural connections and influences should be put back in its true place, at the heart of the subject.'[68] In 1922 the Central Catholic Library was founded in Dublin by Father Stephen Brown SJ with the goal of helping the laity to educate themselves. The collection of books assembled covered the Catholic tradition in history, philosophy, science, art, literature and music. Catholic weeklies from England, the United States, Canada, Argentina, New Zealand, Australia and South Africa were also made available to the reading public at the library.[69]

CELTIC STUDIES AND THE IRISH DIASPORA

MacNeill, a thinker of the decolonising world evolving in the nineteenth and early decades of the twentieth century, was European and global in his cultural and political perspective. He was conscious of Ireland's important cultural place on the world stage. This recognition of the cultural and implicit political strength of the diaspora was essential to the state regenerative drive in the 1920s and 1930s. MacNeill wrote in 1921 that the Irish nation's story should be given 'the place it deserves in the world's history'.[70] He believed that 'a right appreciation of Ireland's place in history disseminated in America must contribute to the cultural and spiritual upbuilding of America.'[71] His efforts to promote Celtic Studies in American universities resulted in his success in acquiring funding for scientific Celtic research in Ireland. The Harvard Mission to Ireland in the 1930s was an expression of diasporic cultural nationalism and an attempt to improve the social and economic circumstances of the Irish in America through Celtic cultural endeavour.

MacNeill was invited to undertake a lecture tour in America by Professors Arthur L.C. Brown of Northwestern University, Tom Peete Cross of the University of Chicago, and Robert D. Scott of the University of Nebraska.[72] He described these scholars as 'of the highest reputation on both sides of the Atlantic as authorities on the mediaeval literatures of Northern and Western Europe'.[73] MacNeill arrived in New York on 2 April 1930. The *New York City Journal* reported that

> detectives from the Bomb Squad, police in uniform, private detectives, Secret Service men were all watching when Dr. Eoin McNeill, Irish patriot and scholar, stepped down the gangplank of the Baltic of the White Star Line today.[74]

MacNeill was escorted from the pier to his car because political threats had been made against him.[75] During his tour, he visited Harvard, Columbia, New York, Yale, Fordham, Notre Dame, and Northwestern Universities. MacNeill's first lecture on early Celtic institutions and law was delivered at New York University (NYU) on 2 April 1930. James McGurrin, president-general of the American Irish Historical Society of New York, was one of the speakers at a dinner given jointly by that society and the University Law School to honour Eoin MacNeill after his completion of a series of lectures there on early Celtic law.[76] Former judge Daniel F. Cohalan, one of the founders of the Sinn Féin League of New York in 1907, also spoke at the dinner. In attendance was Harold O. Voorhis, vice-chancellor and secretary of NYU; Dr James J. Walsh and Dean Frank H. Sommer who announced that a 'MacNeill Alcove' would be established in the library of the NYU School of Law and that a fund had already been established for the purpose. It was the intention to fill the alcove with 'works on Irish history and kindred subjects'. It was during this address that MacNeill revealed that he was unable 'to write an impartial history of Ireland'.[77] Other lectures that he delivered during the course of his American tour included one entitled 'The Story of Irish Culture' in Harris Hall at Northwestern University in Chicago, on 23 April 1930.[78] MacNeill commented: 'I find a very great and growing interest in the cultural side of Irish affairs, and I am doing all I can to stimulate it.'[79]

MacNeill's view of the Celticism of Yeats as inauthentic was shared by some American academics. For example, in 1916, John L. Gerig, one of America's most distinguished linguists and philologists and Professor of Celtic at Columbia University in New York, described the 'so-called neo-Celtic movement consisting of a more or less artificial revival in modern literature of vague Celtic traits'.[80] This idea was discussed many decades later by George Watson, who considers W.B. Yeats to be the 'ultimate Celticist', and '*the* great manipulator of history'.[81] He argues that:

> Like pastoralism or Orientalism, Celticism is a system of representation imposed by a hegemonic group on others with such success that those others begin to accept the truth of that alien representation.[82]

Watson also argues that 'the key to the intellectual strategy of Celticism is the annulment, elision or denial of history'.[83] However, Celticism is a set of cultural ideas and not an absolute reality. The literary Celticism of Yeats and the historical Celticism of MacNeill are different ways to construct a national narrative with divergent emphases, the former on imagination and Irish literature in the English language and the latter on scientific historical analysis and Irish language and literature.

Gerig, in his paper 'Celtic Studies in the United States', made the observation that 'In America the growth of interest in Celtic since 1900 has been marked.'[84] He noted that at the turn of the century only one large institution in the United States offered Celtic as a subject, but by 1916 at least eight universities offered courses. Gerig had been a student of d'Arbois de Jubainville, the famous nineteenth-century French Celticist.[85] MacNeill also acknowledged the work of de Jubainville in his own scholarship and wrote that he was 'guided more or less by the theories of Celtic colonisation set in vogue by D'Arbois de Jubainville and Rhys'.[86]

According to Gerig, the study of Celtic was 'most useful' to the student of history because:

> D'Arbois de Jubainville and others have frequently pointed out that some four centuries B.C. practically all Western Europe was under Celtic domination. In the fifth and succeeding centuries of our era the influence of the Celt was again felt throughout the same section of the continent – this time not by force of arms, but by dint of superior intellectual training. It was then that the erudite Irish monks went forth to establish on the great pilgrimage routes to Rome and other places the monasteries which for centuries were famous as seats of learning.[87]

At the Catholic University of America in Washington DC, attempts were made to establish the teaching of Celtic at the university as early as 1893. In 1896 a Chair of Gaelic Studies was created by the Ancient Order of Hibernians. Harvard and the Catholic University of America were the two institutions at the forefront of the development and promotion of Celtic Studies in the United States in the early twentieth century. MacNeill was awarded an honorary doctorate from the Catholic University in 1930. Other universities involved in the development of Celtic Studies were influenced by the 'unflagging industry and profound scholarship' of Professor Fred Robinson of Harvard enabling what Gerig described as 'this pioneer to exert through his pupils a powerful influence on the development of Celtic research in the United States'.[88] Celtic Studies would not have achieved the position it did in the cultural life of North America without the efforts of Robinson.[89] He was one of the last men to greet MacNeill on his way home from Boston.

A.C.L Brown, one of Robinson's students at Harvard, continued his studies in Paris under Gaidoz and d'Arbois de Jubainville and at Freiburg under Thurneysen. He later became head of the English department at Northwestern University in Chicago. Tom Peete Cross (another of Robinson's students) was described as 'one of America's outstanding Celticists'. He came to Dublin as a travelling fellow of Celtic and Comparative Literature to study Irish palaeography under Professor Bergin at the School of Irish Learning (which had been founded by the German scholar Kuno Meyer in 1903). Cross taught Celtic at the University of Chicago from 1913 until his retirement in 1945.[90] He published widely on matters Celtic, including in 1936 *Ancient Irish Tales*, an anthology of translations from Old Irish with Dr Clark Harris Slover. John L. Gerig contacted the Celtic scholar Edward John Gwynn, provost of Trinity College Dublin, expressing his worry about the future of Celtic Studies in the United States. He noted that 'Professors Robinson, Brown, Cross, and others have chairs in English, Celtic serving only as an uncompensated increment to their work.'[91] After Cross' retirement, his place was taken by Professor Myles Dillon. Dillon also worked at the University of Wisconsin, where he was credited with building up the Celtic holdings of the library there.[92] By the mid-century almost no important Celtic manuscript holdings existed in libraries in the United States with the exception of the Widener Library at Harvard.[93]

The corresponding secretary of the Celtic Society of Columbia University wrote to de Valera on 29 July 1933 requesting that he send a message that could be read out at a public meeting planned for the following month. Included in de Valera's reply was:

> It is world knowledge that the Gaels of Ireland and their descendants number some millions of America's loyal citizens. It is understandable, accordingly, that scholars in American Universities should be interested in the civilisations of the Celts, that race which dominated the Continent of Europe for hundreds of years.[94]

James McGurrin, president-general of the American Irish Historical Society of New York, in a letter published in the *Irish Times*, dated 21 June 1934, expressed the hope that the forthcoming Celtic Congress, which was to be held in Dublin, would give consideration to the growth and progress of Celtic Studies in the United States:

> Men and women of the great Celtic family in America (Irish, Scots and Welsh) are numerous, influential and progressive. They have played an important part in the history and development of this country; they have been pioneers and leaders in the material and cultural progress of the United States.[95]

However, while lamenting the lack of chairs for Professors of Celtic Studies, McGurrin acknowledged the fact that despite this 'handicap' the growing interest in things Celtic had produced a large body of research work, 'and its highest practical expression is seen in the work of the Harvard University Archaeological Mission [to Ireland]'.[96] In 1933, Professor Robinson, Dean of the Faculty of English and Celtic at Harvard University, at the time, visited Ballinderry Crannóg No. 2, County Offaly, where excavations were being carried out by the Second Harvard Archaeological Expedition to Ireland. Robinson examined the possibility of establishing an American School of Celtic Studies in Ireland and spoke to the *Irish Times* about the proposal:

> The Ballinderry investigators might form a nucleus of the school. They would help to promote co-operation between the American Universities and various institutions of learning here.[97]

Professor Clark H. Slover of the University of Texas also came to Ireland in 1933. He expressed the desirability of establishing an American school of Irish archaeology. It was his view that it should be similar to the American school at Rome and the various American establishments for the study of Oriental archaeology and should be under the protection of one of America's learned societies and the National Museum of Ireland.[98] Slover was carrying out research on the Celtic contribution to English culture at the time. He told the *Irish Times* that the increasing interest of America in the Middle Ages was due

> not so much to mere luxuriating in the past as to an increasing tendency to recognise that it is in mediaeval Europe, rather than in classical Greece and Rome, that you find the vital constituents of modern civilisation.[99]

Neither an American school of Celtic Studies nor an American school of Irish archaeology was established at that time but some artefacts discovered by the Harvard Archaeological Mission were displayed in an exhibition entitled 'A Century of Progress', which centred on antiquities from the National Museum of Ireland at the Chicago World's Fair in 1934. Copies of 'Celtic' gold artefacts and Early Christian artefacts; archaeological publications; books in the Irish language; a facsimile of the Book of Kells; stills from the film *Man of Aran*; paintings by Jack B. Yeats and Paul Henry; and items produced by the Cuala Press and the Dún Emer Guild were among the items included.[100] De Valera also sent the *Saorstát Éireann Irish Free State Official Handbook*, which had been commissioned by the Cosgrave government and was edited by William Bulfin. The book contained an article on history by MacNeill and also included articles on archaeology, geology, agriculture, the Irish language, Anglo-Irish literature, folklore, art, education, finance and administration. According to Raymond Gillespie and Brian Kennedy, the book 'offered a window into the philosophy underlying the Irish Free State, the philosophy of an Irish Ireland uncontaminated by its colonial past'.[101] A dramatised version of three and a half thousand years of Irish history was also staged at the Chicago World's Fair. *The Pageant of the Celt*, narrated by Micheál MacLiammóir, was described as a 'richly poetic version of Ireland's history'.[102] The objective of *The Pageant* was 'to present a spectacle worthy of their Celtic past, and reveal to Americans of Celtic tradition a glimpse of their rich racial heritage'.[103]

In 1940, de Valera included a School of Celtic Studies, alongside a School of Theoretical Physics, in the Dublin Institute for Advanced Studies (DIAS). The DIAS was modelled on the Institute for Advanced Studies at Princeton. Celtic scholars of European reputation were attracted to the institute and de Valera succeeded in enticing the Nobel Prize winning physicist, Erwin Schrödinger to the School of Theoretical Physics in 1939.[104]

MacNeill was invited to be an ex-officio member of the board of the DIAS in 1940 as he was President of the Royal Irish Academy at the time and because of his influence and expertise in the area of Celtic studies.

THE 'IRISH CULTURAL REPUBLIC' OF THE FUTURE

At the Celtic Congress in Brittany in 1935, Professor J.E. Daniels of Bangor University in Wales presented a paper in which he lamented the fact that the Celtic peoples 'tended only to have a past' and defined a Celt as:

> one who always has his back to the wall; wherever acquiescence takes place, Celticism ceases to be, so my definition of Celt is psychological and based on this common need of defence against danger.[105]

The perceived danger for the newly established Irish Free State was Anglicisation, interpreted as an expression of imperialism. This fear and the regeneration programme of the state defined by the cultural policy of de-Anglicisation resulted in the creation of a cultural republic rooted in an imagined Celtic past. It had many positive effects in terms of new legislation, cultural policies, institutes and commissions to protect Gaelic-Irish culture and was central to the process of cultural state formation during the tenure of the Cosgrave and de Valera governments.

Terence Brown commented that the Irish Free State was 'notable for a stultifying lack of social, cultural, and economic ambition' in the first two decades of independence.[106] Brown, an Anglo-Irish literature professor, like other commentators on Irish culture, tends to interpret the Irish cultural landscape in the early decades of independence through the lens of the censorship laws. Brian Fallon, however, concedes that the significance of the censorship laws was 'much overplayed'.[107] Peter Martin points out that censorship in the 1920s and '30s was not peculiar to Ireland and can be placed in an international context.[108] The Irish Free State, while practising a form of cultural protectionism, was not isolationist and saw her cultural production as being essential to her place in the world. Cultural protectionism, economic protectionism and the protection of the moral values of the Catholic state can all be seen as part of this tapestry. This had cultural and economic implications for the future of Ireland and, in particular, for potential emigrants to the United States (ironically because they were Anglicised). The myth of the blue-eyed white Catholic Celt, the athletic youth of de Valera's imaginings, was not just part of a nationalist utopian dream but would not have been out of place in eugenic discourse before the end of the Second World War.[109] The institutionalisation of moral purity through legislative processes chimed with the institutionalisation of the racially and culturally pure Celt and the scientific archaeological, anthropological and historical proof for his existence. Gregory Castle points to the pivotal role that anthropology and the study of the past played in the Celtic Revival and argues that it was an essential part of the modernist agenda.[110] After independence, according to Nicholas Allen, 'the discourse of science [was] applied widely in support of cultural, political and economic development in the new state'.[111] What MacNeill in the 1920s and '30s wanted to create was a republic of the mind, the imagined nation validated by academic scholarship underpinned by the latest methodologies. MacGreevy in the 1930s and Kennedy in the 1990s also wanted a republic of the Irish mind, where they as writers and artists and academics felt included.

With independence came state-sponsored Celtic cultural engineering, which saw the institutionalisation of Celtic cultural endeavour. The institutionalisation of history happened with the establishment of an academic framework within which the knowledge of the Irish past was created. The disadvantage of this was that it sometimes predetermined research questions, thus excluding possibilities of more complex results that might be politically disadvantageous at the time. The nation as a bulwark of self-government is a cultural construct, and academic scholarship on the cultural components underpinning and defining the nation served as both a conduit and a shaper of this construct. Smith argues that 'the rediscovery of the ethnic past furnishes vital memories, values, symbols and myths without which nationalism would be powerless'.[112] Cultural institutions such as the Irish Manuscripts Commission, the Irish Folklore Commission, the School of Celtic Studies within the Institute for Advanced Studies and the National Museum of Ireland played their respective parts in the exploration and consolidation of ideas of de-Anglicisation. All these institutions have stood the test of time and made an international contribution to scholarship, cementing Ireland's cultural reputation and giving Irish culture a global resonance within the diaspora.

During this Decade of Centenaries there has been debate about the future Irish Republic and what it should look like.[113] Perhaps less emphasis should be placed on the political nature of the republic and more emphasis on its cultural essence. A future cultural republic does not mean the dismantling of what is in existence at present but encompasses the building upon hard-won success. Kennedy's hope for the future, expressed in 1992, was that:

> It is not too late for an enlightened politician to take up the idea of a cultural Irish republic, to plan for it, to galvanize support for it, and to vigorously encourage every step which would help to realize it.[114]

The Irish cultural republic created under the auspices of the first two nationalist governments was a success on its own terms and of its own time, providing a solid cultural foundation that has served the state well at home and abroad. In 1922, MacNeill, in an article entitled 'Ireland's Future, North and South', said:

> Every year that passes will take us farther from divisions based on old suspicions and enmities for it is only enmity and suspicion, not history or geography, or race or creed, or tradition or culture or economic welfare that decrees a little stream in Omeath to be a dividing line between two Irelands inhabited by one people.[115]

Revolutionary

Countermand and Imprisonment, 1916–17

MICHAEL LAFFAN

U ntil shortly before the Easter Rising MacNeill was consistent. As president and commander-in-chief of the Irish Volunteers he adhered to their official programme: 'to secure and maintain the rights and liberties common to all the people of Ireland. Their duties will be defensive and protective, and they will not contemplate either aggression or domination.'[1] They would fight if the British government reneged on its commitment to grant Home Rule, or repressed them, or tried to impose conscription on Ireland. They should resort to guerrilla tactics if they were attacked.

But in late 1915 and early 1916 he became concerned that some of his colleagues might have another objective: an unprovoked insurrection. Where his approach was rational, theirs was imaginative – and, despite a long, unbroken record of failure, optimistic. When he attended a parade of Volunteers in County Limerick in September 1915 the local commander revealed casually that he had received instructions to 'hold the line of the Shannon in the event of actual hostilities'. The chief of staff was surprised, since 'Nothing nearly so definite had been discussed in Dublin in my presence', but the real significance of this order seemed not to have occurred to him.[2] He simply confirmed the instructions that had been given by Patrick Pearse, the director of organisation.

The Volunteers' policy also faced a threat from outside: James Connolly seemed determined to use his Citizen Army to stage a socialist rebellion. Ominously from MacNeill's point of view, Connolly wrote that 'A revolutionist who surrenders the initiative to the enemy is already defeated before a blow is struck', and (quoting James Fintan Lalor) '*somewhere* and *somehow* and by *somebody*, a *beginning must be made* ... the *first* act of resistance is always, and must be ever, premature, imprudent, and dangerous'.[3]

At the end of December 1915 MacNeill warned the Volunteers about

> 'instances of what may be called unwise impatience ... Impatient action, especially of a detached and sporadic kind, may be a way of relieving this man's or that man's feelings while delaying our country's

deliverance, we do not know for how long. Now, no man has the right to seek relief for his own feelings at the expense of his country.'[4]

In January 1916 he persuaded Pearse to accompany him to a private meeting at which he advised Connolly against any insurrection. According to his later account, when Connolly said that the Citizen Army would fight in Dublin, if necessary alone, he replied that 'if he counted in that event on compelling us to fight rather than stand by & see his men destroyed, he was mistaken'. He concluded: 'We came to no agreement.'[5] Afterwards Pearse assured MacNeill that he could persuade Connolly to abandon his plans, and he soon confirmed that he had done so. But this was no more than technically true. Connolly *did* modify his preparations, but merely to postpone their implementation; he was recruited into the Clarke–MacDermott conspiracy for a rebellion at Easter, and he allied his forces with theirs.[6]

MacNeill's suspicions increased, but they were mild compared to those of the Volunteers' general secretary Bulmer Hobson – who, as an IRB man, had a far deeper understanding of his colleagues. In early February 1916, at the request of Hobson and Seán Fitzgibbon, the director of recruiting, MacNeill prepared a long memorandum expounding the Volunteers' official aims and reiterating his opposition to taking a military initiative. He sent this to Pearse who, in MacNeill's absence, read out the document at a meeting of the headquarters staff. This probably took place in early to mid-February. Pearse and Seán MacDermott denied strongly that they had any intention of launching a rebellion and, according to Hobson, they 'reproached the rest of us for our suspicious natures'.[7]

Hobson wanted a confrontation with those whom he suspected of planning an insurrection; according to MacNeill's later account, 'Hobson constantly insisted that I should demand a clear & binding statement of policy at Executive & Staff meetings, but I had great reluctance to show distrust & preferred to rely on the assurances I had received'.[8] The split of 1914 was still a recent memory and MacNeill was determined to avoid open disunity; to take strong measures, such as dismissing those whom he suspected of conspiracy, would risk dividing and even destroying the Volunteers as an organised force. In particular, he was understandably reluctant to believe that he could be deceived and manipulated by people with whom he had enjoyed a long and close working relationship – with Pearse as a fellow member of the Gaelic League, and with MacDonagh as an academic colleague in University College Dublin. 'He tried to avoid open disunity and gave credit for good faith, as long as it was possible for him to do so.'[9] His trustfulness went to extreme lengths, and for months he procrastinated; a harsh verdict is that he 'usually made Hamlet look the embodiment of ruthless decision'.[10] Hobson wrote scathingly that it was often easier to persuade him to do nothing than to take positive action.[11] MacNeill was a part-time chief of staff and his frequent absences from headquarters, his capacity for ignoring incriminating evidence, and the resulting drift and indecisiveness at Volunteer headquarters all played into the rebels' hands.[12] As one example, even though occasional meetings were held in his house, which was remote and difficult to access, when the police reported the attendance at a series of twenty meetings in the Volunteers' headquarters, his presence was noted at only three of them.[13] He was uneasy and apprehensive but he avoided confrontation for as long as possible.

At the request of Hobson, Fitzgibbon and J.J. O'Connell, the chief of inspection, he drafted a lengthy memorandum, undated but probably written in February 1916, which seems to have incorporated the letter that was sent to Pearse and that was subsequently read out by him. In this document MacNeill revealed an impressive insight into his rebellious colleagues' minds and intentions. He began clearly and forcefully:

> 'The only reason that could justify general active military measures – as distinct from military preparations – on the part of Irish Nationalists would be a reasonably calculated or estimated prospect of success, in the military sense ... The success which is calculated or estimated must be success in the operation itself, not merely some future moral or political advantage which may be hoped for as the result of non-success.'

By Easter Monday, when the rebels' more ambitious plans had been abandoned, partly due to his efforts, future moral or political advantage was precisely what they hoped to achieve. He argued that Britain could crush any insurrection, and he believed that 'If the Government knew that a revolt was about to take place, it would allow the revolt to take place'; it had always wanted to suppress the Volunteers. He was accurate in stressing that the Volunteers' efficiency in Dublin was not matched by their condition in the rest of the country. He argued that 'an armed revolt at present would be wrong and unpatriotic & criminal'. Towards the end of the memorandum he made an obvious objection to a revolt: there was no widespread popular discontent in Ireland. He stressed that he would resist any plan for an insurrection 'with all the force I can, actively & not passively. I will not give way or resign or shirk any trouble in opposing it'.[14]

But he continued to advocate the use of force in certain circumstances. Three weeks before the rising he wrote in the *Irish Volunteer*, 'If our arms are demanded from us, we shall refuse to surrender them. If force is used to take them from us, we shall make the most effective resistance in our power.'[15]

On 5 April, a day-long meeting of the headquarters staff was held in Woodtown Park, beyond Rathfarnham, where MacNeill and his family were living in a house owned by his brother James. Woodtown was without a telephone and it was a considerable distance from the city centre (beyond the modern M50 motorway). Numerous people were to make a remarkable – and at times almost comical – series of journeys to and from the house in the course of the next month. When O'Rahilly was killed during Easter week a sheet of paper was found in one of his pockets, on the back of which was drawn a map showing the route from Rathfarnham to Woodtown Park.[16]

This meeting discussed the Volunteers' policy. By now, MacNeill was convinced that he was 'not in the current of all that was going on' – an obvious understatement. Pearse rejected the idea that he or his colleagues 'contemplated insurrection or wanted to commit the Volunteers to any policy other than that to which they were publicly committed'. MacNeill accepted this assurance and did not bring the meeting to the point of either endorsing or repudiating the Volunteers' declared programme.[17] But it was decided that, apart from routine matters, no order would be sent to the Volunteers without the chief of staff's counter-signature. While 'Pearse no longer lived up to his exhortation to his boys to be like Fianna, who "never told a lie", nor had "falsehood imputed to them"', it has been argued on the other hand that he and his colleagues were as honest with MacNeill as was compatible with planning a revolution.[18]

The following day, 6 April, MacNeill received a letter from an Irish-American, Bernard McGillian, warning that a rising designed to discredit Redmond was planned for the summer.[19] Again, strangely, he took no action. But in the final issue of the *Irish Volunteer*, published on 22 April, he rejected the idea that a rebellion was envisaged; the Volunteers' policy remained unchanged.[20]

On Palm Sunday, 16 April, Hobson made a speech in the Foresters' Hall on Parnell Square in Dublin warning against any precipitate action. The conspirators were outraged and appalled: 'One could see glances passing between those who were probably aware of what decisions had already been taken.'[21] With Hobson proving himself to be dangerous, they felt that it was more necessary than ever to disarm MacNeill. He had often made it clear that an insurrection would be justified if it had a chance of success and if the

British planned aggressive action against the Volunteers. Proof of the second criterion seemed to have been provided by the 'Castle document', shown to MacNeill before it was publicised widely. This seemed to confirm that the British authorities planned to suppress the Volunteers – thereby fulfilling one of his conditions. MacNeill believed the document was genuine and ordered Hobson (who, as always, was more sceptical) to circulate it. The executive held emergency meetings in light of the anticipated British repression and directed the Volunteers to be prepared for resistance. Such heightened tension facilitated the drift towards rebellion.

Decisions were taken in MacNeill's name, behind his back. J.J. O'Connell was ordered to assume control of Volunteers in the southeast, and when Colm Ó Lochlainn, a member of the executive, was dispatched by Joseph Plunkett to Cahersiveen, he was assured that nothing had been done or would be done 'without the absolute approval' of the chief of staff.[22] Pearse sent Seán Fitzgibbon to Limerick and Kerry with orders concerning the anticipated arms landing, and told him that this mission, too, had MacNeill's approval.[23] It is likely that the intention was to get all three men out of the way, and thereby to isolate MacNeill.[24]

It was probably on Thursday, 20 April that a UCD student who was also a Volunteer informed MacNeill that he had been ordered to blow up a large bridge during the Sunday 'manoeuvres'.[25] Astonishingly, no action was taken. But on Thursday evening Hobson learned that orders given to companies could mean only that the weekend marches were to be a cover for a rebellion, and that O'Connell had been given orders without the knowledge of the chief of staff. The two men drove to Woodtown Park and knocked on the door until they roused MacNeill from his bed. When they told him their news he changed from pyjamas into outdoor clothes and they all went to Pearse's school in St Enda's, arriving after midnight and getting *him* out of bed.

Pearse was caught off-guard when confronted with their evidence. He admitted having given orders that railway traffic should be stopped, and he agreed that this amounted to insurrection. MacNeill warned that he would stop a rebellion by every means possible, except (of course) informing the British authorities, and Pearse retorted that he would be powerless to do so. Any countermand would only cause confusion.

MacNeill, Hobson and O'Connell then returned to Woodtown and drafted new orders, overruling any given by Pearse. Hobson was authorised to give directions in the name of the chief of staff, and O'Connell was to take control in Munster. Volunteers were also told to resist by force any attempt to disarm them.

Pearse reported the confrontation to MacDermott, the principal conspirator, who arrived in Woodtown Park some hours later, about 8 a.m. On this occasion MacNeill remained in bed. He listened while MacDermott informed him that a German arms shipment was expected, and that any orders he might send through Hobson and O'Connell would be universally disregarded. News of the impending arrival of German guns, combined with the threat apparently posed by the 'Castle document', persuaded him to change his mind. He now became convinced that the British planned to suppress the Volunteers and that a rising would have a chance of success; thus both of his criteria for insurrection seemed to have been met. He abandoned his earlier opposition and decided to join the rebels. From their point of view, this was the perfect outcome; not merely would they prevent MacNeill from thwarting their plans, but they would be able to recruit his reputation and prestige to their cause. In order to keep him quiet, MacDermott had felt obliged 'to lift just a little more of the curtain',[26] but MacNeill had been given the minimum amount of information to prevent him from disrupting their preparations, and he was 'remarkably unquestioning as MacDermott reeled him in'.[27] Later he wrote, defensively and misleadingly, that this incident was the only foundation for subsequent statements about his change of attitude.[28]

Plunkett and Thomas MacDonagh went to the house separately and the three visitors were entertained to breakfast. After this meeting MacNeill sent Hobson a note directing him to take no immediate action and to await his arrival in the Volunteers' headquarters. He went there, but the two men failed to meet; Hobson had left by the time he arrived, understandably frustrated by his chief's latest reluctance to take a firm stand. MacNeill tore up his papers, sent messages, and complained unfairly that 'Hobson is out joy-riding'.[29]

British repression did not materialise, and the rebels continued with their plans. MacDermott spread the word that MacNeill had resigned as chief of staff and he gave orders that the rising would go ahead; from Cork he received the reply, 'Tell Seán we will blaze away as long as the stuff lasts.'[30] The extent to which MacNeill had been sidelined is indicated in instructions sent by Pearse's brother Willie on Friday, 21 April in which he described himself as 'Acting Chief of Staff'.[31] That evening Hobson was kidnapped by the rebels, but MacNeill may not have learned of this development until the following day. His only action was to issue another circular warning the Volunteers that government suppression was now inevitable and that they should be on their guard.[32]

MacNeill claimed that on Saturday, Plunkett called to Woodtown Park and told him that Pope Benedict XV had sent his blessings to the Volunteers in general and to their chief of staff in particular. (Plunkett's father had gone to the Vatican and passed on news that a rebellion was planned for Easter Sunday.) It has been suggested, perhaps partly in jest, that even the pope knew more about the plans for a rising than did MacNeill.[33] He declined the proposal that he should sign a proclamation, saying that it would depend on the document's terms, and no more was said about the matter.[34] If he had done so he would almost certainly have been executed.

That day the *Freeman's Journal* reported under the heading 'Arms and Ammunition' the discovery of a collapsible boat in Kerry and the arrest of a stranger of unknown nationality.[35] After learning about 'the failure and arrests in Kerry' MacNeill believed that 'the situation was beyond remedy', but he was still prepared to participate in a rebellion despite seeing no prospect of success.[36] He had meetings in his house with MacDonagh and Plunkett and he tried to dissuade them from their planned action, but, not surprisingly, they were unconvinced.[37] He arranged with his friend Dr Seamus O'Kelly (who was both a medical general practitioner and an authority on early Irish history) to meet 'a couple of people' in O'Kelly's house in Rathgar. This was nearly six kilometres closer to the city centre, and therefore a far more convenient location than Woodtown Park. It also possessed a telephone. Despite all the pressures and tensions to which he was subjected, in the course of the afternoon he was able to indulge in a long, scholarly discussion with his archaeologist colleague R.A.S. Macalister.[38]

That afternoon he had other visitors. Ó Lochlainn and Fitzgibbon had met by chance on their train journeys back to Dublin, having already learned that the arms shipment had been intercepted and that Casement had been captured.[39] Ironically Casement, who was presumed by the British to be the leader of the planned insurrection, had come to Ireland to prevent it. He described it as 'the wildest form of boyish folly' and as 'worse than a disaster'.[40] And he imagined that MacNeill, who also wished to avert a doomed rebellion, was actually its leader.

When the two men went to the Volunteer headquarters they found Thomas MacDonagh busily burning documents. For obvious reasons they could not contact Hobson, but they went to O'Rahilly's house and he drove them to Woodtown to tell MacNeill their news. They arrived as Macalister left, and afterwards Ó Lochlainn thought it amusing that MacNeill should have been working on *Lebor Gabála* with him 'while the country was on the brink of revolution'.[41] Fitzgibbon explained that he had been deceived into thinking that his mission had been approved by the chief of staff, and – belatedly – MacNeill became convinced that the 'Castle document' was bogus. By now it was clear that the British had not planned an offensive against the Volunteers, and that there would be no supply of German arms. The circumstances that had persuaded him to change his mind on Friday morning were overtaken by more recent events and revelations, and now, about thirty hours later, he reversed his stance once again.

They all agreed that the rebellion had now no chance of success, and that it should be prevented. They went on another visit to St Enda's for what turned out to be a final confrontation with Pearse – who told MacNeill that the conspirators had used his name and influence for what they were worth, and that any orders he might issue would not be obeyed.[42]

They then returned to Woodtown Park, where more people arrived. Seán T. O'Kelly and Arthur Griffith hired a taxi and came to report that Casement and Austin Stack had been arrested in Kerry, but MacNeill had already been informed of these developments.[43] He invited his latest visitors to join him in Rathgar later in the evening. His brother recorded him as saying that 'a calamity had happened, that Mr. Pearse and others of the Volunteers had deceived him, and that in connection with the landing of arms they had issued orders without his knowledge, and that the result of these orders would be to precipitate a conflict with the Forces of the Crown'.[44]

Then the centre of activity changed to Dr O'Kelly's house on Rathgar Road, which MacNeill commandeered for most of the night. He met various people there – including some who were planning a rebellion and others who were determined to prevent it. Among them were his brother James, Plunkett, MacDonagh, Cathal Brugha, Fitzgibbon, Ó Lochlainn, Griffith, Tom Kelly, Seán T. O'Kelly, O'Rahilly, Paudeen O'Keeffe (the Sinn Féin party secretary), Min and James Ryan, Liam Ó Briain, Eimar O'Duffy, and Joseph Connolly. The house was overflowing, and some of those who arrived sat on the stairs or huddled in the garden. 'People were coming and going; summons being sent out to those whom they required: most coming on bicycles, some in cabs, some in motorcars. There was a row of cars and the like stretching down as far as the door of the church. There was a big collection of bicycles in the garden ... There was never a plot or conspiracy attended by more noise and less concealment.'[45] The bewildered host, who felt that technically MacNeill 'did presume upon my house in utilizing it in the way he did', and that the others who arrived did so without his permission, was described as acting 'like a man awaiting news of the birth of a baby – in and out, fussing, and in an awful state'.[46]

TO THE SENATE, THE NATIONAL UNIVERSITY OF IRELAND.
....

As a Travelling Student engaged in Irish Historical Research and unable to bring the work I have in hand to an end within the stipulated two years I beg to apply for the Senate's special prize(U.C.D.Calendar, 1921-2,P.116,I.) to permit the continuance of my research for a further year.

The subject I am investigating is:-The sources of the early Irish monastic rules and their relation to the rules found elsewhere in the Western Church. Monasticism was common in the Church some 150 years before the introduction of Christianity into Ireland.Whilst the fundamental principles on which it was based remained unchanged its external manifestations varied considerably in different countries.Three chief forms may be distinguished, the Egyptian,the Syrian and the Greek,the last-mentioned the creation of St.Basil the Great.The monastic system when introduced into the West likewise took various forms.The names of St.Eusebius of Vercelli,St.Augustine, St.Jerome,Cassian of Marseilles,St.Honoratus of Lérins and St.Martin of Tours,to mention only the earliest,are all connected with monastic foundations.Whence did our Irish system come?Direct from one of the three Eastern systems,as some ecclesiastical historians hold? Or through Italy or Gaul, as is generally contended?And if this is correct can the Irish system be traced more directly to one or other of the various Continental forms? or is it so different from all others that it can justly be called a native growth? Incidentally a detailed investigation of the Irish system has to be made,and questions of extreme importance arise,like the position of the monastery in the local territory,especially as regards ecclesiastical jurisdiction,its relation to the ruling family or to the Tuath ,its manner of life,its administration.If all or even some of these questions could be solved a step would have been taken in removing the cloud that at present hangs over the early Christian centuries in Ireland.

2

The difficulties in this field of study are enormous.Sources which can be used with confidence from what is still left of ancient literature are meagre(they are chiefly the Regula Monachorum and the Regula Cosnobialis of St.Columban,the Life of St.Columban by Jonas,and the Life of St.Colmcille by Adamnan,and scattered references in Bede).The monastic rules written in Old Irish present many problems e.g.their age,the extent to which they are interpolated,the meaning of what are obviously technical expressions.Prof.Eoin MacNeill has succeeded in bringing order into the chaos of Early Irish political history,but the social history-for research like the present of greater importance-remains still an uncharted sea.With patience,however,and above all with time, much that is of value could,I think,be gleaned from the material at our disposal.

Prof.Thurneysen,under whom I have already had courses in Old-Irish and in Breton,is most ready with his help in all that concerns Irish texts. Prof.Wilhelm Levison,whose work for 24 years in the section of the Monumenta Germaniae Historica dealing with writers of the Merovingian period has given him an exceptional knowledge of the labours of the Irish Missionaries abroad,is also ready with what assistance he can give.From him I have already had courses in historical method.Under Prof. Monsignor Albert Ehrhard I have studied the general ecclesiastical history of the period. Guidance in the stricter sense under a Professor I unfortunately cannot have as the subject is a terra incognita to all the scholars I have met. I have of necessity owing to my profession a life interest in the Philosophical,theological and ascetical studies without an intimate knowledge of which such a work as that here undertaken would be impossible.

I therefore believe that if allowed an extra year in which to pursue my research I would be able in autumn 1924 to have ready for publication matter on the subject indicated which would at least open the way to further progress in that important of early Irish history.In that conviction I beg leave to present my request for the sympathetic consideration of the Senate. Bonn a/Rh. Hofgartenstrasse 9, Germany.   John Ryan S.J. M.A.

9. Letter from John Ryan (Hofgartenstraße 9, Bonn am Rhein) to the Senate of the National University of Ireland requesting an extension to his Travelling Studentship, in which he acknowledges the work of Eoin MacNeill while detailing his own studies in Bonn, including the study of Old Irish with Rudolf Thurneysen, who provides a reference, 13 November 1922 (NUI Archives).

Herr John Ryan hat mir eine regen Selbstbeteiligung und gutem Erfolg bei mir Bretonisch y Alt-Irisch gehört e nimmt auch gegenwärtig an meinem Kolleg über Alt-Irisch Teil.

Bonn, 13. November 1922.   Prof. Dr. R. Thurneysen.

10. 'At liberty again: Professor Eoin MacNeill photographed with his family after his release from Mountjoy Prison', *Freeman's Journal*, 8 July 1921 [newscutting] (L–R standing: Niall, Brian; seated, middle row: Agnes, Eoin, Eibhlín; seated, front row: Róisín, Séamus, Máire (Turlough MacNeill was still in Mountjoy when this photograph was taken) (UCDA LA30/PH/417).

11. Róisín, Brian, Eibhlín MacNeill (seated L–R) with a dog and (standing) Turlough MacNeill in uniform and an unidentified man [*c.*1921–2] (UCDA LA30/PH/359).

12. Photographed on the steps of the Club House and Commercial Hotel, Kilkenny, MacNeill accompanies Cosgrave on the latter's first visit to his constituency of Carlow-Kilkenny since his election as President of the Executive Council. Cosgrave will use this visit to launch Cumann na nGaedheal's 1923 general election campaign. L–R, front row: Vincent White, Mayor of Waterford; Peter de Loughrey, Mayor of Kilkenny; W.T. Cosgrave, President of the Executive Council; Hugh Kennedy TD, Attorney General; Senator John MacLoughlin; MacNeill. Back row (not in order) includes Dan McCarthy TD, Chief Whip and President of the GAA; James Dolan TD; and Colonel-Commandant J. O'Reilly [27 May 1923] (UCDA LA30/PH/395).

13. Members of the Boundary Commission on the first day of their tour, Armagh, 9 December 1924. L–R: Dr Eoin MacNeill, Free State; Mr J.R. Fisher, Northern Ireland; Mr T.E. Read, OBE, JD, Secretary to Armagh County Council; Mr T.E. Montgomery; and Mr Justice Richard Feetham. Photographer: W.D. Hogan (NLI, National Photographic Archive, HOG 181).

14. MacNeill and members of the Catholic University of America, Washington DC [May 1930] (UCDA LA30/PH/398).

15. Máire Sweeney (MacNeill) and Michael Tierney standing underneath a portrait of Eoin MacNeill, 1964 (UCDA LA30/PH/105).

16. Group photograph on the occasion of the publication of *The Scholar Revolutionary: Eoin MacNeill, 1867–1945*, edited by F.X. Martin and F.J. Byrne, 1973. L–R: Thomas Murphy, President of UCD; Éilis McDowell; Francis John Byrne; Máire Sweeney; Séamus MacNeill; Eibhlín Tierney; F.X. Martin; Róisín Coyle (UCDA LA30/PH/377).

Assisted by Griffith, MacNeill drafted orders to Volunteer units throughout the country cancelling the manoeuvres planned for the following day: 'Volunteers completely deceived. All orders for special action are hereby cancelled & on no account will action be taken.' Messengers were sent to deliver them throughout the country (but some of those who did so were unaware of their contents and would later fight in the rising). He told MacDonagh what he had done, complaining that 'I have been grossly deceived all along', and in turn he was informed that no matter what he did, the manoeuvres would go ahead on Sunday; his orders might not be obeyed.[47]

MacNeill rode to the offices of the *Sunday Independent* and persuaded the acting editor to insert a notice cancelling the manoeuvres. It is noteworthy that he, often dismissed as unworldly, was sufficiently practical to disseminate information through the press.[48] He returned to Rathgar and later, at 3 a.m., he cycled back to Woodtown Park. Seán T. O'Kelly claimed that on his way home he met Cathal Brugha and Éamonn Ceannt also riding their bicycles and told them what was happening. Ceannt said that if he had full authority MacNeill would be shot, and Brugha agreed.[49] (Markievicz subsequently expressed the same wish.) At daybreak, shortly after Dr O'Kelly had gone to bed, he heard loud knocking on his front door. He feared that this indicated the late arrival of the 'forces of the law' but the callers were MacDermott and Plunkett, in search of MacNeill.

It is remarkable that the crown authorities had no awareness of what was happening. Yet Dr O'Kelly noted that the night's activities had been observed. The house next door was vacant, but 'A trace of light was noticed in one of its rooms. When everybody had left us and our own house was cleared, an unidentified pair slipped away from that house in the dark. It is not known who they were'.[50] Presumably a courting couple had taken advantage of an empty house and were dismayed to find themselves next door to the equivalent of a public meeting.

After midnight MacDonagh, Pearse and Plunkett all visited MacDermott. (Clarke, Connolly and Ceannt were not available, having stayed away from their homes that night.)[51] They were appalled by MacNeill's decisive action, which they must have seen as being completely out of character; they had earlier countermanded his orders, and now he had retaliated in kind. Considering how they had lied to him and manipulated him, they had no reason for complaint when – most belatedly – he tried to follow a policy that he had advocated consistently until only a day earlier.

The IRB military council decided to modify its plans in light of what had happened, and to postpone the rebellion until Monday. Historians

disagree over whether it was wise to do so. Far more Volunteers turned out
for manoeuvres on Easter Sunday, unaware of the countermanding order,
than did so on Monday. The countermand had dramatic consequences,
and Pearse's earlier confidence that MacNeill's orders would not affect the
rebels' plans was probably more justified than his later caution.[52] On the
other hand, in much of the south and west outside Cork city the would-be
insurgents were virtually unarmed; a rebellion was dependent on the arrival
of German guns. After the interception of the *Aud* the manoeuvres were
cancelled, even before receipt of the countermanding order.[53] In Ulster the
commanders were unaware of the countermand when they decided not to
carry out their (completely unrealistic) tasks, and in Galway a small-scale
insurrection took place despite the cancellation and the interception of the
arms ship.[54] It has even been argued that what happened was 'providential';
the rising in Dublin stood almost alone, in heroic isolation, and thereby had
a greater impact.[55] MacNeill's order never affected the Citizen Army, which
had a fully separate leadership.

There is no doubt that his action, combined with the interception
of the arms shipment and the arrest of Casement (the supposed leader
of the insurrection), removed any British sense of alarm or emergency,
and therefore facilitated the rebels in getting their blow in first. Ceannt
remarked on Sunday night: 'I may thank John MacNeill that I can sleep in
my own house – the cancelling of the manoeuvres will lead the British to
believe that everything is all right.'[56] Whether the authorities would have
remained content to delay their action without the reassurance provided to
them by the countermanding order must remain a matter of speculation.

Pearse accepted that MacNeill, like the rebels, had acted in the best
interests of Ireland, but nonetheless blamed him for the failure of the rising:
'Of the fatal countermanding order which prevented these plans from being
carried out I shall not speak.'[57] But those words, enough to damn MacNeill
in the eyes of many Irish nationalists, were a limited and misleading version
of what happened; they ignored the flaws and failures in the rebels' plans.

On Sunday MacNeill invited members of the GAA council to call
to Woodtown Park and he encouraged them to go to Liberty Hall and
try to dissuade those who wished to stage an insurrection. But he did
nothing more. That evening Pearse wrote to him that MacDonagh had
countermanded the Dublin parade and that he had confirmed this order,
adding that 'the leading men' would not have obeyed it without his
endorsement.[58] He clearly saw himself, rather than the chief of staff, as
the dominant figure in the Volunteers. Naïvely, MacNeill 'then thought

all was settled'; he had prevailed; and the rebels would have to abandon their plans.[59] To confirm this impression MacDonagh called to see him in Woodtown Park, concealing his intention (according to the memorandum he wrote immediately afterwards) 'to act with my own Council, and the position of that Council ... I have guarded secrets which I am bound to keep'. In consequence, his future conduct might 'be different from anything now anticipated by MacNeill and Fitzgibbon, two honest and sincere patriots, though, I think, wrong in their handling of the present situation and in their attitude to military action'.[60] This final deception was the last contact between the two friends.

But on Monday morning Desmond FitzGerald received confirmation that the rising was going ahead. Unable to hire a taxi because of the Fairyhouse races, in the most bizarre of all the many journeys to Woodtown Park he travelled first on a bicycle, which he abandoned when a tyre burst, and then continued by milk cart, on foot, and finally in a jaunting car. On arrival he warned MacNeill that the Volunteers were being mobilised for active service at 10 a.m. and urged him to go to the city. He also suggested that MacNeill try to secure Hobson's release. Even now MacNeill was not fully convinced and wondered whether the manoeuvres might mean either a renewed effort against his orders 'or merely a holiday demonstration to reassure the men after the previous parades had fallen through'.[61] Nonetheless he cycled down towards Dublin, on his way meeting Liam Ó Briain who was travelling uphill on a horse-drawn sidecar to report on his delivery of the countermanding orders.[62] Once more he commandeered the unfortunate Dr O'Kelly's house, this time without giving advance notice, and from there he sent his son and Seán Fitzgibbon to go ahead and see what was taking place. They returned with the news that barricades were being erected on Portobello Bridge. It was now clear that all MacNeill's efforts to prevent a rebellion had failed, and his (short-lived) response was revealing: 'I will return home, put on my Volunteer's uniform and enter the fray.'[63] When he repeated this suggestion some days later Hobson dissuaded him.[64]

Instead, he went home, and briefly took refuge in the Augustinian novitiate in nearby Orlagh, from where he could see the fighting in Dublin. But journeys from Dublin to Woodtown Park continued. O'Rahilly's wife sent two of their sons there for safety.[65] Hobson, after his release on the evening of Easter Monday, made his way there with his fiancée, and he remained in the house for some weeks. Alderman Tom Kelly, Fitzgibbon and O'Connell went there too, and Griffith and a friend cycled by a roundabout route from Clontarf. Only Dr O'Kelly was missing. Charles MacAuley, a doctor who had treated Plunkett in the General Post Office, arrived in the house and found those present 'a rather disconsolate group',[66] but at least MacNeill was not left alone to brood. Most dramatically of all, Desmond FitzGerald, having spent all week in the GPO (despite his earlier efforts to warn MacNeill of the rising), bluffed his way through the British lines and made his way slowly to Woodtown Park, arriving on Tuesday, 2 May.[67]

Shortly before FitzGerald's reappearance MacNeill sent a letter to General Maxwell suggesting that they should meet in an effort to avoid further conflict. Hobson declined to sign the message, arguing rationally that it was an invitation to be arrested, and that while he saw this as likely, he 'was not going to ask for it'. MacNeill pointed out, with perhaps uncharacteristic realism, that they would have no political future unless they were arrested.[68] On the same day Tom Clarke, in his cell awaiting execution, told his wife that MacNeill 'must never again be allowed back into the National life of the country'.[69] (Subsequently she did her best to carry out his wishes.)

They were waiting for the military to arrive in Woodtown Park when FitzGerald turned up, and they urged him to leave before he would be captured. He did, but not before telling them of his experiences; he then went home to Bray, where he was arrested. The British officer who arrived in Woodtown Park to escort MacNeill to Maxwell's headquarters knew Hobson and saw him in the house, but made no sign of recognition. Hobson remained at liberty, with the result that, in contrast to MacNeill, he had no future in Irish public life.

After MacNeill was taken to meet Maxwell he was placed under arrest – and professed to be indignant at this treatment. When he was deposited in Richmond Barracks with other prisoners, MacDermott refused to shake his hand and turned away.[70] He was interviewed by Major Ivon Price, the chief intelligence officer in the Irish Command, and he claimed that Price had tried to lure him into implicating John Dillon and Joe Devlin in the rising. 'His object, in my opinion, was to use a false statement to be made by me, in order to ruin me in the eyes of the public.'[71] He smuggled out his account of their meeting in a matchbox when his wife visited him.[72] Price denied having made any such suggestions.[73] Maxwell was 'a little perplexed what to do about this man McNeill [sic], he is no doubt one of the most prominent in the movement though I believe he did try and stop the actual rebellion taking place when it did. The Priests and politicians will try and save him.'[74]

While he was in jail in Dublin, he could hear the sound of gunfire as some of the condemned prisoners were shot. When he was taken out for exercise he was forced to walk up and down in front of a row of men who were practising aiming with empty rifles. The muzzles were only a few metres away.[75]

He was tried by a full (rather than a field) court martial, which meant that, unlike all the rebels, he was entitled to defence counsel. He was anxious to drag out the proceedings, confident that the pattern of executions would alienate Irish public opinion and that any delay would be to his advantage. He was tried on twelve counts, eight of them under the heading 'Attempting to cause disaffection amongst the civilian population'. The charges included acting as chief of staff of the Volunteers, editing its weekly paper, making a speech in Killarney in May 1915, and prejudicing recruitment to the British army. Most of them had only a marginal connection with the rising. He pleaded not guilty on all counts. The prosecutor made it clear that MacNeill was not charged with taking part in the rebellion, but rather of incitement to rebellion. In practice, however, he was tried for his connections with an insurrection that he had worked hard to prevent; the prosecutor claimed that 'The man who loads the magazines with gunpowder is as guilty as he who ignites the powder and causes the explosion.'[76] As MacNeill pointed out, the prosecution's attempts to connect him with the rising were inevitably feeble; he wrote afterwards: 'Charges 9, 10, 11. All as vague as they could imaginably be. If a charge can fail thro' vagueness these must.'[77] And he argued, reasonably, that 'the men who could give the clearest evidence on that point are now dead'.[78]

He maintained that he had never tried to interfere with army recruitment. The government had never queried the Volunteers' right to organise and had never issued any warning in relation to their newspaper. The Volunteers, as a force, did not take part in the insurrection, and only a very small fraction of its members had done so individually. MacNeill had done everything possible to prevent the rising, and he succeeded in stopping it taking place as planned. Improbably, he claimed that the rebellion would not have taken place but for the government's intention of arresting the Volunteer leaders. By the Sunday afternoon his efforts had succeeded. On Monday morning they had been undone and he

> 'came to the conclusion that something had happened in the meantime which had caused those whom I had overborne the day before to go back of [sic] I believe they had come to the conclusion that their action was inevitable if they did not act themselves it would be forced on them by others'. He described the rebels as 'truthful and

honourable men. They gave me that assurance on the evening of Easter Sunday I had no reason to doubt it. I have no reason to doubt it now.'[79]

This was a tactful, politically astute line to take, but it is hard to imagine that even a man as gullible as MacNeill could have believed what he wrote.

The court martial was a travesty of justice – the judge advocate acted for the prosecution rather than as a neutral advisor – and MacNeill received a life sentence. He wrote later,

> 'I was really tried in a covert fashion for complicity with the rebellion, and of course my sentence – penal servitude for life – was inflicted for the offence for which I was tried though not indicted, & not for the other alleged offences, for which no man has got at any time more than six months imprisonment.'[80]

His brother claimed that his 'acts were similar to Sir E. Carson's. His speeches were at least less defiantly illegal than Sir E.C.'s or Sir F.E. Smith's.'[81] (In 'The North Began' MacNeill had argued that Carson 'has knocked the bottom out of Unionism' and was probably 'at heart a Home Ruler'.) But such parallels were not drawn by the defence as they would have antagonised the members of the court martial.

In a famous incident, when MacNeill joined the Irish prisoners in Dartmoor, de Valera demanded that the others salute him, 'eyes left' (or according to another version, 'eyes right').[82] Accounts differ as to the response given to this order, but it established de Valera as a leader and it gave MacNeill grudging acceptance by some rebels who resented his countermand and blamed him for the limited scale of the rebellion.

He was sent first to Dartmoor and then, in December, to Lewes in Sussex – where the climate and the conditions were much more bearable. His hair was cropped and his beard shaved, with the result that his wife barely recognised him on her first visit. He never grew his beard again. His prison routine consisted of breakfast at 5.15 (gruel), dinner at 11 (boiled beef or thick soup) and supper at 5 (cocoa and bread).[83] He described the food as in general 'repulsive to persons of delicate appetite'. He cared for his health, took exercise in his cell, and – since pipes or cigarettes were not allowed in Dartmoor – he abandoned his long-term habit of smoking. His work consisted of making and sewing postbags and sandbags ('one of the most monotonous tasks imaginable'), weaving hearthrugs on a loom, making floor-brushes, and working in the garden – where he was able to eat plants such as sorrel and dandelion.[84] When he was sent a parcel of shirts he gave one to a less fortunate colleague.[85] He availed himself fully of his leisure time, reading in Greek and learning Spanish and Dutch, discussing with other prisoners topics ranging from food economics to literature, and giving lessons in Irish history and the Irish language. He remarked that study made the time pass more easily and that prison was more bearable for educated men. He tried to keep pace with scholarly affairs, as in requesting the minutes of the Society of Antiquaries and the UCD calendar and booklet of courses. When he was expelled from the Royal Irish Academy he rejoiced that 'Richard Best, an Ulster Protestant, raised his voice against the petty servility of these people'.[86] He sought news from home, about the children's activities and education, about fowl and fruit trees, pigs, poultry and potatoes.[87]

Along with de Valera, Thomas Ashe and Eamonn Duggan, he wrote a petition to the governor, and he was one of the prisoners' spokesmen – speaking more eloquently than de Valera, it was noted.[88] But he was not one of their leading figures in Lewes, and de Valera referred later to a 'triumvirate' of himself, Ashe and Tom Hunter.[89]

He reassured his comrades that their imprisonment would not last beyond the end of the war, but even this estimate was too pessimistic. All those interned without trial after the rising had been freed by the end of 1916, leaving only a small number still in jail. In June 1917 the government decided to release these remaining prisoners and they were able to return to Ireland – as heroes. MacNeill promptly made a contribution of £40 to the society that cared for the families of the rebels killed during or after the rising, and he made it clear that he had no interest in idleness or rest.[90] His gamble in seeking arrest paid off and he was soon able to resume his public as well as his academic career; de Valera, wanting to appeal to moderates as well as to radicals, insisted that MacNeill should accompany him in the East Clare by-election campaign. Even more fully than in the case of de Valera, the military phase of his career was behind him, but – for better or worse – a new phase as a politician now lay ahead. He was elected to the Dáil, became a minister in the 1919 government, was imprisoned again, chaired the treaty debates, served as Minister for Education after independence, and represented the Free State on the Boundary Commission. He also returned to Early Irish History; he was restored to his chair in UCD in 1918 and he remained a professor until his retirement in 1941. He probably regretted that he ever left his world of scholarship for the duties and disillusionments of public life.

Eoin MacNeill and Nationalism

SHANE NAGLE

This chapter examines the published and unpublished works of Eoin MacNeill in order to explore nationalism and its development in his historical writing. In his work, MacNeill drew a distinction between 'nation' and 'state'; this distinction, and the significance of his variant of historiographical nationalism for the broader currents of Irish nationalism in the early twentieth century, will be teased out here. Though MacNeill is mostly remembered for his attempt to halt the Easter Rising and his political career during the periods of the first Dáil and the early years of the Irish Free State, for the first quarter of the twentieth century he stood at the centre of the intellectual culture of Irish nationalism. As a founding member of the Gaelic League, as one of its leading intellectuals and Professor of Early (including Medieval) Irish History at University College Dublin (where he did much to advance the professionalisation of Irish historical research), and as a founder member of the Irish Volunteers, he played a significant role in the development of an explicitly separatist form of nationalism oriented away from Westminster politics. MacNeill's conception of nationalism was fundamental to the development of the militant separatism that led to the Easter Rising and which continued to contour the political and cultural outlook of the Irish Free State in the early years of independence.[1]

MacNeill's engagement with nationalism was inseparable from his conception of Irish history. This chapter will frame MacNeill as an essentially European nationalist, both in his ideas of the purpose that Irish statehood should serve, and the intellectual foundations of his nationalism. In studying MacNeill and his thinking, his influences and how he influenced others, one can arrive at a broader analysis of the nature of Irish nationalism in the critical period between the turn of the twentieth century and the birth of Irish statehood in the early 1920s. MacNeill grew to adulthood and occupied public and intellectual life in an age of clashing ideologies: liberalism, conservatism, socialism, nationalism and fascism. Yet it was *historical* thought that was, above all other 'isms', of the highest importance to nineteenth- and twentieth-century nationalists.[2] 'History' was the pivot not only of MacNeill's intellectual case for separatism, but his idea of what the Irish nation of the future should be.

THE EUROPEAN CONTEXT

Narratives of history centring on peoples and states go all the way back to Ancient Greece and Rome, yet it was not until the early decades of the nineteenth century and onwards that national history became a form of political writing for societies throughout the European continent. The French Revolution, and the myriad reactions to it, redefined sovereignty by making irrevocable the idea that 'the people' had an inalienable right to govern their own affairs. The rise of '*wissenschaftlich*' forms of history writing catalysed the professionalisation and institutionalisation of historical inquiry in the nineteenth and twentieth centuries. As such, historical knowledge, even (and perhaps especially) when combined with nationalist commitment, assumed the status of 'scientific' knowledge, of 'truth'. It was not necessary to argue over abstract concepts, merely use history to determine conclusions for the present and future. National(ist) historians all over Europe were preoccupied by certain themes: origins, territory, religion in the nation's past, the nation's ethnic and cultural basis, and its relationships with its neighbours.

A number of 'canonical' multi-volume works had already appeared by the middle of the nineteenth century, including John Lingard's and Thomas Babington Macaulay's histories of England, Ranke's *Geschichte der romanischen und germanischen Völker von 1495 bis 1514* (Leipzig, 1824), Michelet's *Histoire de France* (17 vols, Paris, 1833–67), the Dutchman Willem Bilderdijk's *History of the Fatherland* (11 vols, Amsterdam, 1832–7), Palacky's *Geschichte des tschechischen Volkes in Böhmen und Mähren* (5 vols, Prague, 1836–67), Juste's *Histoire de Belgique* (Brussels, 1840), and Nikolai Karamzin's *History of the Russian State* (12 vols, 1819–26), to name only a few.[3] These were followed later in the century by Henry Thomas Buckle and his (unfinished) *History of Civilization in England* (London, 1857), E.A. Freeman and his *History of the Norman Conquest* (6 vols, Oxford, 1867–79), Gustav Freytag and his *Bilder aus der Deutschen Vergangenheit* (5 vols, Leipzig, 1859–67), J.A. Froude and his history of England in the Tudor era (12 vols, New York, 1856–70), and Heinrich von Treitschke, probably the most influential and widely read German academic historian of the nineteenth century, and writer of *Deutsche Geschichte im neunzehnten Jahrhundert* (5 vols, Leipzig, 1879–95). In Ireland, as elsewhere in Europe, the process of (national) state formation was accompanied by the development of a historical establishment (which should be considered broadly, to include not just academic institutions but state commissions, commemorative projects and legislative initiatives) that institutionalised, popularised and placed on sound academic footing a nationalist narrative of the nation's history.[4] Ireland was relatively slow to catch up, certainly when it came to professionalisation and institutionalisation in the universities; as in Britain, much of the most influential Irish history writing was done outside these institutions by late eighteenth- and nineteenth-century 'gentleman scholars' such as Eugene O'Curry and John O'Donovan, whose contribution lay principally in descriptive materials, collections of primary sources and (albeit flawed) translations of Old Irish texts.[5] By the 1880s historians such as W.E.H. Lecky and Richard Bagwell were producing multi-volume histories based on primary research that were not fixed in their content and argument by the cultural and political allegiances of their authors.[6] The fact that Lecky, by this time a unionist, would be positively received by Irish nationalists for his history writing attests neatly to the protean character of national(ist) history writing and the futility of attempting to make strict distinctions between 'scientific' and 'partisan' historiography in the nineteenth and early twentieth centuries. MacNeill, for his part, would continue the professionalisation of Irish historical research, while shifting its study away from the early and late modern periods favoured by the likes of Lecky and Bagwell to early and later medieval periods, in which Ireland had developed separately from its larger, eastern neighbour. MacNeill would be known to and respected by prominent European scholars of languages and history including Kuno Meyer, Rudolf Thurneysen and Julius Pokorny. As F.J. Byrne noted, prior to MacNeill, professional historians of Ireland generally commenced with the Anglo-Norman invasion.[7] MacNeill reached the pinnacle of his academic career at a time when the historical profession was still developing in Ireland and pioneered the study of the Irish past through sources from that time while maintaining his nationalist commitment. In his own words, while this commitment was the result of his occupation with history rather than the other way around, he could not 'write an impartial history of Ireland'.[8]

'... OUR COUNTRY IS NOT A POETICAL ABSTRACTION ...'[9]

In February 1916, MacNeill in his role as leader of the Irish Volunteers commented that 'We have to remember that what we call our country is not a poetical abstraction'. MacNeill was signalling his scepticism with the ideological dogmatism of some in the separatist movement, and his worry that the more militant members of that movement were too willing to employ violence over persuasion. Yet when we look at the long span of his career, there is an irony to it. By the time MacNeill had finished university, the dissatisfaction within 'advanced nationalism' at the liberalism and 'utilitarian' bent of the Home Rule movement was becoming apparent. By 1886, the Irish Parliamentary Party (IPP) had become firmly aligned with the Liberal Party in Britain, striving to convince English parliamentarians that Irish Home Rule was no threat to the integrity of the United Kingdom and the British Empire, or a threat to the liberties of Ulster's Protestants. The 1885 'party pledge'[10] ensured unity and discipline within the IPP in Westminster, and in Ireland the Irish National League (a successor organisation to the Land League), in its different functions, ensured that the voters were kept marshalled behind the party.[11] The old tactics of endorsing agrarian militancy and obstructionism in parliament were set aside, and the constitutional strategy for winning Home Rule appeared to be unchallengeable. To the party's critics, however, it seemed much too concerned with persuading British MPs and ministers that Irish autonomy was no threat to them. They claimed it had become an organisation of careerists and conservative Catholics who had hazarded everything on Home Rule, through which they could break down what remained of the Protestant Ascendancy and erect a Catholic one in its place.[12] In the minds of other nationalists, political nationalism was in danger of becoming harmful, not so much because its goal was unattainable but because it was prepared to reach this goal at the cost of the total Anglicisation of Ireland. The IPP's respectability was a problem – as the nationalist polemicist D.P. Moran would put it in 1917, not long before the party's electoral demise, 'extremists of some kind were a long-felt want in the Party and the machine had become rotten'.[13] In this climate, MacNeill was one of the first to posit an 'abstraction' of Ireland, an idea of Irish nationality at least independent of Home Rule politics and a revival of a culture that was, in large part, speedily passing away from or being diluted in the everyday lives of the majority of the Irish people – and an idea of Irishness that could scarcely appeal to unionists in Ulster or elsewhere in Ireland.

This tension between 'nation' and 'state' was pivotal to MacNeill's thinking, and is the basis for his wider relevance in understanding Irish nationalism of the time. It is also relevant to his European context and significance as an Irish contributor to debates on this relationship that were occurring among and between nationalist intellectuals and movements all over the continent during that period. The history of Irish nationalism is as much one of the struggles between its different components over the form that Irishness should take, as the history of separatist and republican politics and revolution. As John Hutchinson has argued, nations are 'zones of conflict' in which competing nationalist groups have used the same cultural and historical resources to elaborate differing and often opposing conceptions of 'the nation', a hypothesis well demonstrated in the course taken by Irish nationalism.[14] MacNeill's significance lies not only in the role he played in this development, but in how the conception of Irishness he elaborated prior to, during, and in the early years after the Irish revolution became an intellectual resource for members of the 'revolutionary generation' in how they conceptualised Irishness and Irish sovereignty in that period. 'History' played an especially important role here, perhaps because it was a more contested area than ideas such as the revival of the Irish language. MacNeill's output as historian did not take the 'grand narrative' form of exhaustive, multi-volume histories across the entirety of Irish history or a particular era, but tended to focus on more specific areas from which a more comprehensive idea of Irish history and its relationship to nationalism took form. In terms of published works, the more prominent included *Phases of Irish History* (1919), *Celtic Ireland* (1921), *St. Patrick: Apostle of Ireland* (1934), and *Early Irish Laws and Institutions* (1935).[15] *Phases of Irish History* is perhaps the most well-known of these works, though in its structure it is a reproduction of twelve lectures given by MacNeill at the Rotunda in 1917 and 1918. It is only after five chapters and 160 pages that the recognisable signposts of the Irish national(ist) historical narrative – the coming of Christianity, the early medieval 'golden age', the coming of the Anglo-Normans, the later medieval 'revival' – appear. As he admitted, the book offered 'no pretence to form a full course of Irish history for any period'; yet to the degree that *Phases* lets us view MacNeill as a 'fully formed' nationalist, study of the book and its arguments is essential.

'EVERY PEOPLE HAS TWO DISTINCT LINES OF DESCENT ...'

In the opening of *Phases of Irish History*, MacNeill claimed that 'every people has two distinct lines of descent – by blood and by tradition'.[16] This is instructive in relation to MacNeill's position on what would come to be called the 'ethnic' vs 'civic' dichotomy in nationalism.[17] In a period when nationalists throughout continental Europe 'racialised' their histories, MacNeill rejected wholesale the idea that 'race' was constitutive of national history: 'There is no existing Latin race, no Teutonic race, no Anglo-Saxon race, and no Celtic race.'[18] Racial nationalism is a hazy concept: given the problematic nature of the term 'race', it can mean anything from an association of nationality with a particular ethnic group, to a conception of immutable bloodlines, nationality as demonstrated by specific physical characteristics, racial hierarchy, superiority and inferiority, and a pathological fear of 'blood-mixing' and 'degeneration'.[19] Irish nationalism, by the end of the nineteenth century, carried a mixture of such ideas, its rhetoric laden with terms like 'Celt', 'Gael', 'Saxon', 'Norman', and so on; but even in its most radical variants, it bore little relation to the *völkisch* nationalism that was taking hold in the rest of Europe. Indeed, the Irish had traditionally been the 'victims' of a racialised conception of (English and subsequently British) nationalism, which very clearly 'othered' them as racially inferior, and, in the more stridently racist interpretations, as ape-like brutes, or white versions of the European image of the indigenous peoples of Africa and the Americas.[20]

MacNeill was clearly rejecting the idea that nationality was exclusively a matter of heredity and bloodline and that 'race' meant anything other than a linguistic category; he was far more interested in the significance of 'tradition' as a 'line of descent' in Irish history.[21] Yet he was not entirely free of the 'racialised' thinking common to history writing of the period, either. Where he praises the advancement of the ancient Irish vis-à-vis the rest of Europe, MacNeill refers to them pointedly as 'European white men', and his hostility to the argument that ancient and early medieval Irish society was organised along 'clan' or 'tribal' lines can be interpreted as a wish to dissociate the Irish from the 'primitive' peoples of the world outside Europe with whom they were sometimes associated. As he put it in *Phases of Irish History*:

> 'I have been reproached with avoiding the word "tribe" ... others have used it with the deliberate intent to create the impression that the structure of society in Ireland down to the twelfth century, and in parts of Ireland down to the seventeenth century, finds its modern parallel among the Australian or Central African aborigines.'[22]

This was not merely an academic debating point. In early twentieth-century Europe, not even MacNeill could escape the associations made between a nation's place in the racial hierarchy, and its capacity for ordered national self-government in the present. Irish nationalists, like their counterparts in most other European societies that had yet to achieve national self-determination in the nineteenth and early twentieth centuries, adopted to a significant degree the language and ideas that had been traditionally used against them, to dismiss their political and cultural claims.[23] Or, they elevated into a national mission the overcoming of the negative qualities that had traditionally been ascribed to them by more powerful and dominant neighbours. By as early as the fifth century, MacNeill wrote in *Celtic Ireland*, 'Ireland stands for the natural early development, according to type, of the European white man ... in this ancient Ireland, perhaps more truly than in the Homeric age of Greece, one may look for the European *juventus mundi*.'[24] Indeed, this may have been a direct answer to W.E. Gladstone, who in his 1869 work *Juventus Mundi* had claimed the glorious inheritance of Homeric Greece for nineteenth-century Britain.[25] MacNeill's distaste for the 'tribal' appellation of early medieval Irish history extended not just to unionist writers but, as Byrne notes, also to nationalist writers who had sought to romanticise the 'clan' or 'tribe' in Gaelic Ireland, mixed with a scholarly impatience with what he regarded as an imprecise and modish historiographical idea.[26] In terms of the 'ethnic' vs 'civic' debate on the definition of Irish nationhood, MacNeill was clearly an ethnic nationalist, but not a racial exclusivist in the mould of, for example, D.P. Moran, the polemicist and editor of *The Leader*. MacNeill clearly believed that Ireland was a Gaelic nation, but not that it was impossible to be Irish without also being Gaelic.[27] There was no single primordial root of Irishness, but a synthesis of different elements in which the Gaelic Irish became most dominant and constitutive of the nation's culture.

In a period when European nationalists associated the 'vitality' of a nation (and its racial component) with the unity and strength of sovereign statehood, Irish nationalists were presented with an obvious problem. There was no institutional historical precedent to Irish nation-statehood comparable to the Kingdom of Scotland, the Kingdom of Hungary, the Kingdom of Poland and the Grand Duchy of Lithuania (formally unified as the Polish–Lithuanian Commonwealth in 1569) or the Italian and German 'petty-states'. MacNeill dealt with this by redefining what 'statehood' had meant in the Irish context. Indeed, he rejected as a matter of principle the straightforward association of nationhood with the possession of a sovereign state. Ireland, in contrast to England and the other nations of Europe, had never been conquered by the Roman Empire and, for that reason, the idea that a nation could not exist without a centralised, militarised state was a foreign one to the medieval Irish mind. 'Ancient Ireland,' he wrote in *Celtic Ireland*, again perhaps with Gladstone in mind, 'has a singular place in the history of Europe ... In ancient Ireland alone we find the autobiography of a people who came into history not shaped in the mould of the East, nor forced to accept the law of Imperial Rome.'[28] As argued in both *Celtic Ireland* and *Early Irish Laws and Institutions*, Ireland had a complex indigenous system of government and, more importantly, a legal and institutional system that encompassed the *entire* island, underpinned by a complex social structure with, the argument went, both aristocratic and democratic characteristics, regardless of which dynasties ruled over the many regional kingdoms of medieval Ireland. This all-island unity of laws and institutional frameworks existed in the context of a society in which each region was able to govern itself with autonomy and due regard to local particularities and conditions.[29] This was in contrast to the uniformity imposed by the Roman Empire and maintained by the kingdoms that arose in the territories it had ruled – including England. This sense of medieval Ireland as a place that had, prior to the Norman invasion, possessed a sophisticated political structure, which to some extent was preserved after the invasion, sometimes by the Anglo-Norman lords themselves, a structure that was more than just 'a prologue' to the historical epoch that began with the Norman invasion, was a riposte to arguments that pre-Norman Ireland had existed in an anarchic state. G.H. Orpen was a notable exponent of this view, and much of the argument of *Phases of Irish History* was a challenge to him, and the implication of his work that the Irish (past and present) had been incapable of governing themselves without British rule.[30]

Between this line of argument, and his aversion to associating 'nation' with 'race', we may be tempted to view MacNeill in at least some respects as a 'civic' nationalist. As he put it of pre-medieval Ireland, the country was 'composed of diverse peoples, but made one by their clear affiliation to the land that bore them – the clearest and most complete conception of nationality to be found in all antiquity'. On the other hand, MacNeill was rather sceptical when it came to the 'Anglo-Irish' tradition of political nationalism, believing that the Protestant 'Patriots' of the eighteenth century had been false models for modern nationalists. The state and political institutions could not make a nation, only be reflective of it. MacNeill's view of the medieval Anglo-Normans is instructive: they had, for the most part, and particularly from the fourteenth century onwards, allowed themselves to be assimilated into the culture of Gaelic Ireland, speaking the language, adopting native customs, and refashioning their fiefdoms into territories more akin to the petty kingdoms of the Gaelic Irish than the duchies and earldoms of the English. In doing so, they had (so the argument went) added to the substance of the Irish nation without diluting its cultural distinctiveness. As Alice Stopford Green, a fellow historian who regarded MacNeill as her intellectual mentor, and did much to popularise his work for a wider readership, put it, 'it is evident that the Norman settlers found a civilisation and culture in which they could adapt themselves'.[31] In this regard, and in this regard only, could they be said to have been Irish. The English and Scottish communities who had come to Ireland in the modern era had, on the other hand, done the opposite, making any claims assumed by members of these communities to leadership of the Irish nation in subsequent generations historically vacuous. Early medieval Ireland had not only been regarded by its own inhabitants as a cohesive and distinctive political unit, as opposed to merely a 'geographical expression', but had also been viewed as such in Europe as well. This was demonstrated, MacNeill argued, by the way sovereignty of the island was 'transferred' from its own kings by Pope Adrian IV to Henry II:

> In virtue of the supposed Donation of Constantine ... the Popes claimed temporal dominion over all the islands of the ocean. In exercise of this temporal claim, Adrian conferred the lordship of Ireland on Henry of Anjou. But in virtue of the same supposed right, Adrian had already an immediate feudatory for Ireland in the person of the king of Ireland – Ruaidhri.[32]

Henry II's signing of the Treaty of Windsor in 1175, by which Ruaidrí Ua Conchobair (King of Connacht) became Henry's vassal, but was still at least in formal terms Ireland's premier Gaelic monarch, was further confirmation of Irish sovereignty in the medieval period prior to the Norman invasions.[33] This idea was not invented by MacNeill but acquired new weight through his arguments for a distinctive Irish idea of law and government. Medieval Ireland, long before 1175 and the first Anglo-Norman incursions, had known a much contested but fledgling political system of its own, which was distinctive and national. Even if not a state in a modern sense, it at least contained the germ of one.[34] The Anglo-Normans led by 'Strongbow', and followed by Henry II and his army, had come under the guise of a mission 'to reform the religion and morals of Ireland'.[35] The reality, however, had been the imposition by violence of a system that was alien to long-established political and legal structures of the Irish and by definition illegitimate. The most important and authentic historical point of reference for Irish nationalism was not the medieval Parliament of Ireland, or the 'Kingdom of Ireland' established by the Tudors, or the Catholic Confederation, or 'Grattan's Parliament', but the early medieval Irish political order. This amounted to a rejection of the idea of Ireland not only as an appendage to England, but also as an 'equal' kingdom linked to England by a common crown, a 'co-ruler' of the empire; an idea that had been part of the historical armoury of Repeal and Home Rule politics and was influential within Sinn Féin until 1917, but which conflicted with the cultural and political separatism of MacNeill's nationalism.

The importance of Anglo-Irish nationalism to the brief period of Irish legislative independence in the late eighteenth century had also been much exaggerated, not least because the 'Patriots' could not cease to think of themselves as 'Englishmen', thus 'the solemn treaty of 1782 failed to rise to the necessity of excluding English political interference at all costs ... Grattan's Irish Constitution ... openly tolerated from the beginning the existence of interference from England'.[36] Whatever progress Ireland had made at the end of the eighteenth century was not simply to be credited to the Irish Parliament. Rather, as MacNeill wrote in an essay on the eighteenth-century parliament and Volunteer movement:

> the prosperity that followed legislative independence must be ascribed rather to the native power, the patriotism of the people, than the virtue of the Parliament ... the English government perfectly understood that the strength of the Irish nation consisted in its armed manhood and in the moral force of its patriot democracy, not in its independent Parliament.[37]

Even the revolutionaries of the United Irish movement were partly at fault, by choosing to define nationhood in terms of ideas imported from France, confusing Irish nationality with abstract or universal politics. This confusion, MacNeill argued, had long-lasting consequences, leading to a preoccupation with political autonomy at the expense of the cultural restoration that the Irish nation required for independence to be worthwhile. He had argued in the conclusion of *Phases of Irish History*: 'What stands for the history of Ireland in that dark time is mainly the history of a government which nobody pretends to have been Irish. We need a new history from the fifteenth century onward, written out of the records of the Irish people.'[38] The effect of MacNeill's argument here, whether in outcome or content, is a complete undermining of the 'common sense' of constitutional nationalism embodied by the Home Rule movement: that Ireland's historically rooted aspiration was to be a contented (junior) partner of Britain in the framework of the empire, governed by its own parliament but subordinate to Westminster's and irrevocably subject to the sovereignty of the British crown.

'NATIONALISM ... HAS MANY CONTRIBUTORY CAUSES'[39]

In MacNeill's time, intellectuals all over Europe, historians and otherwise, were preoccupied with establishing the general criteria and characteristics of 'the nation'. There was, however, more to this than the possession of a common history, yet little certainty as to what were (if there were any) the 'essential' characteristics of 'the nation'. 'The discordant interpretations of nationality arise mainly,' he argued in an essay on the early Irish conception of nationality, 'from a failure to perceive that the foundations of the national consciousness and sentiment may vary in different nations'.[40] He discussed 'nationalism-in-general' at length in an unpublished essay written in 1925 titled 'Nationalism in the Future', in which he acknowledged that 'Nationalism, which I take to be the spirit informing a nation, has many contributory causes.' He noted the historical 'modernity' of nationalism as a mass political phenomenon and its recent significance in the decay of imperialism within Europe.[41] The most important elements that constituted a 'nation' were usually racial kinship, language and religion. As we have already seen, he gave the first short shrift. Racial sentiment was a defining characteristic of 'the primitive forms of nationality', and of lesser importance in 'the most progressive forms'.[42] While distinctive language was not necessary to define the existence of a nation, nonetheless it was of major importance, 'the treasure house of the common tradition of glory and national pride ... the jealous guardian of the heroism which breeds a mystical unity in later generations'.[43]

Religion, also, had a conditional role to play: 'a vigorous element of nationality when it is specially associated with a particular nationality and when it is itself distinctive and vigorous'.[44] Although, as Wycherley notes, the Church as institution is barely mentioned in three of his four principal books, *Phases of Irish History*, *Celtic Ireland*, and *Early Irish Laws and Institutions*, the role of Christianity and, more to the point, Catholicism in

MacNeill's conception of the Irish nation can hardly be underestimated. The mission of St Patrick and the conversion of the Irish represented a point of origin in Irish history and of the Irish people as a nation united not only by a culture, institutions and laws, but by a religion and Church that spanned the entire Ireland and stimulated vernacular Irish learning.[45] The historical figure of Patrick represented the unique receptivity of the ancient Irish to religion, the vitality of a long-standing intellectual culture that did not need to be 'imported', and a link between Ireland and Europe. The elevation of historical religious figures into *national* ones, generally by representing them as embodying national authenticity and defiance to foreign cultural norms or political domination, was common to all nationalists in Europe, whether the figure was St Patrick, St George, St Joan of Arc in France, or Martin Luther in Germany.

MacNeill's argument that the papacy recognised the sovereignty of Ireland as a single unit in transferring it to Henry II has been noted above. In *Phases of Irish History* he draws attention to the linkage between Brian Boru's campaign to establish a single and undisputed High Kingship encompassing the entire island and his elevation of Armagh to primacy of the Irish Church.[46] Elsewhere, disputing the argument that the decay of the Irish Church had justified the Anglo-Norman intervention, he draws attention to the role of Irish churchmen and synods prior to the invasion in reform and establishing structures to bring the Irish Church into line with European counterparts.[47] In the final chapter, he jabs at the moralising nature of the claim that the invasion was necessary to bring Christian civilisation to Ireland: 'They could even use the Church as an instrument of the State, and Mr Orpen boasts that, whereas the Irish bishop of Dublin, Lorcán Ó Tuathail, was only a saint, the English bishops who succeeded him were statesmen.'[48]

Finally, enmity with other national communities inevitably forged nationhood, as the Irish case well demonstrated. In the case of Irish nationalism, in MacNeill's view the primary factor was not one of these or even a combination of them, but instead 'historical sentiment', not just a collective memory of injustice – in this regard he likened Irish nationalism to Polish nationalism – but a particular narrative of Irish history.[49] Ultimately, a nation was created by an act of collective self-will, and defined by whatever cultural constituents were strongest in effect at any given time when this self-will was most keenly felt. It was in this respect that nationalism possessed a 'spiritual' character. MacNeill argued in a speech given in the United States in 1930 that:

> Nationality is a popular consciousness and sentiment of unity and community in a people, peculiar to that people and exclusive of other peoples, and not merely theoretical or traditional but operative as a bond of unity ... When a people possesses a form of civilisation which is, for it, traditional and distinctive, and when it is conscious of this possession, such a people is a nation, whether it be a state or no state, or an aggregate of states or only a portion of a state.[50]

Nations were natural and deeply rooted in history but were also changeable over time. MacNeill was an orthodox European in his view of the causes of nationalism, and how it tended to develop. He criticised 'cosmopolitanism' as having no vitality; but was fully convinced that to be nationalist was not to be isolationist or xenophobic.[51] His concern was with the permeability of Ireland's cultural borders and the possibility of cultural decline.[52] As he put it in *Early Irish Laws and Institutions*: 'Neither Europe nor the world suffers any detriment from the diversity of national civilisations.'[53] The idea of one's own nation bearing unique qualities that could enrich all of human civilisation was a common conceit among nationalists of the period. Ireland, MacNeill had argued in *Phases of Irish History*, had been fulfilling its 'international' duty since the earlies times:

> With all the singularity of its insular character, it maintained the fullest intercourse with other countries, and its written mind exhibits no trace of those international prejudices and hatreds which, for whatever ends stimulated, are the disgrace of our modern civilisation ... You will not find anywhere in Europe during that age any approach towards the definite and concrete sense of nationality – of country and people in one – which is the common expression of the Irish mind in that age.[54]

'THE ANGLO-SAXON ELEMENT IN ULSTER IS OF MICROSCOPIC PROPORTION ...'[55]

Ulster figured largely in MacNeill's historical and nationalist thinking and was, as for many others (up to and including the present day), the greatest challenge to his conception of nationalism. In the early 1920s MacNeill was closely involved in the Free State government's campaign against partition and for an Irish border that would favour the Free State and make Northern Ireland unviable in the long term. He participated in the Boundary

Commission that was established to examine the border with Northern
Ireland, though it was boycotted by the Belfast government.[56] As part of
this campaign the Free State government's North Eastern Boundary Bureau
published the *Handbook of the Ulster Question* (1923), containing a chapter
on the history of Ulster co-authored by MacNeill and J.W. Good. None of
the *Handbook*'s individual authors are named; however, by comparing the
section's content with unpublished notes, proofs, and typescript copies of
the *Handbook* held in the MacNeill papers, and with MacNeill's historical
overview in the *Saorstát Éireann Official Handbook*, we can conclude that
at the very least he closely oversaw its writing, editing and publication.
The argument here, while taking care to dismiss the importance of racial
categorisations, is nonetheless a good specimen of early twentieth-century
European ethnic nationalism, in its denial of the regional minority's right
of collective autonomy, the straightforward identification of national
territory with the ethnic nation, and, for example in his assertion that
the 'Anglo-Saxon element in Ulster is of microscopic proportion', the
'naturalness' of this connection. Religious difference was noted to be of
more importance than 'difference of race' but even here its true significance
was simply as something to be exploited 'by persons and parties whose
interests demanded the frustration of the forces continuously making
for national unity'.[57] The settlers of the seventeenth-century Plantation,
MacNeill argued, had been almost entirely Scottish, and therefore Gaelic.
With this conceit, the 'racial' continuity of Ulster's history could be argued
as unbroken since the distant Irish past. Ulster Protestants were criticised
for assuming that Ulster's history began with the Plantation – 'to rule
twentieth-century issues by seventeenth-century precedents is to block the
road to any hope of progress'[58] – even as MacNeill argued that the history of
Ulster going back to its ancient period was of greater significance. 'The best
defence of the planters, if not the Plantation,' the author of the *Handbook*
added for good measure, 'is that penned by John Mitchel, a man of their
blood, in the preface to his *Life of Aodh O'Neill*.'[59] The author argued for a
continuous 'movement towards unity' that 'was part of a process which had
been at work in Ireland since the day when the Norman invaders became
"more Irish than the Irish"', a process only impeded by English and British
misrule.[60] In this text, there is no sign of that intellectual uncertainty that
MacNeill displayed about the 'reality' or character of nationalism in other
texts. Here, the writer is clear about the traits that *definitely* constitute a
nation:

> a nation is a living organism ... shaped first by geographical conditions, then by history, then by a sense of common interests and purposes ... Ireland as a whole is a nation, and North-East Ulster is merely a small portion of Ireland which for the moment refuses to assent to the political implications of that nationhood.[61]

Despite some eye-catching anticipations of the modern frustration with attempting to categorise forms of nation and nationalism, and admissions of the modernity of the nation as 'a comparatively recent synthesis in which differences of race, religion, character and ideals are resolved', MacNeill, like most other nationalists of his time, simply could not admit the legitimacy of Ulster unionist objections to Irish nationalism.[62] He did not go as far, however, as D.P. Moran, who in summing up his view of the Ulster unionists stated: 'We believe that most of these people are not Irish: they are in relation to Ireland as foreign as born Englishmen.'[63]

It is worthwhile to compare texts like the *Handbook of the Ulster Question* with contemporaneous texts written by nationalists elsewhere in Europe who were faced with the problem of contested or disputed territories. In 1918 the German historian Friedrich Meinecke – who would go on to support, albeit reluctantly, the Weimar Republic, unlike most of his colleagues – wrote a brief pamphlet titled *Geschichte der links-rheinischen Gebietsfragen* protesting the cession of the region of Alsace-Lorraine, under the terms of the Treaty of Versailles, from Germany to France (Germany had annexed the same territory from France in 1871). Meinecke was uncompromising:

> When Germany incorporated Elsaß and a part of Lothringen in 1871 ... she was firmly convinced that it was her sacred duty to win back two peoples originally and essentially of German race, peoples which were a part of the old Empire and which had been torn from it by various historical misfortunes.[64]

French historical claims to German territory were 'dubious and uncertain' if not 'purely arbitrary', designed only 'to limit and to annul the consequential application of the free right of self-determination'.[65] Alsace-Lorraine had been, Meinecke maintained, since the year 1500 – if not earlier – one of the strongest bastions of German culture. The only reason the territory had ever been a part of France was because of the belligerent and unjustified expansion of French rulers. Meinecke described the period of Alsace-

Lorraine's incorporation in the French state as one of 'great misfortune' for 'the German Elsassian', who had been 'forced further and, further away, from a vital connection with the great community of German civilisation'. He confidently asserted that the 'New Germany' would 'have nothing in common with the spirit of national intolerance', while making clear that 'neither can she endure to see children of her own blood torn from her side'. He concluded:

> *an irreparable wrong was committed against German Elsaß and Lothringen when they were forced under the dominion of a foreign nation and alienated from the great body of German civilisation* [Meinecke's emphasis]. This wrong must not be committed again.[66]

While the names of contested territories across Europe in the early 1920s may have differed, the nationalist discourse had a basic blueprint in a range of different societies, centring on the themes of unrepaired historical injustice, the historical inviolability of the national territory, and a 'writing out' of regional affiliations and loyalties as illegitimate and illusory.[67] MacNeill and Meinecke had little in common besides being historians of the same generation whose work hinged on the question of the relationship between nation and state. Nevertheless it is valuable to compare MacNeill's distinction between the two with Meinecke's distinction of *Kulturnation* and *Staatsnation* in his most prominent work, *Weltbürgertum und Nationalstaat* (*Cosmopolitanism and the National State*, 1908). In very broad terms, a *Kulturnation* was defined as a community whose members perceived themselves as united through common culture, language, religions and history; a *Staatsnation* was the political and constitutional state that could encompass one *Kulturnation*, or more than one. Meinecke agreed that nations could not be defined objectively; they were by nature indeterminate, and could be constituted out of several factors of relative importance. An ethnic core 'based on blood relationship' was, however, in Meinecke's opinion, a necessity: 'Only on this basis can a rich and unique intellectual community and a more or less clear consciousness of that community develop, and it is this factor that elevates a union of tribes into a nation and makes it capable of assimilating foreign tribes and elements.'[68] Meinecke distinguished between 'nations that are primarily based on some jointly experienced cultural heritage and nations that are primarily based on the unifying force of a common political history and constitution'.[69] The *Staatsnation*, however, tended to act as a coalescing force for its constituent culture: 'the cases are more frequent in which political communities and political influences have encouraged, if not indeed caused, the growth of a standard language and common literature'.[70] Yet it was of course the case, and here Meinecke cited Switzerland and his native Germany, that the boundaries of *Kulturnation* and *Staatsnation* were seldom one and the same. MacNeill could have at least partially agreed, for all his misgivings about the modern idea of state power, that:

> The lofty insight that the state is an ideal supra-individual personality – this insight that sustains and justifies all our thought and concern about the state – could only come to life when the political feelings and energies of individual citizens permeated the state and transformed it into a national state.[71]

Meinecke believed that modern nations, whether *Kulturnation* or *Staatsnation*, were inherently changeable and unstable because:

> 'As the nation becomes stronger, all the spheres of life within the nation also become stronger. Thus, intellectual, political, and social antipathies entrench themselves more deeply within the nation, and new ones emerge, for all the factions benefit from the vital individual forces stirring at the heart of the nation.'[72]

This is, however, less an expression of existential concern than an appeal for liberal accommodation between these different strands, under one national rubric.[73] It was essential for authentic nationhood that the community be permitted to resolve these differences without the overbearing influence of foreign models and conceptions, and states that were able to achieve this were superior from a national point of view:

> the genuine national state emerges like a unique flower from the particular soil of a nation, and this soil is capable of producing, besides this one unique state, many other political structures of an equally strong and vivid character. This state is not and does not become national through the will of the people or of those who govern it but through ... the quiet workings of the national spirit.[74]

In this fashion Meinecke distinguished between 'national states in the political sense and national states in the national-cultural sense', i.e. states in which the national culture was in large measure a product of centuries of continuous statehood, like England and France, and states in which the national culture (so the claim went) had shaped the form statehood took, such as Germany, Italy and (a generation later) Ireland. Though MacNeill and Meinecke shared the idea that it was necessary to distinguish between the nation as primarily a cultural entity and the state as a political structure that controlled a nation (or nations), they were, of course, approaching the problem from different contexts. Meinecke needed to account for the development of the post-1871 *Kaiserreich* out of a multiplicity of smaller states that were nonetheless governed by German (or at any rate German-speaking) rulers, while MacNeill's conception was shaped by the reality of centuries of rule over Ireland by English and later British monarchs and a need to refute arguments that the Irish had been too primitive and anarchic to govern themselves (as in the debate with Orpen mentioned above). In these two outwardly significant different countries, Ireland and Germany, nationalist intellectuals were preoccupied by a centuries-old disconnect between the 'cultural' nation and the political and constitutional organisation of the nation state that was not fully resolved by the achievement of statehood, whether in 1871 or 1922. Rupture, rather than continuity, had been one of the defining characteristics of both Irish and German history, and had structured in a fundamental way the modern conceptualisations of the national(ist) historical narrative. In a sense, MacNeill's argument about the relationship between 'nation' and 'state' was one of 'heads I win, tails you lose': the absence of a medieval Irish centralised state did not reflect negatively on the Irish because such a system was foreign to them; yet medieval Ireland prior to the Norman invasion possessed political institutions that could have formed the nucleus of a sovereign medieval Irish state comparable to that of England, Scotland or France, and one reflecting the innate genius of the Irish mind, if only these institutions had been able to develop without unwanted foreign influences imported by force. National essentialism, ultimately, was always the final argument.

CONCLUSION

It is a difficult challenge to measure how intellectual influences within and between societies work, and even to judge the extent of MacNeill's influence as a 'theorist' among nationalists in Ireland and elsewhere during his life. Even if we were to exhaust all the relevant archives, it would not leave us with a certain picture.[75] He personally influenced Patrick Pearse, as well as Alice Stopford Green, one of the most prominent popular national(ist) historians of the first quarter of the twentieth century,[76] and probably Éamon de Valera also.[77] MacNeill, and his idea of the decentralised and democratic character of the medieval Irish polity,[78] was directly quoted in the popular history *The Story of the Irish Race*, written by Seamus MacManus.[79] This idea that an authentically 'Gaelic' polity could be a decentralised or federal state had some currency among the more theoretically minded revolutionary writers, such as Aodh de Blácam in his *What Sinn Féin Stands For* and *Towards the Republic: A study of New Ireland's social and political aims*.[80] We can also consider the conceptions of nationalism expressed by supporters of the Irish Free State at its establishment. The speeches and articles of Michael Collins, for example, often feature a frustration with what was perceived as the republicans' arcane obsession with abstract formulae of sovereignty, which he took to be at the expense of a truly nationalist focus on how an authentic Gaelic Irish state was to be restored (*restored*, not created anew). In Collins' words, 'Our ideal of nationality was distorted in hair-splitting over the meaning of "sovereignty" and other foreign words, under advice from minds dominated by English ideas of nationality',[81] such that those minds forgot or could not understand that 'the positive work of building a Gaelic Ireland in the vacuum left has now to be undertaken'.[82] MacNeill was, in the end, perhaps the closest thing the early Free State had to an 'official historian'; serving as Minister for Education, writing a brief historical survey for the *Saorstát Éireann Official Handbook*, making a significant contribution as historian to the *Handbook of the Ulster Question*, and serving as a founding member and first chairman of the Irish Manuscripts Commission (established in 1928).

It is a commonplace idea that the Irish revolution produced little in the way of philosophy or 'great thinkers'.[83] The argument underlying this chapter is that 'history' played the role of political philosophy during the period from around 1890 to 1930 and during the Irish revolution. In this respect – and without considering the more 'active' roles he played within the Gaelic League, the Irish Volunteers, the revolutionary government, and the first Free State government – MacNeill did play a part as one of the foremost philosophers of what Foster has called 'the revolutionary generation'.[84] First, he made a significant contribution to the professionalisation of the study of early medieval Irish history. Second, in establishing an historically grounded distinction between 'nation' and 'state' he helped facilitate a nationalist turn away from the politics of the Home Rule movement without sacrificing the demand for independence. Third, through his work as historian, MacNeill conferred an authoritative, historically grounded status on an ethnic but not racially exclusivist form of nationalism: he fully accepted that to be 'Irish' was to be the inheritor of different 'lines of descent' that had mixed and integrated through history. Though he may have regarded early medieval Ireland as the wellspring of the country's nationality, he understood that there was no point in trying to romanticise the era excessively.[85] Fourth, as an historian he played a prominent role in the Free State's anti-partition campaign up until the 'failure' of the Boundary Commission's efforts to revise the border with Northern Ireland, through his contributions to the *Handbook of the Ulster Question*.

MacNeill presented a distinctively Irish contribution to a broader European debate in the late nineteenth and early twentieth centuries on the relationship between national culture and political sovereignty and the criteria and conditions for how 'nationalism-in-general' could be defined and categorised according to its manifestations in different societies. While some nationalists had romanticised Ireland's 'apartness' as a 'little world unto itself', MacNeill never doubted that Ireland had always been an essentially European country, with a form of nationalism similar and comparable to the nationalisms of other European societies.[86] A focus among historians on the transnational dimension of the Irish revolution, as it continues to develop, will benefit from a renewed and closer attention on how MacNeill conceptualised nationalism and examined its cultural and intellectual constituents, such as ideas on race, ethnicity, religion, and historical forms of government. This will allow historians to fill in one of the more conspicuous gaps in modern Irish historical research: the situating of the history of Irish nationalism, revolution and state-building more analytically within a European panorama.

Eoin MacNeill and the Irish Boundary Commission

TED HALLETT

INTRODUCTION

This chapter examines Eoin MacNeill's role as a member of the Irish Boundary Commission. The focus is on the process of drawing up the Commission's Award and MacNeill's part in it. To provide context, the background to the establishment of the Commission will first be outlined.

British Prime Minister David Lloyd George's proposal for a boundary commission to determine the future border between the two parts of Ireland established by the Government of Ireland Act, 1920 emerged during the Anglo-Irish treaty negotiations when Sir James Craig's Northern Ireland government refused to come under the jurisdiction of an all-Ireland parliament. On Lloyd George's instruction, Thomas Jones, deputy secretary to the cabinet, first put the idea of a boundary commission to Arthur Griffith, leader of the Irish delegation, on 9 November 1921.[1] Griffith told Éamon de Valera that the Commission would 'delimit the six-county area to give us the districts in which we are a majority'.[2] The proposal was included in an outline treaty on 16 November providing that the Commission would determine the boundary 'in accordance with the wishes of the inhabitants'.[3] On 30 November 1921, the Irish delegation were given a formal treaty text, providing for a three-man commission with a chairman nominated by the British government and one commissioner each appointed by the Irish Free State and Northern Ireland governments. There was one significant change: the wishes of the inhabitants were qualified by 'so far as may be compatible with economic and geographic conditions'.[4] The Irish did not challenge the amendment,[5] which was thus included in Article 12 of the treaty.[6] It did not affect Irish expectations of substantial transfers to the Free State, as Michael Collins made clear to Lloyd George on 5 December 1921.[7] Lloyd George did not contradict him at the time, but his subsequent statements about the likely outcome were ambiguous. In the Commons on 14 December 1921, he implied that it would not be in the interests of Northern Ireland's stability to keep Tyrone and Fermanagh against the wishes of their inhabitants,[8] but later in the debate he denied promising the Irish they would get the whole of both counties.[9] There was no ambiguity on the Conservative benches, where the view became firmly established that only adjustments to the border were intended. There was thus the potential for sharply diverging British and Irish expectations of the Boundary Commission outcome.[10]

DELAY IN ESTABLISHING THE COMMISSION

Northern Ireland opted out of the Free State in December 1922, but the Commission was not established until nearly two years later. The Irish Civil War, political instability at Westminster,[11] and the Northern Ireland government's refusal to appoint a commissioner all contributed to the delay. On 20 July 1923, W.T. Cosgrave, president of the Free State Executive Council, requested the British government to set up the Commission and nominated Eoin MacNeill as the Irish member.[12] Cosgrave also outlined his expectations from the Commission, listing Tyrone, Fermanagh and parts of Armagh and Down as areas where 'the majority desire union with the rest of Ireland'. The British government prevaricated by proposing a conference of the three governments to negotiate a border settlement. This met in London on 1–2 February and 24 April 1924, but when no agreement proved possible, Cosgrave renewed his request. There was further delay when the British government's nominee for chairman, Robert Borden, a former Canadian prime minister, withdrew when the Northern Ireland government declined to nominate a commissioner, prompting the British government to seek a ruling from the Judicial Committee of the Privy Council on the implications this raised for establishing the Commission.[13]

On 4 June, the British appointed a new chairman, Richard Feetham, a South African judge recommended by Lionel Curtis.[14] Paul Murray and Kevin Matthews suggest he was selected as unlikely to cause the British difficulty over Article 12,[15] citing Curtis' letter to Churchill of 19 August, which asserted that Feetham could be relied on to reject the Free State's 'preposterous and extravagant claims'.[16] Geoffrey Hand and Nicholas Mansergh, on the other hand, conclude that there is no evidence that Feetham was susceptible to British influence or that he 'deliberately weighted the scales against the Free State'.[17]

On 25 June 1924, the Judicial Committee was asked to rule whether the British government could appoint a commissioner to represent

Northern Ireland and, at Feetham's request, whether the Commission, once established, could proceed by majority. The ruling came on 31 July 1924: legislation in the London and Dublin parliaments was required to empower the British government to appoint a commissioner for Northern Ireland and the Commission, when appointed, could proceed by majority.[18] The legislation was enacted in Britain on 9 October and in the Free State on 25 October. The British government then appointed Joseph R. Fisher as the Northern Ireland Commissioner.[19] Fisher was a Belfast barrister and member of the Ulster Unionist Council, with close links to leading party members. He had edited the unionist *Northern Whig* newspaper from 1899 to 1913.

THE BOUNDARY COMMISSION BEGINS WORK

The Commission was formally established by announcement in the *London Gazette* on 31 October 1924. At their first meeting on 6 November 1924, the commissioners agreed a confidentiality code: 'no Commissioner would consult any of the Governments as to the work of the Commission or make any statement as to such work to any Government or individual without first consulting his colleagues'.[20] Feetham and MacNeill scrupulously adhered to this. Fisher did not. He met regularly with David Reid, leader of the Ulster Unionists at Westminster, keeping him informed of the Commission's progress. Reid passed this information to Craig in a series of letters between July and November 1925.[21] Fisher himself wrote to Robert Lynn, editor of the *Northern Whig*, in November and December revealing details of the Commission's work.[22] MacNeill, in contrast, kept his Executive Council colleagues largely in the dark.[23]

The commissioners appointed two key members of staff to support them: Francis Bourdillon, as secretary, and Major R.A. Boger, as 'chief technical assistant'. Both had experience of boundary delimitation from the German–Polish Commissions of 1920–3.[24] Appointing an 'assistant secretary' from the Free State was discussed, with MacNeill being invited 'to consider the question and bring forward a definite suggestion at the next meeting'.[25] On 17 November, the Executive Council nominated J.J. Hearne to be 'joint secretary'.[26] At the next Commission meeting on 28 November, however, there appears to have been a disagreement. The commissioners discussed 'whether one or two assistant Secretaries, if any, should be appointed', in the light of which, 'Dr MacNeill said he would not proceed with his nomination until the matter had been further considered'.[27] MacNeill informed the Executive Council on 4 December that Feetham 'had objected to the appointment of an Irish representative on the staff' and read out a letter of protest, which he proposed to send Feetham, after clearing it with the Attorney General.[28] What happened thereafter is a mystery. No letter appears to have been sent to Feetham, no further discussion of the subject is recorded and Hearne was not appointed,[29] so it appears MacNeill did not pursue the matter.

'PRINCIPLES OF INTERPRETATION'

The commissioners began work without agreeing an interpretation of Article 12.[30] Feetham soon began to reveal his own thinking, however. At the first Commission meeting, it was decided to invite the three governments to submit statements or appear before it.[31] Only the Free State government took up the invitation.[32] At the hearing, the Irish representatives, Attorney General John O'Byrne and his deputy, Serjeant Henry Hanna,[33] expounded at length the argument that the Commission had no power to transfer territory to Northern Ireland. Feetham appeared sceptical, suggesting that the wording of Article 12 did not support this contention. He also argued that the transfers should not be so extensive as to undermine Northern Ireland's continued existence. The Irish pressed for plebiscites to determine the wishes of the inhabitants, but Feetham said he had no mandate for this. MacNeill was largely silent and did not intervene to support the Free State arguments. Hand assesses O'Byrne's performance as 'not impressive' and suggests that Hanna's arguments were 'more tellingly put'.[34]

After touring the border,[35] the Commission began collecting evidence, inviting written submissions and holding sittings in Northern Ireland between March and July 1925.[36] While they heard nothing from MacNeill, the Executive Council received reports from E.M. Stephens, who attended the sittings. These raised further concerns about Feetham's views, notably his suggestion that Carlingford Lough was 'a good natural boundary'[37] and that transferring Derry city to the Free State would require 'a serious surgical operation'.[38] Disturbed, in particular, by a submission from the Belfast Water Commissioners arguing that south Down should remain in Northern Ireland,[39] the Free State government requested a further hearing, held on 25 August.[40] O'Byrne was supported by Patrick Lynch.[41] As before, Feetham took the lead and, again, MacNeill was largely silent. After contesting the

Belfast Water Commissioners' submission,[42] O'Byrne and Lynch restated their case against transfers to Northern Ireland, but Feetham cut them short saying he was familiar with the Free State position.[43] The Free State performance again seems to have been unimpressive, prompting Cosgrave to tell Chief Justice Hugh Kennedy[44] that, on transfers to Northern Ireland, 'the Attorney General was not at his best and Lynch was weak, very weak'.[45] Cosgrave wanted a more forceful statement of the Free State case and invited Kennedy to assist MacNeill who 'would be available at any time you are in a position to see him'.[46]

FEETHAM'S MEMORANDUM

Feetham finally clarified matters of interpretation on 11 September 1925, when he gave his colleagues a memorandum setting out his views. MacNeill subsequently told the Executive Council that Feetham 'did not think it needed to be replied to formally. It was simply drawn up to show the state of his mind on the subject.'[47] This is confirmed in a preface to the memorandum in the Commission's report,[48] recording that Feetham gave it to his colleagues on 11 September 1925, that it 'formed the subject of private discussion with each of them', but that 'it was not treated as a document formally before the Commission'.[49] Feetham's key points were: the existing boundary should hold good where there was no sufficient reason for altering it; the Commission could shift the boundary in either direction; the changes should not be so extensive as to destroy Northern Ireland's identity; the economic and geographic conditions of an area should be considered in relation to adjoining areas; the wishes of the inhabitants were 'the primary but not the paramount consideration' and must be overruled if incompatible with economic or geographic conditions; the Commission was not empowered to hold plebiscites, so the wishes of the inhabitants should be inferred from the 1911 Census.

In response, MacNeill asked for two matters to be made known if the memorandum were published: that Feetham had asked his colleagues to 'refrain from furnishing written comments and that the subject should be dealt with by verbal discussion'; and that MacNeill had given his colleagues 'the opinion of a high legal authority' that the Commission had no power to transfer territory to Northern Ireland.[50] The first was presumably to enable MacNeill to justify not presenting a formal challenge to Feetham's memorandum. The second presumably refers to Kennedy's paper,[51] though it is clear from a letter MacNeill sent to Cosgrave on 10 October 1925 that he was not happy with it and felt he 'could not use it in its present form, as it contests and impugns a view found in the Chairman's questions and does so in the form of direct criticism of the Chairman's view'. He told Cosgrave, 'I must act on my own judgement and use only so much of the document as I consider proper for the purpose.' While this seems unduly deferential to Feetham, MacNeill explained that, 'nothing is to be gained by antagonising him on the personal ground, but a great deal may be gained by sturdy impersonal argument'.[52] There is no record of MacNeill's private discussion with Feetham, but he subsequently told the Executive Council that he had stated his objections to the memorandum in detail, summarising these in 'outspoken marginal notes' on his copy.[53] He also prepared a summary of Kennedy's arguments against transfers to the North, omitting the criticisms of Feetham.[54] This included the assertion that, 'to read into Article 12 a provision for transferring any part of the 26 Counties to Northern Ireland is to read into it something which is not there, and is not there for the very good reason that no such question arose before signature of the Treaty'. He later informed the Dáil of his points of disagreement and it is reasonable to assume that he put these to Feetham but, without a record, we cannot be sure. We can be sure, however, that none of MacNeill's 'sturdy impersonal arguments' produced any change in Feetham's position.

It is difficult to understand why MacNeill accepted Feetham's approach and did not insist on formal discussion of the memorandum, and he was later to admit that he was at fault in not demanding, 'at the earliest convenient stage, a discussion of the general principles of interpretation and a decision upon those principles'.[55] A possible explanation occurs in his letter to Cosgrave: 'I recognised from the beginning the commanding position of the Chairman. Nothing would weaken it except the improbable event of the other two Commissioners agreeing to differ from him.'[56] Since he knew Fisher would agree with Feetham, he may have concluded that it was futile to pursue the argument, but the consequence was that the opportunity to mount a formal challenge to Feetham's interpretation was missed.

DRAWING UP THE AWARD

After the sittings in Northern Ireland concluded on 2 July, there was a lengthy gap in Commission meetings while the evidence was collated. MacNeill left no record of his thinking at this time, but we have a good idea of Fisher's from Reid's correspondence with Craig. On 7 July 1925, he reported that Fisher found it difficult to gauge the views of his colleagues, which 'seem to vary from time to time', but he was 'certain that the extreme claims are out of court. There will be no interference with Counties.' In light of that, Fisher thought 'it would be possible to arrive at a line which might be accepted [by the Northern Ireland government] apart from Newry. Newry appears to be the whole crux of the situation.'[57] Thus, even before the collation of the evidence, Fisher felt confident that the 'extreme' nationalist demands had been ruled out and that the only major concern for Northern Ireland was Newry.[58] Reid reported again on 15 July: 'Fisher still fears for Newry, as there is no question that the balance of population is against us.' On the other hand, he was confident that 'the East Donegal case [for transfer to Northern Ireland] is very strong'.[59]

On 25 August, the commissioners received a set of documents based on the collated evidence. The most significant were Boger's 'schemes' for different sections of the border,[60] setting out alternative lines providing for different magnitudes of transfer, examining the economic and geographic implications of each line and the proposed numbers of Catholics and non-Catholics transferred.[61] They provided for transfers in both directions and were consistent with Feetham's interpretation of the Commission's remit as subsequently set out in his memorandum.[62] An example illustrating this comes from Section A, regarding Londonderry and Strabane: 'In all the solutions at present under consideration, they remain in Northern Ireland.' It should thus have been clear to MacNeill that an Award based on Boger's schemes would not meet Free State expectations, but there is nothing to indicate that he pressed for more extensive transfers. This may have been due to a failure to absorb the implications of Boger's schemes, or perhaps he had already conceded that more extensive transfers had been ruled out, as Fisher's confident assertion suggests. Boger's schemes were supplemented by Bourdillon's memoranda, summarising the evidence for and against transfer of specific locations.[63] The commissioners thus had a mass of information to assimilate,[64] and MacNeill was clearly at some disadvantage, as his role as Minister for Education prevented him giving full attention to the task.[65] We do not know how thoroughly he had studied the papers before the commissioners began drawing up the Award, but he subsequently indicated his difficulties in his Dáil statement.[66]

On 14–16 September 1925, the commissioners 'deliberated on Boger's schemes'.[67] The minutes do not record the specific points discussed, but can be supplemented by Reid's letter to Craig of 16 September: 'the Free

State contentions as regards the boundary clauses of the Treaty have been definitely turned down and it is now a question of alterations of frontier'.[68] Despite this, Reid warned, 'it is by no means plain sailing' regarding the details of the Award. Craig's reply revealed continuing concern about Newry, as he was meeting leader writers 'from the various important papers and coaching them, especially about the Newry area'.[69] Reid reported again on 21 September: 'while nothing is yet drafted, there has been real consideration of points in detail. On the whole the position is more satisfactory than our friend [Fisher] hoped for at one time, and, so far, our own County [Down] appears safe, which was unexpected.'[70] Craig found this letter 'good reading'.[71]

The commissioners 'continued their deliberations' on 13–16 October. The minutes again contain no details,[72] but Reid reported on 16 October:

> The Commission have begun the discussion of what alterations are to be made. They have begun at the Derry end and so far our friend is satisfied with what has been done. There is no question as to the safety of Derry itself. As regards Donegal, the line adopted is what we were reasonably entitled to. The Tyrone salient will go, but the Florence Court area in Fermanagh is safe. MacNeill, since his long stay in Dublin, is disposed to reopen questions, but so far without effect. I hope the Chairman will remain firm on Newry, but as soon as I hear further I will write again.[73]

THE AWARD IS DECIDED

The commissioners decided the broad terms of the Award on 17 October 1925. The minutes record that Bourdillon 'submitted instructions to the Chief Technical Assistant embodying the result of the Commission's deliberations on 14–16 October'. Boger was asked 'to draft a full description of the line, which has in its general features been approved by the Commission'. The minutes then describe the line, beginning at Lough Foyle and ending at Carlingford Lough, listing the areas and the numbers of Catholics and non-Catholics transferred.[74]

It is necessary to consider the extent of MacNeill's agreement to the new line. As the minutes contain no details of the discussions, we do not know what reservations he may have expressed. Hand (1969) suggests Feetham and Fisher had not fully understood MacNeill's misgivings and assumed they were more unanimous than was the case,[75] but Hand (1973), while noting that 'he seems to have argued somewhat', concludes that 'there can be no doubt that Feetham and Fisher thought, from 17 October, that they had MacNeill's consent'.[76] While MacNeill was later to dispute their claims that the Award had been unanimous, it seems clear that, whatever his doubts, he did acquiesce, as no dissent is recorded.[77] After the decision, the commissioners adjourned briefly and then reconvened to confirm the minutes.[78] Here was a further opportunity for MacNeill to register dissent but, again, he did not do so.[79]

Fisher was quick to inform Reid, who reported to Craig on 18 October:

> The Commission has finished its labours so far as questions of determination go. I have permission to tell you the general result, but our friend is anxious that no hint should get into the press so please regard this as for yourself. Newry and the whole of Co. Down is safe. Derry gets an addition from Donegal on the west side of the Foyle. We get control of the flood gates on the Erne and we get Pettigo. We keep all of Fermanagh which drains into the Erne but lose parts on the west and on the south. We lose south Armagh, but Keady remains with us. We lose no town of any importance. I hope it will represent a line which can be accepted.[80]

On the same day, Fisher wrote a euphoric letter to Carson:

> Although the veil of secrecy is still close (as far as the newspapers are concerned) there is no harm in letting you know confidentially that I am well satisfied with the result which will not lift a stone or tile of your enduring work for Ulster. It will remain a solid and close-knit unit with five counties intact and the sixth somewhat trimmed on the outer edge. It will control the gates to its own waters at Belleek and Newry and the Derry navigation to the open sea. No centre of even secondary importance goes over, and with Derry, Strabane, Enniskillen, Newtown Butler, Keady and Newry in safe keeping, your handiwork will survive. If anybody had suggested twelve months ago that we could have kept so much I would have laughed at him, and I must add that the Chairman and John MacNeill have been throughout models of fair play and friendly courtesy.[81]

The two letters are significant, both in showing that leading unionists knew the broad terms of the Award the day after it was adopted and in containing no indication of any dissent from MacNeill.

On 4 November the commissioners agreed some minor changes suggested by Boger to the 17 October line.[82] On 5 November, a draft of the terms of the Commission's Award was provisionally approved and the chairman undertook to prepare a final version.[83] The meetings on 4 and 5 November thus confirmed the 17 October line with minor adjustments, but no changes of substance. The minutes also record that 'draft rules of interpretation intended for inclusion with the description of the boundary were provisionally agreed'. Once again, there was no dissent from MacNeill. The meeting concluded that letters be sent to the British and Irish governments, stating that it was desirable to confer with them regarding delivery and publication of the Award, proposing 19 November as a suitable date.[84] The commissioners agreed to meet again on 17 November to prepare for the meeting with the governments.

THE MORNING POST 'FORECAST'

The Commission's plans were thrown into disarray, however, when a 'forecast' of the Award appeared in the *Morning Post* on 7 November 1925.[85] Under headlines bound to cause alarm in the Free State,[86] the article gave a broadly accurate description of the new border, though the accompanying map somewhat understated the transfers to the Free State.[87] It has generally been assumed that Fisher was the source, but this has never been confirmed.[88] Two letters written on the day the story appeared betray no sign of guilt. Reid reported to Craig what Fisher had said about the leak,[89] and Fisher himself commented on it to Robert Lynn, without any suggestion that he was the source.[90] Fisher advised Lynn how to present the Award to Northern Ireland opinion: 'If I had anything to do with the [Northern] *Whig* or with Ulster politics, I would accept the settlement as firmly establishing and safeguarding "Carson's Ulster". (This is Carson's own view.)'[91] Fisher's problem was, however, that because Craig's public position on the border was 'not an inch',[92] it would be difficult for him to claim credit for the Award. That he felt credit was due was clear from his next letter to Lynn of 11 November:

> 'The Commission is as good as over, and Ulster comes well out of it. We have got all that is essential and nobody [on the Unionist side] can really quarrel with the result. I fought my best for the North; but I will say that my two colleagues were perfectly loyal and straightforward

and that Ulster had fair play throughout. In another two or three weeks the result will be declared and I am prepared to stand or fall by it, knowing that I have done a good year's work for Ulster.'[93]

MacNeill, in contrast, was in no position to make a similar claim for his year's work for the Free State.

CRISIS IN THE FREE STATE

The *Morning Post*'s 'forecast' provoked a crisis in the Free State, as it revealed the limited scale of the transfers and that there would be some to the North.[94] This must have been an anxious time for MacNeill, as he would have been conscious that he would have to explain to the Executive Council how this had come about and why he had given them no warning. He had some time to reflect, however, as the *Morning Post* article implied that the Award was not final and said nothing about the views of the individual commissioners.[95]

As the crisis developed, Cosgrave concluded that he must prevent implementation of what was, for the Free State, a highly unsatisfactory Award, but the evidence is sparse as to when he reached this decision. There is no hint of it in the conclusions of the three Executive Council meetings between 7 November and the Boundary Commission meeting on 20 November 1925.[96] On 10 November they considered their response to Bourdillon's letter. The Dáil debate on the Education estimates was scheduled for 11–18 November, which required MacNeill's presence in Dublin. Accordingly, the reply said that MacNeill would be unable to go to London for the 17 and 19 November meetings and proposed 24 November as an alternative for the meeting between the two governments. The only indication of the unrest was a reference to Cosgrave's discussions 'with certain members of the Party and a deputation from East Donegal regarding the forecast of the Award'.[97] On 13 November, the Executive Council decided to propose a bilateral discussion with the British government prior to meeting the Commission on 24 November. On 18 November, they discussed the handling of the 24 November meeting, but only regarding who should represent the Free State.[98] The conclusions record nothing about MacNeill's personal position, which suggests that his colleagues remained unaware that the Award had been finalised, with his acquiescence. Patrick McGilligan, Minister for Commerce, saw Cosgrave on 16 November and pressed him to tell MacNeill that transfers to Northern Ireland could not be accepted.[99] Cosgrave met MacNeill on 17 November, but 'what passed between them is unknown', as no record exists.[100]

MacNeill's own communications with the Commission during this period refer only to his availability for meetings and say nothing about the crisis in the Free State, his doubts about the Award or any intention to resign. On 13 November he telegraphed Feetham: 'Delayed by Education debate. Will let you know when I can cross to London.'[101] This prompted an impatient reply from Bourdillon, on behalf of Feetham, urging MacNeill to confirm his availability on 20 November. He replied the following day guaranteeing to be present. When MacNeill appeared at the Commission on 20 November, he announced his resignation.[102] There are two accounts of this meeting, one in MacNeill's statement to the Executive Council the following day, the other in the Commission minutes.[103]

MacNEILL'S EXECUTIVE COUNCIL STATEMENT

On 21 November, MacNeill reported to his colleagues on the Executive Council that he had told the other commissioners on the previous day that a situation of 'extreme gravity' had arisen following the *Morning Post* 'revelations'.[104] Feetham replied that the *Morning Post* article was not accurate, 'but admitted, in response to a question from Dr MacNeill, that it was substantially correct'. MacNeill said he had been in touch with representative people in Ireland whose unanimous opinion was that 'a boundary line such as that indicated in the *Morning Post* would be a violation of the Treaty'. In light of this, he concluded he must resign. Feetham urged him to reconsider, but MacNeill said nothing would alter his decision. Feetham asked whether MacNeill regarded resignation as freeing him from the confidentiality obligation. MacNeill said he did. Bourdillon then turned up the minute recording this commitment, which MacNeill saw as an indication that his resignation 'had not been unexpected'. Feetham suggested MacNeill should be in possession of the maps and documents necessary to make a full and accurate statement, which MacNeill interpreted as 'playing for time' to enable Feetham 'to consult with someone outside the Commission'[105] and replied that 'the facts in his memory were sufficient for the explanation he intended to make to the Executive Council, for which he required no documentary aids'. They then discussed disposal of MacNeill's papers, with Feetham saying, 'I have your copy of that memorandum.' MacNeill explained that this was his copy of the memorandum on interpretation of Article 12, which Feetham had borrowed 'on the plea that he had lost his own, apparently for the purpose of fortifying himself against MacNeill's arguments'. MacNeill offered no objection to Feetham retaining his copy.[106] The meeting concluded with the understanding that MacNeill, no longer bound by confidentiality, was free to make his statement.

THE BOUNDARY COMMISSION RECORD

The minutes of 20 November record that MacNeill announced that he had decided that morning to resign. Feetham urged him to reflect and consult with his fellow commissioners, but MacNeill said his mind was made up and he wished to inform his government of the state of the Commission's work, for which he did not need any written statements or maps. It was confirmed that he was no longer bound by confidentiality and was free to inform his government. In a further attempt to dissuade MacNeill, Feetham then read out a draft statement, which he intended to issue with the Award, recording that, despite their differences of view, the commissioners had been able to record a unanimous decision and they hoped that an Award bearing their three signatures would be accepted by all Irishmen as marking the close of the boundary controversy. No response by MacNeill is recorded. After he withdrew, Feetham and Fisher resolved that the Commission should continue its work.

COMPARING THE ACCOUNTS

There are significant differences between the two accounts. The Commission minutes do not mention the *Morning Post* 'forecast', or MacNeill seeking Feetham's confirmation that it was accurate. There is no reference to Feetham's memorandum or the disposal of MacNeill's papers. The Executive Council record, on the other hand, does not mention Feetham's draft statement on the unanimous adoption of the Award. They also convey very different impressions of the mood of the meeting. The Commission record suggests a reasoned discussion, with Feetham seeking to change MacNeill's mind and preserve the unanimity he believed the Commission had achieved on the Award. The Executive Council statement suggests a contentious meeting, with MacNeill asserting that an Award as described in the *Morning Post* was not compatible with the treaty and implying that Feetham and Fisher were anticipating his resignation because they were aware of his doubts.

In assessing which is more accurate, account must be taken of the process of drawing up the Award described in the Commission's earlier minutes and in the Reid–Craig correspondence. In light of that, it seems clear that MacNeill misled his Executive Council colleagues in implying that he was surprised by the *Morning Post*'s description of the Award and in not revealing that he had been party to it. He did this by emphasising the article's 'revelations' and that he had asked Feetham if it was accurate. But the Award had been decided on 17 October and confirmed on 4 and 5 November, with his acquiescence, so the *Morning Post* article contained no 'revelations' for him and he did not need Feetham's confirmation that it was 'substantially correct' because he knew that it was. MacNeill's resignation letter is consistent with his account in stating that he had resigned, 'since I foresee no likelihood of an Award in accord with the terms of the Treaty'.[107] His version was soon challenged, however, by a press statement issued by the other commissioners.

THE FEETHAM–FISHER STATEMENT

Following MacNeill's resignation, Feetham and Fisher continued finalising the Commission's report. On 21 November they approved the chapter on interpreting Article 12, with 'the Memorandum drawn up by the Chairman' attached as an annex.[108] On 23 November, they issued a statement regarding MacNeill's resignation:

> Our relations with Dr MacNeill in the transaction of the Commission's work have been relations of the closest mutual confidence and these relations continued up to 20 November, when he announced his resignation. In view of the part Dr MacNeill had taken in our proceedings throughout the last twelve months this came as a complete surprise to us. Up to that date Dr MacNeill had made clear his intention of joining with us in signing the Commission's Award embodying a boundary line, the general features of which were approved and recorded in our Minutes on 17 October. It was contemplated that a statement should be issued at the same time as the Award indicating that the Members of the Commission had agreed

to sink individual differences of opinion for the purpose of arriving at a unanimous Award, but not specifying any point on which such differences had arisen. Since October 17 the work of the Commission has proceeded on the basis of the definite understanding between us that our Award embodying the line agreed upon was to be unanimous, and a full detailed description of the line with the necessary maps has been in course of preparation.[109]

A footnote records that it was issued 'to avoid grave misconception'. It was apparently prompted by a speech by Cosgrave at Emyvale on 22 November, which cast doubt on their integrity by suggesting they had been 'swayed in the discharge of their judicial duty by threats and political influences'.[110] Cosgrave exempted MacNeill as

'an honourable man, who had lost faith in the other members of the Commission and felt himself in honour bound to dissociate himself from them because, during the last meetings of the Commission he has been completely satisfied that there was no likelihood that it would result in a report based on the terms of reference in the solemn international agreement under which the Commission was created'.

Cosgrave's remarks confirm that he was still unaware of MacNeill's agreement to the Award. He could hardly have criticised Feetham and Fisher, while exonerating MacNeill, had he known the true position. The Feetham–Fisher statement, contrary to Cosgrave's assertions, made clear their view that, whatever his differences with them, MacNeill had been prepared to 'sink' them to enable the adoption of a unanimous Award on 17 October. The statement thus directly conflicted with MacNeill's account to the Executive Council.

MacNeill's Dáil statement[111]

MacNeill responded in his resignation statement to the Dáil on 24 November. Hand describes the speech as 'a dignified, but not an altogether happy one'. Ronan Fanning says it was 'halting', Eamon Phoenix, less kindly, that it was 'incoherent'.[112]

MacNeill said that the Feetham–Fisher statement, contrary to their claim that it was issued to prevent misconception, was calculated to cause it by claiming unanimity that had not existed. Significantly, however, he did not dispute its factual accuracy: 'Where it states bare facts I do not controvert it, but as to the very decided colouring which it gives to the statement of facts, I do most distinctly controvert it.' He set out his position on unanimity, accepting that the commissioners had agreed on the desirability of an Award signed by all,[113] but insisting that his agreement 'assumed the formulation of an Award based on right principles of interpretation'. It would be wrong to assume that the commissioners were of one mind, as he had profound differences with the chairman on the fundamental principles on which the Award should be based and 'these differences were known to the Chairman when we were engaged upon the consideration of the details of the Award'. He listed his disagreements with Feetham, notably 'that the Act of 1920 had created a status quo which should only be departed from when every factor would compel us to depart from it ... to that position I never assented. It was not in the Article, it was not in the Treaty, and it was only by a constructional effort that it could be brought into play at all.' He had also challenged Feetham's view that, where they conflicted, economic and geographic conditions should prevail over the wishes of the inhabitants.[114]

Having set out his disagreements with Feetham, he had to explain why he had, nevertheless, agreed to the Award. He said that the process of deliberation had placed him 'in a position of exceptional difficulty' as there had been no prior debate on the principles of interpretation and he recognised that he had been at fault in not insisting on this. Instead, 'the details came before us in a very gradual and piecemeal manner and we worked on in that way without decision until a complete boundary line had been presented to us and a draft Award was in existence'. As to why he had agreed to this line on 17 October, he explained that, 'what I agreed to on the ground of avoiding renewed and, perhaps, deepened controversy was not to pronounce unanimity where there was no unanimity, but to sign the Award, in common with the other Commissioners'.[115] MacNeill admitted that 'a better politician, a better diplomatist, a better strategist, than I am would not have allowed himself to be brought into that position'. After 17 October, when the Commission was discussing the presentation of the Award, MacNeill said he had concluded that it would not be possible for him to defend it as a rightful interpretation of the treaty and that he had reached this view in light of the effect produced in the Free State by the *Morning Post*'s disclosure of a version of the Award.

ENDGAME

After MacNeill's resignation, his former colleagues on the Executive Council were restrained in their public comments. In his letter to MacNeill of 22 December, for example, Cosgrave said he was 'personally satisfied that you did what was possible in the most difficult circumstances'.[116] Cosgrave and O'Higgins were, however, strongly critical of him during their negotiations with the British and Northern Ireland governments between 25 November and 3 December to secure the suppression of the Award. MacNeill played no part, but he was frequently mentioned, with Cosgrave and O'Higgins making clear that they felt disadvantaged by their belated awareness that he had agreed to the Award.[117]

On 25 November, Cosgrave informed Baldwin of the serious situation in the Free State following the *Morning Post* leak. Despite this, he said MacNeill had made no statement to the Executive Council until 21 November and 'admitted that MacNeill's agreement on 17 October was a difficult point. Had MacNeill been in touch with border or Free State feeling, he could scarcely have been a party to that agreement.' Thomas Jones recorded Cosgrave's comment more tersely: 'MacNeill's conduct deplorable. He was a philosopher and had been out of touch with the feeling on the border.'[118] Cosgrave said it was clear that 'the intention of Article 12 had not been carried out and some new arrangement should be explored'. Baldwin said he would urge Craig 'to meet you on this matter and would ask the Commissioners to hold up their promulgation'. Cosgrave agreed to see if he and Craig could reach an understanding.

On 28 November 1925, O'Higgins told Baldwin that implementing the Award would bring down the government. Baldwin said he would try 'to get Ireland over her difficulties', but the problem arose because, 'after an Award had been drawn up with the assent of all three Commissioners, one had withdrawn his assent and resigned'.[119] O'Higgins responded that:

> MacNeill agreed in the abstract that the Award should be signed by all three but that this should not imply that there was no disagreement on details. After the *Morning Post* forecast, MacNeill saw that the motive which had made him give his undertaking to his colleagues to sign with them was not going to be realised. For a month he had felt that he ought to stand to the undertaking that he would sign with his colleagues and during that period he was vacillating while the unhappy tendency of the report was becoming more apparent to him.[120]

O'Higgins met Craig the following day. In advance, Baldwin informed him of the details of the Award,[121] suggesting that 'it would be better to base discussion on the real Award and not on the *Morning Post*'s representation'. This prompted a sharp riposte from O'Higgins: 'trifling inaccuracies' did not concern him: 'An Award leaving Newry in the North could not be based on the evidence. Newry is the acid test of the Commissioners' desire to act on their terms of reference undeterred by considerations outside those terms.' When Craig joined the meeting, Baldwin explained that the issue was whether implementation of the Award could be avoided and the existing boundary retained. O'Higgins outlined the Free State position on familiar lines[122] and repeated for Craig's benefit his view of MacNeill's behaviour after the *Morning Post* leak:

> 'MacNeill's attitude of giving agreement in the abstract and yet fighting his colleagues sector by sector was incomprehensible to his colleagues on the Executive Council but finally when the Press exposure came he retracted his engagement and resigned as there was no likelihood of the Award being in accordance with the Commission's terms of reference or the evidence.'[123]

O'Higgins said that the Free State could accept the existing boundary if this were accompanied by 'substantial improvement in the lot of the minority' in Northern Ireland. Discussions then continued between O'Higgins and Craig alone. When Craig made clear he would offer no concessions for the minority, O'Higgins switched to annulment of the financial provisions in Article 5 of the treaty as the Free State's price for accepting the existing boundary.[124] When tripartite discussions resumed, Baldwin concluded that all three governments were agreed that the Award should not be implemented.

Agreement on Article 5 was reached on the evening of 2 December, followed by agreement, on 3 December, to suppress the Award and leave the border unchanged.[125] That evening, Baldwin, Cosgrave and Craig, with Churchill,[126] informed Feetham and Fisher. Feetham responded that the Award had been agreed by all three commissioners in October and requested the report be published, but Cosgrave insisted it be 'burned or buried'.[127] Craig agreed, but expressed sympathy for Feetham and Fisher regarding the charges made against them and suggested an apology. Cosgrave promised to include a passage in a forthcoming speech, which he would clear with MacNeill, accepting that the commissioners' judgements had been honestly made. This prompted a telling remark from Fisher, who 'was sure that Dr MacNeill would admit that no word of bitterness had passed between them. They had worked closely together and he had never complained'. Fisher, inadvertently, had perhaps neatly summed up MacNeill's approach to his role on the Commission.[128]

Feetham remained unhappy, wanting the principles of interpretation to be published to remove the suspicion that the Commission had acted 'under improper influences' and to make clear that 'Article 12 had not been expressed to bear the interpretation put on it by the Free State'. Cosgrave and Craig remained adamant that no part of the report should be made public. A compromise was agreed. The report would be sent to the British government with a letter from Feetham summarising the principles of interpretation on which it was based. The letter, but not the report, would be published.

The 3 December agreement was given effect by legislation in the British and Free State parliaments, providing that the Boundary Commission provisions of Article 12 were revoked, that 'the extent of Northern Ireland' would remain as defined in the Government of Ireland Act and releasing the Free State from the obligations in Article 5. The way was then clear for publication of Feetham's letter, which appeared in *The Times* on 18 December 1925.[129]

FEETHAM'S LETTER AND MacNEILL'S REACTION

Feetham's letter summarised the principles of interpretation set out in his memorandum and emphasised that the Award had been drawn up with MacNeill's agreement:

> 'The line embodied in the draft Award is the line agreed by the Commission before 20 November, the date of Dr MacNeill's withdrawal. The agreement reached by the three members of the Commission with regard to embodying in a unanimous Award the line recorded in the Commission's minutes of 17 October, has already been referred to in the statement issued on 23 November. The report has been compiled subsequent to Dr MacNeill's withdrawal.'

Feetham regretted that 'our decisions are not now to take effect', but hoped that the 3 December agreement 'may bring to the people of Ireland benefits far greater than any which would have resulted from a new determination of boundaries, even if embodied in a unanimous Award'.[130]

MacNeill was evidently angered by Feetham's renewed emphasis on the unanimous adoption of the Award and drafted a statement to the Executive Council asserting that the reference to unanimity in the 23 November statement was 'incorrect and misleading' and that its repetition in the letter was 'evidence of a desire to hold me committed to a particular position with regard to the Award'. He then set out his own view of the understanding on unanimity:

> What was agreed was the desirability of an Award signed jointly by the three members of the Commission, so as to avoid providing material for controversy after the Award had been issued. In accepting this, I expressly stipulated that the Award should be accompanied by a statement making it clear that joint signature did not imply unanimity either as to any part of the Award or as to the principles of interpretation. In effect, the agreement amounted to this, that in the interests of peace and settlement, no minority view should be made public.[131]

AFTERWARDS

After the Boundary Commission episode was over, MacNeill continued to be troubled by criticism of his performance and drafted various statements explaining his position. In these his argument changed from that in his Dáil statement that the failure to meet Free State expectations was due to Feetham's incorrect interpretation of Article 12. He now argued that the problem lay primarily with the 'defective' wording of Article 12, which had doomed the exercise to failure from the start, inferring from this that no other Irish commissioner could have produced a better result. He set this out in a draft election address, almost certainly prepared for his campaign to retain his NUI seat at the June 1927 Dáil election:

> I have been told that the failure of the Boundary Commission to secure an alteration of the Boundary in accordance with the wishes of the inhabitants would be regarded as an adverse factor in my candidature. This provided an additional reason why I seek the opinion of the electors. By merely standing aside, I would give credibility to a false and unjust opinion. It would suggest that some more competent person could have secured a more satisfactory result from the Boundary

Commission. I have never defended myself against such attacks, but refer to them now in deference to the electors of the NUI. What made the Boundary Commission fruitless was the defective character of Article 12, which made the British Government the umpire and deciding judge. Another grave defect was that the requirement for compatibility with economic and geographic conditions did not allow the inhabitants to be the judges of their own economic advantage and made it possible that some undefined economic condition could override their wishes. I was well aware of these defects when I agreed to serve on the Boundary Commission and if I had served my own interests I would not have accepted. I would only add that the task imposed on me and undertaken under a sense of public duty was entirely repugnant to me. It was a barbarous contrivance to draw a line across Ireland based on religious statistics.[132]

MacNeill revisited these arguments in his unpublished memoirs.[133] While reiterating his criticism of Feetham's view that 'any large departure' from the 1920 boundary was beyond the Commission's powers, he said that he had always regarded Article 12 as faulty in qualifying the wishes of the inhabitants by compatibility with economic and geographic conditions, to be 'decided on by the Commission in accordance with any opinion that its members might happen to hold'. He also asserted that Article 12 ensured that the Commission would be dominated by the chairman and that these two factors 'made it impossible to expect satisfactory results'.

On the question of unanimity, he argued that the only basis for the Feetham–Fisher claim that he had agreed with them on the new boundary was that Feetham had represented to him in conversation the desirability of a unanimous Award. He had replied that he did not intend to issue a minority report since that would be a ground for contention, 'but it was not to be understood for that reason that I could accept a majority report either on principles or details'.[134] MacNeill concluded that serving on the Boundary Commission 'was the most disagreeable duty I had ever undertaken' and that he had been glad to escape from politics and get back to his more congenial academic work.

ASSESSMENT

The failure of the Boundary Commission to produce an Award in line with nationalist expectations has ensured that assessments of MacNeill's performance by Irish historians have been predominantly critical. Most take the view that he was the wrong man for the job:[135] a diffident academic, when what was needed was a forceful lawyer-politician, competent to challenge Feetham on the legal issues.[136] J.J. Lee describes him as 'an honourable and guileless man, who seems to have combined integrity with incompetence',[137] while Mansergh concludes that 'he lost his way amid the intractable thickets of partitionist politics'.[138] Murray assesses him 'a largely indifferent, ineffectual Commissioner',[139] and Rankin, as 'out of his depth'.[140] Only his son-in-law Tierney defends him, suggesting, in light of MacNeill's repudiation of the Feetham–Fisher statement, that 'we are entitled to conclude that there cannot have been such a clear-cut "decision" as their statement implies'.[141]

Criticism has centred on MacNeill's 'curiously passive' approach.[142] While he shared his government's view that there should be substantial transfers to the Free State, he did little to achieve this and 'meekly acquiesced' in being overruled on the key issues.[143] He allowed Feetham to dominate, both in the questioning of witnesses and when the Commission was drawing up the Award. He disagreed with Feetham's interpretation of Article 12, but did not press his views with determination, not even insisting on formal discussion of the memorandum.[144] As a result, Feetham's interpretation was allowed to stand as the basis for determining the Award. In the crucial deliberations in mid-October, while he argued about points of detail, he accepted the new boundary line on 17 October and did not dissent when this was confirmed on 4 and 5 November, despite what he later claimed were his growing doubts about the Award's compatibility with the treaty.

MacNeill's quasi-judicial view of his role has also been much criticised.[145] Mansergh argues that he was 'so impressed with what he deemed to be the "judicial" aspect of the Commission's work that he declined absolutely to discuss its progress with his colleagues on the Executive Council'.[146] This had the unfortunate consequence that they were unaware that things had moved decisively against the Free State position until the *Morning Post* leak on 7 November.

MacNeill never convincingly explained his acquiescence to the 17 October line. In his Dáil statement, he said that this had been in the hope of putting an end to controversy over the border, but it is difficult to accept that he could really have believed this. If he did somehow imagine that the new border might be accepted in the Free State, he had indeed, as Cosgrave suggested, become completely out of touch with nationalist thinking.[147]

With hindsight, it seems clear that MacNeill should have made a stand when he realised that an Award corresponding to Free State expectations was not going to emerge. The obvious points for doing so would have been either when Feetham issued his memorandum on 11 September, or during the Commission's deliberations in mid-October, when it became clear that his colleagues were moving towards an Award based on Feetham's interpretation. At either point, he could have made clear that he would not accept such an Award and threatened either to resign or to issue a minority report.[148] Either course would have given Feetham pause for thought and, given his desire for a unanimous Award, he might have agreed to continue the Commission's deliberations in the hope of overcoming MacNeill's objections. MacNeill was not, however, the man to make such a challenge. He had promised Feetham he would not issue a minority report and he appears to have had no thoughts of resignation until after the *Morning Post* leak.

MacNeill can also be criticised for his lack of frankness with his Executive Council colleagues following the *Morning Post* leak. The uproar this produced in the Free State placed him under great pressure and he did not respond well to it. Initially, he said nothing, allowing his colleagues to believe that no Award had yet been adopted and, when he did eventually make a statement to the Executive Council on 21 November, he gave a misleading account in suggesting his resignation had been due to his colleagues' determination to adopt an Award he considered a violation of the treaty. It took the Feetham–Fisher statement of 23 November to bring him to admit that the Award had been adopted, with his acquiescence, on 17 October 1925.

History, Memory, Legacy

Writing Home: understanding the domestic in the life of Eoin MacNeill

CONOR MULVAGH

In 1915, V.L. O'Connor published a book of caricatures among which was an illustration of the bearded Eoin MacNeill in Volunteer uniform. Beside each of the caricatures, O'Connor wrote a brief profile of the figure depicted on the page opposite.

MacNeill's profile read:

Eoin MacNeill (Prof. John McNeill.)

Occupation:	Professor of Irish History.
	President of Irish Volunteers.
	Principal of Omeath Irish College.
Characteristic:	Idealism
Recreation:	running a citizen army.
Favourite pastime:	teaching Irish.
Pet aversion:	answering letters.
At Home:	with children.[1]

O'Connor captured a lot both in his drawing and his pen portrait of MacNeill. It is this last sentence that is of primary interest here. MacNeill's sense of home, and his life within the home, is a significant element of MacNeill's life that has received comparatively little scholarly attention. There he was surrounded by, and took a very active interest in, his eight children alongside his wife Agnes ('Taddie' as Eoin habitually addressed her). In contrast, his life as a scholar, Volunteer and politician is well documented. In perhaps the most intimate of the twelve essays on MacNeill in *The Scholar Revolutionary*, Francis Shaw observed that 'in the bosom of his family, MacNeill was happy to be the absent-minded professor, and as time went on he came to depend more and more on the gracious and very capable lady who was his wife, and on the large family of children with whom their union was blessed'.[2] Shaw is undoubtedly correct about the central role that Agnes MacNeill played in the life of the family. However, Eoin and Agnes' relationship, as this chapter explores, was more symbiotic than Shaw has previously suggested. In place of the 'absent-minded professor', Eoin comes across as a deeply engaged, sometimes paternal, often playful father and husband.

The public and family lives of MacNeill were deeply intertwined during the Irish revolution. To give one vivid example of this, at the Irish Volunteers' St Patrick's Day review in 1916, pulling away from home in the car that would bring MacNeill to the viewing stand in College Green, Eoin wavered in the driveway and beckoned his youngest son Séamus to join him in the car.[3] As Séamus' sister Máire recounted many years later: 'Just before the car drove off, on an impulse he called Séamus into the car. Séamus was then eight. So he was at that historic parade and on the platform, but he was made squat down by some buff who thought it inappropriate to have a child there.'[4]

Memoirs and memories both from MacNeill himself and from his family and friends are essential to telling his story. As a historian, and with a mind to history, MacNeill left a staggeringly voluminous personal archive first for his family and, through them, for the public to explore and interpret. Thus, in scholarship, there has been a tendency to see the MacNeill that is presented in his archive. However, the focus on MacNeill the 'man of action'[5] and MacNeill the scholar has often overshadowed the day-to-day Eoin MacNeill as his wife, his children, and his biographer son-in-law knew him. In some ways, 'the pen and the sword' of this book's title follows in the historiographical tradition of focusing on MacNeill's public life, but this chapter strives to address the sometimes eclipsed side of MacNeill: the son, husband, and father that ran in parallel to the public face. Like Séamus crouched beside him on the viewing stand in March 1916, Eoin's family life was never far from his public profile, even if it was not always in plain sight.

While much scholarly attention has been focussed on the public life of MacNeill, the conclusions that can be drawn from the above is that home life mattered very much to him and that he spent quite a large proportion of his time at home in the domestic rather than public sphere during his political decade.[6]

MacNeill was not, first and foremost, a politician, a commander-in-chief, a cabinet minister. Above all, he was a writer and a scholar. The place in which he conducted these activities was in the home. There is something of a triple intent to the 'writing home' of this chapter's title. One is to write about the home life of the MacNeills. The second is to examine the letters passed between Eoin, Agnes and the children when one or other of them was away from home during the Irish revolution. Finally, 'writing home' considers the fact that much of MacNeill's journalistic and academic writing took place within his home environment. Both the people and things that surrounded him as he wrote mattered to him and shaped both his scholarly and political writings.

The historiographer Bonnie G. Smith has explored the process through which history was written in Europe and North America prior to the professionalisation of the discipline. Her focus is on the period between the mid-nineteenth and the mid-twentieth century. Smith explains how, in the nineteenth century, '[a]s the demands for high-end scholarship and extensive research intensified, historians organized their households into efficient, complex systems'.[7] She describes historians like Eugène Burnouf who had 'four little daughters ... helping him in collecting and alphabetically arranging a number of slips on which he had jotted down whatever had struck him as important in his reading during the day'. François Guizot meanwhile collaborated with both his first and second wives to such an extent that entire chapters of his books had been authored and edited by them. However, when it came to publication, only François' name appeared on the spine and cover.[8] Thomas Frederick Tout meanwhile had his 'wife, sister-in-law, and other female relatives working for him'.[9] In reference to Tout's work, Smith concludes that:

> Such publications were an essential stage in creating the persona of the autonomous historian: the stage in which the wife dismissed her own contribution. Thus, in the periods of both nascent and mature professionalization, history had author-teams that worked in household workshops. Around this complexity arose conventions that formulated authorship as singular and male, as a public and extrafamilial undertaking.[10]

These themes will be revisited later in this chapter, in particular in relation to MacNeill's later life when his adult daughters began to take a more active collaborative role in his work. Before this can be undertaken, it is necessary to look at a less settled phase in the MacNeills' home life, when 'family' included a wider circle of MacNeills (or McNeills)[11] and 'home' was a location that changed with the size and fortunes of the family.

Eoin, Agnes and their children were something of a nomadic family in the first two decades of the twentieth century. As well as being nomadic, the MacNeills were accustomed to accommodating family relatives within their respective households. In the 1901 Census, Eoin (33) and Agnes (28) were living in the home of Eoin's mother and aunt – both widowed – and Eoin's older brother Charles in north County Dublin at Hazelbrook, Portmarnock.[12] Eoin and Agnes began their married life in 14 Trafalgar Terrace, Monkstown, County Dublin but in 1901 they moved to Portmarnock.[13] Hazelbrook had been the family home since 1893.[14] Eoin's mother Rosetta McNeill (née McAuley) was listed as the head of the household.[15] The MacNeill family grew with the addition of Róisín in 1906 and Séamus in 1908.[16] It seems these changed circumstances, with seven children under the age of ten, may have been what prompted the MacNeills to seek out a new home.

From 1908 to late 1915, Eoin and his family were resident in 19 Herbert Park, a newly built house on the edge of the park of the same name. Herbert Park had been developed to host the Dublin International Exhibition in 1907. In the census return for 1911, both Eoin's mother and Agnes' sister were also resident at the MacNeills' Herbert Park home. Eoin's brother Charles, however, was living elsewhere by 1911. By contrast to the census of 1901, Eoin, and not his mother, was now listed as head of household. Michael Tierney records how James McNeill, still a civil servant in India, had bought the house on Herbert Park and then let it to his brother Eoin.[17] The average number of residents in the other homes on the road was six in the 1911 Census but there were then thirteen people, including two domestic servants, living under the MacNeills' roof. The youngest child, Éilis, was born in 1914 and a fifteen-year-old domestic servant was sent from Inis Mór to help Agnes with her now eight children. She, and other girls before her, had been hired for their bilingualism so as to help the MacNeill children improve their Irish.[18]

One of the MacNeills' neighbours was Michael Joseph O'Rahilly, styling himself as 'The O'Rahilly' by this point. A fellow Gaelic Leaguer, The O'Rahilly lived in number 40 and was able to avail of, or exploit, the fact that MacNeill was laid up in bed with the 'flu in October 1913. The O'Rahilly called on MacNeill and asked him to write a piece for *An Claidheamh Soluis*, the paper MacNeill had originally edited and that The O'Rahilly had recently taken over as manager.[19] MacNeill's most famous and arguably most important piece of journalistic writing, 'The North Began', featured in *An Claidheamh Soluis* on 1 November 1913, the first of a new series of the paper produced under O'Rahilly's management.[20]

From 'The North Began' sprung the idea to found a volunteer force to answer the Carsonites. Within the month, the force had been established and enrolments at its inaugural meeting at the Rotunda Rink on Parnell Square were far in excess of anything the organisers had predicted or catered for. The story of the foundation of the Irish Volunteers is so well rehearsed elsewhere that I will not dwell upon it here, but instead focus on November 1913 as a point at which the home life and public life of MacNeill reached a new level of interaction. The moment of decision came in the days following the publication of 'The North Began' when Bulmer Hobson and The O'Rahilly called upon MacNeill. Hobson had asked O'Rahilly to set up the meeting so that he could ask MacNeill if he meant what he had written about founding a volunteer force. MacNeill took Hobson's presence to mean that an overture was being made to him by the Irish Republican Brotherhood of which Hobson, but not O'Rahilly, was a leading member at that point.[21] Agnes MacNeill spoke to her daughter Eibhlín about this moment years later, shortly after Eoin's death. As Tierney recounted it in his first (1964) biographical study of MacNeill:

> ... before giving his consent, he had excused himself from his visitors and crossed the hall to the room where [Agnes] sat sewing. He told her what was proposed and said that his participation would inevitably involve her and the children. It might mean complete loss of security for them all and for himself the danger of imprisonment and even death. He would not go on, he said, without her consent. She said 'Well, John, do you think it is the right thing to do?' He replied 'Yes' and she said 'Then do it.' Her daughter recalls that in giving this account of a fateful decision she appeared to be completely unconscious of the magnitude of her own part in it, taking this for granted as part of the duty of a good wife and an Irishwoman.[22]

Tierney's full-length biography of his father-in-law was posthumously published in 1980. Michael's widow Eibhlín and her sister Máire prepared the text of the book.[23] The passage above appeared almost word for word in the biography but Eibhlín edited the last lines, giving a subtly different reading of her mother's role in the encounter. As it appears in Eibhlín's edited 1980 text:

> This conversation [between Eoin and Agnes in 1913] was recalled to illustrate what 'a just husband' he [Eoin] was. As her daughter listened she noticed how all the emphasis was on her father. There was not

the slightest indication that her mother considered her own response as anything worth comment, and yet it was one of the most fateful consents ever given by an Irishwoman.[24]

By removing the word 'wife' and re-emphasising the idea of Agnes' 'fateful' consent, Eibhlín feminised her late husband's narration of this, her own, memory. In doing so, she deepens our understanding of the relationship between Eoin and Agnes in this crucial but archivally sparse period when the MacNeills lived in Herbert Park.[25] Changes in the life of Eoin's brother James, rather than in his own life, would signal an end to the MacNeills' days in Herbert Park.

In December 1914, in the wake of authoring a report on Indian emigration that had suggested reforms for the welfare of indentured Indians abroad, which 'did not meet the favour of the viceroy', James McNeill retired from an otherwise distinguished career in the Indian civil service at the minimum pensionable age of 45.[26] He returned to Ireland and, in 1915, the MacNeills left Herbert Park for a larger residence, Woodtown Park, which sat on sixty acres about three miles south of Rathfarnham, on the slopes of the Dublin mountains.[27] Here, the entire MacNeill/McNeill family commune of James, Eoin, Agnes and their eight children; and Eoin's mother all moved. It is of Woodtown that the most complete and vivid description of home and family life for the MacNeills survives, albeit in the absence of Eoin, through the letters sent during his incarceration from May 1916 to June 1917.[28]

Following Eoin's release from what was supposed to be a life sentence in June 1917, Eoin's family moved once again, this time to 'Netley' on South Hill Avenue, Blackrock, on Dublin's south coast. It was from here that Eoin and his son Niall were snatched in a raid by crown forces in the wake of Bloody Sunday in November 1920.[29] Eoin was inexplicably and unceremoniously released a few days later although Niall remained incarcerated. However, as he suspected would happen, Eoin was rearrested on 27 November 1920.[30] This time, his third son Turlough was arrested with him.[31] Niall was released after three weeks but both Turlough and Eoin were detained without trial for most of the rest of the War of Independence. Eoin was held in Mountjoy prison after his second arrest until 30 June 1921.[32]

Niall, Turlough, and Brian were heavily involved in the IRA by this point and the house on South Hill Avenue acted both as a safe house for other IRA members and as an arms dump for the South County Dublin IRA (6th Battalion, No. 2 Dublin Brigade).[33] Niall was then battalion quartermaster with the rank of captain and subsequently brigade quartermaster (lieutenant-commandant).[34] Turlough, aged seventeen at the time of his arrest, was then an ordinary Volunteer in E Company of the 6th Battalion, Dublin Brigade but was promoted to assistant company quartermaster after his release in 1921.[35]

It was during this stay in Mountjoy that MacNeill wrote his celebrated paper 'Ancient Irish Laws: The law of status or franchise', subsequently published in the *Proceedings of the Royal Irish Academy* in 1923.[36] It was this piece of prison scholarship that led the famous Celticist Professor Rudolph Thurneysen to propagate an aphorism (first coined by one of Thurneysen's students) that 'any really patriotic government would keep MacNeill in gaol for nine months each year' so that he could continue to produce scholarship of such quality.[37]

The MacNeills were at Netley during the Civil War and the sons, including Brian who was killed in Sligo during the conflict, wrote home to their mother there while on active duty on opposing sides. This was also Eoin's home during his time working on the Irish Boundary Commission and it was from Netley that Eoin departed for mass when he happened upon the assassination of Kevin O'Higgins in July 1927.[38] With the children growing up and having their own children by this stage, Eoin and Agnes moved again, first to Hatch Street in 1932 and for the last time in 1941. The couple's final home was 63 Upper Leeson Street and remained their residence until their deaths in 1945 and 1953 respectively.[39]

Such was the centrality of home life to MacNeill that it is difficult to examine it through the written record during the periods in which MacNeill was comfortably at home. It is through his periods of absence, when he took up his pen to write to Agnes, the children, or one of his siblings, that we get a sense of the centrality of the domestic to MacNeill's life. Only through these letters back and forth can we get a sense of his thinking. Rather than any political allies, Agnes MacNeill was perhaps his closest confidant. Despite the fact that much of their mail in these years passed through censors, even in his prison letters Eoin is more open, honest and self-reflective in his letters to Agnes than in any other set of correspondence. The first and most important series of these letters began in 1916 when he was shipped to Britain as a convict serving a life sentence following the Easter Rising. Eoin's prison letters from England in 1916 and 1917 are filled with a yearning for home. It is to this earlier prison correspondence that this chapter will now turn in search of the insights it gives into what home meant, and felt like, for the MacNeills.

CENSORSHIP AND THE PRISON LETTERS OF EOIN MᴀCNEILL

Before any discussion of MacNeill's prison correspondence can be undertaken, the contextual issue of censorship deserves serious consideration. In evaluating these letters, the fact that they were written in the knowledge that both incoming and outgoing mail would be passing under the eye of the prison censor needs constantly to be borne in mind. It will be argued here that the focus on domestic life is an under-addressed theme in MacNeill's life and that his prison letters are a key source of evidence for this. However, the counter-argument that, given prison censorship, MacNeill chose to focus on safe topics and avoided discussion of politics, the recently suppressed rising, or the Volunteers cannot be entirely disregarded. The strongest evidence of this comes from Agnes MacNeill. In February 1917, she wrote to Eoin:

> Dearest I feel that I have nothing more to tell you, because perhaps am not allowed ~~and~~ of at least public news and at present we are all greatly interested in what is going on and if I got outside home news I might say or tell you something that would be censored & my letters delayed & it is not worth that – so good bye my husband John.⁴⁰

While Agnes may have been anxious about sending 'outside home news', Eoin's constant pleas for domestic news cannot be so easily excused away as representing a fear of the prison censor. Eoin never discussed his prison letters in his memoirs or later correspondence. Thus, the idea that the prevalence of the domestic in these letters stems from a fear of the censor should at least be considered as a factor by the reader as it has been by this author.⁴¹

One notable and somewhat amusing way in which the censor ended up stopping MacNeill's mail was when MacNeill got rather excited about an ogham stone and a hidden souterrain outside Corduff, which a prisoner at Dartmoor had told him about after the rising. When he regained the ability to send letters home following his transfer to Lewes in January 1917, Eoin wrote in great detail to Agnes to describe the location of this site. He was keen that his colleague R.A.S. Macalister, Professor of Celtic Archaeology at the National University, 'may wish to look up these things so near Dublin'.⁴² Back in Rathfarnham, Agnes waited for weeks and wondered why she hadn't received her husband's letter.⁴³ It transpired that it had been held at the censor's office until the presence of a souterrain and not something less innocent at the location described could be confirmed by the authorities in Ireland. Agnes wrote on 12 February 1917 how she had 'just received your letter of the 12th Jan. yesterday I presume it was kept at the Censor's office until they wrote over here to find out all about the ogham stone.'[44] Not only does this incident illustrate the lengths to which the authorities went to ensure that covert information was not coming in or out of the prisons but it also highlights the chilling effect this delay must have had on the contents of the MacNeill family's correspondence. In a later batch of prison letters from November 1920, the same caution is apparent from a younger member of the family behind bars. Turlough sent a veiled warning to his sister Eibhlín not to say anything incriminating in her reply to him, warning her that 'We have to leave the envelopes open, so I suppose they must censor the letters. Apparently, they do the same with the incoming letters.'[45]

After the rising, the MacNeill household had at least one secret that the family definitely wanted to keep from the censor. Woodtown was harbouring two fugitives: Eoin's close ally in the Volunteers, Bulmer Hobson, and Hobson's fiancée, Claire Gregan. Marnie Hay records that the couple were finally married on 19 June 1916 while lying low at Woodtown. James McNeill acted as a witness and hosted a wedding breakfast for the newlyweds. The Hobsons left Woodtown that same day fearing the appearance of their names in the parish register down in Rathfarnham would betray their whereabouts to the authorities.[46]

The constant presence of the censor impacted upon the MacNeills' freedom of expression in other ways during periods of incarceration in that the use of Irish had to be curtailed and almost stopped in their correspondence. In early 1917, a consignment of Irish language books that had been sent to Eoin in Lewes by Stephen Barratt was halted by the censor.[47] Writing to his daughter Eibhlín in March 1917, Eoin asked after one of her teachers at Muckross Park College in Donnybrook, Dublin: 'Tell Sister Dympna that I have been asking for her, & that only for the Censor I wd. write her a nice letter in Irish.'[48] Eoin told Agnes that while he wanted to have 'a line or half line from each of the children' in her letters, 'They had better write in English as before, so as to give no occasion for delay in forwarding.'[49] This restriction on the language of communication meant exchanges outside of the English language were limited to a 'Dear Athair'[50] at the start of the children's correspondence with him. Nonetheless, discussion of the Irish language permeates Eoin's letters home and remained of the utmost importance to the family. In August 1916, Máire and Róisín MacNeill went to live on Inis Mór with a family friend, Una Folan.[51]

Encouraging her to keep on improving her Irish, Eoin wrote to the then ten-year-old Róisín that 'It will be a disappointment when I get back home if I don't find you all as good & better in speaking Irish than when I was taken from you.'[52] The shadow of the censor looms once more in a note Máire sent to her father in April 1917 telling him: 'I am very sorry I can't write to you in Irish.'[53]

'THE CRY FOR HOME'

In June 1916, MacNeill was transported from Dublin to Dartmoor prison along with sixty-four other convicts. Conditions there were harsh and communication among the prisoners, and with the outside world, was tightly controlled.[54] In December 1916, the Easter convicts were concentrated from Dartmoor, Portland, and Wormwood Scrubs and sent to Lewes prison in east Sussex where they were granted certain privileges, including the right to send and receive one letter per month, contingent on good behaviour.[55]

Eoin wrote a long letter home from Lewes in February 1917. In her reply, Agnes told Eoin how 'in every line of it was the cry for home'.[56] With prison visits not possible, more so owing to the costs involved than the threat of submarine warfare,[57] the couple clutched at strategies to make the distance between them seem less great. Agnes wrote:

> Do you remember when I was over seeing you I asked you did you ever see the moon & if so when you looked at it to remember that I was looking at it, it seemed to bring you nearer to me to think that we were both looking at the same object though far apart.[58]

In response, Eoin replied:

> You say that my last letter made you sad because the cry for home was in every line of it. You must not let that make you sad. The cry for home is in every breath I draw. You know I always loved home, & now I love it more than ever. Would it not be sadder if I ceased to love home or loved it less than I do? Do not feel sad on my account. My back is strong enough for its load thank God. Besides I am confident. Every night in my prayers I say ... 'thou, my God, hast singularly established me in hope.'[59]

Eoin's faith allowed him to see his incarceration as a hardship to be endured. He also parsed his suffering in terms of his masculinity: as a trial from which he would emerge strengthened. He also portrayed Agnes' suffering as something to be endured cheerfully. No more than he parsed his own challenges in gendered terms, he also cast Agnes' fortitude in the context of her femininity and motherhood. Following the passage above, he continued:

> You have one or two of Nansen's[60] books in my study. Take a look thro' them and see how men have gone, of their own free will & choice, on a long voyage, suffering separation from home & friends, cut off from all communication with the world, confined to the bounds of a small ship, put on strict rations of food & under a strict discipline, enduring the greatest possible rigours of climate – and all for what? Look around you then and ask yourself whether I, and you too, ought not to be cheerful and confident rather than sad. It is only human and natural that we should feel the pain, but we shall not suffer in vain. The mother of so many children ought to know that the world like the family renews itself in pain and anxiety. So dearest do not allow yourself to be sad. In your first letter to me, after I became a convict, you said 'God is over all.' That is true still.[61]

This sense of stoic forbearance and love of home was reciprocated in the letters Eoin received from Agnes and the children while he was incarcerated. Agnes told Eoin how:

> Niall & I were sitting one evening at the fire together & [word blotted] broke down completely and after some time said 'oh I wish Atair [sic] was home. The house is not like home at all without him everything is different when he is here', and all the children feel like that you were so good & kind to them they felt they could say out what was on their mind and that you never misunderstood.[62]

Even the MacNeills' youngest, Éilis, was developing methods for expressing her hope that her father would be returned to the family. Still learning to talk, she told all around her how she wanted her father home so he could bring her to mass in Rathfarnham. One letter from her elder sister Eibhlín recounts how Éilis had begun a ritual before bedtime in which she would pray "'Sweet Jesus. I love ou [sic] Holy Maily [sic] bling [sic] Daddy home soon.'"[63]

UNDERSTANDING 'HOME'

As to the question of what 'home' meant to MacNeill, the concept seems
fluid to him. It is both a sense of people and of place at different times in his
letters. The move from Herbert Park to Woodtown brought the extended
MacNeill/McNeill clan into a decidedly more rural setting.

One thing which is so prominent in the family correspondence of the
MacNeills that it deserves further discussion is horticulture. The place that
gardening, growing, and news about the latest developments of the sixty
acres around the family home at Woodtown occupied in Eoin's prison
correspondence gives insight into his concept of the word 'home'.

Writing in mid-February 1917, Eoin asked for news about Woodtown
and implored Agnes to

> satisfy that wandering imagination of mine and give it something to
> live on. I don't care how trivial the particulars are, so long as they are
> about home & friends. Tell me how the electric light is working, or
> the vacuum sweeper, or what Siubhán[64] says to Éilis and Eilis [sic]
> to Siubhán. Tell me how many Wyandottes you have & how many
> Indian Runners & Rhode Island Reds, & whether you have gone in
> for turkeys or geese or if James has ventured on beekeeping. James told
> me that Niall was getting too hoary to continue his zeal for rabbits &
> pigeons. I trust all the same that he will find something of particular &
> constant interest, some fad or hobby to occupy him during his hours
> at home, and centre his mind at home.[65]

Later in the letter he continued in the same vein:

> I sh[oul]d like you to realize that I am just hungry for anything you
> can tell me about home, no matter how commonplace the details may
> seem to you. I want to know how you got thro' the severe weather, &
> what James is planning out for his agricultural work this year. He told
> me he was left in the lurch by the timber men. How are your cows &
> poultry doing? What about the fruit trees? I have heard something
> about new regulations regarding tillage of grass lands – do they affect
> Woodtown?[66]

On one hand, Eoin's interest in gardening in this period could be
explained away as a prisoner who pined for news of the outdoors during

his confinement but other references to gardening and horticulture in MacNeill's papers suggest something deeper.

A key component in understanding any scholar's writings from a historiographical point of view is to understand the setting in which they wrote. Evidence suggests MacNeill primarily wrote at home throughout his life, and his surroundings – family, house and garden – constituted important contexts in which he conceived of and perceived the world around him and the past worlds about which he wrote.[67] Shaw observed how 'all his life MacNeill was fond of gardening, and immediately before the Poulaphuca area was flooded, not long before his death, he could have been found making a last check on its flora'.[68]

Gardening was not simply a pastime for Eoin; it became something of a philosophical exercise for him. Tierney suggested that the garden was simply a 'refuge' to Eoin, observing that he spent long hours in it following the '*débâcle* of the Boundary Commission'.[69] However, other sources suggest it was more than a refuge. MacNeill contemplated the complexities of past and present while busying himself with the garden. In 'Vivat!', MacNeill's 1915 exhortation to the students of UCD to see their institution as a 'University College, rather than a College University', MacNeill described the stifling control exercised by the NUI Senate over its constituent colleges as 'mechanical ... It is a unity of death, not of life, a unity without sap or growth, without leaf or blossom or fruit.'[70] These horticultural metaphors went deeper into his pedagogy. In what appears to be the script of a lecture for one of his courses at the National University, MacNeill took up the subject of gardening with his students in an extended metaphor:

> I am fond of gardening and I love to compare civilisation to gardening. I take a piece of ground in its natural or wild state. I surround it with a fence, I remove from it all plants that I do not wish to have in it, I introduce other plants, I mark out plots and beds in it and lay down paths, I dig up the earth, and so on through a hundred different operations, every one of them an interference with the wild, a subjection of wild nature in some measure to the human will and purpose.[71]

If MacNeill thus cast himself in the role of civiliser as he pruned and planted, then his garden was much more than a refuge; it became part of his worldview. It is noteworthy that the civilising aspect of this attitude seems to have been more prevalent than any notion of horticultural nationalism.[72]

In an interesting letter to his brother Charlie from the Aran Islands in 1892, the then twenty-five-year-old Eoin asked his older brother to send a packet of 'American Wonder Peas', explaining that 'These folk never even heard of peas, & haven't a ghost of a notion of them. Pâidîn [sic] is very anxious to try a row in his garden.'[73]

In comparing gardening to civilisation, the other thing that becomes apparent is the sense of control Eoin got from gardening. The prevalence of the garden in his prison letters, when he was deprived both of freedom and power, suggest that news of the garden was a real source of strength to him in prison. At Lewes, MacNeill managed to secure for himself the privilege of engaging in some digging in the prison garden as part of his prison work.[74]

To his daughter Eibhlín, he explained that:

> It is many a year now that I have never missed planting & pruning & sowing till this year. Do you ever take a look to see how the tree peonies & the Sophoras that I planted are coming on? You will have nice fragrant hyacinths by this time as we had last year. The gardener at Muckross, the 'farmer' as some of you used to call him, had a beautiful flowering shrub with exquisite blue flowers in masses. Beg a plant of it – root or cutting – for me from Rev. Mother & plant it at Woodtown. Mrs. Hamilton of Foxrock promised me a root of a very sweet helianthus or rockrose that grows with her. If you ever see her tell her that I look forward to the redemption of that promise.[75]

In the same way that Eoin was keen to share his 'American Wonder Peas' with the inhabitants of the Aran Islands in his youth, throughout his life we see this active sharing economy of cuttings common to avid gardeners. In populating his own garden with plants he had admired on his visits elsewhere, it might not be too far of a stretch to say that Eoin's garden became a sort of memory repository for him, a host of living, blossoming *lieux de mémoire*. The family's garden thus becomes a microcosm of his world with cuttings and plants reminding him of different parts of Ireland, of his life, and of his family that he admired or which held meaning for him.

Gardening seems to have gone hand-in-hand with scholarship as the two chief domestic activities of MacNeill right up to the end of his life. Máire MacNeill recalled how her parents devoted themselves to the small garden of their final home on Upper Leeson Street: '63 was a hard house to run but we were all fond of it ... They [Eoin and Agnes] loved it and used to work and putter in the garden. I can still see the two white heads moving in the greenery there.'[76] Tierney records how, in 1945, the terminally ill Eoin was brought home from St Vincent's hospital and the sunroom facing the garden was converted into a bedroom for him. 'So in his last days he was daily surrounded by the people dearest to him and in sight of the growing, flowering things which seem always to have meant so much to him.'[77]

LANGUAGE LEARNING AND THE ERSATZ FAMILY AT LEWES

If home and garden are one theme that comes out strongly in the MacNeill family correspondence, then the other is language learning. The acquisition and practice of languages was very prominent in Eoin's prison letters during 1916 and 1917. As discussed in the context of censorship earlier, Irish was naturally to the fore, but Greek, Latin, Dutch and Spanish also feature in Eoin's letters. In his earliest surviving letter from Dartmoor, he asked Agnes to ensure that the programme of language learning he had intended for the older children that summer would not be interrupted by his absence:

> I want the boys & Eibhlin to work hard at their studies. I suppose you will all stay at Woodtown during the summer holidays. I wonder if James would find it possible to give Niall and Brian some introductory lessons in Greek. You know I intended doing so. If he thinks well of it, he would perhaps allow a week or two of pure holiday to elapse after the examinations & then ask the boys to do a little Greek each day, always writing something, the alphabet to begin with. You will also take care that all the children keep their own language in good order, especially in conversation with the younger ones.[78]

Back in prison, Eoin was raiding the library for items of interest:

> Before leaving Dartmoor I scrambled thro' the last few pages of the first volume of the Dutch novel I told you of. Dutch is no easy language – very like German in the building of sentences – ... I made greater headway in Spanish without a dictionary than in Dutch with a dictionary having begun both about simultaneously.[79]

It seems Eoin gave up on Dutch after this, but two months later he was pressing on with his Spanish:

> I have fallen in love with Spanish for the time being & am quite delighted with the stories of Fernan Caballero[80] in two volumes in

the prison library – 'Relaciones' (tales of incident) and 'Cuadros de Costumbres' (tales of character). If your sister Maggie could pick up inexpensive copies of any of Caballero's writings, suggest it to her.[81]

Eoin was not alone among the inmates in learning Spanish. Such was the demand for the pocket dictionary of English and Spanish in the prison library that Eoin asked if one could be posted to him from Woodtown.[82] However, Irish was the language that most of the prisoners sought to improve. In this, Eoin was able to take on the mantle of teacher rather than fellow autodidact. He told Agnes: 'There is a general desire among the prisoners here to acquire or improve a knowledge of Irish & I am often engaged during exercise time in giving oral lessons, as are a number of the others who are able to do so.'[83]

Tierney suggests that MacNeill's focus on language was a coping strategy. In a questionnaire that the Prison Reform League sent to MacNeill after his release in 1917, he was asked if prison had 'injured his moral or mental health', to which he replied, 'No ... I applied myself diligently to the study of languages ... had I not done so I have not the least doubt that I should have suffered mental injury.'[84] Thus language learning can be seen as part of MacNeill's strategy for looking after his mental health while in prison. The way he branched out from individual study of language towards teaching other prisoners meanwhile suggests an attempt by MacNeill to replicate both his role as a teacher and a father within the prison system.[85] Eoin sympathised with his son Turlough who, alongside his brother Brian, was then also away from the family home boarding at Blackrock College. Eoin asked Turlough if college was 'very tiresome'. Eoin reflected on his own days as a boarder: 'It is a bit like prison, being at a boarding-school, you have to do what other people tell you nearly all the time & you cannot go where you please, & you are always learning something whether you like it or no.'[86] This connotation of school and prison not only emphasises Eoin's love of home but also further stresses the fact that Eoin saw learning, and teaching, as an intrinsic part of his life within Lewes.

There is a distinct generational quality to MacNeill's attitude to his fellow prisoners, which mimics his attitude to his students at the National University.[87] En route to Dartmoor, MacNeill identified 'another paterfamilias' among his fellow prisoners.[88] MacNeill's paternal bearing towards the younger inmates became particularly evident when the occasion of Desmond FitzGerald's birthday caused Eoin to reflect on his own seniority:

FitzG. had his 28th birthday today, he told me. It seems so queer to think that I was earning my livelihood in Dublin for a year and a half before he was born. I cannot feel myself a bit old, and among these younger men I seem to myself to be as young as they are. The only sign of seniority that obtrudes itself is that I sometimes find myself impatient with their little bits of frivolous & irresponsible doings – I say to myself for aren't they foolish & with that comes the counterthought – am not I foolish to think so? If I in my 50th year feel myself young, what must I expect but boyishness in comrades averaging perhaps less than half my age & some of them as young as my own boys at home?[89]

In teaching, in studying, and in keeping informed about his garden at home, MacNeill thus carved out novel ways in which to build new modes of domesticity for himself while locked up. Without any of our benefit of hindsight, it should be remembered that he thought himself to be embarking upon a life sentence, although the release of internees at Christmas 1916 evidently gave the remaining convicts fresh cause for hope.[90] As coping strategies, MacNeill's prison activities, and the outlook he portrays in his letters, are remarkable to the modern reader. Other inmates, including de Valera, Thomas Ashe and Tom Hunter, seem to have focused on rebuilding their political networks while they were inside the prison system – as did MacNeill to a certain extent. However, all evidence suggests that MacNeill was much more focused on building an ersatz home life for himself during his incarceration: a hybrid of his new prison family and a stream of news from his real family back in Ireland.[91]

BROTHER AGAINST BROTHER: WRITING HOME DURING THE IRISH CIVIL WAR

The older MacNeill boys appear to have always striven to emulate their father. Niall, whether he wanted to or not, followed in his father's footsteps. After the rising, he became a breadwinner at the age of seventeen, going to work for Eoin's old friend, the solicitor John Gore.[92] There Niall encountered many of Eoin's old colleagues from his father's days in the Accountant General's Office at the Four Courts.[93] However, even before this, the older boys in the family were keen to imitate another aspect of their father's life: Volunteering. In an interesting section of his Bureau of Military History (BMH) statement, Niall explained how he and Brian had teamed up with their two younger cousins Hugh (Hugo) and Dermot MacNeill, sons of Hugh Aloysius MacNeill,[94] to establish 'a sort of private Boy Scout organisation of our own, called *Na Ceithearnai[gh] Coille*[95] of which I think we were the only members'.[96] This was before 1915, when the four boys became founder members of the Ranelagh Company of Fianna Éireann.[97] Thus, from the age of perhaps fifteen and fourteen respectively, Niall and Brian were playing at, and training to be, soldiers together. In time, Turlough joined his older brothers. All three were active members of the South County Dublin IRA by 1920 and, as discussed already, both Niall and Turlough were imprisoned following the raids on their home in November of that year.

The Irish Civil War came slowly. The first half of 1922 was a time of tension, standoff and split. According to J.J. O'Connell, when the South County Dublin Brigade of the IRA split in March 1922, the entire brigade staff 'went irregular', except Niall. Niall worked to bring a large number of the Volunteers in his area over to the pro-treaty side.[98] Among these, he succeeded in bringing over Turlough and his cousin Hugh but not Brian. By September of 1922, the Civil War was raging on in the south and west, MacNeill was a minister in the provisional government, and Niall and Turlough were officers in the new National Army. Meanwhile, Brian was in Sligo where he had first been sent as an organiser by IRA GHQ after the July 1921 Truce.[99] It appears Brian stood alone within the family in opposing the treaty. He would be killed alongside three IRA comrades on the morning of 20 September 1922.[100]

One letter from Brian and three from Niall to their mother survive in the MacNeill family papers from this period. Brian's is dated 10 August and Niall wrote home on 18 August, and 1 and 5 September 1922. There is an innocence, and a hint of bravado, to these letters home. The boys keenly related the lighter side of the conflict to their mother, but were parsimonious in their references to personal hardship. From Ballisodare in Sligo, Brian joked about some of the characters he had met and about how the accounts of the campaign in Sligo carried in the *Irish Independent* were favourable to the Free State and not representative of realities on the ground. There is no hint of animosity towards his brothers in his letter. He asks his mother to 'Tell Niall and Tourlough [sic] that I send my best wishes to them', continuing that he 'would take a run up to see you but I have no wish to spend such lovely weather as this in a convict cell'.[101]

From Dundalk, Niall wrote to tell his mother that he and Turlough were safe and in good spirits. He recounted several close shaves and promised to tell his mother about the atrocities he had witnessed in Dundalk when next he saw her.[102] By September, Niall and Turlough had been sent south to County Wexford. En route, Niall called into his cousin Hugh, who was confined to bed in Wellington Barracks after being injured in the fighting.[103] Four days later, Niall wrote again and casually inquired about Brian at the end of an otherwise run-of-the-mill letter, the only reference to Brian within his three Civil War letters.[104] Just over two weeks later, his brother would be dead. While his three comrades were buried in a republican plot in Sligo, Brian's body was brought to Dublin by the family for burial.[105]

STATE FORMATION AND A FAMILY IN TRANSITION

It is tempting to see Brian's death as a watershed in the history of the MacNeill family. The surviving MacNeill children, except Séamus who was elsewhere, went for a family holiday with their mother to Letterkenny, County Donegal, in the summer of 1924. Eoin had to stay on in Dublin and Niall took the opportunity to practise his Irish, writing home to Netley to tell his father all about the fishing in Donegal. He told his father, '*Níl acht rud amháin amú agus sé sin nach bfhuilir fhéin anseo linn, agus tá súil againn nach fada anois go mbéidh tú linn.*'[106]

Eoin's government responsibilities meant that he was often away in the early years of the newly independent state. In 1923, he was part of a Free State government delegation to the League of Nations and, en route, he visited Bobbio for the thirteenth centenary of St Columbanus.[107] This was followed by his work on the Boundary Commission between November 1924 and the Commission's collapse twelve months later.

Work on the Boundary Commission necessitated trips to London. While staying at the Hotel Alwin in September 1925, Eoin wrote of his total isolation there:

> I am as much alone here as if I was living at the North Pole. Outside of the Commission and staff, I have only met one person of my previous acquaintance since I came, and that was no other than Sir A. Cope who ran into me in the Strand yesterday evening as I was walking to the office.[108]

There was, however, some of Eoin's old frivolity in his letters home from his tours of Ulster. He met many old friends there and, still obsessed with nature, he wrote to Agnes in awe of the badgers, geology, and the 'literally millions & millions' of primroses blooming all around Loch Erne in May 1925.[109] Eoin noted he was missing seeing his first two grandsons while he was away. Niall had christened his first son Brian and his second Eoin.[110] Breaking with his strict adherence to the term 'boundary' for the sake of poetic licence, he told Agnes how 'It would be great fun for me to help you keeping them [the grandchildren] in order, but borders is borders, and here I am until further orders.'[111]

In 1930, Máire MacNeill wrote to her father from an impromptu holiday to Donegal with Turlough, Róisín and Séamus. In the midst of an otherwise jovial letter, she turned to a more sombre subject, saying how she and her siblings planned to visit the place where Brian was killed in Sligo if they could manage it.[112] This is a rare reference to Brian in the surviving family's correspondence in the years after his death. Anne Dolan notes how MacNeill 'went proudly to [the 'Collins–Griffith' monument on] Leinster Lawn, left wreaths at Béal na Bláth. He never went to the cross at Benbulben that honoured his dead republican son.'[113] It should, however, be remembered that the commemorations of Collins and Griffith that MacNeill attended were state events. As a member of government, his attendance was neither strictly voluntary nor personal. Meanwhile, the MacNeills had taken Brian from Sligo and interred him in the family plot in Kilbarrack cemetery, on the north Dublin coast where Eoin's mother had been laid to rest in 1917.[114] Thus, while his siblings wished to bear witness to the spot where their older brother had been killed, his parents kept Brian's memory within the geographical and emotional confines of family grief rather than public mourning.[115]

These years saw a transition in the ways Eoin interacted with his children. They became his collaborators in his scholarship, especially Máire. Though her day job at this time was that of a private secretary to the general secretary of Cumann na nGaedheal,[116] she was also her father's *de facto* apprentice and scholarly aide-de-camp. She was liaising on his behalf with Dr R.I. Best in the National Library, corresponding with Eoin's colleagues in the Irish Manuscripts Commission, and arranging the distribution of various papers and articles by post.[117] One letter finds her at home in Blackrock sifting through annual reports from the Department of Education in order to send sections of interest to her father by post while he was on a speaking tour in North America in 1930.[118] On that tour, Eoin's workload increased when he reached Chicago, prompting him to write home to Agnes:

I am to go to the Wisconsin Univ. at Madison also later on. If these engagements keep on increasing I would love to have Máire here. It is hardly practicable just yet, but if it comes to that stage, I'll send a cable, so tell her to be quite ready & see if she can get an option on a *quick* passage without exactly booking it.[119]

When Eoin returned from North America, the lectures he had given there formed the basis of *Early Irish Laws and Institutions*. By then, Máire was working as a sub-editor on Cumann na nGaedheal's newspaper *United Ireland*. However, she left this to become her father's full-time assistant in 1933. She typed both *St Patrick, Apostle of Ireland* (1934) and *Early Irish Laws and Institutions* (1935) from her father's dictations.

This information on Máire's role in her father's scholarship is not new; much of it is contained in Maureen Murphy's biographical study of Máire MacNeill published in 2004.[120] However, such is the gap in time since the last major works of scholarship on MacNeill that it deserves mention here. It should serve as a reminder of the value of oral history and folkloric research methods to the study of modern historiography. Murphy took the opportunity to set the record straight and acknowledge the contribution that Máire MacNeill made not only to Eoin's scholarship but also to the works of both Tierney and F.X. Martin.[121] Murphy goes on to stress how it was not just Máire who played a key role in these later projects. Her sister, Eibhlín Tierney, received no acknowledgement for her central role in the biography of her father. Murphy ensures the record is corrected:

> When the book [Tierney's posthumously published biography of MacNeill] appeared in March 1981 [sic][122] Martin acknowledged Máire's help with proof-reading and the index but he offered no thanks to Eibhlín for her efforts in preparing the manuscript. Let this be a record of her contribution to bring the biography to completion.[123]

Murphy details how, following Tierney's death in 1975, it was Máire and Eibhlín who helped get the manuscript to the publisher. The fact that they brought files of *An Claidheamh Soluis* and the *Irish Volunteer* with them to Máire's home in Poulivaun, County Clare to work on the final typescript in January 1977 suggests that the text as Tierney had left it was far from polished at the time of his death.[124] A very early version of Tierney's biography can be found in his 'biographical study' included in Eoin's posthumously republished *St Patrick* (1964), which was edited by John

Ryan SJ.[125] A close reading of the two texts gives some further insight into the evolution, expansion and editing of the life of MacNeill that occurred between 1964 and 1980.

Thus, in their latter years, as much as in their youth, the MacNeill daughters played a significant role in the production of scholarship within the wider family. In understanding writings *about* MacNeill as much as writings *by* him, therefore, Bonnie G. Smith's characterisation of family members as 'researchers, copyists, collaborators, editors, proofreaders, and ghostwriters' very much holds true for the MacNeill family throughout the twentieth century.[126] Brian Hughes further enhances our understanding of MacNeill's domestic writing process in later years. He records how two journalists, Leila Carroll and Ita Mallon, typed MacNeill's memoir from dictation in 1932–3 and 1939–40 respectively.[127]

MEMORY AND LEGACY: 'THE GIFT OF SILENCE OF THE MacNEILLS'

Much of the scholarship on the Irish revolution that was written between the late 1940s and the 1960s led Eoin's children to feel that he had been misrepresented or, worse still, written out of history. Tierney blamed 'Marxism and mythology' for giving primacy to movements rather than people in the history of Ireland between 1913 and 1921.[128] Máire MacNeill felt her father 'was ignored, a victim of what she called the "silent treatment"'.[129] Privately, Eoin's children strove to understand their late father's role in history as they grew older. In 1958, Eibhlín Tierney wrote to her sister Máire about a visit her aunt-in-law Josephine – by then Irish Ambassador to Switzerland and Austria[130] – had just paid her:

> Jo MacN was here yesterday – she is off again tomorrow.
>   Do you remember Mathair telling of Uncle James annoyance at the mishandling from this side of Athair's resignation from the Boundary Commission? Jo gave me her version of it, which I will give you now as it will serve as a record of what she said …[131]

Depositions of this kind ensured that the generation then passing out of history could leave to the younger MacNeills their memories of the key events in Eoin's life as they recalled them. Eibhlín, her husband Michael, and her sister Máire were to the fore in preserving both the archive and oral memory of their father.

Fortuitously for a more nuanced understanding of history, the 'silent treatment' to which his children felt MacNeill was subjected was substantially redressed in the decades after his death. Both researchers and relatives played their part in ensuring that MacNeill's place in modern Irish history was not occluded. The other great champion of MacNeill and his place in modern Irish history was F.X. Martin. In 1961, Martin published two 'Memoranda' by MacNeill – one from February 1916 and the other written between June and October 1917. This was the first major step in reassessing MacNeill's legacy and rehabilitating him in a more nuanced and complex way into the historiography of the 1916 Rising.[132] For their part, the MacNeill children tried as much as possible to refrain from publicly engaging in the battles over the misrepresentation of their father. In-laws, however, played a significant role, presumably speaking for their spouses who, though hurt, refrained from wading into the fray in a personal capacity.

A good example of this can be found at the height of the commemoration mania of 1966 when Edie MacNeill, wife of the then Col. Niall MacNeill, wrote to the *Irish Times* to complain about the portrayal of Eoin in *Insurrection*, which had just aired on Telifís Éireann. She concluded that she had

> [felt] urged to write this in defence of a great man and patriot who suffered 'the slings and arrows of outrageous fortune' in silence. Not having the gift of silence of the MacNeills so without their knowledge or consent, I send this letter, in defence of my noble and patriotic father-in-law, who was my very good friend, to whom I was devoted, and whose memory I cherish.[133]

The most devoted defender among MacNeill's children-in-law was of course Michael Tierney. As early as 1930, Michael had written to Eoin during the latter's lecture tour of North America. He suggested that Eoin might go on the record about his role in 1916:

> ... being in America might be a favourable opportunity for you to give a true account of the whole affair, perhaps in the form of an interview, apropos of Devoy's book,[134] or in some other suitable way. Your story would be on record anyhow, and might come better if it appeared in a casual sort of way in America. You could get an interviewer to question you about Devoy's version and use that as an excuse for a

brief account of your own. I think it a terrible pity that people who really know nothing about it should be allowed to build up a legend that altogether misrepresents you.[135]

After Eoin's death, Tierney took the cause of rehabilitating MacNeill into his own hands through writing his biography. However, what is notable from the study of the complex authorship and gestation of this biography as discussed above is the way in which, though silent, Eoin's children very much felt aggrieved by his treatment and portrayal in history. They were supportive of, and even complicit in, the efforts of their spouses to defend their father's name and reputation. By contrast, the statement that Agnes MacNeill gave to the BMH in 1949 is decidedly sparse. Beyond putting on record that her husband was never a member of the IRB and knew nothing in advance about the landing of arms at Kerry, she did not give much away. Her statement opens with her telling her interviewer that 'My husband left a lot of papers, but we have not had time to go through them. My son-in-law, Mr. Tierney, intends one day to use them for compiling a life of my husband.'[136]

CONCLUSION: THE SIGNIFICANCE OF HOME

The study of home fills a significant gap in understanding three facets of Eoin MacNeill's life. First, it is a counterpoint to his 'man of action' persona. Second, it is a means of understanding the role of the domestic in his own writing process. Finally, it provides insight into how one of the key families of the Irish revolution crafted their history and reacted to depictions of their father in the aftermath of these years of upheaval.

MacNeill cannot fully be understood outside the context of the domestic sphere in which he spent so much of his time. In a comparative sense, I feel unqualified to comment on whether the MacNeill family were uncommonly close in the context of the wider history of the modern Irish family, but close they were. Eoin transitioned slowly from living with his family of origin to his life with Agnes, to his role as a grandfather. His children, in-laws and grandchildren made a significant contribution to modern Irish history by keeping the study of MacNeill's life the subject of interpretation and reinterpretation, a tradition that continues with Michael McDowell's chapter in the present volume.

It is a challenge to uncover the MacNeill who was '*At Home*: with children'[137] as the caricaturist V.L. O'Connor portrayed him just before the rising. MacNeill the professor, the Volunteer and the politician tend to eclipse him as he appeared to those who knew him best. His extended family were keen that these public personas of the paterfamilias they had known and loved were not omitted from the evolving memory of revolutionary Ireland. However, they were more private and more guarded about the 'Athair' they knew from home. Speaking of the house in which her parents died, Máire MacNeill expressed a fatalism, and even a possessiveness, about the memory of this private side of her family's life. This stands entirely in contrast to her own laconic work to preserve her father's public memory. Of the house, 63 Upper Leeson Street, she speculated that 'It will probably be knocked now and I feel it is right that other people won't move in, and the house ends with our associations.'[138]

His Own Words: MacNeill in autobiography and memoir

BRIAN HUGHES

Eoin MacNeill was no stranger to the pen. 'The North Began', published in *An Claidheamh Soluis* in November 1913, is arguably MacNeill's most famous and influential composition. As well as a contributor, MacNeill served as editor of *Irisleabhar na Gaeilge* (the *Gaelic Journal*) (1894–7), co-editor of *Fáinne an Lae* (1898–9), and editor of *An Claidheamh Soluis* (1899–1901). Over the course of a long and distinguished academic career, MacNeill published widely on Irish history, culture and politics in books, pamphlets and periodicals.[1] A nervous breakdown, brought on by a heavy workload and travel schedule as the volunteer secretary of the Gaelic League, left MacNeill with 'a dislike for writing letters' that he claims he never overcame.[2] He was often an unreliable correspondent, but MacNeill's substantial collection of personal papers, held at University College Dublin Archives with additional material in the National Library of Ireland, suggest that this aversion was not quite as debilitating as it might have been.[3] A prodigious output of public and private writing offers a wealth of valuable, first-hand material for historians of Irish education, the Irish language movement, Irish nationalism, and the birth and difficult early life of the Irish Free State – material that has been used widely, if sporadically, by historians since.[4]

MacNeill was, however, somewhat more reluctant to write about himself. The most significant exception to this generalisation, if still a problematic one, is a *c.*200-page typescript memoir unpublished in his lifetime.[5] MacNeill also occasionally drafted letters strongly setting forth his position on a particular issue without sending them. On other occasions he compiled accounts of significant events that were never intended for publication. An obvious example of this is a memorandum written in 1917 about the events leading up to his countermanding order in 1916, which was never circulated and remained unused by scholars until the early 1930s.[6] These accounts often mirror or complement narratives in MacNeill's memoir and, in a sense, also serve as snippets of autobiographical writing, with MacNeill challenging perceived inaccuracies or misrepresentations of events to which he was a party. This chapter will reassess MacNeill through his memoir and other fragments of (semi-) autobiographical writing.

THE MEMOIR

In 1932, MacNeill sat down to work on a memoir of his public life. He did so reluctantly and only in response to urging from his family to put on record 'an account of his life and particularly the historical events in which he had taken part'. When work began, it was with the proviso that – as his daughter Máire put it – he 'would never write it himself'.[7] Instead, a typist was sent to the family home to receive MacNeill's dictation. Over a number of months in 1932 and '33, journalist Leila Carroll typed the bulk of the surviving memoir. MacNeill spoke directly from memory, with no recourse to notes or papers.[8] After this initial spurt of activity, the text remained unfinished and untouched for several years. The respite is unexplained, but – if not the result of intransigence or prolonged procrastination – might be a result of the pressure of MacNeill's academic work or the difficult early years of the Irish Manuscripts Commission, of which MacNeill was founding chairman.[9] Equally unexplained is MacNeill's decision to resume his dictation, this time to another journalist, Ita Mallon, in 1939. Relatively little ground was covered in this second phase, and that much rather scrappily. Mallon instead seems to have focused on improving the text of the original dictation. In these sittings a rough table of contents was also produced and, on 4 January 1940, a copy of the text was forwarded to MacNeill with the promise that 'I shall be able to clear up any blanks on Tuesday next'.[10] It is not clear if the proposed meeting ever took place, but many blanks certainly remained unfilled.

Mallon undertook a major revision of the text, making substantial manuscript changes to spelling, grammar and syntax, and removing repetitious passages. She also made suggestions for structural changes and items upon which MacNeill might expand. On 7 November 1941, Mallon forwarded the typescript text with her manuscript emendations to MacNeill. She further recommended that an 'alphabetical index' might be of use to the reader and encouraged MacNeill to 'set down more personal recollections of the Boundar[y] Commission': 'If the Commission's report is not published, it will be an invaluable record, and if it is, it will give more interest to your memoirs.'[11] Mallon had also suggested an additional chapter on '"famous men I have met" (and women)' and wrote that by including this 'you could introduce the University and cultural background as well as the political, and give a fuller account of your activities'.[12]

As sensible as Mallon's suggestions may have been – and there was, no doubt, scope for more on both the Boundary Commission and MacNeill's academic career – they were never approved or otherwise by MacNeill. The text was never revised and, after his death in 1945, family and friends agreed that the original typed draft represented 'what he actually dictated', while Mallon's additions 'should not be considered part of his memoir'.[13] As Tierney (who had married MacNeill's daughter Eibhlín in 1923) pointed out in his biography of MacNeill, the memoir that remained would 'require much editing before it could be published'.[14] Many of its themes and topics are underdeveloped, it is sometimes scattered in its chronology, there is little sense of a clear chapter structure, and the text is often repetitive. It certainly needed substantial work and serious revision before a contemporary publisher would have even considered it. But, in some ways, this is what makes it so powerful as a historical document. This is not a carefully sculpted or manicured account of MacNeill's life, framed to meet the needs of a publishing house or the reading public, but something much more immediate. In that sense, it is as much an oral history as a traditional memoir. Indeed, it seems unlikely that MacNeill ever intended it for public release in his lifetime. Having retired in 1941, he died of abdominal cancer on 15 October 1945.

In 1947, the Irish government established a Bureau of Military History, with the aim of gathering together testimony of those involved in the struggle for independence. Between 1947 and 1957, the BMH collected 1,773 'witness statements', a range of ancillary material, and 322 collections of documents (referred to as 'Contemporary Documents').[15] In the summer of 1947, Agnes MacNeill temporarily donated the original typescript of her late husband's 'memoir' to the BMH. Two copies were made (ignoring Mallon's suggested edits), with one returned to Agnes MacNeill and the other kept as part of the BMH's collection.[16] A number of versions of this important piece of autobiography have therefore survived: the original typescript copy of the memoir, as dictated by MacNeill and with handwritten comments by Ita Mallon, is held in the MacNeill papers at UCD Archives;[17] two copies of the BMH's typescript version, with minor handwritten emendations by Máire MacNeill, are also held in UCD;[18] and a final copy, containing some additional, unique typographical corrections, is kept in the BMH Contemporary Documents collection at the Military Archives of Ireland.[19]

An analysis of the contents of this memoir offers some important insights into MacNeill's own thoughts about his role in twentieth-century Irish history, expressed both explicitly and more subtly, several years after his enforced retirement from public life.

EVALUATING MacNEILL THROUGH AUTOBIOGRAPHY

The Gaelic League and revolution

From the outset, MacNeill's memoir makes clear that it was his upbringing in Glenarm, County Antrim that served as the formative influence for his later political and academic interests. Though MacNeill's Irish was learned and perfected as an adult, he opens rather nostalgic reminiscences about his upbringing in Glenarm with the hints of the Irish language to which he had been exposed – even though it had 'become customary' in his grandparents' time for 'parents to conceal their own knowledge of Irish from their children'.[20] Of greater significance in the context of this chapter are MacNeill's reflections – as a northern Catholic who had been deeply associated with the nationalist movement – on inter-denominational relationships in his hometown. 'The local people of different religions,' he insisted, 'got on remarkably well together ... there was hardly such a thing as politics in Glenarm.'[21] As will be seen below, MacNeill remained convinced in his adulthood that religious and political differences in Ireland were not inherent, natural or inevitable, but essentially a deliberate British construct.

The memoir then offers a unique insight into the foundation and early years of the Gaelic League, of which MacNeill was a founding member and driving force. Beginning a day's dictation in September 1932, he outlined that he did not intend to go into detail about the 'growth of the Gaelic League', but rather to 'refer to certain things in which I had special experience'.[22] This is a trope repeated throughout and, importantly, highlights one of the primary purposes that MacNeill saw for his memoir: to record events, conversations and perspectives that were known only to him. A series of anecdotes, ranging from ones about obscure figures like printer Patrick Mahon to others concerning academic colleagues such as Professor R.A.S. Macalister, and national figures like Patrick Pearse and Douglas Hyde, serve the same purpose.

In 1937, MacNeill told Máire of the two decisions in his public life that he had come to regret. The first was pushing the Gaelic League's entry into nationalist politics in 1915 (the second, regarding the Boundary

Commission, is discussed below).[23] This is reflected in passages in MacNeill's memoir, dictated five years earlier. 'I was so strongly convinced that we were in the middle of national crisis,' MacNeill recalled, 'that I thought everyone else as well as myself should throw all our weight into the work of national defence.' MacNeill's views were shared by the 'majority' within the Gaelic League, while others – including the organisation's president Douglas Hyde and his colleague at UCD Agnes O'Farrelly – 'took a different line' and MacNeill later believed that 'those who opposed me were right and that I was wrong'. While MacNeill claimed to have been under no illusion that the Gaelic League had been used as a covert 'recruiting ground' for the Irish Republican Brotherhood anyway, 'the main result was that the political aspect of Irish nationality got the upper hand' within the organisation, 'a complete departure from its whole principles and policy'.[24] Writing in the 1930s, the consequence of this, as MacNeill saw it, was a dramatic fall in the place of the language within Irish nationalism and a consequent reversal in standards of patriotism from a peak at the turn of the century:

> Anyone looking around in Ireland at the present day can see that the standard of patriotism for young and old has drifted back to what it was before 1895. Patriotic duty consists now in voting for the right party or organising for the party vote. As for any sort of national activity on the part of the people themselves doing things for themselves, we hear less of it at present than under the British regime. Even when it comes to things like the language, there is a strong tendency to expect results and try to produce them by action of a purely political kind.[25]

Significantly, MacNeill later returned to this theme, insisting that 'I now think that the Gaelic League ... should have kept entirely clear of politics, and that its failure to do so, for which I am in part responsible, has been bad for the objects of the League and has had other bad results in the time that followed'.[26]

MacNeill had similar problems with the political use of the Irish Volunteers, though he had no such doubts or regrets about the actions for which he is best known, and it is no surprise that a significant portion of the memoir is devoted to 1916. The memoir offers a detailed account of the weeks and days leading up to the countermanding order, MacNeill's attempt to stop the rising, and his week after this attempt had failed.[27] It is clear that MacNeill still believed that his actions had been justified and that he remained firm on his rationale for opposing the plans of Patrick

Pearse and his fellow conspirators. He had first outlined his thoughts on the purpose of the Irish Volunteers and the justified use of physical force in February or March 1916, in a memorandum composed for a meeting of the Irish Volunteer leadership.[28] This pre-dated the rising but after it had taken place MacNeill very quickly realised the necessity of having his own version of events on the record. On 9 May 1916, while in prison, MacNeill compiled handwritten notes on a meeting with Pearse and James Connolly in early 1916, during which he tried to convince Connolly of the folly of a rising, and a day-by-day account of his actions beginning on Good Friday 1916.[29] In 1917, some time after his release from prison, MacNeill again recorded the build-up to Easter Sunday 1916, following the same format – he clearly placed great significance on the meeting with Connolly and Pearse – but this time in greater detail. This second 'memorandum' was written at the behest of Bulmer Hobson, who was then compiling material for a history of the Irish Volunteers, and remained in Hobson's possession until it was deposited in the National Library of Ireland.[30] These accounts are generally consistent in terms of content and argument. Their intention is to set out and contextualise MacNeill's actions, but relatively little time is spent in explicit justification; the actions and their motivations in themselves seem to be deemed sufficient for the task.

By the 1930s, MacNeill remained critical of Pearse's 'notion of heroism on the Cuchulainn model', as he put it.[31] In a letter to author and poet Father Henry E.G. Rope in 1931, which seems not to have been sent, MacNeill lays out a forceful critique of the contemporary principles of 'doctrinaire Republicans': 'activists of the same party murdered Kevin O'Higgins in my sight' and were willing to 'murder' a police officer 'at his own door in the hearing of his wife'. 'Essentially', MacNeill suggested,

> they belong to the very same school as the Imperialists they denounce. For both sets, patriotism means devotion to some form of State absolutism ... The Statists of every variety, Irish, English, French, German, Russian, Italian, and the rest, high and low, of every party, are next to the Devil the worst enemies of mankind. They are the enemies of nationality in the true sense, and their conflict here in Ireland for the last ten years has given Irish nationality a worse set back than the previous 50 years of my memory.

MacNeill defiantly declared that if Pearse 'were alive today and associated with this sort of political doctrinairism, I would tell him as I told him in his lifetime that it was not right'.[32] As Donal McCartney has noted, in the 1930s MacNeill was particularly fond of 'drawing a sharp distinction between "nationality" and "nationalism", between "nation" and "state"', a distinction he had been making throughout his writing career.[33] These sentiments are mirrored – if less forcefully – alongside reflections on the Gaelic League and the rising in his memoir. 'Politics,' he asserts, 'were and have remained to me a secondary and subservient matter as regards Irish Nationality.'[34] 'Nowadays one might think that in the patriotic view, Ireland is only a political entity.'[35] MacNeill also speaks critically of Standish O'Grady's *Story of Ireland* (1894) – 'still highly praised by men of certain literary connection' – as it 'advocated a purely pagan ideal of heroism and held to contempt the heroes of the Irish Christian tradition'; W.B. Yeats' play *Cathleen Ní Houlihan* (first performed in 1902) had similarly promoted a 'mythical view' of Irish nationalism and placed it 'well into the popular mind in general'.[36] Within his memoir narrative, these ideas, which were being articulated elsewhere at the same time, are tied inherently to MacNeill's understanding, indeed his justification, of his actions in 1916 and after.

Both the 1917 memorandum and his 1930s memoir form an important corrective to what MacNeill saw as a deliberately misleading narrative of his role in 1916. MacNeill, for instance, directly contradicts Pearse's assertion to him in 1916 that MacNeill had been 'in some ways difficult to approach', describing this as 'sheer nonsense'.[37] Additionally, significant corrections to publicly pronounced beliefs or perceptions are made in two paragraphs appended to the 1917 memorandum immediately after the Sinn Féin convention in October 1917, where MacNeill was elected to the Sinn Féin executive but also subject to robust criticism from Constance Markievicz and Kathleen Clarke. He was accused of having 'cut the ground from under the feet' of the rising with his countermanding order, of going back on his signature to the first draft of the proclamation, and of causing fatal confusion by repeatedly changing his mind.[38] MacNeill responded directly to the accusation that he had signed the proclamation and then reneged on his signature as 'untrue and without foundation'. The alleged existence of his name among a printed list 'from which it was afterwards removed is obviously no proof at all of my signature'.[39] In his memoir, MacNeill repeated this declaration twice, adding that 'Even with the intention of taking up arms, I would certainly have refused to sign a proclamation containing a delusive statement about alliance with Germany and Austria.'[40] He also argued that it was 'untrue that I changed my mind several times'. MacNeill instead claims that he had believed 'for a few hours that all was

over for our movement and nothing left for us except to sell our lives as
dearly as possible' but once informed that the situation was 'by no means so
desperate' was convinced that 'the rising ought to be prevented'.[41]

Combined, these retrospective accounts make clear MacNeill's desire to
place his perspective on the historical record – if not necessarily to have it
published – and to contradict unfounded or malicious accounts by others.
Writing in the 1960s, F.X. Martin suggested that the 'most noticeable
characteristic' of the 1917 memorandum is its 'dispassionate tone. MacNeill
condemns nobody, though he might easily have considered himself to
have reasonable grounds for resentment.'[42] Though the same might also be
true of MacNeill's memoir, he was much less measured towards those who
wrote histories of the period. A pronounced desire to correct the historical
record is evident in passages where MacNeill directly contradicts recent
publications, particularly those treating his own actions and motivations.
Dictating from memory, these were slights and misrepresentations that
remained fresh in MacNeill's mind. Trinity College Dublin historian
W. Alison Phillips' 1923 book *The Revolution in Ireland*, for instance, is
referred to as a 'volume of so called history' – an accusation prompted by
the use of what MacNeill described as 'concocted' police reports of Sinn
Féin disturbances during campaigning for the East Clare by-election in
1917.[43]

One revealing corrective concerns the meeting between MacNeill,
Pearse and Connolly in early 1916. In his memoir, MacNeill commented
that 'An invented account of this interview has been published based on
ignorant and malicious gossip.' Though it is not named, this may be French
historian Louis Le Roux's biography of Pearse, translated to English by
Desmond Ryan and published some months before MacNeill's comments
(made in December 1932).[44] Le Roux was, in fact, the only writer at that
point with access to MacNeill's 1917 memorandum, but used it selectively
and misquoted MacNeill on one occasion.[45] In his own copy of the book,
MacNeill scribbled 'Mere Invention' and 'More Lies' next to passages
about his reaction to the 'Castle document' and another story about being
shadowed by police on the Tuesday preceding the rising.[46]

MacNeill seems to have been particularly irked by authors commenting
on events or meetings for which he was the only surviving witness. He notes
in his memoir, for instance, that 'a true account' of the January 1916 meeting
'could only have come from Pearse, Connolly and myself and if those
who pretend to know what took place at the interview could show some
authority from any of the three they would not fail to do so. Not having this

they invented what they liked.'⁴⁷ 'In fact,' he later asserted, 'in all the books that have been published, with regard to the happenings from 1913 down, not a single writer has come to me for information though many things have been published about which I was the only living authority better than gossip.'⁴⁸ In a letter to Louis Le Roux in October 1936, presumably referring to the latter's forthcoming biography of Thomas Clarke, MacNeill commented on passages sent to him by Le Roux for review by noting that one sentence in particular 'altogether misrepresents the truth'; Le Roux might have been expected to engage a 'mutual friend' in advance of supplying 'a series of statements concerning my attitude and action in a great national crisis'. In a cutting piece of peer review, MacNeill finished by asking:

> With regard to what follows, and much of what has been written in your book already published [on Pearse], do you recognise any obligation in the interest of truth to enquire upon what kind of evidence these statements of what took place at interviews between me and others who are now dead are based and ought to be based?⁴⁹

MacNeill was similarly critical of Piaras Béaslaí's two-volume biography of Michael Collins, published in 1926.⁵⁰ Many instances in the book were, as MacNeill put it, 'based on nothing better than the gossip of cliques which possess no knowledge of the facts of the case and which seem to have been inserted to show the undercurrent of hostility that I always had to meet among the doctrinaires'.⁵¹ The account that specifically drew MacNeill's ire on this occasion referred to negotiations between Sinn Féin and the Irish Parliamentary Party (IPP) on the northern constituencies during the 1918 general election campaign. To avoid the damage of a split nationalist vote, MacNeill was sent to represent Sinn Féin in discussions with IPP leader John Dillon. Both MacNeill and Dillon agreed that each party would contest four of the eight constituencies, but were unable to come to an agreement on their division (MacNeill's own Derry constituency was one point of contention).⁵² 'At this point,' MacNeill admitted, 'Dillon got the better of me' as it was agreed that Cardinal Logue of Armagh would mediate. Logue, as MacNeill tells it, simply divided the constituencies to ensure that the four encroaching on his diocese would be contested by the IPP. East Down, where the Ancient Order of Hibernians (Board of Erin) (AOH) were particularly strong, was assigned to Sinn Féin, but it soon became clear that the AOH in East Down were intending to run their own candidate. MacNeill described how he had endeavoured to persuade Joseph Devlin, president of the AOH and IPP MP for West Belfast, to bring his followers in line with the agreement only to meet with a 'vague and evasive' response; in the end, 'in the face of a large nationalist majority, the seat went to the Unionist'.[53] Of particular offence to MacNeill, along with the neglect of Devlin's influence in the narrative, is likely to have been Béaslaí's suggestion that MacNeill had – to the 'astonishment of the Sinn Féin Executive, and the anger of [Harry] Boland' – been responsible for an 'undemocratic decision', which was then enforced on the executive, and had 'exceeded his instructions' in doing so.[54]

MacNeill was occasionally provoked to respond to information printed in the press, sometimes sending his rebuttals and sometimes not. In December 1930, for instance, he took issue with the depiction of Roger Casement offered in a review published in the Catholic newspaper *The Universe* of Denis Gwynn's *Life and Death of Roger Casement* and wrote a response to the editor.[55] Much later, in February 1944, he also compiled notes on a series of articles in the *Irish Times* by Cathal O'Shannon on the history of the first Dáil's 1919 Democratic Programme, questioning the credit O'Shannon had offered to Labour leader Thomas Johnson for the programme's text.[56] On 26 May 1933, just before MacNeill resumed work on his memoir after a six-month break, the *Irish Press* published what they described as 'one of the most stirring disclosures ever given to the Irish people', courtesy of a statement by George Noble Plunkett, father of 1916 leader Joseph. The statement detailed how, several weeks before the rising, Plunkett had been sent by the executive of the Irish Volunteers, then acting as a 'provisional government', as an envoy to Rome. After a two-hour audience with Pope Benedict XV, where they discussed 'the question of the upcoming struggle for Irish Independence', Benedict 'conferred his Apostolic Benediction on the men who were facing death for Ireland's Liberty'. Plunkett's statement further suggested that 'John MacNeill will remember that he signed the commission given to this (unnamed) Republican Envoy to Rome'.[57] MacNeill, though, had no such recollection. Moreover, he questioned the contention that the Volunteer executive was acting as a 'provisional government' three weeks before the rising, and the idea that Benedict would offer such absolution in the context of a European war.[58] Plunkett had stated that he was reluctantly publishing the details 'in the interests of truth', but MacNeill was more sceptical on the timing, coinciding with a visit by then Taoiseach Éamon de Valera to Rome: 'There were many occasions during the seventeen years when the same disclosure, if it stated facts, would have been highly opportune. Why was it withheld?'[59] Most of MacNeill's commentary, however, remained confined to his personal papers. A much shorter letter to the editor appeared instead, simply pointing out that the Volunteer executive had never acted as a 'provisional government' before Easter 1916.[60] A letter of reply by Áine Ceannt requesting that MacNeill 'unequivocally' deny that he had 'signed a Letter of Credence to the Vatican' was quickly met with a very firm statement that MacNeill had not signed any document of the kind and had 'no cognisance of any such acts'.[61]

Even with his reluctance to publish, MacNeill obviously recognised the long-term value of his personal papers, as a typescript memorandum and accompanying note among his papers suggests. The memorandum had been delivered by MacNeill to the Boundary Commission and, as the note pointed out, would serve to 'clear up two points' on 'the views taken by me of the main effect of the Treaty as regards the Commission' and 'the view taken by me of the maximum claim put forward on behalf of Northern Ireland'.[62] There was clearly no intention to publish but rather to make sure that this information was available for a future generation of scholars; presumably the desired aim for his memoir too. MacNeill's training as a historian is also evident as he repeatedly points readers of his memoir to the documentary record, in place of much of the published work on the period.[63] Incidentally, by way of contrast, MacNeill was much more favourable towards British army general Frank Percy Crozier's *Ireland for Ever*, published in 1932 and perhaps best known for its searing critique of British policy in Ireland and the conduct of the 'Black and Tans' and Auxiliaries.[64]

MacNeill was clearly conscious of timing when it came to the impact of published work. Even after he had composed his 1917 memorandum on his role in the rising, MacNeill remained reluctant to stoke the fires publicly. In May 1918, many of the leading figures in Sinn Féin (not including MacNeill) were arrested as a result of the British authorities' invented 'German plot'. Sinn Féin was also leading the charge in attempts to oppose the introduction of conscription to Ireland and preparing to contest a by-election in East Cavan (eventually won by Arthur Griffith). At the same time, Bulmer Hobson – by then sidelined from the nationalist movement – was working towards publication of the first volume of *A Short History of the Irish Volunteers*.[65] He had asked MacNeill to provide a preface, but when the manuscript was returned in early June 1918 Hobson 'was extremely disappointed in it'. Hobson had hoped that his book, and MacNeill's preface, would vindicate their position in 1916 and counter-attacks made against those who had stood with MacNeill and suffered the 'grossest of calumny ever since'. It was, Hobson believed, essential to correct the narrative and 'it must be made plain that in acting as we did we were supporting honour and honesty as against deceit'. Instead, what Hobson had received 'carefully refrained from saying anything that could not be said equally appropriately in an introduction to any other book on modern Ireland'.[66] In riposte, MacNeill suggested that he was 'not conscious of having ever agreed to write an introduction in the sense you indicate, and I have no recollection of your mentioning it'. In any case, 1918 'was not the time for clearing up that situation', even if this meant 'disregarding slander and injustice for the time, so far as public refutation goes'; while Hobson's book might 'cause the tortoise to put out its head', in the meantime there would be 'little satisfaction in peppering it on the shell'.[67] It is not clear what was in MacNeill's original draft, but the published version will have done little to appease Hobson's initial complaints. He and Hobson were, he wrote, 'of one accord' in 1916. But, MacNeill continued, 'As to whether those who agreed with us were right or wrong, the Irish people themselves will decide in due time.'[68] For MacNeill, clearly a historian with faith in his successors, published inaccuracies should occasionally be corrected. Otherwise, leaving his words for judgement in the future was enough.

In the same way that MacNeill's critiques of recently published work is revealing, so too is the marked repetition in his memoir, a trait otherwise undesirable in a traditional autobiography. Here, the unprompted retelling of an anecdote or an interpretation – often as an aside to an ongoing narrative trail – gives the reader a real sense of certain ideas on which MacNeill was entirely convinced, the ideas he was most keen to record. In a passage dictated in October 1932, for instance, MacNeill commented that 'due credit has never, in my opinion, been given to Carson for his share in bringing about the changes that have come in Ireland'.[69] On several occasions in the memoir the contention is made that it was – paradoxically – Ulster Unionist leader Sir Edward Carson who had sparked the process that eventually led to twenty-six county independence in 1922. It was, he claimed, Carson's defiance of the British government – first in speeches and then overtly – that began the dismantling of the instruments of British rule. Indeed, this was apparently his response when asked by a journal editor 'about how the strange developments in Ireland had come about.[70]

In his 1917 memorandum, MacNeill related how he had told James Connolly in January 1916 that in the case of a rising the British government 'could easily contrive that the orangemen would make an appearance in arms and then the govt would throw its force against us while pretending to the world that it was saving Ireland from civil war etc'.[71] This is an early example of a sentiment expressed repeatedly in his memoir: that sectarian divisions in Ireland were deliberately fostered to thwart Irish self-determination. In fact, he had already articulated this position in print, in a pamphlet entitled *The Ulster Difficulty*, which, in his own words, 'especially intended to counteract the plan of British politicians to work up and utilise sectarian differences in Ulster for their own political ends'. The pamphlet ended by affirming that 'In an independent Ireland, there will be no "Ulster Difficulty"'.[72] As he dictated his memoir, MacNeill repeatedly insisted that across decades British politicians had stoked up sectarian animosity as a means of denying nationalist aspirations.[73] 'The plan,' MacNeill asserted, 'is to supply provocation and to allow it to come to a head and create bad blood before any attempt is permitted to have a contrary effect.'[74] Ulster unionists were mere puppets of British politicians, while nationalists had been tricked into viewing fellow Irishmen as their enemies.[75]

For an intellectual like MacNeill – a deep thinker, widely read and well versed in centuries of Irish history – this is a surprisingly naïve interpretation of communal differences in Ireland, but one of which he remained utterly convinced throughout his life. It was a belief deeply rooted in his upbringing in County Antrim. The first instance MacNeill records of British malevolence in stirring up sectarian antagonism led to a criminal indictment against his father, who had tried to intervene as British authorities allowed a 'provocative' Orange assembly in Glenarm ('There was no such thing as an Orange Lodge in Glenarm'), leading to 'a scuffle on a very small scale'.[76] Nor was MacNeill immune to an over-simplified or romantic interpretation of the Anglo-Irish conflict between 1919 and 1921. British attempts to suppress the republican movement, for instance, were 'hard to carry out' with 'practically the whole public man, woman and child backing' the Dáil counter-government.[77] He argued that 'Dublin Castle was unable to secure a single informer and hardly able by terror to produce a single squeal'.[78] While composing his memoir, MacNeill would have been unaware of informers now well-known to historians, such as 'Granite' and 'Chalk' in 1916, the conviction here is nonetheless unconvincing. In fact, the Irish Volunteers/Irish Republican Army were often obsessed with uncovering and rooting out (both actual and perceived) informers in their localities after 1919.[79]

Nevertheless, these were not ideas that had been formulated on the spot, but were often repeated in private. Máire MacNeill later asserted that her mother and other members of her father's family and friends had 'often heard him speak of the events treated' in the memoir and were satisfied that the original transcription was an accurate reflection of his thoughts.[80]

The Boundary Commission

If the event in MacNeill's career most indelibly impressed in the public consciousness is the 1916 countermanding order, his service on the Boundary Commission perhaps lies second.[81] MacNeill's only regret, however, was refusing to countenance the release of a minority report.[82] As with 1916, it becomes clear from MacNeill's reflections that the political fallout and personal criticism that followed the Boundary Commission did little or nothing to change his conviction that he had acted correctly and in good faith and it was, instead, the deception or misunderstanding of others that had been at fault.

In his appointment as the Free State's representative to the Commission, MacNeill is cast (again) in his memoir as the reluctant public servant, consenting to act 'for two reasons: because I was asked by the Provisional govt. to act and because no one else could be found to act instead of me'. It was, he insisted, 'the most disagreeable duty I had ever undertaken for to my mind it was nothing short of an outrage on Ireland, and I may say on civilization, to be asked to draw a line across this country dividing it on a basis of religious differences'. From MacNeill's perspective, it was 'impossible to expect satisfactory results' and hopes in this regard were based on 'mistakes about this clause [Article 12 of the Anglo-Irish treaty] in many people's minds in America as well as Ireland that the Boundary Commission was engaged in arriving at a treaty through negotiations': 'Those who thought this had either never read the clause or had forgotten it.' The Commission was never about negotiation, MacNeill believed, but was set up to serve as 'a kind of judicial body to examine the evidence and arrive at a decision'. Tellingly, at this point in his narrative MacNeill once again asserts his belief that British politicians had stoked sectarian disturbances to protect their own interests in Ireland.[83]

Around the same time, MacNeill also articulated his idea that partition was a policy that had been decided upon by the British government in advance of negotiations. In his 1931 letter to Father Rope, MacNeill pointed out that 'not merely Partition but the most indefensible features of Partition were the adopted policy of the British Government, which had the deciding voice under the terms of Clause 12'. Moreover, despite 'having the deepest objections to Clause 12 than any other man as far as I know', he was chosen to put that Clause into operation and was afterwards denounced and defamed for its shortcomings ... I have been denounced as an incompetent negotiator – that was the mildest criticism – when in fact I was appointed one of a tribunal of three to take evidence and arrive at a judicial decision, and not to negotiate about anything.[84]

MacNeill, therefore, remained unwilling to accept that he had fared poorly in his role on the Commission. Instead, he was keen to make clear that the failings of the Boundary Commission were inevitable, and beyond his control: the weakness of Article 12 itself, and allowing the British to act as 'umpire' to boundary discussions by appointing the chair to the committee.[85]

The Civil War

MacNeill's memoir and other fragments of autobiographical writing are almost exclusively reflections on his career as an activist, organiser and politician (with the exception of his time as Minister for Education, which MacNeill declines to comment upon). Regrettably, there is little insight into MacNeill's impressive and pioneering academic career, most obviously as Chair of Early (including Medieval) Irish History at UCD. It might be suggested that by the 1930s MacNeill's academic life was still thriving and thus required little reflection, but a conscious decision was made to record a narrative of his public life after the end of his political career. Even still, it remains an incomplete account, with the reader forced to search for more subtle hints of MacNeill's retrospective position.

The most striking omission is the Irish Civil War (1922–3). Though MacNeill reflected in some detail about the debates in Dáil Éireann on the Anglo-Irish treaty in December 1921 and January 1922 – during which he held the 'troublesome and tiresome job' of speaker of the Dáil[86] – the violent and bitter conflict that followed between anti-treaty republicans and the provisional government and Irish Free State, in which MacNeill held a ministerial portfolio, hardly warranted a mention. There is a vague reference contrasting the good-natured behaviour of Sinn Féin supporters in 1917 and 1918 with 'what was experienced after 1921'.[87] The only other mention serves to downplay the Civil War: MacNeill suggests that, following the Parnell split of the 1890s, 'the bitterness of that time was deeper and sharper and more widespread than anything we experienced afterwards even at the height of the Civil War in '22'.[88]

MacNeill had lived through both crises but his suggestion that the Parnell split was more devastating than the Civil War is remarkable given the personal impact of the latter conflict. But at the same time, his reticence regarding the Civil War is not unusual among those who saw it to its conclusion; the composition of the memoir began less than a decade after 1923 when wounds were still raw (and would remain so for much longer than that). There is little doubt that the Civil War had been personally devastating for MacNeill. When his terminally ill sister Annie McGavock had travelled to Dublin to convince MacNeill to spare the life of Erskine Childers, then under a sentence of death, the siblings quarrelled and were not reconciled. While two of MacNeill's sons joined the National Army in 1922, a third, Brian, remained loyal to his anti-treatyite colleagues in Sligo. On 20 September 1922, he was shot and killed by National Army troops at Ben Bulben. Brian's death had its own unique impact on MacNeill. The family had remained close, despite their political divergence, and MacNeill was a firm devotee (regardless of any evidence to the contrary) of a somewhat idealised version of his son's death: he believed that Brian had shaken hands and laughed with the men who had found him dying. Reports suggesting Brian had been killed after surrendering were, for MacNeill, merely devised to torment him.[89] The last mention of Brian in the memoir comes during MacNeill's narrative of Easter week, cycling to Rathgar, with no mention or hint of what is to come.[90] After 1923, MacNeill would lay wreaths at the cenotaph dedicated to Michael Collins and Arthur Griffith on Leinster Lawn, and the site of the ambush during which Collins was fatally wounded at Béal na Bláth, but never visited the cross at Ben Bulben that marked the death of Brian MacNeill.[91]

Conclusion

What is most significant about MacNeill's public career when reflected upon through the lens of autobiography is the remarkable consistency of his convictions across decades. Two relatively minor personal regrets from a career like MacNeill's might be a surprise to many. This is, perhaps, both a mark of deep thinking and also to some extent of stubbornness, an ability to remain unmoved in the face of often vehement criticism. Recognising the value of having his own perspective on the record, while often simultaneously resisting the temptation to put it in the public domain, is a sign of confidence and a decidedly thick skin for a reluctant politician.

In contrast to silence on the Civil War, for instance, is a poignant and sympathetic account of the shooting of MacNeill's former cabinet colleague and then Minister for Justice, Kevin O'Higgins. MacNeill was asked to prepare a speech for the funeral to be delivered by Richard Mulcahy. MacNeill complied, but, he remembered, 'It all came strangely to me':

> I had always been on the best of personal terms with O'Higgins but in many ways there was not much sympathy between us. I knew that long before this he had been saying to people that it was time the old man got off the tram tracks and it was at his instance and upon his motion that my resignation from the government had been given in.[92]

For MacNeill, ill-will was, perhaps, more naturally directed towards those he considered bad historians than his political opponents. On another level, MacNeill's fondness for an anecdote in his memoir reveals a sense of humour, a playfulness, and a memory for a witty quip, that is not so readily found elsewhere.[93] Not all of the jokes stand up well on paper. In one case, MacNeill tells of a train journey where he was twice asked not to smoke in a non-smoking compartment, firstly by a young man who was being brought 'to a certain institution' and whose companion told MacNeill that he could have his smoke. On the second occasion, a 'man in clerical garb' had just lit a cigar and MacNeill took out his own pipe, tobacco and matches. When another passenger ('a spruce young fellow') again pointed out that it was a non-smoking compartment, the priest leaned out the window while the young man told MacNeill, '"You can go ahead and have your smoke; it wasn't you at all; it was him there."' The moral is, perhaps, that MacNeill politely declined to smoke without approval, but managed to light his pipe in both cases. Or it may be a reflection on attitudes towards the man in 'clerical garb'. Regardless, the outwardly austere and thoughtful academic is complemented here with a droll sense of humour and a (perhaps less surprising) love of storytelling. Indeed, the train anecdote originally won MacNeill a new pipe during a light-hearted break from organising gun-running in 1914.[94] This might well deserve some further reflection in any reassessment of Eoin MacNeill.

The Political Legacy: an insider on the outside

DIARMAID FERRITER

W
ho were the agents of national will in Ireland during the revolutionary decade 1913–23? That question goes to the heart of the political career and legacy of Eoin MacNeill and it was his struggle to answer it that heavily influenced contemporary and retrospective assessments of him. It was also a question that generated a heavy burden for MacNeill and his family as, like others, they were cruelly divided by the Civil War.

The tumultuous events of that era created crises of conscience and confidence for MacNeill that at different stages placed him at odds with both the diehards and the more moderate of the era. Consider, for example, the frustration expressed about MacNeill in September 1914 by Diarmuid Coffey who worked on the staff of the Irish Volunteers and supported John Redmond's attempts to control the Volunteers: MacNeill 'does not stick to a settled course. I liken him to a man trying to swim to Tír na nÓg & thinking each point of the compass is it until he finally swims around in circles. Another man said he always conspires with each man against the man he conspired with last.'[1]

Just over eighteen months later, Constance Markievicz, revelling in her absolutism, heard of MacNeill's decision, as chief of staff of the Irish Volunteers, to issue a countermand to the order for Volunteers to mobilise on Easter Sunday 1916. According to Christopher Brady, a printer on the staff of the *Workers' Republic* who printed the 1916 Proclamation, Markievicz arrived into the machine room with MacNeill's countermanding telegram announcing 'I will shoot Eoin MacNeill', to which Brady recalled James Connolly replying: 'You are not going to hurt a hair on MacNeill's head. If anything happens to MacNeill I will hold you responsible.'[2]

MacNeill's countermand was a crucial intervention born of anger at a serious deception. It was a pivotal moment in modern Irish history and a defining event for MacNeill and his peers. The countermand led to the postponement of what became the Easter Rising until Monday and ensured that fewer Volunteers mobilised than was planned and that the rising was heavily concentrated in Dublin. By issuing this countermand MacNeill denied the IRB cover for a nationwide rising and it ensured considerable hostility towards him from the self-declared republican purists but, as revealed by James Connolly's reprimand to Markievicz, there were always those who, even if they disagreed with his countermand, refused to condemn him for it.

Following a visit to MacNeill on 23 April 1916, Thomas MacDonagh, who himself had been informed relatively late in the day about the rebels' plans but whose involvement was vital as he was Dublin brigade commandant of the Volunteers and co-opted in April 1916 to the IRB's secret military council, left a statement pointedly describing MacNeill as an 'honest and sincere patriot'. MacDonagh was a UCD colleague and something of an intermediary between MacNeill and the conspirators; he was perhaps also feeling guilty because of his lies to MacNeill.[3] Patrick McCartan, another senior member of the IRB, acknowledged in June 1916 that MacNeill's actions had weakened the rising but maintained: 'I think he is to be pitied most of all because he is so misunderstood.'[4]

In keeping with this theme, there was a striking moment in Dartmoor prison after the rising when MacNeill joined his fellow prisoners for exercise and de Valera ordered the prisoners to salute MacNeill: 'Irish Volunteers! Attention! Eyes left.' But as Ronan Fanning notes, de Valera's attitude to MacNeill was 'ambivalent. He admired, even revered' his Gaelic League lineage and scholarship and his role in establishing the Irish Volunteers, 'but admiration stopped short of deference' and de Valera 'resolutely refused to surrender to MacNeill that primacy of place among the prisoners to which he felt himself entitled by virtue of his status as the senior surviving commandant of the rising'. When the prisoners moved to elect a commandant, de Valera was against reinstating MacNeill and insisted that as MacNeill had 'placed himself outside the ranks of those who had fought, he could not hold the position'. MacNeill withdrew and supported de Valera.[5]

De Valera, however, in seeking to build unity of purpose within the Sinn Féin movement in 1917 was mindful that MacNeill needed to be included in the post-rising alliance if it was to succeed in undermining sectionalism. Markievicz attempted again to brandish the countermand as a stick with which to beat MacNeill at the Irish Volunteers convention in October 1917; she objected to him being a candidate for membership of the Sinn Féin executive, but both de Valera and Arthur Griffith spoke in his favour. De Valera urged delegates to 'show by your votes that MacNeill deserves honour from his countrymen'.[6]

MacNeill duly received the highest number of votes in the election of members to the twenty-four-strong executive, though there was also room for Markievicz and it may have been the case, as recorded privately by Liam de Róiste, organiser for Sinn Féin in Cork, that Markievicz 'was strong about the men who have been talking about MacNeill but who had not the courage to stand up there and say what they were saying in private'.[7]

It was a reminder that, for all the public solidarity, wariness remained. MacNeill, it seemed, was an insider on the outside and that sense of him endured despite what can be seen as something of a vindication in 1917, not just because of his election to the Sinn Féin executive, but because a new Volunteers' manifesto launched at that time blamed the failure of 1916 on a 'misunderstanding' (a reference to the countermanding order) but also declared the executive 'would not issue an order to take to the field until they consider that the force is in a position to wage war on the enemy with reasonable hope of success' and that the Volunteers should not 'be called on to take part in any forlorn hope',[8] a sort of backhanded compliment to MacNeill. But MacNeill's election on that occasion was also a reminder of 'the balancing of old and new' in the Sinn Féin hierarchy. Father Michael O'Flanagan, elected joint vice-president of Sinn Féin at that stage, was later keen to stress 'the split was there from the start'.[9] If MacNeill was a 'republican bugbear', who Michael Collins in 1917 wanted to see issuing a statement 'saying that he intends devoting himself solely to literature', there were, nonetheless, quite a few 'MacNeillites'.[10]

MacNeill, however, was not as wily a political operator as his critics, and his perceived pipe dreams and lack of forcefulness have heavily influenced historians' judgements of him; they have frequently bordered their assessments with caveats and qualifications. Joe Lee suggested his influential 'The North Began' article in 1913 that prompted the formation of the Volunteers contained MacNeill's 'customary combination of insight and illusion'; that the Irish Volunteers, 'however genuine MacNeill's protestations to the contrary, had ultimately the logical objective of coercing Ulster unionists. The illusion implicit in this approach would continue to bedevil Irish nationalism for generations.'[11] Roy Foster, in discussing the Irish Volunteer split in 1914, describes him as 'irresolute as ever'.[12] Alvin Jackson views him as someone who was 'hampered not only by his own honest political limitations, but also by the burden of unrealistic public expectations', and that he faced, towards the end of his political career, those who were trained 'in a rather harder school of knocks than he was'.[13]

MacNeill was also privately and publicly full of his own doubts at various stages. According to nationalist MP Stephen Gwynn, MacNeill admitted to him in 1914 'my duty for the future lies in the line of study and teaching ... I have been absolutely forced to the front in this Volunteer movement'.[14] But does that mean he was a well-meaning academic out of his depth in the maelstrom of hard politics and military brinkmanship? Not necessarily; as Tom Bartlett observes, he was not a member of the IRB but he was 'strong-minded enough not to be its stooge'.[15] In the early years of the Irish Volunteers it has been suggested he was more comfortable consorting with IRB members than has been 'commonly supposed', an assertion at odds with Bulmer Hobson's contention in 1947 that he was 'not in any way in touch with the IRB' and that his primary value was as a 'great intellectual figure ... that he quarrelled with nobody and could throw oil on the most troubled waters'.[16]

Hobson's assertion does not correspond to the degree to which the Irish Volunteer movement and its mission were open to multiple interpretations and definitions by contemporaries due to 'the battle of ideas' of that era.[17] Tom Clarke, in a letter to John Devoy in April 1914, suggested MacNeill was 'sound upon the national question generally'.[18] As Patrick Maume sees it, MacNeill's protestations of loyalty to Redmond at the early stages of the Irish Volunteers 'should not be taken at face value since they were accompanied by a refusal to obey Redmond's instructions ... he consistently believed in the existence of a British plot to enslave or even exterminate the Irish'. But he also had too many displaced trusts: a belief in patience to generate a reunification of Irish opinion or misplaced hopes that enduring friendships would trump divisive political or military strategies.[19]

The key question of what constituted a mandate for armed revolt clearly exercised MacNeill. Many would see realism, nobility and democratic sentiment in his assertion in February 1916: 'I am certain that the only possible basis for successful revolution is deep and widespread political discontent. We have only to look around us to realise that no such condition exists in Ireland.'[20] But that was not necessarily the only basis: the rebels were of course ready to act without majority support; in this, suggests Charles Townshend, 'they were hardly different from any revolutionary insurrectionist of the nineteenth or twentieth century'.[21] Some of them were also convinced that a basis for successful revolution involved, not widespread discontent, but sufficient determination by a committed minority to light a spark that would lead to a revolutionary blaze. MacNeill did not brashly trumpet his interpretation of what constituted a mandate for rebellion and 'never tried to vindicate his countermanding order', perhaps because, as he allegedly remarked to Bulmer Hobson during Easter week, 'we would have no political future if we were not arrested'.[22]

MacNeill's reluctance to elaborate on these dilemmas or engage fully with the historicising of his own political career was evident in the tortured evolution of what has been too generously described as his 'memoir'. His career as a cultural activist, scholar, revolutionary and politician could have made for an exceptionally full and revealing autobiography. What he offered in the memoir, however, were just fragments. He began dictating reflections on his life to Leila Carroll in 1932 after he had been urged by members of his family to record his thoughts for posterity.[23] He only agreed under condition 'he would never write it himself', and that compromise ultimately made for a much-compromised manuscript: a sparse, disjointed, incomplete and rambling effort, leaving many blanks.

MacNeill dictated from memory, and on some of the most dramatic and controversial events of his life he offered mere scraps. Brian Hughes, editor of the manuscript that was eventually published in 2016, noted accurately, 'many of its themes and topics are underdeveloped, it is sometimes scattered in its chronology, there is no real sense of a chapter structure and it is often repetitive'. To then assert 'in some ways this is what makes it so powerful as a historical document' is too kind.[24]

For all its shortcomings, however, it includes some frank and revealing assertions and admissions, which, even if they are not always developed satisfactorily, expose much about MacNeill and his unsuitability to political life. Perhaps his moderation – 'I was no doctrinaire whether on behalf of physical force or against it' – often led to him falling between stools during periods when extreme views defined many of his colleagues.[25] He insisted the Gaelic League should have kept entirely clear of politics and that its failure to do so, 'for which I am in part responsible, has been bad for the objects of the League and had other bad results in the time that followed'.[26] He gave much credit to unionist leader Edward Carson 'for his share in bringing about the changes that have come about in Ireland'. His suggestion, however, that the Ulster unionist resistance to Home Rule amounted to 'sympathy to Irish self-government' was a simplification of Carson and what he led, and the contention 'Orange opponents [of nationalism] in Ireland are merely the ignorant tools of a set of English politicians' was equally shallow. MacNeill was apt to overplay the Orange card; in December 1913 at the Ranelagh home of Elsie Henry she recorded having dinner with MacNeill and George Russell and MacNeill acknowledged he had given a recent Volunteer meeting 'too strong a dose' in asking for cheers for the Ulster Volunteers, resulting in disturbances.[27] While MacNeill was reared in Antrim, his dismissal of the depth of many Ulster Protestants' hostility to Catholicism and Irish nationalism was callow, but he was by no means alone in his misconceptions.

MacNeill's essential political moderation seems to have been apparent at an early stage because he distinguished between theory and practice. He wrote in 1904, 'In theory I suppose I am a separatist, in practice I would accept any settlement that would enable Irishmen to freely control their own affairs, and I would object to any theoretical upsetting of such a settlement. If the truth were known, I think that this represents the political views of 99 out of every hundred nationalists.'[28] This was the kind of sweeping statement that was common among activists of that era; a confident, even arrogant sense that they had an instinct for the feelings of most people. That led to exaggeration; what MacNeill did know, however, was the mindset of those he worked closely with and those who deceived him. He was critical of Pearse's preoccupation with the drama of heroism and suggested the meetings plotting rebellion in 1916 were 'councils of despair'.[29] There was certainly truth in that; as 1916 rebel Desmond FitzGerald's son Garret later put it, it was the 'mood of despair within nationalism' that provided the impetus for the rising rather than a confident, popular republicanism.[30]

But neither was the Irish Volunteers' stated objective a model of clarity; its aim was to 'secure and maintain the rights and liberties common to the whole people of Ireland', but there was no proper definition of this and even at the first convention of the post-split Irish Volunteers held at the Abbey Theatre in October 1914 where MacNeill was elected chairman, the declaration of policy – to 'unite the people of Ireland on the basis of Irish nationality' – was similarly ambiguous.[31]

Regardless of the effectiveness of his leadership, MacNeill's decisive role in the formation of the Volunteers is a significant legacy and, given that the Volunteers metamorphosed into the IRA that fought the War of Independence, his stance on violence is particularly worthy of assessment. He insisted in February 1916 'what we call our country is not a poetical abstraction ... it is our duty to get our country on side and not be content with the vanity of thinking ourselves to be right and other Irish people to be wrong'.[32] That contention went to the heart of the controversies of pre-war nationalist Ireland, and MacNeill's 1913 initiative and what followed need to be seen in the context of different and evolving concepts of Irish nationalism; definitions of loyalty and legitimate violence were contested during this period of multiple allegiances and the outbreak of the First World War complicated them further. In relation to his role in the Volunteers, these are the lenses through which we should view MacNeill, his dilemmas and his legacy. He was not a pacifist and insisted he had a right to bear arms in defence of Ireland. Where he differed from some of his colleagues was in relation to the strategy that should underpin use of arms, but such subtleties did not travel well through the decades as the different dimensions to his thinking were lost to absolutes. The later exaltation of MacNeill as 'man of peace'[33] also artificially divorced him from the context in which he emerged as a public figure.

The rehabilitation of his reputation was apparent more than fifteen years after his death with the publication by F.X. Martin of his memoranda from 1916 and 1917.[34] Coinciding with the forty-fifth anniversary of the rising, their publication generated much attention: 'The *Irish Press* and *Irish Independent* displayed posters announcing the publication of the documents and it was included in the lunchtime news bulletins.'[35] There were also calls from academics and politicians for the rejection of a one-dimensional celebration of the fiftieth anniversary of the rising in 1966. The Jesuit periodical *Studies* editorialised that, in relation to MacNeill, 'history has attached to him that most damning label – it tells us that he meant well', but his memorandum on what would justify rebellion, it was asserted, 'is a profound and inspiring profession of Ireland's nationhood. It is the sober, realistic and comprehensive declaration of Irish independence'.[36] Perhaps it was, but it had also been 'put in a drawer' after its composition.[37] Nonetheless, its resurrection in the 1960s robustly challenged the accepted historical narrative and in that sense MacNeill's legacy was quite potent – part of a broader project to 'transfer the Rising of 1916 from the realm of mythology to the sphere of history'.[38] Notwithstanding, the first instalment in Hugh Leonard's *Insurrection* television series in 1966 ended with Eoin MacNeill saying into the camera '"there will be no Rising" ... this worked as a cliff hanger only because the audience knew he was wrong'.[39] MacNeill was still dramatically useful, it seemed, as a lost leader on the wrong side of history.

It was also MacNeill's fate to be sidelined during the War of Independence, appointed Minister for Finance in 1919 only to be replaced by Michael Collins and moved to a 'department' of Industry ('a vast demotion to a token job') and then to be imprisoned from November 1920 until June 1921. He was still, despite holding office and enduring incarceration, 'that perennial object of republican suspicion'.[40]

When it came to the Anglo-Irish treaty, MacNeill was again on the margins; he had 'no connection with the negotiators from first to last', and he elaborated little on the treaty debates that he chaired; he also averred that he had 'no desire' to be a member of the provisional government after the treaty. But he does recall an interesting, spiky, exchange with de Valera who was seeking, in vain, his support for the pact election of 1922. MacNeill was hardly inaccurate in telling de Valera, 'You are lining up with a number of doctrinaire extremists and you do not really agree with them any more than I do.'[41] In a sense this marked a return to the issue of political aloofness and MacNeill was far from alone in insisting Ireland was not a poetical abstraction either in 1916 or in 1922. In a plaintive letter to Cork anti-treaty republican Mary MacSwiney, also in 1922, de Valera admitted 'reason rather than faith has been my master'; he was clearly struggling to make common cause with those who 'keep on the plane of Faith and Unreason and maintain that position consciously'.[42] Frank Gallagher, in contrast, as a trenchant opponent of the treaty and an IRA volunteer in Dublin, insisted Ireland was not land or people: 'Ireland is something else … Ireland is the dead and the things the dead would have done … Ireland is spirit.'[43] No wonder James Connolly, who derided this wading into what he regarded as sentimental slop, did not join in the chorus of derision of MacNeill in 1916. The detachment, however, endured; 'our Ireland', wrote Todd Andrews, who fought with the anti-treaty IRA, 'had in fact become a political abstraction'.[44]

This was not an era when 'schoolmasterish realism',[45] shared, it seemed, by de Valera and MacNeill, would work for de Valera as he was hardly in control of the republican movement, whereas it put MacNeill in line with the provisional government's resoluteness and ruthlessness in 1922 and '23. Notwithstanding, de Valera managed to forge a path to recovery because of his determination and grasp of political strategy, talents that MacNeill did not have as, unlike de Valera, he was too willing to facilitate others. Nor could he generate anything like the electoral appeal of de Valera. When he faced him in the 1923 general election in County Clare, MacNeill was elected as the sole Cumann na nGaedheal candidate with 8,196 first preference votes to de Valera's 17,762. MacNeill had been expected to gain enough of a surplus to elect a running mate, a wildly misplaced optimism.[46] Even in his constituency, MacNeill was seen as too much of an outsider; he did not contest the seat in the June 1927 election[47] which was just as well given that a local priest had suggested the need for candidates to be selected from within 'its own shores and not go outside for them' – MacNeill being criticised as 'an absentee politician who rarely visited the county'.[48]

It seems bizarre that MacNeill would suggest in his memoir that the fallout from the downfall of Parnell in 1890 led to a split 'deeper and sharper and more widespread than anything we experienced afterwards even at the height of the civil war',[49] especially given the way his own family was affected by that war and the squalid, brutal killing of his son Brian, a member of the anti-treaty IRA, in Sligo on 20 September 1922. This was just a day after MacNeill, as Minister for Education, answered Dáil questions on the paltriness of teachers' salaries and a week before the government introduced emergency powers to coldly crush the IRA, inaugurating the cruellest phase of a Civil War that also involved two of his sons fighting with the National Army.[50]

Perhaps MacNeill's refusal to publicly reflect or elaborate on these dark days was one way of externalising the trauma of that war and in such silence he was by no means alone. When he published his book *The Victory of Sinn Féin* in 1924, P.S. O'Hegarty, who took the pro-treaty side, highlighted why that reticence was to become so pervasive. There would be no appetite to recall

> 'that our deep rooted belief that there was something in us finer than, more spiritual than, anything in any other people, was sheer illusion, and that we were really an uncivilised people with savage instincts. And the shock of that plunge from the heights to the depths staggered the whole nation.'[51]

It could be argued convincingly that there was nothing ignoble in the silence that followed the Civil War, but that reticence may also have conveniently helped sidestep moral and political responsibility for some of the desperate things done by the government of which MacNeill was a member in response to entrenched and righteous anti-treaty republicans.

In relation to his period as Irish representative on the Boundary Commission from 1924, MacNeill bleakly admitted in his memoir: 'no one else could be found to act instead of me'. He also regarded it as 'nothing less than an outrage on Ireland, and I may say on civilisation, to be asked to draw a line across this country dividing it on the basis of religious difference'.[52] This was sincere, though melodramatic and in keeping with some of his other grandiose, sweeping statements about the Ulster question and the supposed intrinsic link between the fate of Ireland and the fate of civilisation. MacNeill had been consistently adamant that Ulster Protestant attitudes were a consequence of British duplicity: 'history shows that this present sentiment of theirs is a calculated outcome of persistent and unscrupulous policy of English statesmen pursued purely in the English interest', adding for good measure 'there is no body of people in the world more free from intolerance in matters of religion than the Catholics of Ireland'.[53]

Such reductionism also included the assertion that it was primarily England that had fostered 'religious feuds' in Ireland, but he did acknowledge in an interview with the American journalist Hayden Talbot in 1922 that Irish nationalists carried some of the responsibility too: 'suppose that in view of our own share in aggravating their fanaticism in the past we absolve to abstain from all acts and words of an exasperating kind in the future'.[54]

MacNeill vainly insisted that in an independent Ireland there would be no 'Ulster difficulty'.[55] But most of his colleagues were equally unsophisticated; after all, during the treaty negotiations, Arthur Griffith had similarly insisted that, if Ulster unionists did not have the backing of the British government, 'we could settle the Ulster question'.[56] Ulster Protestant and Sinn Féin TD Ernest Blythe, in contrast, took an independent line. Reared in Magheragall near Lisburn in County Antrim, a strongly unionist area, he believed in a united Ireland but his background, he suggested, prevented him 'ever falling victim to some of the illusions about partition by which many people in political circles in the South are still fantastically misled and which even continue to influence the minds of many good nationalists in the North'. Any notion of coercion, he believed, was counterproductive, and persuasion was imperative.[57]

MacNeill's legacy was greatly tarnished by the Boundary Commission outcome, but the trap had been set long before he took on the role. The section of Article 12 of the Anglo-Irish Treaty that dealt with the Boundary Commission was deliberately ambiguous: in the (inevitable) event of Northern Ireland opting out of the treaty settlement,

> 'a commission of three persons, one to be appointed by the government of the Irish Free State, one to be appointed by the Government of Northern Ireland and one who shall be Chairman to be appointed by the British Government, shall determine, in accordance with the wishes of the inhabitants, so far as may be compatible with economic and geographic conditions, the boundaries between Northern Ireland and the rest of Ireland'.

As early as 16 December 1921, Prime Minister David Lloyd George insisted in the House of Commons that the phrase 'economic and geographic conditions' would not allow for large-scale transfer.[58] MacNeill was not to blame for the vagueness of the wording of Article 12 or the fact that there were no Ulster men included in the Irish delegation that negotiated the treaty.

The hope of unduly optimistic nationalists was that the Commission would 'deliver' Tyrone, Fermanagh and large parts of south Armagh, south Down, Newry and Derry city and that a new mutilated Northern Ireland would not be a viable entity. What was notable after the treaty was signed was the degree of acceptance of the proposed commission as a game-changer by both pro- and anti-treaty sides, evidenced by the relative silence on the issue of the border during the treaty debates. The Irish delegation's legal adviser John O'Byrne viewed the text as ambiguous but, nonetheless, as Attorney General in 1925 he still argued that the commissioners were empowered to transfer large swathes of territory.[59]

In February 1923, MacNeill mused on the general problem of North–South relations and suggested there were three options: to regard the Belfast government as subordinate and open discussions with it; to have direct relationships with the British government; or 'to drift on doing nothing and this promises no advantage'.[60] Ultimately, it was this lethargy that prevailed and came to define his association with the Boundary Commission. He seemed to believe he was involved in a legal rather than a political process and did not enlighten his colleagues: 'I understood that I was, so to speak, a plenipotentiary ... I was not purely and simply the representative of a government nor was I an advocate for a particular point of view'; therefore he 'faithfully observed' confidentiality. The difficulty was, he maintained, that the chairman of the Commission, Richard Feetham, had introduced 'a political consideration which was made a dominant consideration' that was outside the terms of the agreement; that consideration was that if the wishes of the inhabitants created political difficulties for Northern Ireland, 'then the political consideration was to override the wishes of the inhabitants'.[61] But why had he not done more to reject Feetham's interpretation? Why did he elide his responsibility for being party to the controversial recommendations? And why did he not consider authoring a minority, dissenting report?

What was most striking about his explanation to the Dáil was MacNeill's lack of confidence and unsuitability to be 'protector' of northern nationalists, but that was hardly a problem created in 1925. Three years previously, Cahir Healy, Sinn Féin MP for Fermanagh and Tyrone, had written to his friend Kevin O'Shiel, assistant legal adviser to the provisional government and very soon to be director of the Free State's North Eastern Boundary Bureau, to gather data for the Boundary Commission: 'we must look after ourselves, I think'.[62]

They were prescient words and a reminder that northern nationalists had reason to be suspicious of southern political intentions well before the Boundary Commission debacle. In October 1922, a deputation from Northern Ireland arrived in Dublin to the provisional government, including priests, solicitors and local councillors, looking for funds to counteract unionist propaganda. They got short shrift from Kevin O'Higgins: 'We have no other policy for the North East than we have for any other part of Ireland and that is the Treaty policy.' He suggested that what northern nationalists needed was not just funds but 'a great deal of strenuous voluntary work – just the same sort of strenuous work that brought the national position to the stage it has reached'.[63]

The washing of southern hands could hardly have been more apparent; O'Higgins claimed the real problem was the lack of cohesion on the part of nationalists. An interned teacher in Belfast in January 1923 wrote to MacNeill: 'the bitter part is the reflection that when I do get out I shall probably be forgotten'.[64] MacNeill's career will always be associated to an extent with this sense of abandonment of northern nationalists. He also seems to have approached his Boundary Commission role with a degree of self-sacrifice; as Michael Laffan sees it, 'his attitude may have been coldly realistic but such fatalism boded ill for northern nationalists'.[65]

Cahir Healy became more colourful and understandably emotional about what the Boundary Commission fallout meant, accusing MacNeill and his colleagues of having 'cut our cable and launched us rudderless into the hurricane without guarantee or security'.[66] But surely that too displayed a naïvete about what was practically possible? MacNeill, later in 1925, highlighted inconsistencies in Healy's attitude – that he had originally wanted MacNeill to withdraw from the Commission but then denounced his withdrawal.[67]

MacNeill should not be saddled with all the responsibility for this controversial episode; the biographer of W.T. Cosgrave, Michael Laffan, has suggested MacNeill 'acquiesced weakly' at the end of 1924, when the Commission was devoting all its attention to border areas rather than to the heartlands of Fermanagh and Tyrone, making it clear that only minor adjustments to the border were likely. But while Cosgrave 'deplored MacNeill's conduct', he must have been aware 'that in appointing to the Commission someone so unsuitable to the task his own judgement was at fault'.[68] It was 'bizarre' that the government did not see fit to appoint a full-time commissioner, MacNeill continuing his role as Minister for Education in a seven-man cabinet: 'armed with a specialist knowledge of Celtic studies, he was sent to participate on a part-time basis in a quasi-judicial Commission with a supreme court judge and a barrister, both authors of legal textbooks and participating full-time in the work of the commission'.[69] Revealingly, MacNeill had written to Cosgrave on 10 October as the Commission's report was being finalised: 'I am the only one of the three who is not a lawyer.'[70]

In the Dáil on 24 November 1925, MacNeill asserted:

> 'The details came before us in a very gradual and a very piecemeal manner and it may be contended that I was at fault, that I was remiss, that I failed to appreciate the circumstances, failed to see what I might be ultimately up against, when I did not demand, require and challenge, at the earliest convenient stage, a discussion of the general principles of interpretation and a decision upon those principles. That may be so. I think it is probably true that a better politician and a better diplomatist, if you like, a better strategist, than I am would not have allowed himself to be brought into that position or difficulty.'[71]

Independent TD Bryan Cooper's response, after the leader of the Labour party Thomas Johnson spoke of the 'humiliation' the controversy had caused, was balanced:

> 'I think that when we were listening to Deputy Dr. MacNeill this evening there was one feeling, or rather two, in the minds of almost all of us. One was sympathy. For his uprightness of character, the Dáil always has respected and always will respect. The other feeling was one of astonishment that, in his own words, he should have allowed himself to be placed in such a position.'[72]

Cooper further suggested that 'the polished steel of MacNeill's mind was no match for the cudgel play of his fellow commissioners'.[73] But was the entrenchment of partition really avoidable given the strength of unionist resistance, support from London, and lack of a realistic approach on the part of Dublin: what amounted to a combination of 'hope, fear, pressure and illusion'?[74] That combination also amounted to a fair summary of MacNeill's political career.

MacNeill resigned as minister and boundary commissioner in November 1925 and failed to be re-elected in the June 1927 general election. He was relieved to be out of politics, 'glad to escape … and get back to my own congenial work. I had never pushed myself into politics and never taken any prominent part in them except at the request of others. In fact, under urgent pressure from them.'[75] Such an admission is a reminder of how unsuited to politics MacNeill was and why he was often ineffectual and half-hearted. But he remained dignified, a considerable achievement and trait during a divisive era, and he should not be unduly burdened with more than his share of responsibility than the evidence merits. Seán Ó Faoláin later accurately suggested that MacNeill 'was at home with all sorts and conditions of people' and even went as far as to suggest 'he was probably one of the few Irishmen, if not the only Irishman of a period of internecine hates, who has died without an enemy'.[76] That is far-fetched; more credible was Ó Faoláin's assertion that MacNeill 'always retained an extraordinary urbanity in controversy'.[77]

The end of MacNeill's memoir contains a moving account of his witnessing the assassination of Minister for Justice Kevin O'Higgins in July 1927. MacNeill's evidence at the coroner's inquest helped to fashion the legacy of O'Higgins as the hard man of the pro-treaty 1920s government with the forgiving heart, reported under the headline 'Professor MacNeill's Evidence of Dying Minister's Fortitude'. MacNeill told the inquiry, 'When I stooped over him I thought he was on the point of death and I repeated close beside him some of the customary prayers. He then began to speak to me and the first thing he said was, "I forgive my murderers".' But MacNeill, even as he held the dying O'Higgins, was still, in a sense, on the outside; it was Minister for Agriculture Patrick Hogan who then arrived at the scene to take charge of the papers O'Higgins had in his possession.[78] MacNeill had lost his Dáil seat a few weeks previously whereas O'Higgins was not only vice-president of the Executive Council but also Minister for Justice and Minister for External Affairs. Here, yet again, was MacNeill at a turning point in modern Irish history as O'Higgins' assassination can be seen as 'the blood sacrifice that brought the major opposition into constitutional politics'.[79] Here, yet again, was a nonetheless marginalised MacNeill.

Another erstwhile Cumann na nGaedheal colleague, Richard Mulcahy, now Minister for Local Government and Public Health, subsequently asked MacNeill to prepare the speech for O'Higgins' funeral, which 'came strangely to me' as they had not been close, but he assented. It was W.T. Cosgrave who delivered that speech in which he declared that 'the late minister's example of duty, sanity, energy and enterprise would inspire the nation to the end'.[80] It is another reminder that his contemporaries often used MacNeill, and this, rather than his own vision, was what too frequently defined his political career and legacy.

Endnotes

Introduction: reassessing Eoin MacNeill. *Conor Mulvagh and Emer Purcell*

1　See Michael Tierney, *Eoin MacNeill: Scholar and man of action, 1867–1945*, ed. F.X. Martin, (Oxford: Clarendon Press, 1980), facing p. 213; V.L. O'Connor, *A Book of Caricatures* (Dundalk: Tempest, 1915).

2　Eoin MacNeill, *Saint Patrick, with a Memoir by Michael Tierney, and a Bibliography of Patrician Literature by F.X. Martin, O.S.A.*, ed. John Ryan (Dublin: Clonmore & Reynolds; London: Burns & Oates, 1964).

3　Tierney, *Eoin MacNeill*, p. 1.

4　Ibid., p. xvi.

5　F.X. Martin, 'Michael Tierney, 1894–1975', in Tierney, *Eoin MacNeill*, p. vii.

6　Tierney, *Eoin MacNeill*, p. xv.

7　Ibid., p. xvi.

8　F.X. Martin and F.J. Byrne (eds), *The Scholar Revolutionary: Eoin MacNeill, 1867–1945, and the making of the new Ireland* (Shannon: Irish University Press, 1973).

9　Brian Farrell, 'MacNeill and Politics', in Martin and Byrne (eds), *The Scholar Revolutionary*, p. 196.

10　Ibid., pp. 196–7.

11　Michael Tierney, 'Foreword', in Tierney, *Eoin MacNeill*, p. xv. On the subsequent fate of the documents that were taken from the MacNeill household during that raid in November 1920, see Police File PF 91 forwarded to MacNeill by Frank Thornton, New Ireland Assurance Company, 9 Mar. 1942 (UCDA, LA1/G/160–8).

12　Tierney, 'Foreword', p. xvi.

13　MacNeill's is the fifth largest open deposited collection next to Frank Aiken's (225 boxes); Éamon de Valera's (200 boxes); Richard Mulcahy's (100 boxes); and Robin Dudley Edwards' (70 boxes). The deposit of Garret FitzGerald's papers – not currently open to researchers – will constitute the largest collection in the archive to date when it is fully processed and catalogued. The editors are grateful to Kate Manning for her advice on this matter.

14　Brian Hughes (ed.), *Eoin MacNeill: Memoir of a revolutionary scholar* (Dublin: IMC, 2016).

15　F.J. Byrne, 'MacNeill the Historian', in Martin and Byrne (eds), *The Scholar Revolutionary*, p. 17. See also Edel Breathnach, Review article: 'Medieval Irish History at the End of the Twentieth Century: Unfinished work', *Irish Historical Studies*, vol. 32, no. 126, Nov. 2000, pp. 260–71.

16　Donnchadh Ó Corráin, 'Introduction', in Eoin MacNeill, *Celtic Ireland*, ed. Donnchadh Ó Corráin (Dublin: Academy Press, 1981), p. iii.

17　Ibid., p. iv.

18　Colmán Etchingham, 'Early Medieval Irish History', in Kim McCone and Katharine Simms (eds), *Progress in Medieval Irish Studies* (Maynooth: St Patrick's College, 1996), pp. 123–53, at p. 152.

19　Ibid., p. 123.

20　The Lecky Professorship is currently held by Ruth Karras. Seán Duffy holds a personal professorship.

21　Byrne, 'MacNeill the Historian', p. 17.

22　Eoin MacNeill, *Celtic Ireland*, ed. Donnchadh Ó Corráin (Dublin: Academy Press, 1981), pp. 37–8,

23 Byrne, 'MacNeill the Historian', p. 21: 'even his critics had to acknowledge that he seemed to arrive at demonstrably correct solutions to intractable problems by an uncanny power of intuition'; Ó Corráin, 'Introduction' to *Celtic Ireland*, p. iv; Murray, p. 33.

24 Letter from MacNeill to Kuno Meyer, 23 June 1913: printed in Seán Ó Lúing, *Kuno Meyer, 1858–1919: A biography* (Dublin: Geography Publications, 1991), p. 57, n. 16. Quoted in Kevin Murray, p. 36.

25 Murray, p. 33 and Johnston, pp. 70–1.

26 Three maps are included as appendices to *Celtic Ireland*.

27 Paul MacCotter, *Medieval Ireland: Territorial, political and economic divisions* (Dublin: Four Courts Press, 2008).

28 R.A.S. Macalister and Eoin MacNeill (ed. and trans.), *Leabhar Gabhála* (Dublin: Hodges, Figgis & Co., 1916).

29 Colm Ó Lochlainn was to contribute to Eoin MacNeill's festschrift: 'Roadways in Ancient Ireland', in John Ryan (ed.), *Féil-sgríbhinn Eóin Mhic Néill: Tráchtais léigheanta i n-onóir do'n ollamhain Eóin Mac Néill do sgríobh cáirde d'á cháirdibh i n-am a dheichmhadh bliadhna agus trí fichid, an cúigmhadh lá déag de mhí na Bealtaine, 1938* (Dublin: Three Candles, 1940), pp. 465–74.

30 D.A. Binchy, 'MacNeill's Study of the Ancient Irish Laws', in Martin and Byrne (eds), *The Scholar Revolutionary*, pp. 40–1.

31 Byrne, 'MacNeill the Historian', pp. 15–36, at pp. 24–5.

32 'The North Began', *An Claidheamh Soluis*, 1 Nov. 1913, p. 6.

33 Hughes, *Eoin MacNeill: Memoir*, p. 72 and Ferriter, p. 280 in this volume.

34 Dorothy Macardle, *The Irish Republic: A documented chronicle of the Anglo-Irish conflict and the partitioning of Ireland with a detailed account of the period 1916–1923*, 4th edn (Dublin: Irish Press, 1951), p. 95.

35 See, for instance, Desmond Ryan, *The Rising: The complete story of Easter week* (Dublin: Golden Eagle Books, 1949), pp. 63, 90–1, 119.

36 Desmond Ryan puts the time of MacNeill and his delegation's arrival at St Enda's at 'after midnight' (p. 90). Bulmer Hobson, who was also present, puts the time at 'around 2 a.m.': Bulmer Hobson, *Ireland Yesterday and Tomorrow* (Tralee: Anvil Books, 1968), p. 76.

37 Ryan, *The Rising*, pp. 90–1.

38 Tierney, *Eoin MacNeill*, p. 99.

39 Ibid., p. 100.

40 Max Caulfield, *The Easter Rebellion*, 2nd edn (Dublin: Gill & Macmillan, 1995), pp. 33–4. Caulfield notes that he relied upon survivor testimonies when he first wrote his account of the rising in the 1960s (p. ix). There are three written eyewitness accounts of the incident. One is MacNeill's memorandum of the event, another is a letter written by Colm Ó Lochlainn to F.X. Martin on 22 June 1960, and a third is Seán Fitzgibbon's recollection of the event (*Irish Times*, 19 Apr. 1949). A full summary of this is provided in F.X. Martin, 'Eoin MacNeill on the Easter Rising', *IHS*, vol. 12, no. 44, Mar. 1961, pp. 265–6.

41 Eoin to Agnes MacNeill, Lewes Prison, 12 Feb. 1917 (UCDA, LA1/K/142 (9)).

42 Quoted in Geoffrey J. Hand, 'MacNeill and the Boundary Commission', in Martin and Byrne (eds), *The Scholar Revolutionary*, pp. 215–16 quoting an interview between the author and McGilligan conducted on 18 Aug. 1967. See also Tierney, *Eoin MacNeill*, pp. 341–2.

43 Tierney, *Eoin MacNeill*, p. 314 (his appointment as Minister for Education is also given an entry in the chronology of his life on p. 384).

44 Eoin MacNeill, 'Ten Years of the Irish Free State', *Foreign Affairs*, vol. 10, no. 2, Jan. 1932, p. 246.

45 Ibid.

46 *Dáil Éireann Debates*, vol. 2, no. 12, col. 548, 4 Jan. 1923. For further discussion of this point see Farrell, 'MacNeill and Politics', p. 194.

47 MacNeill, 'Ten Years of the Irish Free State', p. 247.

48 Ibid.

49 Farrell, 'MacNeill and Politics', p. 195.

50 MacNeill [n.d.], 'Imperialism', 12ff, NLI, Hobson papers, MS 13,167.

51 On the difference between nationalism and MacNeill's conception of 'nationality', see Donal McCartney, 'MacNeill and Irish-Ireland', in Martin and Byrne (eds), *The Scholar Revolutionary*, pp. 82–6.

52 Ó Corráin, 'Introduction', in Eoin MacNeill, *Celtic Ireland* (1981), p. vi.

53 [North Eastern Boundary Bureau], *Handbook of the Ulster Question* (Dublin: Stationery Office, 1923), p. 43.

54 Donal McCartney, *The National University of Ireland and Éamon de Valera* (Dublin: University Press of Ireland, 1983), p. 15.

55 MacNeill's party colleague and fellow Ulsterman Patrick McGilligan was successful in retaking MacNeill's NUI seat in the ensuing 1923 NUI by-election.

56 John Ryan (ed.), *Féil-sgríbhinn Eóin Mhic Néill: Essays and studies presented to Professor Eoin MacNeill on the occasion of his seventieth birthday, May 15th 1938* (Dublin: Three Candles, 1940).

Eoin MacNeill: a family perspective. *Michael McDowell*

1 'Family of Divided Loyalties that was Reunited in Grief', *Irish Times*, 23 May 2013.

2 'The North Began', *An Claidheamh Soluis*, 1 Nov. 1913, p. 6.

3 F.X. Martin and Eoin MacNeill. 'Eoin MacNeill on the 1916 Rising', *Irish Historical Studies*, vol. 12, no. 47, 1961, pp. 226–71.

4 On Connolly's disappearance for three days in January 1916 during which he was briefed by the IRB's military council of which Pearse was a member, see Michael Foy and Brian Barton, *The Easter Rising* (Stroud: Sutton, 2004), pp. 38–98.

5 Martin, 'Eoin MacNeill and 1916 Rising', p. 239.

6 Ibid., p. 235.

7 Ibid., p. 236.

8 Ibid., p. 239.

9 For recent scholarship of the 'Castle document', including a facsimile of it, see W.J. McCormack, 'What is a Forgery or a Catalyst? The so-called 'Castle document' of Holy Week, 1916', in Lisa Godson and Joanna Brück (eds), *Making 1916: Material and visual culture of the Easter Rising* (Liverpool: Liverpool University Press, 2015), pp. 57–69.

10 Martin, 'Eoin MacNeill and 1916 Rising', p. 245.

11 Ibid., pp. 245–51.

12 Ibid., p. 251.

13 Ibid., pp. 332–3.

14 Michael Tierney, *Eoin MacNeill: Scholar and man of action, 1867–1945* (Oxford: Clarendon Press, 1980), pp. 261–2.

15 Michael Laffan, *The Resurrection of Ireland: The Sinn Féin party, 1916–1923* (Cambridge: Cambridge University Press, 1999), p. 119.

16 Michael Collins and Hayden Talbot, *Michael Collins' Own Story* (London: Hutchinson & Co., 1923), p. 33.

17 Eoin MacNeill to Archbishop Thomas Gilmartin, 2 July 1920 (Tuam Diocesan Archives, B4/8-ii/04-06), cited (partially) in Kieran Waldron, *The Archbishops of Tuam, 1700–2000* (Tuam, Co Galway: Nordlaw Books, 2008), p. 108.

18 Ibid.
19 'Sligo's Noble Six' refers to Brian MacNeill, Seamus Devins, Paddy Carroll, Joe Banks, Tommy Langan and Harry Benson. MacNeill was killed alongside Devins, Carroll and Banks following their capture in an ambush. Meanwhile, Benson and Langan were captured in a separate incident later that day and summarily shot dead. See *Sligo Champion*, 7 Oct. 1922.

Eoin MacNeill's Contribution to the Study of Medieval Irish law. *Kevin Murray*
1 There is an appreciation of Father Hogan by D. Hyde (along with a list of his published works by J. MacErlean) in *Studies: An Irish quarterly review*, vol. 6, no. 24, Dec. 1917, pp. 663–71.
2 These are detailed in E. MacNeill, 'Celtic Studies', in *A Page of Irish History: Story of University College Dublin, 1883–1909*, compiled by the Fathers of the Society of Jesus (Dublin and Cork: Talbot Press, 1930), pp. 186–94. See discussion in R. Dudley Edwards, 'Professor MacNeill', in F.X. Martin and F.J. Byrne (eds), *The Scholar Revolutionary: Eoin MacNeill, 1867–1945 and the making of the new Ireland* (Shannon: Irish University Press, 1973), pp. 279–97, at pp. 279–83.
3 E. Hogan, *Onomasticon Goedelicum Locorum et Tribuum Hiberniae et Scotiae. An Index with Identifications, to the Gaelic Names of Places and Tribes* (Dublin: Hodges, Figgis & Co., 1910). For discussion, see K. Murray, 'Edmund Hogan's *Onomasticon Goedelicum*, Ninety Years on: Reviewers and users', *Ainm*, vol. 8, 1998–2000, pp. 65–75 and the essays in K. Murray and P. Ó Riain (eds), *Edmund Hogan's Onomasticon Goedelicum: Reconsiderations*, Irish Texts Society, Subsidiary Series 23 (London: Irish Texts Society, 2011).
4 Of all his contributions in this area, perhaps the most significant is his 'Early Irish Population-Groups: Their nomenclature, classification and chronology', *Proceedings of the Royal Irish Academy*, vol. 29C, 1911, pp. 59–114, which bristles with information and insights.
5 MacNeill, 'Celtic Studies', p. 193.
6 I will not provide references for these enterprises here. The information is readily accessible in the detailed bibliography by Father F.X. Martin OSA, titled 'The Published Writings of Eoin MacNeill', which is provided as an appendix to Martin and Byrne (eds), *The Scholar Revolutionary*, pp. 325–53. See also idem, 'The Writings of Eoin MacNeill', *Irish Historical Studies*, vol. 6, no. 21, Mar. 1948, pp. 44–62.
7   MacNeill, 'Celtic Studies', p. 188.
8 See Michael Kennedy's contribution to this volume, pp. 80–91, and idem and D. McMahon (eds), *Reconstructing Ireland's Past: A history of the Irish Manuscripts Commission* (Dublin: IMC, 2008). See also Dudley Edwards, 'Professor MacNeill', pp. 291–7.
9 With Introductory Description by R.I. Best and R. Thurneysen. The *Senchas Már* is the largest single collection of Old Irish law tracts. For more information, see L. Breatnach, *A Companion to the Corpus Iuris Hibernici* (Dublin: DIAS, 2005), pp. 268–314; idem, *The Early Irish Law Text* Senchas Már *and the Question of Its Date*, Quiggin Pamphlets on the Sources of Mediaeval Gaelic History 13 (Cambridge, 2011).
10 For what follows, see also D.A. Binchy, 'MacNeill's Study of the Ancient Irish Laws', in Martin and Byrne (eds), *The Scholar Revolutionary*, pp. 37–48.
11 *Early Irish Laws and Institutions* (Dublin: Burns, Oates & Washbourne, 1935), p. 56. However, in the 'Foreword' which MacNeill contributed to the *Senchas Már* facsimile (p. vii), he admits that it was intended that the Book of Lecan would be the first volume to be produced but that this changed 'after consultation with Professor Thurneysen of Bonn'.
12 For example, at the end of the nineteenth century, he had published a number of short notes on a collection of late legal documents in Irish, mostly from the sixteenth century: E. MacNeill, 'Some Irish Law Documents', *Gaelic Journal*, vol. 8, 1897, pp. 74–5, pp. 86–90, pp. 99–100, pp. 114–15.

13 W.N. Hancock, T. O'Mahony, A.G. Richey, W.M. Hennessy and R. Atkinson, *The Ancient Laws of Ireland*, 6 vols (Dublin: Alexander Thom, 1865–1901). Among the major problems with the volumes we may note: the lack of reliable translations, particularly of the older materials; the utilisation of a Gaelic font which did not allow for the deployment of italics, fatal when editing abbreviated manuscript texts; frequent mistakes in transcribing the manuscript materials; the unfortunate death of the two main editors – Eugene O'Curry and John O'Donovan – before any of the volumes were published and their replacement by editors who, with the exception of Robert Atkinson, knew little or no medieval Irish; frequent confusion in the physical presentation of early legal materials versus later legal commentaries; and the over-reliance on inferior manuscript witnesses to a text. See D.A. Binchy, 'Ancient Irish Law', *Irish Jurist*, vol. 1, 1966, pp. 84–92, at pp. 84–5.

14 Published in *Academy*, vol. 28, 1885, pp. 204–5.

15 E. MacNeill, 'The Irish Law of Dynastic Succession', *Studies: An Irish quarterly review*, vol. 8, no. 31, Sept. 1919, pp. 367–82, pp. 640–53 (republished in idem, *Celtic Ireland* [Dublin, 1921; repr. with new introduction and notes by D. Ó Corráin, Dublin, 1981], pp. 114–43). See J. Hogan, 'The Irish Law of Kingship, with Special Reference to Ailech and Cénel Eoghain. With 7 plates', *PRIA*, vol. 40C, 1932, pp. 186–254; D. Ó Corráin, 'Irish Regnal Succession: A reappraisal', *Studia Hibernica*, vol. 11, 1971, pp. 7–39; B. Jaski, *Early Irish Kingship and Succession* (Dublin: Four Courts Press, 2000); I. Warntjes, 'Regnal Succession in Early Medieval Ireland', *Journal of Medieval History*, vol. 30, 2004, pp. 377–410; J. Reid, 'A Case Study in Early Irish Regnal Succession: The kingdom of Osraige, 802–1003' (forthcoming).

16 This lacuna has since been filled by T.M. Charles-Edwards, *Early Irish and Welsh Kinship* (Oxford: Oxford University Press, 1993), pp. 89–166.

17 This analysis is to be found in 'The Family Commune', *Celtic Ireland*, pp. 152–76 (a revised and expanded version of his essay 'Communal Ownership in Ancient Ireland II: The family commune', *Irish Monthly*, vol. 47, 1919, pp. 463–74).

18 For example, N. Patterson, 'Patrilineal Kinship in Early Irish Society', *Bulletin of the Board of Celtic Studies*, vol. 37, 1990, pp. 133–65; Charles-Edwards, *Early Irish and Welsh Kinship*, I: 'The Structure of Irish Kinship'.

19 N. McLeod, 'Kinship', *Ériu*, vol. 51, 2000, pp. 1–22.

20 Thurneysen referred to this time in MacNeill's life as 'a period of involuntary leisure': 'Celtic Law', in D. Jenkins (ed.), *Celtic Law Papers: Introductory to Welsh medieval law and government* (Bruxelles: Librairie Encyclopédique, 1973), pp. 49–70, at p. 64 (translated from 'Das keltische Recht', *Zeitschrift der Savigny-Stiftung für Rechtsgeschichte* (Germanistische Abteilung), vol. 55, 1935, pp. 81–104, at p. 97).

21 E. MacNeill, 'Prolegomena to a Study of *The Ancient Laws of Ireland*', *Irish Jurist*, vol. 2, no. 1, 1967, pp. 106–15 (with an introduction and footnotes by D.A. Binchy).

22 See Binchy's comments in 'Irish History and Irish Law II', *Studia Hibernica*, vol. 16, 1976, pp. 7–45, at pp. 31–2.

23 For example, his suggestion ('Prolegomena to a Study of *The Ancient Laws of Ireland*', p. 112) that 'later scribes ... often seem to have copied from dictation rather than by sight' has been borne out by subsequent scholarship: see D. Ó Murchadha, 'Léitheoir sa Teach Screaptra?', in E. Purcell, P. MacCotter, J. Nyhan and J. Sheehan (eds), *Clerics, Kings and Vikings: Essays on medieval Ireland in honour of Donnchadh Ó Corráin* (Dublin: Fours Courts Press, 2015), pp. 147–54.

24 Letter from MacNeill to Kuno Meyer, 23 June 1913: printed in S. Ó Lúing, *Kuno Meyer, 1858–1919: A biography* (Dublin: Geography Publications, 1991), p. 57, n. 16.

25 E. MacNeill, 'Ancient Irish Law: The law of status of franchise', *PRIA*, vol. 36C, 1923, pp. 265–316. Though *Críth Gablach* has since been re-edited by D.A. Binchy as vol. 11 in the

Mediaeval and Modern Irish Series from the Dublin Institute for Advanced Studies (1941), it has not yet been deemed necessary to offer a re-translation. Robin Chapman Stacey, 'Ancient Irish Law Revisited: rereading the laws of status and franchise', in Katja Ritari and Alexandra Bergholm (eds), *Understanding Celtic Religion: revisiting the pagan past. New Approaches to Celtic Religion and Mythology* (Cardiff: University of Wales Press, 2015), pp. 99–120.

26 See his comments in 'Aus dem irischen Recht IV: Zu MacNeill's "Law of Status or Franchise"', *Zeitschrift für celtische Philologie*, vol. 16, 1926, pp. 197–205. For Thurneysen, see H.L.C. Tristram, 'Eduard Rudolf Thurneysen (1857–1940)', in H. Damico [with D. Fennema and K. Lenz] (eds), *Medieval Scholarship: Biographical studies on the formation of a discipline. Volume 2: Literature and philology*, Garland Library of Medieval Literature (New York/London: Garland, 1998), pp. 201–13.

27 Binchy, 'MacNeill's Study of the Ancient Irish Laws', p. 43.

28 'Ireland and Wales in the History of Jurisprudence', *Studies: An Irish quarterly review*, vol. 16, 1927, pp. 254–8, pp. 605–15; a review of *Welsh Tribal Law and Custom in the Middle Ages* (Oxford: Clarendon Press, 1926). MacNeill's article has been reprinted in Jenkins, *Celtic Law Papers*, pp. 171–92.

29 MacNeill, 'Ireland and Wales in the History of Jurisprudence', pp. 252, 253. See Binchy, 'Irish History and Irish Law II', pp. 31–7.

30 MacNeill, 'Ireland and Wales in the History of Jurisprudence', pp. 605–6.

31 Ibid., p. 613. See now D.E. Thornton, *King, Chronologies and Genealogies: Studies in the political history of early medieval Ireland and Wales*, Prosopographica et Genealogica 10 (Oxford: Unit for Prosopographical Research, Linacre College, 2003), Chapter 5: 'The Déisi Muman in Munster and Dyfed'; T.M. Charles-Edwards, *Wales and the Britons, 350–1064* (Oxford: Oxford University Press, 2012), Chapter 4: 'The Britons and the Irish, 350–800'.

32 MacNeill, 'Ireland and Wales in the History of Jurisprudence', p. 614. See now R. Chapman Stacey, 'Ties that Bind: Immunities in Irish and Welsh law', *Cambridge Medieval Celtic Studies*, vol. 20, Winter 1990, pp. 39–60; eadem, *The Road to Judgment: From custom to court in medieval Ireland and Wales* (Philadelphia: University of Pennsylvania Press, 1994); eadem, 'Law and Literature in Medieval Ireland and Wales', in H. Fulton (ed.), *Medieval Celtic Literature and Society* (Dublin: Four Courts Press, 2005), pp. 65–82; M.E. Owen, 'Some Points of Comparison and Contrast Between Early Irish and Welsh Law', in K. Jankulak and J.M. Wooding (eds), *Ireland and Wales in the Middle Ages* (Dublin: Four Courts Press, 2007), pp. 180–200.

33 Ellis had been a judge in India until his return to Wales in 1921. For further information on Ellis, see the online *Dictionary of Welsh Biography* at http://yba.llgc.org.uk/en/index.html.

34 MacNeill, 'Ireland and Wales in the History of Jurisprudence', p. 608.

35 Stokes, 'Curiosities of Official Scholarship'; D.A. Binchy, 'The Linguistic and Historical Value of the Irish Law Tracts', *Proceedings of the British Academy*, vol. 29, 1943, pp. 195–227, at pp. 196–8 (reprinted in Jenkins (ed.), *Celtic Law Papers*, pp. 71–107, at pp. 74–7). Recently, however, an attempt has been made to partially rehabilitate *ALI* and its editors: see P. Quinn, 'John O'Donovan and Eugene O'Curry's Notes and the Construction of the Ancient Laws of Ireland', *Irish Jurist*, vol. 55, 2016, pp. 166–74.

36 Mention should also be made here of a brief note that MacNeill penned in response to a comment from Henry Morris on 'a surviving trace of the old system of reckoning kin': 'Kinship in Irish Law', *Journal of the Royal Society of Antiquaries of Ireland*, 6th series, vol. 17, 1927, pp. 154–5.

37 E. MacNeill, 'Law: Celtic', in E.R.A. Seligman and A. Johnson (eds), *Encyclopaedia of the Social Sciences* 9 (London: Macmillan & Co., 1933), pp. 246–9, at p. 246.

38 The results of this seminar – which dealt with medieval Irish law relating to women – were later published as R. Thurneysen, N. Power, M. Dillon, K. Mulchrone, D.A. Binchy,

A. Knoch and J. Ryan (eds), *Studies in Early Irish Law* (Dublin: Hodges, Figgis & Co., 1936). The first eighty pages of the volume comprise Thurneysen's edition of the *Senchas Már* tract on marriage, *Cáin Lánamna* 'The Law of Full Couples'. This has since been re-edited by C.M. Eska, *Cáin Lánamna: An Old Irish treatise on marriage and divorce law* (Leiden/Boston: Brill, 2010).

39 MacNeill, 'Law: Celtic', p. 248. On the issue of a matrilinear society among the Picts, see M. Miller, 'Matriliny by Treaty: The Pictish foundation-legend', in D. Dumville, R. McKitterick and D. Whitelock (eds), *Ireland in Early Mediaeval Europe: Studies in memory of Kathleen Hughes* (Cambridge: Cambridge University Press, 1982), pp. 133–61; A.P. Smith, *Warlords and Holy Men: Scotland AD 80–1000* (London: Edward Arnold, 1985), pp. 36–84; W.D.H. Sellar, 'Warlords, Holy Men and Matrilineal Succession', *The Innes Review*, vol. 36, 1985, pp. 29–43; A. Woolf, 'Pictish Matriliny Reconsidered', *The Innes Review*, vol. 49, 1998, pp. 147–67; A. Ross, 'Pictish Matriliny', *Northern Studies*, vol. 34, 1999, pp. 11–22; Nicholas Evans, 'Royal Succession and Kingship among the Picts', *The Innes Review*, vol. 59, no. 1 (2008), pp. 1–48.

40 Vol. 7, 1929–30, pp. 149–265; vol. 8, 1930–1, pp. 81–108, pp. 271–84. The book was published in Dublin in 1935 with the addition of a substantial introduction.

41 Binchy, 'MacNeill's Study of the Ancient Irish Laws', p. 43.

42 M. Dillon, *Lebor na Cert. The Book of Rights*, Irish Texts Society 46 (Dublin: Irish Texts Society, 1962).

43 See, for example, T.M. Charles-Edwards, '*Lebor na Cert* and Clientship', in K. Murray (ed.), *Lebor na Cert: Reassessments*, Irish Texts Society, Subsidiary Series 25 (London: Irish Texts Society, 2013), pp. 13–33.

44 See the various studies of the text in Murray (ed.), *Lebor na Cert: Reassessments*.

45 MacNeill, *Celtic Ireland*, p. 74.

46 Ibid., p. 86.

47 See K. Murray, '*Lebor na Cert*: Language and date', in Murray (ed.), *Lebor na Cert: Reassessments*, pp. 77–102.

48 MacNeill, *Celtic Ireland*, p. 73. See the relevant comments and additional references provided by Donnchadh Ó Corráin, ibid. [1981 reprint], pp. 191–2.

49 As well as *Celtic Ireland* (Dublin: Martin Lester, 1921), mention must also be made of his *Phases of Irish History* (Dublin: Talbot Press, 1919 [repr. 1968]); together these constitute his major works in the field. Outside of the legal material already mentioned, both of these volumes contain much else of interest to students of medieval Irish law: *Celtic Ireland* treats of ownership of land and of the family commune (republished with *addenda* from 'Communal Ownership in Ancient Ireland', *Irish Monthly*, vol. 47, 1919, pp. 407–15, pp. 463–74) while *Phases of Irish History* has chapters on medieval Irish institutions and on the Norman conquest (with a particular focus on legal issues).

50 Published in *Studies: An Irish quarterly review*, vol. 11, 1922, pp. 13–28.

51 Ó Lúing, *Kuno Meyer, 1858–1919: A biography*, p. 70; T. Garvin, *The Lives of Daniel Binchy: Irish scholar, diplomat, public intellectual* (Sallins: Irish Academic Press, 2016), p. 7.

52 See the comments in Ó Lúing, *Kuno Meyer, 1858–1919: A biography*, pp. 131, 154.

53 Binchy, 'The Linguistic and Historical Value of the Irish Law Tracts', p. 199 (reprinted in Jenkins (ed.), *Celtic Law Papers*, p. 77).

54 F.J. Byrne, 'MacNeill the Historian', in Martin and Byrne (eds), *The Scholar Revolutionary*, pp. 17–36, at p. 17.

55 Interestingly, however, Liam Breatnach has shown ('Varia VI: 3 *Ardri* as an Old Compound', *Ériu*, vol. 37, 1986, pp. 192–3) that there was a close compound *ardri* 'high-king' (genitive *ardrech*) which fell out of use at an early stage.

56 In the 'Introduction' to the 1981 reprint of *Celtic Ireland*, p. iv.

Eoin MacNeill and a 'Celtic' Church in Early Medieval Ireland? *Niamh Wycherley*

1 Eoin MacNeill, 'A School of Irish Church History', *Studies: An Irish quarterly review*, vol. 21, no. 81, 1932, pp. 1–6. The year 432 is traditionally celebrated as the date when Patrick arrived in Ireland. This date was deliberately chosen by later medieval authors to blur the lines between Patrick's mission and the activities of a bishop called Palladius, who was sent to Ireland by Pope Celestine in 431, 'to the Irish (*Scotti*) believing in Christ'.

2 MacNeill, 'School of Irish Church History', p. 5.

3 Eoin MacNeill, *Celtic Ireland* (Dublin: Martin Lester, 1921 [repr., Dublin: Academy Press, 1981]); *Phases of Irish History* (Dublin: Gill, 1919); *Early Irish Laws and Institutions* (Dublin: Burns, Oates & Washbourne, 1935).

4 MacNeill, 'School of Irish Church History', p. 4.

5 J.F. Kenney, *The Sources for the Early History of Ireland, Volume 1: Ecclesiastical* (New York: Columbia University Press, 1929 [repr. 1966]).

6 Donnchadh Ó Corráin, *Clavis litterarum Hibernensium* (Turnhout: Brepols, 2017).

7 Some of his best Patrician studies are reprinted along with his biography of Patrick in Eoin MacNeill, *Saint Patrick, with a Memoir by Michael Tierney and a Bibliography of Patrician Literature by F.X. Martin O.S.A.*, ed. John Ryan (Dublin: Clonmore & Reynolds, 1964).

8 Eoin MacNeill, 'The Fifteenth Centenary of Saint Patrick: A suggested form of commemoration', *Studies: An Irish quarterly review*, vol. 13, no. 50, Jun. 1924, pp. 177–88.

9 See, for example, E.A. Thomson, *Who Was Saint Patrick?* (Woodbridge: Boydell, 1985 [repr. 1999]); Liam de Paor, *Saint Patrick's World: The Christian culture of the apostolic age* (Dublin: Four Courts Press, 1993 [rev. edn 1996]); D.N. Dumville (ed.), *Saint Patrick, A.D. 493–1993* (Woodbridge: Boydell, 1993); Thomas O'Loughlin, *Saint Patrick: The man and his works* (London: Triangle, 1999); Dáibhí Ó Cróinín, 'Who was Palladius, "first bishop of the Irish"?', *Peritia*, vol. 14, 2000, pp. 205–37; and a recent controversial reinterpretation of Patrick's motives in Roy Flechner, *Saint Patrick Retold: The legend and history of Ireland's patron saint* (Princeton, NJ: Princeton University Press, 2019).

10 See, especially, T.F. O'Rahilly, *The Two Patricks: A lecture on the history of Christianity in fifth-century Ireland* (Dublin: DIAS, 1942 [repr. 1981]). See also Ó Cróinín in this volume, pp. 53–56.

11 Now readily accessible online at www.confessio.ie.

12 See Patrick's *Confessio* in Ludwig Bieler (ed.), *Libri Epistolarum Sancti Patricii Episcopi*, 2 vols (Dublin: Stationery Office, 1952 [repr. 1993]), I, pp. 56–91.

13 Eoin MacNeill, 'The Hymn of St Secundinus in Honour of St Patrick', *Irish Historical Studies*, vol. 2, no. 6, Sept. 1940, pp. 129–53, at p. 151.

14 MacNeill, *Saint Patrick*, p. 42.

15 Eoin MacNeill, 'Beginnings of Latin Culture in Ireland', *Studies: An Irish quarterly review*, vol. 20, no. 77, 1931, pp. 39–48; Eoin MacNeill, 'Beginnings of Latin Culture in Ireland, part II', *Studies: An Irish quarterly review*, vol. 20, no. 79, 1931, pp. 449–60.

16 MacNeill 'Hymn of Secundinus', p. 148.

17 As evidenced, for example, by Cummian's paschal letter, *c.*632. Maura Walsh and Dáibhí Ó Cróinín (eds), *Cummian's Letter De Controversia Paschali: Together with a related Irish computistical tract De Ratione Computandi* (Toronto: Pontifical Institute of Mediaeval Studies, 1988). MacNeill argues this most clearly in *The Standard*, 30 Jan. 1932.

18 Christiaan Corlett and Michael Potterton (eds), *The Church in Early Medieval Ireland in the Light of Recent Archaeological Excavations* (Dublin: Wordwell, 2014). See also, for example, Tomás Ó Carragáin and Sam Turner (eds), *Making Christian Landscapes in Atlantic Europe: Conversion and consolidation in the early middle ages* (Cork: Cork University Press, 2016), especially chapters by Paul MacCotter and Anne Connon.

19 Teresa Bolger, Colm Moloney and Carmelita Troy, 'Archaeological Excavations at Lorrha, Co. Tipperary', *Journal of Irish Archaeology*, vol. 21, 2012, pp. 113–37.

20 See also Carew's chapter in this volume, pp. 153–70.

21 See, for example, Elizabeth Ashman Rowe, Colmán Etchingham, Máire Ní Mhaonaigh and Jón Viðar Sigurðsson, *Norse-Gaelic Contacts in a Viking World: Studies in the literature and history of Norway, Iceland, Ireland, and the Isle of Man* (Turnout: Brepols, 2019); Elizabeth O'Brien and Edel Bhreathnach, 'Irish Boundary *Ferta*, their Physical Manifestation and Historical Context', in Fiona Edmonds and Paul Russell (eds), *Tome: Studies in medieval Celtic history and law* (Woodbridge: Boydell & Brewer, 2011), pp. 53–64. See also the work of the Discovery Programme www.discoveryprogramme.ie and individual projects such as The Connacht Project: https://www.nuigalway.ie/colleges-and-schools/arts-social-sciences-and-celtic-studies/geography-archaeology-irish-studies/disciplines/archaeology/research/ireland-atlantic-europe/the-connacht-project/.

22 Colmán Etchingham, 'Bishops, Church and People: How Christian was "early Christian Ireland"?', in *L'Irlanda e gli Irlandesi nell'alto Medioevo: Spoleto, 16–21 aprile 2009*, Settimane di studio della Fondazione Centro Italiano di Studi sull'Alto Medioevo, vol. 57 (Spoleto: Presso la sede della Fondazione, 2010), pp. 325–48.

23 MacNeill, 'The Fifteenth Centenary', p. 179.

24 See, for example, Fergus Kelly, *A Guide to Early Irish Law* (Dublin: DIAS, 1988 [repr. 1991, 1995, 1998, 2003, 2005, 2009]), pp. 95–7; Paul Holm, 'The Slave Trade of Dublin, Ninth to Twelfth Centuries', *Peritia*, vol. 5, 1988, pp. 317–45; Janel M. Fontaine, 'Early Medieval Slave-Trading in the Archaeological Record: Comparative methodologies', *Early Medieval Europe*, vol. 25, no. 4, 2017, pp. 466–88.

25 See MacNeill, *Celtic Ireland*; John MacNeill, *Celtic Religion*, Lectures on the History of Religions 1911 (London: Catholic Truth Society, 1935).

26 The so-called 'Viking Age' in Ireland is also being re-evaluated. The title 'Viking' implies a homogenous culture or ethnic group, and one distinct from Scandinavian, which is not borne out by the evidence. See Alex Woolf, 'The Scandinavian Intervention', in Brendan Smith (ed.), *The Cambridge History of Ireland. Volume I: 600–1550* (Cambridge: Cambridge University Press, 2018), pp. 107–30.

27 Elva Johnston, 'Ireland in Late Antiquity: A forgotten frontier?', *Studies in Late Antiquity*, vol. 1, no. 2, 2017, pp. 107–23, at p. 109.

28 He expresses a similar argument in handwritten notes dating to 1932, where he clearly enunciates it as an anti-Bolshevik sentiment (UCD Archives, Eoin MacNeill additional papers LA1/D/613).

29 MacNeill, *Celtic Ireland*, p. 144. See Ó Cróinín, p. 55 and Johnston, p. 71.

30 MacNeill, *Celtic Ireland*, Chapter 9. See also his discussion of property ownership among the extended family in 'Communal Ownership in Ancient Ireland', *Irish Monthly*, vol. 47, 1919, pp. 407–15, 463–74.

31 G.H. Orpen, *Ireland under the Normans, 1169–1333*, 4 vols (Oxford: Oxford University Press, 1911–20). See Stephen H. Harrison, 'Re-fighting the Battle of Down: Orpen, MacNeill and the Irish nation state', in Michael Brown and Stephen H. Harrison (eds), *The Medieval World and the Modern Mind* (Dublin: Four Courts Press, 2000), pp. 171–82.

32 MacNeill, *Celtic Ireland*, p. xi.

33 MacNeill, 'School of Irish Church History', p. 2.

34 See Donal McCartney, 'MacNeill and Irish-Ireland', in Martin and Byrne (eds), *The Scholar Revolutionary*, pp. 75–98.

35 *An Claidheamh Soluis*, 1 Nov. 1913, p. 6.

36 See, for example, T.M. Charles-Edwards, *Early Christian Ireland* (Cambridge: Cambridge University Press, 2000), Chapter 10: 'The Primatial Claims of Armagh, Kildare and Canterbury'.

37 W.S. Kerr, *The Independence of the Church of Ireland* (London: Society for Promoting Christian Knowledge, 1931).

38 *The Standard*, 16 Jan., 23 Jan., 30 Jan., 6 Feb., 13 Feb., 20 Feb., and 27 Feb. 1932.

39 Ibid., 16 Jan. 1932.

40 Ibid., 23 Jan. 1932.

41 Eoin MacNeill, 'Notes on Kerr's Interpretation of the Development of the Early Celtic Church', *c.*1932 (UCD Archives, Eoin MacNeill additional papers LA1/D/614).

42 *The Standard*, 30 Jan. 1932.

43 G.S.M. Walker (ed.), *Sancti Columbani Opera*, Scriptores Latini Hiberniae 2 (Dublin: DIAS, 1957), p. 23.

44 See, for example, Sean McDonagh, 'Columban, the Patron Saint of a United Europe', *Irish Times*, 15 Jan. 2013; 'In the Wings – Saint Columbanus: The first European', presented by Mary McAleese, RTÉ Radio 1, 30 Oct. 2015.

45 Próinséas Ní Chatháin and Michael Richter (eds), *Ireland and Europe in the Early Middle Ages: Texts and transmissions* (Dublin: Four Courts Press, 2002); *Ireland and Europe in the Early Middle Ages: Learning and literature* (Stuttgart: Klett-Cotta, 1996); *Ireland and Christendom: The Bible and the missions* (Stuttgart: Klett-Cotta, 1987); *Ireland and Europe: The early Church* (Stuttgart: Klett-Cotta, 1984).

46 See, for example, Dáibhí Ó Cróinín, 'The Irish Abroad in Medieval Europe', *Peritia*, vol. 5, 1986, pp. 445–52; 'The Irish as Mediators of Antique Culture on the Continent', in P.L. Butzer and Dietrich Lohrmann (eds), *Science in Western and Eastern Civilization in Carolingian Times* (Basel: Birkhäuser Verlag, 1993), pp. 41–52; 'Hiberno-Latin Literature to 1169', in Dáibhí Ó Cróinín (ed.), *A New History of Ireland. Volume 1: Prehistoric and Early Ireland* (Oxford: Oxford University Press, 2005), pp. 371–404.

47 Roy Flechner and Sven Meeder (eds), *The Irish in Early Medieval Europe: Identity, culture and religion* (London: Palgrave, 2016); Emmet Marron, 'The Communities of St Columbanus: Irish monasteries on the continent?', *Proceedings of the Royal Irish Academy*, vol. 118C, 2018, pp. 1–28.

48 See, for example, Alan Thacker, 'Loca Sanctorum: The significance of place in the study of the saints', in Alan Thacker and Richard Sharpe, *Local Saints and Local Churches in the Early Medieval West* (Oxford: Oxford University Press, 2002), pp. 1–46.

49 Easter, the most important feast in the liturgical calendar, was not celebrated at the same time in all parts of the Church in the seventh century. The Synod of Whitby in 664 brought the dispute regarding the correct dating of Easter into sharp focus. See Máirín MacCarron, *Bede and Time: Computus, theology and history in the early medieval world* (Abingdon: Routledge, 2020); Immo Warntjes and Dáibhí Ó Cróinín (eds), *The Easter Controversy of Late Antiquity and the Early Middle Ages: Its manuscripts, texts, and tables. Proceedings of the 2nd International Conference on the Science of Computus in Ireland and Europe, Galway, 18–20 July, 2008*, Studia Traditionis Theologiae 10 (Turnhout: Brepols, 2011).

50 Eric Rebillard, *The Care of the Dead in Late Antiquity*, translated by Elizabeth Trapnell Rawlings and Jeanine Routier-Pucci (Ithaca, NY: Cornell University Press, 2009). For Ireland see Elizabeth O'Brien, *Mapping Death: Burial in late Iron Age and early medieval Ireland* (Dublin: Four Courts Press, 2020); Christiaan Corlett and Michael Potterton (eds), *Death and Burial in Early Medieval Ireland* (Dublin: Wordwell, 2010); Tomás Ó Carragáin, 'Cemetery Settlements and Local Churches in pre-Viking Ireland in Light of Comparisons with England and Wales', *Proceedings of the British Academy*, vol. 157, 2009, pp. 329–66.

51 J.M.H. Smith, 'Portable Christianity: Relics in the medieval West (*c.*700–*c.*1200)', *Proceedings of the British Academy*, vol. 181, 2012, pp. 143–67.

52 Eoin MacNeill, 'A Pioneer of Nations', *Studies: An Irish quarterly review*, vol. 11, no. 41, 1922, pp. 13–28, at p. 13.

53 See, for example, Robin Chapman Stacey, *Dark Speech: The performance of law in early Ireland* (Philadelphia: University of Pennsylvania Press, 2007), p. 91.

54 As expressed in the Irish grammatical treatise *Auraicept na nÉces*. Anders Ahlqvist (ed.), *The Early Irish Linguist: An edition of the canonical part of the Auraicept na nÉces*, Commentationes Humanarum Litterarum 73 (Helsinki: Societas Scientiarum Fennica, 1983).

55 See, for example, Eoin MacNeill, 'Ancient Irish Law: The law of status or franchise', *PRIA*, vol. 36C, 1923, pp. 265-316; Eoin MacNeill, 'Mocu, Maccu', *Ériu*, vol. 3, 1907, pp. 42-9.

56 Eoin MacNeill, 'Beginnings', p. 39.

57 Elva Johnston, *Literacy and Identity in Early Medieval Ireland* (Woodbridge: Boydell & Brewer, 2013); Anthony Harvey, 'Lexical Influences on the Medieval Latin of the Celts', in Maurillo Pérez González and Estrella Pérez Rodriguez (eds), *Influencias Léxicas de Otras Lenguas en el Latin Medieval* (León and Valladolid: Universidad de *Valladolid*/Universidad de *León*, 2011), pp. 65–77; Immo Warntjes, 'Seventh-Century Ireland: The cradle of medieval science?', in Charles Doherty and Mary Kelly (eds), *Music and the Stars: Mathematics in medieval Ireland* (Dublin: Four Courts Press, 2013), pp. 44–72; Elizabeth Boyle, 'Allegory, the *áes dána* and the Liberal Arts in Medieval Irish Literature', in Deborah Hayden and Paul Russell (eds), *Grammatica, Gramadach and Gramadeg: Vernacular grammar and grammarians in medieval Ireland and Wales*, Studies in the History of the Language Sciences 125 (Amsterdam: John Benjamins, 2016), pp. 11–34; Jacopo Bisagni, *Amrae Coluimb Chille: A critical edition* (Dublin: DIAS, 2019); Paul Russell, Sharon Arbuthnot and Pádraic Moran, *Early Irish Glossaries Database*, http://www.asnc.cam.ac.uk/irishglossaries.

58 Nike Stam, *A Typology of Code-switching in the Commentary to the Félire Óengusso* (Utrecht: LOT, 2017); Jacopo Bisagni, 'Prolegomena to the Study of Code-switching in the Old Irish Glosses', *Peritia*, vols 24–5, 2013–14, pp. 1–58.

59 Pádraic Moran, *De Origine Scoticae Linguae (O'Mulconry's Glossary): An early Irish linguistic tract, edited with a related glossary, Irsan*, Corpus Christianorum, Lexica Latina Medii Aevi 7 (Turnhout: Brepols, 2019).

60 For example, David Stifter, 'Chronologicon Hibernicum: A probabilistic chronological framework for dating Early Irish language developments and literature', ERC H2020 Project, no. 647351.

61 MacNeill, *Celtic Ireland*, p. 18.

62 See, for example, Liam Breatnach, *The Early Irish Law Text* Senchas Már *and the Question of Its Date*, E.C. Quiggin Memorial Lectures 13 (Cambridge: Department of Anglo-Saxon, Norse, and Celtic, University of Cambridge, 2011), who argues for a significant Armagh role in the composition of the early Irish laws.

63 MacNeill, *Celtic Ireland*, Chapter 3.

64 See, for example, Eoin MacNeill, 'The Authorship and Structure of the "Annals of Tigernach"', *Ériu*, vol. 7, 1914, pp. 30–113.

65 MacNeill, *Saint Patrick*, p. 80; J.B. Bury, *Life of St Patrick and His Place in History* (London: Macmillan, 1905).

66 Eoin MacNeill, 'Dates of Texts in the Book of Armagh Relating to Saint Patrick', *Journal of the Royal Society of Antiquaries of Ireland*, vol. 58, 1928, pp. 85–101. However, he did unfairly malign Tírechán: see Catherine Swift, 'Tírechán's Motives in Compiling the *Collectanea*: An alternative interpretation', *Ériu*, vol. 45, 1994, pp. 53–82. There have been many evaluations of the Patrician sources in the Book of Armagh since MacNeill. See, for example, Charles Doherty, 'The Cult of St Patrick and the Politics of Armagh in the Seventh Century', in Jean-Michel Picard (ed.), *Ireland and Northern France AD 600–850* (Dublin: Four Courts Press, 1991), pp. 53–94.

67 MacNeill, *Saint Patrick*, p. 80.

68 D.P. McCarthy, *The Irish Annals: Their genesis, evolution and history* (Dublin: Four Courts Press, 2008). See also Nicholas Evans, *The Past and the Present in Medieval Irish Chronicles* (Woodbridge: Boydell & Brewer, 2010); Bernadette Cunningham, *The Annals of the Four Masters: Irish history, kingship and society in the early seventeenth century* (Dublin: Four Courts Press, 2014).

69 Jonathan M. Wooding, 'Reapproaching the Pagan Celtic Past: Anti-nativism, asterisk reality and the late-antiquity paradigm', *Studia Celtica Fennica*, vol. 6, 2009, pp. 61–74, provides a comprehensive overview and bibliographic references.

70 Johnston, *Literacy and Identity*, p. 168.

71 MacNeill, 'Beginnings', p. 48. See also *The Standard*, 6 Feb. 1932: 'Monasticism, introduced on a small scale by St Patrick, developed in Ireland to such a degree in the sixth, seventh and eighth centuries that it brought about a transformation in the administrative system of the Irish Church. While the apostolic tradition of church government remained in theory unchanged, in practice it fell largely into abeyance. Bishops came to be regarded rather as dignitaries and functionaries than as rulers and shepherds of the flock.'

72 MacNeill, *Saint Patrick*, p. 80.

73 Kathleen Hughes, *The Church in Early Irish Society* (London: Methuen, 1966).

74 Patrick J. Corish, 'The Pastoral Mission in the Early Irish Church', *Léachtaí Cholm Cille*, vol. 2, 1971, pp. 14–25; Richard Sharpe, 'Some Problems Concerning the Organization of the Church in Early Medieval Ireland', *Peritia*, vol. 3, 1984, pp. 230–70.

75 Thomas Charles-Edwards, 'The Pastoral Role of the Church in the Early Irish Laws', in John Blair and Richard Sharpe (eds), *Pastoral Care before the Parish* (Leicester: Leicester University Press, 1992), pp. 63–80; Donnchadh Ó Corráin, 'The Early Irish Churches: Some aspects of organisation', in Donnchadh Ó Corráin (ed.), *Irish Antiquity* (Cork: Tower Books, 1981), pp. 327–41; T.O. Clancy, 'Annat in Scotland and the Origins of the Parish', *Innes Review*, vol. 46, 1995, pp. 91–115; Craig Haggart, 'The *Céli Dé* and the Early Medieval Irish Church: A reassessment', *Studia Hibernica*, vol. 34, 2006–7, pp. 17–62; Westley Follett, *Céli Dé in Ireland: Monastic writing and identity in the early middle ages* (Woodbridge: Boydell & Brewer, 2006); Paul MacCotter, 'The Origins of the Parish in Ireland', *PRIA*, vol. 119C, 2019, pp. 37–67.

76 Colmán Etchingham, *Church Organisation in Ireland AD 650–1000* (Maynooth: Laigin, 1999).

77 Kenney, *Sources*, pp. 468–77. See also Peter O'Dwyer, *Céli Dé: Spiritual reform in Ireland, 750–900* (Dublin: Editions Táilliúra, 1981).

78 Note 75 above; Brian Lambkin, 'Blathmac and the Céili Dé: A reappraisal', *Celtica*, vol. 23, 1999, pp. 132–54.

79 Patrick, *Confessio*, §52, p. 86.

80 See, for example, Niamh Wycherley, *The Cult of Relics in Early Medieval Ireland*, Studies in the Early Middle Ages 43 (Turnhout: Brepols, 2015), Chapters 5 and 6.

81 MacNeill, *Phases of Irish History*, p. 238.

82 MacNeill, *Celtic Ireland*, pp. 148–50.

83 Donnchadh Ó Corráin, 'Dál Cais: Church and dynasty', *Ériu*, vol. 24, 1973, pp. 52–63; David E. Thornton, 'Early Medieval Louth: The kingdom of Conaille Muirtheimne', *Journal of the County Louth Archaeological and Historical Society*, vol. 24, 1997, pp. 139–50.

84 Clare Downham, 'The Career of Cearbhall of Osraighe', *Ossary, Laois and Leinster*, vol. 1, 2004, pp. 1–18; Tomás Ó Carragáin, 'The Archaeology of Ecclesiastical Estates in Early Medieval Ireland: A case-study of the kingdom of Fir Maige', *Peritia*, vols 24–5, 2013–14, pp. 266–312. See also Tomás Ó Carragáin, 'Christianizing the Landscape of Mag Réta: Home territory of the kings of Laígis', in James Lyttleton and Matthew Stout (eds), *Church and Settlement in Ireland* (Dublin: Four Courts Press, 2018), pp. 60–85; Paul MacCotter,

'Túath, Manor and Parish: Kingdom of Fir Maige, cantred of Fermoy', *Peritia*, vols 22–3, 2013, pp. 224–74.

85 See Johnston, *Literacy and Identity*, for a modern re-evaluation of the interactions between the secular and clerical power structures in Ireland in relation to communities of learning.

86 See especially *The Standard*, 6 Feb., 13 Feb., 20 Feb. and 27 Feb. 1932.

87 Kerr, *Independence of the Church*, p. 140, quoted by MacNeill, *The Standard*, 6 Feb. 1932.

88 In Smith (ed.), *Cambridge History of Ireland*, for example, there is no discussion of the Church or ecclesiastical politics before the late eleventh century.

89 *The Standard*, 6 Feb. 1932.

90 P.J. Duffy, 'The Shape of the Parish', in Elizabeth Fitzpatrick and Raymond Gillespie (eds), *The Parish in Medieval and Early Modern Ireland: Community, territory and building* (Dublin: Four Courts Press, 2006), pp. 33–61, referenced in Colmán Ó Clabaigh, 'The Church, 1050–1460', in Smith (ed.), *Cambridge History of Ireland*, pp. 355–84, at p. 359. See also Dagmar Ó Riain-Raedel, 'New Light on the Beginnings of Christ Church Cathedral, Dublin', in Seán Duffy (ed.), *Medieval Dublin XVII* (Dublin: Four Courts Press, 2018), pp. 63–80; Paul MacCotter, 'The Exclave Parish and the Geography of Episcopacy in Ireland: 600 to 1300', in James Lyttleton and Matthew Stout (eds), *Church and Settlement in Ireland* (Dublin: Four Courts Press, 2018), pp. 101–18.

91 M.T. Flanagan, *The Transformation of the Irish Church in the Twelfth Century* (Woodbridge: Boydell, 2010); Colmán Etchingham, Review article: 'The "Reform" of the Irish Church in the Eleventh and Twelfth Centuries', *Studia Hibernica*, vol. 37, 2011, pp. 215–37; Donnchadh Ó Corráin, *The Irish Church, Its Reform and the English Invasion* (Dublin: Four Courts Press, 2017).

92 *The Standard*, 27 Feb. 1932.

93 For example, O'Rahilly, *Two Patricks*.

94 MacNeill, *Celtic Ireland*, p. 11.

95 MacNeill, *Celtic Ireland*, p. xv; MacNeill, 'School of Irish Church History', pp. 4–5.

Eoin MacNeill: the scholar and his critics. *Dáibhí Ó Cróinín*

1 Established in 1931 as an organ of the newly founded Fianna Fáil political party, the *Irish Press* (*Scéala Éireann*) ceased to publish on 25 May 1995.

2 A prolific author and Irish language enthusiast, Aodh de Blácam (born in London in 1891 as Hugh Saunders Blackham) was a regular and much-liked columnist with the *Irish Press* (as 'Roddy the Rover') and the author of what is still the only comprehensive survey of literature in Irish, *Gaelic Literature Surveyed* (Dublin: Talbot Press, 1929 [repr, 1974]). For more recent treatments of the subject see J.E. Caerwyn Williams agus Máirín Ní Mhuiríosa, *Traidisiún Liteartha na nGael* (Baile Átha Cliath: An Clóchomhar Tta, 1979) and J.E. Caerwyn Williams and Patrick K. Ford, *The Irish Literary Tradition* (Cardiff: University of Wales Press, 1992).

    De Blácam's survey still makes interesting reading. He anticipated many ideas that became the subjects of later controversy, including the now famous notion (best represented by the 1964 Rede Lecture by the Edinburgh Professor of Celtic, Kenneth Hurlestone Jackson) that the Ulster Cycle stories about Cú Chulainn and the Red Branch 'Knights' at Emain Macha were 'a window in the early Iron Age' (ibid., p. xiii); see Diarmuid Breathnach and Máire Ní Mhurchú, *Beath.áisnéis 1882–1982*, 1 (Baile Átha Cliath: An Clóchomhar Tta, 1986), pp. 25–6.

3 O'Rahilly was, along with Osborn Bergin, one of the two leading authorities on the Irish language at this time; see Breathnach and Ní Mhurchú, *Beathaisnéis*, 2 (Baile Átha Cliath: An Clóchomhar Tta, 1990), pp. 132–4, and Diarmuid Ó Sé, 'Tomás Ó Rathile', *Scoláirí Gaeilge – Léachtaí Cholm Cille*, vol. 27, 1997, pp. 177–210 (though Ó Sé nowhere mentions O'Rahilly's *Two Patricks*).

4 *Irish Press*, vol. XIII, no. 231, 28 Sept. 1943, p. 2. MacNeill's 'reply' had appeared as 'The Other Patrick' in the Jesuit journal, *Studies*, vol. 32, no. 127, 1943, pp. 308–14.

5 Thomas F. O'Rahilly, *The Two Patricks: A lecture on the history of Christianity in fifth-century Ireland* (Dublin: DIAS, 1943). The talk was delivered as the annual statutory lecture of the DIAS, School of Celtic Studies, in Trinity College Dublin on 29 March 1942, under the title 'Palladius and Patrick'. It was the revised title of the published version that caused all the rumpus.

6 O'Rahilly's lecture drew the attention also of the famous Flann O'Brien (Brian O'Nolan and Myles na gCopaleen), who, in his *Irish Times* column *Cruiskeen Lawn* of 10 April 1942, wrote: 'Talking of this notorious Institute (Lord what would I give for a chair in it with me thousand good-lookin' pounds for doing "work" that most people regard as an interesting recreation), talking of it, anyway, a friend has drawn my attention to Professor O'Rahilly's recent address on "Paladius [sic] and Patrick". I understand also that Professor Schroedinger has been proving lately that you cannot establish a first cause. The first fruit of the Institute, therefore, has been an effort to show that there are two Saint Patricks and no God.' Cited in Walter Moore, *Schrödinger: Life and thought* (Cambridge: Cambridge University Press, 1989), p. 378. The Institute sued for libel – and won! The paper was obliged to pay £100 to a nominated charity and all legal costs, as well as undertake that Myles would never again refer to the Institute in his column; Moore, ibid., p. 379.

7 *Irish Press*, vol. XIII, no. 231, 28 Sept. 1943, p. 2.

8 D.A. Binchy, 'Patrick and His Biographers, Ancient and Modern', *Studia Hibernica*, vol. 2, 1962, pp. 7–173, at p. 27.

9 De Blácam noted that 'Only one scholar of weight appears to have supported the attack on tradition – Mr. Gerard Murphy – who writes in *Studies* in favour of Professor O'Rahilly's reasoning, though with manifest uneasiness'; art. cit., 2. See Gerard Murphy, 'The Two Patricks', *Studies: An Irish quarterly review*, vol. 32, no. 127, Sept. 1943, pp. 297–307. On the other hand, Binchy, 'Patrick and His Biographers', p. 29, wrote that 'Osborn Bergin, though far from sharing O'Rahilly's certainty, believed that his thesis was "less improbable" than that of the orthodox school'. For more on Bergin, see further below.

10 *Irish Press*, vol. XIII, no. 231, 28 Sept. 1943, p. 2.

11 See the model treatment in Liam de Paor, 'The Aggrandisement of Armagh', in T.D. Williams (ed.), *Historical Studies* 8 (Dublin: Gill & Macmillan, 1971), pp. 95–110. See now Roy Flechner, *Saint Patrick Retold: The legend and history of Ireland's patron saint* (Princeton, NJ: Princeton University Press, 2018).

12 See *Saint Patrick, by Eoin MacNeill, ed. by John Ryan, with a Memoir by Michael Tierney & a Bibliography of Patrician Literature by F.X. Martin* (Dublin: Clonmore & Reynolds, 1964). For MacNeill's more rigorous scholarly studies, see 'Dates of Texts in the Book of Armagh Relating to Saint Patrick', *Journal of the Royal Society of Antiquaries of Ireland [JRSAI]*, vol. 58, 1928, pp. 85–101, conveniently reprinted in John Ryan (ed.) [Eoin MacNeill], *St Patrick* (Dublin: Clonmore & Reynolds, 1964) pp. 137–57, and 'The Origin of the Tripartite Life of Saint Patrick', *Journal of the Royal Society of Antiquaries of Ireland*, vol. 59, 1929, pp. 1–15, repr. in MacNeill, *Saint Patrick*, pp. 159–77. It must be said, however, that MacNeill's biographical essay on St Patrick in that volume shows him at his least impressive. The piece is pious and uncritical.

13 MacNeill, 'The Other Patrick', *Studies: An Irish quarterly review*, vol. 32, 1943, pp. 308–14.

14 Binchy, 'Patrick and His Biographers', p. 29.

15 Thomas F. O'Rahilly, *Early Irish History and Mythology* [*EIHM* hereafter] (Dublin: DIAS, 1946).

16 The great Italian-Irish scholar Mario Esposito, in his own remarkable essay 'The Patrician Problem and a Possible Solution', *Irish Historical Studies*, vol. 10, no. 38, 1956, pp. 131–55,

at p. 143, reported having received a letter from O'Rahilly in the spring of 1953 (just before O'Rahilly's unexpected death) in which he stated that he had a Life of Patrick running to about 500 pages ready for the press. It is extremely unfortunate that the work has never been recovered.

17 In *EIHM*, p. 538, n. 2 he gives MacNeill credit for having been the first to recognise that the term *Tuath Iboth* represented the *Ebudae*, the ancient population of the Hebrides. Instances of explicit criticism may be found in *EIHM*, pp. 55–6, 57, 473 n. 4, 479 (twice), 481, 482, 504, 507 and 511. I have doubtless missed other such references.

18 *EIHM*, p. 47.

19 *EIHM*, p. 47, n. 4. MacNeill and O'Rahilly had both studied with Father Edmund Hogan SJ, a great pioneering scholar of Early Irish who had in turn learned his Irish from the great nineteenth-century scholar Eugene O'Curry. See Fathers of the Society of Jesus (eds), *A Page of Irish History: Story of University College Dublin 1883–1909* (Dublin: Talbot Press, 1930), pp. 182–4. In the same volume is a memoir (pp. 186–94) by MacNeill of his apprenticeship with Father Hogan and his initiation into what he described as 'the sacred circle of the learned'.

20 See n. 13 above.

21 Osborn Bergin, 'Observations on "The Mythology of Lough Neagh"', *Béaloideas*, vol. 2, pt 3 (Meitheamh, 1930), pp. 246–52. See Eoin MacNeill, 'The Mythology of Lough Neagh', *Béaloideas*, vol. 2, pt 2 (Nollaig, 1929), pp. 115–21.

22 See D.A. Binchy, *Osborn Bergin*. The Osborn Bergin Memorial Lecture 1 (Dublin: University College Dublin, 1970), p. 20, citing an obituary account by Rev. Prof. Francis Shaw (Bergin's successor in the Chair of Old Irish at UCD), *Irish Press*, 7 Oct. 1950, p. 1.

23 Eoin MacNeill, *Celtic Ireland* (Dublin: Martin Lester Ltd, 1921 [repr. Dublin: Academy Press, 1981]), p. 144. For the background to the book, see F.J. Byrne, 'MacNeill the Historian', in F.X. Martin and F.J. Byrne (eds), *The Scholar Revolutionary: Eoin MacNeill, 1867–1945, and the making of the new Ireland* (Shannon: Irish University Press, 1973), pp. 15–36.

24 Bergin, 'Observations', p. 246.

25 Apropos of the seventh-century poet Luccreth moccu Chiara, one of whose compositions was drawn on in his earlier article by MacNeill, Bergin offered the characteristically gnomic comment: 'The credit of originating the metrical experiments of the seventh century may or may not be due to this poet'; Bergin, 'Observations', p. 246, n. 1.

26 Ibid., p. 252.

27 Binchy, *Osborn Bergin*, p. 15.

28 Ibid.

29 On Canon Peter O'Leary [=An tAth. Peadar Ó Laoghaire], parish priest of Castlelyons, Co. Cork, and the leading proponent of the movement to encourage the living language of Irish native speakers (*caint na ndaoine*), see Breathnach and Ní Mhurchú, *Beathaisnéis*, 2, pp. 91–2, and Shán Ó Cuív, 'Materials for a Bibliography of the Very Reverend Peter Canon O'Leary, 1839–1920', *Celtica*, vol. 2, pt 2, 1954, pp. 3–39.

30 For what follows, see especially Shán Ó Cuív, 'Caradas nár Mhair: Peadar Ua Laoghaire agus Eoin Mac Néill', in Martin and Byrne (eds), *The Scholar Revolutionary*, pp. 51–73, which is a synopsis of Shán Ó Cuív, 'An tAthair Peadar agus a Lucht Comh-Aimsire', unpublished MA thesis, University College Dublin, 1956.

31 O'Growney was regarded very much as a founding figure of the language movement; see Agnes O'Farrelly (ed.), *Leabhar an Athar Eoghan. The O'Growney Memorial Volume* (Dublin: Gill, 1904). It was his untimely death that propelled MacNeill into the editorship of *An Claidheamh Soluis*. See MacNeill's 'Reminiscences of Father O'Growney', ibid., pp. 138–40.

32 See Regina Uí Chollatáin, *'An Claidheamh Soluis' agus 'Fáinne an Lae' 1899–1932* (Baile Átha Cliath: Cois Life Teoranta, 2004). Useful also is Andrew Murphy, *Reading and Cultural*

Nationalism, 1790–1930: Bringing the nation to book (Cambridge: Cambridge University Press, 2018).

33 For an authoritative modern assessment of *Séadna*, see Pádraig A. Breatnach, '*Séadna*: Saothar ealaíne', *Studia Hibernica*, vol. 9, 1969, pp. 109–24.

34 *Irisleabhar na Gaedhilge*. vol. 8, 1897–8, p. 27. *Séadna* appeared in book form in 1898.

35 *Notes on Irish Words and Usages* (Dublin: Browne & Nolan, Ltd., 1926), p. 152.

36 'Cad chuige do ghiorróchthá saoghal Shéadna. Tabhair a shlighe féin dó. Mo thruaighe nach féidir tuilleadh réime do bheith aige san *Irisleabhar* gach mí. Acht ná cuir-se cumhgach dá laighead air. Sgaoil leis agus lean é'; Ó Cuív, 'Caradas nár Mhair', p. 60.

37 'Má leigeann tú *Seadna* ar lár as an *Iris Leabhar*, deirim leat go mbeidh dearmhad déanta agat'; in a letter of 1 Apr. 1897, published in Ó Cuív, 'Caradas nár Mhair', p. 61. See now also Tracey Ní Mhaonaigh (eag.), *Tháinig do litir ... Litreacha ó Pheann an Athar Peadar Ó Laoghaire chuig Séamus Ó Dubhghaill* (An Daingean: An Sagart, 2017).

38 See Canice Mooney, 'The Beginnings of the Irish Language Revival', *Irish Ecclesiastical Record*, vol. 64, July 1944, pp. 10–18: 'Four years after its foundation [in 1893] there were already 43 branches established. In another four years the number had leaped up to 120. Three years later it had topped the 600 mark.'

39 For the details of the Cork 'split' (too complex to enter into here), see Traolach Ó Ríordáin, *Conradh na Gaeilge i gCorcaigh 1894–191*, Lúb ar Lár 2 (Baile Átha Cliath: Cois Life Teoranta, 2000) pp. 30–41, 46, 49, 50, 74–5, 84, 139–43, 178–9, 192, 219, 275–6, 280.

40 See Binchy, *Osborn Bergin*, p. 3: '... by the time I first knew him Bergin had long severed his connection with the Gaelic League, and though he could still grow excited when denouncing the then Coiste Gnótha for its treatment of the Lee Branch, which had resulted in a spate of excommunications (or was it secessions?), his words came to me as a mere echo of "unhappy far-off things and battles long ago".

41 From a letter of O'Rahilly's to Bergin in my possession, undated but probably from 1912/13.

42 See above, p. 57.

43 It is greatly to be regretted that the magnificent survey by Philip O'Leary, *Gaelic Prose in the Irish Free State, 1922–1939* (University Park, PA and Dublin: Penn State University Press and UCD Press, 2004) starts when it does. The references in it to Shán Ó Cuív are somewhat unbalanced as a result. An earlier volume by O'Leary, *The Prose Literature of the Gaelic Revival, 1881–1921* (University Park, PA: Penn State University Press, 1994) makes equally little mention of Ó Cuív.

44 *Cork Weekly Freeman*, Christmas Number, Sat. 7 Dec. 1918.

45 The graveside detail is perhaps what prompted later wags to put about the well-known story concerning Bergin's legendary fastidiousness in the matter of correct Irish. See Binchy, *Osborn Bergin*, pp. 6–7: '... the story that Bergin, standing mournfully at the grave-side of his old friend, contrived to detect four mistakes on the name-plate of the coffin, must be dismissed as *ben trovato* [characteristic even if not true]'.

46 Crádh Croidhe Éigeas [= Bergin], 'An tAthair Peadar', *An Branar*, vol. 2, pt 1, Lughnasa, 1920, pp. 2–5. *An Branar* was the Irish language newspaper of the University College Cork student Irish Society. Translation: 'Father Peter is in the grave. Standing by his graveside I said to myself: "We are burying the old world here". What I'm saying is true. It's not that Ireland is without Irish people. The Irish race hasn't died out, and there's no danger that it will. But there have been many changes in the world in the last 100 years. Changes have taken place everywhere, and maybe the change that has come about in Ireland moreso than in any other country in Europe up to the [time of] the First [World] War ... Ireland lost her nobility and her aristocracy and her learned class 200 years before that. Nevertheless, her "little people" remained at home. They had their own old speech and their old customs and the old Irish mindset. Father O'Leary used to say that the life that people lived in the countryside

was the same as that of their ancestors 1,000 years before that, and there was a lot of truth in that ... I sometimes hear people finding fault with Father O'Leary because they don't find in his stories the deep philosophical ideas and the difficult questions that they like [to read] in English and French literature. Let them. There's room in Irish literature for every kind of Irish ... Father O'Leary gave us what he had himself ... He himself is gone now but he has left his Irish after him as an inheritance to the people of Ireland. No other writer has left so great or so good a legacy.'

47 *The Exclusion of Father Peter O'Leary from Irish Education* (Dublin: Irish Book Company, 1907). No author(s) cited but the pamphlet was almost certainly compiled by Norma Borthwick, perhaps with the assistance of Margaret O'Reilly; both were staunch supporters of Father O'Leary. The Irish Book Company was set up specifically with the purpose of printing and publishing his writings.

48 A complete list of the journals and periodicals in which An tAthair Peadar published over the years is given in Shán Ó Cuív, 'Materials for a Bibliography of the Very Rev. Peter Canon O'Leary, 1839–1920', printed as a supplement to *Celtica*, vol. 2, pt 2, 1954. They number 487 in total.

49 Ó Cuív, 'Caradas nár Mhair', p. 58.

50 The history of Canon O'Leary's Bible translation deserves to be treated at greater length than is possible here. Before his recent death, Prof. Pádraig Ó Fiannachta informed me that all of the materials relating to the project, which had been in the possession of Father Shán Ó Cuív, sometime parish priest of Blackrock, County Dublin (and son of the Shán Ó Cuív mentioned above), have now been transferred to the Library in Maynooth University. My father, Donncha Ó Cróinín, collaborated for many decades with Father Ó Cuív on the project.

51 For what follows I am indebted especially to Thomas Mohr, 'Salmon of Knowledge', *Peritia*, vol. 16, 2002, pp. 360–95.

52 The incident was described in graphic detail in the *Donegal Democrat* of 5 June 1925, 2 Oct. 1925, and 5 Aug. 1933; see Mohr, 'Salmon of Knowledge', p. 361, n. 1. See also Peter Leary, *Unapproved Routes: A history of the Irish border 1922–1972* (Oxford: Oxford University Press, 2016).

53 'Ancient Irish Law: The law of status or franchise', *PRIA*, vol. 36C, 1923, pp. 265–316. All three texts were subsequently to be re-edited by Binchy (with corrections of some of MacNeill's interpretations).

54 Mohr, 'Salmon of Knowledge', p. 365, n. 19. There is a complete transcription of the Erne Fishery case in the NAI, CSS papers, CO 3412 Oral Evidence, Book 2, 87–8, 1520–32 (as cited by Mohr, loc. cit.). On Bergin's supposed negative influence on Delargy, see Mícheál Briody, *The Irish Folklore Commission, 1935–1970: History, ideology and methodology*, Studia Fennica Folkloristica 17 (Helsinki: The Finish Literary Society, 2007), p. 82 an exemplary study.

55 Mohr, 'Salmon of Knowledge', p. 366. *Irish Times*, 26 Mar. 2011 reported a dispute over Dublin City Council's legal right to lease out the fishing rights of the Liffey estuary: 'A judge is to look at laws and charters predating the Magna Carta' for the purpose. I am not aware of what decision was arrived at in the case.

56 See Fergus Kelly, *A Guide to Early Irish Law*, Early Irish Law Series 3 (Dublin: DIAS, 1988), pp. 105 ff.

57 'According to Professor Bergin, the *h* in *háe* is silent. He explained that the initial *h* was often used in short words in Old Irish simply as a scribal flourish, in imitation of the Latin *h* when it is silent'; Mohr, 'Salmon of Knowledge', p. 366, n. 24. Comment is superfluous (as O'Rahilly might have said). The term *aí* is defined as 'the time-limit for legal action' by Kelly, *A Guide to Early Irish Law*, p. 152.

58 Mohr, 'Salmon of Knowledge', p. 369.

59 MacNeill had earlier stated his views on private fishing rights in his *Celtic Ireland*, p. 167, and reiterated those views on cross-examination in court, so they would have been familiar already to Bergin.

60 Cited by Mohr, 'Salmon of Knowledge', p. 374, n. 56.

61 See T.M. Healy, *Stolen Waters: A page of the conquest of Ulster* (London: Longmans, Green & Co., 1913).

62 Mohr, 'Salmon of Knowledge', p. 374, n. 58, citing Mr Justice Johnston in the subsequent Moy Fishery case (*Little v. Cooper* [1937] 1 IR 6).

63 Mohr, 'Salmon of Knowledge', p. 383.

64 Ibid., p. 386 and ff.

65 Two other eminent Old Irish scholars, James [Seamus] (later Mr Justice) Henchy and Michael A. O'Brien, later Professor of Celtic in Queen's University Belfast, and subsequently a senior professor in the Dublin Institute for Advanced Studies, did give evidence for the defence. Mr Justice Gavan Duffy, however, refused to allow Binchy the opportunity to respond to their arguments, but they do not appear to have swayed the verdict either way; see Mohr, 'Salmon of Knowledge', pp. 391–2.

66 Cited by Mohr, 'Salmon of Knowledge', p. 393.

67 Mohr, 'Salmon of Knowledge', p. 393, citing the *Dictionary of National Biography, 1945–1950*, p. 565. Binchy was not so critical of MacNeill in his essay 'MacNeill's Study of the Ancient Irish Laws', in Martin and Byrne (eds), *The Scholar Revolutionary*, pp. 37–48.

68 Binchy, ibid., cited by Mohr, 'Salmon of Knowledge', p. 394.

69 See n. 15 above.

70 See, for example, the latest example of the 'revisionist' style of Early Irish History, as reflected in Brendan Smith (ed.), *The Cambridge History of Ireland. Volume I: 600–1550* (Cambridge: Cambridge University Press, 2018), which offers a chapter by Alex Woolf on 'The Scandinavian Intervention', while omitting discussion of whole swathes of material relating to the pre-Viking period.

71 Ó Cuív, 'Caradas nár Mhair', p. 73.

'By blood and by tradition': race and empire in Eoin MacNeill's interpretation of early Ireland. *Elva Johnston*

1 R. Dudley Edwards, 'Professor MacNeill', in F.X. Martin and Francis J. Byrne (eds), *The Scholar Revolutionary: Eoin MacNeill, 1867–1945, and the making of the new Ireland* (Shannon: Irish University Press, 1973), pp. 279–97, at p. 289.

2 See, for example, the comment in Deirdre McMahon and Michael Kennedy (eds), *Reconstructing Ireland's Past: A history of the Irish Manuscripts Commission* (Dublin: IMC, 2009), p. 94.

3 Brian Hughes (ed.), *Eoin MacNeill: Memoir of a revolutionary scholar* (Dublin: IMC, 2016), p. 121.

4 Introductions to MacNeill's career include Patrick Maume, 'MacNeill, Eoin (1867–1945)', in *Oxford Dictionary of National Biography* [*ODNB*] (Oxford: Oxford University Press, 2004) (http://www.oxforddnb.com/view/article/34813; accessed 24 Feb. 2021); Patrick Maume and Thomas Charles-Edwards, 'MacNeill, Eoin (John) (1867–1945)', in James McGuire and James Quinn (eds), *Dictionary of Irish Biography from the Earliest Times to the Year 2002* (Cambridge: Royal Irish Academy and Cambridge University Press, 2009), vol. 6, pp. 150–4. See also Michael Tierney, *Eoin MacNeill: Scholar and man of action 1867–1945*, ed. F.X. Martin (Oxford: Clarendon Press, 1980).

5 Francis J. Byrne, 'MacNeill the Historian', in *The Scholar Revolutionary*, pp. 15–36, at p. 17.

6 Ibid., p. 35. The second quotation is an effective homage to MacNeill's own words in *Celtic Ireland* (Dublin: M. Lester Ltd, 1921 [repr. Dublin: Academy Press, 1981]), p. xiv.

7 Hughes, *Eoin MacNeill: Memoir*, pp. 124–5; John McCarthy, *Kevin O'Higgins: Builder of the Irish state* (Dublin: Irish Academic Press, 2006), provides a biography.

8 Ibid., pp. 49, 81, 88–9, 110–11.

9 Ibid., p. 111. Thurneysen's importance as a scholar is stressed in John Ryan's obituary of him: 'Rudolf Thurneysen: 1857–1940', *Studies: An Irish quarterly review*, vol. 29, no. 116, 1940, pp. 583–90.

10 Examples include Eoin MacNeill (ed.), 'Poems by Flann Mainistrech on the Dynasties of Ailech, Mide and Brega', *Archivium Hibernicum*, vol. 2, 1913, pp. 37–99; idem., 'On the Reconstruction and the Date of the Laud Genealogies', *Zeitschrift für celtische Philologie*, vol. 10, 1915, pp. 81–96; idem., 'The Irish Law of Dynastic Succession', *Studies: An Irish quarterly review*, vol. 8, no. 31, 1919, pp. 367–82; and *Studies: An Irish quarterly review*, vol. 8, no. 32, 1919, pp. 640–63; idem., 'Ancient Irish Law: The law of status or franchise', *PRIA*, vol. 36C, 1923, pp. 265–316.

11 McMahon and Kennedy, *Reconstructing Ireland's Past*, pp. 1–94.

12 See, for example, MacNeill's comments in 'The Fifteenth Centenary of Saint Patrick: A suggested form of commemoration', *Studies: An Irish quarterly review*, vol. 13, no. 50, 1954, pp. 177–88 and idem., 'A School of Irish Church History', *Studies: An Irish quarterly review*, vol. 21, no. 81, 1932, pp. 1–6. McMahon and Kennedy, *Reconstructing Ireland's Past*, pp. 6–7 provide further detail. The *Monumenta* is discussed by David Knowles, *Great Historical Enterprises: Problems in monastic history* (Edinburgh: Thomas Nelson & Sons, 1963), pp. 65–97 and more recently by Gerhard Schmitz, 'Les *Monumenta Germaniae Historica*', in Isabelle Guyot-Bachy and Jean-Marie Moeglin (eds), *La naissance de la médiévistique. Les historiens et leurs sources en Europe (XIXe–début du XXe siècle)* (Geneva: Librarie Droz, 2015), pp. 299–313. See also Michael Kennedy, p. 81.

13 The quote is from Bishop Tírechán's *Collectanea*. For its context see Ludwig Bieler (ed. and trans.), *The Patrician Texts in the Book of Armagh* (Dublin: DIAS, 1979), pp. 132–4 at § 14 (5). The note is reproduced on plate 10 (with no pagination) in *The Scholar Revolutionary*.

14 Maume, 'MacNeill, Eoin (1867–1945)' [*ODNB*].

15 This is the territory of the Uí Amolngada, including the baronies of Tirawley and Erris, described in Thomas Charles-Edwards, *Early Christian Ireland* (Cambridge: Cambridge University Press, 2000), pp. 47–8.

16 A partial exception is Seán Duffy, 'Historical Revisit: Goddard Henry Orpen, *Ireland under the Normans, 1169–1333* (1911–1920)', *IHS*, vol. 32, no. 126, 2000, pp. 246–59, although this is entirely in the context of an apologia for G.H. Orpen. See also Elva Johnston, 'Eoin MacNeill's Early Medieval Ireland: A politics for scholarship or a politics of scholarship?', in Chris Jones, Conor Kostick and Klaus Oschema (eds), *Making the Medieval Relevant: How medievalists are revolutionising the present* (Berlin: De Gruyter, 2019), pp. 211–24.

17 For example, MacNeill's writings on the historical Patrick hold little value. MacNeill has also been challenged on specifics, an example being Donnchadh Ó Corráin, 'Irish Regnal Succession: A reappraisal', *Studia Hibernica*, vol. 11, 1971, pp. 7–39. On the other hand, while subject to important qualifications, MacNeill's analysis of social structures remains dominant. See, for example, the various essays published in Dáibhí Ó Cróinín (ed.), *A New History of Ireland. Volume I: Prehistoric and Early Ireland* (Oxford: Oxford University Press, 2005) and Brendan Smith (ed.), *The Cambridge History of Ireland. Volume 1: 600–1550* (Cambridge: Cambridge University Press, 2018).

18 MacNeill's publications are usefully collated in F.X. Martin, 'The Writings of Eoin MacNeill', *IHS*, vol. 6, no. 21, 1948, pp. 44–62 and idem., 'Appendix 1: The Published Writings of Eoin MacNeill', in *The Scholar Revolutionary*, pp. 325–53.

19 MacNeill, *Phases of Irish History*; idem., *Celtic Ireland* whose lectures were first published in 1906–7 in *The New Ireland Review*, although they are better known from the later book;

idem., *Early Irish Laws and Institutions* (Dublin: Burns, Oates & Washbourne, 1935), with an extra introduction, pp. 5–56. The individual talks were originally published in the *New York University Law Quarterly Review*, vol. 8, no. 7, 1930–1, pp. 149–265; no. 8 (1930–1), pp. 81–108, 271–84.

20 This idea turns up repeatedly. Good examples include MacNeill, *Phases of Irish History*, pp. 1–2, 97, 248; idem., *Celtic Ireland*, p. 17; idem., *Early Irish Laws and Institutions*, pp. 56–7.

21 This is associated with the elevation of the archive by Leopold von Ranke. See, for example, Georg G. Iggers and James M. Powell (eds), *Leopold von Ranke and the Shaping of the Historical Discipline* (Syracuse, NY: Syracuse University Press, 1990) and Andreas D. Boldt, *Leopold von Ranke: A biography* (Abingdon: Routledge, 2019). Influences on Irish scholarship are explored in Ciarán Brady (ed.), *Interpreting Irish History: The debate on historical revisionism, 1938–1994* (Dublin: Irish Academic Press, 1994).

22 Eoin MacNeill, 'Contribution by Professor Eoin MacNeill, M.A., D.Litt', in *A Page of Irish History: Story of University College Dublin, 1883–1909* (Dublin: Talbot Press, 1930), pp. 186–94.

23 Edmund Hogan, *Onomasticon Goedelicum Locorum et Tribuum Hiberniae et Scotiae. An index, with Identifications, to the Gaelic Names of Places and Tribes* (Dublin: Hodges, Figgis & Co., 1910), is still a standard guide. The *Locus* project, based in University College Cork, has produced an online version of the *Onomasticon* as part of its aim to update and expand the material. It can be accessed at https://www.ucc.ie/en/locus/fr-edmund-hogan/. Pádraig Ó Riain, Diarmuid Ó Murchadha, Kevin Murray and Emma Nic Cárthaigh (eds), *Historical Dictionary of Gaelic Placenames*, 8 fascicles (London: Irish Texts Society, 2003–).

24 MacNeill, 'Contribution', p. 191.

25 Donal McCartney, 'MacNeill and Irish-Ireland', in *The Scholar Revolutionary*, pp. 75–97; Regina Uí Chollatáin, *An Claidheamh Soluis agus Fáinne an Lae 1899–1932: Anailís ar phríomhnuachtán Gaeilge Ré na hAthbheochana* (Dublin: Cois Life Teoranta, 2004). The importance of the engaged reading public is highlighted in Andrew Murphy, *Ireland, Reading and Cultural Nationalism, 1790–1930: Bringing the nation to book* (Cambridge: Cambridge University Press, 2018).

26 This complex text, or series of texts, still awaits much work. It was edited and translated by MacNeill's colleague R.A.S. Macalister (ed.), *Lebor Gabála Érenn*, 5 vols (Dublin: Irish Texts society, 1938–56), although MacNeill did not live to see it completed.

27 Joep Theodor Leerssen, *Mere Irish and Fíor-Ghael: Studies in the idea of Irish nationality, its development and literary expression prior to the nineteenth century* (Amsterdam: John Benjamins, 1996), esp. pp. 325–444.

28 MacNeill, *Phases of Irish History*, p. 94. He had already demolished the claim of the synthetic histories to accuracy in idem., *Celtic Ireland*, pp. 25–42.

29 MacNeill, *Celtic Ireland*, p. 144. See Ó Cróinín, p. 55 and Wycherley, p. 43 in this volume for discussion of this quote.

30 See Johnston, 'Eoin MacNeill's Early Medieval Ireland', pp. 222–4.

31 MacNeill, *Phases of Irish History*, p. vi. Mairéad Carew, *The Quest for the Irish Celt: The Harvard Archaeological Mission to Ireland, 1932–1936*, (Sallins: Irish Academic Press, 2018), p. 24, sees his admission that he could not write an impartial history as a black mark, although arguably MacNeill's position was that this was impossible for any historian. MacNeill's phrase is echoed in Paul Holm, 'Beyond Apathy and Antipathy: The Vikings in Irish and Scandinavian history', *Peritia*, vol. 8, 1984, pp. 151–69.

32 Goddard Henry Orpen, *Ireland under the Normans, 1169–1333*, 4 vols (Oxford: Clarendon Press, 1911–20 [repr. in a single volume Dublin: Four Courts Press, 2005]). For commentary see Johnston, 'Eoin MacNeill's Early Medieval Ireland', pp. 215–21; Duffy, 'Historical Revisit: Goddard Henry Orpen', esp. pp. 249–51, offers a more negative assessment.

33 Orpen is mentioned by MacNeill throughout all his book-length studies. Representative examples include MacNeill, *Phases of Irish History*, pp. 227, 240, 300–22; idem., *Celtic Ireland*, pp. 152–76; idem., *Early Irish Laws and Institutions*, p. 6. These can be contrasted with the more positive assessment provided in his formal review of Orpen's published research in Eoin MacNeill, '*Ireland under the Normans, 1169–1333*. By Goddard Henry Orpen', *JRSAI*, vol. 1, no. 3, 1911, pp. 277–82.

34 Typical examples are Orpen, *Ireland under the Normans*, vol. 1, pp. 26, 105.

35 Apart from Orpen's copious use of primary sources throughout *Ireland under the Normans*, he is best known for his edition and translation of an important source for the Norman conquest, published as *The Song of Dermot and the Earl, an Old French Poem from the Carew Manuscript no. 596 in the Archiepiscopal Library at Lambeth Palace* (Oxford: Clarendon Press, 1892); this has since been re-edited by Evelyn Mullally (ed. and trans.), *The Deeds of the Normans in Ireland. La geste des Engleis en Yrlande. A New Edition of the Chronicle Formerly Known as the Song of Dermot and the Earl* (Dublin: Four Courts Press, 2002).

36 See, in particular, Orpen, *Ireland under the Normans*, vol. 1, pp. 19–38 ('Anarchic Ireland: Ninth to eleventh centuries'). Stephen H. Harrison, 'Re-Fighting the Battle of Down: Orpen, MacNeill and the Irish nation state', in Michael Brown and Stephen H. Harrison (eds), *The Medieval World and the Modern Mind* (Dublin: Four Courts Press, 2000), pp. 171–82, provides further political background.

37 There is an extensive literature on this point. See, for instance, the influential article by Archie Mafeje, 'The Ideology of "Tribalism"', *Journal of Modern African Studies*, vol. 9, no. 2, 1971, pp. 253–61. More recent critiques include Vail Leroy (ed.), *The Invention of Tribalism in Southern Africa* (Berkeley: University of California Press, 1989); Felicitas Becker, 'Vernacular Ethnic Stereotypes: Their persistence and change in south-east Tanzania, ca. 1890–2003', in Alexander Keese (ed.), *Ethnicity and the Long-Term Perspective: The African experience* (New York: Peter Lang, 2010), pp. 93–126. The term 'tribal' was adopted by later early Irish historians, for example by Francis John Byrne, 'Tribes and Tribalism in Early Ireland', *Ériu*, vol. 22, 1971, pp. 128–66, but its use remains problematic as shown in Chris Wickham, *Framing the Early Middle Ages: Europe and the Mediterranean, 400–800* (Oxford: Oxford University Press, 2005), p. 51.

38 Eoin MacNeill, 'Early Irish Population Groups: Their nomenclature, classification and chronology', *PRIA*, vol. 29C, 1911, pp. 59–114. This strand of MacNeill's research has proved academically rich. See, for example, Byrne, 'Tribes and Tribalism', and more recently Paul MacCotter, *Medieval Ireland: Territorial, political and economic divisions* (Dublin: Four Courts Press, 2008).

39 Johnston, 'Eoin MacNeill's Early Medieval Ireland', p. 220.

40 MacNeill, *Phases of Irish History*, pp. 98–132; idem., *Celtic Ireland*, pp. 96–113. For *cóiced* (modern Irish *cúigiú*) see eDIL *s.v. cóiced* (dil/ie/10045); His belief in the pentarchy as a political reality has been modified. See Dáibhí Ó Cróinín, 'Ireland, 400–800', in *A New History of Ireland I*, pp. 182–234, at pp. 187–8.

41 MacNeill, *Phases of Irish History*, pp. 274–99; idem., *Celtic Ireland*, pp. 96–113; idem., *Early Irish Laws and Institutions*, pp. 91–118.

42 MacNeill, *Early Irish Laws and Institutions*, pp. 48–9.

43 Ibid., p. 74.

44 MacNeill, *Phases of Irish History*, pp. 292–9; idem., *Celtic Ireland*, 152–76. Harrison, 'Re-fighting the Battle of Down', shows that this dismissal of the over-powerful state was, at least partly, in response to Orpen.

45 MacNeill, *Phases of Irish History*, pp. 275–7.

46 Ibid., p. 275.

47 Maume and Charles-Edwards, 'MacNeill, Eoin (John), 1867–1945' [*DIB*].

48 It was surprising to see Orpen's views recently echoed in Nicholas Vincent, 'Angevin Ireland', in *The Cambridge History, I*, pp. 185–221, at p. 205, where he describes pre-Norman Ireland as Iron Age.

49 This frequently adopted the assumptions of scientific racism, itself emerging from a convergence of medical ideas, anthropology, historicist analysis and museology. Samuel L. Redman, *Bone Rooms: From scientific racism to human prehistory in museums* (Cambridge, MA: Harvard University Press, 2016) explores many of the cross-currents. The Irish context is examined in John Brannigan, *Race in Modern Irish Literature and Culture* (Edinburgh: Edinburgh University Press, 2009) and in detail in Carew, *Quest for the Irish Celt*.

50 MacNeill, *Phases of Irish History*, p. 226.

51 The transcript is reproduced in McMahon and Kennedy, *Reconstructing Ireland's Past*, pp. 89–90. It dates to around 1940.

52 He was also keen to distinguish nationality (and the existence of nations) from nationalism as in MacNeill, *Phases of Irish History*, pp. 1–2, 97, 226. See also the important contribution by Donal McCartney, 'MacNeill and Irish-Ireland', pp. 75–97.

53 Broad context for the acceptance of racial essentialism is provided by Robert Wald Sussman, *The Myth of Race: The troubling persistence of an unscientific idea* (Cambridge, MA: Harvard University Press, 2014); Jessica Blatt, *Race and the Making of American Political Science* (Philadelphia: University of Pennsylvania Press, 2018), traces the role of race-based analysis in academia back to the nineteenth century. For a specific study of early medieval English history see James M. Harland, 'Rethinking Ethnicity and "Otherness" in Early Anglo-Saxon England', *Medieval Words*, vol. 5, 2017, pp. 113–42.

54 MacNeill, *Phases of Irish History*, pp. 1–2.

55 Ibid., pp. 9, 97; idem., *Celtic Ireland*, p. 17; idem., *Early Irish Laws and Institutions*, pp. 56–7.

56 MacNeill, *Phases of Irish History*, p. 2.

57 Ibid., pp. 105, 355.

58 Ibid., pp. 265–6, 273, 322–56.

59 Report by 'Gleó na gCath [Patrick Pearse]', *An Claidheamh Soluis*, vol. 9, no. 29, 5 Oct. 1907, p. 7.

60 MacNeill, *Phases of Irish History*, p. 97.

61 MacNeill, *Early Irish Laws and Institutions*, pp. 56–62.

62 Ibid., p. 57.

63 Ibid., pp. 25–6.

64 MacNeill, *Phases of Irish History*, p. 240; idem., *Early Irish Laws and Institutions*, p. 16, explicitly identifies 'tribe' with 'barbaric society'.

65 MacNeill, *Celtic Ireland*, pp. xi–xii, can be compared with the awkward attempt to talk about Irish racial characteristics in idem., *Early Irish Laws and Institutions*, pp. 59–60.

66 MacNeill, *Early Irish Laws and Institutions*, pp. 56–62.

67 Carew, *Quest for the Irish Celt*, pp. 23–6, outlines the circumstances. See also Mairéad Carew in this volume, p. 163.

68 Included in his publications is *Apes, Men, and Morons* (New York: G.P. Putnam's Sons, 1937), which supported theories of eugenics and degeneracy; Greta Jones, 'Eugenics in Ireland: The Belfast Eugenics Society, 1911–15', *IHS*, vol. 28, no. 109, 1992, pp. 81–92, discusses the introduction of ideas about eugenics to Ireland.

69 Background and development are explored in Jonathan Marks, 'The Origins of Anthropological Genetics', *Current Anthropology*, vol. 53, supplement 5, 2012, pp. 161–72.

70 Anne Byrne, Ricca Edmondson and Tony Varley, 'Arensberg and Kimball and Anthropological Research in Ireland: Introduction to the third edition', in Conrad Arensberg and Solon Kimball, *Family and Community in Ireland* (Ennis: Clasp Press, 2001), pp. 20–1.

71 Brannigan, *Race in Modern Irish Literature*, p. 84; Carew, *Quest for the Irish Celt*, pp. 55–6 (MacNeill) and throughout.

72 Byrne, Edmondson and Varley, 'Introduction', pp. 16–18; Mairéad Carew, 'Eoin MacNeill: Revolutionary cultural ideologue', *Studies: An Irish quarterly review*, vol. 104, no. 417, 2016, pp. 67–75, at pp. 70–2, tends to overstate MacNeill's support for research to prove the existence of a 'Celtic race'.

73 L. Perry Curtis Jr, *Apes and Angels: The Irishman in Victorian caricature*, revised edn (Washington and London: Smithsonian Institution Press, 1997).

74 Aidan O'Sullivan, 'The Harvard Archaeological Mission and the Politics of the Irish Free State', *Archaeology Ireland*, vol. 17, no. 1, 2003, pp. 20–3; Carew, *Quest for the Irish Celt*, pp. 134–54.

75 Anne Byrne, Ricca Edmondson and Tony Varley, 'Arensberg and Kimball and Anthropological Research in Ireland', *Irish Journal of Sociology*, vol. 23, no. 1, 2015, pp. 22–61.

76 MacNeill, *Celtic Ireland*, p. 17. This is echoed as late as idem., *Early Irish Laws and Institutions*, pp. 56–7.

77 MacNeill, *Phases of Irish History*, p. 356.

'Bold and imaginative': Eoin MacNeill's Irish Manuscripts Commission. *Michael Kennedy*

1 This chapter is based largely on material to be found in Michael Kennedy and Deirdre McMahon, *Reconstructing Ireland's Past: A history of the Irish Manuscripts Commission* (Dublin: IMC, 2009).

2 R. Dudley Edwards, 'Professor MacNeill', in F.X. Martin and F.J. Byrne (eds), *The Scholar Revolutionary: Eoin MacNeill, 1867–1945, and the making of the new Ireland* (Shannon: Irish University Press, 1973), pp. 279–97.

3 National Archives of Ireland (NAI), 97/42/1, undated notes in blue type by MacNeill.

4 Eoin MacNeill, *Celtic Ireland* (London and Dublin: Martin Lester Ltd., 1921), pp. xiv–xvi, quoted in R. Dudley Edwards, 'Professor MacNeill', in Martin and Byrne (eds), *The Scholar Revolutionary*, pp. 279–97, at p. 279. A related contemporary suggestion was that of MacNeill's friend Bulmer Hobson to J.J. O'Neill, the Librarian of UCD, and to J.H. Delargy, to found a Manuscripts and Records Society of Ireland.

5 Eoin MacNeill, 'The Fifteenth Centenary of St Patrick', *Studies*, vol. 13, no. 50, June 1924, pp. 177–88, at p. 188.

6 Ibid., p. 186.

7 *Irish Times*, 1 July 1922.

8 *Beyond 2022* Project, Trinity College Dublin, led by Peter Crooks, seeks to create a Virtual Record Treasury for Irish history – an open-access, virtual reconstruction of the Record Treasury destroyed in 1922 (www.beyond2022.ie, accessed 27 Feb. 2021).

9 O'Sullivan and McGilligan were also academic colleagues of MacNeill's in UCD.

10 NAI, DT S5509A, note by Cosgrave, 29 Aug. 1927.

11 Available at https://www.oireachtas.ie/en/debates/debate/dail/1928-03-21/2/ (accessed 2 February 2020).

12 Obituary of MacNeill by John Ryan in *Analecta Hibernica*, vol. 17, 1949, p. 351.

13 NAI 97/42/1, O'Hegarty to MacNeill, 28 Sept. 1928.

14 NAI, DT S5509A, O'Hegarty to Blythe, 17 Sept. 1928.

15 NAI, IMC 97/42/10, Brereton to Carney, 12 Dec. 1952.

16 NAI, IMC 97/42/3, resolution passed at meeting of IMC, 20 Feb. 1930.

17 David Edwards, 'Salvaging History: Hogan and the Irish Manuscripts Commission', in Donnchadh Ó Corráin (ed.), *James Hogan: Revolutionary, historian, political scientist* (Dublin: Four Courts Press, 2001), pp. 116–32, at p. 116.

18 Dudley Edwards, 'Professor MacNeill', p. 297.

19 *The Times*, 27 Mar. 1933.

20 J.R. [John Ryan], 'Eoin Mac Neill' [obituary], *Analecta Hibernica*, vol. 17, 1949, p. 351.

21 NAI 97/42/41, Hogan's draft introduction to *Analecta Hibernica*, vol. 1.

22 Ibid.

23 NAI 97/42/16, An Seabhac (Pádraig Ó Siochfhradha (Patrick Sugrue)) to McElligott, 27 March 1929. An Seabhac was secretary to the IMC from 1928 to 1932.

24 NAI 97/42/17, MacNeill to Blythe, 17 May 1929.

25 Gerard O'Brien, *Irish Governments and the Guardianship of Historical Records, 1922–72* (Dublin: Four Courts Press, 2004, p. 14.

26 Ibid.

27 *Irish Times*, 13 Mar. 1931.

28 NAI 97/42/70, Ryan to Seabhac, 31 Mar. 1932.

29 *The Standard*, 16 Apr. 1932.

30 Later secretary of the Department of Education (1956–68) and the first chairman of the Higher Education Authority (1968–75).

31 Toirdhealbhach Ó Raithbheartaigh (ed.), *Genealogical Tracts I* (Dublin: IMC, 1932), preface.

32 See David Hayton, 'The Laboratory for "Scientific History": T.W. Moody and R.D. Edwards at the Institute of Historical Research', *Irish Historical Studies*, vol. 41, no. 159, May 2017, pp. 41–57.

33 NAI 97/42/146, Simington to Brereton, 5 Jan., 13 Feb. 1939.

34 Ibid., Brereton to Secretary, Dept of Education, 24 May 1939.

35 University College Dublin Archives (UCDA), LA1/J/228, undated transcript of radio broadcast.

36 *Irish Press*, 16 Oct. 1945.

37 NAI 97/42/2, Agnes MacNeill to Brereton, 20 Nov. 1945.

38 NAI 97/42/2, Charles McNeill to Brereton, 20 Nov. 1945.

39 *Irish Independent*, 11 Nov. 1929.

40 Edwards, 'Professor MacNeill', p. 289.

41 Ryan, 'Eoin MacNeill' [obituary], p. 351.

Eoin MacNeill's Pioneering Role in the Irish Language Movement. *Liam Mac Mathúna*

1 Michael Tierney, *Eoin MacNeill: Scholar and man of action 1867–1945* (Oxford: Clarendon Press, 1980), p. 5.

2 Brian Hughes (ed.), *Eoin MacNeill: Memoir of a revolutionary scholar* (Dublin: IMC, 2016), p. 8.

3 John Ryan, 'A Patrician Problem: "Saint Patrick: Bury versus Slemish"', in F.X. Martin and F.J. Byrne (eds), *The Scholar Revolutionary: Eoin MacNeill, 1867–1945, and the making of the new Ireland* (Shannon: Irish University Press, 1973), p. 322.

4 Ibid., pp. 323–4.

5 See Brian Ó Cuív, 'MacNeill and the Irish Language', in Martin and Byrne (eds), *The Scholar Revolutionary*, p. 4; Tierney, *Scholar and man of action*, p. 10; Hughes, *Eoin MacNeill: Memoir*, pp. 17–18.

6 Tierney, *Scholar and man of action*, p. 10; Hughes, *Eoin MacNeill: Memoir*, p. 18.

7 Tierney, *Scholar and man of action*, p. 11; Hughes, *Eoin MacNeill: Memoir*, p. 18.

8 For recent work on Hyde, see Attracta Halpin and Áine Mannion (eds), *Douglas Hyde: The Professor of Irish who became President of Ireland* (Dublin: National University of Ireland, 2016); Brian Murphy, *Forgotten Patriot: Douglas Hyde and the foundation of the Irish presidency* (Cork: The Collins Press, 2016); and Máire Nic an Bhaird and Liam Mac

Mathúna, 'Early Diary Insights into Roscommon's Impact on Douglas Hyde, Ireland's First President', in Richie Farrell, Kieran O'Conor and Matthew Potter (eds), *Roscommon: History and society*, Interdisciplinary Essays on the History of an Irish County (Dublin: Geography Publications, 2018), pp. 515–37. For a recent discussion of O'Growney, see Regina Uí Chollatáin, 'Deisceabail agus Soiscéalta: Ceannródaithe athbheochana agus fóram na hiriseoireachta', *Oidhreacht Uí Ghramhnaigh, Léachtaí Cholm Cille*, vol. 44, 2014, pp. 22–45.

9   Tierney, *Scholar and man of action*, pp. 11–12; Hughes, *Eoin MacNeill: Memoir*, p. 18.

10 Tierney, *Scholarand man of action*, pp. 14–15; Hughes, *Eoin MacNeill: Memoir*, p. 18.

11 Donal McCartney, 'MacNeill and Irish-Ireland', in Martin and Byrne (eds), *The Scholar Revolutionary*, pp. 78–9, records in particular the influence of Hyde's lecture on the language, delivered in New York in June 1891, which MacNeill noted many years later had been fully reported in Dublin. O'Growney had published an article entitled 'The National Language' in the *Irish Ecclesiastical Record* in November 1890: see Tierney, *Scholar and man of action*, p. 13. Hughes, *Eoin MacNeill: Memoir*, pp. 20–1.

12 *Irish Ecclesiastical Record*, Ser. 3, 12: 1099–1108 (Dec. 1891).

13 Tierney, *Scholar and man of action*, p. 14.

14 Ó Cuív, 'MacNeill and the Irish Language', p. 6.

15 McCartney, 'MacNeill and Irish-Ireland', p. 78.

16 *Irisleabhar na Gaedhilge / The Gaelic Journal*, 4 Mar. 1893, pp. 177–9.

17 See ibid., pp. 79–80, and footnote 1; Martin and Byrne (eds), *The Scholar Revolutionary*, p. 357. The article itself is reprinted there on pp. 357–63.

18 On Lloyd, known also as Seosamh Laoide, see Liam Mac Mathúna, 'Seosamh Laoide: Eagarthóir', *Studia Hibernica*, vol. 31, 2000–1, pp. 87–103.

19 See Tierney, *Scholar and man of action*, p. 22.

20 McCartney, 'MacNeill and Irish-Ireland', p. 80.

21 Ibid., pp. 80–1.

22 Leabharlann Náisiúnta na hÉireann, *Athbheochan na Gaeilge: Doiciméid staire* (Baile Átha Cliath: Leabharlann Náisiúnta na hÉireann, 1981), Document 6.

23 McCartney, 'MacNeill and Irish-Ireland', p. 81.

24 Tierney, *Scholar and man of action*, p. 28.

25 Ó Cuív, 'MacNeill and the Irish Language', p. 6.

26 'Important Notice', May 1895:1. Liam Mac Peaircín, '*Irisleabhar na Gaedhilge, 1882–1909*: Gníomh dóchais na teanga', in John Walsh and Peadar Ó Muircheartaigh (eds), *Ag Siúl an Bhealaigh Mhóir: Aistí in ómós don Ollamh Nollaig Mac Congáil* (Baile Átha Cliath: *Leabhair* COMHAR, 2016), pp. 291–312, at p. 299; Liam Mac Peaircín, *Gníomh Dóchais: Irisleabhar na Gaedhilge, 1882–1909* (Baile Átha Cliath: Coiscéim, 2018), p. xiii. Emphasis added.

27 Torna [Tadhg Ó Donnchadha], 'Réumh-Rádh', in E.M. Ní Chiaragáin, *Index do Irisleabhar na Gaedhilge 1882–1909* (Baile Átha Cliath: Faoi Chomhartha na dTrí gCoinneal, 1935), pp. ix–x. Cf. Mac Peaircín, '*Irisleabhar na Gaedhilge, 1882–1909*', pp. 299–300; Mac Peaircín, *Gníomh Dóchais*, p. xiii.

28 Author's translation.

29 Shán Ó Cuív, 'Caradas nár Mhair: Peadar Ua Laoghaire agus Eoin Mac Néill', in Martin and Byrne (eds), *The Scholar Revolutionary*, pp. 51–73. Twenty letters from Eoin MacNeill to An tAthair Peadar relating to the earliest years of their acquaintance were recently presented to Conradh na Gaeilge and are currently being examined by the author. They form part of a larger collection of material relating to An tAthair Peadar Ua Laoghaire that was recently donated to Conradh na Gaeilge. This collection is now known as Bailiúchán an Athar Troy and forms part of the Conradh na Gaeilge Archive, which was deposited at NUI Galway in 2017.

30 Letter dated 3 October 1899, contained in Bailiúchán an Athar Troy.

31 The letters from Eoin MacNeill to An tAthair Peadar in Bailiúchán an Athar Troy, National University of Ireland, Galway, Archives, referred to in note 29, do not seem to include the period and subject in question. Only two of the twenty letters from MacNeill were written after that dated 16 Aug. 1896, and neither of these refers to *Séadna*.

32 On one occasion, MacNeill did allow himself to reply caustically to a particularly abrasive letter from An tAthair Peadar, which took issue with editorial spelling emendations in *An Claidheamh Soluis*. This he did in *An Claidheamh Soluis*, 13 Jan. 1900, p. 701. See Ó Cuív, 'Caradas nár Mhair', p. 67.

33 *United Ireland*, 1 Sept. 1894, cited in Liam Mac Mathúna, 'Réamhrá', in Peadar Ua Laoghaire, *Séadna* (Baile Átha Cliath: Cois Life Teoranta, 2011), pp. vii–lxx, at p. xiv.

34 Author's translation.

35 *United Ireland*, 1 Sept. 1894, cited in Ó Cuív, 'Caradas nár Mhair', p. 51.

36 Author's translation.

37 Letter from An tAthair Peadar to Eoin MacNeill, Meitheamh 1895, quoted in Ó Cuív, 'Caradas nár Mhair', p. 51.

38 Author's translation.

39 Ó Cuív, 'MacNeill and the Irish Language', p. 7.

40 Ibid., p. 10.

41 Tierney, *Scholar and man of action*, p. 47; Hughes, *Eoin MacNeill: Memoir*, pp. 39–40.

42 Tierney, *Scholar and man of action*, p. 45.

43 Regina Uí Chollatáin, *An Claidheamh Soluis agus Fáinne an Lae 1899–1932: Anailís ar phríomhnuachtán Gaeilge Ré na hAthbheochana* (Baile Átha Cliath: Cois Life Teoranta, 2004), p. 36.

44 Tierney, *Scholar and man of action*, p. 48.

45 Ibid., p. 46.

46 Ibid., p. 52.

47 Pádraig Ó Fearaíl, *The Story of Conradh na Gaeilge* (Baile Átha Cliath: Clódhanna Teo., 1975), p. 11; Tierney, *Scholar and man of action*, p. 73.

48 Uí Chollatáin, *An Claidheamh Soluis*, p. 40.

49 Ibid., p. 251.

50 Tierney, *Scholar and man of action*, p. 75.

51 The context indicates that the sense in which the German term is being used is 'people's movement, popular movement'.

52 Tierney, *Scholar and man of action*, p. 63.

53 Ibid. For further consideration of Yorke's influence on the Gaelic League see Regina Uí Chollatáin, 'The Turning of the Tide: Craobh an Chéitinnigh agus coimhlint na Gaeilge i 1916', *Éigse: A journal of Irish studies*, vol. 40, 2019, pp. 305–26.

54 *An Claidheamh Soluis*, 20 May 1899, p. 157; quoted in Tierney, *Scholar and man of action*, p. 66.

55 Tierney, *Scholar and man of action*, p. 67.

56 Tom Garvin, *Nationalist Revolutionaries in Ireland 1858–1928* (Dublin: Gill & Macmillan, 2005 [1987]), p. 139.

57 Cited in Tierney, *Scholar and man of action*, p. 72; 'up' supplied from Hughes, *Eoin MacNeill: Memoir*, pp. 37–8.

58 Tierney, *Scholar and man of action*, p. 72.

59 *An Claidheamh Soluis*, 16 April 1906, p. 6. See Uí Chollatáin, *An Claidheamh Soluis*, p. 112.

60 Tierney, *Scholar and man of action*, p. 78.

61 McCartney, 'MacNeill and Irish-Ireland', p. 92, where the wrong year is cited in footnote 60 for the issue of *An Claidheamh Soluis* in question: it should be 1908, not 1909. Cf. Tierney, *Scholar and man of action*, p. 79.

62 Tierney, *Scholar and man of action*, p. 79.

63 Tomás Ó Fiaich, 'The Great Controversy', in Seán Ó Tuama (ed.), *The Gaelic League Idea* (Cork and Dublin: The Mercier Press, 1972), pp. 63–75, at pp. 70–1.

64 Ó Fiaich, 'The Great Controversy', p. 71.

65 Eoin MacNeill, *Irish in the National University of Ireland: A plea for Irish education* (Dublin and Waterford: M.H. Gill & Son, 1909).

66 MacNeill, *Irish in the National University*, p. [i].

67 Ibid., p. 10.

68 *An Claidheamh Soluis*, 1 Nov. 1913.

69 See, for example, the letter dated 12 Oct. 1914 from Rev. T. Corcoran SJ, Professor of Education at University College Dublin, to John J. Horgan, in which the writer states, *inter alia*: 'From all I can see the effect on the language movement of the situation that has arisen bids fair to be disastrous. Practically all of the Gaelic League forces are now turned away from their proper work ... To my mind the League is already at a low ebb and the new developments will crowd it out or let it die for sheer lack of workers.' Quoted in John J. Horgan, *Parnell to Pearse: Some recollections and reflections* (Dublin: Browne & Nolan, 1948), p. 264.

70 Earnán de Blaghd, 'Hyde in Conflict', in Ó Tuama, *The Gaelic League Idea*, pp. 31–40, at p. 38; 'late in 1916', according to Tierney, *Scholar and man of action*, p. 263.

71 Tierney, *Scholar and man of action*, pp. 178–9; Hughes, *Eoin MacNeill: Memoir*, pp. 35–6.

72 Patrick Maume, 'Douglas Hyde', in Eugenio Biagini and Daniel Mulhall (eds), *The Shaping of Modern Ireland: A centenary assessment* (Sallins: Irish Academic Press, 2016), pp. 41–51, at p. 46.

73 McCartney, 'MacNeill and Irish-Ireland', p. 92.

74 Tierney, *Scholar and man of action*, p. 177.

75 Extract from letter drafted but not sent to an tAthair Peadar in 1903: see Tierney, *Scholar and man of action*, pp. 38–9.

76 See note 16.

77 Martin and Byrne (eds), *The Scholar Revolutionary*, p. 361.

78 John Coolahan, *Irish Education: Its history and structure* (Dublin: Institute of Public Administration, 1981), p. 40.

79 Patrick Maume and Thomas Charles-Edwards, 'MacNeill, Eoin (John), 1867–1945', in James McGuire and James Quinn (eds), *Dictionary of Irish Biography from the Earliest Times to the Year 2002* (Cambridge: Royal Irish Academy and Cambridge University Press, 2009), vol. 6, pp. 150–4, at p. 152.

Eoin Mac Néill: scríobhaí forásach agus iriseoir fadradharcach i bpróiseas na hAthbheochana.
Regina Uí Chollatáin

1 'Strengthen the Weak Points', Eagarfhocal, *An Claidheamh Soluis agus Fáinne an Lae*, 11 Lúnasa 1900, p. 8.

2 Diarmuid Breathnach agus Máire Ní Mhurchú, 'Mac Néill, Eoin (1867–1945)'; https://www.ainm.ie/Bio.aspx?ID=452, 23 Meitheamh 2020.

3 Dúbhghlas de hÍde, 'Litir, 14 Deireadh Fómhair 1938', i Eoin Ua Riain (eag.), *Féil-sgríbhinn Eóin Mhic Néill: Tráchtais léigheanta i n-onóir do'n ollamhain Eóin Mac Néill do sgríobh cáirde á cháirdibh i n-am a dheichmhadh bliadhna agus trí fichid, an cúigmhadh lá déag de mhí na Bealtaine, 1938* (Baile Átha Cliath: Faoi Chomhartha na dTrí gCoinneal, 1940).

4 Féach *Féil-sgríbhinn Eóin Mhic Néill*.

5 Regina Uí Chollatáin, 'Athbheochan Thrasatlantach na Gaeilge: Scríbhneoirí, intleachtóirí agus an fhéiniúlacht Éireannach', i Ríona Nic Congáil et al., *Litríocht na Gaeilge ar fud an Domhain: Cruthú, caomhnú agus athbheochan*, Imleabhar 1 (Baile Átha Cliath: Leabhair Comhar, 2015), pp. 277–309.

6 Eoin Mac Néill, 'Why and How the Irish Language Is To Be Preserved', *Irish Ecclesiastical Record*, eag. 12, Nollaig 1891, pp. 1099–1108.

7 Regina Uí Chollatáin, *An Claidheamh Soluis agus Fáinne an Lae 1899–1932: Anailís ar phríomhnuachtán Gaeilge Ré na hAthbheochana* (Baile Átha Cliath: Cois Life Teoranta, 2004); Regina Uí Chollatáin, 'Deisceabal agus Soiscéalta: Ceannródaithe na hAthbheochana agus fóram na hiriseoireachta', *Léachtaí Cholm Cille*, eag. 44, 2014, pp. 22–45; Regina Uí Chollatáin, 'An Piarsach agus Iriseoireacht na Gaeilge: Iriseoir intleachtúil Victeoiriach agus réabhlóidí machnamhach', i Gearóid Ó Tuathaigh, *An Piarsach agus 1916: Briathar, beart agus oidhreacht* (Conamara: Indreabhán, 2016), pp. 37–58.

8 Mac Néill, 'Why and How the Irish Language Is To Be Preserved', pp. 1100–1.

9 Ibid., p. 1101.

10 Ibid., pp. 1101–2.

11 Ibid., p. 1102.

12 Ibid., p. 1103.

13 Ibid., p. 1108.

14 Fearghal McGarry, *Rebel Voices from the Easter Rising* (Baile Átha Cliath: Penguin, 2011), p. 34.

15 Mac Néill, 'Why and How the Irish Language Is To Be Preserved', p. 1100.

16 Eoin Mac Néill, 'Toghairm agus Gleus Oibre chum Gluasachta na Gaedhilge do chur ar aghaidh i nÉirinn' / 'A Plea and a Plan for the Extension of the Movement to Preserve and Spread the Gaelic Language in Ireland', *Irisleabhar na Gaedhilge / The Gaelic Journal*, eag. 4, uimhir 44, Márta 1893, pp. 177–9.

17 Ibid., p. 179.

18 Ibid.

19 Ibid.

20 Diarmuid Breathnach agus Máire Ní Mhurchú, 'Laoide, Seosamh (1865–1939)'; www.ainm.ie/Bio.aspx?ID=25, 24 Meitheamh 2020.

21 'The Gaelic League', *Irisleabhar na Gaedhilge / The Gaelic Journal*, eag. 4, uimhir 47, Samhain 1893, pp. 226–8.

22 Ibid., pp. 226–7.

23 Ibid., p. 228.

24 'A Memoir Written by Eoin MacNeill, *c.*1932/3', UCDA, LA1/G/372, p. 25, agus Brian Hughes (eag.), *Eoin MacNeill: Memoir of a revolutionary scholar* (Baile Átha Cliath: Coimisiún Lámhscríbhinní na hÉireann, 2016), p. 19.

25 *Irisleabhar na Gaedhilge / The Gaelic Journal*, eag. 5, uimhir 6, Meán Fómhair 1894.

26 Eoin Mac Néill, 'Irish in Co. Antrim', *Irisleabhar na Gaedhilge / The Gaelic Journal*, eag. 6, uimhir 6, Meán Fómhair 1895, p. 96; Féach Mac Néill, 'Irish in the Glens of Antrim', eag. 6, uimhir 6, Meán Fómhair 1895, p. 106.

27 Mac Néill, 'Irish in Co. Antrim', p. 96.

28 Eoin Mac Néill, 'Irish Studies III', *Irisleabhar na Gaedhilge / The Gaelic Journal*, eag. 6, uimhir 12, Aibreán 1896, p. 188; Dubhghlas de hÍde, 'Litir', *Irisleabhar na Gaedhilge / The Gaelic Journal*, eag. 7, uimhir 2, Meitheamh 1896, pp. 17–18.

29 An tAthair Peadar Ó Laoghaire, 'Séadna', *Irisleabhar na Gaedhilge / The Gaelic Journal*, eag. 5, pp. 117, 131, 150, 163, 180; eag. 6, pp. 4, 20, 35, 52, 70, 84, 98, 115, 132, 152, 162, 178; eag. 7, pp. 3, 25, 34, 50, 74, 85, 100, 117, 133, 145, 163, 178.

30 'Father O'Growney in America', *Irisleabhar na Gaedhilge / The Gaelic Journal*, eag. 6, uimhir 10, Eanáir 1895, p. 159.

31 'Gaelic Notes', *Irisleabhar na Gaedhilge / The Gaelic Journal*, eag. 5, uimhir 12, Márta 1895, p. 190.

32 Unsigned 'Important Notice', *Irisleabhar na Gaedhilge / The Gaelic Journal*, eag. 6, uimhir 2, Bealtaine 1895, p. 17.

33 An tAthair Eoghan Ó Gramhnaigh, 'Easy Lessons in Modern Irish', *Irisleabhar na Gaedhilge / The Gaelic Journal*, eag. 4, p. 251; eag. 5, pp. 18, 34, 50, 66, 81, 97, 113, 129, 148, 161, 177, 193; eag. 6, pp. 1, 18, 33, 49, 65, 81, 97, 113, 129, 173.

34 Eoin Mac Néill, 'Irish Studies III', *Irisleabhar na Gaedhilge / The Gaelic Journal*, eag. 6, uimhir 12, Aibreán 1896, p. 188.

35 'Note for the Month', *Irisleabhar na Gaedhilge / The Gaelic Journal*, eag. 7, uimhir 2, Meitheamh 1896, p. 17.

36 'Dr Pederson on the Irish Language', *Irisleabhar na Gaedhilge / The Gaelic Journal*, eag. 8, uimhir 12, Aibreán 1896, p. 191.

37 Dr Holger Pedersen, 1867–1953, teangeolaí, scoláire Ceilteach, agus Ollamh in Ollscoil Chóbanhávan. D'fhoilsigh sé, i measc leabhair eile, *Vergleichende Grammatik der keltischen Sprachen* [Gramadach Comparáideach na dTeangacha Ceilteacha], 2 iml. (Göttingen: Vandenhoeck agus Ruprecht, 1909–13).

38 'Dr Pederson on the Irish Language', p. 191.

39 'An tOireachtas. An Irish Language Prize Meeting', *Irisleabhar na Gaedhilge / The Gaelic Journal*, eag. 7, uimhir 9, Eanáir 1897, p. 1.

40 Ibid.

41 'The Oireachtas', *Irisleabhar na Gaedhilge / The Gaelic Journal*, eag. 8, uimhir 86, Meitheamh 1897, p. 1.

42 'An Irish Weekly', *Irisleabhar na Gaedhilge / The Gaelic Journal*, eag. 7, uimhir 12, Aibreán 1897, p. 192.

43 Ibid.

44 'Past, Present and Future', *Irisleabhar na Gaedhilge / The Gaelic Journal*, eag. 8, uimhir 85, Bealtaine 1897, p. 2.

45 Osborn Bergin, 'Bardic Poetry', in *Irish Bardic Poetry: Texts and translation*, ed. D. Greene and F. Kelly (Baile Átha Cliath: Institiúid Ard-Léinn Bhaile Átha Cliath, 2003 [1970]), p. 4.

46 'Our Eighth Volume', *Irisleabhar na Gaedhilge / The Gaelic Journal*, eag. 8, uimhir 85, Bealtaine 1897, p. 4.

47 'Fáinne an Lae', *Irisleabhar na Gaedhilge / The Gaelic Journal*, eag. 8, uimhir 91, Samhain 1897, p. 1.

48 'The Weekly Organ of the Gaelic League', *Irisleabhar na Gaedhilge / The Gaelic Journal*, eag. 9, uimhir 103, Eanáir 1899, p. 1.

49 'Oireachtas of 1900. VI. Support of *An Claidheamh Soluis* and the *Gaelic Journal* – improved working of branches', *Irisleabhar na Gaedhilge / The Gaelic Journal*, eag. 9, uimhir 108, Iúl 1899, p. 383.

50 'Irish Industries', Eagarfhocal, *An Claidheamh Soluis*, 18 Márta 1899, p. 8.

51 Uí Chollatáin, *An Claidheamh Soluis agus Fáinne an Lae*, pp. 46–51.

52 Eoin Mac Néill, 'The North Began', *An Claidheamh Soluis*, 1 Samhain 1913.

53 Eoin Mac Néill, 'The Blind Pelting the Blind', Eagarfhocal, *An Claidheamh Soluis*, 31 Márta 1900, p. 8.

54 Féach Ó Gramhnaigh, Eoghan, 'The Irish Language', *Irish Ecclesiastical Record*, eag. 11, Samhain 1890; Mac Néill, 'Why and How the Language Is To Be Preserved', pp. 1099–1108.

A Plea for Irish Education: Eoin MacNeill and the university question. *Ruairí Cullen*

1 Eoin MacNeill, *Irish in the National University of Ireland: A plea for Irish education* (Dublin: An Cló-Cumann, 1909), p. 50.

2 Thomas J. Morrissey, *Towards a National University: William Delany SJ (1835–1924): An era of initiative in Irish education* (Dublin: Wolfhound Press, 1983); Thomas J. Morrissey,

William J. Walsh, Archbishop of Dublin, 1841–1921: No uncertain voice (Dublin: Four Courts Press, 2000); Lucy McDiarmid, *The Irish Art of Controversy* (Ithaca, NY: Cornell University Press, 2005), see Chapter 2, 'The Man Who Died for the Language: Rev. Dr O'Hickey and the Irish language controversy, 1908–9'; Brendan Walsh, '"Frankly and Robustly National": Padraig Pearse, the Gaelic League and the campaign for Irish at the National University', *Studies: An Irish quarterly review*, vol. 103, no. 410, Summer 2014, pp. 135–46; and op. cit., no. 411, Autumn 2014, pp. 318–30.

3 MacNeill, *Irish in the National University of Ireland*, p. 3.

4 Senia Pašeta, *Before the Revolution: Nationalism, social change and Ireland's Catholic elite, 1879–1922* (Cork: Cork University Press, 1999), pp. 53–79.

5 Eoin MacNeill, 'Contribution of Professor Eoin MacNeill, MA, D.Litt.', in Fathers of the Society of Jesus (eds), *A Page of Irish History: Story of University College Dublin, 1893–1909* (Dublin: Talbot Press, 1930), p. 192.

6 Gabriel Doherty, 'National Identity and the Study of Irish History', *English Historical Review*, vol. 111, no. 441, Apr. 1996, pp. 324–49.

7 Detailed narratives of the university question are: T.W. Moody, 'The Irish University Question of the Nineteenth Century', *History*, vol. 43, no. 143, June 1958, pp. 90–109; Donal McCartney, *UCD: A national idea: The history of University College Dublin* (Dublin: Gill & Macmillan, 1999); John Coolahan, 'From Royal University to National University, 1879–1908', in Tom Dunne (ed.), *The National University of Ireland 1908–2008: Centenary essays* (Dublin: UCD Press, 2008), pp. 3–18. Another important analysis is Senia Pašeta, 'Trinity College Dublin and the Education of Irish Catholics, 1873–1908', *Studia Hibernica*, no. 30, 1998–9, pp. 7–20.

8 Letters from Michael P. O'Hickey to Eoin MacNeill, and William Walsh to O'Hickey, 1900–1, UCDA, LA1/L/78.

9 The 1899 controversy has been characterised as a coming of age for the Gaelic League as a force in public life and a central voice in the nationalist movement: P.J. Mathews, *Revival: The Abbey Theatre, Sinn Féin, the Gaelic League and the Co-Operative Movement* (Cork: Cork University Press, 2003), p. 44. MacNeill's first editorial on 18 March 1899 in *An Claidheamh Soluis*, during his 1899–1901 stint as editor, dealt with the affair.

10 *Royal Commission on University Education in Ireland. Appendix to the Third Report. Minutes of Evidence Taken in April, May and June, 1902*, 314 [Cd. 1229], H.C. 1902, xxxii, 5.

11 Michael Tierney, *Eoin MacNeill: Scholar and man of action 1867–1945*, ed. F.X. Martin (Oxford: Clarendon Press, 1980), p. 85.

12 Colin Barr, 'University Education, History, and the Hierarchy', in Lawrence W. McBride (ed.), *Reading Irish Histories: Texts, contexts, and memory in modern Ireland* (Dublin: Four Courts Press, 2003), pp. 62–79.

13 George Fottrell, *What Is a National University?* (Dublin: Hodges, Figgis & Co., 1905).

14 Colin Reid, *The Lost Ireland of Stephen Gwynn: Irish constitutional nationalism and cultural politics, 1864–1950* (Manchester: Manchester University Press, 2011), pp. 83–9.

15 *Freeman's Journal*, 20 Jan. 1905.

16 P.H. Pearse, *The Murder Machine* (Dublin: Whelan, 1916).

17 *The Munster News and Limerick and Clare Advocate*, 18 Nov. 1908; handwritten draft of a speech to be given at a feis in Baile an Ghéalanaigh, dated 7 July 1911, UCDA, LA1/E/12.

18 *Irish Times*, 8 Apr. 1905.

19 *Royal Commission on Trinity College Dublin and the University of Dublin. Appendix to the Final Report. Minutes of Evidence and Documents*, 216 [Cd. 3312], H.C. 1907, xli, 87.

20 *Appendix to the Final Report*, p. 211.

21 Ibid., p. 217.

22 Moody, 'University Question', p. 108.

23 *An Claidheamh Soluis*, 9 Feb. 1907.

24 *Royal Commission on Trinity College, Dublin, and the University of Dublin, Appendix to the first report, Statements furnished to the commission in July and August, 1906*, 72 [Cd. 3176] H.C. 1906, lvi, 607. For further discussion see Ruairí Cullen, 'Professor John Wardell and University History in Ireland in the Early Twentieth Century', *PRIA* 117C, 2017, pp. 239–60.

25 *Appendix to the Final Report*, p. 210.

26 This is covered in more detail in Ruairí Cullen, 'Professor John Wardell and University History in Ireland in the Early Twentieth Century', *Proceedings of the Royal Irish Academy*, section C, vol. 117, 2017, pp. 239–60.

27 *Appendix to the Final Report*, p. 255.

28 Máirtín Ó Murchú, 'Irish Language Studies in Trinity College Dublin', *Hermathena*, Quatercentenary Papers, 1992, p. 64.

29 R.B. McDowell and D.A. Webb, *Trinity College Dublin 1592–1952: An academic history* (Cambridge: Cambridge University Press, 1982), pp. 414–15.

30 Tomás Irish, *Trinity in War and Revolution 1912–1923* (Dublin: Royal Irish Academy, 2015), pp. 24–5.

31 John I. Beare, *Trinity College Dublin and the Irish University Question: A non-political memorandum* (Dublin: Hanna & Neale, 1907), p. 14.

32 Eoin MacNeill, 'Memoir', in Brian Hughes (ed.), *Eoin MacNeill: Memoir of a revolutionary scholar* (Dublin: IMC, 2016), p. 42.

33 *An Claidheamh Soluis*, 30 May 1908.

34 Quoted in Reid, *Lost Ireland*, p. 85.

35 Timothy G. McMahon, *Grand Opportunity: The Gaelic Revival and Irish society, 1893–1910* (Syracuse, NY: Syracuse University Press, 2008), p. 74.

36 *Freeman's Journal*, 28 Nov. 1908.

37 *Irish Times*, 8 Dec. 1908.

38 *Freeman's Journal*, 4 Jan. 1909.

39 *Irish Times*, 20 Jan. 1909.

40 David W. Miller, *Church, State and Nation in Ireland 1898–1921* (Dublin: Gill & Macmillan, 1973), p. 242; McDiarmid, *Art of Controversy*, p. 62; R.F. Foster, *Vivid Faces: The revolutionary generation in Ireland, 1890–1923* (London: Allen Lane, 2014), p. 58.

41 Eoin MacNeill to unknown clergyman, c.1907, UCDA, LA1/F/168.

42 Pašeta, *Before the Revolution*, p. 142.

43 *An Claidheamh Soluis*, 12 Dec. 1908.

44 Tomás Ó Fiaich, 'The Great Controversy', in Seán Ó Tuama (ed.), *The Gaelic League Idea* (Cork and Dublin: The Mercier Press, 1972), p. 71.

45 McDiarmid, *Art of Controversy*, p. 75.

46 *Irish Independent*, 20 Sept. 1909.

47 *An Claidheamh Soluis*, 8 May 1909.

48 Morrissey, *Delany*, p. 332.

49 Miller, *Church, State and Nation*, p. 234.

50 See the incendiary essays in publications such as *A Plea for an Irish University: Essays collected and edited by an Irish priest* (Dublin: Sealy, Bryers & Walker, 1909); and 'An Irish Priest' (ed.), *Wanted – An Irish University: Essays on university and kindred subjects* (Dublin: Sealy, Bryers & Walker, 1909).

51 MacNeill, *Plea*, n.p.

52 He had said as much in a letter to the editor of the *Freeman's Journal*, 29 Dec. 1908.

53 MacNeill, *Irish in the National University of Ireland*, p. 51.

54 Ibid., p. 8.

55 MacNeill, 'Memoir', p. 32.

56 *Irish Times*, 24 June 1910. Comprehensive accounts of the controversy can be found in Morrissey, *Delany*, pp. 321–44; and McMahon, *Grand Opportunity*, pp. 73–81.

57 *Irish Times*, 27 June 1910.

58 Reid, *Lost Ireland*, p. 89.

59 Gearóid Ó Tuathaigh, 'The Position of the Irish Language', in Dunne, *National University*, p. 34.

60 Manuscript article on the role of Irish studies in liberal education with particular reference to the University of Dublin and the Royal University, n.d., UCDA, LA1/F/172a.

61 MacNeill, 'Memoir', p. 43.

62 Adrian Kelly, *Compulsory Irish: Language and education in Ireland 1870s–1970s* (Dublin: Irish Academic Press, 2002), p. 18. Irish at Leaving Certificate level is still required for entry into the National University for applicants educated in Ireland.

63 *Irish Times*, 8 Dec. 1908.

64 E. Brian Titley, *Church, State, and the Control of Schooling in Ireland 1900–1944* (Kingston: McGill-Queen's University Press, 1983), p. 92.

65 For the relationship between liberal education and historical studies, see Peter Slee, *Learning and a Liberal Education: The study of modern history in the universities of Oxford, Cambridge and Manchester, 1800–1914* (Manchester: Manchester University Press, 1986).

66 *The Royal University of Ireland. The Calendar for the Year 1900* (Dublin: Longmans, 1900).

67 *The Royal University of Ireland. The Calendar for the Year 1896* (Dublin: Longmans, 1896), p. 183.

68 Arthur E. Clery, 'The Reform of the Royal University', *New Ireland Review*, vol. 27, no. 6, Aug. 1907, p. 324.

69 Manuscript notes on staff meeting, c.1910–13, UCDA, LA1/F/35. The graduates in question were Thomas Arkins and an unidentified Davitt (almost certainly Michael Davitt Jr, (1890–1928), medical doctor, UCD graduate, and son of Michael Davitt MP (1846–1906)).

70 R. Dudley Edwards, 'Professor MacNeill', in F.X. Martin and F.J. Byrne (eds), *The Scholar Revolutionary: Eoin MacNeill, 1867–1945, and the making of the new Ireland* (Shannon: Irish University Press, 1973), p. 287. Dudley Edwards, a UCD graduate taught by MacNeill, was rather cutting in his assessment of his old professor's pedagogical legacy (p. 288): 'His method was much as he had learned from Hogan, but he failed to give anyone the training he had received himself. He was as a teacher more of an inspirer and expounder than a supervisor.'

71 *University College Dublin: A constituent college of the National University of Ireland: Calendar for the Session 1910–11* (Dublin: Browne & Nolan, 1910), p. 52.

72 McMahon, *Grand Opportunity*, p. 81.

73 *University College Dublin ... 1910–11*, p. 62.

74 Ibid., p. 115.

75 Ibid., p. 116.

76 McCartney, *UCD*, p. 70.

77 Philip O'Leary, '"The Dead Generations": Irish history in the Gaelic Revival', *Proceedings of the Harvard Celtic Colloquium*, no. 10, 1990, p. 115.

78 Eoin MacNeill to Charles L. McLorinan, 21 Oct. 1908, UCDA, LA1/J/110.

79 Gaelic League deputation to statutory commission of the Queen's University, Belfast, May 1909, QUB/3/1/3/5/8. I am grateful to Dr Sam Manning for this reference.

80 T.W. Moody and J.C. Beckett (eds), *Queen's Belfast 1845–1949: The history of a university*, 2 vols (London: Faber & Faber, 1959), vol. 1, p. 412.

81 Francis Joseph Bigger to Arthur Jaffe, 21 Apr. 1909, QUB/3/1/3/5/8.

82 L.A. Clarkson, 'James Eadie Todd and the School of History at the Queen's University of Belfast', *Irish Historical Studies*, vol. 41, no. 159, May 2017, pp. 22–40.

83 Carbon copy typed reports from the conference appointed 'to determine how University College Galway can best engage in some work of national importance, such as fulfilling the functions of an Irish-speaking university college, by conducting the teaching of general subjects through the medium of Irish', Apr. 1926, UCDA, LA1/F/50.
84 Dudley Edwards, 'Professor MacNeill', p. 295.
85 McCartney, *UCD*, p. 32.

Eoin MacNeill and the idea of an 'Irish Cultural Republic'. *Mairéad Carew*
1 Correspondence of Thomas MacGreevy, Trinity College Dublin, MS 8003/9 [no pagination].
2 Brian P. Kennedy, 'The Failure of the Cultural Republic: Ireland 1922–1939', *Studies: An Irish quarterly review* vol. 81, no. 321, Spring 1992, pp. 14–22, at p. 15.
3 See, for example, Terence Brown, *Ireland: A social and cultural history 1922–2002* (London: Harper Perennial, 2004 [repr. 3rd edn, 2004]).
4 Gregory Castle, *Modernism and the Celtic Revival* (Cambridge: Cambridge University Press, 2001), pp. 7–8.
5 Douglas Hyde, 'The Necessity for de-Anglicising Ireland', in Charles Gavan Duffy (ed.), *The Revival of Irish Literature* (London: T. Fisher Unwin, 1894), pp. 117–61, p. 121.
6 David Greene, 'The Founding of the Gaelic League', in Seán Ó Tuama (ed.), *The Gaelic League Idea* (Cork and Dublin: The Mercier Press, 1972), pp. 9–19, at p. 18.
7 Breandán Mac Aodha, 'Was This a Social Revolution?', in Ó Tuama (ed.), *The Gaelic League Idea*, pp. 20–30, at p. 23.
8 'N.Y.U. Plans Alcove to honor Dr. MacNeill', from file of news cuttings from American newspapers, 1926–34 including cuttings from newspaper articles in America about lecture tour and the movement in the US to promote Celtic Studies, UCDA, LA1/G/362.
9 See Nagle, this volume, pp. 189–200.
10 Kennedy, 'The Failure of the Cultural Republic', p. 15.
11 Carew, 'Eoin MacNeill: Revolutionary cultural ideologue', pp. 67–75.
12 For an exploration of this idea see Benedict Anderson, *Imagined Communities: Reflections on the origin and spread of nationalism* (London: Verso, 1983).
13 Eoin MacNeill, 'Irish Education Policy', *Irish Statesman*, 17 Oct. 1925.
14 Newspaper clipping, untitled, n.d. from 'File of news cuttings from American newspapers such as *Illustrated Daily News, New York Times, Gaelic American, New York Sun, Chicago Tribune, Boston Post and Boston Traveller*, mainly relating to MacNeill's American Lecture Tour, 1930 and the movement in the US to promote Celtic Studies', UCDA, LA1/G/362.
15 R.D. Edwards, 'An agenda for Irish History, 1978–2018', in Ciaran Brady (ed.), *Interpreting Irish History* (Dublin: Irish Academic Press, 1994), p. 55.
16 A.D. Smith, *Nationalism and Modernism* (Oxford: Oxford University Press, 2000), pp. 22, 45.
17 *Irish Times*, 12 July 1922.
18 Michael Kennedy and Deirdre McMahon, *A History of the Irish Manuscripts Commission: Reconstructing Ireland's past* (Dublin: IMC, 2009), p. xvi.
19 Ibid., p. xviii.
20 T.W. Moody and R.D. Edwards, 'Preface', *Irish Historical Studies*, vol. 1, no. 1, 1938, pp. 1–2.
21 D.W. Hayton, 'The Laboratory for "Scientific History": T.W. Moody and R.D. Edwards at the Institute of Historical Research', *Irish Historical Studies*, vol. 41, no. 159, 2017, p. 41. See also R.F. Foster, 'History and the Irish Question', in *Transactions of the Royal Historical Society*, 5th series, vol. 33, 1983, pp. 197–8.
22 In 1937, the archaeologist Joseph Raftery explained that 'Celtic' La Tène material was 'purely native' even though at different stages it had adopted and adapted foreign decorative motifs: Adolf Mahr, 'New Aspects and Problems in Irish Prehistory', Presidential Address for 1937,

Proceedings of the Prehistoric Society, vol. 3, nos. 1–2, July–December 1937, pp. 409–10. Decades later the archaeologist Barry Raftery stated clearly that 'there is simply no evidence of invading Celts': Barry Raftery, 'Celtic Ireland: Problems of language, history and archaeology', *Acta Archaeologica, Academiae Scientiarum Hungaricae*, tomus lvii, fasciculi 1–3, 2006, pp. 273–9. Hugh O'Neill Hencken, who excavated the 'Early Christian' crannóg at Lagore, County Meath, 1934–6 wrote that 'Another element in the Lagore culture, Christianity, comes from the late Roman world, though there was next to no archaeological evidence of it at Lagore. Still it cannot be doubted that the inhabitants were Christian'. Hugh O'Neill Hencken, with sections by Liam Price and Laura E. Start, 'Lagore Crannóg: An Irish royal residence of the 7th to 10th centuries AD', *PRIA*, vol. 53, 1950–1, pp. 1–247, at p. 16.

23 Smith, *Nationalism and Modernism*, p. 42; see also Ernest Gellner, *Nationalism* (London: Weidenfeld & Nicolson, 1997), pp. 90–101.

24 Quoted in Bruce Nelson, *Irish Nationalists and the Making of the Irish Race* (Princeton, NJ: Princeton University Press, 2012), p. 234.

25 Eoin MacNeill, *Celtic Ireland* (Dublin: Martin & Lester, 1921 [repr., 1981]), p. xi. See also Elva Johnston, this volume, pp. 76–79.

26 Mairéad Carew, *The Quest for the Irish Celt: The Harvard Archaeological Mission to Ireland, 1932–1936* (Sallins: Irish Academic Press, 2018).

27 Edwin Black, *War Against the Weak: Eugenics and America's campaign to create a master race* (New York: Thunder's Mouth Press, 2003), p. 205.

28 Letter from W. Lloyd Warner, Peabody Museum, to Eoin MacNeill, 25 Jan. 1932: 'As you know, I followed your suggestion and gave County Clare my preference in the Survey I made of Ireland last summer and it has been decided by the Division of Anthropology here to concentrate our effort there.' W. Lloyd Warner, UCDA, LA1/H/5.

29 The results of this work were published in two books, Conrad M. Arensberg, *The Irish Countryman: An anthropological study* (London: Macmillan, 1937), and Conrad M. Arensberg and Solon T. Kimball, *Family and Community in Ireland* (Cambridge, MA: Harvard University Press, 1940). Arensberg studied under Eoin MacNeill and acquired a knowledge of the Irish language. See press release 'Harvard University Irish Expedition 1932', E.A. Hooton papers #995–1, Box 21.7, Peabody Museum of Archaeology and Ethnology, Harvard University.

30 Adolf Mahr, 'Our Splendid Celtic Collection', *Irish Times*, 15 Oct. 1927.

31 'Dr Lithberg's Report', NAI, D/TAOIS S5392: Carew, '"The Glamour of Ancient Greatness"', pp. 20–2.

32 Mairéad Carew, 'Politics and the Definition of National Monuments: The "Big House problem"', *Journal of Irish Archaeology*, vol. 18, 2009, p. 129.

33 Smith, *Nationalism and Modernism*, p. 43.

34 Eoin MacNeill, 'Essay Discussing Celtic and Anglo-Saxon "Race Feeling" with Particular Reference to Theories Put Forward by 19th and 20th Century Historians', UCDA, LA1/D/62.

35 Ibid.

36 Julius Pokorny, 'MacNeill's Place in Celtic Studies', in F.X. Martin and F.J. Byrne (eds), *The Scholar Revolutionary: Eoin MacNeill, 1867–1945, and the making of the new Ireland* (Shannon: Irish University Press, 1973), p. 13.

37 John Hutchinson, *The Dynamics of Cultural Nationalism: The Gaelic Revival and the creation of the Irish nation state* (London: Allen & Unwin, 1987), p. 167.

38 MacNeill, *Celtic Ireland*, p. xiii.

39 MacNeill, 'Essay Discussing Celtic and Anglo-Saxon "Race Feeling"'.

40 Hutchinson, *The Dynamics of Cultural Nationalism*, p. 121.

41 Quoted in Brian Ó Cuív, 'MacNeill and the Irish Language', in Martin and Byrne (eds), *The Scholar Revolutionary*, p. 9.

42 Ibid., p. 3.

43 Declan Kiberd and P.J. Mathews (eds), *Handbook of the Irish Revival: An anthology of Irish cultural and political writings 1891–1922* (Notre Dame, IN: Notre Dame University Press, 2015), p. 129.

44 Patrick Pearse, 'About Literature', *An Claidheamh Soluis*, 26 May 1906.

45 Brigittine M. French, 'Linguistic Science and Nationalist Revolution: Expert knowledge and the making of sameness in pre-independence Ireland', *Language in Society*, vol. 38, no. 5, Nov. 2009, p. 608. See also Hutchinson, *The Dynamics of Cultural Nationalism*.

46 Eoin MacNeill, 'Irish Education Policy', *Irish Statesman*, 24 Oct. 1925. MacNeill himself served as Minister for Education between 1922 and 1925 and has been described by John Ryan SJ as 'a reluctant minister who fulfilled his patriotic duty'. John Ryan SJ, 'Eoin MacNeill 1867–1945', *Studies: An Irish quarterly review*, vol. 34, 1945, p. 437.

47 Constitution of the Irish Free State (Saorstát Éireann) Act, 1922, Article 4 and Constitution of Ireland, 1937, Article 8, www.irishstatutebook.ie.

48 Mícheál Briody, *The Irish Folklore Commission 1935–1970: History, ideology, methodology*, Studia Fennica Folkloristica 17 (Helsinki: Finnish Literary Society, 2008), p. 23.

49 In 1936, at the inaugural meeting of the Historical Society of UCD, James Delargy, director of the Folklore Commission, gave an address on the oral tradition entitled 'An Untapped Source of Irish History', *Irish Times*, 11 Mar. 1936.

50 Séamus Ó Duilearga to Eoin MacNeill, 29 July 1928, UCDA, LAI/H/155.

51 Eoin MacNeill to Éamon de Valera, 6 July 1934, UCDA, LA1/H/157.

52 Other founder members included Professor Muehlhausen of Hamburg and Berlin; Dr Bauersfeld of Munich; Dr Weisweiler of Frankfurt-on-Main; Dr Wagner of Berlin; Dr von Tevenar of Berlin; and Herr Clismann of Dublin. See the *Irish Times*, 25 Jan. 1937.

53 *Irish Times*, 25 Jan. 1937.

54 Kennedy, 'The Failure of the Cultural Republic', p. 19.

55 Eoin MacNeill, 'The Historical Saint Patrick', in Paul Walsh (ed.), *Saint Patrick, A.D. 432–1932: Fifteenth centenary memorial book* (Dublin: Catholic Truth Society of Ireland, 1932), pp. 7–30.

56 Edward J. Byrne to Eoin MacNeill, 22 July 1931, UCDA, LA1/G/28.

57 David G. Holmes, 'The Eucharistic Congress of 1932 and Irish Identity', *New Hibernia Review*, vol. 4, no. 1, Spring 2000, pp. 55, 60; see also Rory O'Dwyer, 'On Show to the World: The Eucharistic Congress, 1932', *History Ireland*, Nov./Dec. 2007, pp. 42–7.

58 *The Catholic Bulletin*, vol. 25, no. 4, Apr. 1935, p. 273.

59 'Official Visit of the Cardinal Legate at Government Buildings', in V. Rev. Patrick Canon Boylan (ed.), *Dublin, 1932: The Book of the Congress (XXXIst International Eucharistic Congress)* (Dublin: Veritas Publications, 1932), p. 73.

60 Cyril Fox, Review article, 'Christian Art in Ancient Ireland, vol. 1, Edited by Dr Adolf Mahr, Keeper of Irish Antiquities, National Museum, Dublin, Dublin 1932', *Man*, vol. 32, Sept. 1932, p. 219.

61 Maurice Moynihan (ed.), *Speeches and Statements by Éamon de Valera 1917–73* (Dublin: Gill & Macmillan, 1980), p. 233.

62 Smith, *Nationalism and Modernism*, p. 43.

63 Father P.J. Gannon SJ, 'Literature and Censorship', *The Irish Monthly*, vol. 65, no. 769, July 1937, p. 437.

64 Black, *War Against the Weak*. See also Mairéad Carew, 'Harvard, Celtic Skulls and Eugenics in de Valera's Ireland', *History Ireland*, vol. 26, no. 5, Sept./Oct. 2018, pp. 16–18.

65 Greta Jones, 'Eugenics in Ireland: The Belfast Eugenics Society, 1911–1915', *Irish Historical Studies*, vol. 28, no. 109, May 1992, pp. 81–95, at p. 95.

66 Father Timothy Corcoran SJ, 'How English May Be Taught without Anglicising', *The Irish Monthly*, vol. 51, no. 600, June 1923, p. 272.

67 Father Timothy Corcoran SJ, 'The New Secondary Programmes in Ireland', *Studies: An Irish quarterly review*, vol. 12, no. 46, June 1923, p. 260.

68 Father Timothy Corcoran SJ, 'The Integral Teaching of History', *The Irish Monthly*, vol. 57, no. 667, Jan. 1929, pp. 9–12.

69 Stephen J. Brown, *The Central Catholic Library: The first ten years of an Irish enterprise* [*Messenger* magazine] (Dublin: Central Catholic Library Association, 1932), p. 10.

70 MacNeill, *Celtic Ireland*, p. xv.

71 Eoin MacNeill quoted in the *Irish Times*, 21 June 1934.

72 'Stay at Home: Professor Eoin MacNeill gives advice to would-be emigrants to America, tour of States', newspaper clipping, title unknown, n.d., UCDA, LA1/G/362.

73 Ibid.

74 *New York City Journal*, 2 Apr. 1930.

75 *New York Herald Tribune*, 3 Apr. 1930.

76 'Stay at Home'.

77 Newspaper clipping, untitled, n.d. from 'File of news cuttings from American newspapers such as *Illustrated Daily News, New York Times, Gaelic American, New York Sun, Chicago Tribune, Boston Post* and *Boston Traveller*, mainly relating to MacNeill's American Lecture Tour, 1930 and the movement in the US to promote Celtic Studies', UCDA, LA1/G/362.

78 *Chicago Tribune*, 23 Apr. 1930.

79 Eoin MacNeill to Taddie MacNeill, 7 May 1930, UCDA, LA1/G/79.

80 John L. Gerig, 'Celtic Studies in the United States', *The Columbia University Quarterly*, vol. 19, no. 1, Dec. 1916, p. 30.

81 George Watson, 'Celticism and the Annulment of History', in Terence Brown (ed.), *Celticism* (Atlanta and Amsterdam: Rodopi, 1996), p. 216.

82 Ibid., p. 207.

83 Ibid., p. 208.

84 Gerig, 'Celtic Studies in the United States', p. 30.

85 Roland Blenner-Hassett, 'A Brief History of Celtic Studies in North America', *PMLA*, vol. 69, no. 4, part 2, Sept. 1954, p. 14.

86 MacNeill, *Celtic Ireland*, p. xiii.

87 Gerig, 'Celtic Studies in the United States', p. 34.

88 Ibid., p. 36.

89 Blenner-Hassett, 'A Brief History of Celtic Studies in North America', p. 8.

90 Ibid.

91 'Society of Friends of the Universities of Ireland, Letters Exchanged between Professor J.L. Gerig, Columbia University, New York and Provost E.J. Gwynn, Trinity College Dublin, Irish Are Neglecting Their language, Culture and Ideals', newspaper clipping, title unknown, n.d., UCDA, LA1/G/362.

92 Gerig, 'Celtic Studies in the United States', p. 36.

93 By 1954, it housed the largest single collection of Celtic literary material in the world. Blenner-Hassett described this collection as 'impressive and unique' and representing 'the fruits of Robinson's assiduous attention for almost sixty years'. See Blenner-Hassett, 'A Brief History of Celtic Studies in North America', p. 14. Robinson himself gave an account of the collection in 1946. By then it included 10,000 Celtic books. See F.N. Robinson, 'Celtic Books at Harvard: The history of a departmental collection', *Harvard Library Bulletin*, vol. 1, no. 1, 1946, pp. 52–65.

94 Éamon de Valera, letter dated 18 Aug. 1933, NAI, D/TAOIS 97/9/5.

95 *Irish Times*, 21 June 1934.

96 Ibid.

97 Ibid., 26 Aug. 1933.

98 Ibid., 24 Aug. 1933.

99 Ibid.

100 Mairéad Carew, 'The Pageant of the Celt': Irish archaeology at the Chicago World's Fair', *Archaeology Ireland*, vol. 28, no. 1, Spring 2014, pp. 9–12.

101 Raymond Gillespie and Brian P. Kennedy (eds), *Ireland: Art into history* (Dublin: Townhouse, 1994), p. 145.

102 Quoted in Joan Fitzpatrick Dean, *All Dressed Up: Modern Irish historical pageantry* (Syracuse, NY: Syracuse University Press, 2014), p. 151. 'It was while reading the manuscript and notes of his father's book, *Ireland's Crown of Thorns and Roses* that he became impressed with the dramatic possibilities of Ireland's stirring story. *The Pageant of the Celt* is the result of two years of historical research and preparation by him.' John V. Ryan, *The Pageant of the Celt*, RIA MSS, AP 1934, p. 18.

103 John V. Ryan, *The Pageant of the Celt*, RIA MSS, AP 1934, p. 2.

104 John Gribbin, *Erwin Schrödinger and the Quantum Revolution* (London: John Wiley & Sons, 2012), p. 200.

105 *Irish Times*, 13 Sept. 1935.

106 Terence Brown, *Ireland: A social and cultural history 1922–2002*, 3rd edn (London: Harper Perennial, 2004), p. 4.

107 Brian Fallon, *An Age of Innocence: Irish culture 1930–1960* (Dublin: Gill & Macmillan, 1998), p. 159.

108 Peter Martin, *Censorship in the Two Irelands* (Dublin: Irish Academic Press, 2006), p. xiii. James Joyce's *Ulysses*, 'literary contraband' first published in 1922 and described by Kevin Bermingham as 'a snapshot of a cultural revolution', was not banned in the Irish Free State in contrast to Britain and America. See Kevin Bermingham, *The Most Dangerous Book: The battle for James Joyce's* Ulysses (London: Penguin, 2014), pp. 3, 15. See also Donal Ó Drisceoil, *Censorship in Ireland: Neutrality, politics and society* (Cork: Cork University Press, 1996).

109 Richard Aldous, *Great Irish Speeches* (London: Quercus, 2009), pp. 92–5.

110 Gregory Castle, *Modernism and the Celtic Revival* (Cambridge: Cambridge University Press, 2001), p. 29.

111 Nicholas Allen, 'States of Mind: Science, culture and the Intellectual Revival, 1900–1930', *Irish University Review*, vol. 33, no. 1, Special Issue: new perspectives on the Irish Literary Revival, Spring–Summer 2003, p. 158.

112 Smith, *Nationalism and Modernism*, p. 45.

113 See, for example, Fintan O'Toole (ed.), *Up the Republic! Towards a new Ireland* (London: Faber & Faber, 2012) and Michael D. Higgins, *Renewing the Republic* (Dublin: Liberties Press, 2011).

114 Kennedy, 'The Failure of the Cultural Republic', p. 22.

115 'Ireland's Future, North and South', *Newry Telegraph*, Christmas number, Dec. 1922, UCDA, LA1/K/211.

Countermand and Imprisonment, 1916–17. *Michael Laffan*

1 'Manifesto of Irish Volunteers 25th November, 1913', in F.X. Martin (ed.), *The Irish Volunteers 1913–1915* (Dublin: James Duffy, 1963), p. 100.

2 MacNeill, 'Memorandum on Events Leading up to the Insurrection' (National Library of Ireland (NLI), Hobson papers, MS 13,174 (14), pp. 3–4) (Memorandum); *Irish Historical Studies [IHS]*, vol. 12, no. 47, Mar. 1961, pp. 247, 255, n. 14; Marnie Hay, *Bulmer Hobson and*

the Nationalist Movement in Twentieth-Century Ireland (Manchester: Manchester University Press, 2009), p. 184; Diarmuid Lynch, *The I.R.B. and the 1916 Insurrection* (Cork: Mercier, 1957), pp. 48–9. MacNeill was uncertain about the date of this meeting – 'I think late in 1915' – and Martin argues convincingly that it took place on 5 September 1915 (*IHS*, p. 255).

3   *Workers' Republic*, 4 Dec. 1915, p. 2; 1 Jan. 1916, p. 1 [italics as per original text].

4   *Irish Volunteer*, 25 Dec. 1915, p. 1.

5   Memorandum (NLI MS 13,174 (14), p. 1); *IHS*, p. 246; also MacNeill, 'Notes', 9 May 1916 (NLI, MacNeill papers, MS 43,228).

6   Michael T. Foy and Brian Barton, *The Easter Rising*, 2nd edn (Stroud: History Press, 2011), pp. 35–6.

7   Bulmer Hobson, *Ireland Yesterday and Tomorrow* (Tralee: Anvil, 1968), p. 73. Hobson dates this to 'very early in 1916'.

8   Memorandum (NLI MS 13,174 (14), p. 3); *IHS*, p. 247.

9   Michael Tierney, *Eoin MacNeill: Scholar and man of action 1867–1945* (Oxford: Clarendon, 1980), p. 189.

10 Foy and Barton, *Easter Rising*, p. 63.

11 Bulmer Hobson, Bureau of Military History, Witness Statement (BMH, WS) 81, p. 12.

12 Foy and Barton, *Easter Rising*, pp. 40–1.

13 Chief Secretary's Office, Crime Branch, Dublin Metropolitan Branch. Movement of Extremists 29 May 1915–20 Apr. 1916 (NAI, CSO/JD/2).

14 MacNeill, Memorandum (NLI MS 13,174 (15), pp. 1, 5, 6, 8, 9, 11); *IHS*, pp. 234–40.

15 *Irish Volunteer*, 1 Apr. 1916, p. 1.

16 NLI, O'Rahilly papers, MS 13,019/3/3.

17 Hobson to F.X. Martin, 17 Mar. 1960 (F.X. Martin papers, UCDA, P189/285); *IHS*, p. 230.

18 Ruth Dudley Edwards, *The Seven: The lives and legacies of the founding fathers of the Irish Republic* (London: Oneworld, 2016), pp. 296–7; F.X. Martin, 'Eoin MacNeill and the Easter Rising: Preparations', in F.X. Martin (ed.), *The Easter Rising, 1916 and University College Dublin* (Dublin: Browne & Nolan, 1966), p. 26.

19 MacNeill, Memorandum (NLI MS 13,174 (14), p. 4); IHS, p. 247; Tierney, *Scholar and man of action*, p. 191. McGillian had also written in similar terms to Redmond (McGillian to Redmond, 6 Mar. 1916 (Trinity College Dublin Archives (TCDA)), Dillon papers, MS 6749/609).

20 *Irish Volunteer*, 22 Apr. 1916, p. 1.

21 *The Memoirs of Desmond FitzGerald 1913–1916* (London: Routledge & Kegan Paul, 1968), p. 116.

22 Colm Ó Lochlainn, BMH, WS 751, p. 1; Ó Lochlainn to F.X. Martin, 17 June 1960 (UCDA, P189/285).

23 F.X. Martin, Notes to Memorandum II, *IHS*, p. 265, n. 47.

24 Foy and Barton, *Easter Rising*, p. 51; Hay, *Hobson*, p. 189.

25 Liam Ó Briain, *Insurrection Memories 1916: Cuimhní cinn*, trans. Eoin Ó Dochartaigh (Galway: Ardcrú, 2014), p. 52.

26 MacNeill, Memorandum (NLI MS 13,171 (14), pp. 8–9); *IHS*, pp. 249, 262; Tierney, *Scholar and man of action*, p. 214.

27 Charles Townshend, *Easter 1916: The Irish rebellion* (London: Allen Lane, 2005), p. 136; Foy and Barton, *Easter Rising*, p. 54.

28 MacNeill, Memorandum (NLI MS, 13,171(14), p. 9); *IHS*, p. 249.

29 Kitty O'Doherty, BMH, WS 355, p. 22.

30 James Ryan, BMH, WS 70, p. 3.

31 Willie Pearse to O'Rahilly, 5 p.m., 21 Apr. 1916 (NLI, O'Rahilly papers, MS 13019/3/4).

32 Court Martial Proceedings (UCDA, LA1/G/126, p. 95); Martin, *IHS*, p. 262, n. 40.

33 Townshend, *Easter 1916*, p. 123.
34 MacNeill, Memorandum (NLI MS 13,171 (14), p. 9); *IHS*, p. 249. Tierney argues that this meeting actually took place on Friday (*Scholar and man of action*, pp. 201–2).
35 *Freeman's Journal*, 22 Apr. 1916, p. 5.
36 MacNeill, Memorandum (NLI MS 13,171 (14), p. 9); *IHS*, p. 249.
37 MacNeill, Correspondence and notes re court martial (NLI, MacNeill papers, MS 43,228).
38 Ibid.; Tierney, *Scholar and man of action*, pp. 204–5.
39 Ó Lochlainn, BMH, WS 751, p. 6; Ó Lochlainn to F.X. Martin, 22 June 1960 (UCDA, P189/285).
40 Casement, diary, 28, 29 Mar. 1916 in Angus Mitchell (ed.), *One Bold Deed of Open Treason: The Berlin diary of Roger Casement 1914–1916* (Sallins: Irish Academic Press, 2016), pp. 167, 194.
41 Ó Lochlainn to F.X. Martin, 29 June 1960 (UCDA, P189/285).
42 Colm Ó Lochlainn, BMH, WS 751, p. 6.
43 Seán T. O'Kelly, BMH, WS 1765, part 2, pp. 232–3.
44 James McNeill, Evidence, Court Martial Proceedings (UCDA, LA1/G /126, p. 92).
45 Séamus Ó Ceallaigh, *Gleanings from Ulster History* (Cork: Cork University Press, 1951; repr. Draperstown: Ballinascreen Historical Society, 1994), p. 149.
46 James O'Kelly (Séamus Ó Ceallaigh), Evidence, Court Martial Proceedings (UCDA, LA1/G/126, pp. 107, 106); Mary Josephine Mulcahy, BMH, WS 399, p. 9.
47 *Memoirs of Senator Joseph Connolly* (Blackrock: Irish Academic Press, 1996), p. 99.
48 Maureen Wall, 'The Plans and the Countermand: The country and Dublin', in Kevin B. Nowlan (ed.), *The Making of 1916* (Dublin: Stationery Office, 1969), p. 213.
49 Seán T. O'Kelly, BMH, WS 1765, part 2, p. 239.
50 Ó Ceallaigh, *Gleanings*, pp. 152, 150.
51 Lynch, *The I.R.B.*, p. 52; Lynch, BMH, WS 651, p. 6.
52 Townshend, *Easter 1916*, pp. 143, 138.
53 Fearghal McGarry, *The Rising: Ireland, Easter 1916* (Oxford: Oxford University Press, 2010), p. 228.
54 Wall, 'The Plans and the Countermand', pp. 207, 210.
55 Lynch, *The I.R.B.*, p. 54; Lynch, BMH, WS 651, p. 8; Townshend, *Easter 1916*, p. 142.
56 Áine Ceannt, BMH, WS 264, p. 26.
57 Ruth Dudley Edwards, *Patrick Pearse: The triumph of failure* (London: Gollancz, 1977), p. 299.
58 MacNeill, Charge Sheet and Statement (NLI, MacNeill papers, MS 13,174 (17), p. 17).
59 Ibid., pp. 31, 9.
60 MacDonagh, Memorandum, 8 p.m., 23 Apr. 1916 (NLI, MacNeill papers, MS 43,228/1).
61 MacNeill, Notes for Court Martial (NLI, MacNeill papers, MS 43,228); FitzGerald, *Memoirs 1913–1916*, pp. 125, 128.
62 Ó Briain, *Insurrection Memories*, p. 51.
63 Ibid., p. 55.
64 Bulmer Hobson, 'The Rising', Memorandum, 17 Dec. 1947 (UCDA, P189/300, pp. 19–20).
65 Aodogán O'Rahilly, *Winding the Clock: O'Rahilly and the 1916 Rising* (Dublin: Lilliput, 1991), p. 214.
66 Charles MacAuley, BMH, WS 735, p. 70.
67 FitzGerald, *Memoirs*, pp. 174–5.
68 Hobson, *Ireland*, p. 77.
69 Kathleen Clarke, *Revolutionary Woman 1878–1972: An autobiography*, ed. Helen Litton (Dublin: O'Brien Press, 1991), p. 94.
70 Frank Thornton, BMH, WS 510, p. 24.

71 MacNeill, Notes, 9 May 1916 (NLI, MacNeill papers, MS 43,228).

72 Tierney, *Scholar and man of action*, p. 224.

73 Price, statement, 29 Aug. 1916 (NLI, Redmond papers, MS 15,204); Seán T. O'Kelly, BMH, WS 1765, part 2, p. 272.

74 General Maxwell to Field Marshal French, 4 May 1916 (Éamon de Valera papers, UCDA P150/512).

75 MacNeill, Notes, 9 May 1916 (NLI, MacNeill papers, MS 43,228).

76 Court Martial Proceedings (UCDA, LA1/G/126, p. 14).

77 MacNeill, Notes on Court Martial (UCDA, LA1/G/126(25)).

78 Court Martial Proceedings (UCDA, LA1/G/126, p. 62); see also Seán Enright, *After the Rising: Soldiers, lawyers and trials of the Irish revolution* (Sallins: Irish Academic Press, 2016), p. 105.

79 Court Martial Proceedings (UCDA, LA1/G/126, pp. 64–5).

80 MacNeill, Notes on Court Martial (UCDA, LA1/G/126(25)).

81 Draft, James McNeill to Henry Duke, 7 Apr. 1917 (UCDA, LA1/G/126(27)) (passage not included in final version in NLI, MacNeill papers, MS 13,174 (17)).

82 David Fitzpatrick, 'Decidedly a Personality: De Valera's performance as a convict', *History Ireland*, vol. 10, no. 2, Summer 2002, p. 41; Tierney, *Scholar and man of action*, p. 242.

83 Agnes MacNeill to Alice Stopford Green (NLI, MacNeill papers, MS 43,261/2).

84 Questionnaire for Ex-Prisoners (UCDA, LA1/G/158).

85 Thomas McInerney, BMH, WS 1150, p. 6.

86 MacNeill to his daughter Eibhlín, 12 May 1917 (UCDA, LA1/G/153).

87 See also Mulvagh's chapter in this volume, pp. 233–57.

88 Peadar Doyle, WS 155, pp. 21–2; Fitzpatrick, 'Decidedly a Personality', p. 44; David McCullagh, *De Valera: Rise, 1882–1932* (Dublin: Gill, 2017), p. 114.

89 De Valera to Simon Donnelly, 2 Apr. 1917 (UCDA, P150/512). MacNeill's standing with his fellow prisoners is also discussed by Mulvagh, this volume, p. 276.

90 MacNeill to Michael Collins, 23 June 1917 (NLI MS 43,261/2).

Eoin MacNeill and Nationalism. *Shane Nagle*

1   For a study of MacNeill as a thinker and founder of an Irish 'cultural republic' see in this volume Mairéad Carew, 'Eoin MacNeill and the Idea of an "Irish Cultural Republic"'.

2   Hugo Frey and Stefan Jordan, 'National Historians and the Discourse of the Other: France and Germany', in Stefan Berger and Chris Lorenz (eds), *The Contested Nation: Ethnicity, class, religion and gender in national histories* (Basingstoke: Palgrave Macmillan, 2008), p. 200; Taylor quoted in Tom Garvin, *Nationalist Revolutionaries in Ireland* (Oxford: Clarendon Press, 1987), p. 110.

3   Stefan Berger, *The Past as History: National identity and historical consciousness in modern Europe* (Basingstoke: Palgrave, 2015), p. 100.

4   See Carew in the volume, pp. 153–70.

5   F.J. Byrne, 'MacNeill the Historian', in F.X. Martin and F.J. Byrne (eds), *The Scholar Revolutionary: Eoin MacNeill, 1867–1945, and the making of the new Ireland* (Shannon: Irish University Press, 1973), pp. 17, 18.

6   W.E.H. Lecky, *A History of Ireland in the Eighteenth Century*, 5 vols (London: Longmans, 1913); Richard Bagwell, *Ireland under the Tudors*, 3 vols (London: Longmans, Green, 1885–90).

7   Byrne, 'MacNeill the Historian', p. 17.

8   MacNeill quoted in Carew in this volume, p. 163.

9   Robert Kee, *The Green Flag: A history of Irish nationalism* (London: Penguin, 2000), p. 554.

10 Conor Cruise O'Brien, *Parnell and His Party, 1880–90* (Oxford: Clarendon Press, 1957), p. 143.

11 Conor Mulvagh, *The Irish Parliamentary Party at Westminster, 1900–1918* (Manchester: Manchester University Press, 2016), pp. 2–3, 6.

12 Patrick Maume, *The Long Gestation: Irish nationalist life, 1891–1918* (Dublin: Gill & Macmillan, 1999), p. 14; Mulvagh, *The Irish Parliamentary Party*, p. 5.

13 Quoted in Michael Wheatley, *Nationalism and the Irish Party: Provincial Ireland, 1910–1916* (Oxford: Oxford University Press, 2005), p. 3.

14 John Hutchinson, *Nations as Zones of Conflict* (London: SAGE, 2005).

15 For a comprehensive list of MacNeill's publications see 'Appendix I: The Published Writings of Eoin MacNeill', in F.X. Martin and F.J. Byrne (eds), *The Scholar Revolutionary: Eoin MacNeill, 1867–1945, and the making of the new Ireland* (Shannon: Irish University Press, 1973), pp. 327–53.

16 Eoin MacNeill, *Phases of Irish History* (Dublin: M.H. Gill & Son, 1968), p. 1.

17 See this volume, Elva Johnston, '"By Blood and by Tradition": Race and empire in Eoin MacNeill's interpretation of early Ireland'.

18 MacNeill, *Phases*, p. 2.

19 Bruce Nelson, *Irish Nationalists and the Making of the Irish Race* (Princeton, NJ: Princeton University Press, 2012), p. 6; George L. Mosse, *Toward the Final Solution: A history of European racism* (New York: Fertig, 1985), pp. 45, 77.

20 L. Perry Curtis Jr, *Apes and Angels: The Irishman in Victorian caricature* (Newton Abbot: David & Charles, 1971); R.F. Foster, *Paddy and Mr Punch: Connections in Irish and English history* (London: Allen Lane, 1993).

21 Johnston in this volume, pp. 74–7.

22 MacNeill, *Phases*, p. 289. MacNeill, 'Medieval Irish Institutions', pp. 289–90.

23 Aidan Beatty, *Masculinity and Power in Irish Nationalism, 1884–1913* (Basingstoke: Palgrave Macmillan, 2016), pp. 4–6. This study explores the similarities between Irish nationalism and Zionism during the period.

24 Eoin MacNeill, *Celtic Ireland* (London: Leonard Parsons, 1921), p. xii; Eoin MacNeill, 'History', in Bulmer Hobson (ed.), *Saorstát Éireann: Irish Free State Official Handbook* (London: Talbot Press, 1932), p. 47.

25 William Ewart Gladstone, *Juventus Mundi: The gods and men of the heroic age* (London: Macmillan, 1869), p. 413.

26 F.J. Byrne, 'Tribes and Tribalism in Early Ireland', *Ériu*, vol. 22, 1971, pp. 129–30; Byrne, 'MacNeill the Historian', pp. 29, 32.

27 Donal McCartney, 'MacNeill and Irish-Ireland', in F.X. Martin and F.J. Byrne (eds), *The Scholar Revolutionary: Eoin MacNeill, 1867–1945, and the making of the new Ireland* (Shannon: Irish University Press, 1973), p. 94.

28 MacNeill, *Celtic Ireland*, p. xi.

29 Eoin MacNeill, *Early Irish Laws and Institutions* (Dublin: Burns, Oates & Co., 1935), p. 96.

30 See Stephen H. Harrison, 'Re-fighting the Battle of Down: Orpen, MacNeill, and the Irish nation state', in Michael Brown and Stephen H. Harrison (eds), *The Medieval World and the Modern Mind* (Dublin: Four Courts Press, 2000), pp. 171–82 for a detailed treatment of the Orpen–MacNeill debate. See also Byrne, 'MacNeill the Historian', pp. 24–5; Donnchadh Ó Corráin, 'Nationality and Kingship in pre-Norman Ireland', in T.W. Moody (ed.), *Nationality and the Pursuit of National Independence* (Belfast: Appletree Press, 1978), p. 4.

31 Alice Stopford Green, *Irish National Tradition* (London: Macmillan, 1923), pp. 19–22.

32 MacNeill, *Celtic Ireland*, p. 177.

33 MacNeill papers, LA1/Q/69.

34 As put by Ó Corráin: 'The type of society that was emerging in Ireland in the eleventh and twelfth centuries was one that was moving rapidly in the direction of feudalism, and indeed bears some striking resemblances – in conservatism as well as in innovation – to European

society in the first age of feudalism.' Ó Corráin, 'Nationality and Kingship in pre-Norman Ireland', pp. 32–5.

35 MacNeill, 'History', pp. 53–4.

36 MacNeill papers, LA1/J/258.

37 MacNeill papers, LA1/D/204.

38 MacNeill, *Phases*, p. 346.

39 'Nationalism and the Future', MacNeill papers, LA1/J/146, p. 2.

40 MacNeill papers, LA1/D/64.

41 'Nationalism and the Future', pp. 1, 2.

42 MacNeill papers, LA1/D/64.

43 'Nationalism and the Future', pp. 2–3.

44 MacNeill papers, LA1/D/64.

45 MacNeill, *Phases*, pp. 114, 239–41.

46 Ibid., p. 271.

47 Ibid., p. 283.

48 Ibid., pp. 323–4.

49 'Nationalism and the Future', MacNeill papers, pp. 4, 5.

50 Text of a speech given by MacNeill in the United States, 1930, MacNeill papers, LA1/D/217. On 'nationality' as opposed to 'nationalism', see McCartney, 'MacNeill and Irish-Ireland', pp. 83–4 and Brian Farrell, 'MacNeill and Politics', in F.X. Martin and F.J. Byrne (eds), *The Scholar Revolutionary: Eoin MacNeill, 1867–1945, and the making of the new Ireland* (Shannon: Irish University Press, 1973), pp. 187–8.

51 'Nationalism and the Future', p. 9; Andrew Murphy, *Ireland, Reading, and Cultural Nationalism, 1790–1930* (Cambridge: Cambridge University Press, 2017), p. 112.

52 Murphy, *Ireland*, p. 113.

53 MacNeill, *Early Irish Laws*, p. 54.

54 MacNeill, *Phases*, pp. 227, 244, 246, 248.

55 *Handbook of the Ulster Question* (Dublin: North Eastern Boundary Bureau, 1923), p. 11.

56 For a thorough examination of MacNeill's role in the Boundary Commission, see in this volume Ted Hallett, 'Eoin MacNeill and the Irish Boundary Commission'.

57 *Handbook*, p. v.

58 Ibid.

59 John Mitchel, *The Life and Times of Aodh O'Neill, Prince of Ulster* (Dublin: James Duffy, 1845), pp. v–xii.

60 *Handbook*, p. v.

61 Ibid., pp. 39, 43.

62 Ibid., pp. 39, 40. Eoin MacNeill, 'From the Plantation to "Partition": A brief historic review', in W.G. Fitzgerald (ed.), *The Voice of Ireland: A survey of the race and nation from all angles* (Dublin: Virtue & Co., 1923), p. 201.

63 Quoted in Shane Nagle, *Histories of Nationalism in Ireland and Germany: A comparative study from 1800 to 1932* (London: Bloomsbury Academic, 2016), p. 101.

64 Friedrich Meinecke, *Geschichte der links-rheinischen Gebietsfragen* (Berlin: Reichsdrückerei, 1918), p. 2.

65 Ibid., p. 4.

66 Ibid., pp. 4–18.

67 Nagle, *Histories of Nationalism*, p. 101.

68 Friedrich Meinecke, *Cosmopolitanism and the National State*, trans. Robert F. Kimber (Princeton, NJ: Princeton University Press, 1970), p. 9. The positive connotation of the word 'tribe' in Meinecke's work is another point of contrast with MacNeill. As Byrne notes,

the German word *Stamm* had none of the problematic connotations of 'tribe' in the early twentieth-century Anglophone world. Byrne, 'Tribes and Tribalism', p. 128.

69 Meinecke, *Cosmopolitanism*, p. 10.

70 Ibid., pp. 10–11.

71 Ibid., p. 15.

72 Ibid., p. 16.

73 '... it cannot be the task of the modern national state to nullify these contradictions and reduce the national culture to one level': ibid., p. 17.

74 Ibid., p. 18.

75 There is an illustrating vignette in Ernie O'Malley's revolutionary 'memoir', *On Another Man's Wound*, in which he recalls finding, as a boy, a copy of Wolfe Tone's *Autobiography* in the library of his conservative, pro–Home Rule father. But the pages had not been cut, the book had never been read.

76 Byrne, 'MacNeill the Historian', p. 23. Alice Stopford Green, *History of the Irish State to 1914* (London: MacMillan, 1925), pp. vii–viii.

77 Éamon de Valera quoted in Carew, this volume, p. 161.

78 MacNeill, *Phases*, p. 248.

79 Seumas MacManus, *The Story of the Irish Race: A popular history of Ireland* (New York: The Irish Publishing Co., 1921), p. 385.

80 Aodh de Blácam, *Towards the Republic: A study of new Ireland's social and political aims*, 2nd edn (Dublin: Maunsel, 1919); Aodh de Blácam, *What Sinn Féin Stands For* (Dublin: Maunsel, 1921).

81 Michael Collins, *The Path to Freedom* (Dublin: The Talbot Press, 1922), p. 8.

82 Ibid., p. 20.

83 George L. Mosse, one of the foremost twentieth-century historians of European nationalism and fascism, argued that historians needed to be willing to take seriously 'the thought of minor, often obscure thinkers and novelists', precisely because they were more widely read, popular and influential than the canonical philosophers. This is an insight that is particularly pertinent for the history of Irish nationalism. Karel Plessini, *The Perils of Normalcy: George L. Mosse and the remaking of cultural history* (Madison: University of Wisconsin Press, 2014), pp. 38–60.

84 R.F. Foster, *Vivid Faces: The revolutionary generation in Ireland, 1890–1923* (London: Allen Lane, 2014)

85 '... we must avoid ... insisting that everything in ancient Ireland was perfect, deriving this perfection from the angelic virtue of the national character': MacNeill, *Phases*, p. 247.

86 MacNeill, *Early Irish Laws*, p. 56.

Eoin MacNeill and the Irish Boundary Commission. *Ted Hallett*

1 *Thomas Jones: Whitehall Diary. Volume III: Ireland, 1918–1925*, ed. Keith Middlemas (London: Oxford University Press, 1971).

2 Ronan Fanning, Michael Kennedy, Dermot Keogh and Eunan O'Halpin (eds), *Documents on Irish Foreign Policy [DIFP]*, vol. 1, 1919–1922 (Dublin: Royal Irish Academy, 1998), doc. 192, Griffith to de Valera, 9 Nov. 1921.

3 *DIFP*, vol. 1, doc. 197, Jones to Griffith, 16 Nov. 1921.

4 This was probably for consistency with the boundary commission provisions in the Versailles Treaty: Articles 88 (Upper Silesia) and 95 and 97 (East Prussia) provided for account to be taken of economic and geographic conditions in determining the boundaries between Germany and Poland.

5 It was not mentioned in the Irish cabinet discussion on 3 December, nor in the amendments proposed to the British on 4 December. *DIFP*, vol. 1 docs 209 and 210.

6   John O'Byrne, legal adviser to the delegation, drew Griffith's attention to the wording of
    Article 12 before the cabinet meeting, but neither Griffith nor Collins raised it: Paul Murray,
    The Irish Boundary Commission and Its Origins, 1886–1925 (Dublin: UCD Press, 2011),
    pp. 105–6 and 305. Murray accuses them of 'a lack of diligence' for failing to do so.

7   Collins said: 'we would save Tyrone and Fermanagh and parts of Derry, Armagh and Down'.
    DIFP, vol. 1, doc. 212.

8   *Hansard 5 (Commons)*, vol. 149, cc. 39–40, 14 Dec. 1921.

9   *Hansard 5 (Commons)*, vol. 149, c. 314, 16 Dec. 1921.

10 The Free State government set up the North Eastern Boundary Bureau (NEBB) in October
    1922 to collect evidence for the transfers. The NEBB prepared maximum and minimum
    claims, which the Executive Council considered on 5 June 1923. No specific claim was ever
    put to the Commission, but the Free State hoped to gain Derry city, substantial parts of
    Tyrone and Fermanagh, south Armagh and south Down, including Newry. Eamon Phoenix,
    *Northern Nationalism: Nationalist politics, partition and the Catholic minority in Northern
    Ireland, 1890–1940* (Belfast: Ulster Historical Foundation, 1994), pp. 288–9.

11 The Lloyd George coalition fell in October 1922. The Conservatives then held office until
    January 1924. Following election defeat, they were replaced by MacDonald's minority Labour
    government until the November 1924 election, when the Conservatives returned.

12 Cosgrave statement to the Dáil, 20 July 1923. He said MacNeill, Minister for Education,
    had been chosen 'after long and mature consideration' and had consented 'with great public
    spirit and self-sacrifice'; but given his view that the Irish commissioner should be a Catholic,
    a minister and a northerner, MacNeill was, at that time, the only candidate. Ernest Blythe, a
    minister and a northerner, was a Protestant, while Patrick McGilligan, a northern Catholic,
    did not join the Executive Council until April 1924. Geoffrey Hand ('MacNeill and the
    Boundary Commission', in F.X. Martin and F.J. Byrne (eds), *The Scholar Revolutionary:
    Eoin MacNeill, 1867–1945* (Shannon: Irish University Press, 1973), pp. 215–16) suggests
    that there was then some discussion of McGilligan taking over the role, but Cosgrave ruled
    that MacNeill's greater experience should prevail. Hand's source was McGilligan, from an
    interview conducted in 1967. Michael Tierney, 'Eoin MacNeill: A biographical study' (in
    Eoin MacNeill, *Saint Patrick*, ed. John Ryan SJ (Dublin: Clonmore & Reynolds, 1964),
    pp. 9–34) gives a similar account, citing an unnamed member of the Executive Council,
    again presumably McGilligan.

13 Dominions Office, 'Irish Boundary Negotiations: Diary of principal events, 1921–25',
    D 58509, no. 156. The Judicial Committee was the empire's highest court of appeal.

14 Lionel Curtis, secretary to the British delegation during the treaty negotiations and adviser
    on Irish affairs at the Colonial Office until October 1924. He had previously recommended
    Feetham be engaged to draft the treaty, but this was not taken up (Curtis letter to Jones, LG
    F/25/2/44).

15 Murray, *The Irish Boundary Commission*, p. 199; Kevin Matthews, *Fatal Influence: The
    impact of Ireland on British politics, 1920–25* (Dublin: UCD Press, 2003), p. 155. Both cite the
    'England expects' telegram which Curtis sent to Feetham as indicating that he 'knew his duty
    to those who appointed him'. A neutral interpretation of the telegram is, however, possible.

16 Curtis letter to Churchill, 19 Aug. 1924, Curtis papers MS 89, Bodleian Library, Oxford.
    Curtis also suggested, however, that Feetham had no preconceived view and 'would not allow
    himself to formulate a decision until he had before him the arguments of his two colleagues'.

17 Hand, 'MacNeill and the Boundary Commission', p. 221; Nicholas Mansergh, 'Eoin MacNeill:
    A reappraisal', *Studies: An Irish quarterly review*, vol. 63, no. 250, Summer 1974, pp. 133–40.

18 *Irish Free State (Agreement) Act, 1922. Report of the Judicial Committee of the Privy Council, as
    approved by Order of His Majesty in Council, of the 31st July, 1924, on the questions connected*

with the Irish Boundary Commission referred to the said Committee, 1–5 [Cmd. 2214], H.C. 1924, xi, 351–5.

19 Hand, 'MacNeill and the Boundary Commission', p. 230 suggests this was tacitly approved by Craig.

20 Boundary Commission Minutes, CAB 61/1 Minute 1.

21 Public Record Office of Northern Ireland (PRONI) CAB/9/Z/2/2.

22 PRONI D 3489/59/58.

23 Phoenix, *Northern Nationalism*, p. 290, suggests MacNeill saw his loyalty as being to his fellow commissioners rather than his Executive Council colleagues or northern nationalists, who were disconcerted to find 'they did not have the sympathetic ear of the Doctor'.

24 Bourdillon was Deputy British Commissioner on the Upper Silesia Commission. Boger served on the East Prussia and Upper Silesia Boundary Commissions. Bourdillon was an associate of Curtis and in December 1923 had sent him a memorandum with suggestions on how Article 12 should be interpreted (CO 739/25/60802).

25 CAB 61/1 Minute 2.

26 Executive Council Conclusions, 17 November 1924, TSCH S/1801/K. Hearne was Assistant Parliamentary Draughtsman in the Attorney General's Office. Later, he was a member of the Free State delegation to the 1926 and 1930 Imperial Conferences and assisted de Valera in drafting the 1937 Constitution. His legal expertise would have been valuable to MacNeill and might have stiffened his resolve in his disagreements with Feetham.

27 CAB 61/1 Minute 3.

28 Executive Council Conclusions, 4 Dec. 1924, TSCH S/1801/L. The contents of MacNeill's draft letter are not recorded, so the reason for Feetham's objection is unknown. It may have been a question of status, the Commission Minutes referring to an 'assistant secretary', while the Executive Council nominated Hearne as 'joint secretary'.

29 There is no letter in the Taoiseach's Department files or the Boundary Commission papers.

30 Feetham may have deferred discussion, anticipating that MacNeill and Fisher were unlikely to agree.

31 CAB 61/1 Minute 1.

32 The hearing took place on 4–5 December 1924. In advance, the Free State submitted a memorandum setting out its legal case against transfers to Northern Ireland. Commission report, vol. 2, Appendices 1 and 2.

33 The Free State team also included E.M. Stephens, secretary to the NEBB and Lavery, Lynch and Murnaghan (solicitors engaged by the NEBB), though only O'Byrne and Hanna spoke.

34 Hand 'MacNeill and the Boundary Commission', p. 232.

35 The commissioners' first tour was from 8 to 22 December, staying at Armagh, Enniskillen, Newtown Stewart and Derry. While they met local councillors and other prominent persons, no formal evidence was collected. Boundary Commission report, p. 9.

36 At Rostrevor, Armagh city and Newcastle in March, Enniskillen in April/May, Derry in May/June and Omagh in June/July.

37 Down sittings.

38 Derry sittings.

39 Boundary Commission report, Volume II, Appendix 3. The Belfast Water Commissioners said that a boundary north of the Mournes would put their main reservoir 'under a different jurisdiction' and thus at risk of disruption. The Executive Council were also concerned by submissions from Free State unionists in border areas seeking transfer to Northern Ireland.

40 Reid told Craig about the request in his letter of 30 July 1925, reporting that Fisher did not object because: 'on the previous occasion, they pitched their case so high and took such a long time about it, that they had the opposite effect to what they intended'.

41 Lynch replaced Hanna, who had become a judge. Lavery, Murnaghan and Stephens also attended.

42 O'Byrne argued at length that the wishes of the south Down inhabitants should not be subordinated to the economic concerns of Belfast.

43 Boundary Commission report, Volume II, Appendix 4.

44 *DIFP*, vol. 2, doc. 326.

45 This was as reported to him by Murnaghan. O'Byrne's diffident performance seems confirmed by his own report to Cosgrave: 'The hearing only lasted two hours and was not of a very important character. I spoke mainly on the Waterworks. I then said a few words about the right of the Commission to come on our side of the border, but I did not pursue the matter, as Feetham told me they had a record of what I had said before.' TSCH S/1801/O.

46 *DIFP*, vol. 2, doc. 326. Kennedy drafted a paper for MacNeill, examined below, but there is no record of them meeting to discuss it.

47 MacNeill Statement to the Executive Council, 21 Nov. 1925, *DIFP*, vol. 2, doc. 343.

48 Feetham's memorandum is annexed to Chapter III of the Commission's report.

49 There is no mention of the memorandum in the minutes at this time. The only reference occurs in Minute 29 of 21 Nov. 1921.

50 Commission report, p. 32.

51 *DIFP*, vol. 2, doc. 331.

52 MacNeill letter to Cosgrave, LA1/H/119. MacNeill also addressed Free State concerns about Feetham's views on the extent of transfers, suggesting that it was right to assume, whatever Feetham had said in questions to witnesses, that 'he still has an open mind'.

53 *DIFP*, vol. 2, doc. 343.

54 MacNeill papers, UCD, LA1/F/299.

55 *Dáil Éireann Debates*, vol. 13, no. 9, 24 Nov. 1925.

56 MacNeill papers, UCD, LA1/H/119.

57 'Reid–Craig Correspondence Relating to the Boundary Commission, July–November 1925', PRONI CAB/9/Z/2/2, Reid letter to Craig, 7 July 1925.

58 Fisher's confidence was presumably based on Feetham's questioning of witnesses, as the commissioners had not yet discussed principles of interpretation.

59 Reid letter to Craig, 15 July 1925.

60 CAB 61/1 Minute 16. Boger's schemes are in CAB 61/6. The sections were: 'A) Londonderry and East Donegal; B) Castlederg; C) West Fermanagh; D) South East Fermanagh; E) Monaghan salient; F) Newry and Armagh'.

61 In assessing the economic implications, Boger assumed that the customs barrier imposed by the Free State in April 1923 was a significant obstacle to trade.

62 The minutes do not record Boger's instructions, but he was presumably aware of Feetham's views and drew up his schemes accordingly.

63 Bourdillon's memoranda covered Bessbrook, Fermanagh, Keady and Newtown Hamilton, Londonderry and Strabane, Lough Erne, Newtown Butler and Newry, CAB 61/13.

64 Boger's schemes ran to seventy pages, plus maps, and Bourdillon's memoranda to 120.

65 MacNeill's role as Minister for Education may not have been too great a distraction, however. According to Patrick Maume and Thomas Charles-Edwards, he was 'largely inactive, as he saw the primary responsibility for education as lying with the churches, rather than the State': 'MacNeill, Eoin (John), 1867–1945', in James McGuire and James Quinn (eds), *Dictionary of Irish Biography from the Earliest Times to the Year 2002* (Cambridge: RIA and Cambridge University Press, 2009). MacNeill confirmed this in his article 'Ten Years of the Irish Free State', *Foreign Affairs*, vol. 10, no. 2, Jan. 1932, pp. 235–49. (The article contains no mention of the Boundary Commission, though it does refer to the annulment of the financial provisions of Article 5 of the treaty without saying how this came about.)

66 *Dáil Éireann Debates*, vol. 13, no. 9, 24 Nov. 1925. MacNeill implied that the way the evidence was presented made it difficult for him to see the overall picture.

67 CAB 61/1 Minutes 16, 17, 18 and 19.

68 Reid letter to Craig, 16 Sept. 1925.

69 Craig letter to Reid, 18 Sept. 1925.

70 Reid letter to Craig, 21 Sept. 1925. (Clear evidence here of the importance they attached to keeping the whole of their own county in Northern Ireland.)

71 Craig letter to Reid, 23 Sept. 1925.

72 CAB 61/1 Minutes 20–23.

73 Reid letter to Craig, 16 Oct. 1925. There is no record of the points MacNeill sought to reopen, but they presumably included Newry, which, with a 74 per cent Catholic population, seemed a clear candidate for transfer to the Free State. The letter indicates that MacNeill belatedly sought, unsuccessfully, to reverse some of the decisions that had gone against him.

74 CAB 61/1 Minute 24. The new border gave the Free State south Armagh, the Castlederg salient and parts of west and south Fermanagh, but Derry city, most of Tyrone and Fermanagh and south Down, including Newry, remained in Northern Ireland, which gained part of east Donegal and small areas of Monaghan. Transfers to the Free State were 183,290 acres and 31,319 persons and to Northern Ireland, 49,242 acres and 7,594 persons.

75 Geoffrey J. Hand (ed.), *Report of the Irish Boundary Commission, 1925* (Shannon: Irish University Press, 1969), p. xvii.

76 Hand, 'MacNeill and the Boundary Commission', p. 250.

77 The Conclusion to the Commission's report, completed after MacNeill's resignation, states explicitly that the decisions regarding the new border were recorded 'without dissent' in the minutes of 17 October.

78 CAB 61/1 Minute 25.

79 One feature of the new line illustrates MacNeill's difficulty: the most extensive of Boger's schemes for Section F would have transferred Newry to the Free State, but the Commission rejected this on the grounds that economic conditions favoured Newry remaining in Northern Ireland. MacNeill would have been well aware of his government's expectations but acquiesced in leaving Newry in Northern Ireland.

80 Reid letter to Craig, 18 Oct. 1925.

81 Fisher letter to Carson, 18 Oct. 1925, PRONI D1507/1/1925/6 and Hand, 'MacNeill and the Boundary Commission', Appendix C. Fisher's reference to control of the Erne flood gates and 'the Derry navigation to the open sea' is indicative of northern unionists' anxieties about waters. A particular concern was their claim to the whole of Lough Foyle, based on a charter of Charles II of 1662 which had assigned it to County Londonderry. The Free State maintained a counter-claim to Lough Foyle and all the waters adjacent to Northern Ireland, on the grounds that defining Northern Ireland in the Government of Ireland Act in terms of 'parliamentary Counties' meant that the adjacent waters were not included. The Boundary Commission did not endorse either claim, but in deciding on a boundary in Lough Foyle based on the main navigational channel that ran close to the Donegal shore it awarded virtually the whole lough to Northern Ireland. (See Boundary Commission files CAB 61/17 and /18 and. *DIFP*, vol. 2, doc. 316.)

82 CAB 61/1 Minute 26.

83 CAB 61/1 Minute 27.

84 Bourdillon sent the letters on 6 November.

85 *Morning Post*, 7 Nov. 1925.

86 'No important territory will go to Free State'; 'Changes proposed will consist of adjustments only'

87 The map was crudely drawn, suggesting a verbal rather than cartographic leak.

88 Fisher had given Reid, Craig and Carson a description of the Award and they may have passed on what they knew.

89 Reid letter to Craig, 7 Nov. 1925: 'You will have seen from the *Morning Post* that there has been some leakage in connection with the Boundary Commission. I have seen Fisher and he says he can't imagine how it was done unless the map makers have been got at.'

90 Fisher letter to Lynn, 7 Nov. 1925: 'You will have seen the "forecast" in the *Morning Post*. By dint of steady guessing they are bound to get somewhere near the truth in time. Our report will be ready for final signature in three weeks' time and it will probably be found not to be widely different from that in the *Morning Post.*'

91 Fisher letter to Lynn, 7 Nov. 1925.

92 Craig's public position was that Northern Ireland's territory had been 'finally decided upon' by the Government of Ireland Act, 1920 and could not be altered by a boundary commission. See Craig's letter to Lloyd George, 11 Nov. 1921 (*Correspondence between HM Government and the Prime Minister of Northern Ireland relating to the Proposals for an Irish Settlement*, 4–7 [Cmd. 1561], H.C. 1921, lxxxiii, 86–9, and Jones, *Whitehall Diary*, p. 240.) Fisher evidently feared that this would make it difficult for unionists to take a positive view of the Award, which explains his attempts to persuade Lynn to give it favourable coverage.

93 Fisher letter to Lynn, 11 Nov. 1925.

94 Hand, 'MacNeill and the Boundary Commission', examines how the crisis developed.

95 There was thus, as yet, nothing to indicate that MacNeill had agreed to the new border.

96 TSCH/3/S1801 O.

97 Conclusions of 10 Nov. 1925. These seem odd in the light of the crisis: 'It was decided that a) so far as signature of the Award was concerned, it is a matter for MacNeill's sole discretion; and b) that accordingly, the Council does not require to be kept informed of the proposed line beforehand.'

98 Conclusions of 13 and 18 Nov.

99 Hand, 'MacNeill and the Boundary Commission', p. 254.

100 Ibid. There is no record in MacNeill's papers or in TSCH/3/S1801 O.

101 LA1/H/121. That Fisher was unaware of MacNeill's doubts is suggested by his letter to Lynn of 18 Nov.: 'I have been sitting tight all this week. A publisher sent me a manuscript to read by the weekend. As John MacNeill is over in Dublin trying to get his Education Estimates through I shall just be able to get through it before he returns.' PRONI D3489/59/58.

102 Hand, 'MacNeill and the Boundary Commission', pp. 254–6, speculates on the timing of MacNeill's decision and whether it was made under pressure from Cosgrave, but draws no firm conclusions. MacNeill states in his unpublished memoirs that he resigned 'on instruction' from his government, but there is no record of any such instruction.

103 *DIFP*, vol. 2, doc. 343 (a third-person summary, presumably by the secretary, Diarmuid O'Hegarty) and CAB 61/1 Minute 28, with Feetham's draft statement attached.

104 *DIFP*, vol. 2, doc. 343 notes that he emphasised the word 'Revelations'.

105 This seems an attempt to cast doubt on Feetham's integrity by implying he was subject to external influence. As for the suggestion that Feetham and Fisher were anticipating his resignation, MacNeill appeared to have forgotten this when he drafted his memoirs, as he says there that his announcement 'took them by surprise'. (Brian Hughes (ed.), *Eoin MacNeill: Memoir of a revolutionary scholar* (Dublin: IMC, 2016), p. 120.)

106 This part of MacNeill's statement is puzzling. Could Feetham really have 'lost' his own copy of this key document and why did MacNeill not take back his annotated copy, which recorded his disagreements with Feetham? (MacNeill's copy appears not to have survived. It is not with the Boundary Commission papers, Feetham's papers at the Bodleian, or MacNeill's at UCD.)

107 *DIFP*, vol. 2, doc. 340.

108 CAB 61/1 Minute 29. This is the only reference to Feetham's memorandum in the Commission minutes. It confirmed that it had been given to MacNeill and Fisher on 11 September.

109 CAB 61/1 Minute 30, Annex A.

110 *DIFP*, vol. 2, doc. 345. Cosgrave's speech set out his view of the position regarding the Commission following the *Morning Post* leak. His remarks were clearly based on MacNeill's statement to the Executive Council the previous day. Hand, 'MacNeill and the Boundary Commission', p. 258, regrets Cosgrave's attack on Feetham and Fisher, but excuses his inflammatory language on the grounds that he was 'facing the gravest internal and external crisis since the end of the civil war'.

111 *Dáil Éireann Debates*, vol. 13, no. 9, 24 Nov. 1925.

112 Hand, 'MacNeill and the Boundary Commission', pp. 258–9; Ronan Fanning, *Independent Ireland* (Dublin: Helicon Press, 1983), p. 91; Phoenix, *Northern Nationalism*, p. 330.

113 The understanding on the desirability of a unanimous Award is not recorded in the Commission minutes, so there is no clear indication of its terms or when it was agreed. MacNeill said that the understanding came after the collation of evidence, but before the commissioners began their deliberations on the Award.

114 *Dáil Éireann Debates*, vol. 13, no. 9, 24 Nov. 1925. Feetham's view on the overriding power of economic and geographic conditions was set out in his memorandum. In listing his disagreements with Feetham, MacNeill surprisingly failed to mention transfers to Northern Ireland.

115 Hand describes MacNeill's attempt to answer the Feetham–Fisher statement as 'awkward' and his distinction between 'unanimity' and signing the award 'in common with the other Commissioners' as 'not easy to grasp'. Hand, 'MacNeill and the Boundary Commission', pp. 258–9.

116 *DIFP*, vol. 2, doc. 372. In an earlier letter of 7 December, Cosgrave said he had done 'remarkably well in the circumstances' and that he had been 'grossly unfair' to himself in his Dáil statement. MacNeill papers, LA1/H/126.

117 It is clear that they only became aware of MacNeill's agreement when Feetham and Fisher issued their statement on 23 Nov.

118 *DIFP*, vol. 2, doc. 352 and Jones, *Whitehall Diary*, p. 238.

119 *DIFP*, vol. 2, doc. 353.

120 O'Higgins' account gives insights into MacNeill's state of mind after the leak. *DIFP*, vol. 2, doc. 354.

121 *DIFP*, vol. 2, doc. 356 and Jones, *Whitehall Diary*, pp. 239–43. Bourdillon had given Baldwin the details the previous evening. He had also attempted to give them to the Free State delegation, but O'Higgins declined to see him.

122 Jones describes O'Higgins' statement as 'brilliant' and gives a colourful summary: 'MacNeill had behaved in an extraordinary manner: the Award was to be signed by all three because they desired peace and harmony; however the Award was formulated, it was to be signed by all three; but there was also to be a statement that there was not necessarily agreement. MacNeill was fettered by the undertaking he had given, and became increasingly unhappy. Then press leakage and exposure. MacNeill retracted his engagement to sign and refused to give the sanction and cloak of his name to the proceedings.' Jones, *Whitehall Diary*, p. 240.

123 *DIFP*, vol. 2, doc. 356.

124 Jones, *Whitehall Diary*, p. 242.

125 *DIFP*, vol. 2, doc. 364 and Jones, *Whitehall Diary*, p. 245.

126 *DIFP*, vol. 2, doc. 367. Churchill, Chancellor of the Exchequer, had conducted the negotiations on Article 5.

127 *DIFP*, vol. 2, doc. 367 and Jones, *Whitehall Diary*, p. 245.

128   *DIFP*, vol. 2, doc. 367. MacNeill had formed good relations with his colleagues and appears never to have pressed his disagreements with them to the point of acrimony or breakdown. A good example is his handling of Kennedy's paper on transfers to the North, which he declined to present in its original form, in case its direct criticisms offended Feetham. MacNeill papers, LA1/H/119.

129   Feetham's letter, sent to Baldwin with the report, on 7 December 1925 is in CAB 61/1.

130   *The Times*, 18 Dec. 1925. Feetham's disappointment is evident, both at the questioning of his integrity and that what he considered an objective redrawing of the border in accordance with Article 12 would not be implemented. Fisher, too, was disappointed that his 'good year's work for Ulster' had come to nothing, as revealed in his letter of 8 December 1925 to Lynn, suggesting that the Award would have been 'a legal and permanent decision by a parliamentary tribunal from which there would have been no appeal'.

131   Manuscript of statement to the Executive Council with regard to the proceedings of the Boundary Commission [Dec. 1925], MacNeill papers, LA1/F/300. Described as a draft statement to the Executive Council. There is no evidence that it was actually delivered, as there is no mention of it in the Taoiseach's Department files. It may be an example of MacNeill's tendency, noted by Maume, to draft papers setting out his views, but not sending them.

132   MacNeill papers LA1/F/290. It is in manuscript and it is not clear whether it was intended as a speech or a written statement. MacNeill suggests the Boundary Commission concept was repugnant to him, but the 'barbarous contrivance' had already been drawn by the Government of Ireland Act, 1920 and the Boundary Commission was merely intended to achieve a fairer separation, which he should presumably have welcomed. A variant of the quote appears in MacNeill's unpublished memoirs: '... it was nothing short of an outrage on Ireland ... to be asked to draw a line across this country dividing it on a basis of religious differences'. Hughes, *Eoin MacNeill: Memoir*, p. 119.

133   Hand, 'MacNeill and the Boundary Commission', Annex B, pp. 269–72 and Hughes, *Eoin MacNeill: Memoir*, pp. 118–21. MacNeill's contention that he had always expected that the Boundary Commission would not produce a satisfactory result has received some support from Hand and Tierney. Hand, 'MacNeill and the Boundary Commission', pp. 215–16, mentions a discussion shortly after McGilligan joined the Executive Council in April 1924 in which MacNeill told him that he did not believe the Commission would bring the benefits expected and that the outcome would damage the political career of the Irish commissioner. Hand's source was McGilligan, in a conversation in August 1967. Tierney, *Eoin MacNeill*, 1964, gives a similar account, citing an unnamed member of the then Executive Council, presumably McGilligan. There is room for doubt, however, whether this could really have been MacNeill's view at the time of his appointment. Cosgrave would hardly have nominated him if he had been aware of such doubts. There was, in any case, no reason at that time to take a pessimistic view of the likely outcome, as no chairman had been appointed and it was not known how the Commission would interpret the Article 12 remit.

134   By this stage, MacNeill's recollection of the understanding with his fellow commissioners was merely that he would not produce a minority report.

135   Hand, 'MacNeill and the Boundary Commission': 'he was not a suitable choice'. Michael Laffan, *Judging W.T. Cosgrave: The foundation of the Irish state* (Dublin: RIA, 2014), suggests appointing him was 'an unfortunate decision', p. 201. Murray, *The Irish Boundary Commission*, p. 307, even suggests his appointment was a sign Cosgrave did not take the Boundary Commission seriously but, if so, why would he have pressed the British government so insistently to set up it up?

136   O'Higgins would have been a more effective candidate, but he presumably would not have had the time to combine this with his Justice portfolio. O'Shiel had the legal expertise and knowledge of the border, but Cosgrave wanted a minister.

137 J.J. Lee, *Ireland 1912–1985: Politics and society* (Cambridge: Cambridge University Press, 1989), p. 147.

138 Mansergh, 'Eoin MacNeill: A reappraisal'.

139 Murray, *The Irish Boundary Commission*, p. 307.

140 K.J. Rankin, *The Provenance and Dissolution of the Irish Boundary Commission*, IBIS working paper no. 79 (UCD: IBIS, 2006), p. 26.

141 Tierney, *Eoin MacNeill*, p. 351.

142 Hand, 'MacNeill and the Boundary Commission', pp. 264–5: 'he resisted but he did not initiate'.

143 Maume, 'MacNeill, Eoin' (*DIB*) and Laffan, *Judging W.T. Cosgrave*, pp. 201–5. Maume ('MacNeill, Eoin') and Tierney (*Scholar and man of action*, p. 23) note that, after a nervous breakdown in 1897, MacNeill suffered from 'fits of lassitude', which may explain his passivity.

144 Matthews, *Fatal Influence*, pp. 220–1, is particularly critical of MacNeill's failure to mount an effective challenge to Feetham's memorandum.

145 'The duties of the Boundary Commission were entirely of a judicial character', MacNeill papers LA1/F/290.

146 Mansergh, 'Eoin MacNeill: A reappraisal', p. 140 and Maume, *DIB*.

147 Cosgrave's remark to Baldwin, 25 Nov. 1925; *DIFP*, vol. 2, doc. 352.

148 Hand, 'MacNeill and the Boundary Commission', pp. 264–5, suggests a minority report, or the threat of it, while having no legal effect, might have been a powerful political weapon.

Writing Home: understanding the domestic in the life of Eoin MacNeill. *Conor Mulvagh*

1 V.L. O'Connor, *A Book of Caricatures* (Dundalk: Wm Tempest, 1915) [not paginated]. UCD's copy marked SC 40.D.16 is a bequest of Éilis McDowell, daughter of Eoin MacNeill. For context, Douglas Hyde was described in the book as being 'at Home: All Ireland'; Alice Stopford Green 'in the Past'; Francis Joseph Bigger 'on the warpath'; Dr Starkie, 'At the gates of knowledge'; J.P. Mahaffy 'with his performing Irish bulls'; Dick Fitzgerald ['Dickeen'] 'in the Kingdom'; Patrick Daly 'seldom'; and Count Plunkett 'anywhere'.

2 Francis Shaw, 'MacNeill the Person', in F.X. Martin and F.J. Byrne (eds), *The Scholar Revolutionary: Eoin MacNeill, 1867–1945, and the making of the new Ireland* (Shannon: Irish University Press, 1973), p. 302.

3 In a reference to the delayed promise of Home Rule for Ireland, MacNeill reviewed the parade outside the old Irish Parliament on College Green. There were no speeches: *Irish Times*, 18 Mar. 1916, p. 6.

4 Máire MacNeill, 30 Sept. 1978, quoted in Maureen Murphy, 'Máire MacNeill (1904–1987)', *Béaloideas*, vol. 72, 2004, p. 4. This incident is also referenced in Séamus MacNeill's obituary, *Connacht Sentinel*, 21 Sept. 1993.

5 The subtitle given to MacNeill in his son-in-law's posthumously published biography: Michael Tierney, *Eoin MacNeill: Scholar and man of action, 1867–1945* (Oxford: Clarendon Press, 1980).

6 On MacNeill's decade of political activity, Brian Farrell notes: 'MacNeill was a reluctant political leader. Political activity was an episode in a crowded and productive life; it lasted barely a decade.' Brian Farrell, 'MacNeill and Politics', in Martin and Byrne (eds), *The Scholar Revolutionary*, p. 183.

7 Bonnie G. Smith, *The Gender of History: Men, women, and historical practice* (Cambridge MA: Harvard University Press, 1998), p. 84.

8 Ibid., pp. 83–4.

9 Ibid., p. 85.

10 Ibid.

11 Eoin adopted the spelling 'MacNeill' in preference to his brothers' and mother's 'McNeill' into which he was born. For a full discussion of the use of 'Eoin' and 'John' which MacNeill used interchangeably for most of his life, see Tierney, *Scholar and man of action*, p. 374 [1].

12 1901 Census. Several photographs of Hazelbrook, including family portraits taken on the house's steps, can be found preserved in the Tierney–MacNeill photographic collection. See, for example, Tierney/MacNeill Photographs, UCDA, LA30/PH/334; 339; 347.

13 Tierney, *Scholar and man of action*, p. 44.

14 Manuscript note on verso of 'Photograph of Hazelbrook House, Malahide' (UCDA, LA30/PH/334).

15 There are several inconsistencies in the McNeills' 1901 Census return. For whatever reason, Eoin and Agnes' sons Niall and Brian, b. 1899 and 1900, are not listed as resident. In Form A, Eoin's mother is listed as 'head of household' but in form B1 this position is given to his brother Charles. Presumably, the latter was filled out by the census enumerator. Whoever was head, the house was not owned by the McNeills, as a Mary Gaffney is listed as the owner both of their house and the neighbouring property. 1901 Census return forms A and B for Hazelbrook, Portmarnock, Dublin.

16 Maureen Murphy records: 'The children were given Irish names: Niall, Brian, Eibhlín, Turlough, Máire, Róisín, Séamus and Éilis; however, they preferred the affectionate nicknames they gave each other, some of which lasted a lifetime: Nug, Brug, Babby, Stakeo, Maria, Sasha, Kesk, and Eliza.' Murphy, 'Máire MacNeill', p. 2. Agnes had had eleven live births by 1911 and eight of her children survived infancy: Brian Hughes (ed.), *Eoin MacNeill: Memoir of a revolutionary scholar* (Dublin: IMC, 2016), p. x and 1911 Census return for 19 Herbert Park. Agnes and Eoin's children were, in order, Niall (1899–1969) [m. Edith née Crilly]; Brian (1900–22); Eibhlín (1901–91) [m. Michael Tierney]; Toirdhealbhach (more commonly Turlough) (1903–55); Máire (1904–87) [m. John L. Sweeney]; Róisín (1906–2001) (m. David D. Coyle); Séamus (1908–93) [m. Maribel née Ojembarrena] and Éilis (1914–2002) [m. Anthony McDowell]. Róisín's twin, Giollaspuic, died of a birth defect three days after he was born: *Connacht Sentinel, Connacht Tribune, Irish Times*, https://rip.ie/death-notice/maribel-macneill-galway-city-galway/287701, Civil birth registers, Department of Culture, Heritage and the Gaeltacht, IrishGenealogy.ie (https://civilrecords.irishgenealogy.ie/churchrecords/images/birth_returns/births_1906/01730/1683882.pdf: accessed 2 Sept. 2021); digital image, Róisín and Giollaspuic McNeill [sic] birth registrations, 7 Aug. 1906; filed 3 Sept. 1906 by P.J. Kiernan, Registrar in the District of Malahide in the Union of Balrothery in the County of Dublin, unidentified register, folio 339, "First Page," stamped no. 01683882, entry nos 32 & 33. Civil deaths registers, Department of Culture, Heritage and the Gaeltacht, IrishGenealogy.ie (https://civilrecords.irishgenealogy.ie/churchrecords/images/deaths_returns/deaths_1906/05554/4558659.pdf: accessed 2 Sept. 2021); digital image, Giollaspuic McNeill [sic] death registration, 10 Aug. 1906; filed 3 Sept. 1906 by P.J. Kiernan, Registrar in the District of Malahide in the Union of Balrothery in the County of Dublin, unidentified register, folio 255, "First Page," stamped no. 04558659, entry no. 300.

17 Tierney, *Scholar and man of action*, p. 97.

18 Murphy, 'Máire MacNeill', p. 1 and Eileen O'Brien, 'Woman of Aran [Maggie Dirrane]', *Irish Times* [Supplement], 18 Feb. 1984. In her interview with the *Irish Times* in 1984, Maggie Dirrane notes how her sister had also been sent to Dublin to work for Tom Clarke. Dirrane would later return home to Aran following a raid by British soldiers at Woodtown in 1916. Bairbre Ní Iarnáin (19 and a native of County Galway) is listed as a bilingual nurse and domestic servant on the MacNeill's 1911 Census return for 19 Herbert Park.

19 An account of this is in Tierney, *Scholar and man of action*, pp. 106–13. Tierney describes MacNeill's ailment as a 'severe cold', p. 107.

20 Hughes, *Eoin MacNeill: Memoir*, pp. 45–6.

21 Bulmer Hobson, *Ireland Yesterday and Tomorrow* (Tralee: Anvil, 1968), p. 35. For Hobson's account of his meeting with MacNeill, see pp. 43–4. The O'Rahilly skips over the goings-on in Herbert Park in his retelling of the foundation of the Irish Volunteers: The O'Rahilly, *The Secret History of the Irish Volunteers*, 3rd edn (Dublin: Irish Publicity League, 1915), pp. 3–4. For a modern account from Hobson's perspective, see Marnie Hay, *Bulmer Hobson and the Nationalist Movement in Twentieth-Century Ireland* (Manchester: Manchester University Press, 2009), pp. 111–12.

22 Michael Tierney, 'Eoin MacNeill: A biographical study', in Eoin MacNeill, *Saint Patrick*, ed. John Ryan SJ (Dublin: Clonmore & Reynolds, 1964), pp. 27–8.

23 For a full account of the authorship, editing and publication of *Eoin MacNeill: Scholar and man of action*, see Murphy, 'Máire MacNeill', pp. 20–1.

24 Eibhlín [but nominally Michael] Tierney, *Scholar and man of action*, p. 115.

25 Agnes MacNeill references the visit of Hobson and O'Rahilly to their home in November 1913 in her short statement to the Bureau of Military History but did not mention Eoin having come to speak to her during their visit in this particular deposition (MAI, BMH, WS 213 [Agnes MacNeill], p. 1).

26 Michael Kennedy, 'McNeill, James', in James McGuire and James Quinn (eds), *Dictionary of Irish Biography* (Cambridge: Cambridge University Press, 2009).

27 Tierney, *Scholar and man of action*, p. 98. The date of the move is not entirely certain but the DMP's 'Movements of Dublin Extremists' file for 23 Dec. 1915 notes 'John McNeill has removed from 19, Herbert Park to "Woodtown Park", Rathfarnham. R.I.C. informed.' Owen Brien [Superintendent, 'G' Division, DMP], 23 Dec. 1915 (NAI, CSO/JD/2/166(1)).

28 UCDA, LA1/K/142 contains sixteen family letters between Eoin, Agnes and the children and one from the governor of Lewes prison. The family letters from these months run to over 20,000 words. Letters to Eoin were limited to one folio of paper in Lewes so, in an early letter following his transfer there, he asked that, in replying, Agnes 'use only one sheet of paper – but let it be imperial foolscap at least': Eoin to Agnes MacNeill, n.d. [13 Jan. 1917], UCDA, LA1/K/142(6). There are an additional seven letters between Eoin and Agnes and Eoin and Eibhlín (UCDA, LA1/G/129; 131; 132; 149; 152; 153). These, along with some other letters, are referred to as 'a small sheaf of letters which [Eoin] wrote to various members of his family from Lewes between the end of March and the first half of May 1917', cited in Chapter 17 of Tierney's biography. None of the larger cache of letters now contained in LA1/K/142 of MacNeill's papers are cited by Tierney and it appears he was not aware of them when writing his chapter on Eoin's time in Dartmoor and Lewes. Chapter 17 of Tierney contains four full transcriptions from the LA1/G material: Eoin to Agnes MacNeill, Kilmainham, [29] May 1916 [Tierney, *Scholar and man of action*, pp. 240–1 (UCDA, LA1/G/131)]; Eoin to Agnes MacNeill, 'Railway Leaving Weston Super Mare', 31 May 1916 [Tierney, *Scholar and man of action*, pp. 241–2 (UCDA, LA1/G/132)]; Eoin to Agnes MacNeill, [Lewes], 26 Apr. 1917 [Tierney, *Scholar and man of action*, pp. 248–50 (UCDA, LA1/G/152)]; and Eoin to Eibhlín MacNeill, [Lewes], 12 May 1917 [Tierney, *Scholar and man of action*, pp. 251–2 (UCDA, LA1/G/153)].

29 Hughes, *Eoin MacNeill: Memoir*, pp. 107–8.

30 MAI, MSPC W24SP13724, p. 32.

31 Hughes, *Eoin MacNeill: Memoir*, p. 110. Turlough MacNeill is referred to by this spelling throughout this chapter as it is the version he himself used later in life. However, both in the 1911 Census and in the family's letters during Eoin's time in prison, all members of the family spelled his name in the older form of 'Toirdhealbhach' in seanchló or simply 'Toir' for short. A note on the spelling of his name can be found in Tierney, *Scholar and man of action*, p. 294.

32 Niall was interned for a total of three weeks according to his Military Service Pension application (MAI, MSPC W24SP10285, p. 58). Turlough was held for twenty-seven weeks until around 10 June 1921 (MAI, MSPC W24SP13724, pp. 14 and 32).

33 Turlough MacNeill categorically states that the family home was being used as an arms dump for his battalion in his pension application; his brother Niall, however, was less forthcoming about any such logistical information in both his pension and Bureau of Military History statements. Turlough MacNeill, MAI, MSPC W24SP12724, P. 32; MAI MSPC W24SP10285 [Niall MacNeill], pp. 7, 14, 18, 57–8 and MAI, BMH WS 69 [Niall MacNeill] which, unlike his pension application, does not cover any of his service beyond 1917. A detailed description of the Netley arms dump can be found in MAI, BMH WS 1768 [Andrew McDonnell], p. 68. On Netley being used as a safe house, see Eoin MacNeill's own recollection of two other boys staying with his sons on the night the house was first raided in November 1920: Hughes, *Eoin MacNeill: Memoir*, pp. 107–8. For a history of some other Dublin households that had caches of weapons prior to the 1916 Rising see Lucy McDiarmid, *At Home in the Revolution: What women said and did in 1916* (Dublin: RIA, 2015), p. 43.

34 MAI MSPC W24SP10285 [Niall MacNeill], p. 7.

35 MAI, MSPC W24SP13724 [Turlough MacNeill], pp. 13–14.

36 Eoin MacNeill, 'Ancient Irish Law: The law of status or franchise', *PRIA*, vol. 36C, 1923, pp. 265–316.

37 The most complete account of this anecdote, including its attribution to a student of Thurneysen's and not to the professor himself, comes from Revd Professor John Ryan and can be found in Tierney, *Scholar and man of action*, p. 293. See also Elva Johnston, this volume p. 68.

38 It is notable that a similar-type ambush was laid in an attempt to assassinate Niall MacNeill on his way to mass from Netley in April 1923. However, this earlier attempt was foiled owing to the fact that Niall went to a later mass that day. Tierney, *Scholar and man of action*, p. 313.

39 On the death of Agnes MacNeill, see UCDA, LA1/H/203–4. Maureen Murphy has pieced together the most comprehensive account of the MacNeills' house moves: Murphy, 'Máire MacNeill', p. 9.

40 Agnes to Eoin MacNeill [Woodtown Park, Rathfarnham], n.d. [Feb. 1917] (UCDA, LA1/K/142(11)).

41 For an early instance of letters between Eoin and Agnes being stopped at the censor's office, see Governor, Dartmoor Prison to Agnes MacNeill, 8 Dec. 1916 (IE UCDA, LA1/G/142).

42 Eoin to Agnes MacNeill, Lewes Prison, n.d. [13 Jan. 1917] (UCDA, LA1/K/142(6)).

43 Governor, Lewes Prison [Capt. Marriott] to Agnes MacNeill, 9 Feb. 1917 assuring her Eoin is well and there has been 'some delay in the Censor's office in relation to your husband's letters' (UCDA, LA1/K/142(7)).

44 Agnes to Eoin MacNeill, Woodtown Park, Rathfarnham, 12 Feb. 1917 (UCDA, LA1/K/142(8)).

45 Turlough to Eibhlín MacNeill, 'Friday morning' [3 Dec. 1920], Arbour Hill Military Detention Camp, quoted in full in Tierney, *Scholar and man of action*, pp. 294–5.

46 Hay, *Bulmer Hobson*, p. 201.

47 Agnes to Eoin MacNeill, Woodtown Park, Rathfarnham, 6 May 1917 (UCDA, LA1/K/142(16)).

48 Eoin MacNeill to his children [separate sections to each within single letter], n.d. [Mar. 1917] (UCDA, LA1/K/142(14)).

49 Eoin to Agnes MacNeill [Lewes Prison], 12 Feb. 1917 (UCDA, LA1/K/142 (9)).

50 'Dear Father', written in seanchló. For example, see Agnes and the MacNeill children [various] to Eoin MacNeill, 2 Apr. 1917 (UCDA, LA1/K/142(15)).

51 As Tierney notes, only the eldest, Niall, and the youngest Róisín stayed at Woodtown for the entirety of Eoin's incarceration. For a full account of where the family was scattered during this period and of the various acts of charity offered to the family in their time of need, see Tierney, *Scholar and man of action*, pp. 244–5.

52 Eoin MacNeill to his children [separate sections to each within single letter], n.d. [Mar. 1917] (UCDA, LA1/K/142(14)).

53 Agnes and the MacNeill children [various] to Eoin MacNeill, 2 Apr. 1917 (UCDA, LA1/K/142(15)).

54 William Murphy, *Political Imprisonment and the Irish, 1912–21* (Oxford: Oxford University Press, 2014), pp. 61–2.

55 Ibid., p. 62.

56 Agnes to Eoin MacNeill [Woodtown Park, Rathfarnham], n.d. [Feb. 1917] (UCDA, LA1/K/142(11)).

57 'You know how I would love to see you + have a talk with you but as you say the journey is so expensive and not altogether safe at this time on account of the submarine warfare. Though to be quite candid I would not mind that in the least if there was not the other consideration.' Agnes to Eoin MacNeill [Woodtown Park, Rathfarnham], n.d. [Feb. 1917] (UCDA, LA1/K/142(11)).

58 Agnes to Eoin MacNeill [Woodtown Park, Rathfarnham], n.d. [Feb. 1917] (UCDA, LA1/K/142(11)).

59 Eoin to Agnes MacNeill [Lewes Prison], 12 Mar. 1917 (UCDA, LA1/K/142(13)).

60 Fridtjof Nansen, 1861–1930, Norwegian explorer and, subsequently, humanitarian and League of Nations delegate. It is unclear which book or books MacNeill is referring to but a slew of books on Nansen were published in the late 1890s following his 'Fram expedition' to the North Pole, 1893–6. Notable among these is Fridtjof Nansen and Hjalmar Johansen, *Fridtjof Nansen's Farthest North: Being the record of a voyage of exploration of the ship "Fram" 1893–96 and of a fifteen months' sleigh journey*, 2 vols (London: Archibald Constable, 1897), which appears in at least one twentieth-century Irish private library collection (the Gerard Quinn Frost Collection now held by UCD Library Special Collections. I am grateful to Eugene Roche for his advice on this matter).

61 Eoin to Agnes MacNeill [Lewes Prison], 12 Mar. 1917 (UCDA, LA1/K/142(13)).

62 Agnes to Eoin MacNeill, Woodtown Park, Rathfarnham, 12 Feb. 1917 (UCDA, LA1/K/142(8)).

63 Eibhlín to Eoin MacNeill, Muckross Park [College], Donnybrook, 20 May 1917 (UCDA, LA1/K/142(17)).

64 It is unclear who this Siubhán is but she may have been a domestic servant who helped Agnes with the children. The MacNeills' previous domestic servant, Maggie Dirrane, had left the home in Woodtown, and the MacNeills' employ, after the rising when British soldiers 'burst into the room where she was sitting with the [MacNeill] children': Eileen O'Brien, 'Woman of Aran [Maggie Dirrane]', *Irish Times* [Supplement], 18 Feb. 1984.

65 Eoin to Agnes MacNeill [Lewes Prison], 12 Feb. 1917 (UCDA, LA1/K/142 (9)).

66 Eoin to Agnes MacNeill [Lewes Prison], 12 Feb. 1917 (UCDA, LA1/K/142 (9)).

67 Documents captured from Netley during the raids of November 1920 provide an interesting insight into the contents of Eoin MacNeill's desk at that time that were mainly political in nature. See Police File PF 91 forwarded to MacNeill by Frank Thornton, New Ireland Assurance Company, 9 Mar. 1942 (UCDA, LA1/G/160–8).

68 Shaw, 'MacNeill the Person', pp. 303–4.

69 Tierney, *Scholar and man of action*, p. 368.

70 Eoin MacNeill, 'Vivat!', *National Student*, vol. 5, no. 3, May 1915, p. 11.

71 Eoin MacNeill, Essay on the notion and development of civilisation [n.d.] (4pp) (UCDA, LA1/D/47).

72 For a wider discussion of horticultural nationalism (in the context of Horace Walpole) see Yu Liu, 'Castell's Pliny: Rewriting the past for the present', *Eighteenth-Century Studies*, vol. 43, no. 2, Winter 2010, pp. 254, 256.

73 Eoin to Charles McNeill, Arann [sic] Islands, Galway, 14 May 1892 (UCDA, LA1/G/284). I am grateful to Eileen Hogan for bringing this letter to my attention.

74 Tierney, *Scholar and man of action*, p. 247.

75 Eoin MacNeill to his children [separate sections to each within single letter], n.d. [Mar. 1917] (UCDA, LA1/K/142(14)).

76 Máire MacNeill, quoted in Murphy, 'Máire MacNeill', p. 9. According to Murphy, Eoin's youngest child Éilis lived in the house until 1973 and her son, Michael McDowell, my fellow contributor to this volume, grew up there.

77 Tierney, *Scholar and man of action*, p. 367.

78 Eoin to Agnes MacNeill [Dartmoor Prison], 1 June 1916 (UCDA, LA1/K/142(1)).

79 Eoin to Agnes MacNeill [Lewes Prison], 12 Dec. 1916 (UCDA, LA1/K/142(3)).

80 MacNeill had initially assumed Fernan Caballero was male but later wrote to Agnes that 'the Spanish author, Fernan Caballero, whose stories I got from the prison library here and was captivated by them, is a poetess, therefore Fernan Caballero (= Ferdinand Gentleman) is an assumed name. I would have not suspected that the stories were written by a woman. Among the books James sent me was a collection of short stories by modern Spanish writers. It did not include any by F. Caballero, & to my taste Caballero's are very much superior': Eoin to Agnes MacNeill [Lewes Prison], 12 Mar. 1917 (UCDA, LA1/K/142(13)). Fernán Caballero was the pseudonym of Cecilia Francisca Josefa Böhl de Faber y Ruiz de Larrea [Cecilia Böhl von Faber], 1796–1877, who was born to a German father and a Spanish-Irish mother. See James Fitzmaurice-Kelly, 'Caballero, Fernán', in Hugh Chisholm (ed.), *Encyclopaedia Britannica*, 11th edn (Cambridge: Cambridge University Press, 1913) and Amy Katz Kaminsky (ed.), *Water Lilies: An anthology of Spanish women writers from the fifteenth through the nineteenth century* (Minneapolis: University of Minnesota Press, 1996), p. 415.

81 Eoin to Agnes MacNeill [Lewes Prison], 12 Feb. 1917 (UCDA, LA1/K/142(9)).

82 Ibid.

83 Eoin to Agnes MacNeill [Lewes Prison], 12 Feb. 1917 (UCDA, LA1/K/142(9)), also cited in David McCullagh, *De Valera: Rise, 1882–1932* (Dublin: Gill, 2017), p. 110.

84 Tierney, *Scholar and man of action*, p. 147.

85 For further discussion of MacNeill's standing with his fellow prisoners, see Laffan in this volume, p. 186.

86 Eoin to the MacNeill children [various], n.d. [Mar. 1917] (UCDA, LA1/K/142(14)).

87 For an example of the interest MacNeill took in his students while in prison, see Eoin to Agnes MacNeill, [Lewes Prison], 12 Mar. 1917 (UCDA, LA1/K/142(13)).

88 Eoin to Agnes MacNeill, 'Railway Leaving Weston Super Mare', 31 May 1916 (UCDA, LA1/G/132), reproduced in full in Tierney, *Scholar and man of action*, pp. 241–2.

89 Eoin to Agnes MacNeill [Lewes Prison], 12 Feb. 1917 (UCDA, LA1/K/142(9)).

90 On Eoin's belief that he was embarking on a life sentence, see Tierney, *Scholar and man of action*, p. 240.

91 On political advancement at Lewes, see McCullagh, *De Valera: Rise*, p. 110. Not entirely consumed by politics, MacNeill also noted that de Valera was focusing on science while in prison: Eoin to Margaret MacNeill [sister], Lewes, 26 Mar. 1917 (UCDA, LA1/G/150). David McCullagh records how de Valera spent his various prison spells trying to conquer different topics in mathematics and physics: McCullagh, *De Valera: Rise*, p. 49. One notable

example of de Valera's political ambitions coming to the fore in Dartmoor involved MacNeill. In the often-repeated story of de Valera ordering his fellow prisoners to give an 'eyes left' to MacNeill when he arrived in Dartmoor's main hall, McCullagh argues de Valera was not simply showing respect to MacNeill but also asserting his own leadership and simultaneously firing a shot across the bow of Thomas Ashe and the other IRB men present. Unlike most previous retellings of this episode, McCullagh records that obedience to de Valera's order was underwhelming: McCullagh, *De Valera: Rise*, p. 104.

92 John Gore was also a member of the Provisional Committee of the Irish Volunteers with MacNeill. Tierney, *Scholar and man of action*, p. 118. Tierney identifies Gore as having been loyal to Redmond during the crisis over Redmond's nominees to the Provisional Committee (p. 140). See also Hobson, *Ireland*, p. 61 and Diarmuid Lynch, *The I.R.B. and the 1916 Insurrection* (Cork: Mercier Press, 1957), p. 96.

93 On Niall's work for Mr Gore, see Niall to Eoin MacNeill [Woodtown Park, Rathfarnham], n.d. [Feb. 1917] (UCDA, LA1/K/142(11)).

94 The 1911 Census has Hugh Aloysius MacNeill, who was a year Eoin's senior, living at 6 Sandford Parade. Hugo (Jr) was a year younger than his cousin Brian, and Dermot two years younger again. Like his brother Eoin, Hugh spelled his surname MacNeill in the 1911 Census, unlike Archie, Charles and James. On this less famous branch of the MacNeill family, see 'An Irishman's Diary', *Irish Times*, 16 June 2009, and John Simpson, 'The Reluctant Professor MacHugh', James Joyce Online: https://sites.google.com/site/jjonlinenotes/jioyce-s-people/machugh (accessed 24 Feb. 2021).

95 'The Wood Kerns'. Dinneen also offers the alternative translation of 'outlaws': Patrick S. Dinneen, *Foclóir Gaedhilge agus Béarla, an Irish-English Dictionary being a Thesaurus of the Words, Phrases and Idioms of the Modern Irish Language* (Dublin: Irish Texts Society, 1927 edition), p. 182.

96 Niall MacNeill, MAI, BMH WS 69, p. 3.

97 In a further instance of paternal emulation, just as Eoin became editor of the *Irish Volunteer* newspaper, Niall MacNeill founded and edited a newsletter for his own volunteers in the Fianna. The publication, *The Pioneer*, was of sufficient interest to the authorities that the second issue (and seemingly the sole surviving copy of the publication) is contained in a January 1916 report of the DMP's 'Movements of Dublin Extremists' files. The twelve-page paper contains articles, stories and submissions by Niall, his brother Brian, and their cousins Aodh (Hugo) and Diarmuid MacNeill. The O'Rahilly's son Aodhagan [Aodogán] and a boy named Emmet Mac Amhlaoibh are named in the correspondence column. *The Pioneer*, vol. 1, no. 2, 23 Dec. 1915; Owen Brien [Superintendent, 'G' Division, DMP], 'Movements of Dublin Extremists', 3 Jan. 1916 (NAI, CSO/JD/2/175).

98 Evidence of Col. J.J. O'Connell, 22 Jan. 1926, MAI MSPC W24SP10285 [Niall MacNeill], p. 32.

99 Brian MacNeill was a divisional adjutant at the time of his death according to Philip McConway. Philip McConway, 'TV Eye: A lost son', *History Ireland*, vol. 21, no. 2, Mar./Apr. 2013, p. 50.

100 See also McDowell, p. 28; Johnston, p. 69; and Hughes, p. 273 in the present volume.

101 Brian to Agnes MacNeill, Longford House, Ballisodare, County Sligo, 10 Aug. 1922 (UCDA, LA1/G/338).

102 Niall to Agnes MacNeill, Williams Hotel, Dundalk, 18 Aug. 1922 (UCDA, LA1/G/339).

103 Niall to Agnes MacNeill, Portsmouth Arms Hotel, Enniscorthy, 1 Sept. 1922 (UCDA, LA1/G/340).

104 Niall to Agnes MacNeill, Portsmouth Arms Hotel, Enniscorthy, 5 Sept. 1922 (UCDA, LA1/G/341).

105 *Irish Times*, 23 Sept. 1922, p. 6 and Michael McDowell, 'Family of Divided Loyalties that was Reunited in Grief', *Irish Times*, 27 Apr. 2015.

106 'There is only one thing missing, and that's that you aren't here with us, and we hope it won't be long until you're here with us': Niall to Eoin MacNeill, Leargán Riabhach, Letterkenny, Donegal, 27 July 1924 (UCDA, LA1/O/124).

107 See Eoin to Agnes MacNeill, Geneva, 6 Sept. 1923 (UCDA, LA1/G/215, available in *DIFP*, vol. 2, doc. 115).

108 Eoin to Agnes MacNeill, 6 Clements Inn, London WC2, 10 Sept. 1925 (UCDA, LA1/H/123(19)).

109 Eoin to Agnes MacNeill, Killyhevlin, Enniskillen, 27 Apr. 1925 (UCDA, LA1/H/123(7)); Killyhevlin, Enniskillen, 4 May 1925 (UCDA, LA1/H/123(8)); and 1 St Columb's Court, Derry, 15 May 1925 (UCDA, LA1/H/123(10)).

110 Funeral of Colonel Niall MacNeill, *Irish Times*, 10 Nov. 1969, p. 16.

111 Eoin to Agnes MacNeill, 1 St Columb's Court, Derry, 22 May 1925 (UCDA, LA1/H/123(17)). On a subsequent trip, Eoin's fourth grandson was born to Eibhlín while he was in the United States: Agnes to Eoin MacNeill [telegram], Blackrock, 27 Apr. 1930 (UCDA, LA1/G/71).

112 Máire to Eoin MacNeill, 'Holy Saturday [19 Apr.] 1930, Great Northern Hotel, Bundoran, County Donegal (UCDA, LA1/G/65). The trip was initiated at the last minute when Turlough entered a garda golf tournament at Rosses Point and asked his siblings if they wanted to fill up the car on his drive up.

113 Anne Dolan, *Commemorating the Irish Civil War: History and memory, 1923–2000* (Cambridge: Cambridge University Press, 2003), p. 3.

114 https://www.findagrave.com/memorial/146831102/brian-mac_neill (accessed 6 Feb. 2020).

115 The complex question of what Eoin knew or believed about the circumstances of Brian's death are summarised in McConway, 'TV Eye: A lost son', pp. 50–1.

116 Liam Burke, 1885–1950, general secretary and director of finance, Cumann na nGaedheal, 1925–34 and Fine Gael, 1934–50: 'Minutes exchanged between John A. Belton and Joseph P. Walshe concerning a lunch given by Éamon de Valera for Sir Robert Menzies, Dublin, 8–9 Apr. 1941' [NAI, DFA 235/106], in Catriona Crowe, Ronan Fanning, Michael Kennedy, Dermot Keogh and Eunan O'Halpin (eds), *Documents on Irish Foreign Policy*, vol. 7, no. 39 (Dublin: Royal Irish Academy, 2010).

117 One letter that summarised well the extent of Máire's involvement in her father's work is Máire to Eoin MacNeill, Netley, Blackrock, 28 Apr. 1930 (UCDA, LA1/G/72).

118 Máire to Eoin MacNeill, Netley, Blackrock, 26 Mar. [1930] (UCDA, LA1/G/58).

119 Eoin to Agnes MacNeill, Chicago, 25 Apr. [1930] (UCDA, LA1/G/70).

120 Maureen Murphy, 'Máire MacNeill, 1904–1987', *Béaloideas*, vol. 72, 2004.

121 Tierney, *Scholar and man of action*. Martin worked with the MacNeills in editing Tierney's biography of Eoin. Murphy, 'Máire MacNeill', pp. 18–21.

122 *Eoin MacNeill: Scholar and man of action, 1867–1945* was first published by Clarendon Press in 1980.

123 Murphy 'Máire MacNeill', p. 21.

124 Ibid.

125 Eoin MacNeill, *St Patrick,* ed. John Ryan SJ (Dublin: Clonmore & Reynolds, 1964).

126 Smith, *The Gender of History*, p. 83. The collaboration of Máire and Eibhlín MacNeill in Poulivaun in 1977, though temporary, fits with Smith's characterisation of sister combinations who, alongside 'female dynasties' and 'husband–wife collaborations' pervaded historical scholarship in the era of the 'Great Historians': Smith, *The Gender of History*, p. 84.

127 Hughes, *Eoin MacNeill: Memoir*, p. xii.

128 Tierney takes aim at Desmond Ryan and particularly Max Caulfield's *The Easter Rebellion* (London: Frederick Muller, 1964) for their misrepresentations of MacNeill: see Tierney, *Scholar and man of action*, p. 100.

129 Murphy, 'Máire MacNeill', p. 21.

130 Michael Kennedy, 'McNeill, Josephine', in James McGuire and James Quinn (eds), *Dictionary of Irish Biography from the Earliest Times to the Year 2002* (Cambridge: Royal Irish Academy and Cambridge University Press, 2009).

131 Eibhlín to Máire MacNeill, 23 June 1958 (UCDA, LA1/G/349).

132 F.X. Martin, 'Eoin MacNeill on the 1916 Rising', *Irish Historical Studies*, vol. 12, no. 47, Mar. 1961, pp. 226–71.

133 Edie MacNeill [née Crilly], Leixlip, County Kildare, 'Eoin MacNeill', *Irish Times*, 14 Apr. 1966, p. 11.

134 John Devoy, *Recollections of an Irish Rebel: The Fenian Movement. Its Origin and Progress. Methods of Work in Ireland and in the British Army. Why it Failed to Achieve its Main Object, but Exercised Great Influence on Ireland's Future. Personalities of the Organization. The Clan-na-Gael and the Rising of Easter Week, 1916. A Personal Narrative* (New York: Chas. P. Young, 1929).

135 Michael Tierney to Eoin MacNeill, 23 Apr. 1930 (UCDA, LA1/G/68).

136 MAI, BMH, WS 213 [Agnes MacNeill, 2 Mar. 1949], p. 2.

137 O'Connor, *A Book of Caricatures* [not paginated].

138 Máire MacNeill quoted in Murphy, 'Máire MacNeill', pp. 9–10. Murphy notes that the house was razed in the 1970s after Eoin's daughter Éilis McDowell and her family moved out.

His Own Words: MacNeill in autobiography and memoir. *Brian Hughes*

1 For an extensive catalogue of MacNeill's publications, see F.X. Martin, 'The Published Writings of Eoin MacNeill', in F.X. Martin and F.J. Byrne (eds), *The Scholar Revolutionary: Eoin MacNeill, 1867–1945, and the making of the new Ireland* (Shannon: Irish University Press, 1973); an earlier version was published as F.X. Martin, 'The Writings of Eoin MacNeill', *Irish Historical Studies*, vol. 4, no. 21, 1948, pp. 44–62.

2 Michael Tierney, *Eoin MacNeill: Scholar and man of action, 1867–1945*, ed. F.X. Martin (Oxford: Clarendon, 1980), pp. 54–5.

3 See Eoin MacNeill papers (UCDA, LA1/A–C) and Eoin MacNeill additional papers (UCDA, LA1/D–P); Eoin MacNeill papers (NLI MS 10,874–10,901).

4 The only dedicated biography of MacNeill remains Tierney's *Scholar and man of action*, published posthumously in 1980 several years after Martin and Byrne's collection of essays on MacNeill, *The Scholar Revolutionary*.

5 The memoir has been published as Brian Hughes (ed.), *Eoin MacNeill: Memoir of a revolutionary scholar* (Dublin: IMC, 2016). Subsequent references to the memoir in this chapter only are cited as 'Memoir' and utilise the original pagination from the typescript, which are indicated in bold text and square brackets within the 2016 published edition.

6 'Memorandum by Eoin MacNeill on the events leading up to the insurrection', 1917 (NLI, Bulmer Hobson papers, MS 13,174 (14)). Published as 'Memorandum II' (and hereafter referred to as Memorandum II) in F.X. Martin, 'Eoin MacNeill on the Easter Rising', *IHS*, vol. 12, no. 44, 1961, pp. 226–71. See also undated manuscript memoranda on the Howth Gun Running in 1914 (NLI, Bulmer Hobson papers, MS 13,174 (8)) and on John Redmond, the Irish Volunteers, and the so-called 'Paget Scheme' (NLI, Bulmer Hobson papers, MS 13,174 (8)).

7 Typescript note by Máire MacNeill, 10 Sept. 1947 (MAI, Bureau of Military History Contemporary Documents, BMH CD/7).

8 Ibid. See also Mulvagh in this volume, p. 254.

9 See Deirdre McMahon and Michael Kennedy, *Reconstructing Ireland's Past: A history of the Irish Manuscripts Commission* (Dublin: IMC, 2009).

10 Mallon to MacNeill, 4 Jan. 1940 (UCDA, LA1/G/371).

11 The report was eventually published, with an introduction by Geoffrey J. Hand, as *The Report of the Irish Boundary Commission, 1925* (Shannon: Irish University Press, 1969).

12 Mallon to MacNeill, 4 Jan. 1940 (UCDA, LA1/G/371).

13 Typescript note by Máire MacNeill, 10 Sept. 1947 (MAI, BMH CD/7).

14 Tierney, *Scholar and man of action*, p. xvi.

15 For more on the origins and nature of the Bureau of Military History see, for example, Diarmaid Ferriter, 'In Such Deadly Earnest', *The Dublin Review*, vol. 12, 2003, pp. 36-64; Evi Gkotzaridis, 'Revisionist Historians and the Modern Irish State: The conflict between the Advisory Committee and the Bureau of Military History', *IHS*, vol. 35, no. 137, 2006, pp. 99–116; Eve Morrison, 'Class, Gender & Occupation Among the Bureau of Military History Witnesses & Ernie O'Malley Interviewees Who Were "Out" in 1916', *Saothar*, vol. 41, 2016, pp. 59–67.

16 Typescript note by Máire MacNeill, 10 Sept. 1947 (MAI, BMH CD/7).

17 UCDA, LA1/G/371.

18 UCDA, LA1/G/372 and LA1/S.

19 MAI, BMH CD/7.

20 For MacNeill's family background and early childhood in Glenarm see Memoir, pp. 1–14.

21 Ibid., p. 11.

22 Ibid., p. 58.

23 Tierney, *Scholar and man of action*, p. 350.

24 Memoir, p. 52.

25 Ibid., p. 26.

26 Ibid., p. 68.

27 See ibid., pp. 112–29.

28 Manuscript memorandum by MacNeill, 1916 (NLI, Bulmer Hobson papers, MS 13,175 (15)). Published as 'Memorandum I' in Martin, 'MacNeill on the Easter Rising', pp. 234–40.

29 Manuscript notes by MacNeill, 9 May 1916 (NLI MS 13,175). MacNeill's daughter Eibhlín made a copy of the original pencil notes under the title 'Royal Arms', a reference to the heading on the paper (UCDA, LA1/G/126).

30 Martin, 'MacNeill on the Easter Rising', pp. 230–1. For the original see NLI MS 13,174 (14). MacNeill gave another account to Seán Fitzgibbon on 8 July 1944. Fitzgibbon was a member of the Irish Volunteers and had met with MacNeill in advance of the rising. Michael J. Lennon later published this account, after Fitzgibbon's death: *Irish Times*, 20 Apr. 1949; *Irish Times*, 21 Apr. 1949.

31 Memoir, p. 112.

32 MacNeill to Fr Rope (unsent), 31 May 1931 (UCDA, LA1/J/180).

33 Donal McCartney, 'MacNeill and Irish-Ireland', in Byrne and Martin (eds), *Scholar Revolutionary*, pp. 82–3. See Nagle, this volume, p. 193.

34 Memoir, p. 70.

35 Ibid., p. 26.

36 Ibid., pp. 113–14.

37 Memorandum II, pp. 248–9; Memoir, p. 118.

38 Tierney, *Scholar and man of action*, p. 265.

39 Memorandum II, p. 251.

40 Memoir, pp. 120, 143.

41 Memorandum II, p. 251.

42 Martin, 'MacNeill on the 1916 Rising', pp. 232–3.

43 Memoir, p. 145. See W. Alison Phillips, *The Revolution in Ireland, 1906–1923*, 2nd edn (London: Longmans, Green & Co., 1926 [1st edn 1923]), pp. 132–3.

44 Memoir, p. 115; Louis N. Le Roux, *Patrick H. Pearse*, trans. Desmond Ryan (Dublin: Talbot Press, 1932). The book was originally published in French as *La Vie de Pearse* before being adapted and revised by the author and translated by Ryan.

45 In Le Roux, *Pearse*, p. 239, MacNeill recalls that after the January 1916 meeting Pearse had suggested that 'Connolly was a little too unreasonable, but that he, Pearse, might persuade Connolly'. The memorandum itself states: 'Pearse remained with me after Connolly left, and he told me that he agreed with my attitude. He added that he was confident that he would himself persuade Connolly to abandon his project.' F.X. Martin has suggested this was a deliberate attempt to suit 'the picture of Pearse that he is presenting': Martin, 'MacNeill on the 1916 Rising', p. 252, n. 3.

46 Martin, 'MacNeill on the 1916 Rising', p. 257, n. 25. Martin (p. 231) also accused Le Roux of introducing several inaccuracies about MacNeill, contradicting in parts his earlier work, in a life of Thomas Clarke published in 1936.

47 Memoir, p. 73. See, also, similar comments about another meeting with Pearse and Seán Mac Diarmada in advance of the rising: Memoir, pp. 119–20.

48 Memoir, p. 160.

49 MacNeill to Le Roux, 12 Oct. 1936 (NLI MS 44,694).

50 Piaras Béaslaí, *Michael Collins and the Making of a New Ireland*, 2 vols (London: G.G. Harrap & Co., 1926). It was later revised and republished as one volume: *Michael Collins: Soldier and statesman* (Dublin: Talbot Press, 1937).

51 Memoir, p. 159. MacNeill believed the hostility was not the result of his countermanding order, but because he was not a 'doctrinaire republican' and never joined the IRB: Memoir, p. 143.

52 For more on this, see Eamon Phoenix, *Northern Nationalism: Nationalist politics, partition, and the Catholic minority in Northern Ireland, 1890–1940* (Belfast: Ulster Historical Foundation, 1994), pp. 49–54; A.C. Hepburn, *Catholic Belfast and Nationalist Ireland in the Era of Joe Devlin, 1871–1934* (Oxford: Oxford University Press, 2008), pp. 199–200.

53 Memoir, pp. 157–62.

54 Béaslaí, *Michael Collins*, pp. 248–9.

55 MacNeill to the editor, *The Universe*, 1 Dec. 1930 (UCDA, LA1/F/343).

56 Manuscript notes by MacNeill, 1 Feb. 1944 (UCDA, LA1/F/320); *Irish Times*, 31 Jan. 1944, 1 Feb. 1944, and 2 Feb. 1944. See also a short note in response to a published contribution to the Dáil by Frank Aiken on the killing of Kevin O'Higgins in 1927, to which MacNeill was a witness (UCDA, LA1/L/116).

57 *Irish Press*, 26 May 1933.

58 Manuscript statement by MacNeill, 1933 (UCDA, LA1/J/147).

59 *Irish Press*, 26 May 1933; Manuscript statement by MacNeill, 1933 (UCDA, LA1/J/147).

60 *Irish Press*, 29 May 1933.

61 *Irish Press*, 31 May 1933; *Irish Press*, 1 June 1933. Shortly afterwards, a former member of the Dublin Brigade wrote a letter claiming that he was the last Volunteer to speak to Joseph Plunkett before his execution and that Plunkett had told him, among other things, that the provisional government had sent an envoy to the Vatican and received benediction. Plunkett did visit the pope before the rising but his accounts of the meeting are unreliable. It is not possible at this remove to establish whether MacNeill had signed the order. See Oliver P. Rafferty, 'The Church and the Easter Rising', *Studies: An Irish quarterly review*, vol. 105, no. 417, 2016, pp. 53–5.

62 Manuscript note by MacNeill, 16 Oct. 1925 (UCDA, LA1/F/290).

63 See, for example, Memoir, p. 129; p. 130 [*Hansard*]; p. 149 [article in the *English Review*]; p. 169 [examples in the press]; pp. 186–7 [*Dáil Éireann Debates*].

64 Frank Percy Crozier, *Ireland for Ever* (London: Cape, 1932). See Memoir, pp. 78, 163.

65 Bulmer Hobson, *A Short History of the Irish Volunteers: Volume 1* was published by Candle Press later that year. Hobson never completed proposed additional volumes.

66 Draft letter from Hobson to MacNeill, 3 June 1918 (NLI MS 13,174 (4)). See also Marnie Hay, *Bulmer Hobson and the Nationalist Movement in Twentieth-Century Ireland* (Manchester: Manchester University Press, 2009), pp. 236–7.

67 MacNeill to Hobson, 8 June 1918 (NLI MS 13,161 (1)).

68 Hobson, *A Short History of the Irish Volunteers: Volume 1* (Dublin: Candle Press, 1918), p. v.

69 Memoir, p. 65.

70 Ibid., pp. 65–8, pp. 71–2, pp. 170–1. See also Manuscript notes by MacNeill, 1 Feb. 1944 (UCDA, LA1/F/320).

71 Memorandum II, p. 246.

72 Memoir, pp. 66, 155; Eoin MacNeill, *The Ulster Difficulty*, c.1921, p. 24 (NLI, P2435).

73 See, for example, Memoir, pp. 13–14, p. 93, p. 155, pp. 163–5.

74 Ibid., p. 13.

75 Ibid., pp. 71, 195–6.

76 Ibid., pp. 12–13.

77 Ibid., p. 164.

78 Ibid., p. 173.

79 See, for example, Peter Hart, *The I.R.A. and Its Enemies: Violence and community in Cork, 1916–1923* (Oxford: Oxford University Press, 1998); John Borgonovo, *Spies, Informers and the 'Anti-Sinn Féin Society': the intelligence war in Cork city, 1920–21* (Dublin: Irish Academic Press, 2006); Eunan O'Halpin, 'Problematic Killing during the War of Independence and Its Aftermath: Civilian spies and informers', in James Kelly and Mary Ann Lyons (eds), *Death and Dying in Ireland, Britain and Europe: Historical perspectives* (Sallins: Irish Academic Press, 2013), pp. 317–48; Anne Dolan, '"Spies and Informers Beware ..."', in Diarmaid Ferriter and Susannah Riordan (eds), *Years of Turbulence: The Irish revolution and its aftermath* (Dublin: UCD Press, 2015), pp. 157–71.

80 Typescript note by Máire MacNeill, 10 Sept. 1947 (MAI, BMH CD/7).

81 For a comprehensive account of the origins and work of the Boundary Commission, see Paul Murray, *The Irish Boundary Commission and Its Origins, 1886–1925* (Dublin: UCD Press, 2011). For MacNeill's part, see Geoffrey J. Hand, 'MacNeill and the Boundary Commission', in Martin and Byrne (eds), *Scholar Revolutionary*, pp. 201–75; Tierney, *Scholar and man of action*, pp. 340–55.

82 Tierney, *Scholar and man of action*, p. 350. This is also mentioned in the memoir (pp. 193–4) but MacNeill does not explicitly describe any regrets on this occasion.

83 Memoir, pp. 191–2.

84 MacNeill to Fr Rope (unsent), 31 May 1931 (UCDA, LA1/J/180).

85 Ibid. and Memoir, p. 185.

86 Memoir, p. 186.

87 Ibid., p. 146.

88 Ibid., p. 25.

89 Patrick Maume and Thomas Charles-Edwards, 'MacNeill, Eoin (John), 1867–1945', in James McGuire and James Quinn (eds), *Dictionary of Irish Biography from the Earliest Times to the Year 2002* (Cambridge: Royal Irish Academy and Cambridge University Press, 2009), vol. 6, pp. 150–4.

90 Memoir, p. 124.

91 Anne Dolan, *Commemorating the Irish Civil War: History and memory, 1923–2000* (Cambridge: Cambridge University Press, 2003), p. 3.

92 Memoir, pp. 197–8.

93 See, for example, an anecdote about Douglas Hyde from a Gaelic League meeting: Memoir p. 50; and another relating to Tim Healy: Memoir, p. 172.

94 Memoir, pp. 81–3.

The Political Legacy: an insider on the outside. *Diarmaid Ferriter*

1 Cited in R.F. Foster, *Vivid Faces: The revolutionary generation in Ireland, 1890–1923* (London: Allen Lane, 2014), p. 209.

2 MAI, BMH WS 1766, William O'Brien.

3 UCDA, LA1/G/120, Statement by Thomas MacDonagh, 23 Apr. 1916.

4 UCDA, LA1/G/121, June 1916.

5 Ronan Fanning, *Éamon de Valera: A will to power* (London: Faber & Faber, 2015), pp. 48–9.

6 Michael Laffan, *The Resurrection of Ireland: The Sinn Féin party, 1916–1923* (Cambridge: Cambridge University Press, 1999), pp. 119–20.

7 Ibid.

8 Charles Townshend, *The Republic: The fight for Irish independence, 1918–1923* (London: Penguin, 2014), p. 91

9 Ibid., p. 24.

10 Peter Hart, *Mick: The real Michael Collins* (London: Macmillan, 2005), pp. 138, 155.

11 J.J. Lee, *Ireland 1912–1985: Politics and society* (Cambridge: Cambridge University Press, 1989), pp. 18–19.

12 Foster, *Vivid Faces*, pp. 208–12.

13 Alvin Jackson, *Ireland 1798–1998: Politics and war* (London: Wiley-Blackwell, 1999), pp. 342–3.

14 Justin Dolan Stover, 'Delaying Division: Eoin MacNeill, John Redmond and the Irish Volunteers', *History Studies*, vol. 8, 2007, pp. 111–23.

15 Thomas Bartlett, *Ireland: A history* (Cambridge: Cambridge University Press, 2010), p. 385.

16 Peter Brown, 'How Revolutionary were the Irish Volunteers?', *History Ireland*, vol. 21, no. 6, Nov./Dec. 2013, pp. 32–6; MAI, BMH WS 51, Bulmer Hobson.

17 M.J. Kelly, *The Fenian Ideal and Irish Nationalism, 1882–1916* (London: Boydell, 2006), p. 208.

18 Gerard MacAtasney, *Tom Clarke: Life, liberty, revolution* (Dublin: Merrion, 2013), pp. 272–3.

19 Patrick Maume, *The Long Gestation: Irish nationalist life 1891–1918* (Dublin: Gill & Macmillan, 1999), p. 235.

20 Maureen Wall, 'The Background to the Rising from 1914 until the Issue of the Countermanding Order on Easter Saturday 1916', in K.B. Nowlan (ed.), *The Making of 1916: Studies in the history of the rising* (Dublin: Stationery Office, 1969), p. 160.

21 Charles Townshend, *Easter 1916: The Irish rebellion* (London: Allen Lane, 2006), pp. 347–9.

22 Ibid.

23 See Hughes in this volume, p. 259.

24 Brian Hughes (ed.), *Eoin MacNeill: Memoir of a revolutionary scholar* (Dublin: IMC, 2016), pp. x–xv.

25 Ibid.

26 Ibid.

27 Clara Cullen (ed.), *The World Upturning: Elsie Henry's Irish wartime diaries, 1913–1919* (Dublin: Merrion, 2013), entry for 15 Dec. 1913, pp. 22–3, at p. 22.

28 MacNeill to Fr Convery, 2 July 1904, cited in Michael Tierney, *Eoin MacNeill: Scholar and man of action, 1867–1945* (Oxford: Clarendon, 1980), p. 104.

29 Hughes, *Eoin MacNeill: Memoir*, p. 72: 'It teaches young people to regard their country or their nation not so much as a thing which they should be satisfied to serve, but rather a stage upon which they may expect to play a part in the drama of heroism and that notion has become very widespread ...'

30 Garret FitzGerald, *Reflections on the Irish State* (Dublin: Irish Academic Press, 2002), p. 3; Hughes, *Eoin MacNeill: Memoir*, p. 72.

31 Gerry White, "'They have Rights who dare maintain them": The Irish Volunteers, 1913–15', in John Crowley, Donal Ó Drisceoil, Mike Murphy and John Borgonovo (eds), *Atlas of the Irish Revolution* (Cork: Cork University Press, 2017), pp. 164–72, 183.

32 F.X. Martin and Eoin MacNeill, 'Eoin MacNeill on the 1916 Rising', *Irish Historical Studies*, vol. 12, no. 47, Mar. 1961, pp. 226–71.

33 Patrick Maume and Charles-Edwards, 'MacNeill, Eoin (John)', in James McGuire and James Quinn (eds), *Dictionary of Irish Biography from the Earliest Times to the Year 2002* (Cambridge: Royal Irish Academy and Cambridge University Press, 2009), vol. 6, pp. 150–4.

34 Martin and MacNeill, 'Eoin MacNeill on the 1916 Rising'.

35 Roisín Higgins, *Transforming 1916: Meaning, memory and the fiftieth anniversary of the 1916 Rising* (Cork: Cork University Press, 2012), p. 9.

36 Editor, 'Current Comment: 1966 and After', *Studies: An Irish quarterly review*, vol. 55, no. 217, Spring 1966, pp. 1–4.

37 Maume, *Long Gestation*, p. 176.

38 Higgins, *Transforming 1916*, p. 9.

39 Ibid., pp. 128–30.

40 Hart, *Mick*, p. 187.

41 Hughes (ed.), *Eoin MacNeill*, p. 117.

42 UCDA, P150/657, de Valera to Mary MacSwiney, 11 Sept. 1922.

43 Frank Gallagher, *Days of Fear* (Cork: Mercier, 1967), p. 41.

44 Townshend, *The Republic*, p. 19.

45 Ibid., p. 19.

46 Mel Farrell, *Party Politics in a New Democracy: The Irish Free State, 1922–37* (London: Palgrave Macmillan, 2017), pp. 87–9.

47 MacNeill instead decided to contest the safer option of the NUI constituency where he had topped the poll in 1923.

48 Farrell, *Party Politics*, p. 164.

49 Hughes, *Eoin MacNeill: Memoir*, p. xv.

50 *Dáil Éireann Debates*, vol. 1, no. 7, 19 Sept. 1922.

51 P.S. O'Hegarty, *The Victory of Sinn Féin: How it won it, and how it used it* (Dublin: Talbot Press, 1924), pp. 141–5.

52 Michael Kennedy, *Division and Consensus: The politics of cross-border relations in Ireland, 1925–1969* (Dublin: Institute of Public Administration, 2000), p. 9.

53 Lee, *Ireland*, pp. 18–22.

54 James Carty, *Ireland: From the Great Famine to the treaty of 1921* (Dublin: C.J. Fallon, 1951), pp. 143–4.

55 Eoin MacNeill, *The Ulster Difficulty* (Dublin, 1921), p. 24.

56 Keith Middlemas (ed.), *Thomas Jones: Whitehall diary. Volume III: Ireland, 1918–1925* (Oxford: Oxford University Press, 1971), p. 110.

57 Daithí Ó Corráin, "'Ireland in His Heart North and South": The contribution of Ernest Blythe to the partition question', *IHS*, vol. 35, no. 137, May 2006, pp. 61–80.

58 Diarmaid Ferriter, *The Border: The legacy of a century of Anglo-Irish politics* (London: Profile Books, 2019), p. 33.

59 Paul Murray, *The Irish Boundary Commission and Its Origins, 1886–1925* (Dublin: UCD Press, 2011), pp. 105–7.

60 NAI, Department of Taoiseach (DT) S1730, 27 Feb. 1923.

61 *Dáil Éireann Debates*, vol. 13, no 9, 24 Nov. 1925.

62 Michael Laffan, *The Partition of Ireland, 1911–1925* (Dundalk: Dundalgan Press, 1983), p. 98.

63 NAI, DT S11209, 'Deputation from Northern Ireland to the Provisional Government', 11 Oct. 1922.

64 NAI, DT S5750/2, 25 Jan. 1923.

65 Laffan, *Partition*, p. 99.

66 Eamon Phoenix, *Northern Nationalism: Nationalist politics, partition and the Catholic minority in Northern Ireland 1890–1940* (Belfast: Ulster Historical Foundation, 1994), p. 334.

67 UCDA, LA1/F/302, draft letter of reply to Healy letter in the *Irish Statesman*, Dec. 1925.

68 Michael Laffan, *Judging W.T. Cosgrave: The foundation of the Irish state* (Dublin: Royal Irish Academy, 2014), pp. 203–5.

69 Donnacha Ó Beacháin, *From Partition to Brexit: The Irish government and Northern Ireland* (Manchester: Manchester University Press, 2019), pp. 24–6.

70 Ibid.

71 *Dáil Éireann Debates*, vol. 13, no. 9, 24 Nov. 1925.

72 Ibid.

73 Ibid.

74 Murray, *Boundary Commission*, p. 109.

75 Hughes (ed.), *Eoin MacNeill*, p. 121.

76 Seán Ó Faoláin, 'All Things Considered – 2', *The Bell*, vol. 11, no. 3, Dec. 1945, pp. 761–9.

77 Ibid.

78 *Irish Times*, 12 July 1927.

79 John P. McCarthy, 'O'Higgins, Kevin Christopher', in McGuire and Quinn (eds), *Dictionary of Irish Biography*.

80 *Irish Times*, 14 July 1927.

Bibliography

MANUSCRIPT AND ARCHIVAL SOURCES

Military Archives, Ireland
Bureau of Military History (available at: https://www.militaryarchives.ie/
    collections/online-collections/bureau-of-military-history-1913-1921)
Military Service Pensions Collection (available at: https://www.militaryarchives.
    ie/collections/online-collections/military-service-pensions-collection-1916-
    1923)

National Archives of Ireland
Chief Secretary's Office, Crime Branch, Dublin Metropolitan Branch. Movements
    of Extremists, 29 May 1915–20 Apr. 1916 (NAI, CSO/JD/2)
Department of Foreign Affairs Series
Department of the Taoiseach Series
Irish Manuscripts Commission papers

National Library of Ireland
Bulmer Hobson papers
Eoin MacNeill papers (Ms. 10,874–10,901)
John Redmond papers (collection list no. 118)
Michael Joseph (The) O'Rahilly papers

National Photograph Archive [NLI]
Hogan-Wilson Collection

National University of Ireland, Galway, Archives
Bailiúchán an Athar Troy, Conradh na Gaeilge Archive

Oxford, Bodleian Library
Lionel Curtis papers

Parliamentary Archives, House of Lords, Westminster, London
David Lloyd George papers

Peabody Museum of Archaeology and Ethnology, Harvard University
E.A. Hooton papers

Public Record Office of Northern Ireland
Fisher–Lynn Correspondence relating to the Boundary Commission, Nov.–Dec. 1925 (D3489/59/58)
Northern Ireland Government cabinet minutes
Reid–Craig Correspondence relating to the Boundary Commission, July–Nov. 1925 (CAB/9/Z/2/2)

Trinity College Dublin Archives
John Dillon papers
Thomas MacGreevy papers

United Kingdom National Archives
Cabinet papers
Dominions Office
Foreign and Commonwealth Office

University College Dublin Archives (UCDA)
Éamon de Valera papers (P150)
Eoin MacNeill additional papers (LA1/D–P)
Eoin MacNeill papers (LA1/A–C)
F.X. Martin papers (P189)
Tierney–MacNeill photographic collection (LA30)

NEWSPAPERS AND PERIODICALS

The Bell
Catholic Bulletin
Chicago Tribune
An Claidheamh Soluis
Connacht Sentinel
Connacht Tribune
Donegal Democrat
Freeman's Journal
Irish Independent
Irish Press
Irish Statesman
Irish Times
Irish Volunteer

Irisleabhar na Gaedhilge / The Gaelic Journal
Morning Post
Munster News and Limerick and Clare Advocate
New York City Journal
New York Herald Tribune
Newry Telegraph
The Pioneer
Sligo Champion
The Standard
United Ireland
The Universe
Workers' Republic

OFFICIAL PUBLICATIONS

Correspondence between HM Government and the Prime Minister of Northern Ireland relating to the Proposals for an Irish Settlement, 1–12 [Cmd. 1561], H.C. 1921, lxxxiii, 83–94.

Dáil Éireann ... díosbóireachtaí páirliminte (parliamentary debates); tuairisg oifigiúil (official report). Dublin: Stationery Office.

Irish Free State (Agreement) Act, 1922. Report of the Judicial Committee of the Privy Council, as approved by Order of His Majesty in Council, of the 31st July, 1924, on the questions connected with the Irish Boundary Commission referred to the said Committee, 1–5 [Cmd. 2214], H.C. 1924, xi, 351–5.

Irish Law Reports, *Little v. Cooper* [1937] IR 1.

Royal Commission on Trinity College, Dublin, and the University of Dublin. Appendix to the Final Report. Minutes of Evidence and Documents, i–543 [Cd. 3312], H.C. 1907, xli, 87–643.

Royal Commission on University Education in Ireland. Appendix to the Third Report. Minutes of Evidence Taken in April, May and June, 1902, i–671 [Cd. 1229], H.C. 1902, xxxii, 5–698.

The Parliamentary Debates (Hansard), Fifth Series, House of Commons. London: HM Stationery Office.

SECONDARY SOURCES

Ahlqvist, Anders (ed.), *The Early Irish Linguist: An edition of the canonical part of the Auraicept na nÉces*, Commentationes Humanarum Litterarum 73 (Helsinki: Societas Scientiarum Fennica, 1983)

Aldous, Richard, *Great Irish Speeches* (London: Quercus, 2009)

Allen, Nicholas, 'States of Mind: Science, culture and the intellectual revival, 1900–1930', *Irish University Review*, vol. 33, no. 1, Special Issue: new perspectives on the Irish Literary Revival, Spring–Summer 2003, pp. 150–64

'An Irish Priest' (ed.), *Wanted – An Irish University: Essays on university and kindred subjects* (Dublin: Sealy, Bryers & Walker, 1909)

Anderson, Benedict, *Imagined Communities: Reflections on the origin and spread of nationalism* (London: Verso, 1983)

[Anonymous], *A Plea for an Irish University: Essays, collected and edited by an Irish priest* (Dublin: Sealy, Bryers & Walker, 1909)

Anonymous [editorial], 'Current Comment: 1966 and after', *Studies: An Irish quarterly review*, vol. 55, no. 217, Spring 1966, pp. 1–4

Arensberg, Conrad M., *The Irish Countryman: An anthropological study* (London: Macmillan, 1937)

Arensberg, Conrad M. and Solon T. Kimball, *Family and Community in Ireland* (Cambridge, MA: Harvard University Press, 1940)

Ashman Rowe, Elizabeth, Colmán Etchingham, Máire Ní Mhaonaigh and Jón Viðar Sigurðsson, *Norse–Gaelic Contacts in a Viking World: Studies in the literature and history of Norway, Iceland, Ireland, and the Isle of Man* (Turnout: Brepols, 2019)

Bagwell, Richard, *Ireland under the Tudors*, 3 vols (London: Longmans, Green, 1885–90)

Barr, Colin, 'University Education, History, and the Hierarchy', in Lawrence W. McBride (ed.), *Reading Irish Histories: Texts, contexts, and memory in modern Ireland* (Dublin: Four Courts Press, 2003), pp. 62–79

Bartlett, Thomas, *Ireland: A history* (Cambridge: Cambridge University Press, 2010)

Beare, John I., *Trinity College, Dublin, and the Irish University Question: A non-political memorandum* (Dublin: Hanna & Neale, 1907)

Béaslaí, Piaras, *Michael Collins and the Making of a New Ireland*, 2 vols (London: G.G. Harrap & Co., 1926)

Béaslaí, Piaras, *Michael Collins: Soldier and statesman* (Dublin: Talbot Press, 1937)

Beatty, Aidan, *Masculinity and Power in Irish Nationalism, 1884–1913* (Basingstoke: Palgrave Macmillan, 2016)

Becker, Felicitas, 'Vernacular Ethnic Stereotypes: Their persistence and change in south-east Tanzania, *ca.* 1890–2003', in Alexander Keese (ed.), *Ethnicity and the Long-Term Perspective: The African experience* (New York: Peter Lang, 2010), pp. 93–126

Berger, Stefan, *The Past as History: National identity and historical consciousness in modern Europe* (Basingstoke: Palgrave, 2015)

Bergin, Osborn, 'Bardic Poetry', in David Green and Fergus Kelly (eds), *Irish Bardic Poetry: Texts and translation* (Dublin: DIAS, 2003 [first edition 1970])

[Bergin, Osborn] Crádh Croidhe Éigeas [pseud.], 'An tAthair Peadar', *An Branar*, vol. 2, pt 1, Lughnasa, 1920, pp. 2–5

Bergin, Osborn, 'Observations on "The Mythology of Lough Neagh"', *Béaloideas*, vol. 2, pt 3, Meitheamh, 1930, pp. 246–52

Bermingham, Kevin, *The Most Dangerous Book: The battle for James Joyce's* Ulysses (London: Penguin, 2014)

Best, R.I. and R. Thurneysen (introduction), *The Oldest Fragments of the Senchas Már from Ms. H. 2 15 in the Library of Trinity College*, Facsimiles in Collotype of Irish Manuscripts 1 (Dublin: Stationery Office, 1931)

Bieler, Ludwig (ed.), *Libri Epistolarum Sancti Patricii Episcopi*, 2 vols (Dublin: Stationery Office, 1952 [repr. 1993])

Bieler, Ludwig (ed. and trans.), *The Patrician Texts in the Book of Armagh* (Dublin: DIAS, 1979)

Binchy, D.A., 'Ancient Irish Law', *Irish Jurist*, vol. 1, 1966, pp. 84–92

Binchy, D.A., *Críth Gablach*, Mediaeval and Modern Irish Series 11 (Dublin: DIAS, 1941)

Binchy, D.A., 'Irish History and Irish Law II', *Studia Hibernica*, vol. 16, 1976, pp. 7–45

Binchy, D.A., 'MacNeill's Study of the Ancient Irish Laws', in F.X. Martin and F.J. Byrne (eds), *The Scholar Revolutionary: Eoin MacNeill, 1867–1945 and the making of the new Ireland* (Shannon: Irish University Press, 1973), pp. 37–48

Binchy, D.A., *Osborn Bergin*, The Osborn Bergin Memorial Lecture 1 (Dublin: University College Dublin, 1970)

Binchy, D.A., 'Patrick and His Biographers, Ancient and Modern', *Studia Hibernica*, vol. 2, 1962, pp. 7–173

Binchy, D.A., 'The Linguistic and Historical Value of the Irish Law Tracts', *Proceedings of the British Academy*, vol. 29, 1943, pp. 195–227. Reprinted in D. Jenkins (ed.), *Celtic Law Papers: Introductory to Welsh medieval law and government* (Bruxelles: Les Editions de la Librairie Encyclopédique, 1973), pp. 71–107

Bisagni, Jacopo, *Amrae Coluimb Chille: A critical edition* (Dublin: DIAS, 2019)

Bisagni, Jacopo, 'Prolegomena to the Study of Code-switching in the Old Irish Glosses', *Peritia*, vols 24–5, 2013–14, pp. 1–58

Black, Edwin, *War Against the Weak: Eugenics and America's campaign to create a master race* (New York: Thunder's Mouth Press, 2003)

Blatt, Jessica, *Race and the Making of American Political Science* (Philadelphia: University of Pennsylvania Press, 2018)

Blenner-Hassett, Roland, 'A Brief History of Celtic Studies in North America', *Proceedings of the Modern Language Association*, vol. 69, no. 4, pt 2, Sept. 1954, pp. 3–21

Boldt, Andreas D., *Leopold von Ranke: A biography* (Abingdon: Routledge, 2019)

Bolger, Teresa, Colm Moloney and Carmelita Troy, 'Archaeological Excavations at Lorrha, Co. Tipperary', *Journal of Irish Archaeology*, vol. 21, 2012, pp. 113–37

Borgonovo, John, *Spies, Informers and the 'Anti-Sinn Féin Society': The intelligence war in Cork city, 1920–21* (Dublin: Irish Academic Press, 2006)

[Borthwick, Norma (comp.)], *The Exclusion of Father Peter O'Leary from Irish Education* (Dublin: Irish Book Company, 1907)

Boylan, V. Rev. Patrick Canon (ed.), *Dublin, 1932 The Book of the Congress (XXXIst International Eucharistic Congress)* (Dublin: Veritas Publications, 1932)

Boyle, Elizabeth, 'Allegory, the *áes dána* and the Liberal Arts in Medieval Irish Literature', in Deborah Hayden and Paul Russell (eds), *Grammatica, Gramadach and Gramadeg: Vernacular grammar and grammarians in medieval Ireland and Wales*, Studies in the History of the Language Sciences, 125 (Amsterdam: John Benjamins, 2016), pp. 11–34

Bradshaw, Brendan and Tommy Graham, 'Interview: A man with a mission', *History Ireland*, vol. 1, no. 1, Spring 1993, p. 53

Brady, Ciarán (ed.), *Interpreting Irish History: The debate on historical revisionism, 1938–1994* (Dublin: Irish Academic Press, 1994)

Brannigan, John, *Race in Modern Irish Literature and Culture* (Edinburgh: Edinburgh University Press, 2009)

Breathnach, Diarmuid and Máire Ní Mhurchú, *Beathaisnéis 1882–1982*, 1 (Baile Átha Cliath: An Clóchomhar Tta, 1986)

Breathnach, Diarmuid and Máire Ní Mhurchú, *Beathaisnéis 1882–1982*, 2 (Baile Átha Cliath: An Clóchomhar Tta, 1990)

Breathnach, Edel, Review article: 'Medieval Irish History at the End of the Twentieth Century: Unfinished work', *Irish Historical Studies*, vol. 32, no. 126, Nov. 2000, pp. 260–71

Breathnach, Liam, 'Varia VI. 3: *Ardri* as an Old Compound', *Ériu*, vol. 37, 1986, pp. 192–3

Breathnach, Liam, *A Companion to the Corpus Iuris Hibernici* (Dublin: DIAS, 2005)

Breathnach, Liam, *The Early Irish Law Text* Senchas Már *and the Question of Its Date*, E.C. Quiggin Memorial Lectures 13 (Cambridge: Department of Anglo-Saxon, Norse and Celtic, University of Cambridge, 2011)

Breathnach, Pádraig A., '*Séadna*: Saothar ealaíne', *Studia Hibernica*, vol. 9, 1969, pp. 109–24

Briody, Mícheál, *The Irish Folklore Commission, 1935–1970: History, ideology and methodology*, Studia Fennica Folkloristica 17 (Helsinki: The Finish Literary Society, 2007)

Brown, Peter, 'How Revolutionary Were the Irish Volunteers?', *History Ireland*, vol. 21, no. 6, Nov./Dec. 2013, pp. 32–6

Brown, Stephen J., *The Central Catholic Library: The first ten years of an Irish enterprise* [*Messenger* magazine] (Dublin: Central Catholic Library Association, 1932)

Brown, Terence, *Ireland: A social and cultural history 1922–2002*, 3rd edn (London: Harper Perennial, 2004)

Bury, J.B., *Life of St Patrick and His Place in History* (London: Macmillan, 1905)

Byrne, Anne, Ricca Edmondson and Tony Varley, 'Arensberg and Kimball and Anthropological Research in Ireland: Introduction to the third edition', in Conrad Arensberg and Solon Kimball, *Family and Community in Ireland* (Ennis: Clasp Press, 2001), pp. 20–1

Byrne, Anne, Ricca Edmondson and Tony Varley. 'Arensberg and Kimball and Anthropological Research in Ireland', *Irish Journal of Sociology*, vol. 23, no. 1, 2015, pp. 22–61

Byrne, F.J., 'MacNeill the Historian', in F.X. Martin and F.J. Byrne (eds), *The Scholar Revolutionary: Eoin MacNeill, 1867–1945* (Dublin: Irish Academic Press, 1973), pp. 15–36

Byrne, Francis John, 'Tribes and Tribalism in Early Ireland', *Ériu*, vol. 22, 1971, pp. 128–66

Caerwyn Williams, J.E. and Máirín Ní Mhuiríosa, *Traidisiún Liteartha na nGael* (Baile Átha Cliath: An Clóchomhar Tta, 1979)

Caerwyn Williams, J.E. and Patrick K. Ford, *The Irish Literary Tradition* (Cardiff: University of Wales Press, 1992)

Carew, Mairéad, 'Eoin MacNeill: Revolutionary cultural ideologue', *Studies: An Irish quarterly review*, vol. 104, no. 417, 2016, pp. 67–75

Carew, Mairéad, 'Harvard, Celtic Skulls and Eugenics in de Valera's Ireland', *History Ireland*, vol. 26, no. 5, Sept./Oct. 2018, pp. 16–18

Carew, Mairead. 'Politics and the Definition of National Monuments: the "Big House problem"', *Journal of Irish Archaeology*, vol. 18, 2009, pp. 129–139

Carew, Mairéad. '"The Glamour of Ancient Greatness": The importance of the 1927 Lithberg Report to Irish archaeology', *Archaeology Ireland*, vol. 22, no. 1, Spring 2008, pp. 20–2

Carew, Mairéad, 'The Pageant of the Celt': Irish archaeology at the Chicago World's Fair', *Archaeology Ireland*, vol. 28, no. 1, Spring 2014, pp. 9–12

Carew, Mairéad, *The Quest for the Irish Celt: The Harvard Archaeological Mission to Ireland, 1932–1936,* (Sallins: Irish Academic Press, 2018)

Carty, James, *Ireland: From the Great Famine to the treaty of 1921* (Dublin: C.J. Fallon, 1951)

Castle, Gregory, *Modernism and the Celtic Revival* (Cambridge: Cambridge University Press, 2001)

Caulfield, Max, *The Easter Rebellion*, 2nd edn (Dublin: Gill & Macmillan, 1995)

Chapman Stacey, Robin, 'Ancient Irish Law Revisited: rereading the laws of status and franchise', in Katja Ritari, and Alexandra Bergholm (eds), *Understanding Celtic Religion: revisiting the pagan past, New Approaches to Celtic Religion and Mythology* (Cardiff: University of Wales Press, 2015), pp. 99–120

Chapman Stacey, Robin, *Dark Speech: The performance of law in early Ireland* (Philadelphia: University of Pennsylvania Press, 2007)

Chapman Stacey, Robin, 'Law and Literature in Medieval Ireland and Wales', in H. Fulton (ed.), *Medieval Celtic Literature and Society* (Dublin: Four Courts Press, 2005), pp. 65–82

Chapman Stacey, Robin, 'Ties that Bind: Immunities in Irish and Welsh law', *Cambridge Medieval Celtic Studies*, vol. 20, Winter 1990, pp. 39–60

Chapman Stacey, Robin, *The Road to Judgment: From custom to court in medieval Ireland and Wales* (Philadelphia: University of Pennsylvania Press, 1994)

Charles-Edwards, T.M., *Early Christian Ireland* (Cambridge: Cambridge University Press, 2000)

Charles-Edwards, T.M., *Early Irish and Welsh Kinship* (Oxford: Oxford University Press, 1993)

Charles-Edwards, T.M., '*Lebor na Cert* and Clientship', in K. Murray (ed.), *Lebor na Cert: Reassessments*, Irish Texts Society, Subsidiary Series 25 (London: Irish Texts Society, 2013), pp. 13–33

Charles-Edwards, T.M., 'The Pastoral Role of the Church in the Early Irish Laws', in John Blair and Richard Sharpe (eds), *Pastoral Care before the Parish* (Leicester: Leicester University Press, 1992), pp. 63–80

Charles-Edwards, T.M., *Wales and the Britons, 350–1064* (Oxford: Oxford University Press, 2012)

Clancy, T.O., 'Annat in Scotland and the Origins of the Parish', *Innes Review*, vol. 46, 1995, pp. 91–115

Clarke, Kathleen, *Revolutionary Woman 1878–1972: An autobiography*, ed. Helen Litton (Dublin: O'Brien Press, 1991)

Clarkson, L.A., 'James Eadie Todd and the School of History at the Queen's University of Belfast', *Irish Historical Studies*, vol. 41, no. 159, May 2017, pp. 22–40

Clery, Arthur E., 'The Reform of the Royal University', *New Ireland Review*, vol. 27, no. 6, Aug. 1907, pp. 324–5

Collins, Michael, *The Path to Freedom* (Dublin: The Talbot Press, 1922)

Collins, Michael and Hayden Talbot, *Michael Collins' Own Story* (London: Hutchinson & Co., 1923)

Coolahan, John, 'From Royal University to National University, 1879–1908', in Tom Dunne (ed.), *The National University of Ireland 1908–2008: Centenary essays* (Dublin: UCD Press, 2008), pp. 3–18

Coolahan, John, *Irish Education: Its history and structure* (Dublin: Institute of Public Administration, 1981)

Corcoran, Fr Timothy, SJ, 'How English May Be Taught without Anglicising', *The Irish Monthly*, vol. 51, no. 600, June 1923, pp. 269–73

Corcoran, Fr Timothy, SJ, 'The Integral Teaching of History', *The Irish Monthly*, vol. 57, no. 667, Jan. 1929, pp. 9–12

Corcoran, Fr Timothy, SJ, 'The New Secondary Programmes in Ireland', *Studies: An Irish quarterly review*, vol. 12, no. 46, June 1923, pp. 249–60

Corish, Patrick J., 'The Pastoral Mission in the Early Irish Church', *Léachtaí Cholm Cille*, vol. 2, 1971, pp. 14–25

Corlett, Christiaan and Michael Potterton (eds), *The Church in Early Medieval Ireland in the Light of Recent Archaeological Excavations* (Dublin: Wordwell, 2014)

Crowe, Catriona, Ronan Fanning, Michael Kennedy, Dermot Keogh, Eunan O'Halpin, Kate O'Malley and Bernadette Whelan (eds), *Documents on Irish Foreign Policy / Cáipéisí ar Pholasaí Eachtrach na hÉireann*, 12 vols (Dublin: Royal Irish Academy, 1998–2020)

Crozier, Frank Percy, *Ireland for Ever* (London: Cape, 1932)

Cullen, Clara (ed.), *The World Upturning: Elsie Henry's Irish wartime diaries, 1913–1919* (Dublin: Merrion, 2013)

Cullen, Ruairí, 'Professor John Wardell and University History in Ireland in the Early Twentieth Century', *Proceedings of the Royal Irish Academy*, section C, vol. 117, 2017, pp. 239–60

Cunningham, Bernadette, *The Annals of the Four Masters: Irish history, kingship and society in the early seventeenth century* (Dublin: Four Courts Press, 2014)

Curtis, L. Perry Jr, *Apes and Angels: The Irishman in Victorian caricature*, revised edn (Washington and London: Smithsonian Institution Press, 1997)

de Blácam, Aodh, *Gaelic Literature Surveyed* (Dublin: Talbot Press, 1929 [repr. 1974])

de Blácam, Aodh, *Towards the Republic: A study of new Ireland's social and political aims*, 2nd edn (Dublin: Maunsel, 1919)

de Blácam, Aodh, *What Sinn Féin Stands For* (Dublin: Maunsel, 1921)

de Blaghd, Earnán [Ernest Blythe], 'Hyde in Conflict', in Seán Ó Tuama (ed.), *The Gaelic League Idea* (Cork and Dublin: The Mercier Press, 1972), pp. 31–40

de Paor, Liam, *Saint Patrick's World: The Christian culture of the apostolic age* (Dublin: Four Courts Press, 1993 [revised edn, 1996])

de Paor, Liam, 'The Aggrandisement of Armagh', in T.D. Williams (ed.), *Historical Studies* 8 (Dublin: Gill & Macmillan, 1971), pp. 95–110

Devoy, John, *Recollections of an Irish Rebel: The Fenian Movement. Its Origin and Progress. Methods of Work in Ireland and in the British Army. Why it Failed to Achieve its Main Object, but Exercised Great Influence on Ireland's Future. Personalities of the Organization. The Clan-na-Gael and the Rising of Easter Week, 1916. A Personal Narrative* (New York: Chas. P. Young, 1929)

Dillon, Myles, *Lebor na Cert. The Book of Rights*, Irish Texts Society, 46 (Dublin: Irish Texts Society, 1962)

Dinneen, Patrick S., *Foclóir Gaedhilge agus Béarla. An Irish–English Dictionary being a Thesaurus of the Words, Phrases and Idioms of the Modern Irish Language* (Dublin: Irish Texts Society, 1927)

Doherty, Charles, 'The Cult of St Patrick and the Politics of Armagh in the Seventh Century', in Jean-Michel Picard (ed.), *Ireland and Northern France AD 600–850* (Dublin: Four Courts Press, 1991), pp. 53–94

Doherty, Gabriel, 'National Identity and the Study of Irish History', *English Historical Review*, vol. 111, no. 441, Apr. 1996, pp. 324–49

Dolan, Anne, *Commemorating the Irish Civil War: History and memory, 1923–2000* (Cambridge: Cambridge University Press, 2003)

Dolan, Anne, '"Spies and Informers Beware ..."', in Diarmaid Ferriter and Susannah Riordan (eds), *Years of Turbulence: The Irish revolution and its aftermath* (Dublin: UCD Press, 2015), pp. 157–71

Downham, Clare, 'The Career of Cearbhall of Osraighe', *Ossary, Laois and Leinster*, vol. 1, 2004, pp. 1–18

Duffy, P.J., 'The Shape of the Parish', in Elizabeth Fitzpatrick and Raymond Gillespie (eds), *The Parish in Medieval and Early Modern Ireland: Community, territory and building* (Dublin: Four Courts Press, 2006), pp. 33–61

Duffy, Seán, 'Historical Revisit: Goddard Henry Orpen, *Ireland under the Normans, 1169–1333* (1911–1920), *Irish Historical Studies*, vol. 32, no. 126, 2000, pp. 246–59

Dumville, D.N. (ed.), *Saint Patrick, AD 49–1993* (Woodbridge: Boydell, 1993)

Edwards, David, 'Salvaging History: Hogan and the Irish Manuscripts Commission', in Donnchadh Ó Corráin (ed.), *James Hogan: Revolutionary, historian, political scientist* (Dublin: Four Courts Press, 2001), pp. 116–32

Edwards, Robin Dudley, 'An Agenda for Irish History, 1978–2018', in Ciaran Brady (ed.), *Interpreting Irish History* (Dublin: Irish Academic Press, 1994), pp. 54–67

Edwards, Robin Dudley, 'Professor MacNeill', in F.X. Martin and Francis J. Byrne (eds), *The Scholar Revolutionary: Eoin MacNeill, 1867–1945, and the making of the new Ireland* (Shannon: Irish University Press, 1973), pp. 277–97

Edwards, Ruth Dudley, *Patrick Pearse: The triumph of failure* (London: Gollancz, 1977)

Edwards, Ruth Dudley, *The Seven: The lives and legacies of the founding fathers of the Irish Republic* (London: Oneworld, 2016)

Ellis, T.P., *Welsh Tribal Law and Custom in the Middle Ages*, 2 vols (Oxford: Clarendon Press, 1926)

Enright, Seán, *After the Rising: Soldiers, lawyers and trials of the Irish revolution* (Sallins: Irish Academic Press, 2016)

Eska, C.M., *Cáin Lánamna: An Old Irish treatise on marriage and divorce law*, Medieval Law and Its Practice 5 (Leiden/Boston: Brill, 2010)

Esposito, Mario, 'The Patrician Problem and a Possible Solution', *Irish Historical Studies*, vol. 10, no. 38, 1956, pp. 131–55

Etchingham, Colmán, 'Bishops, Church and People: How Christian was "Early Christian Ireland"?', in *L'Irlanda e gli Irlandesi nell'alto Medioevo: Spoleto, 16–21 aprile 2009,* Settimane di studio della Fondazione Centro Italiano di Studi sull'Alto Medioevo, vol. 57 (Spoleto: Presso la sede della Fondazione, 2010), pp. 325–48

Etchingham, Colmán, *Church Organisation in Ireland AD 650–1000* (Maynooth: Laigin, 1999)

Etchingham, Colmán, 'Early Medieval Irish History', in Kim McCone and Katharine Simms (eds), *Progress in Medieval Irish Studies* (Maynooth: St Patrick's College, 1996), pp. 123–53

Etchingham, Colmán, Review article: 'The "Reform" of the Irish Church in the Eleventh and Twelfth Centuries', *Studia Hibernica*, vol. 37, 2011, pp. 215–37

Evans, Nicholas, 'Royal Succession and Kingship among the Picts', *The Innes Review*, vol. 59, no. 1 (2008), pp. 1–48

Evans, Nicholas, *The Past and the Present in Medieval Irish Chronicles* (Woodbridge: Boydell & Brewer, 2010)

Fallon, Brian, *An Age of Innocence: Irish culture 1930–1960* (Dublin: Gill & Macmillan, 1998)

Fanning, Ronan, *Éamon de Valera: A will to power* (London: Faber & Faber, 2015)

Fanning, Ronan, *Independent Ireland* (Dublin: Helicon Press, 1983)

Farrell, Mel, *Party Politics in a New Democracy: The Irish Free State, 1922–37* (London: Palgrave Macmillan, 2017)

Fathers of the Society of Jesus (eds), *A Page of Irish History: Story of University College Dublin 1883–1909* (Dublin: Talbot Press, 1930)

Ferriter, Diarmaid, 'In Such Deadly Earnest', *The Dublin Review*, vol. 12, 2003, pp. 36–64

Ferriter, Diarmaid, *The Border: The legacy of a century of Anglo-Irish politics* (London: Profile Books, 2019)

FitzGerald, Desmond, *The Memoirs of Desmond FitzGerald 1913–1916*, ed. Fergus FitzGerald et al. (London: Routledge & Kegan Paul, 1968)

FitzGerald, Garret, *Reflections on the Irish State* (Dublin: Irish Academic Press, 2002)

Fitzmaurice-Kelly, James, 'Caballero, Fernán', in Hugh Chisholm (ed.), *Encyclopaedia Britannica*, 11th edn (Cambridge: Cambridge University Press, 1913)

Fitzpatrick, David, 'Decidedly a Personality: De Valera's performance as a convict', *History Ireland*, vol. 10, no. 2, Summer 2002, pp. 40–6

Fitzpatrick Dean, Joan, *All Dressed Up: Modern Irish historical pageantry* (Syracuse, NY: Syracuse University Press, 2014)

Flanagan, M.T., *The Transformation of the Irish Church in the Twelfth Century* (Woodbridge: Boydell, 2010)

Flechner, Roy, *Saint Patrick Retold: The legend and history of Ireland's patron saint* (Princeton, NJ: Princeton University Press, 2019)

Flechner, Roy and Sven Meeder (eds), *The Irish in Early Medieval Europe: Identity, culture and religion* (London: Palgrave, 2016)

Follett, Westley, *Céli Dé in Ireland: Monastic writing and identity in the early middle ages* (Woodbridge: Boydell & Brewer, 2006)

Fontaine, Janel M., 'Early Medieval Slave-trading in the Archaeological Record: Comparative methodologies', *Early Medieval Europe*, vol. 25, no. 4, 2017, pp. 466–88

Foster, R.F., 'History and the Irish Question', in *Transactions of the Royal Historical Society*, 5th series, vol. 33, 1983, pp. 169–92

Foster, R.F., *Paddy and Mr Punch: Connections in Irish and English history* (London: Allen Lane, 1993)

Foster, R.F., *Vivid Faces: The revolutionary generation in Ireland, 1890–1923* (London: Allen Lane, 2014)

Fottrell, George, *What is a National University?* (Dublin: Hodges, Figgis & Co., 1905)

Fox, Cyril, Review article: 'Christian Art in Ancient Ireland, vol. 1, edited by Dr Adolf Mahr, Keeper of Irish Antiquities, National Museum, Dublin, 1932', *Man*, vol. 32, Sept. 1932, p. 219

Foy, Michael and Brian Barton, *The Easter Rising* (Stroud: Sutton, 2004 [2nd edn, 2011])

French, Brigittine M., 'Linguistic Science and Nationalist Revolution: Expert knowledge and the making of sameness in pre-independence Ireland', *Language in Society*, vol. 38, no. 5, Nov. 2009, pp. 607–25

Frey, Hugo and Stefan Jordan, 'National Historians and the Discourse of the Other: France and Germany', in Stefan Berger and Chris Lorenz (eds), *The Contested Nation: Ethnicity, class, religion and gender in national histories* (Basingstoke: Palgrave Macmillan, 2008), pp. 200–30

Gallagher, Frank, *Days of Fear* (Cork: Mercier, 1967)

Gannon, Fr P.J., 'Literature and Censorship', *The Irish Monthly*, vol. 65, no. 769, July 1937, pp. 434–47

Garvin, Tom, *Nationalist Revolutionaries in Ireland 1858–1928* (Dublin: Gill & Macmillan, 2005 [1987])

Garvin, Tom, *The Lives of Daniel Binchy: Irish scholar, diplomat, public intellectual* (Sallins: Irish Academic Press, 2016)

Gaughan, J. Anthony (ed.), *Memoirs of Senator Joseph Connolly (1885–1961): A founder of modern Ireland* (Blackrock: Irish Academic Press, 1996)

Gellner, Ernest, *Nationalism* (London: Weidenfeld & Nicolson, 1997)

Gerig, John L., 'Celtic Studies in the United States', *The Columbia University Quarterly*, vol. 19, no. 1, Dec. 1916, pp. 30–43

Gillespie, Raymond and Brian P. Kennedy (eds), *Ireland: Art into history* (Dublin: Townhouse, 1994)

Gkotzaridis, Evi, 'Revisionist Historians and the Modern Irish State: The conflict between the advisory committee and the Bureau of Military History', *Irish Historical Studies*, vol. 35, no. 137, 2006, pp. 99–116

Gladstone, William Ewart, *Juventus Mundi: The gods and men of the heroic age* (London: Macmillan, 1869)

Green, Alice Stopford, *History of the Irish State to 1914* (London: Macmillan, 1925)

Green, Alice Stopford, *Irish National Tradition* (London: Macmillan, 1923)

Greene, David, 'The Founding of the Gaelic League', in Seán Ó Tuama (ed.), *The Gaelic League Idea* (Cork and Dublin: The Mercier Press, 1972), pp. 9–19

Gribbin, John, *Erwin Schrödinger and the Quantum Revolution* (London: John Wiley & Sons, 2012)

Haggart, Craig, 'The *Céli Dé* and the Early Medieval Irish Church: A reassessment', *Studia Hibernica*, vol. 34, 2006–7, pp. 17–62

Halpin, Attracta and Áine Mannion (eds), *Douglas Hyde: The Professor of Irish who became President of Ireland* (Dublin: National University of Ireland, 2016)

Hancock, W.N., T. O'Mahony, A.G. Richey, W.M. Hennessy and R. Atkinson, *The Ancient Laws of Ireland*, 6 vols (Dublin: Alexander Thom, 1865–1901)

Hand, Geoffrey J., 'MacNeill and the Boundary Commission', in F.X. Martin and Francis J. Byrne (eds), *The Scholar Revolutionary: Eoin MacNeill, 1867–1945, and the making of the new Ireland* (Shannon: Irish University Press, 1973), pp. 199–275

Hand, Geoffrey J., *The Report of the Irish Boundary Commission, 1925* (Shannon: Irish University Press, 1969)

Harland, James M., 'Rethinking Ethnicity and "Otherness" in Early Anglo-Saxon England', *Medieval Words*, vol. 5, 2017, pp. 113–42

Harrison, Stephen H., 'Re-fighting the Battle of Down: Orpen, MacNeill and the Irish nation state', in Michael Brown and Stephen H. Harrison (eds), *The Medieval World and the Modern Mind* (Dublin: Four Courts Press, 2000), pp. 171–82

Hart, Peter, *Mick: The real Michael Collins* (London: Macmillan, 2005)

Hart, Peter, *The I.R.A. and Its Enemies: Violence and community in Cork, 1916–1923* (Oxford: Oxford University Press, 1998)

Harvey, Anthony, 'Lexical Influences on the Medieval Latin of the Celts', in Maurillo Pérez González and Estrella Pérez Rodriguez (eds), *Influencias Léxicas de Otras Lenguas en el Latin Medieval* (León and Valladolid: Universidad de *Valladolid*/Universidad de *León*, 2011), pp. 65–77

Hay, Marnie, *Bulmer Hobson and the Nationalist Movement in Twentieth-Century Ireland* (Manchester: Manchester University Press, 2009)

Hayton, D.W., 'The Laboratory for "Scientific History": T.W. Moody and R.D. Edwards at the Institute of Historical Research', *Irish Historical Studies*, vol. 41, no. 159, May 2017, pp. 41–57

Healy, T.M., *Stolen Waters: A page of the conquest of Ulster* (London: Longmans, Green & Co., 1913)

Hepburn, A.C., *Catholic Belfast and Nationalist Ireland in the Era of Joe Devlin, 1871–1934* (Oxford: Oxford University Press, 2008)

Higgins, Michael D., *Renewing the Republic* (Dublin: Liberties Press, 2011)

Higgins, Roisín, *Transforming 1916: Meaning, memory and the fiftieth anniversary of the 1916 Rising* (Cork: Cork University Press, 2012)

Hobson, Bulmer, *A Short History of the Irish Volunteers*, vol. 1 (Dublin: Candle Press, 1918)

Hobson, Bulmer, *Ireland Yesterday and Tomorrow* (Tralee: Anvil Books, 1968)

Hogan, Edmund, *Onomasticon Goedelicum Locorum et Tribuum Hiberniae et Scotiae. An index, with Identifications, to the Gaelic Names of Places and Tribes* (Dublin: Hodges, Figgis & Co., 1910)

Hogan, James, 'The Irish Law of Kingship, with Special Reference to Ailech and Cénel Eoghain. With 7 plates', *PRIA*, vol. 40, 1932, pp. 186–254

Holm, Paul, 'Beyond Apathy and Antipathy: The Vikings in Irish and Scandinavian history', *Peritia*, vol. 8, 1984, pp. 151–69

Holm, Paul, 'The Slave Trade of Dublin, Ninth to Twelfth Centuries', *Peritia*, vol. 5, 1988, pp. 317–45

Holmes, David G., 'The Eucharistic Congress of 1932 and Irish Identity', *New Hibernia Review*, vol. 4, no. 1, Spring 2000, pp. 55–78

Hooton, Earnest Albert, *Apes, Men, and Morons* (New York: G.P. Putnam's Sons, 1937)

Horgan, John J., *Parnell to Pearse: Some recollections and reflections* (Dublin: Browne & Nolan Limited, 1948)

Hughes Brian (ed.), *Eoin MacNeill: Memoir of a revolutionary scholar* (Dublin: Irish Manuscripts Commission, 2016)

Hughes, Kathleen, *The Church in Early Irish Society* (London: Methuen, 1966)

Hutchinson, John, *Nations as Zones of Conflict* (London: SAGE, 2005)

Hutchinson, John, *The Dynamics of Cultural Nationalism: The Gaelic Revival and the creation of the Irish nation state* (London: Allen & Unwin, 1987)

Hyde, Douglas, 'A Great Irish Scholar', *Studies: An Irish quarterly review*, vol. 6, no. 24, Dec. 1917, pp. 663–8

[Hyde, Douglas] Dúbhghlas de hÍde, 'Litir, 14 Deireadh Fómhair 1938', i Eoin Ua Riain (eag.), *Féil-sgríbhinn Eóin Mhic Néill: Tráchtais léigheanta i n-onóir do'n ollamhain Eóin Mac Néill do sgríobh cáirde d'á cháirdibh i n-am a dheichmhadh bliadhna agus trí fichid, an cúigmhadh lá déag de mhí na Bealtaine, 1938* (Baile Átha Cliath: Three Candles, 1940)

Hyde, Douglas, 'The Necessity for de-Anglicising Ireland', in Charles Gavan Duffy (ed.), *The Revival of Irish Literature* (London: T. Fisher Unwin, 1894), pp. 117–61

Iggers, Georg G. and James M. Powell (eds), *Leopold von Ranke and the Shaping of the Historical Discipline* (Syracuse, NY: Syracuse University Press, 1990)

Irish, Tomás, *Trinity in War and Revolution 1912–1923* (Dublin: Royal Irish Academy, 2015)

Jackson, Alvin, *Ireland 1798–1998: Politics and war* (London: Wiley-Blackwell, 1999)

Jaski, Bart, *Early Irish Kingship and Succession* (Dublin: Four Courts Press, 2000)

Johnston, Elva, 'Eoin MacNeill's Early Medieval Ireland: A politics for scholarship or a politics of scholarship?', in Chris Jones, Conor Kostick and Klaus Oschema (eds), *Making the Medieval Relevant: How medievalists are revolutionising the present* (Berlin: De Gruyter, 2019), pp. 211–24

Johnston, Elva, 'Ireland in Late Antiquity: A forgotten frontier?', *Studies in Late Antiquity*, vol. 1, no. 2, 2017, pp. 107–23

Johnston, Elva, *Literacy and Identity in Early Medieval Ireland* (Woodbridge: Boydell & Brewer, 2013)

Jones, Greta, 'Eugenics in Ireland: The Belfast Eugenics Society, 1911–15', *Irish Historical Studies*, vol. 28, no. 109, 1992, pp. 81–92

Jones, Thomas, *Whitehall Diary. Volume III: Ireland, 1918–1925*, ed. Keith Middlemas (Oxford: Oxford University Press, 1971)

Katz Kaminsky, Amy (ed.), *Water Lilies: An anthology of Spanish women writers from the fifteenth through the nineteenth century* (Minneapolis: University of Minnesota Press, 1996)

Kee, Robert, *The Green Flag: A history of Irish nationalism* (London: Penguin, 2000)

Kelly, Adrian, *Compulsory Irish: Language and education in Ireland 1870s–1970s* (Dublin: Irish Academic Press, 2002)

Kelly, Fergus, *A Guide to Early Irish Law*, Early Irish Law Series 3 (Dublin: DIAS, 1988 [repr. 1991, 1995, 1998, 2003, 2005, 2009])

Kelly, M.J., *The Fenian Ideal and Irish Nationalism, 1882–1916* (London: Boydell, 2006)

Kennedy, Brian P., 'The Failure of the Cultural Republic: Ireland 1922–1939', *Studies: An Irish quarterly review*, vol. 81, no. 321, Spring 1992, pp. 14–22

Kennedy, Michael, *Division and Consensus: The politics of cross-border relations in Ireland, 1925–1969* (Dublin: Institute of Public Administration, 2000)

Kennedy, Michael, 'McNeill, James', in James McGuire and James Quinn (eds), *Dictionary of Irish Biography from the Earliest Times to the Year 2002* (Cambridge: Royal Irish Academy and Cambridge University Press, 2009)

Kennedy, Michael, 'McNeill, Josephine', in James McGuire and James Quinn (eds), *Dictionary of Irish Biography from the Earliest Times to the Year 2002* (Cambridge: Royal Irish Academy and Cambridge University Press, 2009)

Kenney, J.F., *The Sources for the Early History of Ireland. Volume 1: Ecclesiastical* (New York: Columbia University Press, 1929 [repr. 1966])

Kerr, W.S., *The Independence of the Church of Ireland* (London: Society for Promoting Christian Knowledge, 1931)

Kiberd, Declan and P.J. Mathews (eds), *Handbook of the Irish Revival: An anthology of Irish cultural and political writings 1891–1922* (Notre Dame, IN: Notre Dame University Press, 2015)

Knowles, David, *Great Historical Enterprises: Problems in monastic history* (Edinburgh: Thomas Nelson & Sons, 1963)

Laffan, Michael, *Judging W.T. Cosgrave: The foundation of the Irish state* (Dublin: Royal Irish Academy, 2014)

Laffan, Michael, *The Partition of Ireland, 1911–1925* (Dundalk: Dundalgan Press, 1983)

Laffan, Michael, *The Resurrection of Ireland: The Sinn Féin party, 1916–1923* (Cambridge: Cambridge University Press, 1999)

Lambkin, Brian, 'Blathmac and the Céili Dé: A reappraisal', *Celtica*, vol. 23, 1999, pp. 132–54

Le Roux, Louis N., *Patrick H. Pearse*, trans. Desmond Ryan (Dublin: Talbot Press, 1932)

Leabharlann Náisiúnta na hÉireann [National Library of Ireland], *Athbheochan na Gaeilge: Doiciméid staire* (Baile Átha Cliath: Leabharlann Náisiúnta na hÉireann, 1981)

Leary, Peter, *Unapproved Routes: A history of the Irish border 1922–1972* (Oxford: Oxford University Press, 2016)

Lecky, W.E.H., *A History of Ireland in the Eighteenth Century*, 5 vols (London: Longmans, 1913)

Lee, J.J., *Ireland 1912–1985: Politics and society* (Cambridge: Cambridge University Press, 1989)

Leerssen, Joep Theodor, *Mere Irish and Fíor-Ghael: Studies in the idea of Irish nationality, its development and literary expression prior to the nineteenth century* (Amsterdam: John Benjamins, 1996)

Leroy, Vail (ed.), *The Invention of Tribalism in Southern Africa* (Berkeley: University of California Press, 1989)

Lynch, Diarmuid, *The I.R.B. and the 1916 Insurrection* (Cork: Mercier, 1957)

Macalister, R.A.S. (ed.), *Lebor Gabála Érenn*, 5 vols (Dublin: Irish Texts Society, 1938–56)

Macalister, R.A.S and Eoin MacNeill (ed. & trans.), *Leabhar Gabhála* (Dublin: Hodges, Figgis & Co., 1916)

Mac Aodha, Breandán, 'Was This a Social Revolution?', in Seán Ó Tuama (ed.), *The Gaelic League Idea* (Cork and Dublin: The Mercier Press, 1972), pp. 20–30

Macardle, Dorothy, *The Irish Republic: A documented chronicle of the Anglo-Irish conflict and the partitioning of Ireland with a detailed account of the period 1916–1923*, 4th edn (Dublin: Irish Press, 1951)

MacAtasney, Gerard, *Tom Clarke: Life, liberty, revolution* (Dublin: Merrion, 2013)

MacCarron, Máirín, *Bede and Time: Computus, theology and history in the early medieval world* (Abingdon: Routledge, 2020)

McCarthy, D.P., *The Irish Annals: Their genesis, evolution and history* (Dublin: Four Courts Press, 2008)

McCarthy, John, *Kevin O'Higgins: Builder of the Irish state* (Dublin: Irish Academic Press, 2006)

McCarthy, John P., 'O'Higgins, Kevin Christopher', in James McGuire and James Quinn (eds), *Dictionary of Irish Biography from the Earliest Times to the Year 2002* (Cambridge: Royal Irish Academy and Cambridge University Press, 2009)

McCartney, Donal, 'MacNeill and Irish-Ireland', in F.X. Martin and F.J. Byrne (eds), *The Scholar Revolutionary: Eoin MacNeill, 1867–1945* (Shannon: Irish University Press, 1973), pp. 75–97

McCartney, Donal, *The National University of Ireland and Éamon de Valera* (Dublin: University Press of Ireland, 1983)

McCartney, Donal, *UCD: A national idea. The history of University College Dublin* (Dublin: Gill & Macmillan, 1999)

McConway, Philip, 'TV Eye: A lost son', *History Ireland*, vol. 21, no. 2, Mar./Apr. 2013, pp. 50–1

McCormack, W.J., 'What Is a Forgery or a Catalyst? The so-called "Castle document" of Holy Week, 1916', in Lisa Godson and Joanna Brück (eds), *Making 1916: Material and visual culture of the Easter Rising* (Liverpool: Liverpool University Press, 2015), pp. 57–69

MacCotter, Paul, *Medieval Ireland: Territorial, political and economic divisions* (Dublin: Four Courts Press, 2008)

MacCotter, Paul, 'The Exclave Parish and the Geography of Episcopacy in Ireland: 600 to 1300', in James Lyttleton and Matthew Stout (eds), *Church and Settlement in Ireland* (Dublin: Four Courts Press, 2018), pp. 101–18

MacCotter, Paul, 'The Origins of the Parish in Ireland', *PRIA*, vol. 119C, 2019, pp. 37–67

MacCotter, Paul, 'Túath, Manor and Parish: Kingdom of Fir Maige, cantred of Fermoy', *Peritia*, vol. 22–3, 2013, pp. 224–74

McCullagh, David, *De Valera: Rise, 1882–1932* (Dublin: Gill, 2017)

McDiarmid, Lucy, *At Home in the Revolution: What women said and did in 1916* (Dublin: Royal Irish Academy, 2015)

McDiarmid, Lucy, *The Irish Art of Controversy* (Ithaca, NY: Cornell University Press, 2005)

McDowell, R.B. and D.A. Webb, *Trinity College Dublin 1592–1952: An academic history* (Cambridge: Cambridge University Press, 1982)

MacErlean, J., 'A Bibliography of Fr Hogan, SJ', *Studies: An Irish quarterly review*, vol. 6, no. 24, Dec. 1917, pp. 668–71

McGarry, Fearghal, *Rebel Voices from the Easter Rising* (Dublin: Penguin, 2011)

McGarry, Fearghal, *The Rising: Ireland, Easter 1916* (Oxford: Oxford University Press, 2010)

McMahon, Deirdre and Michael Kennedy (eds), *Reconstructing Ireland's Past: A history of the Irish Manuscripts Commission* (Dublin: Irish Manuscripts Commission, 2009)

McMahon, Timothy G., *Grand Opportunity: The Gaelic Revival and Irish society, 1893–1910* (Syracuse, NY: Syracuse University Press, 2008)

MacManus, Seumas, *The Story of the Irish Race: A popular history of Ireland* (New York: The Irish Publishing Co., 1921)

Mac Mathúna, Liam, 'Réamhrá', in Peadar Ua Laoghaire, *Séadna* (Baile Átha Cliath: Cois Life Teoranta, 2011), pp. vii–lxx

Mac Mathúna, Liam, 'Seosamh Laoide: Eagarthóir', *Studia Hibernica*, vol. 31, 2000–1, pp. 87–103

MacNeill, Eoin, 'A Pioneer of Nations', *Studies: An Irish quarterly review*, vol. 11, no. 41, 1922, pp. 13–28

MacNeill, Eoin, 'A School of Irish Church History', *Studies: An Irish quarterly review*, vol. 21, no. 81, 1932, pp. 1–6

MacNeill, Eoin, 'Ancient Irish Law: The law of status or franchise', *Proceedings of the Royal Irish Academy*, vol. 36C, 1923, pp. 265–316

MacNeill, Eoin, 'Beginnings of Latin Culture in Ireland', *Studies: An Irish quarterly review*, vol. 20, no. 77, 1931, pp. 39–48

MacNeill, Eoin, 'Beginnings of Latin Culture in Ireland, part II', *Studies: An Irish quarterly review*, vol. 20, no. 79, 1931, pp. 449–60

MacNeill, E., *Celtic Ireland* (Dublin: Martin Lester Ltd., 1921 [repr. with new introduction and notes by Donnchadh Ó Corráin (Dublin: Academy Press, 1981)])

MacNeill, John [Eoin], *Celtic Religion*, Lectures on the History of Religions 1911 (London: Catholic Truth Society, 1935)

MacNeill, Eoin, 'Celtic Studies', *A Page of Irish History: Story of University College Dublin, 1883–1909*, compiled by the Fathers of the Society of Jesus (Dublin and Cork: Talbot Press, 1930), pp. 186–94

MacNeill, Eoin, 'Communal Ownership in Ancient Ireland, I–II', *Irish Monthly*, vol. 47, 1919, pp. 407–15, 463–74

MacNeill, Eoin, 'Contribution by Professor Eoin MacNeill, M.A., D.Litt', in Fathers of the Society of Jesus (eds), *A Page of Irish History: Story of University College Dublin, 1883–1909* (Dublin: Talbot Press, 1930), pp. 186–94

MacNeill, Eoin, 'Dates of Texts in the Book of Armagh Relating to Saint Patrick', *Journal of the Royal Society of Antiquaries of Ireland*, vol. 58, 1928, pp. 85–101

MacNeill, Eoin, *Early Irish Laws and Institutions* (Dublin: Burns, Oates & Washbourne, 1935)

MacNeill, Eoin, 'Early Irish Laws and Institutions', *New York University Law Quarterly Review*, vol. 8, no. 7, 1930–1, pp. 149–265

MacNeill, Eoin, 'Early Irish Laws and Institutions', *New York University Law Quarterly Review*, vol. 8, no. 8, 1930–1, pp. 81–108, 271–84

MacNeill, Eoin, 'Early Irish Population Groups: Their nomenclature, classification and chronology', *PRIA*, vol. 29C, 1911, pp. 59–114

MacNeill, Eoin, 'From the Plantation to "Partition": A brief historic review', in W.G. Fitzgerald (ed.), *The Voice of Ireland: A survey of the race and nation from all angles* (Dublin: Virtue & Co., 1923)

MacNeill, Eoin, 'History', in Bulmer Hobson (ed.), *Saorstát Éireann: Irish Free State Official Handbook* (London: Talbot Press, 1932), pp. 41–63

MacNeill, Eoin, 'Why and How the Irish Language Is To Be Preserved', *Irish Ecclesiastical Record*, vol. 12, Dec. 1891, pp. 1099–1108

MacNeill, Eoin, 'Ireland and Wales in the History of Jurisprudence', *Studies: An Irish quarterly review*, vol. 16, 1927, pp. 254–8, 605–15. Reprinted in D. Jenkins (ed.), *Celtic Law Papers: Introductory to Welsh medieval law and government* (Bruxelles: Les Editions de la Librairie Encyclopédique, 1973), pp. 171–92

MacNeill, Eoin, *Irish in the National University of Ireland: A plea for Irish education* (Dublin and Waterford: M.H. Gill & Son, Limited, 1909)

MacNeill, Eoin, 'Kinship in Irish Law', *JRSAI*, 6th series, vol. 17, 1927, pp. 154–5

MacNeill, Eoin, 'Law: Celtic', in E.R.A. Seligman and A. Johnson (eds), *Encyclopaedia of the Social Sciences*, vol. 9 (London: Macmillan, 1933), pp. 246–9

MacNeill, Eoin, 'Mocu, Maccu', *Ériu*, vol. 3, 1907, pp. 42–9

MacNeill, Eoin, 'On the Reconstruction and the Date of the Laud Genealogies', *Zeitschrift für celtische Philologie*, vol. 10, 1915, pp. 81–96

MacNeill, Eoin, *Phases of Irish History* (Dublin: Gill & Son, 1919 [repr. 1968])

MacNeill, Eoin, 'Prolegomena to a Study of *The Ancient Laws of Ireland*', *Irish Jurist*, vol. 2, 1967, pp. 106–15 (with an introduction and footnotes by D.A. Binchy).

MacNeill, Eoin (ed.), 'Poems by Flann Mainistrech on the Dynasties of Ailech, Mide and Brega', *Archivium Hibernicum*, vol. 2, 1913, pp. 37–99

MacNeill, Eoin, 'Reminiscences of Father O'Growney', in Agnes O'Farrelly (ed.), *Leabhar an Athar Eoghan. The O'Growney Memorial Volume* (Dublin: Gill, 1904), pp. 138–40

MacNeill, Eoin, *Saint Patrick, with a Memoir by Michael Tierney, and a Bibliography of Patrician Literature by F.X. Martin, O.S.A.*, ed. John Ryan (Dublin: Clonmore & Reynolds; London: Burns & Oates, 1964)

MacNeill, E., 'Some Irish Law Documents', *Gaelic Journal*, vol. 8, 1897, pp. 74–5, 86–90, 99–100, 114–15

MacNeill, Eoin, 'Ten Years of the Irish Free State', *Foreign Affairs*, vol. 10, no. 2, Jan. 1932, pp. 235–49

MacNeill, Eoin, 'The Authorship and Structure of the "Annals of Tigernach"', *Ériu*, vol. 7, 1914, pp. 30–113

MacNeill, Eoin, 'The Fifteenth Centenary of Saint Patrick: A suggested form of commemoration', *Studies: An Irish quarterly review*, vol. 24, 1924, pp. 177–88

MacNeill, Eoin, 'The Historical Saint Patrick', in Paul Walsh (ed.), *Saint Patrick, AD 432–1932, Fifteenth Centenary Memorial Book* (Dublin: Catholic Truth Society of Ireland, 1932), pp. 7–30

MacNeill, Eoin, 'The Hymn of St Secundinus in Honour of St Patrick', *Irish Historical Studies*, vol. 2, no. 6, Sept. 1940, pp. 129–53

MacNeill, Eoin, 'The Irish Law of Dynastic Succession', *Studies: An Irish quarterly review*, vol. 8, no. 31, Sept. 1919, pp. 367–82. Republished in idem, *Celtic Ireland* (Dublin: M.Lester Ltd, 1921 [repr. with new introduction and notes by D. Ó Corráin, Dublin: Academy Press, 1981]), pp. 114–43

MacNeill, Eoin, 'The Irish Law of Dynastic Succession, Part II', *Studies: An Irish quarterly review*, vol. 8, no. 32, Dec. 1919, pp. 640–53. Republished in idem, *Celtic Ireland* (Dublin: M. Lester Ltd., 1921 [repr. with new introduction and notes by D. Ó Corráin, Dublin: Academy Press, 1981]), pp. 114–43

MacNeill, Eoin, 'The Mythology of Lough Neagh', *Béaloideas*, vol. 2, pt 2, Nollaig, 1929, pp. 115–21

MacNeill, Eoin, 'The Origin of the Tripartite Life of Saint Patrick', *Journal of the Royal Society of Antiquaries of Ireland*, vol. 59, 1929, pp. 1–15

MacNeill, Eoin, 'The Other Patrick', *Studies: An Irish quarterly review*, vol. 32, no. 127, 1943, pp. 308–14

MacNeill, Eoin, *The Ulster Difficulty* (Dublin, 1921)

MacNeill, Eoin, 'Vivat!', *National Student*, vol. 5, no. 3, May 1915, p. 11

Mac Peaircín, Liam, *Gníomh Dóchais: Irisleabhar na Gaedhilge (1882–1909)* (Baile Átha Cliath: Coiscéim, 2018)

Mac Peaircín, Liam, '*Irisleabhar na Gaedhilge (1882–1909)*: Gníomh Dóchais na Teanga', in John Walsh and Peadar Ó Muircheartaigh (eds), *Ag Siúl an Bhealaigh Mhóir: Aistí in ómós don Ollamh Nollaig Mac Congáil* (Baile Átha Cliath: *Leabhair* COMHAR, 2016), pp. 291–312

Mafeje, Archie, 'The Ideology of "Tribalism"', *Journal of Modern African Studies*, vol. 9, no. 2, 1971, pp. 253–61

Mahr, Adolf, 'New Aspects and Problems in Irish Prehistory', Presidential Address for 1937, *Proceedings of the Prehistoric Society*, vol. 3, nos. 1–2, July–Dec. 1937, pp. 261–436

Mansergh, Nicholas, 'Eoin MacNeill: A reappraisal', *Studies: An Irish quarterly review*, vol. 63, no. 250, Summer, 1974, pp. 133–40

Marks, Jonathan, 'The Origins of Anthropological Genetics', *Current Anthropology*, vol. 53, supplement 5, 2012, pp. 161–72

Marron, Emmet, 'The Communities of St Columbanus: Irish monasteries on the continent?', *PRIA*, vol. 118C, 2018, pp. 1–28

Martin, F.X., 'Eoin MacNeill and the Easter Rising: Preparations', in F.X. Martin (ed.), *The Easter Rising, 1916 and University College Dublin* (Dublin: Browne & Nolan, 1966), pp. 3–31

Martin, F.X., 'Eoin MacNeill on the Easter Rising', *Irish Historical Studies*, vol. 12, no. 44, Mar. 1961, pp. 226–71

Martin, F.X., 'Michael Tierney, 1894–1975', in Michael Tierney, *Eoin MacNeill: Scholar and man of action, 1867–1945*, F.X. Martin (ed.) (Oxford: Clarendon, 1980), pp. vii–xiv

Martin, F.X. (ed.), *The Irish Volunteers 1913–1915* (Dublin: James Duffy, 1963)

Martin, F.X. and F.J. Byrne (eds), *The Scholar Revolutionary: Eoin MacNeill, 1867–1945 and the making of the new Ireland* (Shannon: Irish University Press, 1973)

Martin, F.X., 'The Writings of Eoin MacNeill', *Irish Historical Studies*, vol. 6, no. 21, 1948, pp. 44–62

Martin, Peter, *Censorship in the Two Irelands* (Dublin: Irish Academic Press, 2006)

Mathews, P.J., *Revival: The Abbey theatre, Sinn Féin, the Gaelic League and the co-operative movement* (Cork: Cork University Press, 2003)

Matthews, Kevin, *Fatal Influence: The impact of Ireland on British politics, 1920–25* (Dublin: UCD Press, 2003)

Maume, Patrick, 'Douglas Hyde', in Eugenio Biagini and Daniel Mulhall (eds), *The Shaping of Modern Ireland: A centenary assessment* (Sallins: Irish Academic Press, 2016), pp. 41–51

Maume, Patrick, 'MacNeill, Eoin (1867–1945)', in *Oxford Dictionary of National Biography* (Oxford: Oxford University Press, 2004)

Maume, Patrick, *The Long Gestation: Irish nationalist life, 1891–1918* (Dublin: Gill & Macmillan, 1999)

Maume, Patrick and Thomas Charles-Edwards, 'MacNeill, Eoin (John) (1867–1945)', in James McGuire and James Quinn (eds), *Dictionary of Irish Biography from the Earliest Times to the Year 2002* (Cambridge: Royal Irish Academy and Cambridge University Press, 2009), vol. 6, pp. 150–4

Meinecke, Friedrich, *Cosmopolitanism and the National State*, trans. Robert F. Kimber (Princeton, NJ: Princeton University Press, 1970)

Meinecke, Friedrich, *Geschichte der links-rheinischen Gebietsfragen* (Berlin: Reichsdrückerei, 1918)

Miller, David W., *Church, State and Nation in Ireland 1898–1921* (Dublin: Gill & Macmillan, 1973)

Miller, M., 'Matriliny by Treaty: The Pictish foundation-legend', in D. Dumville, R. McKitterick and D. Whitelock (eds), *Ireland in Early Mediaeval Europe: Studies in memory of Kathleen Hughes* (Cambridge: Cambridge University Press, 1982), pp. 133–61

Mitchel, John, *The Life and Times of Aodh O'Neill, Prince of Ulster* (Dublin: James Duffy, 1845)

Mohr, Thomas, 'Salmon of Knowledge', *Peritia*, vol. 16, 2002, pp. 360–95

Moody, T.W., 'The Irish University Question of the Nineteenth Century', *History*, vol. 43, no. 143, June 1958, pp. 90–109

Moody, T.W. and R.D. Edwards, 'Preface', *Irish Historical Studies*, vol. 1, no. 1, 1938, pp. 1–2

Moody, T.W. and J.C. Beckett (eds), *Queen's Belfast 1845–1949: The history of a university*, 2 vols (London: Faber & Faber, 1959)

Mooney, Canice, 'The Beginnings of the Irish Language Revival', *Irish Ecclesiastical Record*, vol. 64, July 1944, pp. 10–18

Moore, Walter, *Schrödinger: Life and thought* (Cambridge: Cambridge University Press, 1989)

Moran, Pádraic, *De Origine Scoticae Linguae (O'Mulconry's Glossary): An early Irish linguistic tract, edited with a related glossary, Irsan*, Corpus Christianorum, Lexica Latina Medii Aevi 7 (Turnhout: Brepols, 2019)

Morrison, Eve, 'Class, Gender and Occupation Among the Bureau of Military History Witnesses & Ernie O'Malley Interviewees Who Were "Out" in 1916', *Saothar*, vol. 41, 2016, pp. 59–67

Morrissey, Thomas J., *Towards a National University: William Delany SJ (1835–1924): An era of initiative in Irish education* (Dublin: Wolfhound Press, 1983)

Morrissey, Thomas J., *William J. Walsh, Archbishop of Dublin, 1841–1921: No uncertain voice* (Dublin: Four Courts Press, 2000)

Mosse, George L., *Toward the Final Solution: A history of European racism* (New York: Fertig, 1985)

Moynihan, Maurice (ed.), *Speeches and Statements by Éamon de Valera 1917–73* (Dublin: Gill & Macmillan, 1980)

Mullally, Evelyn (ed. and trans.), *The Deeds of the Normans in Ireland. La geste des Engleis en Yrlande. A New Edition of the Chronicle Formerly Known as the Song of Dermot and the Earl* (Dublin: Four Courts Press, 2002)

Mulvagh, Conor, *The Irish Parliamentary Party at Westminster, 1900–1918* (Manchester: Manchester University Press, 2016)

Murphy, Andrew, *Reading and Cultural Nationalism, 1790–1930: Bringing the nation to book* (Cambridge: Cambridge University Press, 2018)

Murphy, Brian, *Forgotten Patriot: Douglas Hyde and the foundation of the Irish presidency* (Cork: The Collins Press, 2016)

Murphy, Gerard, 'The Two Patricks', *Studies: An Irish quarterly review*, vol. 32, no. 127, Sept. 1943, pp. 297–307

Murphy, Maureen, 'Máire MacNeill (1904–1987)', *Béaloideas*, vol. 72, 2004, pp. 1–30

Murphy, William, *Political Imprisonment and the Irish, 1912–21* (Oxford: Oxford University Press, 2014)

Murray, Kevin, 'Edmund Hogan's *Onomasticon Goedelicum*, Ninety Years on: Reviewers and users', *Ainm*, vol. 8, 1998–2000, pp. 65–75

Murray, Kevin, '*Lebor na Cert*: Language and date', in idem (ed.), *Lebor na Cert: Reassessments*, Irish Texts Society, Subsidiary Series 25 (London: Irish Texts Society, 2013), pp. 77–102

Murray, Kevin and Pádraig Ó Riain (eds), *Edmund Hogan's Onomasticon Goedelicum: Reconsiderations*, Irish Texts Society, Subsidiary Series 23 (London: Irish Texts Society, 2011)

Murray, Kevin (ed.), *Lebor na Cert: Reassessments*, Irish Texts Society, Subsidiary Series 25 (London: Irish Texts Society, 2013)

Murray, Paul, *The Irish Boundary Commission and Its Origins, 1886–1925* (Dublin: UCD Press, 2011)

Nagle, Shane, *Histories of Nationalism in Ireland and Germany: A comparative study from 1800 to 1932* (London: Bloomsbury Academic, 2016)

Nansen, Fridtjof and Hjalmar Johansen, *Fridtjof Nansen's Farthest North: Being the record of a voyage of exploration of the ship* Fram *1893–96 and of a fifteen months' sleigh journey*, 2 vols (London: Archibald Constable, 1897)

Nelson, Bruce, *Irish Nationalists and the Making of the Irish Race* (Princeton, NJ: Princeton University Press, 2012)

[North Eastern Boundary Bureau], *Handbook of the Ulster Question* (Dublin: Stationery Office, 1923)

Nic an Bhaird, Máire and Liam Mac Mathúna, 'Early Diary Insights into Roscommon's Impact on Douglas Hyde, Ireland's First President', in Richie Farrell, Kieran O'Conor and Matthew Potter (eds), *Roscommon History and Society: Interdisciplinary essays on the history of an Irish county* (Dublin: Geography Publications, 2018), pp. 515–37

Ní Chatháin, Próinséas and Michael Richter (eds), *Ireland and Europe in the Early Middle Ages: Learning and literature* (Stuttgart: Klett-Cotta, 1996)

Ní Chatháin, Próinséas and Michael Richter (eds), *Ireland and Europe in the Early Middle Ages: Texts and transmissions* (Dublin: Four Courts Press, 2002)

Ní Chatháin, Próinséas and Michael Richter (eds), *Ireland and Christendom: The Bible and the missions* (Stuttgart: Klett-Cotta, 1987)

Ní Chatháin, Próinséas and Michael Richter (eds), *Ireland and Europe: The early church* (Stuttgart: Klett-Cotta, 1984)

Ní Mhaonaigh, Tracey (eag.), *Tháinig do litir … Litreacha ó pheann an Athar Peadar Ó Laoghaire chuig Séamus Ó Dubhghaill* (An Daingean: An Sagart, 2017)

Ó Beacháin, Donnacha, *From Partition to Brexit: The Irish government and Northern Ireland* (Manchester: Manchester University Press, 2019)

Ó Briain, Liam, *Insurrection Memories 1916: Cuimhní cinn*, trans. Eoin Ó Dochartaigh (Galway: Ardcrú, 2014)

O'Brien, Conor Cruise, *Parnell and His Party, 1880–90* (Oxford: Clarendon Press, 1957)

O'Brien, Elizabeth, *Mapping Death: Burial in late Iron Age and early medieval Ireland* (Dublin: Four Courts Press, 2020)

O'Brien, Elizabeth and Edel Bhreathnach, 'Irish Boundary *Ferta*, Their Physical Manifestation and Historical Context', in Fiona Edmonds and Paul Russell (eds), *Tome: Studies in medieval Celtic history and law* (Woodbridge: Boydell & Brewer, 2011), pp. 53–64

O'Brien, Gerard, *Irish Governments and the Guardianship of Historical Records, 1922–72* (Dublin: Four Courts Press, 2004)

Ó Carragáin, Tomás, 'Cemetery Settlements and Local Churches in pre-Viking Ireland in Light of Comparisons with England and Wales', *Proceedings of the British Academy*, vol. 157, 2009, pp. 329–66

Ó Carragáin, Tomás, 'Christianizing the Landscape of Mag Réta: Home territory of the kings of Laígis', in James Lyttleton and Matthew Stout (eds), *Church and Settlement in Ireland* (Dublin: Four Courts Press, 2018), pp. 60–85

Ó Carragáin, Tomás, 'The Archaeology of Ecclesiastical Estates in Early Medieval Ireland: A case-study of the kingdom of Fir Maige', *Peritia*, vols 24–5, 2013–14, pp. 266–312

Ó Carragáin, Tomás and Sam Turner (eds), *Making Christian Landscapes in Atlantic Europe: Conversion and consolidation in the early middle ages* (Cork: Cork University Press, 2016)

Ó Ceallaigh, Séamus, *Gleanings from Ulster History* (Cork: Cork University Press, 1951; repr. Draperstown: Ballinascreen Historical Society, 1994)

Ó Clabaigh, Colmán, 'The Church, 1050–1460', in Brendan Smith (ed.), *The Cambridge History of Ireland. Volume I: 600–1550* (Cambridge: Cambridge University Press, 2018), pp. 355–84

O'Connor, V.L., *A Book of Caricatures* (Dundalk: Tempest, 1915)

Ó Corráin, Daithí, '"Ireland in His Heart North and South": The contribution of Ernest Blythe to the partition question', *Irish Historical Studies*, vol. 35, no. 137, May, 2006, pp. 61–80

Ó Corráin, Donnchadh, *Clavis litterarum Hibernensium* (Turnhout: Brepols, 2017)

Ó Corráin, Donnchadh, 'Dál Cais: Church and dynasty', *Ériu*, vol. 24, 1973, pp. 52–63

Ó Corráin, Donnchadh, 'Irish Regnal Succession: A reappraisal', *Studia Hibernica*, vol. 11, 1971, pp. 7–39

Ó Corráin, Donnchadh, 'Nationality and Kingship in pre-Norman Ireland', in T.W. Moody (ed.), *Nationality and the Pursuit of National Independence* (Belfast: Appletree Press, 1978), pp. 1–35

Ó Corráin, Donnchadh, 'The Early Irish Churches: Some aspects of organisation', in Donnchadh Ó Corráin (ed.), *Irish Antiquity* (Cork: Tower Books, 1981), pp. 327–41

Ó Corráin, Donnchadh, *The Irish Church, Its Reform and the English Invasion* (Dublin: Four Courts Press, 2017)

Ó Cróinín, Dáibhí (ed.), *A New History of Ireland. Volume I: Prehistoric and Early Ireland* (Oxford: Oxford University Press, 2005)

Ó Cróinín, Dáibhí, 'Hiberno-Latin Literature to 1169', in Dáibhí Ó Cróinín (ed.), *A New History of Ireland. Volume 1: Prehistoric and Early Ireland* (Oxford: Oxford University Press, 2005), pp. 371–404

Ó Cróinín, Dáibhí, 'Ireland, 400–800', in Dáibhí Ó Cróinín (ed.), *A New History of Ireland. Volume 1: Prehistoric and Early Ireland* (Oxford: Oxford University Press, 2005), pp. 182–234

Ó Cróinín, Dáibhí, 'The Irish Abroad in Medieval Europe', *Peritia*, vol. 5, 1986, pp. 445–52

Ó Cróinín, Dáibhí, 'The Irish as Mediators of Antique Culture on the Continent', in P.L. Butzer and Dietrich Lohrmann (eds), *Science in Western and Eastern Civilization in Carolingian Times* (Basel: Birkhäuser Verlag, 1993), pp. 41–52

Ó Cróinín, Dáibhí, 'Who Was Palladius, "first bishop of the Irish"?', *Peritia*, vol. 14, 2000, pp. 205–37

Ó Cuív, Brian, 'MacNeill and the Irish Language', in F.X. Martin and F.J. Byrne (eds), *The Scholar Revolutionary: Eoin MacNeill, 1867–1945* (Dublin: Irish Academic Press, 1973), pp. 1–10

Ó Cuív, Shán, 'An tAthair Peadar agus a Lucht Comh-Aimsire', unpublished MA thesis, University College Dublin, 1956

Ó Cuív, Shán, 'Caradas nár Mhair: Peadar Ua Laoghaire agus Eoin Mac Néill', in F.X. Martin and F.J. Byrne (eds), *The Scholar Revolutionary: Eoin MacNeill, 1867–1945* (Dublin: Irish Academic Press, 1973), pp. 51–73

Ó Cuív, Shán, 'Materials for a Bibliography of the Very Reverend Peter Canon O'Leary, 1839–1920', *Celtica*, vol. 2, pt 2, 1954, pp. 3–39

[Ó Donnchadha, Tadhg] Torna [pseud.], 'Réumh-Rádh', in E.M. Ní Chiaragáin, *Index do Irisleabhar na Gaedhilge 1882–1909* (Baile Átha Cliath: Faoi Chomhartha na dTrí gCoinneal, 1935)

Ó Drisceoil, Donal, *Censorship in Ireland: Neutrality, politics and society* (Cork: Cork University Press, 1996)

O'Dwyer, Peter, *Céli Dé: Spiritual reform in Ireland, 750–900* (Dublin: Editions Táilliúra, 1981)

O'Farrelly, Agnes (ed.), *Leabhar an Athar Eoghan. The O'Growney Memorial Volume* (Dublin: Gill, 1904)

Ó Fearaíl, Pádraig, *The Story of Conradh na Gaeilge* (Baile Átha Cliath: Clódhanna Teo., 1975)

Ó Fiaich, Tomás, 'The Great Controversy', in Seán Ó Tuama (ed.), *The Gaelic League Idea* (Cork and Dublin: The Mercier Press, 1972), pp. 63–75

O'Halpin, Eunan, 'Problematic Killing during the War of Independence and Its Aftermath: Civilian spies and informers', in James Kelly and Mary Ann Lyons (eds), *Death and Dying in Ireland, Britain and Europe: Historical perspectives* (Sallins: Irish Academic Press, 2013), pp. 317–48

O'Hegarty, P.S., *The Victory of Sinn Féin: How it won it, and how it used it* (Dublin: Talbot Press, 1924)

O'Leary, Philip, *Gaelic Prose in the Irish Free State, 1922–1939* (University Park, PA and Dublin: Penn State University Press and UCD Press, 2004)

O'Leary, Philip, *The Prose Literature of the Gaelic Revival, 1881–1921* (University Park, PA: Penn State University Press, 1994)

O'Leary, Philip, '"The Dead Generations": Irish history in the Gaelic Revival', *Proceedings of the Harvard Celtic Colloquium*, no. 10, 1990, pp. 88–145

Ó Lochlainn, Colm, 'Roadways in Ancient Ireland', in John Ryan (ed.), *Féil-sgríbhinn Eóin Mhic Néill: Tráchtais léigheanta i n-onóir do'n ollamhain Eóin Mac Néill do sgríobh cáirde d'á cháirdibh i n-am a dheichmhadh bliadhna agus trí fichid, an cúigmhadh lá déag de mhí na Bealtaine, 1938* (Baile Átha Cliath: Faoi Chomhartha na dTrí gCoinneal, 1940), pp. 465–74

O'Loughlin, Thomas, *Saint Patrick: The man and his works* (London: Triangle, 1999)

Ó Lúing, Seán, *Kuno Meyer, 1858–1919: A biography* (Dublin: Geography Publications, 1991)

O'Malley, Ernie, *On Another Man's Wound*, rev. edn (Tralee: Anvil, 2002)

Ó Murchadha, D., 'Léitheoir sa Teach Screaptra?', in E. Purcell, P. MacCotter, J. Nyhan and J. Sheehan (eds), *Clerics, Kings and Vikings: Essays on medieval Ireland in honour of Donnchadh Ó Corráin* (Dublin: Four Courts Press, 2015), pp. 147–54

Ó Murchú, Máirtín, 'Irish Language Studies in Trinity College Dublin', *Hermathena*, Quatercentenary Papers, 1992, pp. 43–68

O'Neill Hencken, Hugh, with sections by Liam Price and Laura E. Start, 'Lagore Crannóg: An Irish royal residence of the 7th to 10th centuries AD', *PRIA*, vol. 53, 1950–1, pp. 1–247

O'Rahilly, Aodogán, *Winding the Clock: O'Rahilly and the 1916 Rising* (Dublin: Lilliput Press, 1991)

O'Rahilly, The [Michael Joseph], *The Secret History of the Irish Volunteers*, 3rd edn (Dublin: Irish Publicity League, 1915)

O'Rahilly, Thomas F., *Early Irish History and Mythology* (Dublin: DIAS, 1946)

O'Rahilly, Thomas F., *The Two Patricks: A lecture on the history of Christianity in fifth-century Ireland* (Dublin: DIAS, 1943 [repr. 1981])

Ó Raithbheartaigh, Toirdhealbhach (ed.), *Genealogical Tracts I* (Dublin: Irish Manuscripts Commission, 1932)

Ó Riain, Pádraig, Diarmuid Ó Murchadha, Kevin Murray and Emma Nic Cárthaigh (eds), *Historical Dictionary of Gaelic Placenames*, 8 fascicles (London: Irish Texts Society, 2003–)

Ó Riain-Raedel, Dagmar, 'New Light on the Beginnings of Christ Church Cathedral, Dublin', in Seán Duffy (ed.), *Medieval Dublin 17* (Dublin: Four Courts Press, 2018), pp. 63–80

Ó Ríordáin, Traolach, *Conradh na Gaeilge i gCorcaigh 1894–1910*, Lúb ar Lár 2 (Baile Átha Cliath: Cois Life Teoranta, 2000)

Orpen, Goddard Henry, *Ireland under the Normans, 1169–1333*, 4 vols (Oxford: Clarendon Press, 1911–20 [repr. in a single volume, Dublin: Four Courts Press, 2005])

Orpen, Goddard Henry, *The Song of Dermot and the Earl, an Old French Poem from the Carew Manuscript no. 596 in the Archiepiscopal Library at Lambeth Palace* (Oxford: Clarendon Press, 1892)

Ó Sé, Diarmuid, 'Tomás Ó Rathile', *Scoláirí Gaeilge – Léachtaí Cholm Cille*, vol. 27, 1997, pp. 177–210

O'Sullivan, Aidan, 'The Harvard Archaeological Mission and the Politics of the Irish Free State', *Archaeology Ireland*, vol. 17, no. 1, 2003, pp. 20–3

O'Toole, Fintan (ed.), *Up the Republic! Towards a new Ireland* (London: Faber & Faber, 2012)

Ó Tuathaigh, Gearóid, 'The Position of the Irish Language', in Tom Dunne (ed.), *The National University of Ireland 1908–2008: Centenary essays* (Dublin: UCD Press, 2008), pp. 33–43

Owen, M.E., 'Some Points of Comparison and Contrast Between Early Irish and Welsh Law', in Karen Jankulak and J.M. Wooding (eds), *Ireland and Wales in the Middle Ages* (Dublin: Four Courts Press, 2007), pp. 180–200

Padbury, Joyce, *Mary Hayden: Irish historian and feminist, 1862–1942* (Dublin: Arlen House, 2021)

Pašeta, Senia, *Before the Revolution: Nationalism, social change and Ireland's Catholic elite, 1879–1922* (Cork: Cork University Press, 1999)

Pašeta, Senia, 'Trinity College Dublin and the Education of Irish Catholics, 1873–1908', *Studia Hibernica*, vol. 30, 1998–9, pp. 7–20

Patterson, N., 'Patrilineal Kinship in Early Irish Society', *Bulletin of the Board of Celtic Studies*, vol. 37, 1990, pp. 133–65

Pearse, P.H., *The Murder Machine* (Dublin: Whelan, 1916)

Pedersen, Holger (ed.), *Vergleichende Grammatik der keltischen Sprachen* [Comparative Grammar of the Celtic Languages], 2 vols (Göttingen: Vandenhoeck & Ruprecht, 1909–13)

Phillips, W. Alison, *The Revolution in Ireland, 1906–1923*, 2nd edn (London: Longmans, Green & Co., 1926 [1st edn 1923])

Phoenix, Eamon, *Northern Nationalism: Nationalist politics, partition, and the Catholic minority in Northern Ireland, 1890–1940* (Belfast: Ulster Historical Foundation, 1994)

Plessini, Karel, *The Perils of Normalcy: George L. Mosse and the remaking of cultural history* (Madison: University of Wisconsin Press, 2014)

Pokorny, Julius, 'MacNeill's Place in Celtic Studies', in F.X. Martin and F.J. Byrne (eds), *The Scholar Revolutionary: Eoin MacNeill, 1867–1945, and the making of the new Ireland* (Shannon: Irish University Press, 1973), pp. 11–14

Quinn, P., 'John O'Donovan and Eugene O'Curry's Notes and the Construction of the Ancient Laws of Ireland', *Irish Jurist*, vol. 55, 2016, pp. 166–74

Rafferty, Oliver P., 'The Church and the Easter Rising', *Studies: An Irish quarterly review*, vol. 105, no. 417, 2016, pp. 47–57

Raftery, Barry, 'Celtic Ireland: Problems of language, history and archaeology', *Acta Archaeologica, Academiae Scientiarum Hungaricae*, tomus lvii, fasciculi 1–3, 2006, pp. 273–9

Rebillard, Eric, *The Care of the Dead in Late Antiquity*, translated by Elizabeth Trapnell Rawlings and Jeanine Routier-Pucci (Ithaca, NY: Cornell University Press, 2009)

Redman, Samuel L., *Bone Rooms: From scientific racism to human prehistory in museums* (Cambridge, MA: Harvard University Press, 2016)

Reid, Colin, *The Lost Ireland of Stephen Gwynn: Irish constitutional nationalism and cultural politics, 1864–1950* (Manchester: Manchester University Press, 2011)

Reid, James, 'A Case-Study in Early Irish Regnal Succession: The kingdom of Osraige, 802–1003', forthcoming

Robinson, F.N., 'Celtic Books at Harvard: The history of a departmental collection', *Harvard Library Bulletin*, vol. 1, no. 1, 1946, pp. 52–65

Ross, A., 'Pictish Matriliny', *Northern Studies*, vol. 34, 1999, pp. 11–22

Royal University of Ireland: Calendar for the year 1896 (Dublin: Longmans, 1896)

Royal University of Ireland: Calendar for the year 1900 (Dublin: Longmans, 1900)

Ryan, Desmond, *The Rising: The complete story of Easter week* (Dublin: Golden Eagle Books, 1949)

Ryan, John, 'A Patrician Problem: "Saint Patrick – Bury versus Slemish"', in F.X. Martin and F.J. Byrne (eds), *The Scholar Revolutionary: Eoin MacNeill, 1867–1945, and the making of the new Ireland* (Shannon: Irish University Press, 1973), pp. 313–24

[Ryan, John] J.R., 'Eoin Mac Neill' [obituary], *Analecta Hibernica*, no. 17, 1949, pp. 351–3

Ryan, John (ed.), *Féil-sgríbhinn Eóin Mhic Néill: Essays and studies presented to Professor Eoin MacNeill on the occasion of his seventieth birthday, May 15th 1938* (Baile Átha Cliath: Faoi Chomhartha na dTrí gCoinneal, 1940)

Ryan, John, 'Rudolf Thurneysen: 1857–1940', *Studies: An Irish quarterly review*, vol. 29, no. 116, 1940, pp. 583–90

Ryan, John V., *The Pageant of the Celt*, RIA MSS, AP 1934

Schmitz, Gerhard, 'Les Monumenta Germaniae Historica', in Isabelle Guyot-Bachy and Jean-Marie Moeglin (eds), *La naissance de la médiévistique. Les historiens et leurs sources en Europe (XIXᵉ–début du XXᵉ siècle)* (Geneva: Librarie Droz, 2015), pp. 299–313

Sellar, W.D.H., 'Warlords, Holy Men and Matrilineal Succession', *The Innes Review*, vol. 36, 1985, pp. 29–43

Sharpe, Richard, 'Some Problems Concerning the Organization of the Church in Early Medieval Ireland', *Peritia*, vol. 3, 1984, pp. 230–70

Shaw, Francis, 'MacNeill the Person', in F.X. Martin and F.J. Byrne (eds), *The Scholar Revolutionary: Eoin MacNeill, 1867–1945, and the making of the new Ireland* (Shannon: Irish University Press, 1973), pp. 299–311

Slee, Peter, *Learning and a Liberal Education: The study of modern history in the universities of Oxford, Cambridge and Manchester, 1800–1914* (Manchester: Manchester University Press, 1986)

Smith, A.D., *Nationalism and Modernism* (Oxford: Oxford University Press, 2000)

Smith, A.P., *Warlords and Holy Men: Scotland AD 80–1000* (London: Edward Arnold, 1984)

Smith, Bonnie G., *The Gender of History: Men, women, and historical practice* (Cambridge, MA: Harvard University Press, 1998)

Smith, Brendan (ed.), *The Cambridge History of Ireland. Volume I: 600–1550* (Cambridge: Cambridge University Press, 2018)

Smith, J.M.H., 'Portable Christianity: Relics in the medieval West (*c.*700–*c.*1200)', *Proceedings of the British Academy*, vol. 181, 2012, pp. 143–67

Stam, Nike, *A Typology of Code-switching in the Commentary to the Félire Óengusso* (Utrecht: LOT, 2017)

Stokes, W., 'Curiosities of Official Scholarship', *Academy*, vol. 28, 1885, pp. 204–5

Stover, Justin Dolan, 'Delaying Division: Eoin MacNeill, John Redmond and the Irish Volunteers', *History Studies*, vol. 8, 2007, pp. 111–23

Sussman, Robert Wald, *The Myth of Race: The troubling persistence of an unscientific idea* (Cambridge, MA: Harvard University Press, 2014)

Swift, Catherine, 'Tírechán's Motives in Compiling the *Collectanea*: An alternative interpretation', *Ériu*, vol. 45, 1994, pp. 53–82

Thacker, Alan, 'Loca Sanctorum: The significance of place in the study of the saints', in Alan Thacker and Richard Sharpe, *Local Saints and Local Churches in the Early Medieval West* (Oxford: Oxford University Press, 2002), pp. 1–46

Thomson, E.A., *Who Was Saint Patrick?* (Woodbridge: Boydell, 1985 [repr. 1999])

Thornton, David E., 'Early Medieval Louth: The kingdom of Conaille Muirtheimne', *Journal of the County Louth Archaeological and Historical Society*, vol. 24, 1997, pp. 139–50

Thornton, David E., *King, Chronologies and Genealogies: Studies in the political history of early medieval Ireland and Wales*, Prosopographica et Genealogica 10 (Oxford: Unit for Prosopographical Research, Linacre College, 2003)

Thurneysen, R., 'Aus dem irischen Recht IV: Zu MacNeill's "Law of Status or Franchise"', *Zeitschrift für celtische Philologie*, vol. 16, 1926, pp. 197–205

Thurneysen, R., 'Celtic Law', in D. Jenkins (ed.), *Celtic Law Papers: Introductory to Welsh medieval law and government* (Bruxelles: Les Editions de la Librairie Encyclopédique, 1973), pp. 49–70. Translated from 'Das keltische Recht', *Zeitschrift der Savigny-Stiftung für Rechtsgeschichte* (Germanistische Abteilung), vol. 55, 1935, pp. 81–104

Thurneysen, R., N. Power, M. Dillon, K. Mulchrone, D.A. Binchy, A. Knoch and J. Ryan (eds), *Studies in Early Irish Law* (Dublin: Royal Irish Academy, 1936)

Tierney, Michael, 'Eoin MacNeill: A biographical study', in Eoin MacNeill, *Saint Patrick*, ed. John Ryan SJ (Dublin: Clonmore & Reynolds, 1964), pp. 9–34

Tierney, Michael, *Eoin MacNeill: Scholar and man of action, 1867–1945*, ed. F.X. Martin (Oxford: Clarendon Press, 1980)

Titley, E. Brian, *Church, State, and the Control of Schooling in Ireland 1900–1944* (Kingston: McGill-Queen's University Press, 1983)

Townshend, Charles, *Easter 1916: The Irish rebellion* (London: Allen Lane, 2005)

Townshend, Charles, *The Republic: The fight for Irish independence, 1918–1923* (London: Penguin, 2014)

Tristram, H.L.C., 'Eduard Rudolf Thurneysen (1857–1940)', in H. Damico [with D. Fennema and K. Lenz] (eds), *Medieval Scholarship: Biographical studies on the formation of a discipline. Volume 2: Literature and Philology* (New York and London: Garland Library of Medieval Literature, 1998), pp. 201–13

Ua Laoġaire, Peadar, *Notes on Irish Words and Usages* (Dublin: Browne & Nolan, Ltd, 1926)

Ua Laoghaire, Peadar, *Séadna* (Baile Átha Cliath: Cois Life Teoranta, 2011)

Uí Chollatáin, Regina, *An Claidheamh Soluis agus Fáinne an Lae 1899–1932: Anailís ar phríomhnuachtán Gaeilge Ré na hAthbheochana* (Baile Átha Cliath: Cois Life Teoranta, 2004)

Uí Chollatáin, Regina, 'An Piarsach agus Iriseoireacht na Gaeilge: Iriseoir intleaechtúil Victeoiriach agus réabhlóidí machnamhach', in Gearóid Ó Tuathaigh, *An Piarsach agus 1916: Briathar, beart agus oidhreacht* (Indrebhán, Conamara: Cló Iar-Chonnacht, 2016), pp. 37–58

Uí Chollatáin, Regina, 'Athbheochan Thrasatlantach na Gaeilge: Scríbhneoirí, intleachtóirí agus an fhéiniúlacht Éireannach', in Ríona Nic Congáil et al., *Litríocht na Gaeilge ar fud an Domhain: Cruthú, caomhnú agus athbheochan*, Imleabhar 1 (Baile Átha Cliath: Leabhair Comhar, 2015), pp. 277–309

Uí Chollatáin, Regina, 'Deisceabail agus Soiscéalta: Ceannródaithe athbheochana agus fóram na hiriseoireachta', *Oidhreacht Uí Ghramhnaigh: Léachtaí Cholm Cille*, vol. 44, 2014, pp. 22–45

Uí Chollatáin, Regina, 'The Turning of the Tide: Craobh an Chéitinnigh agus coimhlint na Gaeilge i 1916', *Éigse: A Journal of Irish studies*, vol. 40, 2019, pp. 305–26

University College Dublin: A Constituent College of the National University of Ireland: Calendar for the Session 1910–11 (Dublin: Browne & Nolan, 1910)

Vincent, Nicholas, 'Angevin Ireland', in Brendan Smith (ed.), *The Cambridge History of Ireland. Volume I: 600–1550* (Cambridge: Cambridge University Press, 2018), pp. 185–221

Walker, G.S.M. (ed.), *Sancti Columbani Opera*, Scriptores Latini Hiberniae 2 (Dublin: DIAS, 1957)

Wall, Maureen, 'The Background to the Rising from 1914 until the Issue of the Countermanding Order on Easter Saturday 1916', in K.B. Nowlan (ed.), *The Making of 1916: Studies in the history of the rising* (Dublin: Stationery Office, 1969), pp. 157–97

Wall, Maureen, 'The Plans and the Countermand: The country and Dublin', in K.B. Nowlan (ed.), *The Making of 1916: Studies in the history of the rising* (Dublin: Stationery Office, 1969), pp. 201–51

Walsh, Brendan, '"Frankly and Robustly National": Padraig Pearse, the Gaelic League and the campaign for Irish at the National University', *Studies: An Irish quarterly review*, vol. 103, no. 410, Summer 2014, pp. 135–46

Walsh, Brendan, '"Frankly and Robustly National": Padraig Pearse, the Gaelic League and the campaign for Irish at the National University', *Studies: An Irish quarterly review*, vol. 103, no. 411, Autumn 2014, pp. 318–30

Walsh, Maura and Dáibhí Ó Cróinín (eds), *Cummian's Letter De Controversia Paschali: Together with a related Irish computistical tract De Ratione Computandi* (Toronto: Pontifical Institute of Mediaeval Studies, 1988)

Warntjes, Immo, 'Regnal Succession in Early Medieval Ireland', *Journal of Medieval History*, vol. 30, 2004, pp. 377–410

Warntjes, Immo, 'Seventh-Century Ireland: The cradle of medieval science?', in Charles Doherty and Mary Kelly (eds), *Music and the Stars: Mathematics in medieval Ireland* (Dublin: Four Courts Press, 2013), pp. 44–72

Warntjes, Immo and Dáibhí Ó Cróinín (eds), *The Easter Controversy of Late Antiquity and the Early Middle Ages: Its manuscripts, texts, and tables. Proceedings of the 2nd International Conference on the Science of Computus in Ireland and Europe, Galway, 18–20 July 2008*, Studia Traditionis Theologiae 10 (Turnhout: Brepols, 2011)

Watson, George, 'Celticism and the Annulment of History', in Terence Brown (ed.), *Celticism* (Atlanta: Amsterdam, 1996), pp. 207–20

Wheatley, Michael, *Nationalism and the Irish Party: Provincial Ireland, 1910–1916* (Oxford: Oxford University Press, 2005)

White, Gerry, '"They have rights who dare maintain them": The Irish Volunteers, 1913–15', in John Crowley, Donal Ó Drisceoil, Mike Murphy and John Borgonovo (eds), *Atlas of the Irish Revolution* (Cork: Cork University Press, 2017), pp. 164–72

Wickham, Chris, *Framing the Early Middle Ages: Europe and the Mediterranean, 400–800* (Oxford: Oxford University Press, 2005)

Wooding, Jonathan M., 'Reapproaching the Pagan Celtic Past: Anti-nativism, asterisk reality and the late-antiquity paradigm', *Studia Celtica Fennica*, vol. 6, 2009, pp. 61–74

Woolf, Alex, 'Pictish Matriliny Reconsidered', *The Innes Review*, vol. 49, 1998, pp. 147–67

Woolf, Alex, 'The Scandinavian Intervention', in Brendan Smith (ed.), *The Cambridge History of Ireland. Volume I: 600–1550* (Cambridge: Cambridge University Press, 2018), pp. 107–30

Wycherley, Niamh, *The Cult of Relics in Early Medieval Ireland*, Studies in the Early Middle Ages 43 (Turnhout: Brepols, 2015)

Yu Liu., 'Castell's Pliny: Rewriting the past for the present', *Eighteenth-Century Studies*, vol. 43, no. 2, Winter 2010, pp. 243–57

ONLINE SOURCES

Beyond 2022 Project, Trinity College Dublin, led by Peter Crooks: https://beyond2022.ie/

Breathnach, Diarmuid and Máire Ní Mhurchú, 'Laoide, Seosamh (1865–1939)': www.ainm.ie/Bio.aspx?ID=25

Breathnach, Diarmuid and Máire Ní Mhurchú, 'Mac Néill, Eoin (1867–1945)': https://www.ainm.ie/Bio.aspx?ID=452

Census of Ireland 1901/1911, National Archives: http://www.census.national archives.ie/

The Connacht Project: https://www.nuigalway.ie/colleges-and-schools/arts-social-sciences-and-celtic-studies/geography-archaeology-irish-studies/disciplines/archaeology/research/ireland-atlantic-europe/the-connacht-project/

The Discovery Programme, Centre for Archaeology and Innovation Ireland: www.discoveryprogramme.ie

Findagrave: https://www.findagrave.com/memorial/146831102/brian-mac_neill

Irish Statue Book: www.irishstatutebook.ie

RIP.ie (death notices): https://rip.ie/death-notice/maribel-macneill-galway-city-galway/287701

Russell, Paul, Sharon Arbuthnot and Pádraic Moran, *Early Irish Glossaries Database*, http://www.asnc.cam.ac.uk/irishglossaries

Saint Patrick's *Confessio*, Royal Irish Academy: www.confessio.ie

Simpson, John, 'The reluctant professor MacHugh', James Joyce Online: https://sites.google.com/site/jjonlinenotes/jioyce-s-people/machugh

UCC Locus Project: https://www.ucc.ie/en/locus/

OTHER

Stifter, David, '*Chronologicon Hibernicum*: A probabilistic chronological framework for dating Early Irish language developments and literature', ERC H2020 Project, no. 647351

Index